THE CULT
OF VIOLENCE

THE CULT
OF VIOLENCE

Sorel and the Sorelians

Jack J. Roth

University of California Press

Berkeley • Los Angeles • London

University of California Press
Berkeley and Los Angeles, California

University of California Press, Ltd.
London, England

© 1980 by
The Regents of the University of California

ISBN 0-520-03772-3
Library of Congress Catalog Card Number: 78-62857
Printed in the United States of America

1 2 3 4 5 6 7 8 9

To the Memory of
My Father and Mother

Contents

Sorelians after Sorel

Preface

On the night of August 29, 1922, Georges Sorel, in an earlier day known as the "Socrates of the Latin Quarter" but now wearied by years of illness and loneliness, died at the age of 75 at Boulogne-sur-Seine, a suburb of Paris. In the week that followed a reader of the Parisian press would have been somewhat bewildered by the obituaries noting the passing of the old recluse.

The republican press was not without respect. But the *Journal des débats* was quick to point out that Sorel had worked to undermine the Third Republic.[1] The *Action* called him "a man of extremes," who "hated reason" and "hated democracy."[2] The *Temps* suggested that Sorel was happiest when he could find someone at fault,[3] and *Éclair* maintained that his "isolation" had been responsible for his intellectual "deformities."[4]

In quarters unfriendly to the Republic, among extremists of all kinds, the reaction to Sorel's death was far different. The syndicalist *Vie ouvrière* (which had recently added the hammer-and-sickle to its masthead), organ of the Confédération Générale du Travail Unitaire, lamented the passing of "the most learned man of France, if not of the world."[5] The *Humanité,* organ of the Communist party, proclaimed: "Proletarians, exploited everywhere, believe me, one of your most lucid and greatest defenders has passed away."[6] The *Action française,* the monarchist newspaper, carried an article whose author asserted: "I bow and pray before the tomb of the man to whom I owe so much."[7]

In Italy, where substantially the same views were expressed in roughly comparable quarters, there was at least one additional source of homage and indebtedness. It was the *Popolo d'Italia,* organ of Mussolini's Fascist party. Fascism, it declared, was "a movement in which some of the most cherished ideas of the Sorelian conception of life and history are reflected."[8]

This reaction, particularly in the expressions of indebtedness, illustrates why Sorel has continued to be an object of study and wonderment.[9] Both the career of the man and the activities of his following raise troublesome questions. What was the nature of Sorel's political affiliations? What doctrinal gymnastics made them possible? What was the impact of his work, both during his lifetime and after? To understand Sorel and the Sorelians, some have speculated, is to understand something of the cataclysmic character of twentieth-century history.

A respectable body of literature has appeared on Sorel, though it is much smaller (especially in English) than one would suppose and pays far less attention to his following than one would wish. Although clear-cut distinctions are not always possible, this literature is often the work of either partisans or scholars, and much of it has neither been studied nor properly evaluated. Disciples or near-disciples, for example, have often been uncritical in their comments on Sorel: by quoting from an appropriate passage from his multifarious writings, Sorel has all too readily been claimed as the *maître* of this or that movement. But these works, frequently ignored, assume significance only when placed in an appropriate frame of reference. Scholars are not exempt from these criticisms; they have their own shortcomings as well. Few have demonstrated serious interest in the biographical aspects of their subject. Moreover, since the quality of Sorel's written work is not uniform and much of it scattered among little-known periodicals, attention has centered on the sources which are comparatively well known or readily available.

This study attempts a synthesis of the literature by and about Sorel and the Sorelians. Its focus is Sorel's apocalyptic politics; I have attempted to avoid digressions, probably at some cost. Other approaches to the study of Sorel—notably his metaphysics, his ethics, his historical conceptions, and his sociology—have been attempted, and they are not without merit. The argument presented here is that the need for a drastic and total renovation of the social order became (if it was not from the very beginning) the center of Sorel's thought and action. Moreover, attention is directed to the impact of his work in both France and Italy.[10] To be sure, Sorel's work was published elsewhere—*Réflexions sur la violence,* his best-known work, was translated into Italian, German, Russian, English, Spanish, Japanese, and perhaps other languages—but outside of France and Italy, Sorel had no direct or personal involvement in intellectual and political affairs. Only there did a continuing stream of his publications appear during his lifetime. This study aims to establish that after an extended evolution during which he "re-educated" himself, Sorel began a search for movements capable of a politico-spiritual conquest; that though his views underwent important evolution, the basic pattern of his ideas remained substantially unaltered for each of his affiliations; and that the impact of his thought and action initiated in France and Italy a variegated and changing, yet identifiable and important movement that continued after his death until World War II. This study is structured in a way which (while, it is to be hoped, avoiding tedium) will most effectively reveal what is significant in problems involving both change and continuity.

A book must live up to its title; I want no false hopes raised by the title of this one. In *The Cult of Violence: Sorel and the Sorelians* my concern will be with Sorel and his admirers, some of whom were so devoted to him over an extended period of time that they may properly be called disciples, as well as with others who identified themselves with him only briefly. To the extent that any of these venerated Sorel and preserved the essentials of his thought (though in a modified form), their activity may be considered a "cult." That activity, characteristically (though there were exceptions), centered on a periodical, sometimes a newspaper but more often a review. There were not many Sorelians or many Sorelian periodicals—this was no mass movement. Rather, it was a movement which at its core numbered only a handful of intellectuals and those with intellectual pretensions. An explicit statement of indebtedness to Sorel has been required of all those here called "Sorelians," though there are suggestions that the cult may at times have extended to individuals as well as groups well beyond these rather rigid boundaries. As for the cult of "violence," the term is here employed in the Sorelian sense, though vulgarizations (both by Sorel and by his following) are noted. For Sorel, violence was a way in which a movement or a regime asserted itself.[11] To be sure, violence was a technique, but it was also more. "Violence" subsumed almost everything Sorel and his following had to say about revolutionary movements and postrevolutionary regimes. What relation Sorelian violence may have had to earlier, concurrent, or later conceptions of violence, though noted, is not of central concern here.

Various aspects of this study have been presented at American Historical Association meetings since 1962 or have been published in professional periodicals: *Vierteljahrshefte für Zeitgeschichte* (1958), *French Historical Studies* (1963), *Journal of Modern History* (1967), and *Contemporary French Civilization* (1978). This is in no sense, however, a compilation or collection. In both scope and depth, I trust, it stands completely on its own and supersedes anything I have thus far said or written on Sorel and the Sorelians.

I take this occasion to thank those whose aid and assistance over the years have been most helpful in this effort: the numerous (and, for the most part, to me nameless) members of the staff of the Bibliothèque Nationale in Paris and the Biblioteca Nazionale in Florence; the American Philosophical Society; and the University of Chicago, Roosevelt University, and Case Western Reserve University. May I thank personally professors Georg G. Iggers of the State University of New York at Buffalo and Edward T. Gargan of the University of Wisconsin for the aid and advice given to me over the years, as well as innumerable friends and colleagues in the profession (to say nothing of my wife Sheilagh) who have pleaded with me to "finish the damn thing." Thank God, I have finished (I hope).

J.J.R.
Case Western Reserve University
Department of History.

Chapter

1

Introduction

Georges Sorel's family origins, his youth and early manhood, his career in the French civil service, his "marriage"—all this was long shrouded in mystery. He himself wrote virtually nothing of these matters. Even his closest friends in later years knew little. Not until some thirty years after his death was some light shed on a number of perplexing biographical problems.[1]

His parents, established in Cherbourg where he was born on November 2, 1847, were of bourgeois Catholic origin.[2] Gustave Sorel, his father, apparently came from a fairly well-to-do petit-bourgeois family. He was a merchant of wines and spirits who on at least one occasion evidently experienced serious business difficulties. Nathalie Sorel, *née* Salley, was the daughter of a former officer of the Grand Army who had won the Legion of Honor on the battlefield and served for a time as mayor of Barfleur. She was by all accounts a devout Catholic. "Mystical" tendencies, the nature of which are not described, were attributed to her.

Young Georges, the second of three sons (a fourth died in infancy), grew up in Normandy.[3] His summers were spent with a grandmother in the village of Touques. Here Georges and his brothers met their cousin Albert Sorel, the future historian of the French Revolution. We are told that Georges amazed his relatives by his talent in mathematics. In 1864 he received his *baccalauréat* with the highest standing in his class at the Collège de Cherbourg. That same year, at the age of seventeen, he left for Paris, where he attended the Collège Rollin for one year and the elite École Polytechnique for two, completing his studies in 1867 as a civil engineer of bridges and roads. Photographs at 17 and 18 in school uniforms show him to have been an intensely serious blond young man of somewhat haughty appearance. After two years of field work, he took his final examinations in 1870 as an engineer in the civil service. In July 1870, a few days before the outbreak of the Franco-Prussian War, he was assigned to Corsica, where he remained until July of the following year.

We know that during his school years, when the Second Empire flourished, Sorel had become a legitimist, though details of his political views

1

remain fragmentary.[4] As an enthusiastic theatre- and opera-goer in Paris he had no high regard for bourgeois culture. His closest associate of later years, Édouard Berth, was to write that he was an avid reader of the anti-Imperialist *Journal des débats*. In any case, Sorel did not conceal his views: "Vive Henri V," he wrote at the top of his exercise papers. When Sorel left for Corsica he was still a partisan of the Comte de Chambord, but we know nothing of his reaction to the cataclysmic events of 1870–1871. In Corsica he had, of course, no direct contact with the fall of the Empire, the proclamation of the Republic, the siege of Paris, or the Paris Commune. In a biographical essay many years later, however, he wrote that those events had made a profound impression on him, particularly the "imprudence" of the Commune.[5]

With his appointment in July 1871 to Albi as a civil engineer, Sorel began his career as a *fonctionnaire* under the Republic. On sick leave in 1872 he traveled in Spain and possibly in Portugal. In 1876 he began three years of service in Algeria, then in 1879 an appointment in Perpignan lasted until he terminated his career thirteen years later. These years in the civil service were significant primarily for his encounter with Marie-Euphrasie David and his first efforts at "re-education."[6]

In 1875, Sorel, returning to his post after leave in Paris (where his family was now established), fell ill in a hotel in Lyon, where he met a chambermaid, Marie-Euphrasie David. Years later he was to write of her with touching affection and near-reverence as the inspiration of his career, but those of his closest friends who knew there was a woman in his life in all probability never met her, and those few people who did meet her could only guess at the relationship.[7] Marie-Euphrasie came from Chanay, in the Jura mountains, of a family of poor peasants. She had formerly worked in the mountain factories and was virtually illiterate. When they met Sorel was 28 and she 30. She nursed him back to health, and when he recovered he left with her for his post. Sorel apparently asked his parents' permission to marry her. Her relatives have maintained that his parents refused consent, for such a union would have been a *déclassement*. Sorel was now to live somewhat estranged from his family. Possibly bound by some oath, or simply out of respect for his parents' wishes, he never married her.

With Marie-Euphrasie a new life began for Sorel. On several occasions he alluded to this "chance meeting" as having decisively shaped his intellectual development. By all accounts, she was a very pious, sincere, and devoted "woman of the people"; what Sorel may have meant was that she made it possible for him to transcend his own class origins. He endeavored to provide her with an elementary education. For primer he gave her the Bible. On Sundays he required her to read the mass.

During these years, he later recalled, he served his "apprenticeship" as a social critic.[8] His private life may have helped, for it imposed a certain isolation on his household. He wrote later of his sharp dislike of bourgeois society in small towns, yet he did not lead a cloistered life. He frequently attended meetings of local scientific, philosophical, and literary societies, and his reading was omnivorous. A list of books and periodicals he borrowed from the municipal library of Perpignan between 1884 and 1891 indicates a clear preference for philosophy and religion, archaeology, and architecture,[9] but the subject matter of his first literary efforts indicates still broader interests. He must also have read the utopian socialists, the positivists, and, above all, that enigmatic anarchist Proudhon, who had died in 1865, about two decades earlier.

I

Sorel began to publish in 1886, at the age of 39, while still in the provinces. These initial endeavors were not without some interest.[10] His articles revealed at the outset something of the man of science vs. the man of letters in his distrust of the "vices" of rationalism, both ancient and Cartesian. His concern was with the natural sciences, and he speculated on the application of the methods of science to aesthetics and the "moral sciences."

Then in 1889, the year in which the centennial of the great Revolution was widely celebrated in France, Sorel published two books: *Contribution à l'étude profane de la Bible* and *Le Procès de Socrate*. In neither did he demonstrate any direct interest in the Revolution. These curious studies reveal, rather, his identity with the "generation of the 1870s" that had to remake France. His position was either explicitly or implicitly antipolitical: a disdain for monarchists incapable of making a monarchy, for Bonapartists given to plebiscitarian demagogy, for republicans who could establish only an "opportunist" Republic, and for revolutionaries who only dreamed of violence.[11] The thrust of the two studies was moral. With his first major studies he set the tone for all his subsequent work. He began to worry, as did Proudhon, about the "moral decadence" of France. Proudhon's life, too, as Sorel must have known, had been shaped by a deep attachment to a "woman of the people." Sorel became, and never ceased to be, a Proudhonian in his passionate search for moral renewal.

The *Contribution* was a critical study of Biblical sources. Sorel did not question Catholic orthodoxy.[12] Religious experience was founded on a fact beyond scientific argument, "a spontaneous metaphysical creation, a *revelation*." His faith, apparently, was complete. The most significant feature of the study was a preface. Here he urged the *université* that taught the people, and the bourgeoisie who governed them, to give to the Bible a predominant place in general education. The Bible could combat the pernicious effects of utilitarianism and mediocrity. It could evoke in the people the desire to live a "heroic life." Sorel deplored the criticism of the Bible at the hands of Renan and the positivists generally. Their work had corrupted bourgeois and proletarian alike. What Sorel wanted was a return to *"les temps héroiques."*

Shifting from Biblical exegesis to Attic society, *Le Procès* repeated the same theme.[13] He challenged the view that the execution of Socrates was a crime. There were two ethical types in ancient Greece, he maintained, the soldier and the intellectual, and they represented, respectively, heroism and decadence. The faithful interpreters of old Attic society, such as Homer, created a moral order of essentially military virtues. The "myths" of ancient Greece, as long as they were celebrated, sustained a society that was disciplined and courageous. The heroic period came to an end with Socrates and the sophists—Socrates was for Sorel the "anti-Homer." He preached "cosmopolitan indifference." He worshipped the "little and illusory divinity of Reason." He "poisoned" the youth of Athens by shaking their faith in the "sublime." The study of the trial of Socrates had a practical purpose. Sorel saw a parallel between the Socratic "enlightenment" and that of his own time.[14] The system of morals provided by the church had been threatened by the "reveries" of the *philosophes,* by the terror of the Jacobins, by the utopians who envisaged a society based on "talent," and by the positivists who sought the scientific organization of society; but the greatest threat came from democracy. This was a form of society in which power was shared by the wealthy and the talented, who were, in Sorel's opinion, the worst elements. Democracy was dominated by the principles of the stock exchange, which corrupted morals and politics alike. If he took a positive position at all, it was one not far removed from the spirit of Proudhon, whose works he continually cited. Sorel wanted a "society based on work." He denounced the "cult of success" and favored the "revival of pessimistic values" essential to Christian morals. Sorel admired, above all, the perfect integrity of Proudhon's peasant morality, and quoted from his *La Guerre et la paix*: "Temperance, frugality, the daily bread obtained by daily labor, a poverty quick to punish gluttony and laziness: such is the first of our moral laws."[15]

The lack of public reaction to the two studies of 1889 must have dismayed Sorel, but the reasons are easily perceived: Sorel lacked proper academic credentials and the books themselves appeared somewhat amateurish. They seemed to have been constructed by stringing together his notes, a stylistic problem that Sorel never quite overcame. Moreover, the arguments he presented were given no immediacy. There was no discussion of current politics. The Boulanger crisis, for example, went unnoticed. What the studies revealed were the persistence of his traditionalist orientation, a critique of his current reading, and his isolation in the provinces. Although critical of the positivists in general—the relativism of Comte, the determinism of Taine, and the skepticism of Renan—he was nevertheless indebted to them in detail. Even his attraction to Proudhon was qualified. It was not Proudhon's anarchism that drew him, it was his moralism. The failure of these two studies devoted to social criticism may very well have turned Sorel back to his initial interests. For the next several years he was again preoccupied with miscellaneous topics in the natural sciences, aesthetics, mathematics, and engineering.[16] Nevertheless, his nagging critique of the "vices" of rationalism continued very much in evidence.

Not until 1892, in an article on Proudhon, did Sorel again return to a critique of the social order.[17] Sorel attempted to explore further the conception of a "society based on work" by way of Proudhon's idea of justice and his glorification of the Greek city-state, the *polis*.[18] In the *polis*, as Proudhon had observed, the idea of justice was closely bound up with "the reciprocal respect for personal dignity" among soldiers brought up in a cult of virtue and ready to die in the defense of their homeland. Justice was connected with war, "which reveals our ideal to us, ... creates the great epics, reinvigorates nations gone soft." Sorel now transposed the *polis* into a modern industrial setting. The role of the modern industrial worker was comparable in nobility and dignity to that of the Greek warrior. Labor under any system, however, meant man had to toil hard even for a bare living. Poverty would always be the lot of the worker, but poverty, as opposed to pauperism, was decent. He viewed justice in an industrial society in Proudhonian terms, as the individual's consciousness of his personal dignity, his right to be respected, his claim to economic equality with his moral equals. But Sorel rejected Proudhon the revolutionary. Justice was to be attained by education. Education, however, was to be based on the "practices of the workshop," not on the Cartesian "reveries" which still dominated French schools.

At Perpignan in 1892 during a cholera epidemic, Sorel at 45 resigned as a civil servant.[19] The circumstances of his departure are not entirely clear. He had received the rating of chief engineer first class and had been appointed chevalier of the Legion of Honor (he was always to wear the ribbon, even in later years when he had turned fiercely antirepublican). He could have requested unlimited leave, which would have guaranteed his right to a pension, but he preferred, he wrote later, complete "independence." The deaths of his father in 1879 and of his mother in 1887 had provided him with a small income. On departing, the municipal council in Perpignan voted him official thanks for services rendered to the city.

Sorel now moved to Paris.[20] After a few months in the city he established himself at nearby Boulogne-sur-Seine, where a nephew of Marie-Euphrasie resided. There, except for brief periods during the war, he was to live until his death. No new intellectual departures were immediately apparent. Articles in 1892–1893 continued to assail Cartesianism as alien to the scientific spirit and to assert that work was the most noble privilege of man.[21] His writing was now marked by a vituperative element not previously in evidence. Possibly the Panama Scandal may have had some bearing on his work, though he failed to give it serious attention. In 1892, also, he began to rework his notebooks. It was from this date, he wrote later, that he really studied for the purpose of learning.[22] It is also likely that it was from this date, as his friends later recalled, that he became an assiduous frequenter of the Bibliothèque Nationale.[23] There he continued to annotate everything he read, periodically shaping a pile of notes into an article and sending it off to a periodical. It was this method of reading and writing that was in large part responsible for the character of his literary output: a preoccupation with the works of others and a frequently erratic development of his thought.

II

In 1893, Sorel abruptly announced his conversion to Marxian socialism.[24] His work was already marked by a concern for moral renewal and contained some socialist implications. From a "society based on work," moreover, he had not far to go. Thus far he had indicated little interest in current political movements. His proximity to Paris, however, now placed him at the center of that ferment. His attention was undoubtedly drawn to socialist parliamentary successes in the elections of 1893, when their representation in the Chamber of Deputies rose dramatically from the handful of the 1880s to forty. These deputies represented five different parties all more or less Marxist, as well as the Independent Socialists, led by Jean Jaurès, who were vaguely humanitarian and egalitarian.

In a brief but enthusiastic letter to the editor of the *Revue philosophique* in May, Sorel embraced Marxism as an intellectual discipline.[25] He asked that Marxism be given a fair hearing as a science of history; no one, he said, had yet refuted Marx. The great merit of Marx lay in placing the study of society on an empirical basis: there were in Marxism no idealistic reveries. Sorel was as yet reluctant to accept any Marxian program or to identify himself with any faction. He warned that "Jacobin demagogues" (he did not identify them) exploited socialism for their own purposes. Society risked the gravest dangers when abandoned to these agitators.

That same May he published his first article in Italy, on the renowned Italian anthropologist Cesare Lombroso's work on political crime.[26] The essay's publication marked the beginning of Sorel's growing interest in the Italian scene as well as in the Italian tradition of political realism and emphasis on the psychology of politics, but it was significant primarily for revealing the quality of Sorel's new Marxism. He distrusted "audacious minorities" and saw a striking similarity between the "revolutionary type" and the "criminal type."

He denounced both Blanquists and, especially, anarchists whose dynamitings and assaults had reached a peak in the early 1890s. He did not, however, clearly indicate what kind of socialism he preferred.

Sorel soon joined the editorial staff of the Marxist *Ère nouvelle,* the first of many such involvements.[27] The review was founded in late 1893 by Georges Diamandy, a Roumanian student given to public orations in the Latin Quarter. It vaguely supported the views of Jules Guesde, who as head of the Parti Ouvrier Français had assumed the mantle of Marxist orthodoxy in the highly fragmented socialist movement. How Sorel established relations with Diamandy is unknown, but in 1894, just before the demise of the review, Sorel published two lengthy articles in which he clarified the recent transition in his thought.

"L'Ancienne et la nouvelle métaphysique" was remarkable for Sorel's apparently complete identification with the economic determinism of Marx, as well as for his discovery of a young professor at the Collège de France, Henri Bergson.[28] In industrial techniques was to be found, Sorel insisted, man's source of knowledge. The cosmic world can never be known. A new mechanical device which utilized the forces of nature was therefore "an advance into the unknown." Sorel attempted to show the intimate relation between the use of tools and the moral transformation of society.[29] Bergson had demonstrated that man reasoned by means of images or *"supports expressifs"*; Marx before him had said much the same. These images were "in the air," and their quality was determined by the material environment. Sorel concluded that the morals of a social order could not be changed as long as industrial techniques remained unaltered. Capitalism, Sorel was convinced, had failed to utilize all of the opportunities opened by modern technology. Hence his allegiance to Marxian socialism: "Moral progress is dependent upon economic progress.... Science and ethics are nourished by the same soil."[30]

A curiously different slant was to be found in "La Fin du paganisme": it was pervaded far more by the moralism of Proudhon than by the economic determinism of Marx, and it was characterized by an attitude toward Christianity far removed from his 1889 study of the Bible.[31] His concern here, as in his study of the trial of Socrates, was "decadence." Roman society in the first centuries of our era, he maintained, lost its sense of the "seriousness of life." The idea of war became repugnant. This *"sagesse bourgeoise"* was fatal, for the frontiers were indefensible. At this decisive moment appeared the *"mal religieux"*—Christianity. It sowed the seeds of quietism, of despair, and of death. It "emancipated" the individual from the collectivity; everyone became concerned with personal spiritual problems. Contemporary society, Sorel insisted, was in comparable danger.[32] A "bourgeois mentality" had triumphed over the "warrior spirit." Hypocrisy in matters of morals had become an instrument of social preservation. Even the church had failed: its policy had always been one of accommodation, of survival with any and all regimes. Utopian socialism Sorel believed comparable to early Christianity in its pursuit of "personal happiness." Only in Marxian socialism did he perceive a new source of vitality: it was a doctrine which recognized the need for economic progress as a prerequisite to a new order. It was a movement rooted in a source of real energy, the workingman.

The *Ère nouvelle* did not last out the year 1894.[33] Some years later Sorel was to write that the Independent Socialists, notably Alexandre Millerand, one of its leading figures in the Chamber, did not favor the views expressed, particularly in his own articles. It is not clear, however, what objections were raised to Sorel's two articles or what action was taken against the periodical. In any case, the failure of the review soon led to another project.

The new review, *Devenir social,* was also essentially Guesdist.[34] It was founded by Alfred Bonnet, the former secretary of the *Ère nouvelle,* Gabriel Deville, who had produced an epitome of *Das Kapital* in French, Paul Lafargue, Marx's son-in-law, and Sorel. Sorel informs us that the *Devenir social* too was eyed with suspicion by the Independents. Millerand would not permit a notice announcing its appearance to be published in the *Petite république,* the organ of the Independents. From the beginning of 1895 to the end of 1897, however, Sorel's energies were devoted almost entirely to the new review.

For Sorel the years with the *Devenir social* marked an important stage in his apprenticeship.[35] He wrote about a third of the articles and reviews in the periodical. In order to create the illusion of a numerous editorial staff, he made use of various pseudonyms—"X," "David," "F," "B," "E," "E-G," and "G." His book reviews covered a range of literature well beyond the confines of Marxist theory—religion, science, psychology, philosophy, and history. It is likely that during these years he began to attend lectures at the Collège de France.[36] His articles frequently contained references to the lectures of the jurist and historian G. J. Flach and the sociologists Gabriel Tarde and, especially, Émile Durkheim, but Bergson's lectures evidently created the most powerful impact.

Late in 1895 Sorel began to correspond with Benedetto Croce. A letter in December had invited Croce to become a regular contributor to the *Devenir social* (and soon thereafter a similar tie was established with the historian Guglielmo Ferrero).[37] Antonio Labriola, contributor to both the *Ère nouvelle* and the *Devenir social,* had urged Sorel to write to Croce.[38] Labriola, professor of the philosophy of history at the University of Rome, had given considerable impetus to the discussion of Marxist theory in Italy and was widely regarded as Italy's leading theorist. Croce was in 1895 a pupil of Labriola's at the university and passionately interested in Marxism. Sorel's invitation to Croce, his junior by almost two decades, marked the beginning of a correspondence which was to be terminated only by the death of Sorel twenty-seven years later.[39] Their correspondence initiated an "intellectual cross-fertilization" of great moment for both men. Sorel's letters to Croce (published from 1927 to 1930) provide us with a continuing account, from 1895 on, of Sorel's intellectual development.

The studies Sorel began to write for the *Devenir social* from 1895 to 1896 now expressed a more critical attitude toward Marxism. Aroused, possibly, by his recent experience with Millerand (though he had never admired the world of politics) and by his correspondence with the youthful Croce, he undertook to revise his conception of socialism. In a series of articles he questioned the wisdom of relying entirely on socialist deputies.[40] The moral order might remain unchanged if socialism came to power by means of elections. The workers must rely more on their own efforts. Moreover, he attacked current educational practice as being only a preparation for the life of the salon.[41] Socialism had to provide an education which would prevent the revolutionary forces in modern industry from drying up. This was possible only in a factory where real productive relations obtained, where real work was done. He also challenged the "fatalism" in Marxism.[42] There was no necessary evolution toward socialism. There was much in history, he now discovered, that Marx could not account for—traditions, juridical survivals, national dissimilarities. Neither the history of antiquity nor of the Middle Ages, in fact, had ever been explained satisfactorily by Marx or any of his disciples. In these studies and in numerous minor articles and reviews Sorel raised serious doubts about the validity of Marxist doctrine and action.

Late in 1896, Sorel for the first time broached the subject of revolution in an extended study of Vico's *Scienza nuova*. The great eighteenth-century Neapolitan philosopher, he believed, had made a perfect distinction between two types of revolutions. Translated into modern terms, one was the work of a conspiratorial party which had as objective the seizure of the state in order to exploit public power. The other was the work of an exploited class seeking to introduce "new rights." Only when a revolution was a return to the "primitive" in man would it set free moral energies; only then was it a true *ricorso* or renewal. Sorel now adopted Vico's term and viewed the coming of socialism as a *ricorso*, but he noted the Marxist failure to give serious emphasis to the juridical and moral consequences of the class struggle. He still asserted that socialism must not break violently with the past: "The greatest revolution the mind can conceive will be the most peaceful."[43]

In his 1897 preface to Labriola's work on historical materialism, he summarized his conclusions and began to probe in new directions.[44] He saluted Italy as the one country where Marxism was seriously studied and singled out Labriola and Croce as having understood that historical materialism must not be confounded with economic determinism. One could not speak of determinism "since there is nothing determinable." Historical materialism was not a "grand plan" but an instrument of research, a method of historical inquiry. He argued that Marx was not really responsible for caricatures of his doctrine. Marx, he wrote, feared above all leaving behind a system which would be regarded as completed. Sorel urged Marxists to continue his work. At least two aspects of Marxism remained unfinished, its metaphysical base and its psychology. What Marxists must devote themselves to—and here he went beyond Labriola—was not idle speculation about the socialist society of the future but, rather, the action of the proletariat in the present class struggle. In the concept of "class consciousness," he was convinced, lay the key to the required action.

Articles of 1897 in the *Devenir social* and in the *Sozialistische Monatshefte,* a German Marxist review to which he contributed briefly, now set out to demolish what remained of the orthodox position associated with Guesde.[45] " 'Let's return to Marx,' that is my motto," he wrote to Croce in mid-1897.[46] But it was the spirit of Marx that he meant, not the letter. He attacked the Feuerbachian originals of Marxism, to which he attributed the master's failure to recognize the centrality of moral renewal.[47] To support his assertion that the existing bourgeois order could not be transformed by legislation he cited Vilfredo Pareto, the Italian sociologist—Sorel and Pareto had met in Paris that year and had begun to correspond.[48] He saw in the theory of surplus value a mere comparison between an abstractly perfect society and an actual one.[49] He asserted that Marxism would triumph only when it lost all ties with its founder;[50] he denied that under capitalism the rich got richer and the poor poorer;[51] and he observed that socialist intellectuals and politicians were on better terms with the bourgeoisie than they were with workers' organizations.[52]

The last article Sorel was to write for the *Devenir social,* on Saverio Merlino's *Pro e contro il socialismo,* appeared in 1897.[53] Sorel's reading of Merlino, editor of an Italian Marxist review, convinced Sorel that he had to break completely with orthodox Marxism. He now rejected the twofold division of classes; this was merely a symbolic representation of the class struggle. He denied that "dictatorship of the proletariat" could possibly mean direct administration by the masses; this he held "utopian." Sorel embraced Merlino's thesis that socialism must proceed without a doctrine: it must concentrate on development of the austerity and moral fervor which had characterized early Christianity. Socialism meant moral renewal.

In a letter to the editor published in December 1897 Sorel broke with the review.[54] He explained his departure to Croce.[55] The review, he was convinced, had no future. When in 1897 Edward Bernstein, the German Social Democrat, began his revision of orthodoxy in Germany, Sorel wanted the *Devenir social* to take part in the controversy. The periodical could have acquired prominence. Other members of the editorial staff, however, dissented. Lafargue, a pillar of orthodoxy, had, he told Croce, declared him a "heretic."

But Sorel would not be diverted from his attack: "Marx," he wrote, "ought to be translated into a modern language."

Marie-Euphrasie had died in April 1897.[56] Writing in June, he informed Croce that she had been "the companion of twenty-two years of work" to whom he was tied *"per la forza del primo amore."* He was never to forget her. Around his neck he would always wear a religious medal that had belonged to her. All of his letters thereafter were written on black-bordered stationery. He was now to live in Boulogne-sur-Seine with the family of her nephew, a masseur and bicycle racer, whom Sorel had adopted.

Sometime after the death of Marie-Euphrasie but before the announcement of his break with the *Devenir social,* Sorel's attention was drawn to syndicalism as perhaps being the authentic manifestation of the proletarian movement.[57] Following the example of Marx, he began to study the trade-union movement in England, demonstrating particular interest in a recent work by Paul de Rousiers on English trade-unionism. Simultaneously, he discovered French syndicalism.

Toward the end of 1897 Sorel began to frequent Paris regularly to sit and chat at the offices of *Humanité nouvelle,* where members of the staff of *Art social* also congregated.[58] Both reviews were anarchist, but among their number were some of the leading lights of French syndicalism, who had recently converted from anarchism. Sorel's impact on the small group of anarchists, syndicalists, and anarcho-syndicalists, most of them still in their twenties, has been described by Georges Valois. In the group was Fernand Pelloutier, a former anarchist who had become the apostle of anarcho-syndicalism. Since 1895 he had served as the secretary-general of the leading syndicalist organization, the Fédération des Bourses de Travail (FBT). He was dedicated to the principles of complete separation of the trade unions from political parties, revolution by the general strike, and the dissolution of the state and all its works. Paul Delesalle, by profession a machinist, was also an anarchist turned syndicalist. Others included the young Neapolitan anarcho-syndicalist Arturo Labriola, forced into exile in 1898. Valois himself was secretary of the *Humanité nouvelle,* an anarchist soon to become a syndicalist. When Sorel entered the office, Valois recalled some twenty-five years later, there was no more joking.[59] When he spoke everyone listened intently. It was not his age that commanded respect, but his words. He overwhelmed his young listeners by the breathtaking range of his culture, but he asked, wrote Valois, for no mandate, demanded no honor, looked for no influence: "He was the most sincere, modest, self-effacing man one can imagine."

The moment Sorel had digested the work of de Rousiers and studied the aims of Pelloutier, whose moralizing had profoundly impressed him, he revised once again his conception of the socialist movement. The result was the extended article, "L'Avenir socialiste des syndicats," published in the first half of 1898 in the *Humanité nouvelle*.[60] Sorel assailed the idea that socialism would come automatically, that the workers were a mere passive instrument of history. The proletariat had to achieve its emancipation by its own unaided efforts. Pelloutier's syndicalism, he asserted, was the reality of the proletarian movement that had been the subject of Marx's studies.

"L'Avenir" was, in part, an analysis of the methods to be employed by the proletariat. Sorel rejected the notion that the proletariat should achieve its goals solely by political action.[61] Politics was daily becoming more corrupt in France. Perhaps, he suggested, it would be better if political parties disappeared entirely. Politics was the true vocation of intellectuals. They would maintain the "hierarchy of capacities" that now placed workers under their direction. He argued that the transformation of society had to come about by "internal" means and through purely proletarian institutions.[62] The cooperative, the *mutualité*, the *solidarité* all met these requirements, but he considered them as auxiliaries of the trade unions or syndicates: "*The entire future of socialism resides in the autonomous development of workers' syndicates.*" The day-to-day operation of the syndicates would provide the proletariat with the training necessary for the socialist era. Without this preparation the end of the bourgeois order might mean the destruction of civilization. "It is within the fold of capitalist society that the new productive forces must develop, and also the relations of a new social order, what might be called the moral force of the future."[63] Sorel urged the syndicates to win new powers by all "peaceful" means: by interesting the public in their efforts, by denouncing abuses, by demonstrating the incapacity and lack of probity of public administration, and by demanding legislation favorable to their own development.[64] Sorel implicitly rejected Pelloutier's notion of revolution by the general strike. The existing order would be destroyed bit by bit as the syndicates took over everything of value in the existing order. Above all, the syndicates must be regarded as powerful mechanisms for the development of morality, and Sorel introduced a theme of continuing significance in his work: "It is not a question of knowing what is the best moral system, but only of determining if there exists *a mechanism capable of guaranteeing the development of morals.*"[65]

The socialist society of the future was also considered, though vaguely, in "L'Avenir."[66] Sorel rejected any kind of socialism in which the state was to be the master and regulator of industrial life. For this reason he opposed the "state socialism" of the Independents; the Saint-Simonian conception of the state, which he attributed to them, had become dangerously popular. For the same reason he also condemned the "dictatorship of the proletariat" advocated by Guesde; all dictatorships, democratic or otherwise, had in the past led to new abuses. He was at one, however, with Pelloutier's federalism. The federated syndicates would constitute the socialist "government" of the future. The syndicates would absorb only what socialism required in the way of government. Sorel, moreover, believed that socialism would be a catastrophe for intellectuals, notwithstanding their prominence in the movement. Political authority was currently based on the presumed superiority of men of intellect. Differences between persons in the socialist order, however, would be "quantitative," all work having become of the same kind, and hence interchangeable. His attitude toward professionals and women was reflected in his argument that many of the former could be dispensed with by utilization of the latter—women, for example, could serve as lawyers, doctors, and administrators. He saw in the socialist order, finally, a new morality defined in law. The relationship of seller to buyer and lender to borrower would be replaced by those which obtained in the syndicate. The readiness of some syndicates to accept free sexual union on the same basis as legal marriage indicated that "new rights" were already in formation. The syndicates were also capable of eliminating the vices of alcoholism and prostitution.

The study of the future of the syndicates was one of the most important of Sorel's career. It was the first work to command serious attention, though in limited circles. Parisian anarcho-syndicalists now regarded Sorel, notwithstanding his opposition to revolution, as their leading theoretician.[67] After its translation in 1903 Sorel could claim his first sizable following in Italy.[68] From Germany Bernstein wrote to Sorel that though he did not agree with some of the details of "L'Avenir," his attitude toward Marxism was substantially similar.[69] "I do not hate the politican as you do, but I am *en route*." But politics, Bernstein thought, might yet become an effective instrument of propaganda and education. The syndicates, in any case, also had their faults. "L'Avenir" and the reaction it produced convinced Sorel that his future lay with the Marxian "heresy" of syndicalism.[70] His letters to Croce in the first months of 1898 continued to denounce the "idealistic reveries" of Marxism. His articles, now also appearing in German and Italian periodicals, followed in the same vein, attacking "political" socialism, historical "fatalism," and the Marxist theory of value.[71]

III

Sorel abruptly revised his position in 1898 with the reopening of the Dreyfus affair. Initially a question of legal justice, it had become a struggle over the Third Republic itself. Sorel now came to the defense of Dreyfus and the Republic. Doing so required a drastic reversal of some of the crucial arguments in "L'Avenir," notably those on class collaboration and political action on the part of the proletariat. These and other reversals now followed in bewilderingly swift succession.

As early as January 1898 his name appeared among the first on a list of intellectuals demanding a new trial for Dreyfus.[72] Some years later he revealed that he had been very much aroused by the "stupid" socialist manifestoes which received wide publicity in the early days. That of January 19, 1898, had been signed by thirty-six socialist deputies who declared that the Dreyfus affair was a civil war among the bourgeoisie and of no concern to the proletariat. Another of July 24, prepared by Guesde, declared that "fatherland, right, and justice" were words devoid of sense in a capitalist society.[73]

In a preface to a study by Merlino published in France, Sorel urged the workers to enter the political arena and collaborate with the Dreyfusards.[74] The persecution of Dreyfus he thought a great moral issue. Socialists (with the notable exception of Jaurès, who had been won over to the Dreyfusards in July) were blind:

> *Socialism is a moral question* in the sense that it brings to the world a new manner of judging all human acts and, to employ a celebrated expression of Nietzsche, a new evaluation of all values. It is in this way that socialism must be compared with Christianity in the first centuries. . . . It stands before the bourgeois world as an irreconcilable adversary, menacing it with a *moral catastrophe* even more than a material one.[75]

Socialist deputies were fearful of losing their seats.[76] Doctrinaire Marxists wanted to condemn the workers to a sterile class struggle for material interests. The proletariat, Sorel insisted, had to fight for the emancipation of all who suffered—it must be no passive "agent" of history. The proletariat must be the "hero" of history: "the sole soldier, always armed, capable of defending Justice and Truth."

Writing to young Hubert Lagardelle, who in 1899 invited him to collaborate on the projected periodical *Mouvement socialiste,* Sorel was more explicit.[77] He assigned base motives to those who opposed Dreyfus's rehabilitation. If Dreyfus were freed, then the general staff would be dishonored. Some twenty years in officers' circles had made him familiar with the "special mores" of the army. In the anti-Dreyfusards he saw the danger of "caesarism" and an alliance of all elements opposed to the Republic: these included the Catholic clergy, the anti-Semites, the monarchists, and the remnants of the Boulangist movement, as well as high-ranking army officers. The controversies raging among socialists regarding the propriety of intervention convinced him of the utter "futility" of socialist theories. Without abstractions the Guesdists feared they could not justify Marxism as "scientific"; hence their refusal to support Dreyfus on the grounds that the class struggle was not at issue.[78] Only Jaurès and his working-class supporters recognized that socialism had to be based on practical experience, and that the first duty of socialism was to defend the Republic.

The controversy over the revision of Marxism and the battle to secure a new trial for Dreyfus soon became virtually identical for Sorel. In 1899 the "crisis in Marxism," which had been brewing since Bernstein in Germany, Croce in Italy, and Sorel in France had independently assailed orthodoxy, was "formally announced" by Bernstein. Sorel's efforts were now directed toward an exposition of Bernsteinian socialism from a Dreyfusard standpoint.[79] In a series of articles he now came to the defense of parliamentary socialism. He rejected entirely the "catastrophic" conceptions of orthodox Marxism.[80] Instead, he urged the proletariat to concentrate on improvement of its material conditions and to do so by "every" democratic means at its disposal.[81] A marked deterioration in his relations with Labriola ensued. Labriola was widely regarded as the champion of orthodoxy in Italy, as were Guesde in France and Karl Kautsky in Germany. Sorel had been severely critical of Labriola's failure to go far enough in his critique of Marxism. Labriola, aware that both Sorel and Croce had gone far beyond him, now denounced Sorel in his *Discorrendo di socialismo e di filosofia* of 1898 as "a herald of a war of secession" and accused Croce of "literary vanity and political ambition."[82]

Sorel's assault continued. He joined the staff of the Collège Libres des Sciences Sociales, an "adult education" center founded by Dreyfusards.[83] In a series of lectures at the Collège and in his first articles in Lagardelle's *Mouvement socialiste* and Merlino's *Rivista critica del socialismo* he challenged the orthodox conception of the class struggle. He now maintained that the class struggle was a battle between the new rising ethic and the old legal forms.[84] In the rigorously working-class socialist faction led by Jean Allemane, which had heretofore remained aloof but now supported the Dreyfusards, Sorel saw the best possible proof that there was a socialist ethic. He noted approvingly that the Allemanist workers supported that faction of the bourgeoisie which defended Dreyfus and democratic institutions. Sorel also insisted that Marx had been misinterpreted by his disciples.[85] The class struggle had not been for Marx a conflict of interests; at the core of the class struggle was an opposition between decisions made in conformity with existing law and man's eternal moral aspirations. The imperfections of Marxism, to be sure, both in the works of the master himself and in those of his disciples, were troublesome. Sorel nevertheless insisted that he was still a Marxist. Marx alone had attempted "to present a philosophical interpretation of the socialist movement," and the key to that interpretation was the concept of class struggle.[86] Sorel also bitterly assailed the church for meddling in the Dreyfus affair.[87] Christianity had no relevance for modern industrial society. Socialism was a movement of "producers," while the Gospel addressed itself only to "beggars."

Reaction to Sorel's unending critique of socialist orthodoxy was not long in coming. He had published articles denouncing orthodoxy in both socialist and non-socialist periodicals in France, Italy, and Germany, writing often with stinging hostility. He had been denounced by Lafargue. Both he and Croce had already been singled out publicly by Labriola as "heretics." In mid-1899 Sorel heard that *Avanti!*, the official organ of the Italian Socialist party, was attempting to pressure Merlino and Lagardelle into taking some kind of action against him. Sorel bristled. He wrote to Croce in June of his contempt for "official" socialism.[88] He had decided, he said, to break with the two reviews; he would no longer write for any socialist periodical. In brief articles in France and Italy in non-socialist reviews he denounced "official" socialism. He derided the idea of "salvation by a dictatorship of theoreticians,"[89] and he rejected completely the notion that motives of economic interest were decisive in history.[90]

Sorel attacked orthodoxy with renewed vigor with the opening of the *cas* Millerand. A ministry of "Republican Defense," headed by René Waldeck-Rousseau, had been formed on June 22, 1899, after a new trial had been ordered for Dreyfus. It was called to "save the Republic" in the face of a threatened coup. The cabinet included Millerand, the first socialist to accept a post in a non-socialist government. The question of ministerial participation gave a new turn to the quarrel among socialists.

The defense of ministerial participation was Sorel's immediate concern, notwithstanding his previous difficulties with Millerand. In his correspondence he continued to praise Jaurès for his efforts on behalf of Dreyfus, his defense of Millerand, and his leadership in the fight to secure reforms for the workers. "Jaurès has been irreproachable," he wrote to Lagardelle.[91] Guesde and his cohorts, on the other hand, were giving ample proof "that their theories are of no use." In his articles Sorel endeavored to demonstrate that Jaurès and Millerand were receiving their greatest support from precisely those socialists least interested in theory. The French workers in daily street battles with the forces of reaction were covering themselves with glory.[92] Among the "so-called doctors of international socialism," on the other hand, he saw only timidity and a preoccupation with scholastic formulae whose significance was without relevance.[93] As for the university intellectuals now joining the Socialist party, they were doing so because they had perceived that supporting Dreyfus and socialism had become profitable from an electoral standpoint. The workers would have to be on their guard in dealing with these parvenus.

The preface to the French edition of a study of socialism by the Italian deputy Napoleone Colajanni, published toward the end of 1899, and two lectures at the Collège early in 1900 marked a new stage in the development of Sorel's thinking.[94] These were published after the presidential pardon of Dreyfus in September, and they represented Sorel's views at the height of Dreyfusard prestige. Sorel placed himself squarely in the ranks of the defenders of social democracy.[95] The Dreyfus affair had demonstrated that socialism must henceforth work together with other popular parties. Millerand's entrance into the government meant the transformation of socialism from a sectarian to a political spirit, from abstract speculation to real life. Such a passage constituted real progress made under the duress of the affair.

Sorel also reformulated his conception of the impulse behind the socialist movement.[96] The dichotomic division of society Marx had posited, he was convinced, did not exist in the real world, but "it is one thing to make social science and another to inspire men's spirits." The division did exist in the minds and hearts of the militants in all great historical struggles. Marx had recognized this. The notion of class struggle was simply an insight into the method by which the proletariat could best be mobilized for great historic action. Marx was writing "social poetry," but his disciples had transformed his work into an "abstract doctrine." Sorel continued to insist that the question of highest importance in the construction of a socialist society was that of morality.[97] Statesmen considering legislation must always ask themselves what effect it would have on the family. No statement was of greater interest in this regard than the comment, full of Proudhonian overtones, that closed the preface: *"The world will become more just only to the extent that it becomes more chaste;* I do not believe that there is a truth which is more certain."[98] After the preface to Colajanni's study, Sorel could no longer be considered a Marxian socialist in anything but name. Valois recalled some years later that around 1900 he had met Sorel at the Bibliothèque Nationale and confided that he was preparing a study on socialism.[99] Sorel had replied: "You are wasting your time. Socialism is finished."

Sorel must have encountered the young Charles Péguy during the days of the affair; it was Péguy, poet, essayist, and editor, who was to provide Sorel with the opportunity to reach directly an entire generation of young men. There can be no certainty about the time or the place where they met: it may have been at one of Bergson's lectures at the Collège de France, which they both regularly attended; they may have been introduced by Lagardelle, a friend of both since mid-1898; or they may have met at some street *bagarre* when Péguy was the head of a very modest publishing establishment.[100] At the turn of the century Péguy was about thirty and Sorel almost a quarter of a century his senior. Péguy too was an ardent socialist and Dreyfusard and had participated in street brawls with his university friends.[101] He had also attacked "Guesdism" and had quarreled with Lucien Herr, librarian of the École Normale and among the first in the Université to join the ranks of the Socialist party. Péguy soon broke all formal ties with socialism, and in January 1900 he established the *Cahiers de la quinzaine,* soon to be located on the Rue de la Sorbonne in the same building as the Collège Libre. Next to Péguy's *Cahiers* were the offices of a syndicalist periodical, the *Pages libres,* directed by Charles Guieysse.

Undoubtedly Sorel had recognized a kindred spirit in Péguy and his young friends. Péguy had assembled a youthful literary elite for whom the Dreyfusard movement was to bolster a tottering social order—it was not to be used as a ladder to personal success. Péguy's formula printed on the flyleaf of the *Cahiers,* "The Revolution is moral, or nothing," must in itself have been something of a magnet. It was through the *Cahiers* that Sorel personally reached many other young men during the Dreyfus affair, and, more importantly, after it, when its sudden cessation left a void. Through the *Cahiers*

Sorel by 1900 knew intimately Lagardelle, Berth, and Guieysse, and when shortly thereafter he met Jean Variot, René Johannet, Julian Benda, Jean and Jérôme Tharaud, Daniel Halévy, and many others, the first three were already Sorel's followers. They were entirely taken up with the study of the working class. Their masters were "Proudhon in the past, Sorel in the present."[102]

Sorel's attack on orthodoxy continued until mid-1901. He championed Bernstein in his controversy with Kautsky over Marxian fundamentals, a controversy that now dominated international socialist polemics. Bernstein had returned, he believed, to the "spirit of Marx," while Kautsky, in defending the dialectic, was concerned with "the words, the appearances, the fossilized formulae."[103] Jaurès may have declared himself in favor of Kautsky, but Sorel believed Jaurès sided with Bernstein in every practical way. Sorel attacked Kautsky and the German Social Democrats in general for "pretending" to be revolutionary.[104] The German Social Democrats had merely adopted a revolutionary rhetoric; their elaborate organization, their tremendous funds, and their bourgeois-aristocratic leadership had transformed them into an integral part of the imperial regime. He also attacked the "catastrophic idea" in Marxism. A successful proletarian revolution was no longer possible. Barring a surprise attack, the state could defend itself—this had been conclusively established by the Commune. In any case, he did not believe a proletarian revolution was desirable; the employment of violence was incompatible with the introduction of a superior economic system. The transition to socialism required an "economic bridge," not a "political" one. The workers were capable neither of governing themselves nor of managing industry. Should a revolution occur, the proletariat would soon discover that it had merely changed masters.

At the same time, Sorel demonstrated renewed interest in Proudhon and returned to the argument presented in his "Préface pour Colajanni."[105] Proudhon, he charged, had suffered unwarranted neglect at the hands of French socialists.[106] The virtues of the ordinary life and the vanity of vulgar appetites were nowhere discussed in current socialist literature, nor was the social value of art. The destiny of socialist art lay in the identification of the beautiful with the useful. An aesthetic value, he asserted, had to be accorded to the great instruments of production. However, in an introduction to his *Saggi di critica del marxismo,* a collection of articles published in Italy and dedicated to his *"consorte adorata,"* he returned to the subject of "social poetry." Though he did not probe deeply, he began to speak here of "social myths."[107] The dogmatic aspects of Marxism interested him not at all, but he marvelled at the "extraordinary richness" of myths in Marxism. Like Plato, Marx was able to divine more than he had demonstrated: "If Marxism has had so great an influence on the popular masses it is above all because of the attractiveness of its myths."[108] He then dropped the subject of "social myths," not to return to it for several years.

In the meantime, he began to have misgivings about the Dreyfusards. The Republican bloc of radicals and socialists, it soon appeared to him, was not content with rehabilitating Dreyfus and discrediting his detractors. With passionate earnestness, the Dreyfusards were taking advantage of popular reaction against the anti-Dreyfusards. A policy of subordinating the military to civilians, of transferring the higher ranks to republicans, and of encouraging a spirit of pacifism was undertaken. As for the church, the passage of the Associations Law in July 1901 placed the religious orders at the mercy of the Chamber of Deputies. The overwhelming majority that the Republican bloc won in elections shortly thereafter was a mandate to proceed with vigor. In the forefront of those who demanded action was Jaurès.

In his correspondence, in articles, and in revisions of old articles Sorel attacked the bloc in general and Jaurès in particular. He denounced the "socialist fanatics" of pacifism and anticlericalism.[109] He did not take issue with an antimilitarism directed against the army as the instrument of a reactionary state, but antimilitarism was not to be confounded with a vulgar and unrealistic pacifism or antipatriotism. He was still convinced that the workers had nothing to learn from the church, but he cautioned against an anticlericalism that aimed at the church's total destruction.[110] In a society where state and church existed alongside of the bosses, the workers could maintain their independence. But what would happen if the state were all alone, possessing both temporal and spiritual supremacy? Sorel's attack on Jaurès was not yet public, but he was already writing to Lagardelle of "the false socialism of Jaurès." Jaurès was leading the "anticlerical and antipatriotic pack" for purely selfish reasons. Jaurès, by invoking the Declaration of the Rights of Man, pretended that his brand of socialism was superior to all others.[111]

An extended essay, "De l'église et de l'état," published in Péguy's Cahiers, appeared shortly after the passage of the Association Laws. Sorel was critical of the church for having opposed the retrial of Dreyfus but he cautioned against harsh reprisals.[112] The church had stupidly sacrificed the diplomatic work of many years to the interests of a "personal vendetta." It had revealed itself once again as a threat to liberty of thought, while the activities of the religious associations had demonstrated the need for stringent regulation. But he would not go further than Waldeck-Rousseau. The Concordat of 1801, which gave a preferred position to Catholicism, was not to be broken, and the suppression of the associations must not be "complete." The church must not be destroyed. Sorel was no longer a simple Dreyfusard, but he appeared to be saying that he was still a socialist.[113] The methods of democracy, he asserted, were essential to the progress of socialism. "The contradiction between democracy and socialism is essentially economic; their agreement . . . is spiritual." The threat to socialism and to liberty, however, came as much from the "caste" of "journalist-professors" who had rallied to the defense of Dreyfus as from the caste of priests. The "politico-scholastic" party, inspired by the "narrow ideas of the eighteenth century," had exactly the same spirit. The *université* was, in fact, an "antichurch" and the conflict between church and state was in reality a struggle between these two parties. Moreover, the motive for the journalist-professors' actions was, he maintained, simple revenge.

Dreyfusard espousal of what appeared to be a vulgar anticlericalism and antipatriotism had by now also repelled Péguy and many of his associates at the *Cahiers*.[114] In October 1901 the *Cahiers* moved to its historic home, 8 Rue de la Sorbonne. By then Sorel and Péguy possessed, according to the Tharaud brothers, parallel ideas on Dreyfus and the Dreyfusards, on socialism and *Jaurèsisme,* and on democracy and those who exploited it.

"Thursdays" at the *Cahiers* were a revered institution for the collaborators and friends of Péguy. Every Thursday Péguy opened the door and let his friends flock in. Facing Péguy, seated on a straw chair in the corner of the room which no one would have dared usurp, was "M. Sorel," as they all called him. As Halévy points out, it was his white beard, his immense experience, and his 54 years which were venerated in 1901 by young men who were, for the most part, in their mid-twenties and whose experience was nil. The Tharauds have described Sorel during these years:

> I liked *"le père Sorel,"* as we called him among ourselves, immensely. He was a robust old man, with a complexion fresh as a child's, white hair, a short white beard, and remarkable eyes, the color of Parma violet, which suggested to me the Vikings, his Norman ancestors.[115]

At the *Cahiers* office Sorel continued the "talks" begun in 1897 at the *Humanité nouvelle.* "Besieged by a pack of friendly young people who fired questions" at him, Sorel improvised rapid answers: "Everything which occurred in the universe was weighed, criticized, husked, analyzed, reduced to wafers, to pellets, and prepared with a thousand different sauces."[116]

If Thursday was the day Péguy and his friends devoted to Sorel, on Fridays the crowd, accompanied by Sorel, paid homage to Bergson at the Collège de France.[117] Bergson was very much in vogue during the first decade of the century, drawing to his lectures men of widely differing political persuasion. He attempted to expose the weak spots in positivist thought, in the determinism and scientific dogmatism of the day. Sorel found in Bergson's philosophy a justification of his own. What appealed particularly to Sorel, as well as to many others in the audience, was Bergson's effort to transform the whole conception of reality by placing the accent on intuition as the key to truth and on the creative forces of life, a life whose course was often unforeseeable and irrational. Perhaps Sorel had begun to perceive during these years affinities between Bergson's "intuition" and his own scarcely probed notion of "social myths."

Sorel's faith in parliamentary socialism faded rapidly through the final months of 1901 into early 1902. He now confided to Croce that Millerand's entrance into a bourgeois cabinet had not aided the proletarian cause. To Lagardelle he wrote that Jaurès's hypocrisy as a socialist had been fully demonstrated by his daughter's communion.[118]

A series of prefaces revealed the extent of his disenchantment. In a new edition of "L'Avenir" he protested the invasion of the workers' movement by "socialists of the chair" (socialist professors).[119] He urged the syndicalists to combat the program of Saint-Mandé that Millerand in 1896 had proposed as the minimum reform to be achieved by the ballot. He now accepted completely Pelloutier's notion of the general strike free from the direction of politicians. The same theme appeared in a preface to a study by Giuseppe Gatti, the Italian socialist deputy, where Sorel deplored the state of socialism in France, but looked hopefully to Italy.[120] Italy seemed to him the only country where Marxist criticism was worked at seriously. "Italy," he wrote, "has been the educator of Europe; she could well assume that role once again." He also speculated on the possibility of a "psychological interpretation of history":

All our current psychology has been imagined in order to describe the life of the upper classes, and the ordinary psychological interpretation of history is wholly superficial because it assumes that almost everything in history depends on the feelings of high society.[121]

A preface to Pelloutier's posthumous study of the FBT reveals Sorel's complete disillusionment with both the Bernsteinian revision of Marxism and the methods of the Dreyfusards.[122] Bernstein too had raised false hopes. The day the socialists acquired a particle of power they became indistinguishable from other political parties. The socialist politicians, furious at government opposition to them in the Dreyfus affair, went to the people, their speeches full of hatred against the church and the army, and conquered the masses by demagogy. Now in office, they, and the Dreyfusards in general, used their power with the same selfish immorality as those whom they had displaced. The workers alone had covered themselves with glory. He recalled his consideration in 1896 of Vico's *ricorsi*—"recommencements," he called them here—and he saw just such a renewal in Pelloutier's movement. He expressed the hope that the Confédération Générale du Travail (CGT), which was on the point of fusion with the FBT, would maintain the course set by Pelloutier before his untimely death in 1901.

There was repeated probing in new directions by 1902. He traced the "democratic prejudices" in socialism to the "utopians" who had carried eighteenth-century illusions into the nineteenth century.[123] In opposition to the concept of "citizen" he raised the concept of "worker." The "citizen" was an eighteenth-century abstraction; the "worker" was a "living instrument" fashioned by the historic conditions of capitalism. In opposition to a democratically determined "general will" he asserted the concept of "class struggle." Collaboration of classes necessarily meant that class differences could be resolved only by morally questionable "bargains"; class struggle was the path to liberation and triumph. The social sciences, he asserted, ought to be devoted to the determination of what social action was currently possible.[124] The purpose of the social sciences was to distinguish between freedom and necessity. There was no necessary evolution toward socialism; capitalism was still capable of producing new productive forces. Socialism was only a possibility, but the material bases for socialist production, he argued, already existed.[125] What remained was to win the workers over to socialism. And he quoted Engels: "To let loose a tempest in the masses one must present to them their own interests in a religious guise."[126]

The policies of the ministry of Émile Combes produced an even sharper reaction. When Combes came to power after the election of May 1902, he proceeded to enforce the Associations Law with a vigor at which Waldeck-Rousseau had balked. Almost all religious orders except those engaged in missionary and hospital work were denied authorization and were formally dissolved. Combes was also giving serious attention to an even more startling proposal—the separation of church and state by the abrogation of the Concordat of 1801. Jaurès, the leader of the parliamentary socialists, led the demand for "reprisals."

Somewhat paradoxically, Sorel came simultaneously to the defense of the traditional church and to that of orthodox Marxism. The material losses of the church did not greatly distress him; what did disturb him were the arguments of Catholics who counselled the church not only to submit but to "modernize" in accordance with the "progressive" ideas of the day.[127] Catholicism, he asserted, must be treated with respect. There was nothing in science that could be regarded as anti-Catholic, no demonstrable proof either for or against miracles. He urged Catholics not to give way in favor of modernism. The "mystique" in Catholicism would save the church, just as it always had in the past.

As for orthodox Marxism, Sorel once again collaborated briefly on a review that expressed the views of Guesde and Lafargue, the *Études socialistes*. These articles, for the most part, possessed little that was "orthodox."[128] Their primary concern, a theme which also appeared in his correspondence in 1903, was to link "reformist" socialism and "moderate" Catholicism as debasers of their respective doctrines, prepared to compromise with a common enemy—democracy.[129]

In April 1903 Sorel wrote to Croce: "I have never asked myself the question, 'What would be the synthesis of my diverse writings?' I write from day to day according to the needs of the moment."[130] That was to remain true to his death. But since he had started to write, notwithstanding the often erratic and contradictory development of his thought, at least one theme had never been dropped, the theme of his preoccupation with decadence and his search for moral renewal. With the publication in 1903 of the *Introduction à l'économie moderne,* the first work of book length to appear since 1889, the central problems to be discussed in this study came into sharper focus. This work clearly committed Sorel to the support of a revolutionary *ricorso,* to revolutionary syndicalism.[131] His first fully developed theory of revolution was presented here. Moreover, Sorel's following in both France and Italy had by 1903 crystallized into recognizable groups committed to a "cult of violence."

Revolutionary Syndicalism

Sorel's attraction to revolutionary syndicalism coincided with its "heroic" period, the first decade of the twentieth century. The movement developed with peculiar force in France and Italy, where the virtues of great strikes, work stoppages, sabotage, violent manifestations, and collisions with the police and army were both preached and practiced by workingmen. The movement reflected in many ways the persistence of localist and artisanal traditions, in contrast to the more disciplined and organized trade-union movements in industrially advanced Britain and Germany. It was impelled by stagnation in real wages, by unemployment, by the harshness of employers and the repression of the state, and, possibly, by the growing threat of industrial concentration and mechanization. As it emerged, revolutionary syndicalism tended to develop on two more or less distinct levels. There was, first, the practical day-to-day operation of the syndicates as conducted by its working-class militants, and there was also theoretical exposition of the methods and purposes of the movement by "intellectuals" who endeavored to find in syndicalist life the embodiment of their syndicalist doctrines.

Revolutionary syndicalism in France took concrete form in 1892 when the non-Guesdist syndicates founded the FBT. Under Pelloutier as secretary-general in 1895, the FBT pursued two ideals: emancipation by direct action (as opposed to political action) and federalism or anarchism (as opposed to "statism"). The FBT was not destined to enjoy a monopoly of the forces of labor. Apart from the Guesdist unions, there were still towns that possessed syndicates but no labor exchanges, there were national federations of craft and industry, and there were many ardent syndicalists who objected to both revolutionary methods and anarchist goals. The CGT was established in 1895 as an organization which, with no intention of superseding the FBT, attempted such comprehensiveness as to include it (if it cared to join), as well as all other groupings that stood aloof from political parties. It posed as the guardian-in-chief of the laboring class. It urged the workers to fight and to do so without the aid of the bourgeoisie or their institutions. There can be little doubt that up to 1900 the FBT constituted the chief stronghold of the labor movement, which explains its attraction for Sorel in 1898. The CGT could accomplish little, for Pelloutier's organization had already enrolled the most active organizations; it was compelled to rely principally on the national federations, the majority of which were still in an embryonic and precarious state. In fact, Pelloutier regarded the CGT as a hostile organization. The doctrinal differences between the two were, however, minimal. Both were dominated by ideas of revolution, repelled by political action, and convinced that a general strike alone would bring down the hated regime and introduce a society based on the trade unions.

The merger of the two groups was finally attained through the force of circumstances. When in June 1899 Millerand had accepted a post in Waldeck-Rousseau's cabinet, the theory of political action was put to the severest test.

The efforts of Millerand, once in office, were devoted to raising the standard of working-class life and averting class war. Violent protests were soon raised by revolutionary socialists: they decried Millerand's work as an attempt to turn the syndicates into administrative machines at the service of the government. They railed at the "democratic peril" and professed to see no difference between the work of Millerand and that of the most bourgeois of the bourgeoisie. All this was pure loss to the socialists, but the syndicalists reaped no little advantage from the hostility to Millerand and to parliamentary socialism in general. Many who had expected much from political activity were at last disillusioned. Socialism was being hopelessly wrecked by politics. The offices of the CGT were now invaded by revolutionary socialists like Victor Griffuelhes and anarchists like Émile Pouget and Sorel's young friend Paul Delesalle. They combined to overwhelm whatever tendencies there may have been toward reformism. Their *Voix du peuple* became the tribune of the CGT, registering its complaints and affirming its demands. With such a spirit animating the CGT, union with the FBT was only a matter of time. When Pelloutier died in 1901, it was only a question of satisfying the amour propre of both parties. Agreements were soon reached, and were sanctioned by congresses of both organizations in the autumn of 1902. After January 1, 1903, organized labor in France was represented in a single body, a new and revised CGT, in which the labor exchanges on the one hand and the industrial federations on the other, though keeping their individuality and autonomy, united to pursue a common policy— and that policy was revolutionary.

The CGT was controlled by men who preached war against the bourgeoisie and war against the state, but it did contain a not inconsiderable element inclined to more moderate methods. In fact, after 1902 within the CGT was waged an almost incessant struggle between reformists and revolutionaries. The Congress of Bourges, however, in September 1904 sealed, for some years at least, the fate of reformists. The control of the CGT (claiming then a mere 158,000 members), was vested in the more revolutionary syndicates. The eight-hour workday became their immediate goal, and it was to be achieved by means of direct action. One might say that it was at the Congress of Bourges that revolutionary syndicalism was adopted by the CGT as a guiding principle in the struggle against the bourgeois order. The movement had thus far been the work of its working-class militants. In 1903–1904, after revolutionary syndicalism in France had become a reality, it began to win the serious attention of "intellectuals." Among the contributors to Lagardelle's periodical, the *Mouvement socialiste,* were some who began to see in the movement possibilities as yet unsuspected by its militants.

Revolutionary syndicalism in Italy did not develop along the same lines as the French movement. The Italian working-class organizations at the end of the century included the *camere del lavoro* (labor exchanges comparable to the *bourses du travail*) and the national trade federations. Organized locally, the *camere* were, as in France, stronger and more numerous than the national unions. When they grew to prominence during the decade 1890–1900, the former were naturally concentrated in the more industrialized north of Italy. Their purpose was to provide a central local organization for the various leagues already in existence, for purposes of resistance as well as for dealing with practical working-class problems.

The syndicalist movement in Italy was on all levels more active, variegated, and subtle than its French counterpart, something Sorel had, perhaps, taken into account in his "Preface" to Gatti in 1902. There was a deeper discontent with democratic processes in Italy; "Giolittismo," a synonym for the flagrant abuse of electoral and parliamentary practices, was at its height. The labor movement exhibited considerably greater differentiation, stemming from local differences and emphasis on local autonomy as well as from divergences among industrial and agricultural organizations; agricultural syndicates were to play a particularly important role in the development of revolutionary syndicalism in Italy. There was, moreover, far deeper involvement by university intellectuals and socialist politicians in the affairs of workers, giving to Italian syndicalism greater doctrinal and tactical subtlety; though incompatible with his own view of syndicalism, Sorel was obliged to accept this fact of life in Italy.

The Segretariato Nazionale della Resistenza was formed in Milan in 1902 in an effort to coordinate the activities of all local and some twenty-four national unions claiming a membership of about 480,000, about half of which was agricultural. Intellectuals representing the various schools of socialist thought attempted to influence and control the Segretariato Nazionale. Among them were those who, though formally members of the Socialist party, were essentially syndicalist in outlook. Their principal organ was the *Avanguardia socialista* of Milan. They passionately desired to launch in Italy a syndicalism comparable to that which had appeared in France, seeing in a revolutionary labor movement extraordinary possibilities for the future. To a far greater extent than the CGT, the Segretariato Nazionale was an organ in which theoreticians and militants were working allies.

The collaboration bore fruit in September 1904, when there occurred the first successful general strike the world had ever witnessed. A strike among agricultural workers in Sicily was the spark. The fiery Arturo Labriola, the leading Italian theoretician and co-director of the *Avanguardia socialista* (not to be confused with Antonio Labriola, the orthodox Marxist), won over the Milan *camera* to a proclamation of a general strike. The outbreak spread like wildfire from Milan through the rest of Italy, though the strike had been called in opposition to reformists both in the Socialist party and in the Segretariato Nazionale. The successes of September 1904 worked in Italy an effect similar to

28

that of the Congress of Bourges. The revolutionary syndicalist movement was now launched in Italy also as a current of the first magnitude aimed at the destruction of the bourgeois order by the general strike.

What Sorel had already begun to say, and was about to develop further, appeared to be relevant to the labor movements in France and Italy rather than to the more highly industrialized societies he really did not understand.

Chapter

2

The Man

Beginning in 1903, Sorel's hopes for renewal were grounded in his perception of the methods and purposes of revolutionary syndicalism. He had been drawn to the movement ever since the publication of "L'Avenir" in 1898, but his attention and, indeed, the thrust of his thinking had been diverted by the Dreyfus affair. Lagardelle's 1899 offer of collaboration with the *Mouvement socialiste* was still open.[1] For the time being, however, Sorel envisaged other projects.

His *Introduction à l'économie moderne,* published in 1903, was an attempt to formulate a theory of revolution consistent with the "spirit of Marxism."[2] Sorel endeavored to demonstrate that "reform" could influence only the most superficial aspects of the social order.[3] Fundamental changes, those involving *morale,* could be altered only by revolution—he returned to a theme of his 1896 study of Vico. History must be viewed as a series of epochs, each characterized by a value and juridical system, each dominated by an essential principle. "Revolutionary myths" were popular representations of a catastrophic transformation of this principle. In revolutionary syndicalism he saw such a movement. The workers were determined to destroy capitalist democracy. They had resolved to establish a "society of producers." They aimed at political neutralization of the community, analogous to the "suppression of friction in a machine."

The *Introduction* was no great success as a publishing venture, even though it included Sorel's first extended analysis of revolutionary myths.[4] The work was poorly structured and frequently abstruse; Sorel himself had no high hopes for it. He wrote to Croce that the socialists would undoubtedly stifle it by silence and savants in general would be scandalized by his "aesthetic" approach to history.

Though deeply involved from 1903 to 1905 in the preparation of two long studies,[5] Sorel found time for his usual diversions. He regularly took the tram from Boulogne-sur-Seine to visit his favorite haunts in the Latin Quarter. He regularly appeared at Péguy's bookshop on the Rue de la Sorbonne on Thursdays and assiduously attended Bergson's lectures at the Collège de

31

France on Fridays.[6] He appears to have attended other lectures and meetings as well:[7] at an October 1905 meeting of the Société Française de Philosophie, for example, he spoke at a session devoted to the mysticism of St. Theresa.[8] The herald of the workers' revolution by the general strike must have startled his audience by coming to the defense of the "miraculous" in Catholicism. Visions, he asserted, should not be dismissed as "psychological disorders." The door must be left open to "other explanations." Paradoxically, he also continued to maintain his ties with the Dreyfusard École des Hautes Études Sociales, the former Collège Libre.[9] These were, nevertheless, financially difficult years. His books were not selling well. Perhaps to supplement his meager income, he prepared numerous brief items for a bibliographical review.[10]

Sorel's correspondence and briefer articles reveal him to have been dismayed by events in France but heartened by the activities of the Italian syndicalists. To Croce he wrote early in 1904 that he sensed a profound decadence in Socialist parties throughout Europe; the French and Italian parties, particularly, were becoming an "*exercise de clown*."[11] In two articles he discussed for his Italian readers the consequences of the Dreyfus affair.[12] The conservative parties in France, the republican elite, had been completely discredited, he asserted, and the affair had climaxed with a "Jacobin restoration." The conquest of the state had been from the very start the sole objective of the Dreyfusards. He was elated by the Italian general strike of September 1904.[13] At the head of the movement was Labriola, one of his Italian admirers. The Milanese syndicalists, he asserted, really understood what Marx meant by the class struggle. Events in France early the following year threw him into a rage. He had nothing but contempt, he told Croce, for the world of politics.[14] He was disgusted by the Syveton scandal, which revealed the role of the Freemasons in the campaign to "republicanize" the army, and by the *Guerre sociale,* Gustave Hervé's weekly, which promoted desertions from the army. Both, he thought, were characterized by a vulgar antimilitarism.

Sorel's two major works of 1905 were published in Italy and France, respectively. The first was devoted to the rising syndicalist movement, the second to the origins of Christianity. Both studies were pervaded by a theme that had appeared in his work in 1902–1903: the virtues of intransigence. The *Insegnamenti sociali della economia contemporanea* was a rather drastic revision, for his Italian readers, of the *Introduction* of 1903. He repeatedly made invidious comparisons between his own France and Italy. The French, for example, were too much preoccupied with scandal, while the Italians demonstrated a genuine interest in Marxist theory. Though the *Introduction* had received little attention in his native land, he hoped that "in the land of Vico" he would find "more competent judges."[15] The French syndicalist movement languished, but its Italian counterpart demonstrated far greater vigor—the French, he feared, had undergone a moral and material decline as a result of the long period of peace since 1871. In the *Insegnamenti* he presented for the first time a conception of revolutionary violence that would maintain class divisions between proletariat and bourgeoisie.[16] He opposed as a relapse into reformism the agitation among French syndicalists for the eight-hour workday. He now once again insisted on the value of the "catastrophic idea" in Marxism as essential to the formation of revolutionary myths.

The same general notions appeared in *Le Système historique de Renan*. Though harshly rejecting much, Sorel took what he needed from Renan's work on the origins of Christianity.[17] At the same time, he included what had been "worthwhile" in the *Contribution* of 1889. Sorel viewed the origins of Christianity as a problem in the psychology of the masses. His attention was primarily centered upon the uncompromising character of early Christian literature and upon the influence of the Christian persecutions in the development of a revolutionary mythology. He returned again to Vico—the rise of Christianity was the classic example of a *ricorso*. The Christian conquest was for him also something of a standard against which contemporary social movements were to be measured. Primitive Christianity provided him with a principle of revolutionary action which he believed applicable to the proletarian movement, "*la scission chrétienne*":

> There is a great analogy between gnosticism and the socialism of the cultivated of today; *the big question is still that of scission*; but it does not seem that socialism has nearly the resources that primitive Christianity had to maintain its separateness. Violent strikes have the same value as the ancient persecutions.[18]

Someday, he hoped, he would treat these matters from the point of view of the workers' movement.[19]

The two studies of 1905 made little impression on either the socialist world or the general public. Sorel, in fact, had anticipated as much. In a correspondence with the young student of politics, Roberto Michels, that began in 1905, Sorel complained that "official" socialists were boycotting his books and had been doing so for years.[20] The official attitude had always been to maintain silence about anything that did not carry the seal of their approval. The *Ère nouvelle* and the *Devenir social* had been destroyed in this way. The same tactic was now being employed against the *Mouvement socialiste*. Moreover, he warned Michels that the socialists would boycott him also if he insisted that Sorel write a preface for one of his works. For a projected Italian edition of "L'Avenir," Sorel's preface of 1905 considered still other reasons for his failure as a writer—the stylistic ones of disorderly exposition frequently confounded by obscure language.[21] These defects, he recognized, were fatal in France, where clarity of expression was often equated with soundness of thought. He avoided precise terms, he said, because he believed they distorted the ideas he was attempting to convey. Too great exactitude in language "would be in contradiction with the fluid character of reality, and in this way language would be deceptive."

Notwithstanding their shortcomings, Sorel's publications and the heightened activity of syndicalist movements in France and Italy had by mid-1905 given rise to an active school of writers who looked to Sorel as their *maître*: in France, they called themselves the Nouvelle École, and in Italy, Neo-Marxismo.[22]

Lagardelle's *Mouvement socialiste* became the organ of the group in France. When founded in 1899, the review had at Sorel's own bidding taken a Dreyfusard and reformist position. Lagardelle's experience as a Dreyfusard had paralleled Sorel's, so that when in September 1904 at the Congress of Bourges the CGT decided in favor of a revolutionary program, Lagardelle indicated that he too was prepared to adopt a "serious" program. Since the foundation of the review Sorel had a standing invitation to make regular use of it; several of his articles had already been published in it. In July 1905 Sorel began regular publication.[23] With a number of other "theoreticians" he hoped to establish a "seminar" in which leading militants of the CGT were included, though the theorists resolved not to mix in the internal politics of the CGT. Sorel immediately assumed the role of leading spokesman for the *Mouvement socialiste*.

In Italy the *Divenire sociale* of Rome, which began publication in January 1905 under the direction of professor of political economy and journalist Enrico Leone, was generally regarded, especially after the demise of Labriola's *Avanguardia socialista,* as the leading syndicalist doctrinal review in Italy. Here, as in the *Mouvement socialiste,* Sorel's articles in mid-1905 received the lead position.[24] Here also, a group of Italian writers whose articles also appeared frequently in the *Mouvement socialiste* looked to him for guidance as they attempted to instill in the militants under the Segretariato Nazionale confidence in their mission of emancipation.[25]

Sorel's association with the *Divenire sociale* and the *Mouvement socialiste* was highlighted in 1905–1906 by the appearance of a series of articles on the merits of violence in general and the general strike in particular; this was the first version of the celebrated *Réflexions sur la violence,* which appeared in book form two years later.[26] The articles were written in the atmosphere of battle prevailing in syndicalist quarters during those years.[27] In France the CGT was fighting for the eight-hour workday and planning a general strike for May 1, 1906. In Italy the syndicalists were fighting the army and the police in city streets and in the countryside. The labor movement was on the verge of unification, and syndicalist intellectuals within the Socialist party were about to achieve the height of their influence at the party congress planned for October 1906. The immediate consequence of the publication of Sorel's articles on violence was his retirement from the post of administrator at the École des Hautes Études

Sociales.[28] Their publication produced an "uproar" in this bourgeois and Dreyfusard institution, subventioned by the state, that Sorel had urged the workers to destroy. Sorel was disturbed by the reaction and at first refused to resign.[29] He wrote to Lagardelle in January 1906, defending his right to belong to an organization whose views he did not hold, but he shortly afterward decided to withdraw in order to save the institution embarrassment.

Michels, who attended their gatherings around 1906, has described the truly international circle of syndicalists and their sympathizers in Paris with whom Sorel had established social as well as intellectual ties.[30] There was little about them that could be considered subversive. For a number of years they met with their wives at Lagardelle's for Sunday afternoon tea, with Lagardelle's aristocratic Russian wife acting as hostess. Frequent guests (besides Sorel) were young Berth, a contributor to the *Mouvement socialiste* and Sorel's closest friend; the militant Delesalle, a leading figure of the CGT; Griffuelhes, the secretary of the CGT; Alphonse Merrheim, also an official of the CGT; Salvatore Piroddi, translator of Sorel's articles for the *Divenire sociale* and himself a contributor to the Italian periodical; and Georges Weill, the historian of socialism. Now and then others would attend: Labriola, Paolo Mantica, and Alfredo Niceforo, all Italian syndicalists; Edward Beneš, later president of Czechoslovakia; and Christian Racowski, later Soviet ambassador to France.

Sorel, according to Michels, was invariably the center of attraction at these affairs. He was "very bourgeois" and "old-fashioned" in his appearance. He was by temperament a man of letters rather than a revolutionary, and, oddly enough, always wore the ribbon of the Legion of Honor in his buttonhole. Sorel was adored by his group; they hung on his every word. He was intransigent and intolerant and very distrustful of the Jews (a distrust not yet in evidence in his writings). He repeatedly attacked the "impure," declared himself against the "inveiglers of women," and insisted on premarital chastity for both sexes. "I was struck," wrote Michels, by his *"fondo cattolico."* The final victory, Sorel believed, would go to the class that was "most integral, most concentrated, and most moral."

The "heroic" period of revolutionary syndicalism reached its climax in France and Italy almost simultaneously in 1906: membership in the CGT had reached about 300,000, and Italian syndicalists numbered about 200,000, but, events revealed the limits of the two movements' revolutionary potential.[31] Sorel, disheartened by the developments, reacted most sharply to events in France.

The general strike in France on May 1, 1906, had been called to secure the eight-hour day. From the start Sorel opposed its objective.[32] The idea of a shortened workday he believed utopian and alien to the spirit of a "society of producers." Moreover, the strike had brought about a reconciliation between syndicalist officials and socialist politicians that infuriated him.[33] Before the strike and immediately preceding the general elections that followed, the story of a syndicalist-monarchist plot against the Republic had been circulated in the press. This story, he was convinced, was an invention of the police. He denounced the Clemenceau government for attempting to make political capital of the charges. In a letter to Lagardelle late in May he demanded that Lagardelle protest publicly in the *Mouvement socialiste*.[34] Lagardelle promptly did so, but the CGT militants Griffuelhes and Émile Pouget, whose need was to reach the great mass of the workers, had no organ other than the weekly *Voix du peuple* in which to defend themselves against the charge of being secret allies of the monarchists. They consequently accepted Jaurès's offer to defend themselves in the *Humanité,* the organ of the Socialist party, Section Française de l'Internationale Ouvrière (SFIO), unified the preceding year. To Sorel, this collaboration was treacherous.[35] He saw in the *Humanité* a campaign designed specifically to ensnare the CGT into a policy of joint action with socialist politicians. He was convinced, moreover, that Jaurès was out to destroy both the syndicalist movement and the influence of the *Mouvement socialiste*. By the end of 1906 Sorel's contempt for French socialist politicians knew no bounds, as his public statement in December testifies.[36] In democratic politics he saw only a struggle for public spoils, a struggle he called "criminal." His patience with French syndicalism had been severely tried.

Events in Italy in 1906 were equally discouraging. Among leaders of the Segretariato Nazionale, to say nothing of the reformist national trade federations, the long-run effect of the rampantly uncontrolled general strike of 1904 was a perceptible swing to reformism, notwithstanding the continuation of syndicalist militancy.[37] Through the efforts of reformists in the labor movement and with the sympathetic support of reformists in the Socialist party, the "unification" of labor (at first, some 200,000) was achieved at a congress in Milan late in September with the formation of the Confederazione Generale del Lavoro (CGL), modelled on the CGT. The CGL was born almost simultaneously with the party congress of Rome that met in October. At the congress, syndicalist intellectuals reached the height of their influence within the party, but to no avail—the party remained solidly in the hands of reformists. With these defeats in 1906, syndicalists found it difficult to decide whether to oppose the CGL and the Socialist party from outside or within their respective organizations. Sorel was now clearly distraught by these setbacks.[38] When some syndicalists left both the CGL and the Socialist party, he speculated about the possibility of the formation of a syndicalist party. He now had doubts about the future of the movement in Italy as well.

Notwithstanding his doubts, the published output of Sorel in 1906, whatever the immediate subject at hand, continued the assault on democracy in general and political socialism in particular. In an article in the *Mouvement socialiste* he attacked "internationalist" socialism as a futile abstraction.[39] In another he held Lassalle, the nineteenth-century German socialist, responsible for introducing "scholastic abstractions" into socialism.[40] He also published a series of articles (two years later reshaped into book form) exploring Marx's notion of the idea of "progress" as a bourgeois doctrine.[41] A number of briefer articles in the *Divenire sociale* explored such varied matters as the tenacity of Judaism, the "Owenist mentality" of English trade-unionism, the triumph of the anticlericals in the French elections of 1906, the religious quality of the syndicalist movement, and the "errors" of Catholic modernism.[42]

Signs of new interests appeared in 1907 and 1908 as Sorel passionately pursued the movements of pragmatism and modernism in his correspondence.[43] The popularity of William James, having in Italy become something of a craze, especially commanded his attention. Giuseppe Prezzolini and Giovanni Papini, associated with the newly established *Voce* of Florence, were considered the leading exponents of pragmatism. They belonged, Sorel told Croce, as much to the Renaissance as to pragmatism, but he was fascinated by this new current in Italian thought: "There is something frightening in the idea of making success the proof of the legitimacy of a belief." The future of modernism also concerned him. He returned often in his letters to the notion that modernism threatened the church as reformism threatened socialism. He was intensely pleased that he and Croce were in agreement concerning the *Pascendi,* the papal encyclical against modernism. Articles reflected these and related interests. The *Mouvement socialiste* published two articles deploring the influence of "commercialism" on socialist thought[44] and of "intellectualism" on the history of the church.[45] An extended essay in the form of a letter to Daniel Halévy, frequenter of the *Cahiers* and Sorel's friend, considered at length the role of myths, elites, and violence in history.[46] A review of a work by Charles Maurras, the French monarchist leader, noted that Maurras had "men of great faith" about him, though the future was not favorable to his cause—Sorel was to return soon to the subject of the monarchists.[47] A series of articles on Bergson's recently published *Évolution créatrice* argued that Bergson had confirmed his own views concerning the nature of reality; Sorel, moreover, perceived in intuitive methods a particularly valuable instrument for the study of mass movements which had embarked on a revolutionary course.[48] The *Divenire sociale* also published numerous articles, generally somewhat more vituperative: an attack on the theories of liberty and equality, another scathing denunciation of the Dreyfusards, a critique of the "ethics of moderation," an array of arguments in favor of extremism, and, finally, a discourse on the ineptitude and corruption of parliamentary institutions.[49]

During the period 1907–1908 Sorel also prepared the manuscripts of three studies published in 1908; these works constituted his major effort on behalf of revolutionary syndicalism. *La Décomposition du Marxisme* was based on a lecture Sorel delivered on April 3, 1907, at an international conference on syndicalism in Paris. Among the participants were not only Lagardelle, Kritchewsky, and Griffuelhes, Sorel's associates on the *Mouvement socialiste,* but Labriola, generally recognized as his leading Italian disciple, and the young Michels. *Décomposition,* a history of Marxian criticism in which Sorel identified the rejuvenation of Marxism with the appearance of his own movement, was published early in 1908.[50] The "decomposition" of which he wrote was the breakdown of Marxism into three movements: Bernsteinian evolutionary socialism, Blanquism, and the Nouvelle École.[51] Bernsteinian evolutionary socialism, he wrote, rejected revolutionary methods completely and obliged the workers to pursue their aims as other political parties did, modifying their attitudes to meet electoral needs. Blanquism rejected the notion of the revolutionary class in favor of a revolutionary high command leading the poor against the rich and hoping to achieve its objectives by means of a coup d'état. It was the Nouvelle École, revolutionary syndicalism, that was grounded in the "Marxism in Marx." Marx, Sorel reiterated, was not to be taken literally. Marx was passionate in his beliefs, and his passion prevented him from recognizing realities very clearly. "We are in the presence of what I have called a 'social myth.'" The proletarian myth was the reality of the workingmen's movement. This fact had been most clearly established by the Nouvelle École, which maintained not only the Marxian legacy that the iconoclastic zeal of the Bernsteinians had failed to preserve but also the proletarian character of the movement as one of workers rather than Blanquist "conspirators."

Sorel's most important and widely known work, the *Réflexions sur la violence,* was dedicated to Marie-Euphrasie; it was, he wrote in the dedication, "completely dominated by her spirit."[52] The study had grown out of articles on proletarian violence published in France and Italy in 1905–1906.[53] In 1908, after further revision, the *Réflexions* made its appearance: the first edition was published by Guiyesse's *Pages libres,* Péguy's neighbor. Sorel evidently encountered some difficulty in securing its publication. His books made little money; he himself could not finance the venture.[54] Halévy came to the rescue by advancing some 6,000 francs, while André Spire, also an habitué of Péguy's establishment, put up the rest. Halévy edited the manuscript, giving it somewhat greater clarity and polish than Sorel's other works.

The introduction, in the form of a letter to Halévy, asserts that the study was born of conversations with Halévy, whose views "fitted so well into the system of my own ideas."[55] The roots of the *Réflexions* actually reached back to 1889, to the work on Socrates in which he had first written of the social significance of myth and legend.[56] In other studies, notably the preface to Colajanni in 1900 and the *Introduction* of 1903, he had returned to the subject of "social poetry." More recently, he had been concerned in the *Système* with the development of an apocalyptic mythology in primitive Christianity. The *Réflexions* revealed no single source of inspiration. As in his other works, Sorel indiscriminately invoked a wide variety of intellects—Plato and Aristotle, Pascal and de Maistre, de Tocqueville and Le Bon, Taine and Renan, Proudhon and Marx, Nietzsche and Bergson.

The *Réflexions* proved to be a significant statement not only of Sorel's conception of revolutionary syndicalism but also of his method.[57] His method, he maintained, was "psychological," but he rejected all current psychological interpretations—as he had in the preface to Gatti in 1902—as having been devised to describe the feelings of the upper classes: "I want to find out how... the masses are moved." He concluded that the masses intervene dramatically in history only when impelled by "revolutionary myths." The myth was their reality. He saw in the proletarian myth the vision of an "absolute and irrevocable transformation" of the social order to be achieved by violence culminating with the general strike. But he insisted that he had invented nothing:

We have limited ourselves to defining the historical bearing of the notion of the general strike. We have tried to show that a new culture might spring from the struggle of the revolutionary syndicates against the employers and the state.[58]

The theme of the *Réflexions* was morality. When Croce published a critique of Sorel's work in 1907 which later served as the preface to the Italian edition of the *Réflexions,* Sorel commented in a letter, "You especially have really recognized the great preoccupation of my whole life: the historical genesis of morality."[59] For Sorel, as for Proudhon, "France has lost her morals," and the plight of France was symptomatic of what prevailed everywhere in Europe.[60] France was dominated by a bourgeoisie that had lost every feeling of class. Two "accidents," he noted significantly, might yet restore to the bourgeoisie something of its former energy: a great foreign war might bring men to power who had the will to govern, or a great extension of proletarian violence might disgust the bourgeoisie with the humanitarian platitudes that currently put them to sleep. Sorel's faith, however, lay in a total renewal of society by the aims and methods of revolutionary syndicalism.

Les Illusions du progrès was also an expanded version of articles appearing in 1906. It drew on the work of de Tocqueville, Taine, and Renan.[61] Its text was the argument raised in the *Communist Manifesto* that the theory of progress was received as a dogma at a time when the bourgeoisie was the dominant class.[62] What Sorel attempted, therefore, was an analysis of the theory of progress as an historically limited doctrine. The idea of progress, he argued, arose in the seventeenth century as the world-view of a class that believed itself perfectly prepared to assume power and eager to undertake great projects of reform. "Progress," under the influence of eighteenth-century rationalism, became essential democratic dogma and continued to be cherished in the nineteenth century because it permitted the bourgeoisie to enjoy its privileges in peace. Socialism had long followed in the wake of what had become a bourgeois democratic tradition, but syndicalism was now obliged to purge itself of all utopian fantasies based on the idea of progress. The *Illusions* may be regarded, consequently, as in some respects the necessary complement of the *Réflexions*. The "creative" and "intuitive" proletarian concepts of "myth" and "violence" were here placed in opposition to the "unitary" and "rationalist" bourgeois constructions of "democracy" and "progress."

Sorel's activities on behalf of revolutionary syndicalism reached their climax in 1908. Thereafter, his criticism of the movement mounted rapidly, though his disenchantment with the French movement was much more rapid. Somewhat paradoxically, his work appeared to receive attention in unexpected quarters.

The reaction to the *Réflexions* and the *Illusions* was again disappointing. The press greeted their publication with silence or outrage (of the two, Sorel possibly preferred the latter).[63] In an article in the *Matin* on May 18, he admitted the "grave responsibility" that must attend a philosophical justification of violence, but he insisted that without violence the proletarian movement could not exist.[64] In the *Petite république* on June 12, he repeated his attack on the idea of progress and noted sarcastically that the "natural employment of intelligence" did not consist in "inventing plans for the future happiness of mankind."[65] The reaction in syndicalist circles was mixed.[66] If French syndicalists knew of the work, they said little of it. Italian syndicalist leaders were clearly more interested. Curiously, in both France and Italy the *Réflexions* and the *Illusions* won greater attention in nationalist than in syndicalist circles.

That neither the public in general nor the syndicalists in particular (especially in France) seemed to respond to his work undoubtedly vexed Sorel. Possibly for this reason, he permitted a monarchist review, the *Revue critique des idées et des livres,* to republish an article in August 1908 which some ten months previously he had published in the *Divenire sociale.*[67] The *Revue critique* had for some months demonstrated more than casual interest in his work. The article was on "modernism" in socialism and Catholicism, and it attacked moderates in both camps. Sorel was well aware that syndicalist circles might be outraged by his publishing in a monarchist review, but, as he wrote to Croce in September (somewhat apologetically), "These young people are very intelligent. Since they cite my books constantly, I could not refuse collaboration of this type."[68]

Sorel was soon distressed once again by what he suspected was treachery among syndicalist leaders.[69] The *Action directe,* a weekly founded by CGT militants in January 1908, had attacked the Clemenceau government for its heavy-handed manner in dealing with strikers. This campaign was supported by several contributors to the *Mouvement socialiste,* including Lagardelle. But Jaurès, having become the foremost defender of the strike activities of the CGT in the Chamber, had undertaken in the *Humanité* a similar campaign against Clemenceau. In a letter to Lagardelle in March 1908 Sorel confessed his suspicion of some sort of intrigue between Jaurès and the CGT.[70] The CGT, he wrote, should be exclusively a center of propaganda, but instead it had been placed by Griffuelhes at Jaurès's disposal. The salvation of the proletariat did not lie, Sorel insisted, in the cunning maneuvers of politicians. By June 1908 he confided in Croce that he was considering withdrawal from Lagardelle's review.[71] He could not approve what he believed was the transformation of the *Mouvement socialiste* into a "courtesan" of any political faction, socialist or otherwise.

The bloody strikes of June and July 1908 among quarry workers at Draveil and Villeneuve-St. Georges, as well as the Socialist Congress of Toulouse in October, further distressed Sorel. He was shocked by the clashes between strikers and troops at Draveil, which had resulted in a number of deaths.[72] With the news of actual bloodshed, he became "withdrawn and troubled." "He's a gentle man," an acquaintance observed. He reacted even more strongly to the shootings at Villeneuve-St. Georges.[73] That strike had been organized by provocateurs. The CGT heads, who at first opposed the strike, supported it only with reluctance. The ensuing riot, however, led to their arrest and imprisonment. Jaurès "declared war" in the Chamber on the Clemenceau ministry because of the bloodshed, the suppression of the strikers, and the arrests. The CGT had found itself again dependent on Jaurès.

Sorel fiercely opposed any collaboration, asserting that CGT leaders would be playing Jaurès's game. Moreover, Sorel was now embittered by Lagardelle's maneuvering at the Congress of Toulouse.[74] Jaurès defended the CGT against attempts of the Guesdists to subject it to the recently unified Socialist party; he upheld its autonomy and asked only that it surrender its revolutionary views. On the eve of the congress Sorel had counselled Lagardelle, who was to attend, not to become involved in the affairs of the Socialist party, but once at Toulouse Lagardelle, accompanied by several contributors to the *Mouvement socialiste* and posing as the head of a "syndicalist group," supported the Jaurèsists against the Guesdists. Sorel denounced this tactic: "I perceived that there were politicians around Lagardelle who desired that Berth and I give them free rein."[75]

The *non-lieu* delivered in favor of the jailed syndicalist leaders finally brought about Sorel's break with the *Mouvement socialiste*. On October 31 he wrote to Lagardelle announcing his immediate withdrawal.[76] He suspected collusion. He could not approve of any act directed against Clemenceau if that meant falling in with Jaurès's plan to topple Clemenceau's government. He charged Lagardelle with complicity in the maneuvers that had led the CGT into "the Jaurès-Combes morass." Several days later Sorel explained his decision to Delesalle.[77] The liberation of the workers, he insisted, could be achieved only by the workers themselves. Had the CGT remained what it was supposed to be and what it had been for a long time, an "office of revolutionary propaganda," he would not leave the *Mouvement socialiste*. But the day the "politicians" were able to exert the slightest pressure, the CGT became "statist" in outlook and began to function as a political party. "*Je me retire dans mon trou.*"[78] Lagardelle did not deny Sorel's charge, but Sorel, he said, wanted to impose his opinions rather than convince the youthful staff of the review. These young men would not follow him—a humbler man was necessary. Many years later, Lagardelle was to write, "I was obliged, if I wanted to act, not to isolate myself from my generation."

The collaboration between Sorel and the *Mouvement socialiste* came to a close early in 1909. In a series of brief articles in mid-1908 and with characteristic versatility, he attacked Jews in American politics, deplored the signs of decadence in the Augustan age, and upbraided "intellectuals" in ancient Athens.[79] A final booklet, *La Révolution dreyfusienne,* was published with the *Mouvement socialiste* press the following year. This brief study was the first public confession of a repentant Dreyfusard. Other confessions by Halévy and Péguy were soon forthcoming. Here, Sorel indicated a clear lack of enthusiasm for all previous revolutions and for the Dreyfus "revolution" in particular.[80] He lauded the Action Française as the sole organization that had protested against the "illegal" decree setting aside the judgment of the second court-martial at Rennes. He insisted again that the Dreyfus affair had discredited a "republican aristocracy," the mainstay of liberal parliamentary government in France—the country had fallen into the hands of rogues and demagogues like those surrounding Napoleon III at the beginning of the Second Empire.

The break between Sorel and the *Mouvement socialiste* produced no cataclysmic repercussions in the ranks of French syndicalism. His writings had, indeed, constituted the principal statement of theoretical revolutionary syndicalism in France, and he himself had been the most widely learned and cultured exponent of the movement, but by 1908 the differences between Sorel and the militants of the CGT, marked from the very start, could no longer be glossed over. The break revealed his virtual isolation from the movement. Hardly anyone followed the *maître*. When Sorel left the *Mouvement socialiste*, his close friend Berth alone departed with him.[81]

Sorel did not immediately break his ties with the Italian movement; he had, in fact, reacted with enthusiasm to the Parma general strike of 1908.[82] But his primary response was to events in France and what he wrote made clear his continuing disarray and disillusion. Events, moreover, served only to confirm his conviction that even in Italy revolutionary syndicalism was not destined to fulfill his expectations.

The collaboration in 1909 between Sorel and Italian syndicalism was marked by still another incident involving the French monarchists. He continued to address himself primarily to Marxian criticism[83] and in particular to the failure of French syndicalism,[84] but his articles in the *Divenire sociale* were now punctuated by brief but highly complimentary comments on the French monarchists. The *Action française,* the Parisian monarchist daily, republished, with his permission, one of these articles.[85] Sorel had discussed the strike at Villeneuve-St. Georges and dismissed as ludicrous the charge that monarchists had given financial aid to the heads of the CGT. He had gone on to commend the monarchists: he had words of praise for Maurras personally; he spoke of the "great service" of the *Action française* to the nation. These were strange comments, indeed, coming from the foremost champion of the workers' revolution by the general strike, and in a monarchist newspaper, to boot! If Sorel was discomfited by the appearance of the article in such ultra-bourgeois surroundings, he did not reveal it, but it would not be long before there were serious doubts in Italian syndicalist circles concerning the genuineness of his sympathies for the workers.

The Ferrer affair furthered these doubts.[86] In Barcelona during July 1909, in the course of a general strike called to protest inequalities in military service, rioters had turned against the church and massacred priests and nuns. Francisco Ferrer, the anticlerical anarchist, was thereupon seized by the government. Though he was not implicated in the rising, he was executed in October. With the news that Ferrer, who was well-known abroad, was to be executed, Parisian anarchists staged a giant demonstration in his behalf. They were supported by many syndicalist militants. Like the anarchists, the syndicalists regarded Ferrer as a victim of vindictive clericalism and obscurantism and as a martyr to free thought. Sorel opposed syndicalist participation, but he chose to reveal his wrath in an interview granted on September 29 to the *Action française.*[87] He described Ferrer as an "adventurer," one of the "last vagabonds of the Renaissance." He likened the agitation to that of the early days of the Dreyfus affair—both were "shrouded in mystery." He suspected a "conspiracy," this time of Freemasons and anarchists. He held the Briand government responsible for an uproar which it could stop if it wanted to, but which it encouraged in the hope of maneuvering the syndicates into an alliance with the government. Sorel's attack on Ferrer and his sympathizers in a monarchist newspaper hardly increased Sorel's popularity in syndicalist circles in either France or Italy.[88] The interview was greeted with stinging insults by anarchists and syndicalists alike. Yet Sorel insisted in a letter to Agostino Lanzillo, a leading Italian disciple, that the anarchist Ferrer should never have become the concern of syndicalists.[89] Syndicalism was the spontaneous organization of the workers. Anarchism was, in a sense, its opposite, a movement of "intellectuals" who viewed the worker as their instrument.

The final break with revolutionary syndicalism came late in 1910, when Sorel abandoned all hope for the movement in Italy. He was to the end, evidently, reluctant to cut himself off completely. In a preface written early in the year for a study of the CGT by Griffuelhes and Louis Niel (who followed Griffuelhes as secretary-general in 1909), he expressed his lingering hopes.[90] In "Unité et multiplicité," an essay concerned with the methods of social science, which was appended to the second edition of the *Réflexions,* he still wrote, though vaguely, as a partisan of a proletarian movement. Here, incidentally, he discussed his own method of "*diremption,*" arbitrary abstractions from reality, a tentative yet useful tool of historical study.[91] But there was little in these efforts of the polemical zeal of former years. Moreover, the Italian CGL had by 1910 demonstrated substantially the same shortcomings as the CGT.[92] There was in Italy, to be sure, an active and enthusiastic syndicalist movement led by men devoted to Sorel, but it was clear that they could exercise only limited influence on the great mass of Italian workers organized in the CGL. In "Le Confessioni," published from March to May in the *Divenire sociale,* Sorel announced his break with the Italian movement.[93] The study, he said, was destined to be his last on syndicalism.[94] The French movement, which he discussed at length, had not brought to realization his expectations of it. It had been won over to democracy. He said virtually nothing of the Italian movement. In any case, he asserted, nothing could ever come from a workingman's movement that entered the political arena. In a letter to Lanzillo in October published in the *Giornale d'Italia,* he declared his intention "to devote myself to studies, foreign to socialism, which have always interested me."[95]

At the CGL Congress of Bologna on December 10 2 and 11, 1910, a letter was read to the assembled delegates in which Sorel renounced once again both French and Italian syndicalism.[96] He restated his desire to dedicate himself to new pursuits. He had, in fact, already embarked on these new studies. He also recalled his remarks in "Le Confessioni": "Many people hope that the future will correct the evils of the present; but the author is too old to live in distant hopes."[97]

Chapter

3

The Idea

The focus of Sorel's political interests during the period 1903 to approximately 1910 was revolutionary syndicalism, represented in France by the CGT and in Italy by the Segretariato Nazionale and its successors. This most prolific period in his career permits a certain systematization of his ideas, but it should be borne in mind that Sorel was himself no systematizer.[1] Moving from one study to another, he was given to abrupt and sometimes startling changes in subject matter or argument or both. Further complicating his work was a tortuous prose style and a text cluttered with innumerable allusions drawn from the entire range of human history, from all the arts, and from all the sciences, and added to this was the cloudy spirit of Pascal. Yet, the need to give definition to his writing is imperative, even at the risk of losing something of the complexity of his thought. What Sorel wrote on revolutionary syndicalism was written largely with the French movement in mind, even in studies published in Italy. He described tendencies he saw or pretended to see in the movement. Above all, he warned against the hazards that might divert the movement from its historic mission.[2]

I

Revolutionary syndicalism was for Sorel the organization of workingmen in their syndicates dedicated to the destruction of the bourgeois order by means of the general strike. The rise of the movement was for him what Vico had called a *ricorso*.[3] The movement was capable of bringing about a drastic and total transformation of the moral and social order.

What impelled revolutionary syndicalism, according to Sorel, was an apocalyptic mythology, the outlines of which could be detected whenever the masses had been deeply moved.[4] The Greeks believed in "glory" as a value without equal, a conviction that bore fruit in the pursuit of "the good" and "the beautiful." The myths of ancient Rome evoked those extraordinary virtues of the Romans who resigned themselves to "frightful inequality and suffering" in order to conquer the world. The Christian myths looked to the return of Christ, the destruction of the pagan world, and the inauguration of the kingdom of the saints. The deliverance did not take place, but without these myths, he asked, would Christianity have triumphed? Only the myths of the Reformation, the dream of Christian renovation, can explain the religious upheaval of the sixteenth century. The myths of the French Revolution evoked the enthusiasm of its first champions. The Napoleonic myth alone can account for the sacrifice of life that the soldiers of France were prepared to make in order to take part in "immortal deeds." Far more than Cavour and all the politicians of his school, the myths of Mazzini and his followers had finally brought unity to Italy.

The myth of the proletariat longing for emancipation was the "general strike."[5] It was the body of images capable of evoking "instinctively" all the sentiments produced by the war undertaken by the proletariat against modern society. This myth dominated all truly working-class movements.

The deepest convictions of the proletariat were embodied in these images.[6] Myths expressed the strongest inclinations of a people, party, or class. Those of the proletariat "recur to the mind with the insistence of instincts" and "in all circumstances of life." Their roots, Sorel believed, were to be found in the long and bitter war the proletariat had waged against the bourgeoisie. To the great majority of men history appears as a series of legends impressed on the memory at such a tender age and with such force that they cannot be uprooted by reason when maturity is reached. Memory counts for more in determining the character of action than does appraisal of present facts. The convictions of the proletariat had their source in the popular legends of the exploits of the *sansculottes,* in the bitter "June Days" of 1848, in the dream of revenge for "Bloody Week" of May 1871, and in the painful memories of the daily conflict between the workers and society: "The general strike groups them all in a coordinated picture, and by bringing them together gives to each one of them its maximum intensity."[7] Marx's originality, Sorel asserted, lay in his happy intuition of the psychic needs of the proletarian movement.[8] His doctrines were not to be taken literally as statements of historic fact. Marx had set out to construct a proletarian mythology. His ideas were to be valued for the convictions they so perfectly expressed and the images they evoked. The law of the increasing misery of the proletariat, the law of capitalist concentration, the law of the correlation between economic and political power—all this was "social poetry." Militants considered these axioms beyond all controversy, regardless of what savants might think, and that was as it should be.[9] The accuracy of a myth was irrelevant. A doctrine was open to criticism because it was a representation of the intellect, but not a myth. A myth was a "whole," an historical force. It was not a description of things, but an expression of wills. It could not be refuted, for it was beyond criticism. A myth was at bottom identical with the convictions of a group, being the expression of these convictions in the language of the movement. Some scholars had concluded that the proletarian myth was a religion,[10] but there was in the myth no faith in the supernatural and no metaphysic of the soul. Nevertheless, a revolutionary myth was capable of evoking those sentiments which ordinarily were expressed only in religion: "Bergson has taught us that it is not only religion which occupies the profounder regions of our mental life; revolutionary myths have their place there equally with religion."[11]

The myth of the general strike was an expression of the "hopes" of the proletariat and of its "way of looking at the future."[12] Myths, Sorel recognized, could not possibly be free of utopian conceptions. The utopian elements, however, were not really crucial. The text of Marx with regard to the future society, for example, was not to be taken literally; no particular detail was to be regarded as historically foreseeable. It was fortunate, in fact, that the third volume of *Das Kapital* remained unfinished, for the obscurity of Marxism on the subject of the socialist order had thereby been enhanced. The workingmen's movement, Sorel maintained, was independent of theories regarding the society of the future. Theories were, in any case, born of "bourgeois reflections" (though he excepted what he considered essential in Marxism). With the myth of the general strike,

We are no longer compelled to argue learnedly about the future, we are not obliged to indulge in lofty reflections about philosophy, history, or economics; we are not on the plane of theories, and we can remain on the level of observable facts.[13]

The determination to act that was embodied in the revolutionary myth was derived from the impatience for deliverance and the hope behind it.[14] Revolutionary myths made men act before they could calculate; like Plato's "noble lies," they stirred men to heroic and sublime action. There could be no great historic action, according to Sorel, without the aid of warmly colored images. Those who wished to influence the masses must, therefore, speak the language of the men being addressed and not the language of abstract truth:

There is probably in the mind of every man, hidden under the ashes, a quickening fire, and the greater the number of ready-made doctrines the mind has received blindly, the more is this fire threatened with extinction; the awakener is the man who stirs the ashes and thus makes the flame leap up.[15]

The myth of the general strike, Sorel believed, contained everything needed to move the proletariat to action.[16] Workers regarded themselves as an army of truth fighting an army of evil. The myth raised a barrier against attempts at reaction and gave the actors in the drama the confidence to win: "Once it has entered the minds of the people, they can no longer be controlled by their leaders, and ... thus the power of the deputies will be reduced to nothing."[17]

The revolutionary myth sustained the desire for a catastrophic overthrow of the existing order.[18] As long as no myths were accepted by the masses, one could go on talking revolt indefinitely without provoking revolutionary action. Only an apocalyptic mythology, as Bergson had indicated, could destroy an order sanctioned by centuries. Such a breach with the past, Sorel asserted, was possible only because of the historical pessimism implied in the myth. Historical pessimism denied automatic progress. Society was viewed as a whole and so was its destruction. History was conceived as a "march toward deliverance." The pessimist viewed history, therefore, as a perpetually fresh creation. Pessimism was an inextinguishable source of creativity. Optimism, on the other hand, was dangerous because it took no account of the great difficulties which might be encountered:

> In primitive Christianity we find a fully developed and completely armed pessimism: man is condemned to slavery from birth—Satan is the prince of the world—the Christian, already regenerated by baptism, can render himself capable of obtaining the resurrection of the body by means of the Eucharist; he awaits the glorious second coming of Christ, who will destroy the rule of Satan and call his comrades in the fight to attain the heavenly Jerusalem. [19]

Sorel saw a threat to the movement in the attempt to reduce proletarian aspirations to programs. [20] "The man who draws up a program for the future is a reactionary," he quoted Marx. Programs must be expressed in words, and words can readily be deflected from their original meaning so that certain parts of a program can with adjustments be fitted into approaching legislation. Not so the myth. The nature of the myth is such that the specific direction in which it leads cannot be determined beforehand. The myth is an instrument at once historical and metaphysical. It is a vision of the proletariat engaged in a battle, "which, like the Napoleonic battle, is to annihilate completely a condemned regime." It implies an "irrevocable transformation" from one historical era to another.

The organization of revolutionary syndicalism was, according to Sorel, based on an elite; the truly great movements in history had been led by "fighting institutions." [21] His theory of elites was as haphazard as his theory of myths. He wrote of Homer's "Achaean type" as the indomitable hero confident of his strength, putting himself above all rules. [22] He extolled the virtues of the Roman legions. He found particularly significant the role played by monastic institutions in the history of Catholicism. The "master type," he noted, still existed in the "captains of industry" who led the extraordinary technological advances of the United States.

The syndicate was such an organization of the elite; the great mass of workingmen did not belong, but only the most militant. [23] He viewed the character of the syndicate in terms of its selectivity and isolation, and he saw in these qualities an attempt to fashion the new order in microcosm.

The syndicates, he asserted, must be limited to the most trustworthy elements. [24] The history of the church demonstrated that it was the politicians and intellectuals who repeatedly placed the church in jeopardy. Popes and priests trafficked with princes and with temporal authorities generally. Theologians reduced Christian mysteries to "reasonable" doctrines. He urged the syndicates to have nothing to do with either politicians or intellectuals. His anger was directed particularly against socialist politicians of the Jaurès and Millerand variety—"socialist Escobars," he called them, after the seventeenth-century Spanish Jesuit. By attempting to divert the workers from the idea of class struggle, they were the greatest enemies of the proletariat. Politicians were entirely dominated by the idea of personal success; they did nothing for nothing. He attacked intellectuals with equal vigor. The syndicates were cautioned to have nothing to do with "that section of the middle class" that had embraced "the profession of thinking for the proletariat." This was the great misfortune of Marxism. A Marxist vocabulary had been preserved by people completely estranged from the spirit of Marx. Intellectuals were not, in any case, "thinkers." "*They are people who have adopted the profession of thinking,* and who take an *aristocratic salary* on account of the nobility of this profession."[25] What Sorel wanted in the syndicates was an elite:

It is with elite troops, perfectly trained by the monastic life, ready to brave all obstacles, and filled with an absolute confidence in victory, that Catholicism has been able, until now, to triumph over its enemies.[26]

The religious orders, by the rigor and austerity of their lives, saved the church repeatedly when threatened.[27] The syndicates also required men who would devote themselves wholeheartedly to the revolutionary cause. These men would know that they would always remain poor, but would nevertheless be prepared to carry on their work in obscurity.

The syndicates, moreover, must be isolated from the bourgeois order.[28] The recent experience of the Allemanist party, Sorel contended, was proof of how fatal alliances might be for the proletariat. Since the Dreyfus affair the Allemanists had become increasingly dependent upon bourgeois parties. The anarchists had been correct all along—revolutionaries ran the risk of being transformed into reformists if they used bourgeois institutions. The concept of *solidarité,* Sorel argued, Léon Bourgeois's notion that classes should work together cooperatively, was equally hazardous. Solidarity implied that the rich had the social duty of aiding the poor. This was a philosophy of "hypocritical cowardice" on the part of the bourgeoisie and an acknowledgment of inferiority on the part of the proletariat. There must be no confounding the workers with the "poor." The syndicalist movement must present itself as representing the "proletariat" and nothing else.

The ideals of the proletariat were to be cultivated in the syndicates.[29] In the history of the church he again found an important parallel, for it was a comparatively small number of regular clergy who maintained and perfected the ideals of the church: "The elite, which bore the assault on the enemy positions, received material and moral assistance from the masses, which saw in it the reality of Christianity."[30] If it did not develop this same specialization, Sorel suggested, the proletarian movement would risk becoming an inert mass.[31] Only an elite could serve as a myth's custodian, a role that was essentially aristocratic. The great movements of history had invariably been led by enthusiastic minorities in whom the ideals of the movement were actually experienced. Catholicism would long have been dead were it not for such groups. By virtue of this specialization, Catholicism found itself to this day in far less danger than Protestantism. The syndicates, Sorel argued, must also be convinced that their work was "serious, formidable, and sublime." The duality of classes might not exist in fact, but it could exist in the minds of the militants. This was of vital importance. The syndicates had to be able to bear the innumerable sacrifices imposed on them and to accept duties which could procure them neither honors nor profit nor even immediate intellectual satisfaction. So rigorous was the analogy between the syndicate and the monastery, in Sorel's thinking, that he compared deviation toward "trade unionism" with the relaxation of monastic rules.

The administrative and organizing capacities of the workers were to be developed in the syndicates.[32] The syndicates must, therefore, learn to attend exclusively to working-class matters. They must avoid the practices of "pseudo-proletarian" institutions. Cooperatives and mutualities, for example, were not truly proletarian. What struck one in these organizations was their tendency to breed functionaries who lacked the spirit of revolt. The syndicates, Sorel insisted, must be engaged in a continuing search for new practices. These must be perfected by ceaseless criticism. The greatest threat to syndicalism was the danger of imitating existing institutions and values: "It would be better for it to remain content for a time with weak and chaotic organizations than . . . to copy the . . . forms of the middle class."[33]

What Sorel saw as essential in the technique of revolutionary syndicalism—that is, its mode of action—was violence.[34] It was not a question of justifying violence but of understanding its role in history. For Sorel, great historic action was inevitably marked by violence. The whole of classical history was dominated by the idea of war conceived heroically. The republican institutions of Greece were rooted in the organization of armies of citizens. Greek art reached its apex in the citadels. The greatness of the Romans lay in their conquest of the known world and its submission to Roman law. The Christian conquest was the work of a "holy army" which saw itself constantly exposed to the attacks of the accomplices of Satan. The Protestant reformers, nourished on the reading of the Old Testament, strove to imitate the exploits of the Hebrew conquerors of the Holy Land. The wars of the French Revolution "filled the French soul with an enthusiasm analogous to that provoked by religions."

The violence exhibited by syndicalism was symptomatic of a movement with a great historic mission.[35] It was to the credit of the anarchists who, when they were admitted to the movement, taught the workers that they need not be ashamed of acts of violence. No apologies need be made for it.

Violence was normal in history, a normal expression of the war waged by the proletariat against the bourgeois state.[36] The distinction between force and violence was important for Sorel. Force aimed to bring about absolute and automatic obedience. It had been used by the state since the beginning of modern times. Its object was the imposition of authority. Violence "would smash that authority." It was not to be confused with those Jacobin acts of savagery engendered by the cult of the state. It was violence without hate and without the spirit of revenge. It was war carried on in broad daylight,

without hypocritical attenuation, for the purpose of ruining an irreconcilable enemy.... It excludes all the abominations which dishonored the middle-class revolutions of the eighteenth century.[37]

Proletarian violence, Sorel argued, was only partly physical.[38] Physical violence took the form of strikes and those clashes with public authorities that normally accompanied strikes. Even certain "criminal acts" could be considered proper. It might be useful, at times, he suggested, "to thrash the orators of democracy and the representatives of the government." In this way there would be no illusions about the character of proletarian violence. These acts, however, could have historic value only if they were clear and brutal expressions of class war. He therefore condemned sabotage as it was ordinarily practiced by the syndicates. Sabotage was not in keeping with the principle that the employer was to be hurt and not the consumer. Sabotage, moreover, was not compatible with the advance of production. Violence was also intransigence, the refusal to compromise in word and deed. Early Christianity afforded the best illustration of this practice. The cleavage between Christian and pagan society was extraordinarily well marked: the chasm between the two was maintained by the persecutions and explained by the doctrine of the Anti-Christ. Syndicalism could profit from this experience. The strike had to be supported by uncompromising propaganda in which even the daily circumstances of life were viewed by militants as incidents in the epic struggle of the workers against bourgeois society. The propaganda of the proletariat must neither be "prudent" nor "skillful." The proletariat was to surrender nothing—nothing is surrendered in war.

Violence was a "training school"—Bergson had written of the enormous obstacles that confront revolutionary movements.[39] These obstacles could be traced to the egoism of individuals, to their tendency to avoid any special effort. Violence had to be employed, Sorel asserted, to remove every mark of weakness. In the Wars of Liberty, after they had been defeated, the soldiers of the revolution felt no pity for the officers whom they saw guillotined on the charge of dereliction of duty. In the syndicates defeated workingmen should also attribute their failure to the base conduct of those who had not done all that was expected of them. A defeat is to be explained by "treason alone" and "will therefore be accompanied by many acts of violence." Violence, Sorel contended, maintained revolutionary morale. By making an appeal to the honor which developed naturally in all organized armies, class war could eliminate those "evil feelings" against which every revolutionary movement had to struggle. Class war weeded out the pacifists who would undermine elite troops.

The role of violence was social scission—violence maintained the idea of the dichotomic division of society in the minds of the militants.[40] In arguing the merits of scission, Sorel repeatedly turned to primitive Christianity. The Christians could have obtained toleration as the mystery cults did, but their leaders were determined to isolate the movement. By doing so they provoked hostility and persecution. The strikes and propaganda of the proletariat achieved the same result. Hierophants of social peace, of course, did not want two rigorously separated worlds. The Catholic ethic of "social duty" (most recently, in the form expressed by the sociologist Le Play) was a device calculated to confuse the masses and to conceal from them those who really possessed power. The democratic ethic artificially divided society into political parties engaged in a mock struggle but united by a deeper solidarity. Proletarian violence, however, effectively maintained the separation of classes. The strike separated the interests and ways of thinking of the two classes. The employing class was forced to assume its traditional role: "This kind of violence compels capitalism to restrict its attention solely to its material role and tends to restore to it the warlike qualities which it formerly possessed."[41] The cowardice of the middle class, Sorel observed significantly, prevented true social scission.[42] The middle classes had permitted themselves to be led by "the chatter of preachers of ethics and sociology" into correcting the "abuses" of the present order. They surrendered before every threat of violence:

> One of the things which appears to me to have most astonished the workers during the last few years has been the timidity of the forces of law and order in the presence of a riot; magistrates who have the right to demand the services of soldiers dare not use their power to the utmost, and officers allow themselves to be abused and struck with a patience hitherto unknown to them.[43]

The politics of cowardice hindered the development of the class struggle.[44] A capitalism resuming its robust, vigorous, and selfish advance would be able to reach perfection. A bourgeoisie rich and hungry for conquest would be confronted by a united and revolutionary proletariat. Society would then be "plainly divided into two camps, and only two, on a field of battle."

The role of violence was to heighten expectations of a catastrophic revolution.[45] Primitive Christianity again provided Sorel with a lesson of great importance. As Renan observed, the renewal of Roman persecutions revived the idea of the advent of the Anti-Christ, and, as a consequence, of all the apocalyptic hopes relative to the reign of Christ. Though the Second Coming did not take place, "we know by innumerable testimonies . . . what great things the march toward deliverance can bring about." The Christians were more "Roman" than the Romans. The courage with which they died won for them the respect of their enemies and lent credence to their belief in the presence of the living Christ: "Today we see that it is because of these madmen that Christianity was able to form its ideas and become master of the world when its time came."[46] The expectation of the general strike, constantly rejuvenated by the sentiments evoked by proletarian violence, also produced an almost "epic state of mind."[47] Sorel observed, however, that the general strike could not be reduced to a great organized plan; it could not follow a direction determined in advance. He rejected, therefore, the "political" general strike which at a signal would bring the government to its knees by a stoppage of all essential operations. Such tactics had to be commanded by a party, and the strike would be over when that party had signed a compact with the government. He also opposed a "Blanquist conspiracy." A coup by "red Jesuits" would not, in the long run, change anything. One set of masters would be replaced by another. He rejected civil war as impractical. Introduction of new weapons and the cutting of rectilinear streets in capitals had made effective resistance difficult. Every strike, he concluded, however local it might be, was to be viewed as a skirmish in the great battle of the general strike. Each was a "partial *ricorso,*" for it generated a little syndicalist current which might be conserved and increased with others. Each was "a reduced facsimile, an essay, a preparation for the final upheaval," and no one could foresee what would arise from any one such engagement. The great battle never came to a head, but the movement was everything, as Bergson had observed, the final aim nothing. Every time they struck a blow, the strikers could hope that it was the beginning of the great "Napoleonic battle" which would crush the condemned regime. In this way recurrent strikes would engender the notion of a catastrophic revolution. Though not the most appropriate method of obtaining immediate material advantages, proletarian violence was in the "immemorial interests of civilization."

II

Revolutionary syndicalism was also considered by Sorel as a functioning revolutionary order, though he rejected the possibility of any extended speculation. The character of the new order could not be predicted. The future was what man would choose to make it within the limits of physical and economic possibilities. Nevertheless, Sorel's work was punctuated by frequent comments on the socialist society of the future. The proletarian revolution would in any event be no mere change in personnel or form of government. This new order Sorel generally, though by no means consistently, called "socialism."[48] "National traditions" would, he said, play an important role, though he did not elaborate.[49] "International" socialism, in any case, he held to be a utopian abstraction.

A new *morale* would provide the impulse behind the socialist order.[50] Human creativity had its roots in moral values. With Christian belief in decline, what would replace it? As Renan had observed, the "sublime" was "dead" in the bourgeoisie, liberal and Catholic alike. Sorel was given to invidious comparisons between the current social order and what would be required under socialism, but he was not without concern: "If the contemporary world does not contain the roots of a new ethic, what will become of it?" This fear was at the center of his thought. What distinguished the syndicalist movement from all other forms of socialism was that syndicalism alone recognized the danger. Sorel therefore assigned to syndicalism the almost sacred mission of providing new moral values, of raising socialism to the level of a religion.

The new *morale*, according to Sorel, would derive from proletarian myths, now reinforced by myths engendered by the general strike.[51] Neither "mild preaching" nor the "ingenious constructions of theorists" would avail. Nor was anything to be expected from existing sources of *morale;* liberal bourgeois sources Sorel thought worthless.[52] For a long time the Declaration of the Rights of Man was regarded in an almost religious light: the struggle in defense of the institutions deriving from the Declaration provided the basis of a moral order. But the Dreyfus affair had demonstrated conclusively that bourgeois morals had degenerated to the standards of the stock exchange. Catholic sources were no better.[53] Catholicism had become a "deteriorated religion." Everywhere the idea of "the mission of the church" had disappeared. When the papacy spoke of these matters, the bourgeoisie regarded this as "barbaric nonsense." The people who today professed Catholicism were chiefly preoccupied with mechanical rites more or less related to magic, which they believed would assure them present and future happiness. Syndicalism alone could produce a renovation of morals.[54] Moral values had their origin in convictions sustained by a "state of war": in the present circumstances this would be the war of the proletariat against the bourgeois order.

The new moral values must correspond to the needs of a socialist order.[55] More than fifty years ago Proudhon had made this quite clear. *"Liberté, Égalité, Fraternité"* seemed now only a colorless collection of abstract and confused formulae without practical bearing on twentieth-century industrial society. What did these formulae have to do with the advance of production?

Neither was Catholic morality relevant.[56] The economics of Catholicism were Aristotelian, oriented in favor of the consumer. The church viewed economic life in terms of haggling over prices and the responsibilities of the rich toward the poor. There was no connection between morality and production in Catholicism. "I do not think," Sorel wrote, "that there exists a class less capable of understanding the economics of production than priests."[57] Socialism had no need to borrow from an insolvent system. The worker had to be able to judge himself in accordance with values proper to a proletarian society.

A principal role of *morale* was the curbing of the passions.[58] Human nature, when left to itself, always tends toward evil. Bourgeois and Catholic morality both failed in this regard. Bourgeois morality was rooted in the eighteenth century, when morals were "relaxed." The theories of the *philosophes* were contrived to justify a society that wished to amuse itself without respect for chastity or fear of sin. Catholicism too had developed a deplorable indulgence in matters of morals; the church saw in marriage only an accord of financial and mundane interests. It permitted divorce under the guise of annulment when the parties were prepared to pay the price. Only in syndicalism did Sorel see a serious consideration of the sexual problem, though he was struck by its absence in Marx:

> Morality depends in so intimate a way on sexual relationships that we have the right to say that a class that has no clear idea about the family has none either about morality. It seems that Marx had never gone deeply into such questions.[59]

Marx, he wrote, was a Manchestrian hypnotized by economics, who relegated moral problems to a minor role.[60] Socialism, as conceived by the syndicalists, considered matters of sex to be of the gravest importance. Socialist society would act as a brake on the passions, would discipline the instincts and direct them along socially constructive lines. The triumph of the proletariat would depend in large part on their "heroic renunciation" in matters of sex. Women could play a role of inestimable importance in the moral development of men. "Love...can produce that sublimity without which there would be no effective morality."[61]

A socialist *morale* must be a "*morale* of producers," a *morale* that would induce men to act freely in the interests of their comrades before they had time to reflect on their own.[62] For Sorel, little of this capability was in evidence in the existing regime. The bourgeoisie were no longer animated by their former warlike spirit; they were concerned solely with increasing their personal wealth and comfort. The "worn-out" Christian ethic was even less appropriate to the needs of modern industrial life. For Sorel, the workers had to have within themselves a source of conviction that would dominate their being. Socialism had to borrow from religion something of its inspiration and driving force. The essence of all religions worth having was their appeal to the heroic. The emotions which morality had to call up were those which inspired the perfection of machinery and increased the productivity of labor: "We must give," he wrote, "a socialist significance to our lives."

From the practices of the syndicates would emerge the organization of socialism. The syndicates were now constructing their own institutions, autonomous development of which was essential. The capitalist order united and disciplined the proletariat in the syndicates: "From *discipline* we march toward *organization,* that is, toward a juridical constitution of the proletariat."[63] The network of syndicates would take over all functions of capitalism which still had viability. The syndicates would be in full control of the social order, which was therefore to be regarded in an essentially economic light. The structure of socialism, a problem once vainly explored by the utopians Fourier and Owen, will have been resolved, at least initially, by capitalism.

The socialist order would be a "society of producers," a society devoted to work.[64] As he had in another context, Sorel warned against a political system that bred a class of professional politicians. Politicians were "practitioners of the easy life." They performed no truly productive role, but merely exploited the opportunities of public office: "This takes us far from the road to the sublime; instead, we are simply on the one that leads to the practice of politico-criminal societies."[65] Nor did Sorel see any need for intellectuals.[66] They were parasites, regardless of the regime to which they might attach themselves: they were parasitical because of their detachment from the world of productive work. As the world became more industrialized, he noted, more people came directly under the influence of the factory, and men were increasingly bound to one another in a common creative effort, with the measure of their value to society determined by their productivity. The socializing tendency of modern industry was the fundamental fact of modern times, the key to the problem of creating new social structures.

The state could be replaced by a federalist system. Whether in its traditional form or in the form of a "dictatorship of the proletariat," the state could serve no purpose in the proletarian society. The state, Sorel thought, had always been an evil institution. "Syndicalists do not propose to reform the state.... They want to destroy it."[67] The history of the state both in antiquity and in modern times had always been marked by a ferocious struggle between parties seeking to secure the advantages possessed by those with political power. As long as the state existed, it would invite conspiracies, since conquest of the state would always be the easiest way to obtain power and fortune. The army, moreover, was the clearest and most tangible of all possible manifestations of the state and the one most firmly connected with its origins and traditions. There was, therefore, an "absolute opposition" between socialism and militarism, but antimilitarism had nothing to do with humanitarian considerations. There was in the state, in the struggle for its control, and in the army, its instrument of defense and conquest, a "cloud" that concealed what was essential in the community—its economy. Moreover, the "dictatorship of the proletariat" suggested by some socialists, Sorel thought, would in practice become a "dictatorship of intellectuals." Such a dictatorship, which he accused the Jaurèsists of favoring, would be reminiscent of the Inquisition or the Terror. None of the present powers of the state would disappear. Authority would be transmitted periodically from one privileged group to another, and the mass of producers would merely change masters. In opposition to statism of any kind, Sorel appeared to favor an economic federalism based on Proudhon's ideas, though its nature was not spelled out in detail.[68] Society would presumably be divested of all central "political" authority. Socialism would then proceed to operate essentially on its economic foundations, "just like a factory." Thus would the political neutralization of society be achieved. He recognized, however, that Proudhon's federalist ideas might not be completely realized in our time, for the workers of the cities did not readily grasp them. But, he added obscurely, the "hypothesis" of federalism constituted a convenient way of representing "mythically" the realization of such a system in law. "The reality of federalism is not absolutely necessary for the realization of federalist tendencies."[69]

The organization of socialism would be substantially resolved by its continuity with capitalism.[70] Such standard socialist formulae as the "socialization of the means of production," therefore, Sorel thought unintelligible. Socialization of this type would presumably aim at establishing a permanent communist collectivism the day after the revolution. Socialist intellectuals were in gross error; communism would more than likely be a point of departure, not a terminal point. Collective property, moreover, would lack meaning unless a great deal of private property existed at its side. The "socialization of distribution," that is, by cartelization, Sorel viewed in a comparable light.[71] In the organization of socialism there could be no doctrinaire utopianism, no preconceived plans. The revolution would place all resources at the disposal of the community. The ultimate disposition of property in all its forms would depend upon the requirements of production.

The "administration of things" was the role assigned to socialist organization.[72] Socialism would be no "government of men." The idea of the general will and the institutions which derived from it, according to Sorel, could only confound a role that was purely functional. The general will of the community was presumably expressed by means of parties, campaigns, and elections; the parties supported those who were most valuable to its projects and the electorate selected those whose policies corresponded with its opinions at the moment of election. But these matters concerned party sentiments and fluctuations in public opinion. They had no particular bearing on the economy. Sorel especially berated parliamentary democracy for failing to bring to the fore men competent in matters of economics. The representatives of the people invariably displayed an astounding ignorance whenever economic matters were discussed. They had no practical experience with such matters. Socialism could dispense with everything that preoccupied liberals: public opinion, elections, parliamentary eloquence, and political alliances. Socialism

has nothing to do with the rights of men, absolute justice, political constitutions and parliaments; it repudiates not only the government of the capitalist bourgeoisie, but also every hierarchy more or less similar to the bourgeois hierarchy.[73]

The supervision of production should be the responsibility of agents of the syndicates, charged with specific duties.[74] What was alone important was to know whether those duties had been carried out effectively. The removal of all administrative arbitrariness was of vital importance. *"Actions populaires"* might be effective in this regard. Syndicates could act as judicial bodies in dealing with administrators who failed to meet their responsibilities.

Essential to the technique of a socialist order was the creation and support of a cult of work.[75] The conquests of capitalism were to be safeguarded, and the intensive character of capitalist production was to be renewed. Sorel's post-revolutionary cult of work was an unending effort at "conquest," comparable to the prerevolutionary cult of proletarian violence.

The primacy of production was essential to the operation of socialism.[76] It was the merit of Marxism that it based all its investigations on considerations of production. It was this emphasis that separated genuine socialism not only from capitalism but also from bourgeois caricatures of socialism. Sorel saw the material basis of a socialist society in production.[77] Capitalism viewed man not as a producer but as a consumer who, like the Polynesian savage, worked only when he had to. Politicians and financiers were shamelessly permitted to misdirect and exploit industry. Capitalism, moreover, was far too subject to the caprice of those who saw in science only a means of satisfying their curiosity. Utopian socialism, Sorel complained, assumed that the factory of the future would resemble "drawingrooms in which ladies meet to do embroidery." It ascribed to the proletariat feelings closely resembling those which the eighteenth century attributed to savages: goodness, simplicity, and an anxiety to imitate the bourgeoisie. It was only necessary, according to the utopians, to make the rich better and the poor more enlightened. The "primacy of production," Sorel argued, recognized the principle that the machine was the ultimate expression of man's ability to understand and control the forces of nature.[78] The construction of machines was an expression of man's freedom that could be understood and participated in by everyone who had to do with production. Through industrial production man triumphed over the arbitrary forces of nature. The constructive, the creative, the socializing forces of man could thereby be uncovered and brought to mature expression. Sorel also saw in production the cultural basis of socialism: "I am persuaded that work may serve as the basis of a culture which will make no one regret bourgeois civilization."[79] The sentiments necessary to the creation of a socialist culture were, for the most part, still absent among workers. Their education had thus far served to make them more bourgeois; they did not take seriously *idées de métier*. The utopian socialists, however, presented a conception of work which contained an intuition of a truly revolutionary principle: they had proposed that each should produce according to his abilities. The implications of this principle, however, had not been fully explored. Their utopias had been devised for a preindustrial society. According to Sorel, socialist society would be rooted in the conception that art was the highest form of work:

> Whenever we consider questions relative to industrial progress, we are led to consider art as ... the highest and technically most perfect form of production, though the artist with his caprices often seems to be at the opposite pole from the modern worker.[80]

The analogy was sound, because the artist disliked reproducing accepted types. His inexhaustibly inventive turn of mind distinguished him from the ordinary worker, who was mainly successful in the unending reproduction of models not his own. The "worker-inventor" too was an "artist" who "wears himself out in pursuing the realization of ends which practical people generally declare absurd."[81]

The centrality of production required juridical support; that is, the construction of the requisite institutional and legal apparatus.[82] Bourgeois jurisprudence was still based on eighteenth-century notions of a logical and coherent social order, but the so-called "laws of nature" had in fact been employed by the bourgeoisie in their own interests and against those of their opponents. Sorel based the argument that a socialist order required a unique juridical structuring on the assumption that justice was for all practical purposes dependent upon force. Pascal had effectively demonstrated this principle when he said that:

> Justice is subject to dispute; might is easily recognized and is not disputed. Thus it is not possible to attribute might to justice, because might has often contradicted justice, and said that it itself was just. And since it was not possible to make what was just strong, what was strong has been made just.[83]

Pascal was correct, Sorel believed, though he had confounded the various manifestations of force.[84] In economics was to be found a type of "force" which should have absolute sway and could be clearly identified with what was "just"—the imperatives of production. A perfect juridical order therefore existed when economic and intellectual circumstances converged. Sorel did not, however, consider the nature of the new forms in detail, an omission justified on the grounds that analysis and rational deduction were completely inadequate to deal with production, the most mysterious of all aspects of economics.[85] But the thrust of what he foresaw was clear. The social order was not to be governed by humanitarian considerations; he opposed, for example, the eight-hour workday, since there was no evidence that it would increase production. He favored piecework, which had brought about a gradual but uninterrupted industrial advance. The workers, in any case, were not to be treated as children and corrected with gentleness. Socialism was not a "morality of the weak." The socialist worker would be characterized by the total absorption of his personality in his work. Beyond these brief comments Sorel did not venture.

The advance of production was for him something of an ultimate goal.[86] Marx had maintained that capitalism would be struck down when all the conditions necessary for socialism had been brought to maturity. Advances in production, accordingly, would continue with the inception of the socialist era. Sorel presented a more pessimistic view: there was nothing inevitable in this advance. He saw periods of transition in history when economic productivity and industrial techniques were in real decline. He compared the effect of the two great revolutionary waves on economic advance. That economic progress had attended the French Revolution had been due to the economic setting of that upheaval:

It was because the *ancien régime* was attacked with rapid blows, at a time when production was on the road to great progress, that the contemporary world has had a relatively easy birth and has been able to be assured so quickly of a lusty life.[87]

But the triumph of Christianity came under entirely different circumstances.[88] It took place in a period of real economic decline, a decline that was not arrested. When the Roman Empire became Christian everything continued to go as badly as in the past. Still more disheartening was the spread of immorality to the church itself. Even the conversion of the barbarians did not check this downward trend:

Economic decadence was accentuated under these barbarian kings. . . . At least four centuries of barbarism were required before a progressive movement showed itself; society was compelled to descend to a state not far removed from its origins, and Vico was to find in this phenomenon an illustration of his doctrine of *ricorsi*. Thus a revolution which took place in a time of economic decadence forced the world to pass again through a period of almost primitive civilization and stopped all progress for several centuries.[89]

Such a decline, Sorel suggested, was not impossible today.[90] Should the proletariat fail to replace the moribund institutions and values of the bourgeoisie with their own new creations, then the danger would be imminent.

In that case, the proletariat would be corrupted and stultified as the Merovingians were. Socialism had to work to reverse the current and restore its impetus. The continued advance of production would be assured only if technological inventiveness could be combined with an "ethic of good work." Herein lay the key to a successful socialist order. The renewed emphasis upon invention of machinery and improvement of industrial techniques would free a socialist society from the dangers which presently beset the world of capitalism.

The creation of a "society of heroes" would parallel the advance of production.[91] Heroism was a "striving for perfection" without hope of securing a reward equivalent to the expended effort. Sorel compared the armies of the French Revolution with those of the Empire. The soldiers of the Wars of Liberty would never have performed acts of heroism if each soldier had been permitted to claim a reward proportionate to his deserts:

> When a column is sent to an assault, the men at the head know they are being sent to their death, and that the glory of victory will be for those who, passing over their dead bodies, enter the enemy's position. However, they do not reflect on this injustice, but march forward.[92]

The need for reward, which made itself actively felt in the armies of Napoleon, signaled the decline of revolutionary idealism.[93] Officers were amazed to see the fuss made about feats of arms which would have passed unnoticed in the days of their youth. "A soldier," Sorel quoted Renan, "is not made by promises of temporal rewards. He must have immortality. Instead of paradise, there is glory, which is itself a kind of immortality." Socialism, Sorel argued, had to adopt the same attitude.[94] He united in a trilogy the warrior, the artist, and the producer: they were all "heroes." In all he perceived a striving for perfection; all shared a desire to work primarily for future generations. But the producer, the "worker-inventor," was his principal concern. In every industry important advances could be cited which had originated in small changes made by workmen endowed with the artist's taste for innovation. Here was a selflessness that had nothing to do with reward. Sorel had in mind the identification of work and art to be found among medieval craftsmen. Among the architects and stonecarvers of the thirteenth century were men of extraordinary talent who seemed always to have remained anonymous. They produced masterpieces even though their genius was developed in silence and obscurity. Under socialism the same devotion to work was possible:

> This striving for perfection, which manifests itself in spite of the absence of any personal, immediate, and proportional reward, constitutes the *secret virtue* which assures the continued progress of the world.[95]

The present era, "which seems to many to presage the darkest future," could give way to a "society of heroes."

Chapter

4

The Impact

The impact of Sorel, of his personal activities and his writings, on revolutionary syndicalism presents more than the usual complexities. He did not write for the workers, and he disclaimed any interest in founding a "school." On the contrary, his declared ambition was to make his conceptions a faithful reflection of the tendencies which appeared to guide a movement in being. Whether intended or not, however, the question of his influence or lack of it can legitimately be raised. His work in both France and Italy produced a reaction that was peculiar to the development of syndicalism. In each country, the movement was compounded of various kinds or levels of activity and reaction to Sorel's work varied accordingly. One may distinguish an official level—that is, the activities of the principal organizations of the movement directed by its leaders; a supporting level, of the organs of the movement, which were, for the most part, related publications reflecting special interests or tendencies; and, finally, an individual level, of the partisans of the movement (workers, organizers, journalists, and sympathizers on all intellectual levels), who either directly or marginally identified themselves with the aims and methods of revolutionary syndicalism. In addition to the kinds of problems stemming from a consideration of these various levels are others that arise when ideas are misunderstood, distorted, or otherwise put to purposes unintended by their author. The main fact that emerges from any appraisal of these varied factors is that the impact of Sorel's work was both more marked and more variegated in Italy than in France.

I

One is struck by Sorel's failure to win any appreciable attention in France, let alone a following there. The explanation probably lies in the fact that the movement on all levels was not for long, if it ever had been, projected in the direction Sorel designated. The methods and purposes that he attributed to revolutionary syndicalism in France, in fact, were not generally characteristic of the movement. Except for the *Mouvement socialiste*, in whose activities he had been directly involved (and that was only for a few years), Sorel's influence on supporting groups and publications was extremely limited. From the origins of Guieysse's *Pages libres* in 1901 to its demise in 1909, occasional contributors such as Lagardelle and Halévy, as well as Guieysse himself, demonstrated serious interest in Sorel's work. Sorel himself only published one article here after 1901 (apart from excerpts from his books).[1] The *Pages libres* remained essentially a review of general culture, only vaguely proletarian and never explicitly syndicalist or Sorelian (that is, never dominated by Sorel's conception of a proletarian *ricorso*).

By January 1904 the *Mouvement socialiste* had, indeed, turned Sorelian.[2] The articles of such socialist luminaries as Bernstein and Jaurès, as well as those of Émile Vandervelde, Morris Hyndman, Beatrice and Sidney Webb, Karl Kautsky, Wilhelm Liebknecht, Rosa Luxembourg, and Leonida Bissolati, had by then disappeared from its pages. Lagardelle had been convinced by Sorel of the need for a "revolutionary" rather than a "Bernsteinian" revision of Marxism and had accordingly transformed his periodical into a "school" where syndicalism, viewed as a spontaneous manifestation of the workingmen's movement, could be studied with sympathy and in depth by intellectuals who had rallied to the movement. Sorel began to publish his articles and reviews in quantity here in mid-1905 and continued to do so well into 1908.[3] He was unquestionably the chief spokesman of the period, writing more articles and reviews than any other contributor. With Sorel sounding the "main theme"— and it was apocalyptic—various contributors to the periodical provided the "variations."

The *Mouvement socialiste* became an international review of *haute culture révolutionnaire*. Militants and theoreticians of France met here on common ground. The articles of those directly involved in CGT affairs, however—Griffuelhes, Pouget, Delesalle, Merrheim, and Yvetot—beyond occasional references to Sorel revealed little interest in his theorizing.[4] Those of Ernest Lafont and André Morizet exhibited some degree of dependence, but only the contributions of Lagardelle and Berth really breathed the spirit of Sorelian violence. Among foreign contributors, the Italians alone exhibited the same bent. A variety of journalist-academicians intimately involved in syndicalist affairs, such as Arturo Labriola, Enrico Leone, Paolo Orano, Angelo O. Olivetti, Sergio Panunzio, and Agostino Lanzillo, were Sorel's most devoted supporters.[5] Essays by others—especially Croce, Pareto, and the "Italianized German," Michels—whose influence on Italian thought extended well beyond socialism or socialist circles were also published in the review.

As editor, Lagardelle conducted a number of surveys, notably the one in 1905–1906 on "the fatherland and the working class."[6] Replies were solicited, for the most part, from CGT officials. The inquiry revealed general agreement between workers and Hervéistes (followers of Gustave Hervé, renowned for his spectacular attacks on militarism and patriotism). Lagardelle concluded that antimilitarism and antipatriotism were "an integral part of revolutionary syndicalism."[7] The survey was significant, however, in its failure to reveal anything like the "proletarian nationalism" which concurrently had begun to appear in some Italian syndicalist circles, and, in fact, in the work of some of the Italian contributors to the *Mouvement socialiste.*

Two periodicals, the *Avant-garde* and the *Action directe,* briefly extended Sorelian activities elsewhere into the proletarian movement. The weekly *Avant-garde* of Paris from 1905–1906 on placed Lagardelle and Berth in association with Hervé, who was shortly to launch the celebrated *Guerre sociale.*[8] The collaboration was in a way a follow-up of the inquiry into working-class patriotism. Sorel himself thought Hervé a demagogue. Beyond a common aversion to traditional militarism and patriotism, no real rapport could be established between Hervé and Sorel's friends. The *Action directe* was also a Paris weekly, which appeared only briefly in 1908.[9] Since it had no official ties with the CGT, its contributors, who included some of the regulars of the *Voix du peuple* as well as of the *Mouvement socialiste,* were afforded considerably more scope in matters of theory than they were in the *Voix du peuple.* Lagardelle and others frequently discussed Sorel's theory of violence; an extended discussion of the *Réflexions* in August 1908 was interrupted, however, by the announcement that four members of the editorial board, all officials of the CGT, had been arrested in connection with the Villeneuve-St. Georges affair and that the periodical would cease publication.

The failures of both the *Avant-garde* and *Action directe* were, possibly, indicative of Sorel's inability to extend his influence significantly beyond his immediate following, that is, beyond Lagardelle and Berth. Sorel established close friendships with a mere handful of militants in the CGT, who often mentioned him as a sincere friend of the workers. Delesalle, for one, was a self-educated worker who had turned from anarchism to syndicalism to become an official of the CGT.[10] Robert Louzon was also a self-educated worker with journalistic pretensions.[11] Though their concern was with practical problems, they reflected Sorelian attitudes in matters concerning the merits of working-class scission and the *"morale* of producers." It cannot be said, however, that their articles in the *Voix du peuple,* the *Mouvement socialiste,* and the *Action directe* explored Sorel's formulations either in depth or with originality.

Sorel did impress others less directly associated with the syndicalist movement, but for the most part, only those in his immediate circle of friends. Péguy, for example, frequently referred to Sorel as his *"maître"* "in all things which touch on techniques, industry, the relation between science and industry."[12] With characteristic pomposity, he noted that Sorel's conception of morality was "its highest expression, its definitive expression. ... There can be no other." There is more than a suggestion of parentage between Sorel's version of Vico's *ricorso* and Péguy's notion of the degeneration of *"mystique"* into *"politique,"* by which he characterized the Dreyfus affair. Halévy, too, was a young man disenchanted with the bourgeois world who admitted his intellectual debt to Sorel at a time when he also looked to a "society of producers."[13] These professions of admiration and indebtedness came from men who, though caught up in the same intellectual and political currents, were oriented toward literature and were distinguished (especially Péguy) by considerable independence of mind.

Lagardelle, however, the young editor of the *Mouvement socialiste* who had been trained in law and had written his *doctorat* on the evolution of French syndicates, had come under Sorel's influence in 1898 while still in his early twenties.[14] Up to 1908, though in a somewhat irregular fashion, paralleled in his writings the ideas of his master. In a contribution to an inquiry of 1905 which he directed, he viewed the general strike in an almost mystical light.[15] The world could be renewed, he insisted, only by a total rupture with the past, and that required the cultivation of a revolutionary myth and violence. A new note appeared in his work in 1906, destined to reappear almost three decades later in another context—a distinction between *l'homme abstrait* and *l'homme réel*.[16] The abstract man was an invention of political democracy, the "citizen" without class identity. Far superior was the socialist conception of "producer," the man who organized in defense of his material and moral interests. Elsewhere Lagardelle drew attention to Sorel's argument that the future of the proletarian movement depended on the militancy of the syndicates, and he warned of their becoming "political clubs" and playing the parliamentary game.[17] No "parasites" were to be admitted. No traffic with the democratic state or with any other "tyranny" was to be tolerated. In *Le Parti socialiste et la C. G. T.* of 1908, however, although he adopted Sorel's battle-cry, *"Retour à Marx,"* he now believed "political weapons" useful.[18] This pronouncement was an indication of Lagardelle's growing separation from Sorel. The Charte d'Amiens of 1906, he asserted, had implied that, provided political methods were considered "secondary," political weapons could be valuable. He had employed the same argument when he defended his activities at the Socialist Congress of Nancy in 1907, against which Sorel had protested.[19] After Sorel left the review, Lagardelle became more deeply involved in the affairs of the Socialist party. By January 1911, in fact, the break with Sorelian violence was complete. Lagardelle was now prepared to admit that syndicalism was not incompatible with the spirit of parliamentary democracy.[20]

Perhaps Sorel's most devoted friend and disciple was Berth, who had been diverted from a university career by the Dreyfus affair.[21] Financial distress subsequently forced him into a second career with the Paris Assistance Publique, where he served for many years as a hospital administrator. Berth retained from his days at the university a penchant for Hegel and Bergson, as well as for Sorel. It was Sorel, however, who had induced him to continue his career as a publicist, begun during the Dreyfus affair. In his first articles in the *Mouvement socialiste* Berth revealed an overriding hostility to the modern state.[22] "The state is dead," he asserted simply. This he believed a "dynamic truth." The "ideal curve" of history demonstrated that the "era of states" would be supplanted by the "era of classes." He railed as much against Guesdist statism as against the bourgeois variety. *Les Méfaits des intellectuals,* a collection of articles published in the *Mouvement socialiste* from 1905 to 1908, turned to a related theme: the role of "nonproducers" in general and "intellectuals and merchants" in particular, who fought over the spoils that possession of the state made possible.[23] The intellectual who pretended to be scornful of the merchant was himself something of a merchant. Berth pushed to the limit Sorel's scorn of professional intellectuals: there would be no place for them in the new order. Society would be stateless, with "no traditions, no routines." It would possess an economy firmly in the hands of those who labored, an economy in a perpetual state of revolution and heroism.

Sorel's theory of myths was the subject of Berth's *Les Nouveaux aspects du socialisme,* published in 1908.[24] Man needs to believe that the entire universe has joined him in his efforts before he will act decisively. The discovery of revolutionary myths by Sorel had saved the catastrophic tradition in Marxism. The "iron law of wages," for example, though it had little claim to scientific validity, was a vivid illustration of the hopelessness of labor, and therefore served to keep the proletariat from the morass of reformism and social peace. For syndicalism, class war was a symbol of life, while social peace was a mark of atrophy and death. Berth drew from the metaphysics of Hegel and Bergson to support Sorel's conception of the socialist order of the future and arrived at conclusions similar to those of Lagardelle. The bourgeois order was "geometric," he wrote, statist, intellectual, and governmental, while the proletarian order would be "vital," founded on the "technical discipline of labor." The "universal abstract" would give way to the "universal concrete." A final article by Berth in Lagardelle's review on Proudhon looked hopefully to the formation of Sorel's "*morale* of producers."[25] Bourgeois morality was finished. It had become a mere "degeneration of the sentiment of honor." When Berth broke with Lagardelle's review in 1908, he explained that revolutionary syndicalism had not justified the hopes he had placed in it.[26] The movement had fallen into anarchism or political socialism. The myth that Sorel had discovered in syndicalism had been dissipated within a few years.

The efforts of Sorel, Lagardelle, and Berth produced no serious response in the syndicalist movement—their influence on the CGT was virtually nil.[27] The Nouvelle École, with the *Mouvement socialiste* as its organ, was supposed to bring militants and theoreticians into close harmony, but the project never bore fruit. The leading militants of the movement and their organs seem hardly to have taken cognizance of Sorel's work. Pataud's weekly *Voix du peuple* of Paris, the chief organ of the CGT, rarely mentioned Sorel.[28] Though violent and passionate in tone, it was concerned with practical day-to-day problems. There were publications of local organizations throughout France, for the most part monthlies, ranging from revolutionary to reformist, but here, too, there was little or no interest in theory, and Sorel's name rarely appeared. Even the "manifesto" of the Nouvelle École, the *Réflexions,* "fell flat" in workingmen's circles. The sensation it created was in a totally different quarter, one not without some embarrassment to its author.[29] When Griffuelhes, the secretary-general of the CGT (who considered himself a worker) was asked about Sorel's influence among workers, he replied, "I read Alexandre Dumas."[30] Others have also testified to the fact that Sorel's work and Sorelian conceptions in general were unknown to the workers.

The CGT, moreover, as it developed during the first decade of the century tended to lose much of its initial intransigence.[31] There were no severe economic dislocations. Eventually, as Sorel had feared, the CGT turned to the recently unified Socialist party when it required protection and support. When Sorel had first been drawn to the CGT in 1903, strikes and violent demonstrations had followed one another almost without interruption.[32] The organization had only recently been invaded by anarchists. Under the leadership of Griffuelhes, Pouget, Merrheim, Yvetot, and Pataud, the CGT, tainted with anarchism, declared virtual war on capitalism and its socialist collaborators in parliament. The Congress of Bourges in September 1904 had officially proclaimed a revolutionary posture, antimilitarist and antipatriotic. As a guiding principle, however, revolutionary syndicalism reached its zenith with the general strike of 1906 called in favor of the eight-hour workday. The strike, attended by considerable violence and repression, failed in its immediate objective. In October the more conservative federations at the Congress of Amiens urged cooperation with the Socialist party. The move was briefly blocked by the radical syndicates—who succeeded in voting the Charte d'Amiens, reaffirming the autonomy of the CGT with respect to political parties and the state and again sanctioning antimilitarist and antipatriotic propaganda—but the revolutionary elements nevertheless weakened after 1906.[33] The general strike of 1906 had been their most comprehensive undertaking, and it failed because only a comparatively small minority of workers could be persuaded to support it for long. It brought disillusionment and disappointment to revolutionaries and gave wider scope to the activities of reformists. The consequences of the strikes of 1908 at Villeneuve-St. Georges and Draveil effected the turn toward reformism during the prewar years.

The leaders of the CGT (and this is perhaps more to the point) had all along conceived of revolutionary syndicalism in terms far more mundane and not at all Sorelian. Even when its revolutionary posture and rhetoric were most pronounced, Sorel had pretended to see in the movement attitudes that were not really there. The divergence was particularly striking with respect to methods.[34] The militants of the CGT had no taste for the pessimistic nuances of the Sorelian myth; the general strike was for them no "myth" but a weapon, practical and concrete. With energy and patience it could be effective as an instrument of immediate gain or even of revolution. The CGT militants certainly considered themselves the elite of the workers. Some may have viewed the syndicates as the society of the future in microcosm, but when embattled they were not averse to accepting aid from the Socialist party. Moreover, the militants did not view violence in Sorelian terms: it played for them a more vulgar, if not a more brutal, role. Strikes and sabotage (which Sorel condemned) would bring, they were convinced, immediate and material advantages as well as the ultimate destruction of the wage system.

The socialist society was also envisioned very differently by the militants.[35] They would have viewed the stern Sorelian *morale* as "reactionary." The militants had no interest in social pessimism or in chastity, but wanted a constant amelioration of material living conditions. They wanted such things as female emancipation and greater liberty in sexual relations—the syndicates were, in fact, centers of birth control and sex-for-pleasure propaganda. The militants viewed the society of the future in an anarchist and individualist light. Essentially optimists and ingenuous believers in the native goodness of men, they wanted no constraints of any kind, which explains their very hostile antimilitarist and antipatriotic propaganda. They on no account sought to establish Sorel's "society of heroes"—what they wanted was a shorter workday, greater wealth, and a maximum of consumer goods. There is no evidence that militants would have been interested in the severe moral obligations Sorel foresaw in a future socialist society.

The evolution of syndicalism in France during the two years following the departures of Sorel and Berth only confirmed their suspicions.[36] In March 1909 Louis Niel became secretary-general of the CGT; he was replaced in July by Laon Jouhaux. With Griffuelhes, who had led the organization since 1902, in the background, reformism triumphed. The CGT now acquired a departmental, federal, and confederal structure. The conservative federations exercised the preponderant influence. Though another rash of strikes broke out in 1909 and 1910, the CGT turned to the Socialist party in the prewar years for help in defending itself and implementing its demands. The "heroic" period of revolutionary syndicalism in France was over.

II

In Italy Sorel's efforts on behalf of revolutionary syndicalism reaped a more substantial reward. The response to his work can be attributed to a mood of rebellion far more pronounced than that in France. Apart from a deeper level of working-class discontent, there was exasperation with Giolittismo and a conviction that the Risorgimento had fallen short or had been diverted from its goals, either social or national or both. That mood of rebellion was exemplified by the popularity of the Marxian theory of class struggle, the will-to-power philosophy of Nietzsche, and the pragmatism of James. "Sorelismo," as it came to be called, was symptomatic of the Italian mood of revolt.[37] Sorel, consequently, received far wider attention than he did in France. Far more was written about him, written by men of the first intellectual rank. In labor circles his impact on those of anarcho-syndicalist, syndicalist, or even socialist persuasion was also far more pronounced. A number of groups and related periodicals of varying tendencies appeared, explicitly identifying themselves as "Neo-Marxist" or Sorelian. The mainstream of the syndicalist movement, though with significant exceptions, could not, however, be persuaded to follow the rigorous path Sorel and his Italian followers had charted.

The impact of Sorel's ideas upon a small number of writers whose work commanded national attention gave Sorel access to an Italian reading public well beyond the limits of the syndicalist movement. Croce was the most enthusiastic, but Pareto and Michels did not lag far behind in their admiration for Sorel's work. All three, moreover, published in syndicalist reviews, had met Sorel in Paris, and had corresponded with him.

Croce encountered Sorel when at the close of the century he had undertaken a deep study of Marxian socialism; their correspondence, begun in 1895, led eventually to a meeting in Paris in 1902.[38] By 1905 Croce's interests had shifted to history, literary criticism, and social ethics. He had acquired prominence in intellectual circles, by means of his review, the *Critica,* extending his influence far beyond his own Naples. Perhaps more than anyone else Croce was instrumental in popularizing Sorel in Italy; he secured publication of Sorel's major works and lent the prestige of his name to Sorel's efforts. An article on Sorel's *Système* written in 1907 was revised and republished as the preface to the Italian edition of the *Réflexions.* Croce's endorsement of Sorel's work was most flattering: "I have never ceased to read the publications of Sorel, because of the trust [in his work] that he, with his singular penetration and supreme integrity, has inspired in me."[39] The *Réflexions* were "in perfect accord with an immanentist view" of history.[40] Sorel might not have shared this opinion, for he considered his method scientific rather than metaphysical. In any case, Croce believed the work itself to be something of a *ricorso,* that is, a return of historical writing to its "intimate" nature, and as in every *ricorso,* there was in the *Réflexions* something "barbaric" and "spontaneous."[41] Sorel's prime concern was the discovery of the source from which moral values spring; hence his theory of violence. Croce, too, looked to new values to replace the optimism, the pacifism, the humanitarianism, and all the other "trashy ideals" of the eighteenth century. He accepted Sorel's conception of morality as one which "rules all the actions" of life. "*Morale,* being universal, is not outside any action."[42] In an article on Marx in 1910, Croce declared that he no longer considered Marxism to be philosophy or economic theory.[43] It was not thought, but action; the "acute perception" of Marx had been "practically and morally inventive." His theories had operated and would continue to operate in modern society: "And its new action is today called syndicalism, and its new will, Georges Sorel." Marxism, he also wrote in the *Giornale d'Italia,* was in conflict with Freemasonry, the "principles of 1848" against the "principles of 1789."[44] The final victory would go to one or to the other. The conflict between the two systems guided the labors of "the greatest representative" of Marxism, Sorel.

As early as 1901 Sorel had invited Pareto to present a series of lectures at the École des Hautes Études Sociales. The following year Pareto, professor of political economy at Lausanne, published his *Les Systèmes socialistes,* in which he recognized the originality of Sorelian syndicalism and its essential agreement with many of his own views.[45] The *Manuale di economia politica,* which first appeared in 1906, gave continuing evidence that Pareto's admiration for Sorel had not diminished. Pareto thought the *Réflexions* "the most remarkable scientific work which since many a year had seen the light of day."[46] It was concerned with "scientific realities" and not at all with "empty humanitarian declamations devoid of sense." Though Sorel may have had France largely in mind, what he wrote applied equally well to Italy. A "new elite will follow the old," and Sorel's exposition of syndicalism permitted one to see something of its "force and dignity." The theory of myths Pareto thought Sorel's most original discovery: to understand a social movement one must understand the language and the forms by which it expresses its aspirations. Sorel's greatest merit, however, lay in his discovery that the problem of modern collectivism was principally one of production.[47] Pareto was also intrigued by Sorel's observations on the cowardice of the bourgeoisie. Sorel, he noted, had written that a great war or a great extension of proletarian violence might restore to the bourgeoisie something of its former vigor. Pareto thought the first possibility more likely, but he did not rule out the prospect of a bourgeoisie defending itself against the threat of proletarian violence, for this was precisely where Pareto's sympathies lay. Though intellectually attracted to Sorelian syndicalism, he nevertheless hoped that the bourgeoisie might still save itself. In a letter of 1907 to his publisher he asserted his intellectual identity with Sorel: "Sorel and I," he wrote, "starting from opposite points, have reached identical conclusions."[48] Two years later he wrote to Sorel, notwithstanding the apparent failure of syndicalism, that the movement might some day be transformed and reappear under another name.[49]

By no means on the same intellectual level as Croce or Pareto, Michels during the first decade of the century completed his studies and began a career as professor of political economy at various Swiss and Italian universities. He had barely started the development of a sociology of politics when he met Sorel at a Lagardelle "Sunday tea" and a correspondence ensued.[50] Though not directly involved in the movement, he published in leading French and Italian syndicalist periodicals. In a 1906 study on the German Social Democratic party marked by frequent allusions to Sorel's "society of producers," Michels foresaw the establishment of a social order which would end the "chaos of production" by rendering the authentic "producers" masters of production.[51] In 1908 in *Il Proletariato e la borghesia nel movimento socialista italiano,* which received wide attention, he urged that full use be made of a parliamentary group working on behalf of a revolutionary movement.[52] Such political action he did not believe incompatible with Sorelian scission. Socialism, he was convinced, could be reborn only with the aid of revolutionary syndicalism.[53]

The most important centers of Sorelismo, however, were to be found in a variety of syndicalist publications of varying tendencies.[54] Regionalism added to the variety; major publications appeared in numerous cities throughout Italy, whereas in France they were to be found almost exclusively in Paris. They were organs of working-class information, propaganda, theory, or some combination of the three. Here were assembled an assortment of writers attracted to Sorel's views. Some, at least until 1906, belonged to the Socialist party and participated in elections. In fact, little differentiation was made before 1906 between "revolutionary syndicalism" and "revolutionary social-ism." All denounced the party for its cowardice and attempted also to work closely with militants of the labor movement to promote more or less Sorelian objectives.

The first such publication was the *Avanguardia socialista,* a workers' weekly of Milan (also briefly of Bologna) published from late 1902 to 1906, that aimed to strike at socialist reformism at its center.[55] It was directed by Labriola, a university tutor in political economy who was widely regarded as Sorel's foremost Italian disciple, and by the journalist Walter Mocchi. As the tribune of the intransigent fraction of the Socialist party and the Camera del Lavoro of Milan, the weekly was devoted far more to syndicalist organization and practice (particularly to the railroad workers, after 1905) than to doctrine.[56] Labriola had discovered that the "ammunition" employed by Sorel against Jaurès and Millerand could be used by *Avanguardia socialista* with even greater effectiveness against Turati and Treves, the leading socialist reformists. Sorel's "L'Avenir" was translated and published here in 1903, and subsequently became almost a bible of Sorelian syndicalism;[57] Italian revolutionary syn-dicalists thereafter usually dated the origins of their movement with its publi-cation in Italy. It was Labriola in the *Avanguardia socialista* who inspired the general strike of 1904. The weekly preached "heroic violence" and a workers' republic dedicated to production: "Our thinking coincides with that of

Sorel."[58] The contributors to the weekly included Leone, Orano, Panunzio, and Emanuale Longobardi, all either present or future academicians. The journalists Mocchi, Tomasso Monicelli, and Roberto Forges-Davanzati published here, as well as the elder Costantino Lazzari and the young Benito Mussolini,[59] both revolutionary socialists. Directly or indirectly, all, including Mussolini, proclaimed their adherence to Sorel's "catastrophic revolution" and "*morale* of producers."[60]

Devoted primarily to theory, the *Divenire sociale* was a monthly founded by Enrico Leone and the journalist Paolo Mantica that took the name of the Parisian review with which Sorel had been associated.[61] It was published in Rome from 1905 to 1911 as the organ, at least initially, of the syndicalist faction of the Socialist party. After the demise of Labriola's weekly in 1906 it became the leading syndicalist organ, widely regarded as the Italian equivalent of the *Mouvement socialiste*. The *Divenire sociale* attempted to instill in Italian youth an antipolitical, antimilitarist, and antipatriotic orientation, all within a Sorelian framework. Sorel's articles, especially the series on violence in 1905–1906, dominated the review. Appearing in great profusion from 1905 through mid-1910, many of these articles had never been published in France. Here, too, Sorel was studied, quoted, praised, and defended against all possible defamers.[62] One regular contributor styled himself "Soreliano." Croce, Pareto, and Michels published here, as did many of the contributors to the *Avanguardia socialista*. The lawyers Olivetti and Lanzillo, the academicians Alfonso de Pietri-Tonelli and Francisco Arcà, and the nationalist *literati* Giuseppe Prezzolini and Giovanni Papini, as well as several of Sorel's French disciples and friends, also contributed, but Sorel, by acknowledgment and by the preponderance of his own articles, was undisputed *maestro*. When established in 1905 the review was categorically antinationalist, but by 1910, as discussion intensified concerning a possible Libyan war, Mazzinian, irredentist, and even imperialist ideas were discussed; various contributors to the *Divenire sociale* inveighed against the pacifist internationalism of the Socialist party, though Leone's editorial policies remained unchanged. Sorel's articles by then frequently included comments favorable both to the French monarchist and to the Italian nationalist movements.[63] The review did not long survive Sorel's break with Italian syndicalism and the controversies in syndicalist and socialist circles over the question of war in Libya.

At least a dozen additional newspapers and reviews with a working-class orientation published from about 1903 to 1910 exhibited a Sorelian accent, modified by a special tendency. Sorel, Lagardelle, and Berth wrote with some regularity for these publications, which proliferated particularly between the general strike of 1904 and the attempted unification of the labor movement in 1906. The *Lotta proletaria* of Mirandola, directed by Ottavio Dinale, favored direct action and was rigorously "apolitical,"[64] while the *Sindacato operaio* of

Rome, directed by Romolo Sabatini (with Leone and Alceste de Ambris), was more politically oriented, unwilling to exclude "*astensionisti*" from its pages.[65] The *Azione* and its successor the *Azione sindacalista* of Rome, the *Propaganda* of Naples, and the *Lotta di classe* of Milan were all at various times directed by Labriola or Leone or both. All were organs of the revolutionary faction of the Socialist party and explicit adherents of Neo-Marxism.[66] The *Guerra sociale* of Turin (in which both Sorel and Lagardelle published briefly) was modelled and named after Hervé's Parisian antimilitarist journal,[67] while the *Bandiera del popolo* of Mirandola, directed by the organizer Edmondo Rossoni, was the organ of the local *camera del lavoro*. Still others were imbued with the Sorelian conception of violence: the *Internazinale* of Parma, the *Difesa* of Florence, the *Gioventù* of Milan and its successor (under a new name) the *Gioventù socialista* of Rome, directed by Michele Bianchi and Orano, respectively.

Until Sorel's break with Italian syndicalism and as long as his comments on the French and Italian nationalist movements appeared to be no more than incidental, editorial policy in these periodicals remained more or less Sorelian, that is, dedicated to the pursuit of Sorel's "catastrophic idea" by way of the strike. Sorel occasionally published here; more often, however, his works were excerpted. He was always praised, and was defended against all detractors. His opposition in 1909 to syndicalist involvement in the Ferrer affair evoked a flurry of criticism, especially among anarchists,[68] but even in this instance he was not without defenders, of whom Lanzillo was foremost. These periodicals reveal not only the extent of the diffusion of Sorelismo but also the number of syndicalist organizers Sorel apparently reached: de Ambris, Bianchi, Rossoni, and Filippo Corridoni, who was not yet twenty.

The *Pagine libere* of Lugano in Italian Switzerland, founded in late 1906 by the exile A. O. Olivetti with Orano and then Labriola as co-director, was possibly the most unusual of the Sorelian reviews; it too took the name of a Parisian review with which Sorel was associated.[69] From the start, although rigorously proletarian, it was nationalist. Its "Presentazione" of December 1906 favored a "national syndicalism."[70] The *Pagine libere* attempted to link the proletarian *ricorso* with a renewal of the Risorgimento. The nation was declared to be the "*massimo sindacato*." The workers were to be raised simultaneously to the "summit of history" and a restoration of their "*italianità*." The contributors to the periodicals included virtually all the regulars of the *Divenire sociale,* as well as Monicelli, Forges-Davanzati, Maurizio Maraviglia, and Luigi Federzoni, who (Olivetti boasted some years later) were to constitute the editorial board of the *Idea nazionale,* organ of the nationalist movement established the following decade. Still others were Rossoni, Corridoni, and Mussolini.

Publications aside, at the heart of Sorelismo were academicians, journalists, and organizers serving revolutionary syndicalism at Socialist party congresses as well as on syndicalist publications or in labor agitation. Virtually all corresponded with Sorel, though their views were by no means identical in all matters. Among the most active were Neapolitans (Labriola, Leone, Lanzillo, Longobardi, Mocchi, and Mantica) and young academicians-to-be trained in political economy, law, or philosophy (Labriola, Leone, Orano, Olivetti, Panunzio, Lanzillo, de Pietri-Tonelli, and Longobardi). Most were under thirty during the first decade of the century.[71] What significance is to be attached to these matters is not at all clear, but it may be hazarded that coming from the rural south, Neapolitans would give special emphasis not only to violence but to antiauthoritarian traditions in general. Moreover, they were more likely to sound a responsive chord among agricultural laborers in north and north-central Italy than among workers in industrial cities. It may also be speculated that academic syndicalism may have been more closely attuned to the latest intellectual currents than to the realities of working-class life. Their youthful enthusiasm, in any case, may have made up for any deficiencies. Contrary to Sorel's doctrines, they remained in the Socialist party; Labriola ran for parliament as early as 1904. Such a group had hardly existed in France. The Italian syndicalists had good reasons for their socialism, however. It was clear by 1905 that they could not control the trade-union movement, while the party still provided opportunities for action. The party had a strong hold on a large part of the labor force and possessed considerable parliamentary representation. The syndicalist leaders, moreover, had been party members before notions of Sorelian violence came into vogue. They were to remain in the party until they were expelled in 1908.[72]

Arturo Labriola was a young tutor at the University of Naples who had attended Pareto's lectures in Lausanne and Sorel's "talks" in Paris during his exile. Returning to Italy to serve in Milan as director of the *Avanguardia socialista,* he published widely in both Italian and French reviews.[73] His tempestuous eloquence had been a factor of no small importance in promoting the general strike in 1904. Shortly after the establishment of the *Avanguardia socialista,* he wrote that Sorel was "the most penetrating and most original of present-day socialist writers."[74] Labriola too saw in Marxism only an artifice, an "abridged exposition of reality." He warned also of the danger of "professional thinkers" who, when they could no longer be supported by the dominant class, looked to the proletariat for possible victims of their exploitation. This warning, he noted, had also been issued by Pareto. Labriola's *Riforme e rivoluzione sociale* of 1904 was an attack on parliamentary democracy and reformism.[75] He took up Sorel's plea that the "Marxism in Marx" be preserved. He dedicated himself to the cause of transfusion of Sorel's doctrine of violence into Italian workingmen's organizations. In 1908 came his expulsion from the Socialist party—a blow, because he had always viewed the parliament as a center of revolutionary action. As co-director of the *Pagine libere* from 1907 to 1909 his syndicalism took a nationalist turn.[76] (He was to write many years later that his outlook had been somewhat nationalist even as director of the Milan weekly.) Labriola had never been an admirer either of the pacifist internationalism of socialism or of Hervé's antimilitarism, and he saw no conflict between socialism and patriotism. By 1910 he was clearly expressing nationalist ideas, but from a "proletarian" standpoint: "Whoever finds illogical the sentiment of national independence must find equally illogical the sentiment of class independence."[77] He now fused the two: not only was the proletariat a victim of history, but so was Italy. Labriola had become an exponent of an "imperialism of the poor."

The director of the *Divenire sociale* and the *Azione,* Enrico Leone was also an academician. As professor of political economy at Rome, he was first drawn to Sorel by an interest in industrial productivity. His *L'Economia sociale in rapporto al socialismo* of 1904 had declared that "private" enterprise would have to give way to "social" enterprise if a new advance in productivity were to be achieved.[78] What was required was the release of new energies, available only in the proletariat. Leone (with some show of independence) provided the preface to Sorel's *Lo Sciopero generale e la violenza* of 1906, an early version of the *Réflexions.*[79] Sorel had presented the general strike as "the key to modern socialism." But Leone denied that violence could be a source of "rights"—rights would be the "automatic product" of economic development. Violence could not be an end in itself. Nevertheless, he saw in the general strike "genuine creative powers." The success of the general strike would in itself constitute proof of the historic readiness of the proletariat to assume the direction of a syndicalist order without an extended dispersal of energy and without suspension of social life. A study of 1907 further noted that proletarian violence would diminish with the growth of proletarian institutions—Leone and Sorel had identical views on the reformist "illusion" of the political conquest of power, on the need for a rigorous isolation of the proletariat, and on Marxism as an "instrument" to be applied in the present setting in which "the contingent and the variable must be reconciled with the typical and the constant."[80]

A native of Bologna practicing law and journalism in Lugano, Angelo O. Olivetti had founded the *Pagine libere* in 1906. In articles published from 1906 to 1911, he asserted that Sorelian syndicalism ruled out any "international utopias." Sorel implied that the hierarchy of syndicates must culminate in the "nation";[81] indeed, the nation could be viewed as a super-syndicate. But the "nationalization" of the syndicates did not mean that the proletariat should be any less hostile to the bourgeois state or to bourgeois nationalism. Olivetti, in fact, accepted Sorel's conception of violence without reservation. The syndicalism taught by Sorel, in any event, possessed no formal content. It was a philosophy "of action, of life, of energy."[82] There was no reason why syndicalism could not be national, why workers could not be patriots. The proletariat was obliged to act within the confines of the nation even though the immediate objective was social revolution.[83] Reformism Olivetti thought the greatest danger, because it would strengthen bourgeois institutions.[84] Only if the syndicalists were truly "aristocratic" in mind and in spirit, not like the legal or monied aristocracy but one of "blood and sinew," "open to all the brave," could the danger be averted.[85] He insisted, above all, that the truly great traditions of the Italian people had not entered into unification.[86] The unification had been "partly Piedmontese, partly French, partly Austrian," but not at all "Italian." The Italian tradition was republican and federal. The completion of the Risorgimento in its real sense would be the work of revolutionary syndicalism.

Paolo Orano, trained in philosophy, was a high school teacher. In 1903 he served briefly on the editorial staff of the *Avanti!* With Labriola and Leone he became a leading promoter of Sorelian syndicalism.[87] Orano was among those who left the party in 1906; he then worked as a labor organizer in Ferrara and Parma. During that period he directed the *Gioventù socialista* and the *Azione sindacalista,* two workingmen's publications. From 1907 to 1908 he also served as co-director of the *Pagine libere.* In articles in these and other publications he dispensed the usual fare of syndicalists on the bourgeois state, on intellectuals, and on the Socialist party, all in a Sorelian "sauce." A major scholarly effort was his *Cristo e Quirino,* in which he commented at length on Sorel's *Système.*[88] Sorel, he said, had made a unique contribution to both the history of Christianity and the theory of syndicalism by viewing primitive Christianity as a revolutionary movement. The comparison with Christianity had revealed not only the character but the potential of syndicalism. By 1910, as discussion concerning the merits of war in Libya grew more intense, Orano was preparing to go beyond the *Pagine libere* in attempting to accommodate Sorelian syndicalism with a proletarian nationalism.[89]

A practicing lawyer and a member of the Socialist party until 1908, Sergio Panunzio also contributed to syndicalist periodicals in Italy and France, attempting to explore the juridical implications of Sorelian violence both in a revolutionary movement and in a functioning social order.[90] A 1907 article (written when he was in his early twenties) explored further Sorel's conception of a working-class elite.[91] Throughout history vigorous, homogeneous, and conscientious minorities invariably triumphed over complacent, heterogeneous, and unorganized majorities. These minorities were the bearers of new rights imposed by "conquest." Panunzio's *La Persistenza del diritto* of 1910, on the origins of law, went further.[92] He viewed conflict as the most persistent of all social facts: from conflict came power, from power came law. Syndicalism, based as it was on direct action, would mean the emergence of a new juridical and institutional configuration. Panunzio went beyond Sorel: syndicalism was antistatist only in appearance. Unlike anarchism, it opposed only the traditional state. A regime operating on the imperatives of industrial production would of necessity, he maintained, be "authoritarian." Accepting the distinction Sorel had made in the *Réflexions* between violence and force, he asserted that the triumph of syndicalism would come with the transformation of syndicalist violence into syndicalist force.

Agostino Lanzillo, a young lawyer and journalist in Rome, trained in both law and economics, was expelled from the Socialist party in 1908.[93] He replied in the *Mouvement socialiste* with a stinging denunciation of the "moral and intellectual decadence" of the party.[94] He published frequently in the *Divenire sociale* and the *Pagine libere*. Lanzillo had met Sorel at Péguy's and had provided the preface to the Italian translation of the *Illusions,* where he claimed Sorel as his *maestro*.[95] Sorel's theory of myths he called a "philosophy of the fist." Sorel's critique of the democratic idea—the rights of man, the social contract, the theory of progress—he pronounced "final." A brochure he published in 1910 nevertheless conceded the failure of revolutionary syndicalism in Italy as well as France.[96] He ascribed this failure to the backwardness of the proletariat and to its inability to provide its own leadership; its weakness had opened the door to domination by a class of parasitical politicians and intellectuals. That same year Lanzillo published the first biography of Sorel, defending Sorel's position on the Ferrer affair as well as his recent attraction to the Action Française.[97] The focal point of Lanzillo's thinking was still, however, a proletarian syndicalism, the finest expression of which he found among the agricultural workers of Parma and Ferrara, where there had been a number of particularly bitter and bloody strikes. Lanzillo viewed the Action Française as a bourgeois movement and believed Sorel's interest was serious. Sorel was in pursuit of the "sublime." The monarchists shared with the syndicalists the same hatreds: they were antibourgeois, antidemocratic, and antiunitary. Both movements were also "intuitive," "mystical," and "religious" in character. Should the monarchists become more "warlike," the French proletariat might respond in kind.

What has been said of the foregoing academic syndicalists could be said of others: Arcà, for example, and Longobardi, and de Pietri-Tonelli.[98] Each in his own way adhered to Sorel's catastrophic conception of syndicalism. Though "carriers" of his ideas, they were not as prominent as Labriola, Leone, or Olivetti either during that period or during the evolution of Sorelismo in later years. There were other "carriers" among agitators and organizers—de Ambris, Bianchi, and Rossoni, though their effect was more by virtue of their activities and the circles in which they moved than by an explicit acknowledgment of intellectual indebtedness to Sorel.[99] Two such activists, however, were fairly explicit.

Among organizers and agitators, Corridoni was in spite of his youth a striking figure. A young man of thought and action, he repeatedly passed into and out of the ranks of the Socialist party, organizing strikes in defiance of the reformist CGL.[100] Moreover, he was a passionate admirer of Sorel. Corridoni had begun to read Sorel in 1907 at the age of nineteen, while still a student, and had corresponded with him briefly.[101] Frequently employing the pseudonym "Leo Celvisio," his articles appeared in Bianchi's *Gioventù socialista* and Rossoni's *Bandiera proletaria*. Although an admirer of the heroes of the Risorgimento, he was also profoundly influenced by Sorel's pessimism, his emphasis on the necessity of violence and suffering, his theory of the moral degradation of the bourgeoisie, and his vision of a "society of heroes." Four articles in the *Bandiera proletaria* in 1909 on the revolutionary strike revealed Corridoni to be interested not so much in the betterment of working-class conditions (although he was much distressed by Italy's poverty) as in the formation of a "school of heroism" for the worker.[102] He went beyond Sorel in his insistence that the triumph of the proletariat would also be a national triumph. He dreamt not of a stateless society but of *"una nuova primavera, un nuova Maggio"* for Italy.[103]

Mussolini, who turned twenty in 1903, was, at least formally, a revolutionary socialist who (unlike Corridoni) did not take part in syndicalist agitation and organization.[104] He favored participation in elections and approved of parliamentary action, but he was otherwise scarcely distinguishable from the revolutionary syndicalists; indeed, his relations with such figures as Olivetti, Panunzio, de Ambris, and Corridoni became intimate in the prewar years. What he saw in syndicalism was the most vigorous opponent of reformism, with an emphasis on direct action that might serve as a source of renewal for a movement he believed to be debilitated. He was a fairly regular contributor to Labriola's *Avanguardia socialista* from 1903 to 1905 and for a time was its regular Swiss correspondent, submitting a number of anticlerical and antimilitarist articles and occasionally commenting favorably on Sorel.[105] As the reformists increased their control over the party, Mussolini's articles turned more explicitly to the subject of Sorelian violence. Writing in 1908—at times under the pseudonym of "Vero Eretico"—for the *Lima* of Oneglia, he applauded the Italian general strikes of 1904 and 1908.[106] He praised the efficacy of "muscular" violence and berated, as had Sorel, "professional intellectuals." In the *Lima* Mussolini republished Sorel's "Apologie de la violence," which had shortly before appeared in the *Guerra sociale*.[107] A prefatory note asserted that he found in Sorel "a sufficiently authoritative confirmation" of his own views on violence—views that undoubtedly stemmed from Mazzinian, anarchist, and Marxist sources, as well as the traditions of his own Romagna. In the Trentino, where he acquired a sensitivity to the problem of irredentism, he wrote two articles on Sorelian syndicalism in 1909 for the *Popolo* of Trent. In the first, an extended review of a recent study by Prezzolini on the doctrines of syndicalism, Mussolini demonstrated considerable enthusiasm for Sorel's theory of the proletarian myth, his antipathy to parliamentary and humanitarian socialism, and his emphasis on the "moral value" of violence.[108] In the other, on the Italian edition of the *Réflexions* with a preface by Croce, he expressed admiration for both thinkers who avoided "learned verbal manipulations," who taught that life was a struggle that required a "continuing surpassing of oneself."[109] In the *Popolo* in 1909 he wrote: "As Sorel states, our mission is terrible, grave, sublime!"[110] And so it continued well into 1910, when Mussolini began to publish in the *Lotta di classe* of Forlì and with shock and outrage discovered that Sorel had become involved with the French monarchists.

Though a significant number of syndicalist writers and agitators under Sorel's influence may have had equally effective access to rank-and-file workers by way of publications and organizational activities, the amount of influence they may have exercised on the workers remains difficult to gauge. Sorelian syndicalism was fundamentally a doctrine "about" the proletariat and not "for" them. If the workers were to become aware of the mythical character of their aspirations, presumably they would not be inspired to action. Notwithstanding an overriding hostility to intellectuals, what the Sorelians purveyed was, in fact, a doctrine for an intellectual elite of propagandists and agitators. There is implied both distinction and distance between the workers who act in pursuit of their deepest convictions and a minority who view these constructions as myths. Nevertheless, syndicalist spokesmen offered a good deal of admonition and practical advice to workers in their endeavor to cultivate the myth of the general strike. One can legitimately raise questions, therefore, concerning the proletarian movement's receptivity to Sorelian tactics. In France, of course, neither group existed in significant numbers—there were hardly any Sorelians and no significant number of workers prepared to follow—but in Italy the situation was different. Italian syndicalism was in many respects even further removed from Sorel's model than its French counterpart, but its very complexity opened the possibility of a more varied response.[111] There were connections with both the intellectuals and the party. Though preoccupation with proletarian resentment was dominant, irredentist and national currents were also present. There were not only regional differences but also a differentiation between industrial and agricultural syndicates. Nevertheless, except for a small but significant segment of the movement, what was true of the CGT was substantially true of the CGL from its commencement in 1906.

The Segretariato Nazionale and its successor, the CGL, turned markedly reformist by the end of the first decade of the century; as the CGL drew closer to the Socialist party, only a segment of the Italian labor movement could be persuaded to detach itself and assume a frankly revolutionary and syndicalist posture.[112] The general strike of 1904 did at first have a leavening effect on the revolutionaries. Such activists as Labriola, Leone, Orano, Lanzillo, Arcà,

Mocchi, Mantica, de Ambris, and many others who had been directly involved in the 1904 strike continued their efforts with renewed zeal. Numerous periodicals displaying a distinctly Sorelian tone continued the assault on the moderates of the Socialist party as well as those in the Segretariato Nazionale, but the response to these efforts in labor circles was by no means uniform.

The *camere* rather than the national unions tended to be susceptible to Sorelian ideas (though the *ferrovieri* constituted an important exception), and among the *camere* those in rural areas were most receptive.[113] The legitimacy of the national unions was as yet only grudgingly accepted, while the *camere* remained in many areas the traditional home of labor. It was the persistence of localism that gave relevance to revolutionary syndicalism. Localism made possible the tactic of solidarity and sympathy strikes which were spread over as wide an area as possible. For the most part, only those workers who lacked organizational experience and who sought dramatic answers to their resentments against the social order were receptive. A fiery revolutionary appeal evoked more enthusiasm among them than the sober preaching of the national unions urging restraint and responsibility, "coupled with pleas for high dues and slow evolution of strong organizations." A dramatic strike and the attendant "heartwarming emotional spree" meant more than winning specified and limited demands. For these reasons the most spectacular successes of syndicalist agitation and propaganda took place in those north and north-central areas dominated by large-scale use of farm labor, rather than in the industrial cities. Parma was the heart of the movement, though syndicalists had considerable influence in wide areas of the Po Valley and in Emilia and Romagna. Such a group did not exist in appreciable numbers in France. As for the railroad workers (the Sindacato Ferrovieri Italiano), although they had evolved from local, to regional, to national organization they had become intensely aware of the central role they might play in a general strike on the national level, and they made much of this. The railroad workers threatened to bring the life of the nation to an abrupt halt and the government dealt with them as though they would in fact do so.

The year 1906 was a critical one for syndicalism.[114] The long-run effect of the general strike of 1904 on the leadership of both the Segretariato Nazionale and the Socialist party was a perceptible swing to reformism. Through the efforts of labor leaders and with the sympathetic support of reformists in the party, the Segretariato, now in disarray, was succeeded by the CGL at a Congress of National Union held in September of 1906 in Milan. Some of the syndicalist unions had refused to participate. Those representatives who did attend walked out after the approval of the resolution establishing the CGL. Committed to a policy of moderation, the confederation elected Rinaldo Rigola as its secretary-general the following year. At the end of 1907 the CGL had some 200,000 paid adherents, though the figure is undoubtedly an understatement of actual strength, for payment of dues was a rare practice. In October, several days after the CGL was established, the Socialist Party Congress met in Rome. Croce noted that during the congress Sorel's name was to be found in all the newspapers as the most authoritative spokesman of syndicalism.[115] The meeting was tumultuous: the revolutionary faction, inspired also by the recently formed CGT in France, had reached the height of its influence within the party. At the congress the syndicalists were castigated by the reformist Turati as "mystics, Messianists, who want a kind of apocalypse." But the "integralist" Enrico Ferri, who exercised a controlling position in the party, would not countenance their expulsion and attempted a temporary delicate balancing of the reformist and revolutionary wings.

The syndicalists were in a state of rebellion after 1906 against what they deemed unwarranted interference by the party in the affairs of the workers. They sensed what a powerful arm the CGL could be for their reformist antagonists. Some lesser figures began to leave the party in disgust that year: Forges-Davanzati, Maraviglia, Federzoni, and Monicelli.[116] They were drawn to Olivetti's *Pagine libere* and then, beyond to the newly formed nationalist movement.[117] Their aversion to an internationalist and reformist socialism had prevailed over their attachment to a proletarian movement. Others, remaining in the party, attempted in 1907 to consolidate their forces and to organize in Parma a countermovement to the CGL, the Comitato Nazionale della Resistenza.[118] The organization claimed about 200,000 members, but the figure is probably an exaggeration. There was a reorientation of their doctrines and organs of propaganda. Without joining the nationalist movement and while remaining anchored in syndicalism, they raised the torch of "proletarian nationalism" with Mazzianian overtones. They were led by young Corridoni and were supported by Labriola, Leone, Orano, and the organizer de Ambris. The group saw in the strike a technique for generating "enthusiasm rather than immediate gain." This was Corridoni's "school of heroism." Limited to a few centers in the north, it experimented with revolutionary methods on the occasion of the agricultural workers' strike in Parma in the summer of 1908.[119]

Both the CGL and the party fought the Parma strike. Rigola at the CGL Congress of Modena in September 1908 asserted:

It is noteworthy that syndicalism has made progress more easily in agriculture. The industrial proletariat rejects it in toto. The farm laborer is still a mystic who needs to go through a stage of faith in miracles.[120]

The suspicion and hatred of syndicalism came to a head at the Socialist Party Congress of Florence in October of that same year.[121] At Florence the leadership of the party was transferred from Ferri to Turati. Syndicalism was described in Turati's address as the "stone age of socialism," and he declared the two to be incompatible. The remaining syndicalists were expelled from the party, and closer cooperation with the CGL was voted. Thereafter until 1910, the Italian labor movement as a whole continued to gravitate in the direction of reformism. Having gotten rid of the syndicalists in 1906, the CGL embarked on an openly reformist tactic.[122] As in the past, it proclaimed its independence of all political parties, but in fact it became increasingly dependent upon the parliamentary efforts of the Socialist party.

The syndicalist unions, however, soon found themselves engaged in a parallel movement. Syndicalist agitators and propagandists might fulminate against the loss of revolutionary ardor, but without effect. At the CGL Congress of Bologna in December 1910 the syndicalist unions returned to the fold.[123] Some returned with the hope of conquering from within, others with the realization that their cause was, at least for the time being, hopeless. It was to this congress that Sorel sent his letter announcing that he had abandoned all activity on behalf of Italian syndicalism.[124] The movement had been won over to democracy. Nothing, he said, could be expected from a workingmen's movement which entered the political arena.

Integral
Nationalism

The "heroic" period of integral nationalism in France and Italy followed closely the heyday of revolutionary syndicalism—Sorel's interest in integral nationalism rose as his hopes for revolutionary syndicalism waned. The movements in France and Italy, spurred by the heightened danger of war, especially after the Moroccan Crisis of 1905, had much in common. Both drew sharp distinctions between their brand of nationalism and the democratic variety. Both asserted that the future of the nation was threatened or compromised, its status in international society as well as its institutional and cultural heritage. That threat came primarily from parliamentary democracy and its "heir apparent," pacificist and international socialism. In the origins of both was a marked literary component, a quality that persisted to a surprising degree during the prewar years. With appropriate differences, the principal weapon in their arsenal of arguments against the existing regime was the juxtaposition in sharpest outline of an ideal past against a sordid present. Their rhetoric, as the rhetoric of revolutionary syndicalist writers, was "totalist." Their concern was with the "whole" nation. They demanded a drastic reordering of the existing system of institutions and values, a transformation, they indicated either implicitly or explicitly, that might be achieved by direct action.

Integral nationalism in France was represented by the Action Française. The organization had its origin during the Dreyfus affair, emerging from the anti-Dreyfusard Ligue de la Patrie Française formed early in 1899. The Ligue was not a political organization, nor was it capable of effective intervention in public affairs. Moreover, it included both republicans and antirepublicans. The Action Française began as a small group of intellectuals who broke with the Ligue that same year, determined to challenge more directly the sway of the Dreyfusards. It was led by Charles Maurras, Henri Vaugeois, and Lucien Moreau, who were joined shortly by Maurice Pujo, Jacques Bainville, Léon de Montesquiou, the Marquis de la Tour du Pin, and Léon Daudet. Their organ, characteristically, was a review, the *Action française*. Adherents and supporters came primarily from the bourgeoisie of royalist, Bonapartist, or clerical persuasion. It was the Dreyfus affair that rapidly gave the organization national prominence and created out of Maurras, whose background was literary, a political pamphleteer of the first order. Maurras took the offensive against the Dreyfusards, unshaken by the discovery that Colonel Henry was a forger. Indeed, he was first to state the doctrine of "forgery for patriotic reasons." It was he also who introduced the charge that the Dreyfusards were a combination of four "alien estates" within France: the Jews, the Freemasons, the Protestants, and the *métèques,* or naturalized foreigners. With the publication of his *Enquête sur la monarchie* in 1900, Maurras convinced the Action Française that salvation for France lay in the restoration of the monarchy.

The first decade of the century saw the Action Française take on some of the appurtenances of a revolutionary movement, spurred by fierce resentments against the manner in which the affair had been liquidated by the Republic and the apparent unwillingness of the regime to undo the humiliation of the Franco-Prussian War. The organization expanded rapidly. By 1905 literary figures of some distinction were engaged in its propaganda and it enjoyed considerable support from conservative elements. In 1908 the review became a daily newspaper and the *camelots du roi,* news-hawkers and student members, were organized into paramilitary units available for direct action. The exposition of doctrine was primarily the responsibility of Maurras, who was universally recognized as the *maître.* His immediate objective, he wrote, was to destroy a regime based on the false principles of the Revolution and run by non-French cosmopolites. The army, the clergy, and the bourgeoisie were to be "re-educated." The creation of a royalist state of mind in these quarters would prepare the way for a coup. Maurras's ultimate goal was the restoration of the power and glory of France, a France once again pursuing a policy of *"politique d'abord."* Such a restoration required the revival of the institutions and values of the Old Regime, particularly those of the seventeenth century. These were an hereditary monarchy headed by a dictator-king and supporting secondary institutions: Catholicism, decentralization, traditionalism, and classicism.

Integral nationalism in Italy began to take shape in 1903, though it did not assume a formal character until 1910. The first signs of the new nationalism, distinct from the democratic idealism which had impelled the Risorgimento, appeared shortly after the humiliating defeat of an Italian army at Adowa in 1896 at the hands of primitive Ethiopians. But nationalism fed not only on the setback to Italian colonialism but also on a variety of grievances left unsatisfied by Italian unification: failure to establish little more than an administrative and bureaucratic fusion, the hostility of the church, the deplorable state of the national culture, the weakness of the economy, continued emigration from the impoverished and backward south, and the *Italia irredenta.* It was Gabriele D'Annunzio who translated these resentments into novels, plays, and poems, and thereby seized the popular imagination at the turn of the century. He became the anti-Giolittian par excellence. While Giolitti attempted to keep passions within the bounds of prosaic reason, D'Annunzio declaimed on the beauty of fire and destruction and the voluptuous attractions of power and glory.

The current generated by D'Annunzio was the most powerful element to enter the nationalism which became a school and eventually a party under the aegis of Enrico Corradini. Young Corradini fell under the spell of D'Annunzio's lyrical nationalism after the catastrophe of 1896, and in 1903 he undertook to launch more systematic propaganda. He established a fiery review in Florence, the *Regno,* which he edited with the aid of Prezzolini and Papini. Although in an organizational sense hardly significant, the small band of writers nevertheless adopted the rhetoric of revolution. The group was confined largely to young middle-class students and intellectuals and reached only a limited circle of readers. When the original trio parted company in 1906, the review was abandoned.

Italian nationalism for several years thereafter possessed neither a *maestro* nor a central organ. This circumstance opened the movement to diverse new influences and eventually gave impetus to two amorphous groups of propagandists. Prezzolini and Papini founded the *Voce*—also in Florence—in 1908, a review dedicated to a moral and cultural nationalism, while Corradini continued to develop his original D'Annunzian themes, though incorporating new ideas. The Italian nationalism which became a party stemmed from Corradini's activities. In 1910 he considered the movement sufficiently strong and clearly enough oriented to call a national congress at Florence. Here, finally, was established the Associazione Nazionalista Italiana, dedicated to the reordering of the current regime. Adherents of nationalism initially refused to organize themselves as a political party, ostensibly because they opposed party politics and claimed to represent no particular clientele or class.

Although Italy already possessed a king, Italian nationalists asserted that the regime was not authoritarian enough. Nationalism favored a regime that displayed a vigorous and adventurous spirit in both domestic and international affairs. Italy's history as a nation-state, to be sure, went back no more than two generations. If the effort to invoke a glorious past were extended to the Renaissance or to ancient Rome, the relevance of past glories became somewhat vague, but that uncertainty provided Italian nationalists with wider scope than the Action Française (to which many looked with admiration) had for speculation about the future.

Chapter

5

The Man

Sorel first began to demonstrate interest in integral nationalism in 1908, though the way had been well prepared many years before. At the beginning of his career, it should be recalled, his work had exhibited a profoundly conservative quality.[1] Eventually this conservatism gave way to the hope for a proletarian *ricorso,* first by the methods of reform, and when these appeared to him discredited, by the methods of revolution. Conservative implications had been present, however, even in his conception of revolutionary syndicalism. To the proletariat had been assigned the duty of establishing moral values that smacked strongly of traditional morality; the syndicates were urged to absorb everything in the existing order which demonstrated continuing viability; and the collective energies of the proletarian order were to be devoted to a "renewal" of the advances of the capitalist era. Moreover, the bourgeoisie, he had suggested, might yet save itself. It might be "revived" by a great foreign war which would bring to power men with the "will to govern," or it might be restored to its former energy by striking back against proletarian violence.[2] When revolutionary syndicalism failed to meet his rigorous demands Sorel began to draw away from the movement. At the same time, the wholly unanticipated reaction to Sorel's ideas in nationalist circles in France and Italy tended to draw him into their orbit. Now the older, conservative strain in his thinking began to reappear in a new form.

In France the activities of Georges Valois and Paul Bourget brought Sorel to the attention of the Action Française.

Valois had been a member of the *Art social,* a group of young anarchists much impressed by Sorel's "L'Avenir" of 1898. He had left school in 1892 at 14, worked his way around the world (including Russia and India) and was largely self-educated.[3] Some years later, Valois was to write that it was Sorel who had delivered him from his "democratic prejudices," for after reading Sorel's "L'Avenir" he had turned from anarchism to syndicalism. A brief experience as a member of a syndicalist publishing house, Armand Colin, was enough to convince him that Sorel had been in error. The trade unions, he discovered, had been transformed during the Dreyfus affair into "democratic clubs."[4] Attracted by the vigor and *élan* of the Action Française in 1904–1905, Valois undertook to extract from Sorel's work a "realistic syndicalism" which would meet the requirements of monarchism. The two antirepublican movements, he was convinced, were the only virile forces in French society. In 1906 he was seeking a publisher for *L'Homme qui vient*, his first effort at an accommodation between syndicalism and monarchism.[5] He called for a dictatorial regime which would provide both a restored monarchy and the autonomous organization of labor. He saw in Sorel the "French Nietzsche" and in his ideas the inspiration of a regime that would take "work and prayer" for its motto. That same year Valois joined the Action Française and became a convert to Catholicism.[6]

The monarchist novelist and playwright Bourget brought Valois's manuscript to the attention of Maurras.[7] Valois and Maurras then engaged in a series of heated interviews during which Valois presented his adaptation of Sorelian syndicalism: the violence of the workers would restore the bourgeoisie in their former vigor; the bourgeoisie would thereupon rise in defense of traditional institutions and re-establish the monarchy. The bourgeoisie, however, was not to use its power against the workers. The king would act as an arbiter in a community in which sentiments proper to each class had been revived.[8] Maurras was enthusiastic. He had vaguely sensed the need for labor support and had already made overtures in this direction, though how realistic they were is open to question.[9] One of the economic theorists of the Action Française, La Tour du Pin, had devised a plan whereby the workers in the restored monarchy would be organized in "corporations"; but these were little more than medieval guilds, more suited to a handicraft economy than to modern industry. A number of "yellow syndicates" led by Pierre Biètry had been approached in the spring of 1906 with the hope of winning them over to monarchism. But Biètry had no connections with either the syndicalist or socialist movement and his organization, which he ran somewhat as a "racket," was made up of strikebreakers. The possibility of serious syndicalist support for the Action Française evidently appealed to Maurras, and Valois, after all, appeared to have syndicalist connections. The Nouvelle Librairie Nationale, the monarchist publishing house, gave Valois a job and accepted *L'Homme qui vient* for publication. "Let's experiment," Maurras told him.[10]

Valois announced his project in a series of articles in the *Action française* from September to December 1907.[11] The monarchist *Revue critique des idées et des livres* was to serve as the organ of the proposed *rapprochement*. The *Revue critique* appeared in April 1908. René de Marans, its director, though under the influence of La Tour du Pin, had also viewed Sorel's work with great favor. Valois was the principal contributor; others included Maurras, Bainville, La Tour du Pin, and Pierre Gilbert. The *Revue critique* announced to its readers that the purpose of Valois's "Enquête sur la monarchie et la classe ouvrière" was to investigate the possibilities of a merger between antidemocrats of the left and those of the right.[12] Valois's survey was addressed to leading theoreticians and militants of the CGT. The inquiry was conducted from April 1908 to May 1909.

Sorel's reply appeared in May 1908.[13] He had just published the *Réflexions* and the *Illusions* and was still the leading contributor to the *Mouvement socialiste*. Valois, however, presented Sorel to the readers of the review as one who was better known among monarchists than among socialists.[14] Sorel, he asserted, was engaged "in an effort parallel to ours . . . to destroy the Republic." Valois addressed to him the question of the possibility of syndicalism "in a form other than that of the social myth." Sorel's reply was not encouraging.[15] The difficulty in bringing the syndicalist movement over to monarchism, he answered, lay in "the legend of the Commune," which had dominated the thinking of the French proletariat since 1871. The Commune, according to the workers, was a revolt against royalists that ended in a bloody massacre of the workers in the name of royalism. Though this was a legend, the workers had continued to believe that royalism was their mortal enemy. Sorel's response, the first of some fifteen published interviews with syndicalists, was not unique: the CGT and the Action Française were pursuing parallel courses only to the extent that they desired the destruction of bourgeois republicanism. Beyond that, they were separated by all of French history since the Revolution. Although Berth and Lagardelle also received inquiries, neither responded. Berth, however, was progressively drawn to Valois's venture, while Lagardelle viewed it with disdain.[16]

The coolness of Sorel's response, however, did not lessen the esteem in which he was held by the young men of the *Revue critique;* his work continued to be discussed in its pages. His popularity in these quarters, albeit embarrassing, was not entirely unwelcome to him. Perhaps it was for this reason that he consented to the republication of an article which had appeared originally in Italy in the *Divenire sociale*.[17] "Modernisme dans la religion et dans le socialisme" was published in August 1908 and accorded most admirably with the editorial policy of the review, attacking as it did moderates in both camps. The failure of socialists to heed the "Marxism in Marx" was roughly comparable to the failure of present-day Catholics to exercise a rigorous doctrinal orthodoxy.[18] Sorel's comments on the church were of special interest.[19] The new rationalist apologetic and the attempted *ralliement* to the Republic, he believed, had done great harm to Catholicism. The church, he also suggested, could be served today by Bergson as it had once been by Aristotle.

Valois later maintained that the inquiry had been a success, if only because it established intellectual communication between Sorel and Berth on the one hand and the monarchists on the other.[20] It is true that Sorel submitted his last article to the *Mouvement socialiste* in September 1908 and Berth followed suit in January, but Sorel's collaboration with the monarchists had not extended beyond his reply and article on modernism, while Berth did not publish in the *Revue critique* at all. Several members of the Action Française did reveal considerable interest in the inquiry—notably de Marans, Gilbert, Albert Vincent, Octave de Barral, and Henri Lagrange—but a "bond" had by no means been established between antidemocratic extremists. Significantly, Maurras's articles indicated no personal interest either in Sorel or in syndicalism.[21] As Valois's inquiry proceeded, and as it became increasingly clear that it would fail in its primary objective, the articles of the other contributors tended to become more literary both in subject matter and in flavor.[22] By May 1909, when the series came to an end, Valois's project was dropped entirely from the pages of the review.

Nevertheless, from late 1908 on, Sorel's interest in the monarchist movement mounted. Indeed, shortly after he broke with the *Mouvement socialiste,* Jean Variot records that he began to speak privately of the Action Française as "the scientific form of patriotism."[23] Variot was a young contributor to Hervé's *Guerre sociale* who met Sorel one Thursday in October 1908 in Péguy's bookstore. He began to record Sorel's comments at Péguy's and, in fact, wherever he encountered Sorel. Variot records in the *Propos de Georges Sorel* that Sorel was convinced that Maurras's monarchism was "concrete" and "realistic." It was rooted in an institution that had possessed a "real" historical existence. It was not at all concerned with a "rational" or "good" society.[24] The monarchist movement appeared to be something of a bourgeois *ricorso,* initiated, possibly, by an "instinct of self-preservation."

By mid-1909, however, Sorel was prepared to go further. His letters to Croce discussed at length the work of Maurras and Valois. Maurras might fail to restore the monarchy, he stated, but he would undoubtedly have considerable influence in the future.[25] Valois's survey, he thought, was marked by "high intelligence" and "acuteness," and he suggested that Croce read it.[26] To Maurras himself Sorel wrote in July, after a reading of the second edition of *Enquête sur la monarchie,* of his agreement with Maurras's fundamental argument:

In modern France the traditional monarchy has been the sole institution capable of executing the immense labor that present-day theorists of the state assign to the governance of a great power.[27]

Sorel's attraction to the Action Française was by now so advanced that in August of 1909 the *Action française* republished an article by Sorel that had appeared recently in the *Divenire sociale,* and in September printed an interview with him.[28] The subject of the article in August was the Villeneuve-St. Georges affair. He was introduced to the readers of the newspaper as "the brilliant and profound theoretician of antidemocratic socialism," who, though he believed a monarchist restoration improbable, had "no serious objection to it." Sorel was here extremely generous in his praise of the Action Française. He challenged Jaurès to accept Daudet's offer to debate publicly "the lie of the innocence of Dreyfus." He took comfort in the existence of the *camelots du roi,* who served, he said, as a warning to democrats everywhere. He admitted that the "friends of Maurras" might not succeed in restoring the monarchy, but in their struggle against decadence they rendered a great service to the French nation. The interview by Gilbert was on the Ferrer affair.[29] Gilbert introduced Sorel as one commonly identified with the "extreme léft" but noted for the independence of his judgment. Sorel remarked that he would not take offense if he were charged with having "sold out to reaction."

The appearance of a play on the Parisian stage based on the *Réflexions* brought Sorel brief national prominence and drew him still closer to the orbit of integral nationalism. *La Barricade* opened at the Vaudeville Theatre on January 7, 1910. It was written by Bourget, a member of the Académie Française and one of the most illustrious literary figures in the Action Française; it was Bourget who had introduced Valois to Maurras in 1906. The play was based on the chapter in the *Réflexions* entitled "La Décadence bourgeoise et la violence."[30] It proved to be an immediate success. Bourget had been struck by Sorel's idea that the role played by violence in history was singularly grand, "provided that it was *a brutal and direct expression of the class struggle.*"[31] He gave Sorel's conception of violence an interpretation designed for the use and edification of the bourgeoisie. He called upon the bourgeoisie to defend itself against attacks by the workers. The "employer" Breschard in the fourth act, for example, asserted:

No, the worker is not a brute, but he is excitable and it is necessary to control him. It is our duty to lead [the worker]. . . . Social classes are like nations. They have not the right to own what they no longer have the energy to defend. Let's be strong and let's defend ourselves.[32]

The audience, however (according to reviews), regarded "old Gaucheron," the Sorelian "worker," as the hero of the play. He was the enemy of sabotage, a veritable model of probity and energy.[33]

The triumphant success of *La Barricade* suddenly brought Sorel and his *Réflexions* into the limelight—he had finally been discovered by the press. Several days after the opening of the play he was interviewed by the conservative *Gaulois.*[34] He explained that the *Réflexions* had been an attempt at "scientific observation." He had observed that society was at war, but thus far only one side was fighting. He would be happy if the bourgoisie would abandon its cowardly resignation and arm itself. Again, he suggested two possibilities might yet save the bourgeoisie: a great war might restore its energies and bring to the fore men who possessed the will to govern, or a great extension of proletarian violence might induce the bourgeoisie to abandon its humanitarian platitudes. The Parisian press expressed amazement that Sorel had not been discovered until then, that he possessed such a "remarkable originality," that "everyone [was] talking about him," and, curiously enough, that he was not "an anarchist with a knife between his teeth."[35]

In Italy a movement parallel to that in France was under way: Corradini and Prezzolini were performing the role that Valois and Bourget had undertaken in France.

In 1903 Corradini founded the Florentine nationalist review, the *Regno,* with Prezzolini and Papini as his chief contributors.[36] With passion and no little bombast its program called for the end of democracy, a reassertion of the principle of authority, and the fulfillment of Italy's imperial destiny. The *Regno* was the first indication of right-wing interest in Sorel. Corradini urged the Italian bourgeoisie to react with vigor to the proletarian danger and demanded that the regime embark on a program of imperial expansion. Prezzolini, on the other hand, displaying somewhat greater solicitude for the proletariat, called for a social order of workers' syndicates and frowned on power, authority, and war as ends in themselves. These differences led to a clash among the founders during the general strike of 1904 (Prezzolini was sympathetic to the strikers) and a decision to disband after two years of publication.

With the failure of the *Regno* Papini, Corradini, and Prezzolini went their separate ways. Papini turned to literary and philosophical pursuits; Corradini busied himself with propaganda and organizational activities; and Prezzolini became a contributor to the *Divenire sociale,* prepared a study attacking modernism (which he sent to Sorel for comment), and planned a new review.[37]

Corradini's efforts were now directed toward the formation of a "national syndicalism" as the only solution to the labor problem compatible with the new nationalism.[38] In 1906 he was joined by a small group of syndicalists, former associates of Labriola and Leone, who had left the socialist party and briefly collaborated with the *Pagine libere*: Forges-Davanzati, Maraviglia, Federzoni, and Monicelli.[39] These had not expressed an explicit dependence on Sorel, though in tone and argument they differed little from syndicalists who did. In lectures and discussion in numerous Italian cities, Corradini and his group explored further the possibilities of national renewal.[40] Syndicalism and nationalism, Corradini observed, had a common "love of conquest": they were both "imperialist." Moreover, Italian imperialism was that of a "poor nation." The workers, therefore, in fighting for Italy were fighting also for themselves. Corradinian nationalism by 1908 had arrived at a national syndicalism for "all producers" and an imperialism of a "proletarian nation." Corradini's lectures—especially "Sindacalismo, nazionalismo, imperialismo," first delivered at Trieste at the end of 1909—breathed the spirit of the *Réflexions.* Sorel wrote to Croce that the "remarkably intelligent" Corradini understood "exceedingly well the value of my ideas."[41]

Corradini's efforts had some practical results. In Turin a small band of nationalists, blatantly monarchist and expansionist, began publication of the

weekly *Tricolore* in April 1909.[42] Its director, Mario Viana, and his group, with
the support of Corradini and Mario Missiroli, attempted the same kind of
endeavor concurrently undertaken in Paris by Valois and his monarchist
friends: recruitment of workers in the name of a nationalist syndicalism. Sorel
was invited to submit articles. For Viana, nationalism was a movement open to
all classes. While the class struggle was not excluded, it was to be contained
within the limits of national solidarity.

The establishment of the *Voce* in Florence by Prezzolini in December 1908
was an attempt to fashion a nationalism on a more spiritual and moral plane
than the Corradinian variety—the *Voce* was to become a major influence in
prewar Italian culture.[43] Its leading contributors included many of the leading
literary lights of the day: Croce, Papini, Gaetano Salvemini, Luigi Ambrosini,
Giovanni Amendola, and Antonio Anzilotti. It was open to all views. It too was
characterized by an appeal for renewal, a concern with the "southern question,"
and, initially, considerable interest in Sorel. In December, Prezzolini wrote to
Sorel describing the review and in the following February he asked him to
become a regular contributor.[44] Sorel did not reveal why he turned down this
request, though he complained to Croce that he had neither the time nor the
inclination to write any more articles.

Prezzolini, nevertheless, maintained his enthusiasm for Sorel's work, an
enthusiasm amply reflected in the review.[45] In a leading article on Sorel in the
first issue, Prezzolini announced Sorel's abandonment of the French syndicalist movement and declared that Sorel had paved the way for the moral and
cultural renewal of Italian life. In an interview, Sorel expressed the conviction
that an Italian national renewal was, in fact, already underway. Other articles
during the next several months (plus the publication of the first bibliography of
Sorel's work) were in much the same vein. Still others demonstrated interest in
Maurras, Bergson, and Péguy and the culture of French nationalism in general.
Prezzolini lectured on Sorel and published an extended study of syndicalist
theory.[46] It appeared in 1909 (Mussolini reviewed it) with a chapter entitled,
"Notre maître Sorel." Prezzolini had great respect for Sorel's "fanatical love of
truth" and his "Protestant-like view of life"; he compared Sorel and Bergson
and found them both to be theoreticians of "movement" as opposed to
"mechanical rigidity" and "cold intellectualism."[47] But Prezzolini was convinced the syndicalist movement was still in its infancy. Ultimately it would
shed its proletarian garb and become an instrument of social integration and
conservation. Sorel read the work. He thought Prezzolini "too literary," but he
was flattered by the comparison with Bergson.[48] For the moment, he said
nothing about a syndicalism extended to "all producers."

It was Corradini's work, however, that proved to be the focus around
which Italian integral nationalism eventually crystallized.[49] The D'Annunzian
nationalism that he had originally asserted had been modified after 1906 by an

invasion of syndicalists. The influx of irredentists after 1908 who had despaired of parliamentary parties added a third component. By December 1910 the nationalists considered themselves ready for a national congress; they met in Florence to establish the Associazione Nazionalista Italiana.[50] The themes of the *Regno* were voiced again, but had been modified by elements that had entered the movement since 1906. The principal address was presented by Corradini. He spoke of a "national syndicalism" which would include all groups, and attempted to justify Italian expansion as the imperialism of a "proletarian nation."[51] The rhetoric of the congress, resounding with appeals both social and national, suggests that the ideas of Sorel and his admirers were not unknown to its participants.

The intellectual ties between Sorel and Italian nationalism were certainly well established by 1910. Though he had not yet published in any Italian nationalist periodical, he did not conceal his interest in nationalist activities. In Prezzolini's work he saw a "serious pragmatism,"[52] while in Corradini's he perceived a "remarkably intelligent" adaptation of his own ideas.[53] In Italian pragmatism and nationalism he found in 1909 the inspiration for a lengthy article on William James. Sorel was now almost as enthusiastic about James as he had been about Bergson.[54] He found most attractive the idea of the pragmatic value of a religion which could excite to the point of heroism, a heroism, he believed, that would redound to the benefit of the nation. In the *Divenire sociale,* where his articles continued to appear until the first months of 1910, there were now frequent comments favorable to nationalism, comments which did not go unnoticed among syndicalists.[55] In the meantime, Sorel's name had become virtually a password for the initiates of small avant-garde Italian reviews in which his theory of myth, elites, and violence were widely discussed.[56] His work was far more widely known in Italy than in France, for the Italian syndicalists had also done much to popularize his ideas. Though Giuseppe Borgese, the young scholar and critic, was himself not attracted to Sorel, he wrote in 1910:

> It is difficult to find, since the time of Frederick Nietzsche, a man of intellect who has so strongly and tumultuously become popular among the intellectual aristocracy.... A prophet of the proletariat ... has raised his standard among the aristocracy.[57]

Sorel had recognized signs of a national renewal in Italy, but he had been most reluctant, thus far, to state publicly that he saw evidence of a true national *ricorso* in France—and what took place in his own France was decisive for him. That conviction finally came early in 1910. Péguy had published *Le Mystère de la charité de Jeanne d'Arc* in December 1909,[58] after he had become very much alive to the dangers of a war with an aggressive Germany. Jeanne d'Arc was to Péguy a symbol of France simultaneously fighting for its own Christian liberty and for the Christian liberty of the world. Pacifism, antimilitarism, and internationalism were now treason in his eyes. Jeanne d'Arc, however, was not only a national hero but also a saint. Bergson's philosophy made possible Péguy's rediscovery of his religious faith. It was Bergson who had made him aware (as for so many others of that day) of a dimension of human nature hardly explored by scientific rationalism. Sorel read *Jeanne d'Arc* shortly after its appearance, and in February 1910 he wrote to Croce that Péguy's work was a sign of a genuine "reawakening" of patriotic and religious sentiments in France. Sorel had found another *ricorso*,[59] of which *Jeanne d'Arc* was both the inception and the inspiration. The Christian idea, he wrote, had been put brilliantly to work in the interests of the nation. In April he published an article on Péguy's work that appeared simultaneously in the *Action française* and the *Voce*.[60] Sorel now publicly greeted Péguy's masterpiece as the beginning of a "renaissance" of French nationalism. Once again he wrote to Croce, elated that the success of *Jeanne d'Arc* was assured.[61] Bergson had found it "very beautiful," and Bergson had also "strongly approved" of Sorel's own article on Péguy.

His enthusiasm for Péguy's work was unqualified, but throughout 1910 Sorel retained lingering doubts as to the potential of the nationalist revival in France and the desirability of associating with it publicly. When Berth indicated in May an interest in publishing an article on Proudhon in the *Revue critique,* Sorel cautioned against it and urged, as a "last resort," that Berth employ a pseudonym.[62] In June Variot asked Sorel if he thought the Republic would be overthrown by "Marxism" or by "Maurrasism." He replied that the advantage still lay with Marxism.[63] Though the Action Française possessed men of great intellectual merit, their talents could, in the long run, prove fatal. The Action Française needed more "doers" and fewer "thinkers." The war which was coming would, in any case, resolve the problem: after foreign war would come internal war, and the choice would be between the two extremes. Yet, he frankly admitted, parliamentary democracy might continue to "vegetate" indefinitely: Marxism might come to nothing in France, and the Action Française might be preaching in a desert. In a lengthy essay, "Grandeur et décadence," written in July for the second edition of the *Illusions,* however, he was somewhat more hopeful.[64] The present time, he feared, might not be favorable to great historic achievement, but other times would come which would take "the incomparable treasures of classical culture and Christian tradition" as their point of departure.

In mid-1910 Prezzolini arranged for Sorel to publish in the *Resto del Carlino,* an independent liberal daily of Bologna.[65] The *Resto del Carlino* was edited by Missiroli, one of Sorel's new admirers, with whom Sorel was to correspond until mid-1921. Sorel's prewar association with the daily was of short duration (it was to be resumed after the war); however, in articles for his Italian readers Sorel presented his views of the Action Française with considerable candor. He admired Maurras and his followers; but at the same time he continued to be suspicious of the "intellectuals" who abounded in the monarchist movement.[66] The Action Française, he thought, might some day come to the same ignominious end as the Boulangist movement.[67] He attributed the rising spirit of nationalism in France not only to the Action Française but to a Republic that would not permit Maurras to reap all the advantages that accrued from patriotic propaganda.[68] He nevertheless denounced the hypocrisy of republican nationalism, particularly its program of "francisation" in the colonies.[69]

Sorel's methodological predispositions were given somewhat new emphasis late in 1910.[70] In his letters to Croce he had urged a study of Hegel which would emphasize not the mechanics of the dialectic (which he thought useless) but the "vital elements." In a long essay, "Vues sur les problèmes de la philosophie," he undertook that study himself. Sorel saw a great similarity between Hegel and Bergson: for different reasons, both considered abstract understanding and discursive intelligence to touch only the surface of the real; they both had qualitative and dynamic conceptions of the spirit; and they were at one in negating the substantialism and atomism which would isolate and fix the moments of the life of the spirit. Sorel, like his friend Croce, was drawn to the Hegelian "universal concrete," which he considered a happy transition from the out-of-date dogmatic philosophies of Descartes and Leibnitz to the new modes of thought. The new metaphysics of Bergson and James was not reasoned but intuitive. It was, essentially, the inspirer of inventive activity:

> Philosophy should renounce the pretense of bringing solutions.... A philosophy is only valuable by virtue of the indirect results that it provokes.... In a word, a philosophy is only valuable as a means of promoting invention.[71]

Notwithstanding his doubts, late in 1910 Sorel attempted to found a review that would provide him with an opportunity to express his new views and to facilitate, if possible, a "fusion" of antidemocrats from the right and the left.[72] He was probably unaware that the ephemeral *Terre libre* founded in late 1909 was attempting the same thing. Variot, in any case, has written that Sorel wanted to publish extensively in the *Cahiers,* but Péguy, aware of Sorel's new interests, feared that such collaboration might antagonize his clientele, which was still largely Dreyfusard, socialist, antimilitarist, and anticlerical.[73] Péguy finally gave Sorel to understand that he would not countenance a *"Cahier Sorel."* Thus during the summer of 1910 was the idea of the *Cité française* born.[74] Valois, who had been informed by Maurras that the *Revue critique* was no longer at his disposal, approached Berth,[75] but Valois was really after Sorel. Valois and Berth decided to establish the review. Variot, who had recently been an associate of Hervé's, and Gilbert, poet and editor of the *Revue critique,* completed the editorial board. Since only Valois and Gilbert were declared monarchists, the *Cité française* board allayed Sorel's concern at being compromised. Valois and Berth asked Sorel to serve as the director.[76] The project was acceptable to Sorel, but he insisted that he and Berth act as co-directors, for Sorel wanted to advance Berth's career as a publicist. As soon as the review was well underway, Sorel planned to retire and leave its direction entirely to Berth. In September Sorel mailed copies of a prospectus to his friends, and urged Croce and Pareto to submit articles. The first issue was scheduled for November 1, 1910.

The prospectus of the *Cité française* contained a "Déclaration" signed by Sorel, Berth, Variot, Gilbert, and Valois.[77] It stated that, though the undersigned represented diverse points of view, they all agreed that "it is absolutely necessary to destroy democratic institutions." Sorel in his own statement asserted that the new review would be addressed to all who were "sickened by the stupid arrogance of democracy, by humanitarian nonsense, and by foreign ideas."[78] Though he denounced the negation of social classes and the ideal of ultimate social reconciliation, the thrust of Sorel's argument was nationalist. The nation was to be freed from "alien" influences. The path to be taken, wrote Sorel, was the noble one "opened by the masters of nationalist thought." He said nothing of the Action Française. The familiar philosophical pessimism and invocation of Proudhonian moralism followed. Berth underscored Sorel's arguments, but went further.[79] Democracy was a regime of "pure destruction" from the standpoint of both the national interest and the needs of production. The union of the national and the social was symbolized in the merger of monarchism and syndicalism. Gilbert and Valois hailed Sorel as their *maître* and embraced simultaneously the doctrines of integral nationalism and revolutionary syndicalism.[80]

The appearance of the prospectus announcing the *Cité française* produced a scandal. In some quarters Sorel's impending association with members of the Action Française was taken to mean that a rapprochement among antirepublicans of all sorts was taking place.[81] At the *Cahiers* it was assumed that Sorel had been converted to monarchism. Péguy's Dreyfusard patrons did not conceal their displeasure (Sorel still came every Thursday to Péguy's shop).[82] Sorel's former syndicalist colleagues had the same reaction. Lagardelle was outraged. He published portions of the prospectus in the *Mouvement socialiste* and disclaimed any responsibility for the rapprochement. In any case, an alliance between the two extremes was out of the question: "Two swallows do not make a summer."[83] Syndicalists were critical of democracy, "not in order to suppress it, but to surpass it."

Sorel was disturbed by these reactions. In a letter to Lanzillo in October which was published the following month in the *Giornale d'Italia* (some of Sorel's Italian admirers—Mussolini, for one—were also critical), Sorel defended his right to participate in the project.[84] He protested that free research was becoming increasingly difficult in France. His specifically socialist writings, he asserted, did not constitute the greatest portion of his work; moreover, his ties with monarchism were no closer than they had been with socialism:

> The mission of the philosopher is to examine and to understand the movements which seem important to him; he is not necessarily obliged to support the men in the movement.[85]

To be a sound judge, he insisted, one must place oneself "within the movement and acquire an intellectual love for it." There was no other way to get to "the bottom of things." In letters to Croce in January and February 1911 he agreed with the Italian philosopher that socialism was finished.[86] The personal attack by Lagardelle was proof enough. He noted that Lagardelle, who had often derided "parliamentary cretinism," was now seeking election as a deputy. The essence of socialism, whether of the syndicalist or the party variety, was pure demagogy; both he and Berth had resolved never to write again in its behalf. A short time later, in a preface to the French edition of Edwin Seligman's study of the economic interpretation of history, Sorel condemned socialist intellectuals and gave little sign that he identified himself in any way with Marxism.[87]

The Cité française never saw the light of day. Sorel was displeased with the arrangements from the beginning:[88] he complained about the work; he fretted over the quality of the review; he did not want his name to appear among the directors; and he insisted on Marcel Rivière as the publisher (Rivière published a great deal of syndicalist literature, including virtually all of Sorel's major works). Moreover, a quarrel broke out among the sponsors of the review before its scheduled November 1 appearance.[89] Valois tried to get rid of Variot, but Sorel would not agree for fear of being outvoted by the monarchists on the board. Sorel abruptly resigned as director in favor of Berth, instructing him to retain Variot. Under these circumstances, it was decided to disband the review entirely. Sorel, strangely, wrote to Maurras explaining why he insisted on Variot, possibly in order to embarrass Valois.[90] As for Valois, having failed to persuade Sorel and Berth to fall in with his plans, he publicly invited Lagardelle to discuss a similar project. Lagardelle would have none of it.[91]

Sorel encountered new difficulties during the years 1910 and 1911, as his relations with Péguy began to deteriorate.[92] There is no reason to believe that serious personal difficulties had arisen between them since their meeting at the turn of the century. Sorel continued to appear every Thursday at the Cahiers, where he was still the center of attention. He had seldom mentioned Péguy before 1910 in his written work, though he thought highly of him. He had greeted the publication of Jeanne d'Arc, however, with the most lavish praise. Péguy, for his part, had always demonstrated great esteem for Sorel.[93] He may have been piqued occasionally (as some have suggested) by the way Sorel dominated the Thursday afternoon gatherings but he never failed to treat Sorel with great deference. However, the subscribers to the *Cahiers,* many of whom were Dreyfusards and Jewish, had begun to regard Sorel and Péguy with distrust and apprehension.[94] By 1910 they were convinced that Sorel was a "reactionary." They pointed to his new ties with Valois and Variot, as well as to his articles in the *Action française.* Péguy's new orientation was also a cause for alarm. They were afraid of anything that smacked even remotely of nationalism and clericalism, and Péguy, they feared, had embarked on such a road. There were open hints that subscriptions to the *Cahiers,* upon which Péguy's livelihood depended, might be cancelled.

Sorel's response to all this was to urge Péguy to break with his Dreyfusard past.[95] Since 1908 Sorel had become increasingly concerned with the "Jewish problem." He often identified Jews with his familiar *bêtes noires:* parliamentary politics, Freemasonry, high finance, socialist theory, and "professional intellectuals." He expressed these sentiments (which did not yet extend to Bergson) not only in his correspondence and articles but also in his conversation. According to Variot, he began to object openly in 1910 to Péguy's dependence upon a clientele which was largely Jewish. He told Variot shortly after the appearance of *Jeanne d'Arc:* "We must defend Péguy against the attacks of his former partisans. The man has children; Catholics must form a group to support him."[96] He suggested that the financial assistance of the Comte de Mun, the prominent Catholic layman, be sought.[97] When Variot informed Péguy of Sorel's suggestion, Péguy "hit the ceiling." Péguy would renounce nothing of his past and would not turn his back on his subscribers. Sorel continued to insist, however, that *Jeanne d'Arc* had turned Péguy toward nationalism and Catholicism and that he had to choose between his Dreyfusard subscribers and his new orientation.

Péguy's choice hardly pleased Sorel: it was to attempt to show that his new patriotism was not incompatible with his former Dreyfusism. In 1910 Halévy had published his *Apologie pour notre passé* at the *Cahiers,* an eloquent statement by a repentant Dreyfusard in much the same vein as Sorel's *La Révolution dreyfusienne* of the previous year. Some three months after Halévy's book appeared, Péguy published a retort "and a downright virulent one."[98] *Notre jeunesse* was in part a blast against some of his closest friends: Halévy was criticized for having written what Péguy himself had often spoken; Variot was berated for not admiring universal suffrage; and Sorel was reproached for monopolizing Thursdays at the *Cahiers.* The misunderstandings between Péguy and his subscribers were all redressed. He wrote a long eulogy of the Jews. He pronounced himself "republican," republicanism constituting for him a certain way of life and not a form of government. Both Halévy and Sorel agreed that *Notre jeunesse* had been designed to flatter Péguy's Dreyfusard clientele and that it was an excuse for *Jeanne d'Arc.*[99]

Halévy ceased to attend the Thursday gatherings and saw Péguy only occasionally. Sorel too was distressed. In December 1910 he prepared a preface for the second edition of *La Révolution dreyfusienne* and took note of the recent studies by Halévy and Péguy. He considered Halévy's to be a confirmation of his own views, but he said virtually nothing about Péguy.[100] For the time being, however, Sorel remained on amicable terms with him.

Shortly after the decision to abandon the *Cité française* Sorel began to plan a new review, the *Indépendance*.[101] Variot, who suggested the project, had the money. He asked Berth to join, but since Berth had conceived the original scheme with Valois he would not accept. The review, published by Marcel Rivière, made its appearance on March 1, 1911. A foreword announced its editorial policies.[102] The *Indépendence,* it was declared, would not be the organ of a political party or of a literary group and would make no demands on its contributors that would in any way circumscribe their independence. It would take as its "general line" (and this no more than three years after the publication of the *Réflexions*) the proposition that France had inherited and enriched the classical traditions of Greece and Rome. Aberrations and impurities had compromised this heritage. All those who were prepared to combat the detractors of that heritage were asked to support the review: "Negation of the past and regret for the past are equally sterile, but tradition, far from being a fetter, is the necessary fulcrum which assures the most daring innovations."[103]

The literary talents at the disposal of the *Indépendence* were truly formidable. They clearly attest to Sorel's renown in conservative and rightist circles. Many contributors were distinguished literati of the Action Française or figures associated with the Catholic "literary renaissance" which had followed the publication of *Jeanne d'Arc.* Sorel had been introduced to Bourget in 1910 shortly after the opening of *La Barricade.*[104] He met the well-known nationalist Maurice Barrès in May 1911, after the latter had indicated to Variot that he wished to meet the celebrated author of the *Réflexions.*[105] He probably encountered the dramatist Paul Claudel in 1912, having twice read both *L'Otage* and *L'Annonce faite à Marie.*[106] He was introduced by Variot to the poet Elémir Bourges; this was probably in October 1912.[107] All these men became regular contributors. The original editorial board included the novelists Émile Baumann and René Benjamin and the composer Vincent d'Indy, as well as Paul Jamot, Ernest Laurent, Émile Moselly, and the brothers Jérôme and Jean Tharaud (virtually all of the Action Française), plus Variot and Sorel. The board was enlarged in October 1912 to include Barrès, Bourget, and Maurice Donnay (all three of the Académie Française) and Elémir Bourges, Henri Clouard, René-Marc Ferry, and Francis Jammes. Others who had been associated with Sorel in the past, both on French and Italian syndicalist reviews, also contributed.[108]

The *Indépendance* was far more active than the *Mouvement socialiste* had ever been. A small group of young monarchists of "ardent and subversive mind" came regularly from 1911 to 1913 to chat with Sorel at the office of the review on the Rue Jacob.[109] The Oeuvre de Défense Française was formed to agitate in favor of the abrogation of the law of 1889 on naturalization.[110] The review gave wide publicity to the lectures of General Bonnal at the Institute of the Action Française on "the disasters of 1870."[111] Young Variot, who had become an ardent monarchist, engaged in a number of heated polemics. He challenged Jacques Copeau and then André Gide to a duel in defense of an article written by Copeau in the *Nouvelle revue française* for which he held Gide, its editor, responsible.[112] He also threatened Imbart de la Tour, the director of the *Bulletin de la semaine,* as having inspired an anonymous article attacking Sorel.

As they had once dominated the *Mouvement socialiste,* Sorel's views now dominated the *Indépendance* in 1911 and 1912. He wrote more articles and book reviews than any other contributor. These covered, characteristically, a wide range of subjects: historical, political, and literary.

The articles of 1911 assailed the Third Republic, but from a standpoint which reflected his new orientation. He deplored Ferry's anticlericalism and the decline of the sentiments of "revenge" that attended the acquisition of the second French colonial empire.[113] A study of the relations between Gambetta and a German secret agent convinced him of Gambetta's treason in giving up the idea of revenge.[114] He attacked the historians Lavisse, Liard, Lanson, Seignobos, and the "Sorbonnards" in general for having imported German pedantry into France.[115] Responsibility for the defeat of 1870 was laid to the liberal policies of Émile Ollivier.[116] He scolded the sociologist Gustave Le Bon for failing to distinguish between magic or superstition and religious belief.[117] The disappearance of religion, he asserted (in an article reminiscent of his syndicalist writings), would be paralleled by a great moral and intellectual decline.[118] He ridiculed the endless critique of social theories—the destiny of a doctrine did not at all depend on scholarly exercises.[119] The mathematician and economist Antoine Cournot, he thought, deserved a more prominent place in the history of philosophy, for Cournot was a precursor of James.[120] In a final article in 1911, on Halévy's study of the Dreyfus affair, he attacked those intellectuals (including Halévy himself) who had made possible the "Dreyfus revolution"—the "parasites of politics" had alone profited from the affair.[121]

The articles of 1912 were in much the same spirit, though Sorel seemed to be directing his attack principally against Jews and Jewish influence. He came to the defense of Urbain Gohier, one of the more virulent anti-Semites of the Action Française.[122] Arthur Meyer, a converted Jew who directed the conservative newspaper, *Gaulois,* was assailed for harboring republican sentiments.[123] He idealized the virtues of Lucien Jean, the worker-writer of the turn of the century whose moral strength, he asserted, derived from his poverty.[124] The Italian novelist and historian Alfredo Oriani was compared with Proudhon.[125] He attacked Jewish particularism throughout history, and decried the "Jewish spirit," which had triumphed with the Reformation.[126] The "vile and unscrupulous" Dreyfusards were accused of having plotted with Germany to discredit the French military.[127]

During the years when Sorel directed the *Indépendance,* little of his work was published in Italy, notwithstanding his interest in Italian affairs. He regularly read the *Voce* and the *Resto del Carlino.* He followed passionately the polemics precipitated by Italy's Libyan venture, which he discussed with sympathy and understanding in letters to Croce and Missiroli,[128] and he frequently asked Croce for information about D'Annunzio, on one occasion requesting an article and on another inquiring if D'Annunzio were a Jew.[129] But he published only one article in Italy: he saluted the Macedonian conquerors who conserved the finest traditions of ancient Greece; the world once again needed such a power, one capable of performing a comparable civilizing mission.[130]

These were troubled years for Sorel. He appeared uncomfortable with his new associates and apologetic about his new orientation.[131] Undoubtedly he was disturbed by Berth's continued association with Valois. The two were organizing a "study group" at the end of 1911, as well as still another review, the *Cahiers du cercle Proudhon.* Although the Cercle Proudhon looked to him as a *maître,* Sorel would have virtually nothing to do with it. He frequently asked Variot what was being said about "the violent one."[132] When he attempted to clarify his position, he was not always clear or convincing. In July 1911 he explained to Variot that his profession of nationalism was not to be interpreted as a complete rejection of syndicalism.[133] He was still concerned with the lot of the workers, but the syndicalism which he now put forward was no longer exclusively proletarian. He considered the latter "demagogic syndicalism," whereas he was now exploring the possibilities of a syndicalism applicable to the whole of society. In 1912, however, he published a third edition of the *Réflexions* in which he stated (rather paradoxically) that he was now "more than ever convinced of the value of this philosophy of violence."[134] To Édouard Molléans, a Thursday visitor at the *Cahiers* and an historian of the labor movement, he wrote in October 1912 that he had no objection to being called a "traditionalist."[135] For some sixteen years he had taken the side of Vico against Descartes: in that sense he was a traditionalist, but to believe that he was a Maurrasian monarchist was a "gross error." Still another self-appraisal was implied in his publication in the *Indépendance* of a letter Bergson had written to a mutual friend:

Georges Sorel is, it seems to me, a mind too original and too independent to enlist under the banner of any particular school; he is not a disciple. But he accepts some of my views, and when he cites me, he does so as a man who has read me carefully and who has perfectly understood me.[136]

Sorel and Péguy finally came to the parting of the ways in December 1912; the formidable gap that had in recent years developed between them finally became critical. Péguy's refusal to break with his subscribers had led Sorel to suspect the genuineness of his conversion to Catholicism. The Tharauds, for example, recalled that Sorel in 1912 once asked them a question he undoubtedly asked of others: "Do you think he's a Catholic? Does he go to mass? He doesn't go. Well then, is all this serious!"[137] Sorel did write, in fact, that he knew of "no one" who believed in Péguy's conversion. The Catholicism of Péguy, he said, "is shrouded in the mysterious regions of his inner life."[138] The freethinkers and Jews did not believe in his conversion, and surely they ought to know, for the slightest sign of a Catholic renaissance terrified them. Sorel began to demand that Péguy demonstrate publicly that he was no longer the man he had been before he had written *Jeanne d'Arc*.[139] He insisted on the publication of Péguy's pilgrimage to Chartres, deeming absolutely necessary a "public act of conversion." He expressed these views both in his correspondence and in his conversation. Péguy was aware of Sorel's doings.[140] He did not like them, and he did not tolerate them for long.

The occasion for the break came with the "Benda affair," when Péguy would no longer tolerate Sorel's anti-Semitism and what he deemed unwarranted interference in a matter that vitally concerned the *Cahiers*. Julien Benda, a frequenter of Péguy's establishment and a friend of Sorel, was Jewish.[141] There is no evidence that Sorel had ever harbored any ill will toward Benda since they had met early in the century. In fact, Benda had written the preface to Sorel's *Préoccupations métaphysiques des physiciens modernes* in 1907.[142] It was generally believed at the *Cahiers* that Sorel was a great admirer of Benda's wit. In mid-1912, however, Benda published *Le Bergsonisme, ou une philosophie de la mobilité*, in which he attempted to demolish Bergson's philosophy. Sorel wrote to Croce shortly thereafter that Benda was really without competence. Having failed to become popular as a writer of "pornographic tales," he was now attempting to attract attention by attacking Bergson.[143] He wrote again to say that the Jews and their allies, the academicians, were determined to shatter Bergson's influence:

Powerful forces are today combatting the spread of Bergson's ideas. I believe that in Italy few persons realize the role of the Jews.... The Jews cannot pardon Bergson's leading the present-day world toward realism.[144]

Late in 1912 Benda published a novel, *L'Ordination,* at the *Cahiers,* and there was talk that it might be awarded the Prix de Goncourt.[145] Péguy earnestly hoped that it would: he liked Benda, and he believed the award would be in the interests of the *Cahiers*. It was not long, however, before he heard rumors that Sorel was engaged in an intrigue with members of the Académie Goncourt against Benda. Sorel did in fact speak openly and harshly of *L'Ordination* to many of his friends.[146] He talked to Bourges, a member of the editorial board of the *Indépendance* and the one judge on the Goncourt jury that he knew, ten days before the awards were announced. He did not conceal his dislike of Benda's book. When *L'Ordination* was turned down for the Prix de Goncourt (Bourges and Daudet, both of the Action Française, had voted against it),[147] Péguy's retort came at once: he sent Sorel a *petit bleu* early in December: "I recognize your hand in all that is being done against the *Cahiers*. I beg you in the future not to come on Thursdays."[148] With Sorel went his faithful friends Variot and Berth; indeed, Variot also received a violent letter from Péguy.[149] Berth gave up his subscription: "Since you choose between Sorel and Benda, keep your Benda and keep my copies too."[150] Benda now inherited Sorel's straw chair in Péguy's bookstore.

Péguy's decision to break with Sorel was witnessed by several frequenters of the *Cahiers*. By the end of 1912, Romain Rolland has written, Péguy felt terribly isolated and persecuted.[151] He bristled "like a wolf in the forest." He sensed everywhere about him *"l'ennemi, la trahison."* By coincidence, Delesalle was present at the writing of the *petit bleu*.[152] He attempted to dissuade Péguy. When Péguy left his office to mail the note, Delesalle accompanied him, and for more than two hours they walked around the Latin Quarter while Delesalle pleaded with him not to send it, but in vain. On a Thursday afternoon several days later, Halévy walked into Péguy's office and inquired why Sorel was not there. He recorded Péguy's reply in his diary:

> I had to break with him. Because of the prize he made Benda lose. Variot and he conducted a fierce campaign against it. I am more and more against anti-Semitism. . . . If people want to start the *Affaire* . . . again, we will set to work. . . . I'm on the side of the Jews, because with the Jews I can be the sort of Catholic I want to be; with the Catholics I couldn't.[153]

Sorel's reaction to his "excommunication" revealed that he never quite understood what had produced it. Berth many years later told Marcel Péguy, Péguy's eldest son, that Sorel believed the sole cause of the break to have been Péguy's conviction that he had caballed against Benda.[154] Variot received the same impression: "I can still see him repeating maliciously, 'Péguy imagines that it is because of me that Benda was blackballed by the Goncourt jury! That's ridiculous!' "[155] Sorel, it would appear, did not understand Péguy. He did not comprehend the nature of his conversion or his sensitivity to anti-Semitism. Nor did he exhibit any solicitude for Péguy's feelings. For two years he had been going to Péguy's gatherings while he spoke and allowed others to speak so poisonously about him.[156]

The rupture between Péguy and Sorel initially meant for Sorel only a change of bookshops. Some observers of these events have maintained that he was deeply grieved and that there was in his exclusion from the *Cahiers* something of "tragic grandeur."[157] It would be difficult to establish that this was immediately the case. The best evidence suggests that instead of going to Péguy's on Thursday, Sorel went to another bookshop which his old friend Delesalle had established.[158] He found at Delesalle's an even greater audience than he had known at the *Cahiers*. He was not at all "in mourning":

Old Socrates that he was, he needed a corner of his own to sit and talk somewhere in the Latin Quarter. If there were books to turn over and two or three people to listen to him, it was a satisfactory afternoon.[159]

The affairs of the *Indépendance* took Sorel frequently to the office of Rivière, its publisher. There too he held forth, surrounded by the editorial board, a few young monarchists and an occasional visitor—Bourget, Barrès, or Jammes.[160]

After his break with Péguy Sorel's doubts about the "reawakening" of religious and national sentiments in France mounted rapidly. Early in 1913 he began to question the genuineness of the whole Catholic literary renaissance. To Joseph Lotte, Péguy's friend, who was also a recent convert, he wrote that the movement had fallen into "paganism." He criticized its failure to maintain "a Christian view of sex."[161] He questioned the sincerity of Claudel, of Jammes, and of Lotte himself.[162] To Croce he wrote that Claudel and Péguy were not extensively read, that Claudel might really be Catholic but Péguy was not at all.[163] A religion, moreover, whose adherents encouraged its detractors and attacked Bergson could not count for much: "What blindness!"[164] Elsewhere, however, he wrote that the possibility of miracles, ruled out by Renan, was now admitted by science—"Pascal is winning over Descartes every day." But Sorel had also become dissatisfied with French nationalism (and in no uncertain terms). He frankly told Barrès, probably early in 1913, that French nationalism was hollow, that it possessed neither doctrine nor profound conviction.[165] It was represented by a party composed solely of "reactionaries." It understood nothing of the "social question." Barrès, who had joined the editorial board of the *Indépendance* in October 1912, replied by terminating his affiliation with it.

The *Indépendance,* Sorel was soon convinced, was no longer a viable enterprise. As early as November 1912 he had confided to Croce that he was going to plead illness and leave the review.[166] He was, indeed, suffering periodically from a kidney stone, but he now also found the spirit of his young collaborators "too compromising for an old man." From October 1912 to March 1913 his contributions were limited to book reviews. At Easter 1913 he called Variot to Boulogne-sur-Seine and in his tiny room told him that he was going to leave the *Indépendance.*[167] The review, he complained, was labeled "nationalist and reactionary," and that displeased him. It was, furthermore, of no great consequence—a review with a monthly circulation of 500 copies was not likely to achieve much:

> Do I pretend that I can warn people with books that sell a thousand copies...? I write because I can do nothing else. But I am under no illusions as to what my work can do.... One is believed when one has been dead fifty years![168]

Variot and his friends on the *Indépendance* were desolate. Without Sorel, said Variot, the review would be "a land without the sun."[169] In July 1913 the editorial board of the *Indépendance* was changed, and later that year the review ceased publication.

The break with the *Indépendance* greatly saddened Sorel. He now took refuge in the Delesalle bookshop on the Rue Monsieur-le-Prince, where he came to sit and chat.[170] There were few clients at Delesalle's, however, and his young friends no longer came to listen to him. Shortly before the war, one could see him there often, talking to the woman in charge, Delesalle's wife Leona, who listened to him intently, for she was almost deaf. As for his recent experience, his correspondence early in 1914 reveals him to have been greatly disillusioned. He no longer had a good word for anyone in the nationalist camp, even in Italy.[171] He was delighted to hear that Catholic influence had failed to prevent Bergson's election to the Académie Française.[172]

When his young friend Berth, who had not yet lost faith in integral nationalism, published a book in 1914, Sorel prepared a preface.[173] The despair Sorel now expressed was almost complete. Both the bourgeoisie and the proletariat were, he wrote, "under the direction of Mammon."[174] Yet the future was not entirely without hope. He linked Pascal, Bergson, and James. Their genius would "yet triumph in our time," he insisted. The world had been tyrannized long enough by "intellectualist" dogmas: "It is in heroism... that the mystery of life is to be found. A man counts for nothing if he is incapable of making any sacrifice."[175]

Chapter

6

The Idea

Sorel's major political interest after 1908 was "integral nationalism," a term he himself employed.[1] This attraction had by 1910 deepened into a more or less enthusiastic collaboration with members of the Action Française, as well as engendering a sympathetic interest in the affairs of the Italian nationalist movement. To mid-1913, however, he did not so much construct new theories as adapt former ones to new needs. The focus of his attention appeared to shift from the proletariat to the bourgeoisie, though the role of class was at times obscure. More clearly, however, it had shifted from the social to the national. Although it was the Action Française that had captured his attention, his "conversion" did not extend to the specifics of Maurrasian monarchism. He was on the lookout for a revolutionary movement impelled by traditionalist sentiments, and it was in the Action Française that he saw the most serious contender in the field. His commitment to the monarchists was never as deep as his syndicalist involvement. Sorel tended to address himself to nationalism in general rather than specifically to Maurras's movement. By far the most interesting of his comments appeared in the *Propos,* but his articles in the *Indépendance* also reflected this preoccupation. In his discussions of integral nationalism one sees at its clearest the duality of observer and partisan in Sorel's writing.[2]

I

Sorel was convinced that a national renewal was underway in France. Its appearance was symbolized by the publication of Péguy's *Jeanne d'Arc* and was expressed concretely by the activities of the monarchists: "Ardent young men are turning toward what Republicans call reaction, because only there do they perceive some signs of vitality."[3] There was much in Péguy, as well as in Maurrasian monarchism, however, that displeased him. Sorel's discussion of nationalism therefore had the quality of perceptions that had not quite jelled because the movement itself had not crystallized, at least not in the way he had anticipated. All this was reflected in his exposition of the case for a nationalist *ricorso.*

He returned to the theory that what impelled a nationalist renewal was a myth or myths, but there was nothing in his work on nationalism that corresponded precisely to the myth of the general strike. Sorel spoke of an "instinct of preservation" that came into play whenever a group was threatened with extinction.[4] He saw in this instinct the power to evoke sentiments in which both the dangers threatening the group and the manner by which these might be overcome were expressed.

The deepest convictions, in any event, were in evidence in the myths of the nationalist movement.[5] All the nations of Europe had lived for centuries in a constant state of fear. In their insecurity was to be found the root of nationalist sentiments. France, according to Sorel, after a long and brilliant history had become convinced that her very existence was in jeopardy.[6] The Franco-Prussian war was a catastrophe of the first order, but too short, too lacking in events for legends to take form. It terminated in a series of disasters too frightful for the constitution of the French mind to be modified. The Dreyfus affair was more than a "second Sedan." It revealed a threat to the entire fabric of French life: the state, the church, the entire cultural and institutional heritage. The danger of the renewal of war with Germany gave further weight to the conviction that France was in peril. Religious themes, he maintained, were not required to accompany this anxiety for the future of France, but it was incontestable that it was when they did that nationalism proved capable of moving the masses profoundly.[7] French nationalism had its most powerful ally in Catholicism: state and church were intimately related in French history. Catholicism, by virtue of its mystical elements (monasticism, sacraments, and miracles) gave to the believer absolute certitude. In Péguy's *Jeanne d'Arc* Sorel found an admirable fusion of fear for the future of France with the mystical elements in Catholicism. The Maid of Orléans was both hero and saint. The "mystery of lamentation, of supplication and of lyrical praise" had been brilliantly employed to create a mythological representation entirely national in its import. He saw in Péguy's work a demonstration of what the full awakening of the French national spirit required: the fusion of the patriotic with the religious idea.

The essence of nationalist myths was the conviction that the nation needed to be "restored" in its purity and vigor. In French nationalism was the notion of an "order" that had to be called "true."[8] It was true because its fecundity had been established by French history:

When there exists an ancient tradition fertile in grand achievements and distinguished by men of genius, these expressions constitute, at the very least, *pragmatic truths* which the intellectual is always obliged to control, but which cannot be rejected on the sole pretext that they are not *scientifically* demonstrable.[9]

That order was to be found in the seventeenth century, the century of Henry IV, Richelieu, and Louis XIV, of Corneille, Pascal, and Bossuet, the century in which the two great traditions, the classical and the Christian, merged with the genius of the French people.[10] French nationalism was also marked by the conviction that what was vital in that order had in the course of time become debilitated by impurities and aberrations.[11] The fear of "decadence" stemmed from the belief that foreign elements and vulgar impulses were sapping the vitality of that order.

A determination to act was implicit in nationalist myths, but Sorel here issued a warning to Maurras. What were required were "warmly colored images."[12] Scholastic abstractions were of no avail. Herein Sorel perceived the great merit of James.[13] James's significance lay in his demonstration of what was needed to evoke the heroic: the ethics of infinite and mysterious obligation from on high released every sort of energy and endurance, of courage and capacity to deal with the obstacles of life. Victory on the battlefield of history always went to "religion." Faith was necessary to avoid the confusion of ethical skepticism and relativism. "Religion" would always drive "irreligion" to the wall. A nationalism rooted in the glorious traditions of France and the mysteries of Christianity, Sorel urged Maurras, would evoke that nobility of life and spirit of sacrifice that led to "action."[14] He warned Maurras that modernists and intellectualists were the hidden enemies of his movement—the Jews were behind their activities. Maurras, moreover, had erred in declaring himself a disciple of Comte. Positivism was the negation of the mystical, and the church would never accept it.

Nationalist militants had resolved to purify the nation.[15] A national order, for militants, "has its exact laws." These are fixed. There is no progress for that order. If the order is threatened, it is only because its purity has been compromised. It might be argued, Sorel speculated, that aberrations in French traditions were no more numerous today than they had been at any other time, but nationalists were nevertheless convinced that the enemies of the nation were now in positions of such great prominence that they were capable of reducing the country to helplessness.[16] Sorel agreed: French politicians, out of ignorance, fear, or an illusory desire for novelty, were weakening France by unremitting propaganda in favor of political anarchy, antimilitarism, and anticlericalism. French thinkers, poets, and artists were confounding liberty with disorder and originality with lack of taste. In reaction to this, the fear of foreign elements, Sorel thought, had become especially acute, a fear manifest in the rise of anti-Semitism.[17] Anti-Semitism was rooted in the conviction that there were foreigners in high places urging absolute emancipation from national traditions. The vision of a terrestial paradise emerging from a catastrophic revolution was, he asserted, an invention of the Jews. The Messianic myth had continued to maintain in simple minds an infinite confidence in magical political forces. Anti-Semitism had now become "fundamental" for France.[18] There had been a religious antipathy toward the Jews even before the Dreyfus affair; Drumont and the anti-Semitic *Libre parole* gave to that antipathy the force of real hatred. Maurras had demonstrated that the "Jewish spirit" threatened national traditions. Anti-Semitism was now widespread among the French masses; not because it was an "idea" that had been successfully propagated, for the masses hardly had any intelligence or subtlety, but they did have "instinct," and anti-Semitism was an "instinct." "The French must defend their state, their mores and their ideas against the Jewish invaders who wish to dominate everything."[19]

The nationalist movement was composed of an elite.[20] The movement, Sorel recognized, was essentially bourgeois, but the bourgeoisie did not become nationalist automatically, any more than the proletariat became syndicalist. Sorel's comments concerning the organizational aspects of the nationalist movement remained fragmentary. He hardly discussed the role of class in the nationalist movement beyond the argument in the *Réflexions* of bourgeois revival by way of proletarian violence or a great war. His scattered and brief comments were limited to the role of the leadership and the following of the movement.

The role of leadership was given an emphasis in Sorel's work totally absent in his discussion of revolutionary syndicalism, and the discrepancy was nowhere explained.[21] In recent years, Sorel observed, the nationalist movement had produced a variety of commanding figures, but he was disquieted by the absence in France of true "men of action." Drumont was a great journalist, an excellent writer, but "half-mad." Déroulède electrified crowds, but there was little in him beyond noisy insulting talk. Barrès was a superb poet and Bourget had a great love of ideas, but they were not leaders. In Maurras Sorel found elements of genuine leadership. Maurras was the most eminent theoretician that monarchy had yet produced, superior in dialectical skill to any of his predecessors, but was Maurras a "man of action"? Sorel doubted it.[22]

A dedicated minority had been recruited into the ranks of the Action Française.[23] Young men of courage and ability, he observed, were especially in evidence in the *camelots du roi,* who were a sort of private army. For Maurras to achieve his goal, however, that "army" would have to be sizable: "I know very well that the *camelots du roi* go to prison, but I have the impression, notwithstanding their courage, that they constitute a group of rather limited proportions."[24] Moreover, the Action Française would have to ward off all influence from "conservatives" who had been recruited into the movement.[25] Some conservative groups were so ferociously jealous of the popularity of the monarchists that they would like nothing so much as to use them for their own ends. Conservatives posed as advocates of "order," but were, in fact, defenders of the parliamentary regime. Apart from his doubts concerning the limited character of the *camelots,* Sorel also doubted that Maurras realized how serious his organizational preparations must be.

What Sorel saw as essential in the technique of nationalism was, once again, violence. He asserted that violence was not retrograde; it was an explicable social phenomenon, as understandable in the history of a people "as the abrupt movement of a glacier on which the sun had been beating for centuries."[26] He failed to explore the relation between proletarian violence and the bourgeois variety. The nationalist movement, moreover, had nothing comparable to the general strike either in mystery or grandeur.

Violence was a normal manifestation of the social order.[27] Society was at war but thus far in France only one side had, for the most part, genuinely obeyed "the grand human law of struggle." The bourgeoisie had been lulled to sleep by humanitarian platitudes about "social peace," but it had nothing to gain from social peace and it was no more obligated by "social duty" than were the workers. If it were to take up the challenge posed by the proletariat, the bourgeoisie might yet be saved. The final victory would go to one or the other. The bourgeoisie, therefore, must fight to survive:

A policy founded on bourgeois cowardice, which consists in always giving way to threats of violence, cannot but engender the idea that the bourgeoisie is condemned to death.[28]

The bourgeoisie must learn to consider as belonging to it only that which it had taken by force of arms. It must protect its possessions in the same way.

Violence, to be sure, was the hallmark of the *camelots*.[29] The young monarchist militants understood the principle of "action and nothing but action," but their attack on the Republic, both open and secret, must be relentless—beyond this, and the comment that the *camelots* constituted "a group of rather limited proportions" Sorel did not venture.

A commitment to violence, moreover, prevented the nationalists from taking a place alongside of republican political parties.[30] Democracy was a virus that had infected the whole of French political life. It was an error to assume that it was confined solely to the parties of the left. The conservatives, in fact, were the real enemies of the Action Française. They were to monarchism what parliamentary socialism was to revolutionary syndicalism. The monarchists alone among bourgeois groups had the courage to say that they were against democracy.[31] Violence would keep it that way.

Seizure of power, Sorel declared, must be the ultimate objective of revolutionary nationalism, but he seriously doubted whether Maurras understood what was required:

Take all the possible examples of revolutions or of seizures of power: you will see that the men who achieved their goals acted without writing. Bonaparte did not write. The man who was one day to become Napoleon III acted. . . . The encyclopedists wrote; they did not act. The men who made the Revolution really went to war.[32]

He feared that the Action Française would not pass from theory to action.[33] The books and articles of Maurras, he warned, would hardly suffice to overthrow the Republic. The *Action française* was remarkable for its moral courage but "if

Maurras is successful, it will be the first time that a newspaper will have achieved the results which only direct action could be expected to obtain."[34] Sorel specified no method for the seizure of power.[35] The possibility of a coup d'état, however, was implied in his assertion that the *camelots* ought to be "strong enough to hold in check" the military forces of the Republic. The ultimate objective, in any case, was quite clear: genuine revolutionaries did not discuss power; they *took* it.

II

Sorel speculated on the general character of the order to emerge from a nationalist movement. "Bourgeois," he said, was the essence of all that was to be destroyed, but he saw no necessary contradiction in the destruction of the "bourgeois order" by a bourgeois elite.[36] What was to be destroyed was a system of values and institutions that had infected the entire order—it was not at all, he wrote somewhat paradoxically, a matter of class. The bourgeois order was to be replaced by a society rooted in what was most authentic in French tradition.

What would impel a nationalist order, he observed, would be traditional morality.[37] France had been diverted from her sources of moral energy by the major historical currents of the eighteenth and nineteenth centuries. The sarcasm of the Encyclopedists, the utopianism of the revolution, the dissolvent forces of romanticism, the social messianism of the nineteenth century, the vengeance of the Dreyfusards—all this had brought nothing but arbitrariness and disorder. France's traditional moral values must be restored. Disappearance of traditional values would leave her virtually amoral. How this restoration was related to nationalist myths, and how all this was to come about, was apparently not considered in any depth.

Outside of the nationalist movement there were no sources capable of evoking either patriotic or religious sentiments.[38] From the laic morality of the Republic nothing less could be expected than the destruction of Catholicism and its replacement by "tiresome 1prattle." That prattle was rooted in the notions of "progress" and "reason." Progress was an illusion, "an infantile encouragement" that men had allowed themselves, and rationalism was a mixture of half-baked reasoning and personal feeling that made for arrogance and anarchy. From parliamentary socialism had emerged utopian internationalism devoid of love for the fatherland.

Much of what he objected to he now attributed to Jewish influence. He had been hostile to the Jews even during his syndicalist period, though not in his published work.[39] Their activities, he now charged, had done much to trouble the "French spirit": "The Jews would be . . . wise to limit themselves to being peaceful merchants instead of attempting to light the way for mankind's journey to messianic lands."[40] It was Jewish exegesis that had "illuminated the road to impiety" from the Reformation to the most radical freethinkers.[41] Their influence had not only triumphed with Luther and Calvin but was also the cradle of the Grand Orient. The Jews were now attempting to destroy the influence of the Action Française. A people base enough to sacrifice their traditions lightheartedly to "Jewish ironists" deserved the "worst catastrophes."

The role of *morale* remained largely unchanged for Sorel. As in his syndicalist writings, its role was, at least partly, to overcome the arbitrary and destructive forces of sex and to project them into socially constructive channels.[42] In sexual relations the true measure of man's moral nature stood revealed. Sorel denounced contemporary France, consequently, for the laxity prevalent in sexual matters. He deplored the widespread infidelity on all social levels, and bewailed the fact that the prostitute was regarded as the natural companion of the man of culture. He condemned the emancipation of women and the interference of the state in family matters. Nationalism, he believed, had a "magnificent trump" in the form of monasticism.[43] Widespread development of religious congregations in France during the nineteenth century could have arrested the decline of morals. The Republic, however, suppressed the congregations before the significance of this act was understood. The energies released by the sex drive, he thought, must be channeled by a conscious application of custom and tradition.[44] Again he argued for premarital chastity for both sexes, stressed the role that conjugal love played in the moralization of man, and called for the integrity of the family and the indissolubility of marriage.

Morale would also overcome the inclination to act in one's own interests.[45] The tendency toward individualism, which was a constant menace to the social order, threatened relapse into mediocrity and materialism. Mediocrity played a powerful role in history. Society tended toward mediocrity when men abandoned themselves to the advancement of their own interests. Complacency in matters of collective concern had become an outstanding characteristic of contemporary society:

> Of all the feelings that characterize our epoch, there is probably none so tenacious as the hatred of the majority of our citizens for those audacious men who speak to them of the superior interests of their fatherland.[46]

Respect for the law was the test, for the law was the supreme instrument of the collectivity,[47] but the prestige of the law had declined throughout the nineteenth century and the nadir was reached with the Dreyfus affair. The pretended concern of the Dreyfusards for legality was a mere hoax. Their object from the very start had been to make political capital at the expense of the church and army. There was currently also an overriding preoccupation on all social levels with the accumulation of material goods.[48] A fallacious metaphysics had assured humanity of a vulgar progress, that some day there would be sufficient riches to pass around to all. To all this he opposed a Proudhonian eulogy of the modest life: "Humanity must work prodigiously... to meet modest needs; the just society will be one which will accept the law of poverty."[49] Daily life was to be raised to the heroic level. The *homo proudhonianus,* the "man of old France," was for him the highest moral type. He was patriotic and pious; he possessed dignity but was not proud; he was pliable to the constraints of custom and to the obligations of the law; and he was a worker, a warrior, and a lover of justice. With such people "Cyrus and Charlemagne founded empires, Saint Louis and Henry IV a kingdom."

The organization of the social order must be based on the state. Here his hostility to the state, so marked in his syndicalist writings, was nowhere in evidence. The danger of war and internal disorder he believed to be the "original sin" of society. Pacifists, both international and social, were either imbeciles who did not recognize the obvious, or else demagogues.[50] Internal disorder, like war, was always latent in society and was very agreeable to certain human inclinations.[51] With these considerations in mind, Sorel explicated the requirements of the state, although he was rather more concerned with principles than with structures.

Leadership was essential to the organization of the state.[52] The leader, a king or dictator, for example, was the personification of the will of the state. Sorel was not especially concerned with the form taken by such leadership. Should the monarchy be restored, a thoroughgoing application of the monarchical principle would be in order.[53] The Comte de Chambord, he believed, had a "sure and sound instinct." The tricolor had been unacceptable to him; he had insisted that with a monarchist restoration the fleur-de-lis should be restored. In the eyes of many of his followers, he had been insisting on a mere detail, but his moral position was irreproachable. The count could no more have accepted the standard of the Revolution than any of its other institutions:

> There is a monarchical truth, there are not monarchical truths. There is but one process possible in a monarchy: to be openly monarchist from the moment of taking power.... Do you find the monarchy useful? Accept it completely.[54]

The agitation of Maurras, he thought, might very well prepare the way for a Bonapartist restoration or, possibly, "another Boulanger."[55] It was the quality of leadership that essentially concerned Sorel. Whatever the form of the regime, authority must be absolute and unitary. The political institutions of the Republic were accordingly berated for the "anarchy" they produced. The following maxim he laid down as a general rule:

> Power must be exercised only in accordance with the judgment of the one to whom it is entrusted, and not in accordance with a generalized critique.[56]

Decentralization such as regionalism or federalism was the necessary concomitant of authoritarian rule at the center.[57] Like the sociologist Le Play, whom he frequently cited, he saw in the supreme authority the head of a hierarchy, the members of which, because they embodied a passionate feeling for the duties imposed by tradition, served as local "social authorities." A sound system of decentralization, therefore, required an aristocracy of traditional families, but the French hereditary aristocracy no longer truly existed.[58] It had lost its traditions, and having done so, it had lost the respect of the masses. A "republican aristocracy" was to be found in the last representatives of the old provincial bourgeoisie.[59] It had once been worthy of the highest respect, for it had attempted to maintain the traditions of the judiciary of the Old Regime, but it had given way to parvenus of the Gambetta type. In point of fact, Sorel was not hopeful about the future of decentralization of any kind.[60] It had been suppressed by democracy and replaced by a Parisian oligarchy "hallucinated by the idea of despotism." This oligarchy flattered the masses in order better to dominate the state. It had sacrificed the future of the country to its vanity, its hates, and its interests.

The administration of the state must be conducted with the utmost discipline.[61] General Jomini's teachings on the military Sorel thought applicable to the state. "A discipline that was hard without being humiliating" was required, as well as "a spirit of subordination and punctuality." The overriding duty of the functionary was to serve the state.[62] A regime was entirely guilty if it allowed its civil servants to believe that their obligations were less severe than those of its soldiers. The state would surely perish, perhaps more certainly than after military defeat, if its servants combined suddenly to stop working. The Third Republic was censured for its failure to impose hard discipline or to require any real dedication to duty.[63] The result was the republican bureaucracy. "Behind a wicker cage, when it is not closed, one often finds a face which is." For this he held the democratic regime responsible. The Republic dared not be firm with its civil servants because it abused them: it did not pay them well, and it denied them the right to defend their collective interests. The civil service, moreover, suffered a great deal from the favoritism, the wickedness, and the insolence of politicians.[64] It was no longer respected. Its situation was "miserable," and the entire nation was obliged to suffer the consequences. There was, he maintained, only one principle in public administration. The authority of the state must be absolute and unitary and every conferred rank must be a visible delegation of that authority. "Extend this idea to all branches of public administration, and you will have an exact idea of what the administration mores should be."[65]

The corporate organization of the social order—as well as regionalism—was, presumably, what Sorel desired of a nationalist order, though he apparently did not use the term "corporate" and did not delineate the relationship.[66] The organization of society, he urged, ought to be designed to evoke feelings which made for local, class, and professional consciousness. He therefore deplored the mingling of classes in the "democratic marsh":

It is necessary to reawaken the consciousness which classes must possess . . . and which is at present stifled by democratic ideas. It is necessary to revive the virtues proper to each class.[67]

The same was true of professional sentiments. Those "who encourage workers to see no more in their professions than the source of their wages commit a crime against social morality."[68] Everywhere he saw Frenchmen divided into mutually antagonistic groups devoid of common purpose:

When one says "France," what does it mean? Parties that detest each other, an aristocracy without mandate, growling and reactionary . . . ; a bourgeoisie . . . which is opportunist; a lower bourgeoisie of avaricious shopkeepers . . . ; peasants who do not look beyond their fields. . . . I repeat: nothing but political interests. No public spirit.[69]

A "syndicalism" applicable to all social and professional categories appeared eminently capable of achieving unity in diversity, though Sorel evidently did not use the term "national syndicalism," either.[70] The proletariat would no longer be the irreconcilable enemy of the bourgeoisie; it would find its proper place in relation to other groups. The bourgeoisie would have to recognize that without a social doctrine which provided an honorable place for the workingman no social stability was possible in an industrial age. The professions too must defend their interests, animated by a spirit appropriate to each case. Such an order possessed historic roots in France. It would provide the framework within which all Frenchmen, whatever their region, class, or profession, could be joined in a common purpose.

The best description of the technique to be pursued by a nationalist order might be the propagation of a "cult of the nation."[71] Though Sorel did not use the phrase, he implied as much. He thought it would be in keeping with Bergson's doctrine of the *élan vital*—traditional forms and norms would serve as a continuing point of departure for cultural and political creativity. Bergson, he recognized, had not yet taken up historical problems and had said nothing of traditionalism, but his conception of the *élan vital* was perfectly compatible with "the more fruitful ideas of enlightened traditionalists." Sorel once again had in mind a "society of heroes."

Traditional sources of inspiration could again sustain the creativity of the French people.[72] The most vigorous defenders of these sources were Maurras and the Action Française, while their greatest detractors were the educational institutions of the Republic. He particularly assailed the Sorbonnards for importing German pedantry after 1870 as a means of restoring the nation.[73] German methods had only succeeded in creating devoted and loyal subjects of the Republic. Moreover, German scientism undermined religion among the youth. He also took note of the many Jews on the Sorbonne faculties. Jewish intellectuals were violent adversaries of traditionalism: they encouraged revolutionaries and agitators, wrote obscene literature, and clamored for persecution of the church. He also attacked the Republic for attempting to impose a lay and bourgeois culture by way of primary and secondary education.[74] "Neutrality" in the schools had only encouraged teachers to attack the church. Deputies insisted on an education that flattered the masses (without meeting their real needs) in order better to dominate them. As for the traditional sources of French culture, Sorel's formula was classicism and Catholicism.[75] The maintenance of classical studies at a high level had provided England, for example, with a really cultured elite whose education might be compared with that received by the patricians of ancient Rome. The coexistence of Catholicism and modern science presented no problem so long as they conformed to their respective principles and maintained mutually exclusive boundaries. For the workers Sorel's formula was "work and religion." Their needs could be met by vocational training and Christian instruction.

The national interest was the only sure foundation of political action.[76] Under pain of extermination, man since the beginning of history had been forced to create groups with conventions of existence. Inherent in the division of the civilized continents into nations was an important principle: from the standpoint of survival, the nation was the most effective unit. The nation was, nevertheless, perpetually in danger. A continuing concern with its power and prestige was therefore imperative. The prominence of the Jews was symptomatic of the abandonment of the national interest on the domestic scene. The Jewish "invaders" had conquered the social citadels; they ruled finance; they were predominant in the university, the army, and the government. They were the principal protectors of anticlericals and modernists. They had succeeded everywhere in blending themselves into the general population, but their particularism had hardly disappeared and their loyalty to the nation remained questionable. The rights of the Jews were not in question, he asserted, but he believed a monarchist regime would "put certain Jewish political agitators in their places."[77] The threat from without lay in the fact that Europe was a continent of "hereditary enemies."[78] Germany's interests did not parallel those of France, nor did the interests of Russia parallel those of Austria-Hungary. The attitude of European socialists when war finally came, Sorel thought, would be revealing. Their pacifism and internationalism were hypocritical. At the zero hour they would rally to their respective nations. "It will not be ... with *bavardages socialistes* that the events will be faced. It will be with the principles of nationalism."[79] Like Achilles, a nation might die through neglecting to protect the vulnerable areas of its national life.

A cultural renaissance would attend the revival of national traditions.[80] The apogee of nations, he observed, was always the period of the greatest flowering of the arts. The correlation between weakness in politics and deterioration of the arts was well established: "To write poorly, paint poorly, compose poorly, build poorly is all very much related to ... poor management

. . . in the domain of the state."[81] He objected to the idea of "progress" in the arts in the sense that art "advanced" as it became increasingly comprehensible to the masses.[82] There could not exist, he wrote, an art that was base. Art that had real merit might be popular, but art contrived in order to please the mob could only be ephemeral. The current indulgence of mediocrity he found deplorable. It was partly a consequence of the egalitarian spirit that affected high places but it was also due to the tendency toward artistic overproduction that resulted in commercialization and the lowering of standards. He argued also against the idea of "art for art's sake."[83] Aristotle rightly condemned the flute and Asiatic melodies because he believed them to be incompatible with civic virtues. Sorel felt that art should be the highest expression of a professional skill—an idea he had put forth in his syndicalist writings. "The first thing I attempt to discern in a worker of quality, a writer, a musician, a painter, an architect, an engineer, is the conception which he has of his *métier*."[84] Art must also be regarded as the highest expression of the genius of a nation:

A people belonging to the . . . great races must . . . make continual efforts, aided by the legacy of the past, to create anew. It may attempt diverse routes but it will ultimately select one which will permit it to add to its traditions [those] achievements destined to be especially fecund.[85]

The pursuit of *"la grande politique"* was the only way a great nation could live.[86] "It was conducted like war." It allowed natural genius to play the leading role—nothing was more likely to obstruct genius than the imposition of some pedantic theory that claimed politics to be a "science." Needless to say, the Republic was incapable of pursuing such policies either at home or abroad.[87] The democratic regime was a product of both the revolutionary and the reactionary spirit. When it attempted to be "advanced," its bourgeois followers created difficulties. When it wished to be "reactionary," its revolutionary origins stood in the way. The Republic was therefore obliged to follow a path of systematic deception, raising foolish hopes of riches falling from heaven for all and sundry. It was "really a 'monster'; it does not know what it wants and cannot, moreover, know it. It has no head and cannot have one."[88] Only a nationalist society—only "definitive regimes"—could meet the need for order and justice.[89] As Proudhon had observed, these needs require "juridical sentiments" tempered by war and warlike ideas. Only with these sentiments was it possible to construct institutions that endured. As for the foreign policy of the Republic, it had been marked by a repugnance for conflict and a relationship with Germany bordering on treason.[90] The policies of Ollivier, Napoleon III's "liberal" minister, had been "republican" in their effort to facilitate the triumph of a "peaceful and cultured" Germany. France was weakened in advance of her defeat not only by growing manifestations of republicanism but also by a German espionage system that penetrated Parisian financial circles, especially the Jewish ones. After 1871 the country became engrossed in the pursuit of material prosperity.[91] Nevertheless, he recalled, the young men of that day rushed into military service, thinking only of *revanche,* hoping earnestly for an opportunity to "gut" the Prussians. Gambetta, however, at the behest of German agents, abandoned that attitude and created the "republic of Bismarck." The election of 1877, a plebiscite on *revanche,* and the failure of Boulanger in 1889 were due to occult powers in the Republic that were unalterably hostile to the renewal of the German war. Sorel attributed the Dreyfus affair to a carefully prepared agitation by Germany.[92] The connivance of the Dreyfusards guaranteed its success. What followed was the humiliation of the French military and indefatigable antimilitarist propaganda. More recently, the forced resignation of Delcassé during the Moroccan crisis of 1905 was a humiliation without precedent in French history and a clear indication that the Republic had not yet broken its ties with Germany.[93] Sorel saw war coming, and he believed France to be unprepared.[94] The Entente Cordiale, he asserted, was useless so long as the British refused to commit themselves to military action. If war came, the British would make the French do the fighting. In sharp contrast with this record of debility and humiliation, a nationalist regime would restore the greatness of France as a great power. France, he was convinced, was in a better position than Britain to pursue a policy of imperial expansion.[95] Unlike Britain, she had no lack of soldiers. She was eminently qualified to govern the Moslem world. German foreign policy struck Sorel as particularly significant. When William II proclaimed Germany's future to be on the seas, he demonstrated that he understood perfectly the nature of historical greatness in the future. If Germany's world situation today was extraordinary, it was due to her war fleet and merchant marine. France should follow suit. In short, the object of "*la grande politique,*" both internally and externally, was the creation of a society of heroes fashioned after the Roman prototype: "Rome was not only the *cité* of the legions; it was also the *cité* of jurists. These two, jurist and warrior, as Proudhon recognized, are inseparable."[96]

Chapter

7

The Impact

The impact of Sorel's work and activities in France and Italy became even more complex during the period from 1910 to 1914. By 1910 his ideas had become operative in two movements, integral nationalism and revolutionary syndicalism. Valois and Bourget in France and Prezzolini and Corradini in Italy had attempted an accommodation between their own nationalism and various aspects of Sorelian syndicalism. At the same time, Sorel and Berth in France had moved tentatively in the direction of nationalism, while a number of syndicalist writers in Italy had done so more affirmatively. The movement of nationalists toward syndicalism and that of syndicalists toward nationalism had begun both in France and in Italy independently of Sorel. The development had, however, centered around him and his work. Moreover, there were passages in the *Réflexions* and elsewhere that may have encouraged the tendency. Essentially, Sorel added the prestige of his name as well as his efforts, however tentative, to a development already underway, a development which was to continue under its own momentum after Sorel withdrew. During these years Sorel's support of integral nationalism had been measured and equivocal. His literary efforts in its behalf had been something less than passionate. In fact, his impact during this period was due as much to the continuing influence of the *Réflexions* as to his current articles in the *Indépendance* and elsewhere.

I

In France Sorel's ideas were to be found at work primarily among nationalists, a "Sorelian right"—during the immediately prewar years the "Sorelian left," though it did exist, was almost invisible. Among monarchists there were some who saw in Sorelian syndicalism qualities they deemed essential to their own movement. With Maurras's blessing, a genuine, if limited, rapprochement was effected.

That rapprochement was most clearly evident in activities (some have called them "pre-fascist") centering on a number of reviews.[1] The *Revue critique* was the first such effort, though it did little more than establish contact.

The *Terre libre,* though it appeared on and off from 1909 to 1914, was inspired largely by Maurras. Had the *Cité française* ever appeared, it is likely that with Valois's participation it might have fared better than its predecessor. As for the *Indépendance,* it too had limited success. Sorel's articles and those of Variot, Berth, Pareto, and Missiroli revealed a common orientation, but the participation of prominent monarchists gave the review, almost from the start, a primarily literary quality. The monarchists' participation certainly attested to Sorel's prestige in those circles, but their contributions hardly suggest that they were under his influence. The *Cahiers du Cercle Proudhon* provides the most striking evidence of Sorel's new influence.

The Cercle Proudhon was established late in 1911 by Valois and Berth.[2] The idea of the group emerged from discussions between Valois and Lagrange, an associate on the *Revue critique* and secretary of the Étudiants d'Action Française.[3] A common admiration for Proudhon provided a convenient patron. Berth, because of his syndicalist background and close ties with Sorel, was given "great visibility." The Cercle held its first meeting on December 16, 1911, at the Institut d'Action Française and thereafter met regularly each week.[4] It was composed of some twenty to thirty young men, most of them members of the Étudiants d'Action Française who had served on the *Revue critique.* Many were enrolled at the École des Sciences Politiques, the "Sciences Po," a prestigious private institution that prepared students for the highest grades of the civil service; other participants included Gilbert Maire, René de Marans, André Pascalon, Marius Riquier, and Albert Vincent.[5]

Berth and Valois had convinced the group of the necessity of continuing attack on the democratic regime from both nationalist and syndicalist standpoints. When publication of the *Cahiers* began in January 1912, its "Déclaration" recognized the differences in the points of view which still existed among some participants, for not all had been converted to monarchy. All agreed, however, that the nation must be organized in accordance with French tradition and the ideas of Proudhon. They also asserted that democracy was the greatest obstacle to the realization of this goal:

> Democracy is the greatest error of the past century.... If we wish to conserve and to extend the moral, intellectual, and material capital of civilization, we must without fail destroy democratic institutions.... Democracy thrives on gold and the perversion of intelligence.[6]

The Cercle looked to Sorel and Maurras for guidance. At a dinner in Sorel's honor on May 27, 1912, at the Café de Flore (where the Action Française had been born), Berth, the oldest and most faithful of Sorel's friends, presided.[7] Lagrange and Valois of the Action Française presented testimonials and a letter from de Marans was read to the assembly. Even Barrès honored Sorel with his presence. The affair had been called to express the gratitude of the

Cercle to its *maître*. In the words of Lagrange: "Without Georges Sorel the Cercle Proudhon could not exist: he will always be honored and admired as the *maître*"[8] The May/August issue of the *Cahiers* was dedicated to Sorel.

Neither Maurras nor the *maître* himself attended the dinner in his honor. Indeed, Sorel's attitude toward the organization remains something of a mystery. Notwithstanding repeated efforts to secure his involvement (Lagardelle was also courted unsuccessfully), and although he was a subscriber, Sorel did not once submit an article to the *Cahiers,* nor did he attend any of the meetings of the Cercle. Although he informed Berth that he did not believe it possible "to annex Proudhon to the Action Française," he published two letters in the *Cahiers* challenging the *Mouvement socialiste*'s claim to Proudhon. When he learned of Berth's deep involvement in the organization, he urged him to await an "understanding" between syndicalism and monarchism "that could yield better results."[9] Maurras also played an obscure role. At the first meeting of the Cercle, he presented a paper on Proudhon, subsequently published as the lead article in the first issue.[10] He claimed Proudhon for integral nationalism, but made no mention of Sorel. Maurras's participation in the affairs of the Cercle was apparently limited to this one effort. Shortly thereafter, according to Valois, Maurras began to look with disfavor on the activities of the group.[11] He would not permit any mention of its activities in the *Action française.*

Since neither Sorel nor Maurras interfered, the *Cahiers* proceeded on its own. The articles appearing from 1912 to 1914 breathed the spirit of Sorel. He was eulogized along with other "great liberators of the human spirit," Maurras, Barrès, and Bergson.[12] The nature of the "liberation" was conceived in terms Sorel could hardly have rejected, given his own writings on nationalism. The usual republican deities were denounced, as were the conspiratorial elements— Jews, Protestants, and Freemasons. A revitalized bourgeoisie was called upon to restore traditional values and institutions and undo the shame of Sedan. All this was demanded, but with a solicitude for the worker and a concern for "modern economy" not generally found in monarchist quarters. Generally speaking, however, economic analysis did not go very deep. There was more than a suggestion that for these young men Maurras's conception of monarchy was viewed as somewhat of a "myth," something that would have horrified Maurras himself.

The contributions of several members of the Cercle, all young men and monarchists, indicate something of the nature of their interest in Sorel. Maire, for example, who possessed a penchant for philosophy, had been drawn to both Sorel and Bergson.[13] Sorel's method, he asserted, derived from a Bergsonian anti-intellectualism that recognized the limitations of abstract or logical reasoning. The theory of myths and the concomitant theory of violence were both products of this method. Sorel's astounding frankness regarding the creative value of myth and violence Maire thought "brilliant." The "point of suture" between the two was Sorel's rejection of natural law and his moral pragmatism that led to a "society of heroes." Sorel's philosophy was one of "pure action" that banished all absolutes from metaphysics and politics alike. This, Maire thought, explained the comparative ease with which Sorel could move from syndicalism to nationalism. Lagrange, a *camelot* at 15, expelled before 20 for his independence of mind, and dead on a battlefield at 21, viewed the Cercle as an organization obligated to voice all spontaneous protests against democracy and capitalism.[14] That syndicalists and monarchists did not yet agree on the final form of the state disturbed him not at all.[15] The antipatriotism of syndicalism, he maintained, was symptomatic only of its hostility to the bourgeois Republic. When re-established in accordance with the traditions of the monarchy, the state would be the necessary complement of a society organized along national syndicalist lines involving all social and professional categories. Like Lagrange, de Marans of the Association Catholique had contributed to the *Revue critique*; he claimed to be the first of his group to announce publicly his interest in Sorel.[16] What appealed to him most were Sorel's moralism and pessimism, but Sorel had also clarified for him the concepts of "state" and "society." "Monarchist state" and "syndicalist society": one would limit the other. In this way those institutions which had once made France so diversified and yet so powerful might yet be revived.

Though its review never possessed more than a few hundred subscribers, the Cercle continued to thrive until the outbreak of the war, when it was obliged to suspend meetings and publication.[17] Whatever differences existed in 1911 had been resolved by 1914. Its members had embraced a monarchism based on tradition, and they recognized Sorel and Maurras as "the two masters of French and European regeneration." In the 1930s the novelist Pierre Drieu La Rochelle, who had been a member of the group, recalled the "fascist atmosphere" of the prewar Cercle:

> There were young men . . . who were animated by a love of heroism and violence. . . .
> The marriage of nationalism and socialism was already projected. Yes, in France, about
> the Action Française . . . there existed the nebula of a kind of fascism. It was a young
> fascism that feared neither difficulties nor contradictions.[18]

Drieu wrote of other groups of young men in Lyon, for example, who then called themselves "royalist-socialists" and were similarly inspired by Maurras and Sorel. Most members of the Cercle, however, were young men who might have continued along the lines of the "Déclaration" of January 1912, but within the next few years most had been killed as front-line soldiers during the war.[19]

Those on the right who appear to have been seriously drawn to Sorel were not numerous. Lagrange, Maire, and de Marans have already been mentioned; others may have been deeply touched but, like Drieu, did not yet publish. Two additional "conversions," however, may be cited; both were literary rather than political. Variot had turned from Hervé to Sorel to Maurras. He had participated in the founding of the *Cité française* and served as acting editor of the *Indépendance*. Although he wrote little during these years, an essay on the virtues of "heroism" clearly indicated his indebtedness to Sorel.[20] From the Action Française came Bourget, whose *La Barricade,* it will be recalled, had been inspired by the *Réflexions* and gave wide publicity to the idea of bourgeois revival through proletarian violence. Bourget's articles in the *Indépendance,* however, were limited to literary exercises, and with the exception of Bourget, none of the original founders of the Action Française seems to have been touched significantly by Sorel.[21] Berth and Valois alone can be counted as true disciples; in their work Sorel's imprint was deep, long visible, and freely acknowledged.

Sorel's closest friend and disciple in the days of the *Mouvement socialiste* had been Berth, who had not only experienced the same disillusionment as his *maître,* but went well beyond him in his involvement with the Action Française. Berth pronounced himself a monarchist and devoted himself, under the name "Jean Darville," with zeal to the activities of the Cercle. His first article in the *Cahiers* discovered in both Proudhon and Maurras the spirit of classical antiquity, as well as that of seventeenth-century France.[22] Proudhon was both revolutionary and counterrevolutionary. Proudhonian moralism was the antithesis of the "vain" and "cowardly" democracy controlled by "merchants of the Pen, the Stock Exchange and the Urn" against which Maurras was struggling. Berth also attempted in the *Indépendance* to develop Sorel's contention that societies require a mystical sentiment to impel them to great deeds—"something mysterious which does not offend reason."[23] Catholicism was at once the most eminent form of mysticism and its best discipline. It was, moreover, the "faith of our fathers." The lay state was devoid of all mystique, substituting a "pseudo-scientific and sociological" culture for one that was "real," opting for the "social" rather than the "sacred." In another article Berth championed Proudhon against Marx in an attack on German intellectual dominance as well as German social democracy. He applauded Italy's war in Libya and the warlike spirit of the Balkan peoples, but he deplored the fact that "the most plutocratic of modern nations ... had tranquilly permitted forty-two years to go by without wiping out the shame of the Sedan."[24] Most of Europe was "suffocating" from bourgeois materialism.[25] Only the nationalist and syndicalist movements, "parallel and simultaneous," could lead to the "triumph of heroic values." In a foreword and introduction written in 1913 for a collection of articles dedicated to Sorel which had appeared in the *Mouvement socialiste* as well as in the *Cahiers,* Berth hailed the Cercle Proudhon and the rapprochement underway between monarchism and syndicalism.[26] The two movements appeared to be in opposition, yet from their antagonism, he was convinced, a new equilibrium would emerge, "a perfect, fundamental convergence." Proudhon had demonstrated that authority and liberty were the two poles around which society revolved. The conflict between tradition and revolution would produce the social order of the future, a politically neutral state standing above all social and economic categories.[27] In Maurras, Berth perceived a preoccupation with the "beautiful," and in Sorel, the "sublime." In Nietzschean terms, Maurras was "Apollonian" and Sorel "Dionysian." "This alliance is not only possible and fruitful; it is ... necessary."[28] The convergence of an heroic bourgeoisie and an heroic proletariat would produce a fusion of *"réalisme classique"* and *"réalisme ouvrier."* The Republic was bankrupt. What socialists had in mind (he recalled Sorel's appellation) was a "Polynesian regime." The new France, "warlike and revolutionary," was to mark the beginning of a new historic era.

Having taken the lead in the *Revue critique* in the attempt to merge syndicalism and monarchism, Valois continued his enterprise in the Cercle. An article in the *Cahiers* posed the question: how could one restore the finest traditions of France and yet equip her to meet the demands of a modern industrial economy?[29] Valois's solution was corporatism. In "Sorel et l'architecture sociale" he asserted that Sorel had brought about the conjunction of two movements, nationalism and socialism, that had opposed each other in the nineteenth century.[30] Sorel's disciples, he noted, came from a variety of political and intellectual backgrounds; since Sorel provided no precise directions, his disciples were likely to continue on their own. Herein, Valois noted, was the secret of Sorel's influence: "He has given us ... new ways of understanding the world, of penetrating its darkest corners." Again, in an article on the capitalist bourgeoisie, Valois returned to the theme he had expressed in 1906 in *L'Homme qui vient.*[31] A new bourgeoisie had appeared after the French Revolution, without the corporate identity or traditions of the old. This new bourgeoisie had been swamped by Jewish capital that simultaneously threatened national interests and exploited and impoverished French workers. It was the syndicalists who were saving France:

The revolutionary action of French syndicalism has forced the bourgeoisie to return to its traditions, to rediscover the traditional values of French culture.[32]

Valois published a novel, *Le Père,* in 1913 in which he argued, as Sorel had, that a return to tradition would enable the family to become once again an institution within which the passions would be disciplined in the interests of both the individual and society.[33]

Notwithstanding the efforts of the Cercle Proudhon, the influence of Sorel on the French right, in quarters where, presumably, he and his followers had received a serious hearing, remained circumscribed.[34] In 1908–1909 Maurras had, apparently, given Valois a free hand in an effort to entice syndicalists into the monarchist camp. By 1910 Sorel had declared his interest in a national revival by way of the Action Française, and the monarchist newspaper had pronounced Sorel "the most penetrating and most powerful of French sociologists." But Sorel had never declared himself a monarchist. Only Berth and Variot, recent arrivals from the left, so declared themselves, and no segment of the syndicalist movement could be persuaded to follow. What remained of the Sorelian ferment was confined to the Cercle Proudhon, a group of young dissident monarchists. Sorel's influence extended no further on the right, because Maurras had changed his mind concerning the merits of a proposed monarchist-syndicalist merger.

After 1911 the Action Française, as far as it was able to do, directed enthusiasm for Sorel into limited channels.[35] Valois tells us that Sorel's name and the activities of the Cercle Proudhon were no longer mentioned in the monarchist newspaper. Valois himself was refused permission to write in the *Action française*. The reasons for this about-face are not entirely clear. Valois has maintained that Maurras would not tolerate a rival for leadership, either intellectual or organizational, and that he probably saw in Sorel (or, possibly, in Valois himself) a potential rival.[36] It is also true that an intellectual abyss separated Sorel and Maurras, notwithstanding their common hatred of the Republic. Maurras's nationalism was based on positivism and rationalism. He had turned from literary criticism to monarchism in order to restore a society that had been in harmony with the classical tradition of French literature and faithful to the Greek principles of beauty. He was an aesthete before he was a nationalist. His nationalism was cultural before it finally became political and it never really became economic, that is, he never spoke in terms of a modern industrial society. Maurras conceded that Sorel's intellect was truly "remarkable," but he likewise contended that it lacked "discipline."[37] He had a profound disdain for anything that smacked of Bergson's intuitionism. He was "horrified" by the obscure and bizarre qualities of Sorel's ideas and writing style. He could never fully accept the support or permit the widespread influence, as in the Cercle, of someone who in his thinking and writing flouted so flagrantly the classical ideal. And Maurras dominated the French right.

Moreover, the provincial following of the Action Française opposed any collaboration between syndicalism and monarchism.[38] The attempt initiated by Valois in 1908 to effect such collaboration had continued, but without serious application. To be sure, at monarchist national congresses Valois addressed delegates on the continued growth of working-class support. In December 1910, for example, the delegates were told that syndicalist leaders were becoming more and more antirepublican as a result of the repressive policies of the Briand government. From 1909 to 1912 the monarchists intensified their propaganda in certain working-class sections of Paris by holding public meetings at which Daudet made fiery speeches against Jews and employers.[39] These practices, however, brought protests from the provincial branches of the Action Française, where there were relatively few students and intellectuals and where there was little interest in working-class problems. The Action Française began to lose support. Objections were made in the provinces to any ties with a syndicalism tainted with revolutionism. La Tour du Pin, the monarchist theoretician of corporatism, raised similar objections and withdrew his patronage. Simultaneously (and for other reasons), a new danger arose—condemnation by the papacy. In 1913 the Action Française ended its flirtation with syndicalism, and attempted to win back lost ground. "Social" themes were officially dropped and exclusively "national" ones asserted. The Cercle Proudhon was allowed to wither on the vine.

In French syndicalist quarters there was little sign of a Sorelian left during the period—not at all surprisingly, in view of the very limited influence Sorel exercised before 1910. There were, however, indications of more than casual interest in a small group of intellectuals that was marginal to syndicalism. Jean-Richard Bloch's *Effort* was initially fervent in its profession of Sorelian syndicalism, though it had neither local nor national ties with the syndicalist movement.

Effort was a bi-monthly review of literary and artistic criticism that appeared in Poitiers in June 1910. Young Bloch, a twenty-six-year-old Jew from Alsace, had been drawn belatedly to Sorel's conception of the activating myth and its implications for modern art. "We live in an era between two myths," he asserted. The moral adherence commanded by Christ no longer existed. The void left by Christianity could be filled only by a myth of proletarian revolution. Bloch saw the syndicalist myth as a way by which people would rise again to "sublime" and "heroic" existence in a "society of producers."[40] A reading of Sorel's "La Valeur sociale de l'art" of 1901 had first suggested to him that the destiny of a socialist art lay in the identification of the beautiful with the useful, that an aesthetic value must be given to our great instruments of production. The *Réflexions,* moreover, had viewed art as the highest form of labor. Bloch addressed the *Effort* to the study of the implications of a "society of producers" for art. In August 1910 Bloch published a letter from Sorel in which the latter provided assurances that, notwithstanding his interest in nationalism, he had not reversed his position on syndicalism and was, in fact, planning to republish some of his syndicalist writings.[41] The *Effort*'s contributors included Émile Herzog, Augustin Hamon, Charles Albert, Romain Rolland, Henri Franck, and André Spire, several of them members of Péguy's circle, and the Italians Prezzolini, Papini, and Ardengo Soffici, all at the time associated with the *Voce*. The *Effort,* in fact, was similar to the *Voce* in its cultural nationalism. In "L'Irredentisme française" Bloch argued that no one "listened" to France any longer.[42] The curve of French culture was descending. He rejected the nationalism of the Action Française. Those who were of the people could have nothing to do with Maurras.[43] What *Effort* asserted was an "*impérialisme spirituel français.*"

What happened to the *Effort* after 1911, according to Bloch, "happened to France."[44] Revolutionary syndicalism turned out to be no more than "an element of maneuver in the play of material interests." The myth "that Sorel had revealed to us ... no longer existed." Moreover, there had been an apparent revival of the bourgeoisie. In October 1911 Bloch introduced a new series and in the following year changed the title to *Effort libre*.[45] Though he continued to be concerned with "social passions, hopes, and suffering" as expressed in the arts, the review identified with "no school." The goals of the review were now more modest: "to vanquish the rancor and distrust of workers for artists and to dispel the aristocratic and scholarly prejudices of the latter." Sorel nevertheless remained a subject of serious discussion. Franck, for example, supported Sorel's attack in the *Indépendance* on the Sorbonne.[46] Albert (in an article of 1914 that suggests that he was not aware of Sorel's recent disillusionment) noted that Sorel and his antidemocratic associates of the right had scoffed and derided the art of the comparatively recent past, an art that was still full of vital forces.[47] Instead, they acclaimed a past that was "distant, empty, and dead." The *Effort libre,* which never had more than a few hundred subscribers, continued publication until the war.

II

In Italy from 1910 to 1914 the nationalist and syndicalist movements continued along parallel paths. Both despised Giolittian democracy. While nationalists heaped abuse on bourgeois parties, syndicalists leveled their deadliest charges against parliamentary socialists. Both groups had adopted the cult of voluntarism, activism, and heroism. Nationalists viewed the elite as the elect of the nation; syndicalists declared it the elect of producers. Both endeavored to transcend their doctrinal origins. Nationalists turned toward syndicalism, and syndicalists tended toward nationalism. The extent of their rapprochement during the prewar years must not, however, be exaggerated. Though intellectually the lines between them were breaking down, organizationally, except in isolated cases, they continued to hold firm. It is likely that the origins and class composition of the two movements served to maintain their separation. In this setting, after 1910, Sorelismo developed in an increasingly diffused way. In spite of various claims, Sorelismo in fact belonged to no particular faction. Moreover, Sorel's ideas were no longer novel in Italy; others, with or without acknowledgment, were saying much the same thing.

The interest in Sorel's work displayed in the past by Croce, Pareto, and Michels persisted without diminution. Sorel's ideas, in one form or another, continued to serve as a spur to their own intellectual development.

By 1911 Croce had turned tentatively toward a Vocist nationalism— Marx's vision, "for the second time seen by Georges Sorel," was dead.[48] Engaged primarily in literary and philosophical pursuits that took the form of a revolt against German philosophical systems, Croce published his *La Filosofia di G. B. Vico* in 1911. It was Sorel, he confessed, who had urged him to undertake the study.[49] It was Sorel also, more than any of his contemporaries, who had demonstrated the fecundity of Vico's *ricorsi* by applying the concept to primitive Christianity as well as to contemporary movements. Croce was lavish in his praise of Sorel. His work, he asserted, was in accord with the discoveries of nineteenth-century historiography regarding the importance of spontaneous historical developments, the psychology of primitive man, the barbaric quality of early civilizations, and the aristocratic character of their institutions.[50] Croce saw in Sorel's conceptions of the class struggle, of revitalization of societies by a return to a primitive state of mind, and of a "new barbarism" the influence of Vico. Sorel was, in fact, "Vico in twentieth-century garb."

Meanwhile, Pareto continued to elaborate his sociological system, noting on occasion the parallel development of Sorel's thought. Observing in 1910 that Bourget's *La Barricade* had finally drawn attention to Sorel, he wrote to his publisher:

Poor science, that needs literature to make itself known! . . . Bourget knows only Sorel, and so he says that he had been inspired by him. But without knowing it, he was even closer to my *Manuale*.[51]

Pareto was a contributor during these years to the *Indépendance*, speculating on one occasion on the consequences of defeat in modern war.[52] His *Il Mito virtuista* in 1914 dealt more directly with a Sorelian theme. Sorel, he maintained, had successfully demonstrated the capital importance of the "ideal" which became manifest in the form of a myth capable of exciting and sustaining great historic action.[53] Pareto was quick to point out the paradox. Mere renunciation had never made a people strong and potent. Societies in which monastics, anchorites, or ascetics were in the majority had eventually become the prey of the first conqueror to appear on the scene. Nevertheless, great historic achievement, as Sorel had observed, had always been joined with a religion, a faith, or a myth. In the life of a people there was nothing so real and practical as the "ideal."[54] The logical or pseudo-logical content of the ideal, he concluded, counted for little; the reality of the ideal was in the psychological state it produced.

In 1911 Michels published his celebrated study of political parties, in which he perceived in Sorelian syndicalism the prototype of the kind of movements soon to supersede bourgeois political parties.[55] The merit of Sorel's syndicalism, he thought, lay in its recognition of the weaknesses of bourgeois democracy: the incompetence of the masses, the mechanical impossibility of government by them, and, most important, continued exploitation of the masses by an oligarchy of intellectuals. Michels asserted that the "iron law of oligarchy" was characteristic of large organizations, syndicalist included (as Sorel himself had come to see).[56] "Youthful syndicalism," notwithstanding its origins, "is thus quite unable to escape the oligarchical tendencies which arise in every organization." Michels turned to other studies just before the war. In *L'Imperialismo italiano* in 1914, he seemed less interested in Sorel himself, though he explained Italy's Libyan venture in terms similar to those currently employed by the nationalist Corradini and the syndicalist Labriola.[57] Italian imperialism was "the imperialism of a poor people," based as it was on feelings of inferiority with respect to the great powers and the yearly loss of 600,000 nationals leaving the homeland.

As for the Sorelian ferment in the nationalist movement, the very successes of the movement after 1910 appeared to work against Sorelismo. By 1910 such periodicals as the *Tricolore* and the *Voce,* as well as the activities of Corradini (to say nothing of Sorelian activities in syndicalist circles), had all heightened interest in and discussion of Sorelian ideas. But the dynamics of Italian nationalism would not long sustain an explicit Sorelismo after the formation of the Associazione Nazionalista Italiana in December 1910.

The following March, on the anniversary of Adowa, Corradini with Federzoni, Forges-Davanzati, and Francisco Coppola established the *Idea nazionale,* the weekly organ of the association. From the start, the *Idea nazionale* demonstrated little or no interest in Sorel.[58] To be sure, it was preoccupied with creating a state of mind receptive to war in Libya. Sorel's views on the subject were well known and Labriola, regarded as his leading disciple, was lauded for supporting the war of 1911,[59] but there was no indication that nationalism owed anything to Sorel. The fate of the *Tricolore* was also symptomatic.[60] The weekly did not long survive the establishment of the association. Viana wrote that his efforts were "sacrificed" by the leadership of the association, who were increasingly receptive to pressures from industrial interests that were hostile to anything that possessed the slightest taint of proletarianism. The *Tricolore* was to be the last effort to establish an explicit link between Sorel and the nationalist movement.

Prezzolini's review, the *Voce,* also tended to lose its distinctly Sorelian quality within a few years of its foundation. Though it continued to be interested in Sorel, and it explored his involvement with the Action Française, other French interests were soon introduced: those of Barrès, Péguy, and Maurras.[61] Moreover, though Vocists could find in the war in Libya neither values nor goals capable of producing a national renewal, after the war Corradinian and Vocist nationalism drew closer.[62] By 1914 neither demonstrated much interest in Sorel. The review now became more militantly "Italian," a proponent of Giovanni Gentile's idealism and activism. *Lacerba,* an offshoot of the *Voce,* followed the same course.

The nationalist writers who explicitly identified themselves with Sorelismo after 1910 were few indeed. Sorel's ideas were by now very much "in the air."

Moreover, the nationalist movement was aggressive in its denial that any but Italians had played a role in its intellectual formation. Corradini was a case in point: it was around him that the movement of integral nationalism had tended to crystallize, and it was his *Idea nazionale* that became a popular and powerful organ of the younger generation.[63] The Sorelian origin of the argument presented in his *Il Volere d'Italia* of 1911 is indisputable—it was that war had the same moral value for the nation that violence had for the proletariat.[64]

Just as socialism has been the method utilized for the redemption of the proletariat from the bourgeois classes, so nationalism shall be for us Italians the method of redemption from the French, the Germans, the British, and the North and South Americans who are our bourgeois.[65]

Notwithstanding the argument, there was no recognition here of indebtedness to Sorel, nor was there in his novel *La Patria lontana* of 1911 or in *Il Nazionalismo italiano* of 1914.[66]

Prezzolini, the leading exponent of a nationalism devoted to spiritual awakening and internal improvement, continued to pay homage to Sorel. The national syndicalism he projected was one for all classes and professions. Articles in the *Voce* continued to reaffirm his indebtedness to Sorel, though he rejected his views on the war in Africa.[67] By early 1914, however, he had drawn closer to Corradini's position. A preface to a collection of articles that year saw in nationalism a reaction to the dangers of moral decline, as well as an expression of pride in the material betterment of Italy.[68] Within a few months he had gone the full distance: war was direct action in international society, comparable to class violence on the domestic scene. War between nations produced all of the beneficent moral consequences of the class struggle.[69]

Missiroli, editor of the *Resto del Carlino* of Bologna, was a Sorelian enthusiast of more recent origin.[70] An article of 1911 in the *Indépendance,* to which Missiroli was a contributor, denounced "Jacobin democracy," the corruption of its politics, and the vulgarity of its institutions.[71] His interest in nationalism was more than casual. He recognized the "advantages" possessed by the French national movement, based as it was on a monarchical tradition associated with the greatness of France. In Italian nationalism there was no such tradition, a factor that might make it all the more dynamic and creative. Missiroli had neither a Vocist nor a Corradinian background and, in fact, published in Orano's syndicalist weekly, the *Lupa,* as well as the *Tricolore.* Italian nationalism, Missiroli noted, was being put forward by both proletarian and bourgeois movements. A national order, therefore, would be the crowning achievement of the class struggle or it would be nothing. The revolution would be the work of the most noble element and the one whose class interests most closely coincided with those of the nation. A eulogy of Oriani in 1912 linked Oriani with Sorel.[72] Oriani in his "brilliant" *Rivolta ideale* had described the family, the state, and Christianity as civilizing forces, had talked about the dawn of a greater Italy, and had praised Sorel's *Système,* in which he had found many of his own ideas. Sorel, on the other hand, had likened Oriani to Proudhon in his moralism, in his defense of tradition, and in his attack on democracy, positivism, and the tyranny of the state. Missiroli concluded that Sorel was fundamentally, like Oriani, a "man of order"—not a radical or a Jacobin, but profoundly conservative. His was a "creative" and not a "destructive" conception of revolution. Since his principal achievement was the annihilation of both Marxist and liberal sophisms, Sorel was rightly called *maestro* by both syndicalists and nationalists.

Developments in the nationalist movement go far to explain why Sorel's name gradually dropped out of sight in the right-wing writings, except in the works of a handful of devotees. The nationalists, though remaining antiliberal and antidemocratic as well as fiercely authoritarian and imperialistic, eventually turned increasingly toward a "conservative respectability." As they did so, the movement endeavored to ground its doctrines in "Italian" sources. Like the Action Française, it also attempted to remove from its doctrines any taint of socialist or proletarian origin.

The Congress of Florence of 1910, it should be recalled, was dominated by elements having important contact with the ideas of syndicalism—even irredentists and republicans had participated.[73] But the program of the *Idea nazionale,* begun the following March, was already marked by an emphasis on the monarchy and the church as traditional institutions essential to a national renewal. Moreover, the Libyan war, when it finally came, did not serve to radicalize the movement. The war of 1911–1912 cannot be credited exclusively to the emotions aroused by nationalist propaganda, nor did the nationalists reap all the benefits from it. It was Giolitti's regime that had made the war. Virtually all political groups, except the revolutionary socialists and syndicalists and the "Vociani," had supported it.

The nationalists who had rallied around Corradini and the *Idea nazionale* in 1911 triumphed at the two subsequent party congresses, at Rome in December 1912 and at Milan in May 1914, where the process of domestication continued.[74] In 1913 the nationalist movement was transformed into a political party, and in the following year the *Idea nazionale* became a daily. Doctrines were attributed variously to Machiavelli, Vico, D'Annunzio, Oriani, Mosca, and Pareto, rather than to foreigners.[75] The organization, moreover, stressed the "traditional" character of proposed institutions.

The new orientation appeared strikingly in the reports presented to the third congress in 1914.[76] A "mixed syndicalism" was now proposed by the nationalist economists Alfredo Rocco and Filippo Carli. It was a syndicalism, they asserted, rooted in Italian medieval tradition and the Christian socialism of Leo XIII's *Rerum novarum,* a syndicalism "cut loose from its socialistic trunk" and "denuded of its revolutionary and anarchistic tendencies." In fact, said Rocco:

we propose ... to substitute our name for the foreign one and speak ... of Corporations.... In the Corporations, we have not an absurd equality, but discipline and differences. In the Corporations everyone participates in production; [there exists] ... a genuine and fruitful fraternity of all classes.[77]

In revolutionary syndicalist circles Sorel's impact was not only more substantial but also more readily acknowledged. Moreover, if nationalism had turned toward a form of syndicalism, so too elements in syndicalism had turned increasingly toward varieties of nationalism. For syndicalism also, the crucial issue during these years was the war in Libya.

The *Pagine libere* of Lugano, edited by Olivetti, had propagated a proletarian nationalism since its origins in 1906. Its nationalism, in fact, had now turned irredentist as well—Olivetti was to be expelled from Switzerland in 1912 as an agitator.[78] War in Libya was urged before it began and glorified after its inception.[79] The war was viewed as a "revolt" of proletarian Italy against her bourgeois oppressors, but also as likely to advance the revolutionary prospects of the proletariat. On domestic issues the program of the review remained unchanged. Its nationalism was rigorously republican as well as proletarian, and there was no talk of "mixed syndicalism." Prominent among the contributors were Labriola, Orano, Lanzillo, Panunzio, and Michels; Corridoni and Mussolini, and the syndicalist organizer Rossoni also contributed occasionally. Interest in Sorel continued generously. Sorel was defended after he had been "stupidly" attacked by the *Mouvement socialiste*.[80] French syndicalism, it was asserted, had never grasped the *maestro*'s conception of scission. Even Sorel's ties with the Action Française were viewed with sympathy and understanding: French monarchism in its devotion to realism and heroism had objectives that paralleled those of Sorelian syndicalism.

Symptomatic of the "new tendency" in syndicalism was the *Lupa*, founded by Orano in Florence in October 1910. The weekly was an attempt to do from the left what the *Tricolore* had undertaken from the right. Though it lasted no more than a year, it identified itself as the Italian exemplar of Sorel's new orientation; Sorel was listed as one of its contributors although, for reasons that remain unclear, he did not in fact publish there.[81] The syndicalists Labriola, Mantica, Arcà, and de Pietri-Tonelli joined here with nationalists, Corradini the most prominent among them; Missiroli was also a contributor. The *Lupa* was primarily devoted to doctrine. The relevance of the *Réflexions* to the new ideological tendency as well as Sorel's involvement with the Action Française were studied here, but not all commentators reached the same conclusions.[82] The structural aspects of a "national syndicalism" were considered; a "proletarian" and a "mixed" syndicalism were found to be incompatible. On one issue, however, there was complete agreement: "proletarian Italy" and the "imperialism of a poor nation," the glories of war, and the likelihood of national renewal in a Libyan war—"Dobbiamo avere Tripoli," wrote Orano.[83] But on the desirability of a proletarian revolution, syndicalists and nationalists could not agree.

Elsewhere in syndicalist circles, where in the past Sorel had been highly regarded, his ties with the monarchists were now denounced as a betrayal of the proletariat. These were reviews in which syndicalist organizers played a leading role and were addressed primarily to workers. The Libyan war was condemned as a bourgeois venture in colonialism. Here, also, hostility was marked toward anything that appeared to dilute a rigorously proletarian revolutionism. This was substantially the case with the *Demolizione,* the *Conquista,* and the *Avanguardia* (all of Milan), the *Gioventù socialista* (Parma), the *Bandiera del popolo* (Mirandola), and the *Propaganda* (Naples).[84] Nevertheless, the persistence of Sorel's influence was unmistakable. Articles breathed the spirit of the *Réflexions*—it was an earlier Sorelian position that was presented. Frequent contributors included the organizers Corridoni and de Ambris and the revolutionary socialist Mussolini.[85] Notwithstanding their support of the Libyan war, leading Sorelian theoreticians such as Labriola, Lanzillo, and Orano also published here. Though Sorel no longer enjoyed favor and his influence was rarely acknowledged, the renunciation of the *maestro* of syndicalism was not in all instances to be permanent.

The most steadfast of Sorel's disciples were still to be found among a syndicalist elite of theoreticians and commentators. Most had long since left, or been expelled from, the Socialist party, though Labriola was elected to parliament in 1913 as an "independent" socialist. With the exception of Leone, who remained director of the *Divenire sociale* until its demise in 1910, all had by now turned toward a proletarian nationalism, and even Leone looked to the general strike "to continue" the work of the Risorgimento.

Even before the issue of war in Libya arose, syndicalist intellectuals— Labriola, Orano, Lanzillo, Olivetti, Panunzio, and de Pietri-Tonelli—had already, for the most part, "understood" and defended Sorel's new ties with the Action Française. What it was that they perceived in the Action Française of 1910 tended to vary.[86] Some saw in the monarchist movement a response by the bourgeoisie to a proletarian challenge, from which the proletarian revolution would ultimately benefit. Others saw in the Action Française and its leadership warlike and heroic virtues that even proponents of a proletarian revolution could admire. Still others believed French syndicalism by its failure to understand Sorel had failed to understand its own purposes and that Sorel's monarchist followers were his authentic heirs and disciples. On the issue of war in 1911 something of the same pattern of views appeared:[87] war might lead to revolutionary opportunities for the proletariat as yet unsuspected; war by breaking treaties and throwing aside international law was a school of virility and courage; Italy's war was that of a "proletarian nation" struggling against the world's plutocracies to protect her national interests; or, the problems of the *mezzogiorno* would be solved through immigration to Libya.

Though syndicalist intellectuals asserted their independence from the nationalist movement, events were, nevertheless, steadily reducing the doctrinal distance that separated them from it. Labriola's view, that the mass of Italian workers had demonstrably failed to become genuinely revolutionary, was shared by others.[88] So too was de Pietri-Tonelli's argument that *"il caso Sorel"* (Sorel's involvement with the monarchists), the full implications of which were still uncertain, was of crucial importance for the future of Italian syndicalism, if it was to have one.[89] All accepted, or were not far distant from, Lanzillo's position that a true syndicalist was also a nationalist, and Panunzio's notion that syndicalism was antistate but not antiauthoritarian, and Orano's argument that Italian national prestige was the concern of all Italians.[90] In the final analysis, they shared Olivetti's view that syndicalism was not a doctrine at all but "a state of mind."[91] Leone alone took exception to these views. During this period he appears not to have commented on Sorel's recent activities, but he categorically rejected both irredentism and colonialism as being bourgeois in inspiration.[92]

If the theoreticians were generally sympathetic to Sorel's new ties and supported the Libyan war, this was true neither of Corridoni nor of Mussolini: Corridoni seemed indifferent to the former and opposed the latter; Mussolini objected vigorously to both.

By 1910 Corridoni had developed into an intense proletarian nationalist. Although he wrote with some regularity in 1910 and 1911 for *Conquista* and *Bandiera del popolo,* he appears not to have commented on Sorel's activities; these were periodicals, however, that had turned hostile to Sorel. An article of 1911 on the class struggle nevertheless possessed marked nationalist overtones.[93] Corridoni drew a distinction between the "historic" and "economic" proletariat. The Italian bourgeoisie, he contended, was a remnant of the degenerate yet powerful Europe which for centuries had dominated Italy and from which the Risorgimento had only partially freed her. Only the "historic" proletariat, as distinguished from the "economic," was an "heroic aristocracy" dedicated to a continuation of this struggle. He viewed the Sorelian general strike as a "revolutionary war for liberty." The form the new Italy would take, however, was for him a matter of indifference. Though his partisans were overwhelmingly republican, he wrote:

I am not a ferocious anti-monarchist. I am a republican more by intellectual sympathy ... than by conviction. In truth, for me, syndicalist and revolutionary, the monarchy is no better or worse than a republic.[94]

When the war came in Libya, Corridoni would not support it.[95] For years the poverty of Italy and her subjection by the great powers had been a constant theme in his work, but he associated the Libyan war with "Giolitti's dictatorship," and from it, he was convinced, only the bourgeoisie would benefit. It was "Giolitti's war." After the formation of the Unione Sindacale

Italiana (USI) in 1912, he continued to preach the historic mission of *"la grande proletaria,"* ready and willing to fight and suffer for the regeneration of Italy.[96] He continued, as head of the Unione Sindacale Milanese, to organize strikes as a "school of heroism," and he continued to view himself as the successor of Mazzini, Pisacane, and Garibaldi.

Mussolini developed a rather abrupt aversion to Sorel late in 1910 when he first heard rumors of Sorel's activities on behalf of French monarchism and his decision to break with syndicalism. Though he himself had turned sympathetic to irredentism in the Trentino, Mussolini was in no sense an "Africanist" or "imperialist."[97] He bitterly assailed Sorel in the *Lotta di classe* of Forlì for "flirting with the most reactionary forces of the past":

Here comes Georges Sorel, the comfortable bourgeois-minded *pensionné,* decorated with the Legion of Honor, who censures the general strike, and describes Ferrer as "one of the last vagabonds of the Renaissance." ... This man has a nostalgia for the ancien régime. And he returns to it in the company of the *camelots du roi.* For us, no surprise. We have known Georges Sorel for some time. We have never believed in the revolutionism of this pensioned bookworm. His syndicalism was nothing but a movement of reaction. It was a mask. Today it has fallen.[98]

He greeted Sorel's decision to break with the Italian syndicalists with a sarcastic "bon voyage"—Sorel had "passed definitely over to the service of the ancien régime and of the gibbet."[99] Mussolini's attacks continued. In July 1911 he denounced Sorel for his "intellectual deformation" of syndicalism.[100] He attacked Sorelian syndicalism again in his address at the Socialist Congress of Reggio Emilia on July 8, 1912.[101] The isolation that Sorel had decreed for proletarian syndicalism was neither practicable nor desirable. The syndicalists erred in viewing the proletarian problem from an "abstract" point of view. Moreover, the new ties between Sorel and the French monarchists had revealed his true colors—Sorel was a "Bonapartist" at heart. As for the war, Mussolini and the revolutionary socialists generally were "violently pacifist" in their opposition. He and Pietro Nenni attempted to raise the workers in a general strike in October 1911, but were sent to prison for their pains. Mussolini's opposition to the war, however, led to a striking change in his political fortunes. Late in 1912 he assumed the editorship of the Socialist party newspaper, the *Avanti!* Notwithstanding the prominence of Sorelian syndicalists who soon collaborated, in Mussolini's first important article he dwelt on the fact that Sorel had granted several press interviews recently—he called this "interviewmania":

I am beginning to believe that the accusation being made against him to the effect that he is vain and a *poseur* (for example, he cares much about the Legion of Honor decoration) is not exaggerated or unfounded.[102]

Mussolini again attacked Sorel in March 1913.[103] Syndicalism had exaggerated Marx's error in attributing excessive importance to economic factors.

Socialism, he insisted, viewed man as a whole, not solely as a "producer." To all appearances Mussolini had completely rejected Sorel, but this rejection was more apparent than real. Nenni recalled years later, for example, that when the two shared a prison cell in 1912, Mussolini had read aloud "with feeling" passages from the *Réflexions*.[104] Essentially, Mussolini had turned only against Sorel's "deformations": his emphasis on the workers as "mere" producers; his antipolitical conception of syndicalist tactics; and his involvement with the Action Française. He had not rejected what had originally drawn him to Sorel, the myth of an "heroic and historic day." In May 1914, a few weeks before the bloody riots of Red Week in which he participated, Mussolini declared his faith in voluntarism.[105] Behind historical progress, he said, was "human faith." The belief that the socialist era would arrive automatically was "fatalism," the deadliest of socialist sins. A socialist era was only "possible." If it came to pass, it would be the work of "disciplined socialists endowed with courage, faith and moral energy."

Following the CGL Congress of Bologna in December 1910, revolutionary syndicalism was in considerable disarray. As a consequence of the Libyan war, however, the Italian trade-union movement was to re-emerge, this time as an independent national confederation. This development was not without Sorelian overtones, though it did not take place under Sorelian auspices.

The syndicalist unions, having returned to the CGL at Bologna, were at first fragmented and disorganized.[106] Their center in Milan was under Corridoni's direction and their following was to be found largely in Lombardy and Emilia. Their bid for control of the trade-union movement had failed. In the meantime, the intellectuals had been expelled from the Socialist party and were now unable to plead for syndicalism at party congresses. The reformists had taken over control of the party and had, in fact, explicitly declared syndicalism incompatible with socialism. The party, moreover, maintained a strong hold on a large part of the CGL.

Nevertheless, the syndicalists were to profit greatly by the overturn of the Socialist party leadership as a result of the Libyan war. In preparation, Giolitti hoped to draw the socialists into participation with the government by introducing universal manhood suffrage and by offering a cabinet post to the socialists. The revolutionary socialists in the party, however, bitterly opposed the "imperialist war." At the Socialist party Congress of Reggio Emilia in July 1912, the revolutionaries, headed by the old Lazzari,[107] won control. Bissolati and Bonomi, moderate socialist stalwarts, were expelled because they had collaborated with the government. Turati and Treves remained but were uncomfortable. Mussolini by succeeding to the editorship of the *Avanti!* now rose to first rank in the party hierarchy.

The revival of revolutionism within the party was soon followed by a comparable transformation in the CGL. Though the reformists retained control, revolutionary syndicalists in the CGL now found new opportunities not only for attacking the leadership but for expanding their movement.[108] Although Corridoni's organizations were dedicated to proletarian nationalism, they too had condemned the war, as had rank-and-file syndicalists and anarchists generally. For the first time in many years Italian syndicalism found its propaganda closely in accord with that of the Socialist party leadership. Once old animosities had been attenuated in the common opposition to the war, Corridoni, who was a close friend of Mussolini, began to extend the membership and the influence of revolutionary syndicalism both within and outside the CGL. Syndicalist intellectuals, to be sure, had drifted away from rank-and-file syndicalists; they and their organs, the *Lupa* and the *Pagine libere,* conducted a vigorous agitation in favor of the war. But in cooperating with the revolutionary socialists, revolutionary syndicalism had found a powerful new ally.

The Unione Sindacale Italiana, a national confederation (which included anarchists) was founded at Modena, with de Ambris as secretary-general, in November 1912, after the conclusion of the Libyan war.[109] For the first time, all revolutionary syndicalist unions were outside the CGL. Moreover, competitive chambers of labor were set up in many centers—including Milan, Bologna, and Piacenza—providing stiff competition for CGL affiliates. The new organization signified the reappearance of a serious revolutionary syndicalism. The USI numbered about 80,000 adherents. Though reduced in number by about half since the formation of the Comitato Nazionale della Resistenza in 1907, the new organization was concentrated to a greater extent in northern industrial centers. The USI was inspired by Corridoni (who still sang the praises of Sorel) with a sense of the historic mission of the Italian proletariat. With Corridoni at Milan, de Ambris at Parma, and Bianchi at Ferrara, the organization was dedicated to a continuation of the struggle, both social and national, that had begun with the Risorgimento.[110] Expert at seizing the initiative, they sustained an uninterrupted round of strikes and demonstrations. Afraid of "losing contact with the masses," the local CGL leadership felt compelled to follow suit. The "general strike" projected by the syndicalists was viewed as the sole weapon capable of creating a rejuvenated Italy. Mussolini, whose position in the party needed trade-union support, offered an alliance.[111] In November 1913 in informal discussions in Bologna, he attempted to persuade the syndicalists to return to the Socialist party and join in a common assault against reformists in the party, against the CGL, and against the state. This effort was significant even though it failed.

The eruption of "Red Week"—June 7 to 11, 1914—displayed the temper of the USI and its allies in the party (republicans and anarchists were also involved).[112] The culmination of an intense campaign of agitation and demonstration since 1912, the disorders began as an antimilitarist protest at

Ancona. Supported by Mussolini's *Avanti!* and the party revolutionaries, the violence spread rapidly to all of Italy, presenting in some areas the aspect of civil war. (Sorel, curiously, blamed it all on a Masonic plot.) In Milan the partisans of Corridoni marched through the streets waving the national Tricolor and singing the hymn of the Risorgimento. Crying "Viva l'Italia," they proclaimed the beginning of Italy's revolutionary war of redemption. What has come to be known as "Red Week" offered a taste of things to come.

Bolshevism

The events of 1914 began with war and ended with revolution that both hastened and shaped the closing of an old era and the beginning of a new. The First World War and postwar conditions created multiple opportunities for drastic transformations, among which were the hopes and aspirations raised by the Bolshevik Revolution in Russia and the nascent communist movements that appeared almost worldwide soon afterward. Sorel's political interests and expectations shifted accordingly.

Total war had dealt the final blow to tsarism. When it collapsed in March 1917, the liberals in the Duma established the Provisional Government, but in the state of anarchy that followed, the bolsheviks saw opportunities for further upheaval. The movement had appeared with the split in Russian Marxism, the Social Democratic Labor party, in 1903. The bolsheviks represented revolutionary methods, while the mensheviks espoused a more moderate program. In the years that followed, Lenin, as leader of the bolshevik faction, urged a rigidly disciplined and highly centralized party organization that would not be too large for secrecy but would be large enough to provide leadership for the less class-conscious but potentially revolutionary masses. He organized the party into a "staff organization" for the proletariat. He made Marxism the creed that held the party together, the guide of its actions, and the means by which it sought to extend the circle of class consciousness. Lenin shrewdly sensed the revolutionary possibilities created by the war, especially the situation produced by the collapse of the old regime. Returning from exile shortly thereafter, he seized power from the Provisional Government in November 1917. Immediately he proclaimed the establishment of the "dictatorship of the proletariat."

The regime created by the bolsheviks was the first avowedly based on Marxian socialist principles. During its first years, from 1917 to 1921, it proceeded to introduce "War Communism." The forcible dissolution of the Petrograd Constituent Assembly in January 1918 was the first blow struck against the "bourgeois" institutions of representative government and free speech. The entire hierarchy of classes was inverted; all political power was theoretically transferred to the proletariat. The state became the owner of the means of production. The workers were given control of the factories. The peasants partitioned the large estates. Like the Jacobin government of 1793, however, the new regime was almost immediately threatened both from within and without. The counterrevolution raised its head in Siberia and in the Cossack country. The Entente powers, infuriated by Russia's withdrawal from the war, began an armed intervention that eventually joined the counterrevolution. A hideous famine reinforced the unsettling effects of intervention and civil war.

The bolsheviks by their successful coup had transformed Russia (if the new regime survived) from the most backward of the great powers into a world revolutionary force of first magnitude. There arose an alarm in Europe unknown since the days of the French Revolution. Though the war had ended ostensibly as a triumph for liberal democracy, it introduced an era of disorder and disillusionment in its wake. The gravest problems of political, economic, and social reconstruction confronted statesmen and peoples. Bolshevism threatened to take advantage of this situation. In the collapse of central Europe were unexpected opportunities for revolution. For the unfulfilled proletarian movements even among the victorious nations of Europe, the new regime provided a source of inspiration and a model to be emulated. And beyond Europe was a colonial world becoming increasingly restive. In the Third International established in Moscow in 1919, these revolutionary currents appeared to join forces.

The contest between Russia and the great powers was eventually fought to a standstill. The bolsheviks were obliged to give up any immediate hope of world revolution, while the great powers gave up intervention. The new regime settled down to an uneasy truce with the rest of the world. Internal conditions were so appalling that War Communism was abandoned and temporary concessions in favor of prerevolutionary practices and institutions were made. The new turn was signalized by the introduction of the New Economic Policy in 1921.

Against the background of a war he detested from the start and a Europe he was convinced was "rotten," Sorel was drawn to the new regime in a country in whose history he had never demonstrated any interest. The regime, he was eventually convinced, though fighting for its very life, possessed revolutionary potential of global dimensions.

Chapter

8

The Man

Sorel returned to his first love, the proletarian revolution, early in 1914. He had decided to republish some of his early articles on socialism in a collection to be entitled *Matériaux d'une théorie du prolétariat.* Though not published until after the war, a dedication and foreword were completed in July 1914.[1] He declared himself "a disinterested servant of the proletariat" and reaffirmed his faith in the proletarian movement, while insisting that the arguments against the democratization of syndicalism, presented in the *Confessioni* of 1910, still held.[2] He again called on the proletariat to create a new social order on the ruins of capitalism. Anticipating criticism for still another reversal, he declared that his "contradictions" were proof of his good faith.[3] His "explorations," in fact, had given him an advantage over those "observers" who viewed contemporary history from a "unilateral" position.

The outbreak of war in August 1914 produced a profound reaction in Sorel. Berth has written that Sorel was plunged into the darkest despair, while Johannet held that his revolutionary expectations rose immediately.[4] There is something to both views. Sorel detested the "stupid war" from the outset, but he expressed the hope that from it a *ricorso* might spring. In September of his sixty-seventh year, as the German armies neared Paris, he fled Boulogne for Malix, a small hamlet in the Jura in the district from which Marie-Euphrasie had come. His state of mind was mirrored in a letter he now wrote to Croce: He charged that "the Jacobin politicians, the financiers, and 'big-city high-livers'" had produced the bloodbath.[5] A victory of the Entente would destroy what was left of the "Roman" in Europe. He predicted that the war would shake Europe to its foundations:

Events overwhelm me: I sense that we are entering an era more novel than that of the Revolution; . . . all Europe is in the process of rejecting all that remains of the institutions that Renan loved. . . . I am a man of the past. . . . It seems to me that Proudhon in the last years of his life must have had feelings analogous to mine: you are younger and you must provide the philosophy of the new revolution.[6]

Following the "miracle of the Marne," Sorel returned to Boulogne in October. His correspondence with Croce and Missiroli makes clear that his initial excitement had passed. Scanning the horizon, however, he saw no sign of renovation.[7] The war, he feared, might "liquidate" socialism entirely, for the latter had little to say that was original—the great problem, he agreed with Croce, was "living without religion."[8] Moreover, the war had brought no nationalist upsurge of any real merit. D'Annunzio was "miserable." But D'Annunzio was a "genius" compared with Barrès. There was hope neither for France nor for Europe.[9] Though the Entente had declared itself for universal democracy, this he thought pure hypocrisy. He confided to Croce that he did not look forward to a French triumph—until the Bolshevik Revolution, in fact, Sorel appeared to be something of a Germanophile:

> The victory of France means the definite triumph of "the school of Godlessness"; it means the end of Christianity and a peace which can be signed only with a republican Germany.[10]

The war, he asserted, was a Masonic war.[11] Everywhere men demanded only to be received as auxiliaries of the Masons. Moreover, the censorship in Europe was oppressive; it was worse than under Louis XV.[12]

Letters to Croce, Missiroli, and Pareto soon revealed that Sorel was greatly troubled by Italy's possible intervention.[13] Sorel applauded the declaration of neutrality, but Italy's situation he thought extremely grave. Her position in the Mediterranean was threatened not by the Central Powers but by the Entente in general and the South Slavs in particular. His high expectations for Italy he believed doomed by mounting sentiment in favor of intervention on the side of the Entente. He deplored Mussolini's interventionist agitation.[14] He was disturbed by the activities of Prezzolini and Papini, who supported Mussolini, and, even more so, by the theatrical prowar antics of D'Annunzio and Marinetti.[15] Fifteen years of effort to develop in Italy something "serious" appeared to him to have been fruitless. Italian nationalism as well as French, he wrote early in 1915, had revealed its true character. Its leaders were basically demagogues who complained of democracy only when the circulation of their newspapers fell off.

In May 1915, at the zero hour, Sorel was interviewed and published an article in *Avanti!*[16] The newspaper was now in the hands of the antiwar Socialist party, after Mussolini's expulsion from the *Avanti!* and the party. Here Sorel vigorously opposed Italy's entrance in the war. The interventionists, he argued, were either anticlericals or intellectuals who had become "drunk with words." From the standpoint of Adriatic hegemony, Dalmatia, which the interventionists were disposed to abandon to the Slavs, was far more important than Trieste. Moreover, no one would accept Italy's conquests as final if they were secured with Russian aid. After a few years Austrian armies would once again be marching on Milan and Bologna. When the news came that Italy had taken up arms, Sorel wrote sadly to Croce: "Let us hope that she will not have to suffer too much for her folly."[17]

Sorel now saw little sign of "rejuvenation" from any quarter. Some kind of socialism might yet emerge from the war, but it would be a kind for which he had no liking.[18] The war, he observed, had made necessary a large number of controls, the memory of which would long remain. But there was no *ricorso* in the offing:

Whoever believes in the doctrines of Vico looks everywhere in vain in an endeavor to find the direction from which rejuvenation may come.... The Slavs are alien to the ideas which have directed our civilization. By succumbing to decadence we become Slavs: we are ripe for Russian domination.[19]

He did take comfort in the Italian antiwar socialists, who were displaying an unexpected sagacity.[20] They were saving themselves, he thought, for "the hour of the debacle"; they might yet profit from the war. He saw nothing comparable in France.[21] In Italy there was some independence of thought; in France he saw nothing but a "most profound intellectual decrepitude."

From mid-1915 through 1916 Sorel wrote little. He prepared two prefaces for studies by Missiroli. The first attacked those Italian intellectuals since Crispi who had supported the interests of France against those of their own country.[22] The second preface was intended for a projected Italian translation of Renan's *La Réforme intellectuelle et morale* (which did not appear until 1931).[23] In it he discussed at length the introduction of "Germanism" into French culture. Sorel was now prepared to recognize the need in France of a system of solid virtues which Renan had called "Germanic" but which embodied what had survived that was still "Roman" in Europe. An extremely revealing article appeared in 1916 in an inquiry concerning the German wartime mobilization, *L'Allemagne a-t-elle le secret de l'organisation?*[24] What the world needed, he wrote, was a "catastrophe" capable of hurling it into a "new Middle Ages." Society had arrived at one of those moments in history when profound reforms were no longer possible. The catastrophe would fulfill its purpose if it removed the liberal bourgeoisie from power and reduced intellectuals to the status of "performing clowns." A "fourth century" need not follow. Today's economy differed profoundly from that of the era of Roman decadence. Uninterrupted technological advance was therefore assured. The "new Middle Ages" would be one in which myriads of obscure workers would provide both the means of existence and moral grandeur:

A severe medieval penitence would give birth to a civilization rich in quiritarian virtues. What the German philosophers call *individualism* would be vanquished by what they call *organization*.[25]

Although he took note of the revolutionary upheaval in Russia, through 1917 and as late as February 1918 Sorel gave little indication in his correspondence with Missiroli or Croce that he believed anything new was impending—he was so poorly informed on Russian Marxism that as late as

September 1916 he identified Lenin as a "German socialist."[26] In March 1917 he wrote a foreword for *De l'utilité du pragmatisme,* a collection of purely philosophic essays he had published in previous years.[27] In it he vigorously condemned, as he had so often in the past, the *"préjugés scientistes."* He enlisted himself as the disciple of James and viewed pragmatism as an instrument in the pursuit of the "sublime" and the "freely heroic." In his correspondence he made only passing references to events in Russia.[28] In fact, he was looking in another direction—toward Italy—but with faint hope. If Italy did not save herself from the current "universal stupidity," Europe would find itself "on the edge of an abyss."[29] The thinking of Europeans, he feared, ran the danger of "sinking to the American level." As late as January 1918 he demonstrated no particular interest in events in Russia; he was preoccupied largely with personal matters.[30] His physician would not permit him to make the trip into Paris because of a recently developed heart condition, and he complained bitterly that Bergson had not sent him an invitation to his reception into the Académie Française. Bergson, he wrote, now expressed the views of rich Parisian society, and particularly of the Jewish world.[31] Bergson wanted on this occasion to be "surrounded by the solicitations of the *grands Juifs.*" This was the first time he had ever turned on Bergson.

Sorel acclaimed Lenin's dissolution of the Constituent Assembly on January 19, 1918, evidently the first act of the Bolshevik Revolution to command his serious attention. To Delesalle in February he wrote that this was an act of "powerful originality."[32] He doubted Lenin's ultimate success, however: "Everything may end in an immense disaster." Letters in March suggested the nature of his doubt. Although convinced of Lenin's integrity, he distrusted Trotsky. Trotsky must resemble, he speculated, the Russian Jewish revolutionaries one met in Paris, "talkative, braggarts, half-hallucinated, on the lookout for some popular dictatorship which will make Caesars of them." Trotsky was possibly in the pay of the Entente. Jews attracted to bolshevism were not, in any case, capable of understanding its "sublime aspects." Nevertheless, he conjectured, events in Russia seemed to constitute "the funeral of the socialism of bourgeois orators."[33]

Within the next several months he became convinced that the Bolshevik Revolution was indeed a *ricorso.*[34] In June 1918 he wrote to Delesalle that for a long time he had been asking himself what good his thirty years of work for the advancement of the proletariat had been.[35] He did not yet know the nature of bolshevism or how it was to be adapted to the Western mind, but he declared himself convinced that European socialism was doomed in view of events in Russia. "I see only one solution: forget our hopes which are obviously vain and attach ourselves . . . to the bolsheviks." Though the bolsheviks were faced with "terrible" difficulties, they showed amazing tenacity. The regime, notwithstanding repeated announcements that it was on the verge of collapse, had not been betrayed by its leaders: "Lenin," he said, "seems to be as incorruptible as Robespierre, and, astonishingly, he has been able to maintain himself in the midst of Jews who cannot all be too pure."[36]

As his admiration for Lenin soared, his letters reveal that his detestation of the "Western bourgeoisie" now knew no bounds.[37] He was convinced that the Entente was plotting with the Russian Social Revolutionary party. He accused the European press of distorting the true picture of events in Russia, "It is because of this . . . that I have so much sympathy for Lenin and his followers."[38] The entire bourgeoisie, European and American alike, had two great hatreds: Prussian militarism and Russian bolshevism.[39] They did not know which to hate more. They saw in bolshevism, perhaps, the gravest danger yet to the bourgeois order.

As for the significance of the Bolshevik Revolution, Sorel was still uncertain.[40] What could have been said of the French Revolution if it had ended with the Convention? The principle promulgated by the Fifth Congress of Soviets in July 1918 reserving political rights solely to "producers" was clear enough. The regime was unmistakably opposed to bourgeois democracy. This act suggested something of the outlook of Allemane's *manuellistes*:

I recollect having read somewhere that in Russia the red guards proclaim unhesitatingly: "Death to the Intellectuals." It is incontestable that Russian intellectuals have done their country considerable harm. . . . There again one may say that the friends of Lenin are pushing the Allemanist tendencies to the hilt.[41]

Bolshevism, he was now convinced, might bring about a "Socialist renaissance." If only it could hold out, Bolshevism would mean that social problems in the West would henceforth be regarded in an entirely new light.[42]

By early December Sorel was reading final proofs of the *Matériaux*.[43] The volume was composed of articles written during various stages of his career, though for the most part they dated from his syndicalist period. Inconsistencies abounded, as Sorel was well aware. But he preferred, he said, to reveal his innumerable "variations" himself rather than allow his enemies the glory of discovering them.[44] Even then, he doubted that he would be understood. A postscript added to the foreword of 1914 commented on the victory of the Entente in November and its intervention in Russia. The "stupid bourgeoisie" would "howl," he wrote to Delesalle, when they read it. He had written:

The victory of the Entente has been a triumph of demagogic plutocracy. The latter wishes to complete its work by suppressing the *bolsheviks* who frighten them: their military forces are substantially adequate to execute this operation; but what will the plutocracies gain by the extermination of the Russian revolutionaries? Will not the blood of the martyrs once again be fertile? . . . One must be blind not to see that the Russian Revolution is the dawn of a new era.[45]

In 1919 Sorel became more active in his defense of the Bolshevik regime. He wrote to Croce and Delesalle of his determination to defend Lenin, who had shown himself to be "a really practical man".[46] American journalists had said that there was constant improvement in conditions in Russia. He also planned to attack the victory of the Entente as the triumph of bourgeois plutocracy. He found particularly contemptible the demand that the kaiser be tried as a war criminal. He met Variot on the Pont de la Concorde on the day the Treaty of Versailles was signed. Variot recorded that Sorel told him: "Europe will be the shame of the living world for this useless war. And it is not over. You are still young ... believe me."[47]

During that year his health had recovered sufficiently to permit him to earn some badly needed funds (he had invested, curiously, in Hungarian, Russian, and Austrian bonds before the war).[48] He became a regular correspondent for two Italian newspapers, the *Resto del Carlino* of Bologna and the *Tempo* of Rome, as well as a contributor to the *Ronda,* the Roman literary review, publications which were hardly pro-bolshevik. The *Resto del Carlino* was enlightened, critical, and liberal—Missiroli, its director, now became, in effect, the principal agent between Sorel and Italian culture. The *Tempo* was a conservative daily of considerable repute. Both were greatly concerned with what Italy was to receive at the Paris Peace Conference. The *Ronda* was an exponent of a Leopardian, neo-classical revival. That Sorel could publish in these organs, notwithstanding his unconcealed sympathies for the Bolshevik regime, testifies to his continuing popularity. He was widely regarded as an unsparing critic of his own France, to say nothing of Entente policies generally, and as a "friend of Italy."

Sorel's articles during the first half of 1919, characteristically, covered a wide variety of matters, and were frequently shrewd in their perceptions and sharp in their criticism. He surveyed the horizon and affirmed his faith in the revolutionary potential of Russia and Germany.[49] He challenged the "myth of Belgian neutrality."[50] He wrote critically of Péguy and his "conversion," and of the prewar traditionalist revival.[51] In a series of articles on bolshevism he questioned Lenin's statement that Russia could be raised to the level of the Western powers in five years—it would, he felt, take much longer.[52] The Western powers did not realize that Russia, threatened with disintegration, could take but one of two courses, tsarism or bolshevism. Sorel thought a "bolshevik imperialism" might someday replace that of the tsars. In other articles he deflated Clemenceau's reputation for his Italian readers;[53] he explored the role played by "revolutionary armies," from Cromwell's Ironsides to the Red Army;[54] and he praised Italian revolutionaries for supporting the bolsheviks.[55]

He continued to applaud the bolsheviks throughout the year, while he struck out in all directions against his enemies, both recent and long-standing.

The German Social Democrats, he believed, were well on their way to creating a gigantic political and bureaucratic machine.[56] Lenin's address of May 1918 on the power of the Soviets was as important for the future of Marxism as was the work of Marx on the Commune.[57] The possibility of France's moral regeneration by either left or right was categorically ruled out.[58] Agitation among the Entente powers for the trial of the kaiser was an attempt to create a precedent that could be used against the bolsheviks.[59] The Okrana was responsible for the assassination of Jaurès—Gohier and Daudet were blameless.[60] A brief article on modern art asserted that once they were liberated from bourgeois influences, artists would rediscover the "idea of liberty."[61] A comparison between Max of Baden and La Fayette concluded that both "saved" their country by betraying it.[62] A new perspective on Proudhon convinced Sorel that he was the authentic precursor of Bergson and James.[63] A number of articles revealed again his despair over his own France.[64] Both socialists and conservatives, he was convinced, were dedicated to the defense of the status quo. Yet he hoped French socialists would be able to amass sufficient strength to prevent Foch's election to the presidency, which would be a victory for clericalism. The French bourgeoisie, he feared, was attempting to establish a "Byzantine" regime, an inert conservatism which would, like Byzantium, outlast the Rome of the Caesars. Again he returned to the bolsheviks: he flayed Kautsky for objecting to Lenin's conception of the dictatorship of the proletariat, and he deplored the failure of French socialism to follow the example of the Italian movement in its support of Lenin—in no other country did socialism have better prospects than in Italy.[65]

Sorel prepared two new editions of earlier works, the *Réflexions* and the *Introduction,* during 1919. The fourth edition of the former contained the celebrated "Pour Lénine."[66]

The "Pour Lénine" had its origins in an article on Sorel written by Paul Seippel, a Swiss journalist and professor, which appeared on February 4, 1918, in the *Journal de Genève*—Sorel had long been a reader of the daily.[67] Seippel expressed the fear that the Bolshevik Revolution was a mere prelude to a great revolutionary wave about to engulf all Europe. Moreover, during their exile in Switzerland Lenin and Trotsky, he maintained, must have come to know the *Réflexions.* Bolshevism was a "terrifyingly logical" application of Sorel's doctrines on violence. To these charges Sorel replied that he had no reason to believe that Lenin had employed the ideas put forth in his study on violence, but if that were true, he would be uncommonly proud to have contributed to the intellectual formation of a man who seemed to be at once "the greatest theoretician that socialism has produced since Marx" and "the head of a state whose genius recalls that of Peter the Great."[68] In any case, he had not presented in the *Réflexions* an apology for absolute ruthlessness. It was absurd, therefore, to see in the study, as Seippel did, a brief for terrorism.[69] He expressly regretted the use of brutality by the bolsheviks. The revolution's excesses, he maintained, could be understood only by keeping in mind the "Muscovite character" of bolshevism and the large number of Jews attracted to the movement.[70] The number of people shot by the bolsheviks was, in any event, considerably smaller than the number of victims of the blockade organized by the democratic Entente.[71] The real significance of the conflict between Russia and the Entente transcended these considerations. What was transpiring could be compared only to the struggle between Rome and Carthage.[72] Russia was "Rome." She was bringing to the world a new civilization. She was, therefore, destined to triumph in the end. He closed on an ecstatic note:

May the plutocratic democracies which are starving Russia be cursed! I am only an old man whose life is at the mercy of trifling accidents; but may I, before descending into the tomb, see the humiliation of the arrogant bourgeois democracies, today so shamelessly triumphant.[73]

Prewar themes dominated the foreword and appendix to the third edition of the *Introduction*. The foreword acknowledged the disdain with which the *Introduction* of 1903 had thus far been treated by the "professionals of economics."[74] This Sorel attributed to his "juridical" approach to the study of the syndicates; the Bolshevik Revolution, he asserted, had vindicated this method. The future of socialism depended on the proper operation of the soviets, which, he now averred, were not unlike syndicates. The appendix was a refashioned version of a preface prepared in 1905, but his argument remained unchanged. He saw humanity condemned by a "law of nature" to pain and grief.[75] Only by work and productivity was man capable of transcending nature and raising human activities to an "heroic level."

Throughout 1920 Sorel was haunted by the possibility that the "socialist renaissance" initiated by the Bolshevik Revolution might be suppressed, particularly by France. From February to May, France was torn by a series of strikes marked by considerable sympathy for the Soviet regime. The leadership of the CGT endeavored to settle the strikes before May Day. This "meddling" outraged Sorel, for it undercut the revolutionary mood of the workers.[76] In August, when the Quai d'Orsay decided to recognize General Wrangel's counterrevolutionary regime in Russia, he charged that France had become the "citadel of reaction."[77] The decision was, nonetheless, a stupid one, for it would make the French workers all the more determined in their support of Lenin. That same month Sorel wrote to Croce that there was no sign of good faith anywhere among socialists. He was disgusted by both the French and Italian movements. He feared their leaders would betray Lenin at the next congress of the Third International because they really feared bolshevism: "In a word, everything is rotten in Europe."[78] When Millerand decided that France should come to the aid of the Poles in their struggle against the Red Army, Sorel again took heart.[79] The example of the German workers who prevented the transport of French munitions to Poland would be, he thought, a powerful one. The Third International would eventually profit from Millerand's error.

That year Sorel began to contribute to the new *Revue communiste*. He had, in fact, been asked to join the staff of *Humanité,* but he refused because he thought the responsibilities too arduous.[80] The *Revue communiste,* which began publication in March 1920 under the direction of Charles Rappoport, pronounced itself in support of "Integral Communism and the Third International."[81] In his contributions Sorel explored the broader implications of the Bolshevik Revolution. He suggested, for example, that the penetration of bolshevik ideas into China could have a profound effect on the future of the West.[82] Once armed with bolshevism, a much-to-be-desired "Mongol conquest" of the West might follow. In an article on Egypt, he argued that the bolsheviks had proved possible the overthrow anywhere of a regime rotten with "*Parisienisme*" if workers and peasants were led by a few determined revolutionaries.[83] The Bolshevik Revolution, in any event, had now become the model for revolutionary movements in all backward countries. He asserted that Lenin's emphasis on rapid technological advance made comparison between the new regime and societies of antiquity difficult.[84] The Bolshevik Revolution was the sole revolution in history based on the idea of technological advance.

Articles that appeared in the *Resto del Carlino* continued to present familiar arguments: the soviet was an institution that could be readily imitated elsewhere; French intellectuals were seeking a vulgar popularity by attempting to discredit German culture and philosophy; "absolutism" was sweeping across Europe sponsored by France (by absolutism he meant "the suppression of forces that arise spontaneously in the masses"); parliamentary governments were developing into regimes of personal power—he perceived this particularly in the England of Lloyd George; and the Nitti government in Italy demonstrated unique good sense in abandoning intervention and establishing diplomatic and commercial relations with Russia.[85] Two articles followed on the current French political scene: he was convinced by the elections of November 16, 1919, that there was no longer any real sentiment in favor of a monarchist restoration, and he applauded the decision of the Socialist Federation of the Seine to adhere to the Third International.[86]

What was striking about his articles in the *Resto del Carlino* as they continued into 1920 was the way in which, at every turn, he reviled France. He asserted that the French bourgeoisie, because it no longer personally directed production, was historically "finished."[87] In French foreign policy he saw only a bourgeois compulsion to strangle the infant Bolshevik regime.[88] The French conservatives, he asserted, supported Millerand's presidency because "fear of socialism is the very soul of the bourgeoisie."[89] He railed against arguments in the French press that the road into Europe must be blocked against the "Asiatic barbarism" of bolshevism; on the contrary, Sorel welcomed the "barbarians."[90] Bergsonian philosophy still commanded his respect, and Bergson, he thought, might yet become for the future what Aristotle had been for the Middle Ages.[91] The renewed attack on the doctrines of Marx in postwar France he found intellectually contemptible.[92] He concluded, moreover, that the Bolshevik regime would have aroused in Jaurès, had he lived, "the most profound disgust."[93]

An opportunity to comment at greater length on matters of a more theoretical nature was provided in new editions of the *Matériaux* and the *Illusions* prepared in 1920. "Exégèses Proudhoniennes" was appended to the second edition of the *Matériaux*—Sorel believed it to be "as scandalous" as the "Pour Lénine."[94] He was concerned here, as he had been with the prewar Cercle Proudhon, lest Proudhon be taken for a nationalist.[95] The Action Française, he wrote, despite its professed admiration for Proudhon, could not accept his obvious esteem for Prussia and her Protestantism, nor could it overlook his admiration for the proletariat. Sorel was convinced that Proudhon would count for more than Marx in the annals of socialism.[96] Marx had revealed the role played by the class struggle in history. Proudhon's superiority lay in his demonstration of how the class struggle could "regenerate social and political mores."

"La Marche au socialisme," appended to the fourth edition of the *Illusions*, attempted to explain the obvious inconsistency between the Marxian notion that socialism was the necessary sequel to a highly developed capitalism and the appearance of a socialist society in economically backward Russia—a problem already considered in "Pour Lénine."[97] The "march to socialism," he insisted, was not as simple as Marx had described it. Socialism, as he had argued in the *Réflexions* many years ago, did not depend upon the "excellence" of Marxist theories; it relied upon convictions held by the workers. The innumerable controversies raging in socialist circles regarding Lenin's "orthodoxy" were without relevance.

A preface prepared for a collection of his Italian newspaper articles (which did not then appear) proclaimed his faith in the Third International.[98] The Second, he said, had been a mere "academy" of socialist politicians who proved their impotence in 1914. The Third was fashioned along new lines. Russia had now assumed the leadership of a world revolutionary movement because she had given to the revolutionary idea a reality it had heretofore lacked. Support of bolshevism was now the only proper focus of proletarian propaganda. Workers were more powerfully moved by realities than by academic abstractions.

By 1921 Sorel was frequently bedridden and unable to write. Leaving Boulogne for Paris again with the approval of his physician, he visited former haunts and old friends: Delesalle's bookshop, Variot's home, Bourget's study. Years later Bourget, the dean of nationalist writers, was to recall Sorel, the champion of Lenin, coming to visit him: "I can see him now entering my study as he did so frequently in the mornings, and begin to talk, or rather to think out loud."[99] When Sorel met Variot one day in January, Sorel proceeded to tell him that Europe offered an astonishing spectacle.[100] Here was the elite of savants, writers, and artists, but not one of them had really attempted to understand Lenin. He suspected a conspiracy of intellectuals, both of the left and of the right, to conceal the real nature of events in Russia. Socialist intellectuals were no different than other varieties. Lenin, he thought, had every right to suppress intellectuals: "Oh! how I understand Lenin."[101] A true servant of the proletariat was one who served without the Sorbonnard's air of superiority or the politician's passion for self-advancement.[102] In March Sorel met Variot again. This time Variot told him that it was widely bruited about that Lenin's regime and Mussolini's Fascist party were inspired by Sorel's doctrines.[103] Sorel replied that he had heard the same thing and was greatly flattered, but he doubted that a single individual could be that influential. Besides, he had not invented anything new; his doctrines were "in the air." He did not think that it was necessary for a man of Lenin's genius to have read his books. Lenin had at the beginning of the century also taken part in the "decomposition of Marxism" and had attempted to restore Marxism to its pure form. Lenin was a proponent of "violence," that is, of Marxism "to the hilt."

In July Sorel wrote to Delesalle with great concern that his physician had once again prohibited his trips to Paris.[104] He feared this interdiction meant that his heart illness was far more serious than had been intimated. He was troubled by other matters as well: "I am on the way to becoming an outcast." He believed himself "persecuted" by the printers of Villeneuve-St. Georges, who were not pleased with his books. Anyone who wrote favorably of the bolsheviks, he was convinced, ran this risk. That same month he wrote to Croce:

The war has not made men more serious. . . . What a sad future we have before us. It is true that I am 74 years and that, with my heart trouble, I cannot have many more years to live; I will not see the worst days.[105]

What Sorel published in France in 1921 was confined to the *Revue communiste.* "Lénine d'après Gorki," a critique of Gorki's brief biography of Lenin published by *Humanité,* ranks with the most important essays he had ever written; it appeared the following month in Antonio Gramsci's *Ordine nuovo,* the organ of the Turinese communists.[106] Sorel took Gorki's study as a confirmation of the views he himself had expressed in "Pour Lénine." He discussed "bolshevik myths" in general and compared the formation of the "Lenin legend" with that of the Napoleonic legend. Sorel did not conceal his pride when Bergson, who had read the "Lénine d'après Gorki" (as well as the *Pragmatisme*) wrote to him: "You give the pragmatic criterion a precision and a universality that it has not yet received."[107] A reading of Barrès's work demanding the Rhenish provinces for France aroused his wrath; he denounced Barrès, and French nationalists in general, as "bands of partisan fanatics."[108] He followed with a critique of the church in France in which he branded the Society of Saint Vincent de Paul a "clerical Okrana."[109]

In the *Resto del Carlino* in 1921, articles followed one after another with by now predictable views on widely varied subjects: the Catholic opposition to Bergson, the reaction of the Moslem world to bolshevism, and the celebration of the centenary of Napoleon's death.[110] He also took note of the new role played by the United States in world affairs.[111] Wilson he described as the "quintessence of political Calvinism." His administration, Sorel asserted, was the most arbitrary and corrupt in American history. Again he turned on his bêtes noires, some old, some new: the parliamentary socialists who had accorded to Kerensky what they denied to Lenin; the role of Belgian politics in the German violation of Belgian neutrality; and the inability of Bertrand Russell, an "authentic Englishman," to discern greatness in Lenin, an "authentic Muscovite."[112] Sorel devoted two articles to the pronouncements of the historian of Rome, Ferrero (with whom he had resumed his prewar correspondence): bolshevism would triumph in Europe if democracy did not heal the wounds of the war and the victors did not overcome their blindness toward the vanquished; and bolshevism would end in a "Napoleonic despotism."[113] Still others followed in bewildering confusion: the growth of bureaucracy was explained by the passion of intellectuals for jobs; the rapid disappearance of the "heroic" in war was due to the new military technology; the commemoration of the Commune by the Communist party demonstrated what was required to revive French working-class militancy; the collapse of the prewar Catholic renaissance was due to its failure to make proper use of Bergson's philosophy; and the destruction of the monarchical idea in Europe was assured with the fall of the Hapsburgs.[114] Sorel often demonstrated considerable insight as, for example, in an article on the possible rapprochement between Russia and Germany and in another on the way in which socialist controversy would in the future be dominated by questions concerning the new Russia.[115]

Sorel was gravely ill at the beginning of 1922. He could no longer meet the responsibilities of a regular correspondent, but he nevertheless continued to write. He prepared the second edition, with a new foreword, of *La Ruine du monde antique*. Ferrero had recently compared the coming of bolshevism with the disasters which shook the Roman Empire in the third century. Sorel accepted the analogy but argued in his foreword as well as in his correspondence with Ferrero that it did not follow that the West was about to enter a primitive era which would last several centuries. Ferrero, he said, demonstrated all the errors of "historical scientism". He viewed the history of antiquity as a "completed" system, a determinism. By not taking the contingent and the voluntaristic into consideration, he had arrived at wholly unwarranted conclusions.[116]

The news of Sorel's grave illness prompted *Humanité,* now (since the Congress of Tours of December 1920) the official organ of the French

Communist party, to publish an interview on March 9 at which Bernard Lecache, its editor, and Charles Rappoport, the editor of the *Revue communiste,* were present.[117] Lecache wrote that Rappoport had to lead him by the hand. Lecache had not the courage to enter Sorel's tiny room in Boulogne by himself. Then, finding Sorel so poor and ill, Lecache was seized by an "adolescent timidity" before *"le maître."* During the interview Sorel turned repeatedly to the subject of Russia. He had complete faith in Lenin; the difficulties of the regime were to be expected. He thought the Italian situation "grim" and he was critical of the German Independent Socialists. Returning to the bolsheviks, he feared that Russia might yet succumb: "We must go forward! That is the sole objective! We must save her!"

Sorel's stamina must indeed have been remarkable, for Michels, now professor at the University of Basel, met him in Paris in March at Delesalle's bookshop.[118] On this occasion Sorel had expressed confidence in the vital energies of the Russian, the Italian, and, perhaps, the German people. He asked Michels to send him as many of the writings of Lenin and Trotsky as he could obtain in Switzerland; little of this literature, he asserted, was readily available in France. When Michels expressed the belief that these writings might "set the world aflame," the conversation "threatened to become difficult." Michels noted in his diary:

I confess that the prospect appealed to me very little, and using the first opportunity to extricate myself . . . , I saluted my old friend and *maestro* respectfully and took my leave. I never saw him again.[119]

The last article written by Sorel appeared in April in the *Mercure de France* and concerned an abstract drawn up in 1828 by Jeremy Bentham for Mehemet Ali suggesting how Egypt could achieve both her independence and the blessings of constitutional government. Sorel had become interested in the postwar Egyptian nationalist movement, urging the cultivation of *"Egyptienisme"* and violence against the British.[120] Characteristically, he attacked the "rationalism" and "utopianism" implied in Bentham's endeavor.[121] Bentham, he charged, knew nothing of Egyptian conditions or of the desires of the Egyptian people. Mehemet Ali, as a constitutional monarch, was an absurdity. Besides, constitutions did not make nations.

The summer of 1922 was Sorel's last. On June 11, Bertrand de Balandes of the Action Française wrote to Valois that he had just visited Sorel and that he found him near death.[122] He asked Valois if it would not be possible to turn Sorel's thoughts to God, to find a priest or nun who might approach him. Valois evidently failed to do so. On his deathbed Sorel was visited by Johannet of the Action Française and Delesalle of the staff of *Humanité.* Johannet has written that with a voice barely audible, "I heard him gasp: *'Il faut aider la Russie.'* "[123] Sorel died on August 29, 1922.

Chapter

The Idea

From early 1918 to his death in 1922 Sorel's allegiance went principally to bolshevism. Though in 1914 he had pronounced himself once again a "disinterested servant of the proletariat," there was until 1918 no sign of the "sublime" to which he could dedicate his energies. In the Bolshevik Revolution he finally perceived not only vindication of his prewar syndicalism but the possibility of a *ricorso* of the first magnitude. Bolshevism was no mere national phenomenon like revolutionary syndicalism or integral nationalism. To be sure, the bolsheviks had restored to Russia its "Muscovite character," but the revolution had also become the symbol and model for revolution everywhere. It was, therefore, not only "national" but "civilizational" in its significance. Notwithstanding elements in the bolshevik *ricorso* which were "new," there was much in Sorel's conception of bolshevism that smacked of the *Réflexions* and his "first love," revolutionary syndicalism. Lenin's revolution had come as the unexpected triumph of a frustrated old man who had given up all hope of a *ricorso*. It is significant that Sorel appended the "Pour Lénine" to the *Réflexions,* written on behalf of revolutionary syndicalism. In doing so, however, Sorel did not become a bolshevik; rather, Lenin was made out to be a Sorelian. Indeed, what one sees in Sorel's conception of the soviets is his prewar idea of a self-governing elite of producers, now with Lenin as their leader. So great was Sorel's long-standing aversion to politicians and intellectuals that he did not see, or refused to see, the Bolshevik party, the reality behind the soviets. His interpretation of bolshevism, therefore, was unique: it was not only in conflict with Marxism but also with Leninism.

I

Though power had been seized in November 1917, bolshevism remained in danger. Sorel apparently had little knowledge and demonstrated only occasional interest in the movement before the November coup. It was the operation of bolshevism in what appeared to be a continuing revolutionary situation that intrigued him.

Again, as in the past, he was convinced that revolutionary myths provided the impetus to bolshevism.[1] He found these best expressed in the writings of Gorki, whose skill as an interpreter of what was in the hearts and minds of the masses was equal to the best of the ancient poets. Gorki had no interest in "ideologies," which were, after all, only translations of myths into an abstract form. Bolshevik myths, though they had a distant and obscure origin in Russian history, had only recently appeared—they arose out of a veritable "explosion."[2] Their rapid appearance could be compared only with the myths of primitive Christianity. Their development had undoubtedly been favored by Russia's conflict with the Entente and her isolation from the bourgeois world.

Sorel noted that both the social and the national discontents of the Russian masses had shaped the character and quality of bolshevik myths. The workers's hatred of the bourgeoisie was only one component, part of the universal struggle against plutocracy.[3] The great proletarian myths of the past—the "June Days" of 1848, the Paris Commune, the syndicalist battles earlier in the century—had all merged with the struggle in Russia in the consciousness of the workers. To their credit, the bolsheviks had created the first socialist state. Regardless of what might happen in Russia, the bolshevik example would henceforth provide singular confidence for the partisans of socialist intransigence. But the character of bolshevik myths, Sorel asserted, was due even more to the protest of the "real Russia" against ideas and institutions imported from the West.[4] Tsarism, he contended, was not really Russian. In the last two centuries only one tsar, Nicholas I, had endeavored "not to be European." Upper-class culture was French and its greatest concern was not to appear Russian. Even the resources of the country were in the hands of foreigners: the petroleum fields of Baku were controlled by Germans and English; the electrical industry was run by Swedes; and most of the great factories were run by French engineers, French foremen, and even French and German skilled workers. Bolshevism, as Gorki had perceived, sprang from the hatred of the Russian masses for the "rich foreigners" who had succeeded in infiltrating the "Republic of the Poor."[5] Bolshevism was an expression of the Russian spirit. Whether this spirit was of Slavic or of Mongol origin was of little importance. Russia patiently endured the revolution because she felt herself again ruled by a true Muscovite.

Everywhere in bolshevik myths were visions of a new world in formation.[6] In Gorki, for example, was the passionate desire to see new usages, new customs in the world of the future. This desire was often vague, ambivalent, and incoherent, but to introduce greater precision or logic into these myths in order to analyze tendencies or determine trends would vitiate them. In Gorki's works there were visions "worthy of the Hebrew prophets." Russia was a land dedicated to "justice, liberty, and beauty." It was a "kingdom of labor" in which man's effort, no longer to be expended on "coarse and dirty work," was transformed into "spiritual energy." Russia was a "gigantic emerald, adorned with the facets of the labor of a free humanity." In Gorki's vision, furthermore, was the notion that Russia was called upon to fulfill a Messianic mission. Sorel quoted Gorki:

It is today clear that to the Russian people, to this people starved and tortured by three centuries of slavery, history has entrusted this great mission (of saving the world), notwithstanding the possibility of her being crushed by brigands.[7]

One might charge Gorki with fanaticism, but his was not the fanaticism of a clever manipulator of words. It was the vision of a man who has the right to use poetry "to express a thought which fills his entire soul."[8]

The bolsheviks were not afraid to act.[9] A mystique, as Péguy had observed, was an indispensable lever of energies. It was a sort of "love for an idea," and love was the most powerful of forces. In Gorki was confirmation of the view that men had an absolute need to believe in order to undertake great historic action.[10] Revolutionary movements were not, however, religions.[11] Militants were without doubt "mystics" if one understood by that term men completely devoted to a cause, but they did not observe "états d'oraison." The "logical pantheism" which posited a common basis in social and religious movements not only overlooked the concrete historical differences between the two but also the nature of the salvation sought—Sorel went no further. Lenin, in any case, had transformed the "potential energies" in Russian myths into a "religious-like enthusiasm." This enthusiasm sustained the action of the militants and made it possible for them to face the greatest difficulties revolutionaries had ever encountered.

A cataclysmic transformation of the social order was clearly implied in Gorki's vision of the revolution.[12] Gorki too was a "pessimist" who viewed history as a "march toward deliverance." The pessimist viewed society as a "system" that could only be destroyed by a catastrophe involving the whole, while the optimist naively believed in "progress" or "evolution." Gorki also expressed a view of "expiation" which struck Sorel as particularly significant. Gorki had seen and felt deeply the bloody scenes of the revolution, suffering that was the consequence of the evil regime imposed upon the Russian people for centuries.[13] His conception of the revolution as a "day of expiation" was, Sorel thought, no rhetorical device but a necessity demanded by the "noblest sentiments . . . in the soul of an oppressed people." Gorki called for the complete destruction of the present order. The following passage in his work on Lenin Sorel considered among the finest in the literature on revolution:

It is the Russians who are going into battle for the triumph of Justice, the vanguard of the peoples of the world—the Russians—the warriors the least warlike, the feeblest, the people of a country backward from the point of view of both economy and culture, a people whose past will torture them more than any other. Only yesterday the world considered them half-savage, and yet today, almost dying of hunger, they are marching to victory or death, ardent and brave like old warriors.[14]

Sorel gave scant attention to bolshevik organization. He viewed the soviets as performing substantially the same role as the syndicates. Rather curiously, he demonstrated no knowledge or even interest in the Bolshevik party as such— a serious omission, to say the least. He regarded the revolution as the work of an elite in which Lenin's leadership was of central importance.

The role of charismatic leadership received an emphasis which had been totally absent in Sorel's consideration of revolutionary syndicalism or even of the Action Française. Lenin was for him a personal rather than an institutional model and authority.[15] He was a theoretician and leader, a "doctrine in action." He quoted Gorki:

Lenin speaks in extremely simple terms, in a language of iron, with the logic of an axe; but in his rude words I have never heard any coarse demagogy, or any banal search for the beautiful phrase.... One feels how calm is his faith; it is the faith of a fanatic, but of a *wise fanatic,* and not that of a metaphysician or mystic.[16]

Moreover, Sorel observed that Lenin possessed something of the "saint" about him—the quality of saintliness was not confined to religious leaders.[17] His temperate, almost ascetic life set him apart from the masses. According to Gorki, he had already become a legend in India, and Sorel noted that Asia was a good judge in matters of sainthood. Again he quoted Gorki:

Respect for the ascetic life, disinterested devotion to the cause of the poor, a sincere pity for human misery, these are things which have become very rare; but we have the right to hope that now, as in the past, these qualities will still win for the men who possess them the... respect of their fellows; the world still wants these heroes to lead the way to liberation.[18]

Allusions to Lenin as a "model revolutionary" suggest that for Sorel this was Lenin's primary role.

An elite of worker and peasant producers organized in the soviets stood behind Lenin.[19] The soviets were the most zealous, prepared to accept all the hard and implacable realities of the revolution: "disinterested..., enthusiastic, ready to sacrifice their own lives." The role of the soviets struck him as in many ways comparable to that which he had earlier assigned to the syndicates.[20] Both were class organs and both, ideally, set themselves apart from other elements in the community. Events had indicated that the soviets had thus far demonstrated far greater rigor than the syndicates in maintaining a sense of their revolutionary mission. Not only the institutions but the mores of a great nation, as Proudhon had once observed, could be profoundly changed by a revolutionary elite. What Sorel had written of the syndicates he now said of the soviets: by maintaining their integrity, the soviets would be better able to develop their administrative and organizing capacities.

The violence employed by the bolsheviks could never be employed, Sorel asserted, in accordance with some preconceived plan.[21] Yet Jean Grave in the name of the "anarchist papacy" and Karl Kautsky in the name of social democracy had with great solemnity "excommunicated" Lenin for failing to make use of "scholastic formulae." Events in Russia had demonstrated once again that reality is fluid, complex, and often contradictory. Revolutionary techniques were incompatible with fidelity to some orthodoxy. Violence required the determined pursuit of a goal and a readiness to explore all possible modes of action: "A revolution is never the holiday that historians, more poets than historians, have promised us. It is a storm in which the unforeseen triumphs."[22]

Bolshevik violence was a clear expression of social war against the condemned order and the danger of its restoration.[23] The French Revolution, Sorel said, had never really aroused his admiration, for precisely this reason. The *guillotinades* and *noyades* were directed against individuals, not against classes. There was no "real violence" in the sense of going "to the limit of an idea." The French Revolution, consequently, "replaced one state of things by another state of things." Bolshevik violence was far different. It "inspired and excited the instincts" of the workers against their enemies. "All the fearful consequences, all the risks involved and sacrifices imposed," were seen as "inevitable and necessary4.4.4.4to the achievement of this renaissance of humanity."[24] He drew distinctions between terrorism and violence, but he failed to make clear just what the difference was. The terrorism and the proscriptive measures that had disfigured the Bolshevik Revolution he attributed variously to the "Muscovite character" of bolshevism or to the Jews. He also conceded that the design of history, which obliged Lenin to kill some for the good of others, might bring "torments which crush the soul," but that could not be avoided. He quoted Gorki: "One cannot demand of someone who has not known justice that he be just."[25]

Bolshevik violence was the readiness to accept the will-to-power as the only philosophy capable of dealing with a hard and inexorable reality.[26] The difficulties confronting the bolsheviks—the wreckage left by the war, the civil war, the allied intervention—were, he declared, of monumental proportions. Their success thus far had amply demonstrated the foresight of those who had argued for an "absolute socialism" ready to make use of whatever means might be necessary to achieve its ends. Violence was the mark of "powerful minds that know where they are going."[27] It was pointless, therefore, to compare bolshevik police and tribunals with European institutions bearing the same names. Their roles were far different. The bolsheviks could not recoil from the most terrifying severities in order to deal effectively with assassins and conspirators. The bolsheviks were to be judged solely in the light of what was necessary to prepare the way for the construction of a socialist society.

An essential purpose of violence was the maintenance of scission—the separation of a movement from the corrupt world about it.[28] Only by scission could the purity and integrity of a movement be maintained. Only by scission could the idea of social war be made clear to the masses. Scission, he thought, was still best illustrated by nascent Christianity. He recalled the closing passage of his *Insegnamenti* written in 1905:

> Nascent Christianity, like so many of the other exotic cults, would have been able, very likely, to obtain tolerance, but it attempted to isolate itself; it thus provoked suspicion and even persecution. It was the intransigent doctors of the church who prevented the new religion from taking a normal place in Roman society.... Today, we see that it is thanks to these so-called madmen that Christianity was able to form its ideas and become the master of the world when its hour came.[29]

But it was the bolsheviks whom he now had in mind.

The role of bolshevik violence was to secure the revolution.[30] With fearful clarity Lenin had demonstrated that the coup of November 1917 was hardly enough. The new regime could still be easily overwhelmed. It was the creation of the Red Army, a "revolutionary army," that saved the revolution.[31] The value of such an army had been first demonstrated by Cromwell's Ironsides. The hard necessity of forming it had been immediately recognized by the bolsheviks. Unique in its creation was the idea of the "worker-soldier." The bourgeois "nation-at-arms" still maintained the military traditions of the old monarchies, but the sources of morale of the Red Army were unique. It drew on revolutionary sentiments in which were joined the class struggle and the war of national liberation.

II

Bolshevism, though still fighting for its life, Sorel viewed as a functioning postrevolutionary order. He hardly took note of the introduction of the NEP in 1921, and he did not hedge as to the significance of the Revolution.[32] It had already gone well beyond anything achieved by the French Revolution. It was, he said, "the greatest revolution which had taken place in two thousand years."

The new regime was impelled by a new *morale,* which Sorel called "mass-force."[33] The tsarist regime, so hard and violent, had none. There was an appearance of authority, but in reality there was little more than brute force. There was an appearance of justice, but what in fact existed was servile obedience to the orders of a brutal despotism. There was an appearance of an army, but it was, in fact, a badly organized mass of poorly equipped and poorly trained men subjected to an iron discipline. There was the appearance of a church, but Russia was really a spiritual vacuum. When Lenin appeared, the people of Russia were broken in spirit, "strangled in a net of barbed wire." The masses soon began to listen to and then to follow this "poor theoretician of Marxism." His incomparable achievement had been the overnight creation of a revolutionary *morale* that released new and powerful energies among the masses.

This new *morale* had emerged from the revolutionary struggle of the masses against their bourgeois and foreign oppressors.[34] The remarkable successes of the bolsheviks could be explained in no other way. Certainly, the apparatus of constraint did not maintain the regime, nor were its military and economic achievements to be credited to the exercise of Lenin's absolute authority. The moral energies released by the revolution were what had really saved the regime from destruction—and that more than once.[35] These energies were, moreover, reinforced by agitation and propaganda which endlessly asserted the rights of those who labored. The formerly amorphous "Russian people" had been transformed by these efforts into a "dictatorial mass."

The new *morale* was, accordingly, anticapitalist and anti-Western.[36] To create a society free from capitalist and alien influences required enormous effort. The problems, as Lenin had asserted, were "a thousand times more difficult than the most difficult military campaign." The conditions Marx had considered necessary for the passage from capitalism to socialism existed only in the Western countries; Russia was attempting to construct a socialist society from a technological level that was almost primitive. In the past, revolutionaries had only had to destroy certain reputedly harmful institutions; economic reconstruction had been left to the initiative of domestic or foreign capitalists motivated by the desire for personal profit. This new regime was obliged simultaneously to destroy and to construct in such a way that the Russian people would not find themselves enslaved by new oppressors, and it was necessary to attempt this in the face of the murderous hostility of the entire world. The Russian workers were acquiring immortal glory in their efforts to realize what until now had never been attempted.

Morale, Sorel contended once again, held in check a natural tendency toward moral laxity. Sorel believed Lenin's personal life to have been so exemplary that it might serve as a powerful model to the masses.[37] He was still convinced that democracy failed to instill a "profound love for home and hearth." His views on the subject of sex, moreover, remained unchanged. He conspicuously did not address himself to the new moral code in Russia. Sorel also cautioned Russian workers not to deride what might appear to be "bourgeois" advice: "Be honest in money matters, be economical, do not be lazy, do not steal, observe the strictest discipline in work."[38] These rules, he maintained, were "always valid." They had, in fact, become the most important orders of the day in the Bolshevik regime.

Bolshevik *morale* would prevent the formation of a bourgeoisie "hallucinated by the mirage of becoming wealthy by a stroke of fortune."[39] The bourgeoisie were not at all interested in participating in "the construction of a great historic edifice." Lenin was teaching the Russian masses not to be bourgeois, "the aim of old and decrepit people."[40] To be sure, much was being sacrificed in order to pioneer in the construction of socialism, but the efforts of the Russian masses deserved history's greatest rewards.

The organization of the Bolshevik regime was based on Lenin's conception of the "dictatorship of the proletariat."[41] In the preface to the Russian edition of the *Communist Manifesto* of 1882, as well as in notes that were discovered in 1888, Marx had clearly indicated that Russia was not obliged to follow in the wake of the more advanced capitalist countries in establishing socialism. He believed that Russia could skip full-blown capitalism, that she could avoid "the tortures of the system and appropriate all of its fruits while developing her own historic institutions." In Lenin's dictatorship was the apparatus of a "state" designed to "force" this transition to socialism.[42] But the "withering away of the state," Lenin's declared goal, would be no easy matter. The bolsheviks were deceiving themselves if they believed the power of the state would disappear by any natural process. At the same time, the use of "Jacobin methods," though expedient, would not in the long run establish a durable basis for socialism. It was to be hoped that the regime would ultimately resolve the dilemma by evolution in favor of a stateless "society of producers" which (except for the special role assumed by Lenin) was similar to Sorel's conception of prewar syndicalism.

Lenin's preeminence in the dictatorship of the proletariat did not disturb Sorel at all. For Sorel, Lenin stood virtually alone—he made no reference to Lenin as head of a party.[43] Kautsky had charged that the role assumed by Lenin was not "orthodox," but what Kautsky had in mind was a proletarian revolution from which such institutions as universal suffrage and representative assemblies would emerge. Marx himself had condemned this faith in democracy as a "miserable Lassallian superstition." Lenin was justified, Sorel argued, in rejecting the "democratic supernatural."[44] Democracy was the child of the "Calvinist mythology" that had inspired Rousseau. The Calvinists believed that the Holy Spirit illuminated the faithful when they met to invoke Christ. The democrats of today believed that the representatives of the people were similarly inspired when they were called upon to give the law. The "general will" and similar metaphysical fantasies, happily, had no roots in Russia. Bolsheviks recognized the incompatibility of their goals with European democracy. The experience of the French revolutionaries, divided into parliamentary parties, had not been lost on them. The suppression of the Constituent Assembly and of the innumerable socialist parties in Russia had been among the most beneficial consequences of the revolution. The regime was not now likely to degenerate into "the can of worms" the Convention had become. Lenin, Sorel asserted, had resuscitated Marxism from the "decomposition" of parliamentary socialism.[45] Lenin was a "government of one," the very negation of democracy. He did what democratic assemblies were incapable of doing. He was a kind of "king," a "genius in politics." For that, democrats could not forgive him. They refused to believe that a man could become a "doctrine in action." Lenin, however, brought to this task the most impressive understanding of socialism since Marx, with statesmanship which recalled that of Peter the Great or Nicholas I. Lenin resembled the second more that the first because he was so profoundly Russian. In any case, he was to be judged "from the standpoint of *Russian* history," to be compared "with tsars and not with presidents of the United States."[46]

Managerial control of large-scale industry was to Sorel an indication that the bolsheviks proposed to give primary consideration to production.[47] He was by no means clear, however, about the relationship between workers and management. Bertrand Russell (who had visited the new regime), Sorel observed, had recognized in Lenin a talent for engaging the services of men of the "American type" as managers of industry. Such men were far more interested in the satisfactions that come from power and material achievement than they were in the accumulation of personal wealth. Qualified managers who were constantly on the lookout for greater industrial efficiency, who inculcated in the workers attitudes of application and probity, constituted an element indispensable to a socialist society. Factory workers' subordination to the will of one man was, therefore, essential. Such subordination might, if necessary, take the acute form of dictatorship, "but, in one fashion or another, absolute subordination to one will is indispensable to the successful employment of labor in large-scale industry."[48] The hierarchy of responsibilities in evidence in Russian factories (manager, engineers, foremen, and workers) testified to the authoritarian character of the bolshevik conception of production.[49] Sorel counselled, however, that its purpose was to seize upon the smallest improvements in production and substitute them for less efficient methods. All those who had anything to do with production must consider themselves in "perpetual apprenticeship."

Workers' control of the state was one of the greatest discoveries of the Bolshevik Revolution.[50] Sorel said nothing of possible conflict between workers' control and Lenin's preeminence and ignored entirely the role of the Bolshevik party. The administrative problems Lenin initially faced had been enormous: an inherited personnel distinguished for its laziness, ignorance, and dishonesty; the dangers inherent in placing adventurers in positions of responsibility; and the risks inherent in creating a privileged bureaucracy. The discovery of the "worker-administrator" solved these problems. Lenin himself provided the model.[51] Lenin ordered the masses to toil, but they knew that he toiled as well. He was unconcerned with personal aggrandizement—he worked for all. He constituted, therefore, a powerful example to all those who labored with him in behalf of socialism. The gratuitous fulfillment by workers of their obligations as administrators struck Sorel as uniquely creative. In these circumstances, the workers had no reason to fear the dictatorship of the proletariat. They now saw in the state not an enemy but their own instrument in the construction of a socialist society:

We know today, thanks to the Russian Revolution, what the Marxist "dictatorship of the proletariat" implies: it is the Republic of the Soviets, appointed solely by the workers.[52]

A "society of producers" was being formed by the dictatorship of the proletariat—again, Sorel ignored the role of the party.[53] The emergence of a society of producers was a fact visible to all who took the trouble to look. The influence of non-productive elements had been destroyed. More than twenty years ago, he recalled, he had written that socialism would constitute a "disaster for intellectuals."[54] The bolsheviks had affirmed this principle by suppressing all those who wished to "live largely and magnificently without being of any use to production." The new regime would have nothing to do with the former "luminaries of the duma" or the "innumerable Jouhauxs" who were so ready to offer their services to the proletariat. The Red Guards shouted, "Death to the intellectuals!"

The cry "Death to the intellectuals" . . . will perhaps someday be heard from the workers the world over. One must be blind not to see that the revolution is the dawn of a new era.[55]

Moreover, as he had argued in the past, the capitalist was no more a producer than was the intellectual.[56] The role of the capitalist might readily be performed by others—he merely provided the financial requirements for his enterprise. He bought the machines, the raw materials, and the labor, and then sold the manufactured product. He added nothing of value. Lenin had recognized him for what he was: an intermediary who saw in his factory only an instrument designed to "sweat profits," who desired to improve his machines so that he might dispense with his higher-salaried workers, and who frequently undertook to create scarcity in order to raise prices. Capitalism was prevented from exploiting the full potential of modern industry by its usurious and commercial origins. Socialization of the means of production, by eliminating the capitalist, removed from the economy an element which threatened to limit its progress.[57] Once liberated from the parasitical influence of intellectuals and capitalists, Sorel declared, the society established by Lenin would belong indisputably to those who participated in the productive process:

The Soviet dictatorship . . . will no longer have any reason for being when the working masses of Russia realize that their . . . rights are based on their merits as producers.[58]

Sorel saw the essence of bolshevik technique in Lenin's idea of the "general line," that is, a "pragmatic Marxism, exactly informed and free from prejudice"; the general line was the "method of violence."[59] Marx, said Sorel, had devised his doctrine from the point of view of a German of the mid-nineteenth century. He could not have foreseen his doctrine in action. He did not recognize, nor had most Marxists, that the application of Marxism required absolute freedom of action. Lenin was not one of those theorists who believed his genius placed him above the evidence of reality. He was quick to learn by practical experience how the Marxist idea was to be implemented. Lenin did not do what so many other Marxists would have attempted—he refused to use what remained of the old regime.[60] Certain well-wishers who believed that everything had its utility had counselled him to do so, but to "replaster," to make new from old, was not for a revolutionary genius. Lenin was a revolutionary to the hilt, a "revolutionary-inventor." The "intransigent Lenin goes where he must, that is, *to the limit of his ideas!*"[61] He had held his head above water under conditions considerably more difficult than those which confronted the Convention and had thereby demonstrated that under other circumstances socialism might be attained with much less difficulty.

Bolshevism was a "pragmatic Marxism."[62] Again Sorel stressed, as he had in his syndicalist writings, the primacy of production. The bolsheviks were aware that their ultimate fate depended upon their economic achievements.[63] The Taylor system had been introduced as a method by which capitalism might be overtaken. Reward and punishment had been employed with the same purpose. Though he had been accused of cynicism, Lenin's insistence on the payment of "capitalist wages" to specialists and technicians, as well as on the general establishment of piece-work, had already cut labor costs in half. As for punitive measures, it was well known that the great plague of Russian industry was workers' laziness and absenteeism—the problem had been met without hypocrisy. Lenin's policy toward the peasants revealed the same approach.[64] The regime had refused to allow the old system of landed property to be replaced by another in which a new category of egotistical and rapacious landowners, the *kulaks,* would replace the old. After having laughed secretly at their maneuvers, Lenin had by a few salutory examples made clear that the peasants were to work on the land as the workers did in the factories. The problem of the *kulak,* Sorel thought, despite the difficulties inherent in the mores of the peasant, would in a few years be a distant memory. Lenin, in short, was proceeding by trial and error. The fact that the bolsheviks had at times employed certain bourgeois ideas was all to their credit. The possibility that Lenin might be obliged to employ foreigners as engineers and specialists, a prospect that scandalized Western socialists and democrats, did not disturb Sorel. The juridical formation of socialist institutions paralleled in importance, Sorel asserted, the primacy of production.[65] The genesis of law was a social phenomenon which always had the closest relation to production. The

Bolshevik regime could therefore be expected to promote the growth of juridical structures that supported the advance of production. These structures had not yet emerged. The institutions which had been introduced, such as the soviets, were basically designed to determine on the basis of experience which practices were beneficial and which were harmful to production. The regime was obliged to do everything it could to facilitate the growth of a new legal system which, he suggested, might center around the basic concept of the "right to work." This concept he believed to be the proletarian equivalent to bourgeois property rights. In a socialist philosophy of law it was destined to play an important role. Juridical sentiments were, however, fragile, and the revolution might yet lead to ruin. Old institutions had been destroyed and the new ones remained weak. That was why the dictatorship of the proletariat was necessary.

By virtue of its startling successes, bolshevism served also as a model and an inspiration to revolutionaries elsewhere. The bolsheviks had produced a renaissance of intransigent socialism everywhere in the West.[66] Prewar syndicalism had failed in its mission and parliamentary socialism had been discredited by the war. The myth of the proletarian revolution had now been powerfully reinforced. Everywhere in Europe the partisans of the proletarian revolution looked to Russia. Moscow had become the "Rome of the proletariat." America and England were "modern Carthage." What remained of European socialism that was vital was, therefore, urged to join the Third International. He found the conditions of adherence, the "Twenty-One Points" (launching frankly revolutionary propaganda, recourse to illegal as well as to legal action, adoption of the "dictatorship of the proletariat," and acceptance of the leadership of Moscow) acceptable. Sorel saw in the Third International an instrument designed to organize active international support for the Bolshevik government. Unlike the Second, the Third International would be no "academy of rhetoric." It would be in perfect accord with Lenin. Those who did not support his dictatorship were not socialists, and Lenin had every right to exclude them. Among non-Western people, moreover, the bolsheviks had given heretofore unknown reality to the revolutionary idea.[67] The non-Western world was ruled by a decadent Westernized ruling class. The Bolshevik Revolution, as anti-Western as it was antibourgeois, had already led patriots to look to Russia for assistance. The isolation imposed on Russia by the Entente would draw Russia even closer to the non-Western world. Bolshevism alone, therefore, would profit from anti-Western sentiments in Asia and in the Near East—and Sorel urged Lenin to take advantage of the opportunities. In China and India, for example, his regime already enjoyed considerable prestige, for here the ground had been well prepared. Sorel was convinced that this was also true in Moslem countries—Egypt, in particular.

Bolshevism's domestic advance required pursuit of economic and juridical goals whose attainment must be viewed as conquests. "Invention," Sorel argued, was the key to economic conquest.[68] Socialism must take over from capitalism its capacity for making constant inroads on the unknown. Such advances would be assured in a regime that provided production with "a freedom of choice which approaches that of art." The "most perfect state" would be attained if the most original and highest kind of "work" were regarded as "art." The "worker-inventor" would then be placed on the same plane as the "artist." In the Bolshevik regime artists and workers already understood that they were both victims of the bourgeoisie and had come to regard each other as "brothers." A new era had commenced for both in Russia, where for the first time a regime had been established which understood the historic role of production. If "invention" was the key to greater productivity, the pursuit of "justice," Sorel was convinced, was the principal instrument in the construction of a socialist order.[69] The most effective institutions in this pursuit were the local soviets. Their administration of justice had already served to educate and to discipline the workers. They had also exercised a kind of "*justice supplétive*" that Proudhon had long ago proposed. He had viewed "private justice" as a necessary complement to "official justice." Actually, a system of private justice, even to the imposition of the death penalty, had existed among some groups in the early days of the French trade-union movement. Such methods had a greater chance of success today in Russia than they had had in Proudhon's time. Workers in Russia were more keenly aware of the issues at stake, and traitors to the working class were more readily recognized. In the hands of the soviets, administration of justice promised to become a formidable instrument. The soviets were "true social authorities." By acclaiming practices favorable to production while punishing those that were harmful, they were engaging in an enterprise that was in the immemorial interests of civilization.

Expansion of bolshevism beyond Russia was also to be viewed as conquest.[70] The modern world was under the influence of an effete and decadent West that deserved to be destroyed. Sorel saw a parallel between the state of the Roman Empire during its decline and the condition of the contemporary world.[71] "Just as ancient Rome merited its fall, so too the crimes of the contemporary world justify its destruction." The West had succumbed to a plutocratic bourgeois ideal that had also infected the ruling elements of non-Western peoples. The West no longer had any high ambitions—it felt no need for the "sublime." The extraordinary longevity of Byzantium had given to the West no reason to despair of the future. The Eastern Empire had been able to withstand repeated assaults because it had possessed material resources that were, for its time, enormous. Modern capitalists hoped that they too could continue to produce goods in great abundance and thereby last indefinitely. Sorel assigned the destruction of the West to bolshevik imperialism, which was fundamental to the Russian spirit.[72] Russia had for centuries looked upon Europe as a prey which would some day be hers—she hated the West. The Revolution did not lessen these sentiments; indeed, it had reinforced them.

Lenin's followers, in their bitter polemics against leaders of Western social democracy, had long made clear their hatred of the West. Bolshevik Russia would never forgive the attempts of foreign powers to dismember her. Once internal difficulties had been overcome, she would once again menace Europe. It has been argued that the bolsheviks were the "Mongols" of the twentieth century. No one feared them more than the French diplomats, who had nightmares of their some day crossing the Rhine. A bolshevik conquest would, in fact, suppress all the "conventional lies," socialist as well as bourgeois.[73] It would be "violent." Western "stupidity" would have to submit:

History, according to Renan, rewarded the military virtues by giving to Rome a Mediterranean empire; despite the innumerable abuses of conquest, the legions accomplished what he calls "the work of God." If we are grateful to Roman soldiers for having replaced abortive, stray, or impotent civilizations by a civilization whose pupils we still are in law, literature, and monuments, how grateful will the future have to be to the Russian soldiers of socialism! How lightly will historians take the criticism of the orators hired by the democracies to denounce the excesses of the bolsheviks. New Carthages must not triumph over what is now the Rome of the proletariat.[74]

Chapter

10

The Impact

Though we are most directly concerned with Sorel's impact on the nascent French and Italian communist movements, that on the Russian movement is not without some interest. A cursory examination, however, suggests that information is at best fragmentary; some of it is contradictory, and evaluations are uncertain.

Sorel was certainly known to the Russian revolutionaries in the decade before 1917. The *Réflexions* had been translated into Russian in 1907 and the *Insegnamenti* and *Introduction* in 1908.[1] His articles, and articles about him, in French and Italian periodicals were undoubtedly available in Switzerland, where Russian revolutionaries in exile might have encountered them. Lenin read Sorel, but his response was hardly flattering. He listed as a source the Russian translation of the *Insegnamenti* in a "Bibliography of Marxism" that followed a study of Marx.[2] A brief passage in his *Materialism and Empirio-Criticism,* a vigorous polemic against revisionism published in 1909, commented directly on Sorel. Addressing himself to the mathematician Henri Poincaré, Lenin wrote without elaboration: "Your works prove that there are people who can give thought to absurdity. To that category belongs the notorious muddlehead, Georges Sorel."[3]

After the Bolshevik coup, persistent references appeared in French sources to the formation of "Cercles Sorel" in Petrograd.[4] A bust of Sorel's "splendid Socratic head" was said to dominate certain committee rooms in the Kremlin. In an article published shortly after his death in the organ of the Executive Committee of the Communist International, Sorel's work was critically reviewed:

Notwithstanding its errors, its exaggerations, and its obscurities, it anticipates with a sure instinct everything essential . . . in our program, which is aimed at preparing the soul of the proletariat for revolutionary action.[5]

Without considering the question of Sorel's influence in Russia, the writer went on to charge that Sorel was neither a "Marxist" nor a "consistent communist."[6]

He reflected the "fractured and contradictory social structure" of France with its magnificent revolutionary tradition and economic backwardness. His was a "profound and prophetic insight into the soul of the proletariat and its [historic] role." But this Sorel attained with "a petty-bourgeois ideology which is naive and absolutely wrong." He attempted to reconcile the most heterogeneous currents of modern French philosophy with the fundamentals of Marxism, and he did not succeed.

I

Sorel did not figure directly in the events leading to the formation of the communist movement in France.[7] The movement originated with those socialists who despised the Second International for failing to stop the war and who condemned former colleagues who had participated in bourgeois governments during the war. When the bolsheviks seized power in November 1917, the antiwar socialists were greatly encouraged. What had been rhetoric in Paris had become reality in Petrograd; now the bourgeois state no longer seemed so formidable. The appearance of the Bolshevik regime, however, initiated a bitter conflict within both the Socialist party and the CGT between those who wanted victory for France in the war and those who gave priority to liberation of the proletariat after the Russian model. With the arrest of the minister Louis Jean Malvy and the great strike in the Paris munition works in March 1918 the gap widened. Allied intervention in Russia powerfully reinforced the pacifist and revolutionary wave.

The controversy soon reached its climax. While the new rulers of Russia were busy organizing the Third International, disputes raged within the French Socialist party and the CGT over the adoption of the methods and goals of the bolsheviks. In February 1920 a delegation led by Marcel Cachin and L. O. Frossard was sent to Moscow to learn of the conditions for admittance to the Third International. Moscow handed down the Twenty-One Points.

The Socialist Congress of Tours in December 1920 voted adherence to the Third International. The French Communist party, which inherited Jaurès's *Humanité,* was born. The minority, which included most of the leadership of the socialist movement, left the party and reconstituted itself as the SFIO. The trade-union Congress of Lille in July 1921 also split into the new Confédération Générale du Travail Unitaire (CGTU), affiliated with the Red International of trade unions in Moscow, and the CGT, which remained syndicalist and vaguely associated with the Socialist party.

The name of Sorel was not forgotten in these developments. Neither his prewar efforts on behalf of the proletarian revolution nor his current defense of bolshevism went unrecognized. The communist press claimed him as one of their own, especially in articles written by former syndicalist associates who now embraced the new cause, but there was no sign that these periodicals were in any sense under his sway.

It should be recalled that Sorel had been asked by *Humanité* in April 1920 to serve as a regular contributor.[8] He was honored in March 1922 in an interview by its editor, Bernard Lecache, who paid tribute to him as the untiring friend of the workers and as one of the first intellectuals to come to the defense of Lenin. In announcing his death, *Humanité* pronounced the *Réflexions* the "equal" in "ideological importance" to *Das Kapital* itself.[9] Extravagant eulogies soon followed. Delesalle declared that his name would be forever inscribed in the annals of the proletariat.[10] A few days later, an excerpt from Sorel's "Letter to Daniel Halévy" of 1907, which had served as the introduction to the *Réflexions,* appeared.[11] The excerpt quoted Sorel on the trials of early Christianity and on the relation between philosophical pessimism and the *"marche vers la délivrance."* Louzon, like Delesalle a former syndicalist, claimed Sorel for bolshevism but also found it necessary to protest against the counterclaims of Italian fascists.[12] The response to Sorel's death in the *Vie ouvrière,* organ of the CGTU, was similar. Louzon here described Sorel's Marxism as "authentic" Marxism, not a "vulgar caricature."[13] Excerpts from various of Sorel's writings were introduced with the comment that what Sorel had written many years ago was still true.[14]

The *Revue communiste,* which numbered Sorel among its contributors, also reveals that Sorel was honored there as a "friend of the proletariat." The *Revue* was directed by Charles Rappoport, a former Guesdist, and it addressed itself to communist sympathizers.[15] Among its most frequent contributors were the Russian leaders Lenin, Trotsky, Zinoviev, Bukharin, and Radek. The French writers Griffuelhes, Henri Barbusse, and Boris Souvarine, who despite their rather diverse intellectual origins were nevertheless drawn to the new regime, also contributed. Sorel's publications were limited to about five articles and a somewhat greater number of reviews. There is no evidence that editorial policy was influenced by his participation.

The review *Clarté,* however, was another matter. It had been founded in 1919, under the direction of the novelist Barbusse, as the organ of a "league of internationalist intellectuals in opposition to nationalist intellectuals." In 1921 it declared itself a "review of proletarian culture." Its intent during these years was to establish liaison between intellectuals of widely differing views who shared an admiration for Russian communism.[16] Though Sorel did not contribute to the periodical, his close friend Berth was appointed to its editorial board a few months after Sorel's death, and Berth began to introduce Sorel's ideas.[17] When in 1923 he was joined by other admirers of Sorel, *Clarté* began to take on a distinctly Sorelian cast.[18]

The number of Sorel's followers, either new or old, who joined the communist camp during these years was not impressive. Indeed, there is no reason to believe that anyone of intellectual stature other than Berth did so. Delesalle and Louzon were working-class militants turned journalists, little interested in doctrine, whose attraction to Sorel was primarily personal.

Berth's development had most closely paralleled Sorel's, but as late as 1919 Berth was still writing in praise of Maurras.[19] What finally produced a break was Maurras's attack on Sorel for having come to the defense of Lenin that year.[20] In a foreword to a brief study on Sorel by an Italian admirer and in articles published between 1919 and 1922, Berth came to Sorel's support as a defender of Lenin, and he attacked Sorel's former monarchist associates.[21] Sorel's argument that bolshevism had brought about a rebirth of socialism had been amply justified. The choice for Europe henceforth would be federation under French or under Russian hegemony: "Paris or Moscow," "Maurras or Lenin." In 1922 Berth began to contribute to periodicals devoted to the intellectual defense of communism—*Clarté* in France and the *Rivoluzione liberale* in Italy.[22] On the occasion of Sorel's death Berth appraised the career of his friend and teacher. He described him as a "soul of fire," a "believer" for whom a revolutionary myth had taken the place of religion. Sorel's work on behalf of the proletariat he thought equal in importance to that of Proudhon or Marx. Several months later Berth wrote that for his master primitive Christianity had always been the prototype for all truly revolutionary movements.[23] It was the "Christian scission" of Tertullian that had given the early Christian church its discipline. This Christian intransigence and separateness was to Sorel all-important in a revolutionary movement. In the new Soviet regime Sorel had finally found the *ricorso* for which he had been searching throughout his entire career.

II

Within the newly established communist movement in Italy after the war, Sorel's ideas found somewhat wider currency, but here, too, he was influential only in limited circles. His Italian following was, for the most part, centered in another political quarter.[24]

Sorel was known to those who organized the communist movement, although he did not figure in the events leading to its formation.[25] The Italian Communist party was born out of the two great events of the autumn of 1917, the defeat at Caporetto and the Bolshevik Revolution. The military disaster brought Italy very near to the collapse which had overtaken Russia a few months earlier. It brought the first great wave of disgust with the war, leading to the reappearance of revolutionism on the left. Moreover, it produced a wide break in the Socialist party. Turati and Treves urged continuation of the war, but the left wing of the party urged Italian soldiers to desert, like the Russians, with arms in hand. The Bolshevik Revolution gave further stimulus to the revolutionary or "maximalist" elements in both the CGL and the Socialist party. A national congress of the CGL in January 1919 voted to introduce a "producers' parliament" based on the chambers of labor and modelled after the Russian soviets. Though the moderate leadership in the CGL and in the party opposed revolution, the workers grew more restive.

During the greater part of 1919 and 1920 strikes spread throughout Italy. "Soviets" appeared in Romagna and Tuscany; the anarchosyndicalist USI (which had opposed intervention in 1915), now under the direction of Armando Borghi, briefly adhered to the Third International; and some socialist deputies reverted to a most uncooperative attitude in parliament.[26] In September 1920 came the high-water mark of proletarian revolutionism, with the occupation of the factories in the north by metallurgical workers. The nucleus of the movement was in the Fiat works of Turin. It was led by Antonio Gramsci and Palmiro Togliatti, far closer to Sorel than the Socialist party regarding the significance of the soviets, more revolutionary-minded than their superiors in the CGL, and less fearful of the Communist party and statist tendencies in the new Russian regime than the USI. Seizing the factories proved to be the last serious revolutionary effort on the left—no effective collaboration between the USI and the nascent Italian communist movement proved possible.

At this moment, when the party was disheartened and divided, the Twenty-One Points arrived from Moscow. The Socialist Congress of Leghorn met in January 1921 to consider the conditions of adherence to the Third International. The congress voted adherence but not at the cost of a split in the party and not on dictated terms. Thereupon the "pure communists," led by Gramsci and Togliatti, left the Socialist party and founded the Communist party. Within six months, therefore, under the twin blows of the failure of the occupation of the factories and the controversy over the Twenty-One Points, the Italian socialist movement had fallen apart.

The split at the Congress of Leghorn spread down to the smallest party group and the remotest chamber of labor. Rival communist and socialist organizations, both political and syndical, now emerged, but they never had time to crystallize during the years of battering persecution to which they were now to be subjected.

A new center of Sorelismo, meanwhile, had arisen during these years among a group of young intellectuals in Turin. The *Ordine nuovo* was founded in 1919 by the twenty-eight-year-old Gramsci, the leader of the communist minority of the Turinese section of the Socialist party, after the party decided to suppress the Piedmontese edition of the *Avanti!* This group (accused of "Bergsonism" as early as the 1917 Socialist party congress) proposed to reconstitute the party on a rigid class basis.[27] Its aims were political, not syndical—its goal was conquest of power and establishment of an "ethical-political" state. The group stimulated the proliferation of "soviets" which were to provide the foundation for a workers' state. The *Ordine nuovo* became the official daily organ of the Communist party after the Congress of Leghorn, and although it was burned out in November 1922 by the fascists, it continued publication intermittently until 1925. Gramsci's leading associates were Togliatti and Angelo Tasca; all three admitted to Sorel's influence in their intellectual formation. Togliatti saw in Sorel an historian above events, who had fathomed the psychology of classes by his theory of myths; Tasca too viewed the imminent liberation of the proletariat as a "Sorelian myth."[28] Gramsci was possibly drawn to Sorel even more than the others.[29]

The young Gramsci had discovered Sorel by reading his article in the *Resto del Carlino* in October 1919 on Turinese factory councils.[30] Already drawn to Croce and Bergson, he admired "the precision, the originality and the... faculty of penetration" in Sorel. Though he did not doubt Sorel's sincere love of the proletariat, he would not accept everything in Sorel. He did accept a great deal: the spontaneous origin of popular revolutionary movements; the idea of primitive Christianity as the prototype of the proletarian movement; the centrality in the revolutionary myth of a catastrophic transformation from one epoch to another; the proletarian movement as imminent in modern industrial society; the "religious" character of the class struggle; and the need for spiritually creative violence. He applauded Sorel's willingness to discard the syndicates and accept workers' or factory councils.[31] Sorel's conviction that the proletarian impulse must express itself without interference had made this flexibility possible—Gramsci admired the antibureaucratic as well as the antireformist aspects of Sorel's conception of the workers' councils. Gramsci was no admirer of Sorel's Italian disciples, however. He accused them of "spiritual meanness and crudity." Sorel himself was blameless,

... just as Karl Marx was not responsible for the absurd ideological pretensions of the "Marxists." Sorel is, in the field of historical research, an "inventor." He cannot be imitated. He does not place at the service of his aspiring disciple a method that can be applied mechanically, always and by everyone, and result in intelligent discoveries.[32]

The *Ordine nuovo* frequently republished articles by Sorel that had appeared elsewhere in Italy, and it had several translated from ones published in the *Revue communiste*.[33] At Sorel's death his obituary in the *Ordine nuovo* proclaimed: "Italian revolutionaries bow before the great man."[34] The review, it continued, had "followed" Sorel not as his "disciple," but as the *maestro* would have had it—as a "rigorous and respectful critic." Other articles followed, including an excerpt from the *Réflexions* headed "Pessimismo e rivoluzione."[35]

Only two Sorelians of former years, however, remained devoted to Sorel and to the proletariat, and they could give only qualified approval to the regime in Russia. Leone had been one of the foremost proponents of Sorelian syndicalism in the prewar years; he remained, as Sorel had been, opposed to the war, and at war's end he came to the defense of bolshevism. In an article in the *Resto del Carlino* in 1919 he, too, likened the Russian workers' soviets to the syndicates.[36] At the Socialist Congress of Bologna that same year he defended the regime, and in March 1921 he wrote to Delesalle that he had not registered with the Socialist party.[37] The party had "started its crusade against the communists." It did so, he believed, "in order to gain absolution from the fascists for its past sins." Leone's admiration for the Russian regime was to be short-lived—he already had doubts about its "statist and dictatorial" nature, as a study of 1923 was to reveal.

Labriola, who had been a vigorous partisan of intervention in 1915, had been elected to parliament in 1913 as an independent socialist and remained a deputy until 1921. He accepted the ministry of labor in Giolitti's postwar cabinet from June 1920 to June 1921. His prewar revolutionism had by then become a thing of the past. During his ministry (when Labriola was also a power in the CGL), the organization became one of the mainstays of the government during the occupation of the factories, attempting to discourage communist revolts in local chambers of labor. How does one explain his transformation? Some years later he was to explain: "*L'essenziale era . . . mettere le mani sul governo.*"[38] Labriola, in any case, continued to look with favor on Sorel. As late as 1922 the establishment of a socialist republic of workers in Italy was still Labriola's goal.[39] His admiration for prewar revolutionary syndicalism continued undiminished. Prewar syndicalism was a form of "working-class imperialism," exhibiting the same tendencies of "energy" and "conquest" found in capitalist imperialism, but he too looked to a socialist order based on postwar experiments with "factory councils." These institutions were capable of releasing unforeseen energies in the proletariat and in modern industry. His position was now not far removed from "official" socialism. Though he was drawn to the Bolshevik regime, such a society, he was certain, had not yet been established in Russia.[40] Lenin, to be sure, had saved the "moral and historical unity of Russia," but the price—establishment of a party dictatorship which modestly called itself that of the "proletariat" was too high. What socialism needed was a republic freed of parties and intellectuals. A study Labriola completed in 1922 commented on Sorel at length.[41] He rejected fascism's claim on Sorel. Sorel's career, he wrote, had come to an end with "Pour Lénine,"

which is his real political testament and the final confession of faith in the proletariat, in its revolution and in the force of renovation which exists in the proletariat.[42]

All that Sorelian syndicalism had in common with fascism was its critique of reformism and democracy. Labriola also wrote of the "spiritual deceit" which had led many former syndicalists into the fascist movement.[43] He believed them absolutely sincere but was convinced that they would soon be disillusioned. The Fascist party had started out antibourgeois but would eventually become antiproletarian. A fascist absolute state in Italy with a private army at its disposal, he was certain, would be far more onerous than its liberal predecessor.

Fascism

The fascist movement arose in Italy as a direct consequence of the First World War and conditions immediately postwar. Sorel's political interests during these years were not limited to bolshevism. After 1919 he fixed his attention increasingly on the emerging fascist movement.

The immediate origins of Italian fascism are related to the political transformation of Mussolini and his following after the outbreak of war. The events of August 1914 found Mussolini, as editor of the socialist *Avanti!*, in favor of "absolute neutrality." Among non-socialists, however, interventionism grew rapidly: the nationalists, both the "Vocist" and Corradini variety, soon favored involvement; the syndicalist Corridoni and a number of his colleagues joined the Garibaldi Brigade for service in France; and the futurist Marinetti organized prowar demonstrations. Due possibly to the influence of his friends Corridoni and Panunzio and the sincere conviction that war might hasten the coming of revolution, Mussolini passed from neutrality to intervention by mid-October. For this about-face the Socialist party removed him from the *Avanti!* and expelled him from the party in November 1914.

The *Popolo d'Italia,* subtitled "A Socialist Daily," appeared a few weeks later. It was edited by Mussolini and urged intervention on the side of the Entente. Its contributors were a mixed lot: syndicalists, nationalists, republicans, and futurists. In his first editorial Mussolini hinted darkly that war would be merely a prelude to a proletarian revolution. Early in 1915 he organized his supporters into a national organization, the Fasci d'Azione Rivoluzionaria. In the months that followed, Mussolini's Fasci and Corridoni's Comitato Sindacale Italiana organized street demonstrations and violence against antiwar socialists in particular and neutralists in general. It was not an irredentist war for which they called, but one impelled by the most elevated idealism, one whose outcome would produce an Italian moral and social renovation.

With the declaration of war in May 1915, Mussolini turned to an editorial policy of military victory and aggrandizement in the eastern Mediterranean. He was drafted in the fall of 1915, served until wounded in the spring of 1917, and was then discharged. He returned to his paper protesting that the war was not being prosecuted with sufficient vigor. He denounced as treasonable the bargaining for portfolios, the debates on civil liberties, and the rights demanded by labor. Early in 1918 he launched on the masthead of the *Popolo d'Italia* the formula "Sindacalismo nazionale."

The conclusion of the war brought little satisfaction and increased rather than diminished social tensions in Italy. Failure to obtain at the Paris Peace Conference all that the Entente had promised embittered most Italians. Parliamentary politicians, incapable of coping with postwar problems, impaired the already sinking prestige of the liberal parliamentary regime. Radical socialists, encouraged by the Bolshevik Revolution, intensified the class struggle by strikes and riots in industrial centers and in the countryside. The reaction of Mussolini was to call together on March 23, 1919, the survivors of the Fasci of 1915 (who were, in the main, syndicalist) to form the Fasci di Combattimento. What Mussolini's group said it feared was not "economic" bolshevism but Russian, international, antiwar bolshevism. Fascism also professed to be revolutionary, not merely the defender of the existing order and vested interests. Reliance was placed on the "proletariat of the trenches," the veteran who was both patriotic and revolutionary. The subtitle of the *Popolo d'Italia* was now changed to "A Daily for Fighters and Producers." Its program included little more, however, than a demand for national syndicalism and annexation of Fiume and Dalmatia. "Formal principles," wrote Mussolini, "are iron and tin fetters."

The fascist movement grew much more rapidly in 1919 and 1920, as the Italian government continued to show weakness. When the poet D'Annunzio pounced upon Fiume in September 1919 with a few adventurers, but was subsequently forced to abandon it by the government, Mussolini promptly denounced the puerile and weak-kneed authorities who interfered thus with Italian destinies. In September 1920, when the workers seized the factories and the government did little to expel them, Mussolini's group began to accept funds from the terror-stricken employers. The Trieste speech made on September 20, 1920, marked Mussolini's break with his exclusively proletarian and republican nationalism of 1919. He attacked not only the Treaty of Versailles and the League of Nations but the "bolshevik" seizure of the factories as well, and he declared himself free from all prejudice toward existing institutions—meaning, primarily, the monarchy.

The violence of the fascists, now organized in "Blackshirt" squads, increased sharply after September 1920. Violence was directed against both socialists and communists in agrarian as well as industrial settings. Strikes were broken up, parades were turned into street battles, and chambers of labor were sacked and burned. By the spring of 1921 the fascists had won wide popularity with the middle and upper classes, posing as the defenders of public order and private property; an electoral alliance with the Nationalist party that year won them thirty-five seats in parliament. To maintain his independence, however, Mussolini again announced himself to be republican and broke his ties with the nationalists. Along with an increase in popularity went a temporary decrease in radicalism. In July Mussolini called off squadrist violence, only to break the truce in November.

The Partito Nazionale Fascista was established that same November. During the following months Mussolini broadened the base of his following while at the same time strengthening his grip on party machinery. In January 1922 he asked for and received the moral and material support of a variety of national syndicalist groups organized in the Confederazione Nazionale delle

Corporazioni Sindacali. On September 20 at Udine, Mussolini reestablished a common front with the Nationalist party by announcing that a change in regime could be brought about without disturbing the House of Savoy. Early in October the fascists entrenched themselves in the north. They took possession of prefectures and police headquarters and "guarded" railroad and telegraph offices. They also spread their influence to southern centers. A few weeks later, an armed "March on Rome" was begun by fascist Blackshirts and by a sprinkling of nationalist Blueshirts. On October 30 Mussolini was appointed prime minister by the king. Fascism had come to power.

The appearance of fascism in Italy was paralleled by the rise of similar movements elsewhere in Europe. These movements were sustained by the widespread disruption which followed the war and were supported by a middle class too powerful to be driven to the wall by proletarian revolutionism. These movements assumed different forms wherever they appeared, but they were to receive from Italian "fascism," by virtue of its priority, its leadership, and its spectacular success, not only their name but also many of their ideas.

Chapter

11

The Man

Sorel had "divined" the role that Mussolini was to play in Italian history long before the March on Rome. Variot recalled that in 1912, when Mussolini had risen to party leadership and was appointed editor of the *Avanti!,* Sorel had told him:

> Our Mussolini is no ordinary socialist. Believe me: you will see him one day, perhaps, at the head of a sacred battalion saluting the Italian flag with the sword. He is an Italian of the fifteenth century, a *condottiere!* The world does not know him yet, but he is the only energetic man capable of redressing the feebleness of the government.[1]

It is remarkable that Mussolini should in 1912 have been regarded by anyone as a socialist who would someday raise the standard of nationalism. Little in Mussolini's previous career justified such a prophecy.[2] Only recently, at the Congress of Reggio Emilia, he had attacked the Libyan war, the monarchy, the church, and the aristocracy. Sorel may have had the potential of the Italian proletarian movement in mind rather than Mussolini's personal development. Variot also recorded that in December 1912 Sorel had stated that he did not believe Italy's future would come about by an "evolutionary process."[3] He expected great things from the Italian syndicalists. He believed them to be "the most serious in Europe" and profoundly patriotic. Lanzillo also recalled that in 1913, when Sorel was a regular reader of the *Avanti!,* he had followed Mussolini's editorials "with sympathy," notwithstanding the fact that Mussolini appeared to be personally hostile toward him.[4] Sorel also discussed Mussolini's future in a letter to Barrès shortly before the war:

> Italy has the first, the best diplomacy in the world. We shall see great things—either a terrible war or a not less formidable revolution, perhaps both. Italy will never lose her compass. The common sense and balance of the Italian mind is often ignored in France. To continue to ignore it will cost us dear. In any case, I know a young man, a certain Mussolini, a Socialist, who is the only Socialist I know today incapable of making a fool of himself. He will know, indeed, how to lead his countrymen toward their own interests.[5]

When war broke out in Europe, Sorel opposed Italian intervention on the side of the Entente and expressly deplored the formation of the Fasci of 1915.

To Pareto he wrote that Mussolini was the "principal agent" of the French government in Italy.[6] Sorel objected to an irredentism which he identified with Freemasonry and democracy, and he bitterly denounced Prezzolini and the Vocists. He was outraged by the antics of some of the promoters of intervention who were neither morally nor politically "serious," notably D'Annunzio and Marinetti. His interview and article published in May 1915 in the *Avanti!* objected strongly to all "demagogic efforts" to bring about intervention.[7]

During the war he was critical of the monarchy and continued to be interested in revolutionary possibilities in Italy, though Mussolini no longer enjoyed his favor:

I believe Italy is marching toward a republic. . . . The socialists act with a sagacity of which I would not have thought them capable, by keeping themselves in readiness for the hour of collapse.[8]

He blamed the king for bringing Italy into the war.[9] The Piedmontese monarchy, Sorel suggested on one occasion, had completed the work of the Spaniards by imposing a deadening bureaucracy on the nation. In May 1918 he wrote to Delesalle that the nationalist leader Corradini had sent him one of his pamphlets.[10] In it he had read: "Will the syndicates destroy parliamentarism? That is our belief." To Delesalle Sorel wrote, "Truth is on the march!" Sorel included in the *Matériaux* of 1918 an article in which he had declared his faith in Russian bolshevism, but he seemed to imply that in the more technologically advanced countries of Europe the field of revolutionary opportunities was not limited to proletarian movements.[11] The argument he now presented recalled the attempt in the *Réflexions* to demonstrate the beneficent effects of proletarian violence on proletariat and bourgeois alike. Two possibilities were now open: the proletariat could embark on the road leading to the destruction of capitalism, or it could accommodate itself to a new bourgeois order. During the war years Sorel never lost confidence in the revolutionary future of Italy. In December 1918 he wrote to Croce: "In your country there is still a public capable of listening to your teachings; here there is nothing but the most absolute emptiness of thought."[12]

After the war Sorel hoped for a rapprochement in Italy between syndicalism and nationalism—but it was Italy's national interests that were uppermost in his mind. He wrote of Italy's betrayal by the Entente.[13] He complained that the Yugoslavs were receiving the support of the Entente in matters concerning the annexation of Dalmatia. He took heart from D'Annunzio's demonstrations and protestations in regard to Fiume. The efforts of D'Annunzio, he told Croce, were now of great value. "It becomes difficult not to take him into account."[14] Sorel was perplexed, however, by the syndicalists' failure to take advantage of the controversy with the Slavs—they had not taken up the cause of Dalmatia. Their failure to do so had lost them a "magnificent opportunity" to revive their movement.[15]

Sorel began to follow the activities of fascism during the course of 1919–1920, though that was not his primary interest.[16] He was delighted by the great wave of strikes, but mystified by the Socialist party's failure to take advantage of its truly remarkable revolutionary opportunities, especially after the seizure of the factories in September 1920. When Blackshirt rioting and "punitive raids" began, Sorel's interest in the fascists deepened. Though for some months uncertain of its character, by July 1920 he had identified fascism with "bourgeois reaction":

It seems to me that more than one incident recalls ... the last days of the Roman Republic. The same disorders commanded by the magnates of finance we see in the time of Crassus.[17]

His articles of 1919, for the most part in the *Resto del Carlino,* reveal him as an untiring champion of Italy's national interests abroad and still hopeful that Italian workers would create a "society of producers." Again and again he returned to the nationalist plaint that Italy was being treated like a defeated power.[18] Wilson's readiness to grant the Trentino to Italy Sorel explained as an attempt by the "cunning Yankee" to create a "German irredenta." France, he complained, had received from the Treaty of Versailles considerably more than she had had any right to expect in 1915. The Italian decision to leave the peace conference won his enthusiastic approval. The world powers, he observed, could now be classified as either "bourgeois" or "proletarian": France, Britain, and the United States fell under the first heading, while Russia, Germany, and Italy represented the latter. French hostility to Italian aims was due to fear of a powerful Italy who would threaten France's future. Italy, Sorel asserted, was entitled to receive not only what had been promised by the Treaty of London— that was not enough—but Fiume, Spalato, and the Adriatic coast to the Narenta. He attacked Italian "intellectuals" who had gloated over Italy's failure in Abyssinia, who had opposed the Libyan war, who had demanded war in 1915, but who were now prepared to permit Italians to live under an alien and inferior Serbo-Croatian regime. He thought Sonnino's retirement a "tragedy" for Italian foreign policy. On the domestic scene, he continued to attack parliamentarians, socialist and conservative alike.[19] He examined in detail an address by Giolitti in which the latter had candidly recognized the declining prestige and effectiveness of Italian parliamentary institutions. Italian agricultural workers alone, Sorel observed, were showing the way: organized in producers' associations, they had contributed more to the development of a society of producers than had all the efforts of theoreticians. Sorel was in 1919 looking for a proletarian *ricorso*; he praised the Italian socialists at the Congress of Bologna for voting adherence to the Third International. Ironically, in his first discussion in the press of fascist doctrine he found its two principles, the authority of the state and the "right to work," marked by "high originality."[20]

The search for a *ricorso* on the domestic scene and in Italy's international status continued in his 1920 articles.[21] He attacked the "Popolari," liberal Catholics who had entered the political arena in 1919, as a party demonstrating neither originality nor ability to defend the interests of the church. In any event, all parliamentary governments in Europe were in decline, tending everywhere toward regimes of personal power exercised by commanding political figures. He turned frequently to the powerful example of the "soviets" as institutions which could be used to enforce the idea of nationality. His search was still on the left. What he was looking for was a "national bolshevism." He found some comfort in Italian foreign policy. Nitti's proposal to abandon intervention, to end the blockade, and to re-establish commercial and diplomatic relations with Russia he considered to be a blow to the Quai d'Orsay, which had expected Italy to follow blindly the leadership of France. Turning to Wilson's solution to the problems of Fiume and Trieste, Sorel observed that Italy would have spent her blood and treasure for the benefit of "Anglo-Saxon speculators." Again he wrote of "bourgeois" and "proletarian nations." When it was announced that an Italian ambassador would shortly be sent to Russia, Sorel declared that France's "Latin sister" had thereby placed herself at the head of the "proletarian nations." He described, with some extravagance, the role that Italy might play in the future as the center of a "Mediterranean civilization."

Sorel began to reveal a rather curious inconsistency in his correspondence in 1921 on the subject of Italian fascism. Writing in February to Delesalle (whose sympathies were with the communists), he expressed fear that the fascists were growing ever more powerful.[22] Italian communists were being pursued by the Blackshirts, as Irish republicans were hounded by the Black-and-Tans. Giolitti's efforts alone prevented a fascist triumph. As for the real head of the fascists, he speculated, it might be the king, who was determined to destroy socialism.[23] The impending elections of May 15 were frightening to Sorel. The new chamber, he warned in March, might see the socialists considerably weakened—the Blackshirts were already "masters of the streets." "Things seem to be going very badly in Italy; the fascists are getting more important every day."[24]

However, when Variot, who was a monarchist, met him on a street in the Latin Quarter that same month, Sorel did not hesitate to express a far more favorable view of fascism.[25] Variot had remarked that it was being said that not only Lenin but Mussolini, too, was Sorel's disciple. Sorel replied, "It is possible, it is even probable, if I can believe trustworthy persons, that Benito Mussolini has read my work."[26] Mussolini, he thought, was a "political genius" no less extraordinary than Lenin.[27] Though Mussolini might have read his books, it was, perhaps, only the theory of violence which had influenced him, and even that was "in the air." Moreover, Mussolini was the inventor of something which was not in the books: "the union of the national and the social, which I studied but which I never fathomed."[28] The problem of "influence," Sorel suggested, was very complex, but he added:

It goes without saying that I would be rather proud if the reading of my books had been able to interest a Lenin or a Mussolini. To interest is quite enough and I do not ask for more, especially where such men are concerned. . . . It is nevertheless rather curious that after having been so little read, so many grandiose things are being said about me.[29]

Writing to Delesalle from April to July, Sorel again expressed his fear of a fascist triumph.[30] The rise of fascism convinced him that all Europe was destined to experience a new "Thermidorianism." The Giolitti ministry, he believed, would be overpowered by the fascists. The peasants in certain regions were already abandoning the Socialist party in order to place themselves under their protection: "You have no idea of the sad situation in which our Italian *prolos* find themselves; one must read, as I have, Italian newspapers every day in order to understand the extent of the disaster."[31]

Peace was temporarily made between the Fascist and Socialist parties from July to November 1921. In his correspondence with Delesalle, Sorel took this as tacit recognition by the socialists that they could no longer hold their own in the face of Blackshirt violence.[32] He suggested that the socialists (and this was a remarkable reversal) should come to an understanding with Giolitti's government in order to protect proletarian institutions from the fascist onslaught. But when he wrote to Croce in August, he did not conceal his admiration for fascism: "The adventures of fascism are, perhaps, at the present time the most original social phenomenon in Italy; they seem to me to surpass by far the devices of the politicians."[33] To Missiroli Sorel was even more open in his praise. In April he wrote that the "fascists were not entirely wrong" in invoking his name and that "their power demonstrated rather clearly the value of triumphant violence."[34] In September he contended that fascism was defending the Italian national heritage.[35] It was a consequence of the failure of the state to protect the bourgeoisie from the socialists. It was also the result of the failure of Italy to receive her just demands at the Paris Peace Conference:

We are at the beginning of a movement that will completely destroy the parliamentary edifice, which becomes less useful each day. I foresee that one day or another the fascists will change this state of affairs radically.[36]

There had been little indication of Sorel's interest in fascism in his published writings until 1921—only in his conversation and correspondence is there evidence of attraction. In his last articles published in 1921, there were finally hints that he was moving publicly in a direction compatible with Mussolini's movement. He argued the merits of bolshevik institutions for Italy, but nevertheless insisted that the regime which put them to use should remain "profoundly Italian."[37] He also praised the agreement which brought to an end the seizure of the Italian metallurgical industries. Of central importance was the provision for workers' participation with management in matters of technical, financial, and administrative control. This experiment in "mixed syndicalism" he believed to be perfectly in accord with proletarian interests.[38] He now saw in fascism a middle-class revolt which took into account the discontents of the workers, but which was directed essentially against the abuses of utilitarian social democracy.[39]

All evidence seems to indicate that Sorel's attraction to fascism continued to mount until his death in 1922. Michels recorded that when on March 22 Sorel spoke highly of Lenin at Delesalle's shop, he also exhibited "great sympathy" for Mussolini. "Does anyone know where he will go? In any case, he will go far."[40] Variot recalled that at Delesalle's Sorel also stated that:

The two capital facts of the postwar era are: the action of Lenin, which I believe lasting, and that of Mussolini, who will certainly triumph in Italy, notwithstanding the coalition of the left and the revolutionaries.[41]

On October 30, two months after Sorel had died and following the successful March on Rome by armed Blackshirts, Mussolini was named prime minister by the king. One wonders what Sorel would have said of that event had he lived to hear of it.

Chapter

12

The Idea

The quality of Sorel's interest in Italian fascism suggests that he saw in the movement, particularly by mid-1921, the likelihood of still another *ricorso,* like bolshevism (though less clearly so) on a "civilizational" level of significance. Italy, he believed, had taken the revolutionary initiative in Western Europe:

France has lost her ... leadership. ... Many reasons led me long ago to the conclusion that what an Hegelian would call the *Weltgeist* is today looking to Italy. Thanks to her, the light of a new age will not go out.[1]

His conception of the fascist movement's character and potential, however, can be reconstructed only with difficulty. There are neither private nor public sources in which he discussed the movement at great length or with full knowledge of its changing character. Furthermore, his virtually concurrent support of bolshevism and fascism was left unexplained except for the comment that fascism was part of a "Thermidorian reaction" about to sweep over Europe, a reaction (in part) to the danger of disorders and the spread of bolshevism.[2]

One may suggest, however, that Sorel assumed implicitly, if not explicitly, a complex of postwar revolutionary possibilities that included both bolshevism and fascism. Some such complex had been implied in his prewar move from revolutionary syndicalism to the Action Française. To be sure, for Sorel, bolshevism and fascism also had much in common, but, basically, similarities were beside the point. Sorel was drawn to bolshevism and fascism not so much because he thought them similar as because he saw them as alternatives. To posit, as he did (especially during the postwar years), the "decline of the West" was to raise the possibilitiy of at least two revolutionary choices: one could be on the side of the barbarians and start all over again, or on the side of an equally barbaric reaction that would initiate the rejuvenation of an aging civilization. One could conceivably be enthusiastic about either *ricorso* or even about both. It was unfortunate that Sorel's comments on fascism were for the most part private and fragmentary, that he never explicitly endorsed it, and that he never quite clarified its "European" significance. But others were to attempt to fill these gaps.

I

Sorel viewed fascism as a movement actively engaged in a revolutionary effort; like bolshevism, it was opposed to the parliamentary regime. Revolutionary myths, he appeared to say, impelled the fascist movement. Although he did not discuss fascist myths as such, his assertion that fascism was a "union of the national and the social" is significant. "This national and social 'discovery,' which is the base of his method, is purely Mussolinian."[3]

The character of the national and social fears operative in fascism were stated clearly enough. Fascism was an effort to defend "the national independence conquered by Garibaldi," and more immediately, a reaction to the "disaster" of the Treaty of Versailles.[4] Elsewhere he wrote that Italy was a "proletarian nation," as much a victim of the plutocratic powers as Russia or Germany.[5] She was "imprisoned" in Europe. Lacking enough territory to meet the needs of a growing population, she had been obliged to colonize in the lands of others. She needed above all, he asserted, to obtain favorable conditions for her immigrants. France, "the rock of reaction," had taken the lead in the "Holy Alliance" organized against the "proletarian nations" in general and Italy in particular. Italians in Tunisia were prevented from acquiring land or preserving their language. Furthermore, Italian efforts at expansion were repeatedly blocked by France. From the "social" standpoint, fascism was a reaction to the failure of the government to prevent socialists from "foolishly terrorizing the bourgeoisie."[6] Fascism was impelled by the fears of a bourgeoisie threatened by a "catastrophe" at the hands of industrial and agricultural workers. Sorel may have known of the subventions provided by the great consortium of metallurgical enterprises to Mussolini's movement.[7] He did write of the subsidies fascism received from the great landed proprietors.

The national and social discontents that impelled fascism had raised the hope of Italian renewal.[8] The myths engendered by these discontents constituted an indispensable lever for revolutionary energies. The regime that fascism aimed to destroy was viewed as one in which the apparatus of parliament, having out-lived its usefulness, stood in the way, a regime in which socialist agitators had usurped power over the workingmen.

Fascist organization received no systematic discussion, but in scattered comments Sorel again seemed to place emphasis on the role of personal leadership.[9] A great *condottiere* might end the disorders that threatened Italy. Both D'Annunzio and Mussolini were "modern *condottieri*"; Mussolini he considered especially gifted. Sorel admired his "astonishing comprehension of the Italian masses": "He is also a political genius who stands head and shoulders above all other political men living today, except Lenin."[10] With the exception of occasional comments about Mussolini, Sorel said little about the composition or structure of the fascist movement, though he did recognize that the movement was no ordinary "political party."[ee]

The technique employed by fascism, he observed, was violence: that is, "the will of a powerful intellect who knows what he wants."[12] The violence of fascism took into account the unforeseen. The "genius of Mussolini" lay in his ability to find "unexpected solutions to resolve unforeseen problems."[13]

Fascist violence was a manifestation of social war.[14] By defending the interests of property, Sorel asserted that the fascists were substituting their "violence" for the "force" of a state which could no longer protect these interests. The town and countryside of Italy were now the scene of a social war in which the fascists harried socialists and trade unionists the way the Jacobins had been by the Thermidorians. Mussolini might be employing some of the ideas in the *Réflexions*: "I say that every doctrine, whatever it may be, bourgeois or proletarian, in order to be stable and in order to attain its objectives, must have violence for its method."[15] In any event, Mussolini clearly understood this principle.

Fascist violence served as "a school of heroism."[16] The "historic value" of its violence had already been amply demonstrated by events. It was by violence, moreover, that the fascists would eventually come to power: "The action of Mussolini would certainly triumph."[17] Elsewhere, Sorel wrote that the bourgeoisie was "Bonapartist at heart,"[18] but his discussion of the Bonapartist *coup* was not explicitly related to the methods of fascism.

II

Sorel also commented on the regime fascism might undertake to establish. In fascism, he asserted, Italy possessed a movement which would shake the entire existing edifice to its foundations.[19] Though not expressly with reference to Mussolini's movement, Sorel had suggested elsewhere that "national energies" in Europe could be restored only if they were "reinforced" by bolshevik ideas and institutions.[20]

The motivation of a fascist order would derive, presumably, from new moral values.[21] Fascism was already characterized, he observed, by "high idealism." The new *morale* (one suspects) would bear the stamp of the "national" and "social" origins of the movement, but Sorel evidently failed to discuss the quality or function of this new *morale*.

Sorel made it quite clear that, as in the bolshevik victory, the state would not be destroyed but that a fascist triumph would entail the destruction of the existing structures.

The new structures, he anticipated, would be characterized by a leader operating in a state conceived along radically new lines. The role of personal leadership, he observed elsewhere, had appreciably increased in recent years.[22] Even well-established democracies tended to develop into regimes of personal power led by outstanding political figures. Lloyd George, for example, was an "uncrowned king," more powerful than any Bourbon had ever been. The old ruling families of England were daily losing their political influence. Since the days of Napoleon III, despots had successfully set aside parliamentary control of public affairs without suffering much opposition from the bourgeoisie.[23] Mussolini was following in the Bonapartist tradition, but he was superior even to the great Napoleon. The latter had established a new aristocracy modelled on the old; his military glories had been sacrificed to the interests of the bourgeoisie. Mussolini, on the other hand, was a "leader of the people." His comprehension of the masses and his "disinterestedness" were no less astonishing than Lenin's:

> Lenin and Mussolini, so different from each other in their social conceptions, coincide almost perfectly as leaders of the people, whom they serve and of whom they do not make use.[24]

The state, Sorel suggested, might undergo a fundamental change under Mussolini's leadership.[25] The traditional conception of the state as the foremost juridical entity derived from the association of landed property with the notion of strict allegiance. The fascists had acted independently of the state to protect the interests of property-owners. Moreover, they were known to harbor ideas on the "right to work," a right which, as they were aware, occupied a position analogous to the right of property in the minds of the bourgeoisie. The fascists might fashion a regime which recognized both the right to work and the right to property. The assertion of these principles would not only establish a sound basis for production but also provide an honorable place for the proletariat.

The new structures would give renewed vigor to Italian institutions. The role of leadership is to lead; a fascist order would be authoritarian.[26] The old ruling elements had renounced their right to exercise political power. They had brought Italy to the verge of ruin. A fascist triumph would surely destroy parliamentary and related structures and would replace them with institutions both more responsive and more decisive.[27] Sorel noted that the "mixed councils" planned by Giolitti—they provided for workers' participation in the administration of the Italian economy—admirably met this need.[28] In Belgium, he observed, similar councils had reduced strikes and had increased production. The mixed councils compared favorably with the workers' soviets in Russia: "The men who have at heart the interests of Europe must be thankful ... for ... a vast experiment which seems to correspond perfectly with the attitude of the proletariat."[29]

The technique of a prospective fascist order also received only brief and fragmentary consideration. Again, "social" and "national" criteria appeared to be of central importance to Sorel.

A fascist regime would be characterized by a concern for both the juridical development and the power interests of the state. A new period in Italian juridical history might begin with the triumph of fascism (presumably because of fascism's recognition of both the right of property and the right to work).[30] Although he asserted that the construction of fascist institutions would require the appropriate "juridical sentiments," he offered no elaboration. A fascist regime would be marked by concern for the national interest in the conduct of foreign affairs.[31] Mussolini had already announced his determination to inaugurate, "finally," an "Italian foreign policy." Such a policy, said Sorel, was certain to receive the support of the Italian people, who had long resented Italy's willingness to accept the leadership of France. He wrote that Italy should accept no limitation on its national sovereignty nor should she recognize in the League of Nations "the so-called superior interests of humanity."[32] Italy should not consider herself bound by any specific obligation undertaken in the form of a treaty. The decision to break with the Central Powers and to enter the war on the side of the Entente in the name of Italy's "sacred egoism" was a case in point. The Italians were urged to look to their own interests.

A fascist regime would be dedicated to conquest both at home and abroad. The advance of production, Sorel frequently noted, would be required of any Italian revolutionary regime. His hopes were high.[33] Italy, like Germany, was one of the few countries where the idea of industrial advance was respected, where labor was disciplined, and where work was marked by a high inventive capacity. Italy, he felt certain, was soon to experience a "renaissance" in industrial productivity. The pursuit of power and prestige abroad, he reiterated, would be the goal of a rejuvenated Italian nation. Though he nowhere spoke expressly of fascist intentions, several possibilities, all imperialistic, were discussed. There was, first, the notion of an Italy leading the "proletarian nations" of Central and Eastern Europe against the "plutocracies" of the West.[34] There was also the prospect of an Italy expanded to include not only Fiume and Trieste but the entire eastern Adriatic coast, an Italy conceived, moreover, as the center of an empire with a civilizing mission in Africa.[35] There was, finally, the possibility of emergence of a "new Mediterranean civilization" uniting "East and West" and dedicated to "work, liberty, and justice."[36]

Chapter

13

The Impact

The war was of crucial importance for the origins of fascism. On the home front, fighting the war had everywhere promoted the union of the "national and social." Moreover, wherever the war had been lost or was thought to have been lost, prewar elites, values, and institutions fell into discredit. France, for the moment, gloried in her "victory," for the war had, in the eyes of many, "legitimized" the Republic; but France had been deeply wounded. Italy, too, had "won" the war, but the conviction that the peace had been "lost" was widespread, and postwar conditions approached those in the defeated nations. The rise of fascism was not limited to the Italian scene. There were movements in postwar France as well that called themselves "fascist." Among these fascists in both France and Italy, there were some who admitted varying degrees of indebtedness to the work of Sorel.

I

Sorel's ideas continued to enjoy at least limited circulation on the French right, particularly among some of his prewar partisans in the Action Française. They had been distressed by his enthusiasm for bolshevism, but eventually explained away that attachment as an aberration and preferred to see his influence really at work elsewhere. Valois was foremost among these men.

The Action Française continued for some years after the war to provide Valois with a platform on which to present his wares. Valois's prewar efforts, however, had already pointed to eventual conflict. He had never ceased to regard Sorel as his foremost teacher, but his attempt to adapt Sorel's ideas to what he presumed were the needs of the monarchists and to provide them with a working-class following had met with very limited success. Maurras, possibly jealous of his organizational talents and suspicious of his activities, had denied Valois any real freedom of action. Valois, in any case, joined the colors in 1914.[1] He has since maintained that when Maurras "extorted" funds from his *librairie* in 1915, he almost left the movement, but remembered that Daudet, Maurras's closest associate, "had saved my life" by providing a surgeon when he was badly

194

wounded. Late in 1917 Valois was discharged from the army. He recommenced his activities for the monarchists in the spring of 1918.

Valois now began to develop a doctrinal and practical "integral syndicalism" based on the experiences of the war. Appearing first in the form of articles in the monarchist newspaper, *L'Économie nouvelle* was an attack on both "economic liberalism" and "economic communism," which he viewed as related—a "plutocratic barbarism" was giving way to a "Marxist barbarism."[2] The war had confirmed the need for "coercion" in economic and social life, as well as the Maurrasian precept, "Politics first." "Integral syndicalism" was the answer. It was corporatist: employers, managers, technicians, and workers in each industry would form their own syndicate. It was hierarchical: the syndicates would culminate in a "national economic council."[3] All parties would operate in accordance with a system of "mutual coercion." This structure required men nurtured by patriotic and religious sentiments who would elevate themselves above crass materialism. Valois wanted men in whose view the social and economic hierarchy reposed on "heroic," not "economic," sentiments—he had not forgotten Sorel. Such a system, he maintained, would operate best under a monarchy which would maintain Frenchmen in their appropriate "functions,"[4] but whether another form of government might also meet this requirement was unclear. Valois's doctrinal position was clearly antiparliamentarian and authoritarian, but not necessarily monarchist.

The wave of strikes in France in 1919–1920 aroused Maurras's fears of the dangers of communism. To meet this threat he again enlisted the talents of Valois. In the spring of 1920 Valois and some fifty friends, including a number of businessmen such as Jacques Arthuys and Eugène Mathon, launched the Confédération de l'Intelligence et de la Production Française, renamed in 1924 the Union des Corporations Française.[5] Based on the ideas of *L'Économie nouvelle,* it was an organ of the Action Française under Valois's direction. It aimed at the corporative organization of industry on both a professional and a regional basis. Valois began his campaign with a series of *"semaines,"* conferences designed to promote industry and sales in publishing, building trades, foreign commerce, and agriculture. A *"Semaine de la Monnaie"* in 1922 dealt with the current inflation. The conferences met with some success. There were favorable responses from the conservative press and in industrial circles. The Confédération published the *Production française,* a weekly addressed primarily to commercial and industrial interests, though it professed concern for the workers. There were scarcely any references to the Action Française and Valois seemed increasingly drawn to the Italian fascist movement.[6] Valois, as director, appeared to be on his own.

During these years, however, Valois grew increasingly impatient with Maurras. By 1922 Valois had become the recognized spokesman of the Action Française in matters economic. He wrote a daily column, "L'Action française économique et sociale," on the first page of the monarchist newspaper. His organizational activities were prodigious. Indeed, in some quarters of the Action Française he was regarded as "the equal of Maurras."[7] But Valois's relations with Maurras, and indeed with the monarchist leadership in general, had become strained. Valois complained that while he was "constructing institutions," the organization did nothing; that the Action Française was frightfully ignorant of social and economic affairs; that it no longer attracted men of really revolutionary temperament but only those who feared communism.

In 1922 Valois asked Maurras if he really intended to seize power.[8] The movement, he said, was too much devoted to literature and not enough to action. The restoration of the monarchy was out of the question. Maurras was evasive and no break occurred, but Valois began to act even more independently. He began a "tour of the right-wing middle classes." He delivered dozens of lectures before veterans, chambers of commerce, and employers' associations. Looking back on these years, he observed: "It was *fascisme du moment*. I was making it another way: in Italy, the Mussolinian socialists were going from socialism to nationalism; I was doing the opposite."[9] At Sorel's death it was Valois who wrote the obituary in the monarchist newspaper. He admitted that Sorel's defense of bolshevism had led to their estrangement, but, he wrote, "I bow and pray before the tomb of the man to whom I owe so much."[10]

There were others on the French right who after the war continued to search for "renewal" and who remained as convinced as before the war that Sorel had shown the way. Although they all tended to gravitate toward the Action Française, they were not numerous, and they by no means constituted a school. One was Bourget who, though a monarchist, professed his admiration for Italian fascism. On the eve of the March on Rome he observed, "The fascists are at this very moment following the counsels of Georges Sorel."[11] Almost simultaneously Variot, whose sympathies were also with the fascists, observed that both bolshevism and fascism derived, at least in part, from the *Réflexions*.[12]

René Johannet, a newcomer to the Sorelian current, was also sensitive to Italian events. Johannet had met Sorel in 1911 at Péguy's. During the postwar years he was effecting a transition from Catholicism to the Action Française and Italian fascism. His *Itinéraires d'intellectuels* of 1921 dealt at length with the development of Sorel's thought and concluded that Sorel's primary concern had been the origin and nature of "heroism."[13] The "Sorelian hero," however, was by no means plebeian; he could be found in "all vanguards." In a series of articles first published in 1920 (which appeared in 1924, expanded and modified, as *Éloge du bourgeois français*) Johannet was to demand a resurgent bourgeoisie led by a "French Mussolini."[14]

Drieu La Rochelle had also encountered Sorel around 1911 when as a "Sciences Po" student he had been attracted to the Cercle Proudhon. The experience had left a deep impression. "Prewar fascism," he observed later, had been "killed by the war."[15] The war itself had renewed fascism for him, however, by providing him with an aesthetic experience of violence: "On August 23 and October 29, 1914, in the course of two bayonet charges, I experienced an ecstasy... I consider equal to those of St. Theresa."[16] His first book (apart from war poems), published in 1921, revealed an interest in the heroic, especially in the works of Nietzsche and Gobineau.[17] The following year *Mesure de la France* demonstrated his deeply rooted revulsion and disgust with "decadence" and his renewed interest in Sorel.[18] Drieu, like Johannet, invited the French bourgeoisie to consider the Italian fascist example—the Action Française had become a *"monarchisme du salon."* What Drieu wanted was "something more profound" than a revolution or a restoration; he called it a "renaissance." He linked Sorel with Maurras, Barrès, and Péguy—his admiration for Sorel was by no means exclusive—as the "originators," who had prepared the way.

The postwar Sorelian ferment on the French right was limited to no more than a handful of enthusiasts. Valois's activities, however, were shortly to mature with the formation of a French fascist movement. Valois required the stimulus and example of Italian fascism and a domestic situation that provided opportunities for action.

II

Sorel's ideas had long been known to the various currents in Italy which combined to form the fascist movement. He had published extensively in the Italian press during the postwar years, but it is unlikely that these articles had a direct bearing on the rise of fascism, though they may have contributed to the mounting dissatisfaction with the parliamentary regime. What appears to have been a more than casual interest in fascism was expressed largely in conversation and private correspondence. It was the continuing influence of Sorel's work and his following in Italy from former years, rather than his postwar efforts, that were apparently operative in the formation of Italian fascism. The *Réflexions,* for example, continued to be the most widely quoted of all of his studies; his "prophecy" of 1912 regarding Mussolini's future in Italian politics also received considerable attention in the press.[19] In any case, the fascist movement was during the years of its origin a composite, the major components of which admitted varying degrees of indebtedness to Sorel. Some elements continued to proclaim their indebtedness (though they may have exaggerated), while others denied it (and may also have exaggerated). Still others were genuinely unaware of it—by 1914 and certainly by the war's end the most original of Sorel's ideas had become common intellectual property, and in some form may even have touched the masses. For all these reasons, therefore, Sorel's impact on the Italian fascist movement entails more than the usual difficulties.

Sorelismo was sustained during these years by the continuing interest in Sorel demonstrated by Croce and Pareto, who now enjoyed first intellectual rank, and (to a somewhat lesser degree) by Michels. All three revealed that Sorel's writings remained a point of reference in their own work. All, in one fashion or another during these years, eventually came to the support of or found it possible to accept the new fascist regime.

By 1914 Croce's principal concerns had become literature and philosophy rather than politics. He had developed a system of ethics which tended toward a "cautious liberalism" in its political conclusions. There were lapses, however. An article shortly after the outbreak of war expressed regret that the syndicalist socialism of his "venerated friend" Sorel had failed to achieve any positive results in Italy.[20] Croce hoped for a proletarian movement which would resolutely defend the national traditions, a "socialism of state and nation." The action of the German social democrats convinced him that Germany, rather than Italy, France, or Britain, might some day provide the model for such a movement. In 1915 and 1917, he appeared to be looking for a regime "devoted to and for labor."[21] Socialism had possessed only two original thinkers, Marx and Sorel, "both full of warlike and yet, in a sense, conservative spirit."[22] What appealed to him most in Sorel, he wrote in 1918, was an "ideal of labor and justice,"

a strong consciousness of moral problems, a fact not immediately apparent to the superficial reader, for Sorel fights shy of all ostentatious moralizing. He would never make [morality] the title of any of his books.[23]

In 1919, when Croce published a collection of articles of the war years, he selected those which constantly reiterated antiliberal ideas—the amorality of politics and economics and the doctrine that force alone was the basis of domestic and international politics.[24] He attacked democracy as an inferior "Latin" concept, the product of eighteenth-century humanitarianism and Freemasonry. He declared himself to be in favor of the "Germanic" idea of the struggle for survival which ultimately assured the ascendancy of the fittest, within each society and among nations. In 1920 Croce did lend the prestige of his name to the tottering liberal regime by accepting the Ministry of Education in Giolitti's last government. With the March on Rome, however, he accepted fascism as both inevitable and beneficial. The idea that Croce was an intransigent antifascist from the start has little basis in fact. He pronounced fascism the only alternative to the "anarchy of 1922," although he saw no contradiction in still calling himself a "liberal."[25] Liberals ought now to recognize that they had failed to save Italy. They could best serve the nation by acting as a friendly and understanding elder generation.

During and after the war Pareto elaborated a sociological system which at critical points incorporated many of Sorel's ideas. In 1916 he published his greatest work, the *Trattato di sociologia generale*. Drawing distinctions between "residues" (religious sentiments in the widest sense of the term) and "derivatives" (rationalizations of these sentiments), he arrived at conclusions which Sorel had already presented in embryo.[26] Residues chiefly determined the form of society and were susceptible to only the most gradual modification. Derivatives or theories were pseudo-logical reasons invented and applied by men to justify their sentiments and actions; they were much more pliant and responsive to pressure. What counted in forming the strength and prosperity of a people was religion, faith, myth, devotion to some common ideal. An "aristocracy," constantly renewed from below, was the custodian of this ideal. This was the active element in history. On the subject of violence, however, Pareto took issue with Sorel.[27] He disputed the argument that in order to be effective proletarian violence necessarily required retaliation by the ruling class. He maintained that theories designed to justify the use of violence by the governed were almost always combined with theories condemning the use of force by public authorities. "People who use illegal violence would ask for nothing better than to be able to transmute it to legal violence."[28] Pareto also rejected Sorel's notion of the moral value of violence. It was the "utility" of violence that concerned him, not at all its legality or morality. For him it was a question of the relative merits of employing shrewdness or force in any given situation.[29] Pareto's *Trasformazione della democrazia* of 1921, a study of postwar democracies, revealed considerably less interest in Sorel,[30] but at Sorel's death Pareto commented at length on his relations with him, both personal and intellectual.[31] No cloud, he asserted, had ever darkened their friendship since it began in 1897.[32] There was in Sorel's work and in his own "a fundamental identity" of view, even though Sorel was a "man of faith inclined toward metaphysics" and he a practitioner of the "purely experimental method." Sorel's work had fully demonstrated the emptiness of democratic and humanitarian dogmas and the weakness of "pseudo-scientific intellectualism" which maintained that in social action reason prevailed over sentiment:

Hence our agreement, hence our common attempt . . . to treat as a special aspect of the theory of Residues the celebrated doctrine of the Myth, which Sorel had arrived at independently.[33]

Among those who gladly welcomed some of Sorel's arguments without accepting all of them, Pareto continued, were the fascists.[34] They had detached the theory of violence from the proletariat, for the two were not joined by any intrinsic logic. The fascists, moreover, had confirmed "in a splendid way the uniformity of the empirical laws observed by Sorel, without endorsing in the least his admiration for the proletariat."[35]

While teaching at Basel during and after the war, Michels continued to explore the nationalist phenomenon. A 1921 appendix to his earlier study of the Italian socialist movement credited Sorel with the leading role in shaping the quality of the syndicalism of the Italian professors.[36] The idea of "proletarian Italy" had capped the development and bridged the gap between syndicalism and nationalism, between Labriola and Corradini. When Michels met Sorel in March 1922 in Paris, he noted in his diary that Sorel spoke with sympathy of his old friend Pareto as well as of Mussolini.[37] Despite their disagreement on bolshevism, in the years following the March on Rome Michels's admiration was to grow both for Sorel's work and for the new fascist regime.[38]

Both the syndicalist and nationalist movements were characterized during the war and the years immediately postwar by continuing tendencies toward national-syndicalist solutions. It was the emergent fascist movement, however, that was to provide the common ground by which important elements in the two currents were finally joined. Sorelismo was to play a significant role in this evolution.

Italian syndicalism of the temper represented by Corridoni's interventionist group (notably the Unione Sindacale Milanese) broke with the USI (about a third of their 100,000 membership left) on the issue of intervention; in November 1914 they embarked on a course that for many led to the nascent Italian fascist movement.[39] After Corridoni was killed on the battlefield in October 1915, a sacrifice which was to become legendary for fascism, Rossoni became (along with de Ambris, who had converted Corridoni to intervention) one of the leading figures of the Comitato Sindacale Italiano—the successor in 1916 to the syndicalist interventionist groups, an opponent of both the antiwar USI and the CGL. Rossoni had been Corridoni's close friend for a time during the prewar years; he had also spent several years as an organizer of the Italian Industrial Workers of the World in New York.[40] Though his rhetoric suggests that Sorel may have been known to him, he was rarely mentioned in Rossoni's writings. Rossoni returned to Italy late during the war years. His experience as an organizer in the United States, he later related, was crucial in the development of this thinking:

The fortunes of Italian workers are indissolubly bound to the fortunes of the Italian nation.... We have seen our workers exploited and held in contempt not only by capitalists but even by their revolutionary comrades of other countries. Hence we know by experience that internationalism is but a fiction and hypocrisy.[41]

In June 1918 the Comitato (which included Corridoni's Unione Sindacale Milanese) was transformed into the Unione Italiana del Lavoro (UIL), with Rossoni as its head.[42] The UIL immediately claimed some 137,000 adherents, mainly among agricultural workers and small proprietors, especially in the Romagna and Tuscany. It was fiercely prowar and anticommunist, but it also declared war on wage capitalism. A campaign of recruitment was undertaken in the center and north. Although it grew during the next two years, the UIL nevertheless remained (even more so than the USI) a minority movement overshadowed by the CGL. Its syndicalism was republican and nationalist. It aimed at proletarian management of all aspects of national life—the "nation" was not to be "rejected" but "conquered."[43] Its principal enemies were the reformists and the communists in the CGL; over struck establishments the UIL flew not the red flag but the tricolor. Moreover, in two Milanese reviews, the *Italia nostra,* founded in May 1918 by Rossoni and Olivetti, and, particularly, the *Pagine libere,* revived in 1920 and directed by Olivetti and Orano (both publications supporters of the UIL), Sorelismo flourished once again, linked with a "neo-Mazzinian idealism."[44]

When Mussolini sought labor support in the summer of 1919, he turned to the UIL as the only labor movement that had expressed an interest in fascism, but when he suggested an alliance it was rejected. The UIL suspected that he might be harboring monarchist sympathies.[45] Mussolini then attempted the formation of his own syndicates, also under the tricolor. In 1920 he persuaded Rossoni (who seemed near to breaking with the UIL) to set up the Confederazione Italiana dei Sindacati Economici at Ferrara. The 50,000 adherents who came from the UIL were to constitute the genuinely syndicalist nucleus of fascist labor support, though Rossoni held out for syndicalist autonomy.[46] The syndicates were "mixed," that is, they contained peasants and landowners, workers and proprietors. They were not at all unlike D'Annunzio's syndicates, which had recently arisen. D'Annunzio had seized Fiume in September 1919 and, aided by de Ambris, had organized the Comitato Nazionale d'Azione Sindacale Dannunziana. D'Annunzio had planned to organize citizens of the "State of Fiume" into a system of corporations.

At the invitation of Rossoni, the leaders of these groups (fascist, syndicalist, and D'Annunzian), all intensely patriotic and opposed to the CGL as well as the communist labor federation, met in Ferrara in October 1921 to discuss common action.[47] They planned a national congress for Bologna in January. In this way the stage was set for amalgamation and union with the fascist movement: fascism needed labor support, and syndicalism needed political weapons. The recently named secretary-general of the Fascist party, a prewar syndicalist, Bianchi, was sent to Bologna to make an offer of union. Bianchi's maneuvers led to the formation of the Confederazione Nazionale delle Corporazioni Sindacali, whose program and platform, the resolution of the Bologna convention asserted, were "essentially the same as the program and platform of the Fascist party"—Rossoni had accepted party control.[48] The resolution of the Bologna convention that January called for a system of national corporations. It dwelt on the dignity of "labor," "labor" being interpreted to mean virtually every form of useful activity—"the process of creating, perfecting and enhancing whatever constitutes the material, moral and spiritual welfare of man":

> The nation, regarded as the highest synthesis of all the material and spiritual values of the race, is above individuals, occupations, and classes. Individuals, occupations, and classes are the instruments which the nation employs to attain its greater glory. The interests of individuals, of professions and of classes acquire the stamp of legitimacy when they come to be embodied in the plan of the higher national interest.[49]

The following month in Milan, Rossoni joined the party and became the secretary-general of the consolidated organization.[50] It numbered about 500,000 by June 1922, with a membership drawn from the UIL, the fascist, and the D'Annunzian syndicates. It was renamed the Confederazione Sindacale Fascista after the March on Rome, and became an integral part of the fascist regime.

To summarize the fascist encounter with revolutionary syndicalism: only a fraction (50,000 members) of the UIL under Rossoni's direction could initially be persuaded to join the fascist syndicates (which were themselves early in 1922 comprised largely of socialist and Catholic agrarian leagues that had been beaten, fragmented, and frightened by squadrist violence into forming or joining the fascist syndicates). The majority of the UIL remained adamantly hostile, but it was so weakened by subsequent losses to fascism that in 1925 it was absorbed by the CGL. The USI, the largest syndicalist organization, was destroyed in 1923. The rump-CGL survived only until 1926, when it was absorbed by the fascist labor syndicates. Rossoni's defection in 1922 is not easily assessed. It was typical only of nationalist and interventionist revolutionary syndicalism and it was not entirely conclusive. Even though he became head of the rapidly expanding fascist labor syndicates, these were largely refugees from squadrist violence directed against the UIL, USI, CGL, and the fascist opposition in general. As time would show, Rossoni was to fight for syndicalist autonomy even within the fascist regime.

The syndicalist periodical that most clearly expressed Sorelian sentiments during these years was the revived *Pagine libere,* which reappeared in February 1920 (the *Italia nostra* appeared only intermittently in 1918 and 1919). The two prewar series edited by Olivetti had been followed briefly by a third in October 1914, following the outbreak of war. Olivetti, joined by Lanzillo and Libero Tancredi, called for intervention "to coordinate the social revolution with the *fatto nazionale.*"[51] The review, moreover, published and gave full publicity to the manifesto of Mussolini's first Fascio, though it terminated publication in March 1915.

Early in 1920 the *Pagine libere* reappeared for a fourth time to engage in postwar political and intellectual debate. Again the review was under Olivetti's direction. Although Orano (already a fascist) served as political editor, divergent tendencies were clearly in evidence. The review maintained a distinctly Sorelian cast by virtue of its direction, as well as its principal contributors—Olivetti, Panunzio, Labriola, and a newcomer, Max Ascoli. Once again the revolutionary and national-syndicalist themes of its "heroic" prewar series reappeared.[52] The review was against German social democracy and Russian communism (though not without admiration for Lenin). Though favorably disposed toward fascism, it was nonetheless suspicious of Mussolini's statist tendencies. Ostensibly republican, Olivetti and Panunzio emphasized Mazzinian nationalism and political "indeterminacy," but theirs was no longer an exclusively proletarian syndicalism. They appealed to "all who produce." The war as well as the more recent bolshevik experience with "workers' control" had conclusively demonstrated the utopian character of prewar proletarian syndicalism. Sorel, in any case, was still regarded here as *maestro*.[53] Corridoni was the finest exemplar of Sorelian syndicalism— Corridoni was a "Sorelian hero." Sorel had established the basic psychology of revolutionary movements and the centrality of the *"morale* of producers." Sorelian syndicalism of the prewar years had, however, been "too rigidly" proletarian. Ascoli nevertheless insisted that Sorel had never wavered in his faith in the proletariat.[54] Labriola, too, at Sorel's death proclaimed him a faithful servant of the workers whose career had terminated with the "Pour Lénine."[55] Olivetti's reservations regarding fascism persisted: "Fascism wants to swallow national syndicalism the way the whale swallowed Jonah."[56] By mid-1921 the review was becoming recognizably less militant and more "cultural" and, in fact, broke all ties with fascism. It survived only until the end of 1922. By then Panunzio and Orano had joined the ranks of the fascists; Olivetti was to join in 1924.

The Sorelians with syndicalist origins exhibited much the same pattern of development during these years. All of the leading figures (with the notable exception of Leone) had been interventionists and members of the Fasci of 1915. All had been profoundly influenced by the character of the war and the Bolshevik Revolution. All drifted toward the postwar fascist movement, each at his own pace.

Lanzillo had been Mussolini's lieutenant on the *Popolo d'Italia* since its establishment; he maintained close ties with fascism while professor of economy and finance at the University of Bocconi from 1920 to 1922. In 1918 his *La Disfatta del socialismo* asserted that he wanted above all to be a "postwar" rather than a "prewar" man. The failure of socialism he attributed to its "illusion" of reformism, its internationalism, and the "predominance of the political over the moral."[57] The moral value of violence had been amply demonstrated, he asserted, in the events of the Bolshevik Revolution. His hopes for Italy were more than ever focused on a national syndicalism free from all "international prejudices." In *Le Rivoluzioni del dopoguerra* of 1922 Lanzillo discussed the multifaceted character of the fascist movement at length.[58] He attacked bolshevism as a form of "terrorism" in the "French eighteenth-century style," and not at all in the manner of the *Réflexions*. The Third International he viewed as an instrument of Russian expansion; he noted that Sorel had long been opposed to "internationals of all kinds." Fascism, however, was eminently Sorelian in its heroic and creative qualities: "In the present-day victory of fascism we see an instance of *force which creates right*." Lanzillo found in fascism the middle classes at work in an effort to defend a complex of general Italian interests which most closely approximated those of the nation. He expected the class struggle to continue. Fascist syndicates would obey "the ineluctable law of all working-class organizations." He wrote in an article in which he maintained that Sorel had provided the "spiritual" foundation of fascism:

Fascism will tear the proletariat away from the domination of the Socialist party, reconstruct it on the basis of spiritual liberty and idealism, animate it with the breath of creative violence. That will be the true revolution which will give shape to the Italy of tomorrow.[59]

As professor of law at the University of Rome, Panunzio was also among the early contributors to the *Popolo d'Italia,* convinced that war would have revolutionary consequences, and a fascist of "the first hour." He too in postwar articles in the *Pagine libere* continued to regard Sorelian syndicalism as the "only authentic socialism."[60] Lenin, he thought, had borrowed much from Sorel, though Panunzio failed to specify exactly what that "much" was. But Lenin had attempted to implement Sorel's ideas "in Russia in 1917"; hence his failure. The *Diritto, forza e violenza* of 1921 endeavored to formulate a new system of jurisprudence.[61] Sorel had drawn a distinction in the *Réflexions* between the "force" of the state and the "violence" of those who sought to destroy it. Panunzio here undertook to elaborate a theory of jurisprudence based on Sorelian violence as the instrument by which new rights are fashioned. Articles and speeches during 1919–1923 described fascism as a regime dedicated to the establishment of an "integral" or national syndicalism.[62] The unity of nationalism and syndicalism had been forged by the war experience for Italy. Sorel had been the first and foremost exponent of "integral syndicalism." What Sorel had contributed was his vision of a "society of producers" and a "cult of production" as vital to the modern world.

Orano was a member of both the prewar and postwar Fasci and had been throughout one of Mussolini's chief aides.[63] Neither as political editor of the *Pagine libere* from 1920 to mid-1921 nor in his articles in the *Popolo d'Italia,* the *Gerarchia,* and elsewhere did he reveal much of his prewar interest in Sorel. His arguments, though containing marked national syndicalist overtones, now took on the character of little more than exercises in fascist propaganda.[64]

The Bolognese lawyer Olivetti who edited the *Pagine libere* also served during the postwar years as secretary of the UIL, and was a partisan of

D'Annunzio; by 1924 he had become a Fascist party member. He repeatedly emphasized "National syndicalism," as distinguished from its "anarchist predecessor."[65] The new syndicalism recognized the nation as an "immanent historical reality" and did not rule out a continuation of the class struggle. It retained from the earlier syndicalism Sorel's idea of elevating the workingman to a "superior revolutionary idealism." Though fearful of a statism that would lead to dictatorship, Olivetti was even more critical of communist or socialist internationalism.[66] Internationalism, he argued, corresponded to no reality whatsoever. Its source of strength lay in the weakness of the proletarian movement. The future of syndicalism would be resolved only within the framework of the nation.

Italian nationalism also entered into the mainstream of fascism, but what nationalism brought with it that had Sorelian roots is difficult to assay. The tendency in nationalist quarters was to identify Sorel with proletarian syndicalism, which had reached its climax with his defense of Lenin. Nationalists had sought in prewar Sorelian syndicalism (if they looked there at all) Sorel's "society of producers," stripped of its proletarian revolutionism and open to all economic and professional categories. Sorel's influence in nationalist quarters during the war and postwar years, needless to say, was more often denied than acknowledged.

As soon as the possibility of war against the Entente vanished, the Nationalist party turned against the Central Powers—the nationalists saw in war, any war, an opportunity for national renewal. Early in 1915 nationalism made its first contact with the future elements of fascism,[67] and during the war the accord between the *Popolo d'Italia* and the *Idea nazionale* was at least tacit. In December 1918 the nationalists founded the doctrinal review *Politica*. It opened with a ringing manifesto announcing the notions which during the war had produced a "corruption of ideology": democracy, individualism, peace, self-determination, and internationalism.[68] The review announced instead a "philosophy of Rome," of the empire and of the church: "Everything calls Italy to the resumption of her imperial mission."[69]

The differences between nationalism and fascism were for some time serious and in some regions there was rivalry between local Blueshirts and Blackshirts. Nationalism was unalterably monarchist, while fascism was at first republican. Nationalism, never a mass party, recruited its force mainly from the upper middle classes, while the fascists from the outset in 1919 sought mass support. In March 1919 the Nationalist party held a national convention at Rome. Corradini proposed again the "organic, unitary, integral" organization of the social order.[70] Rocco demanded the "integral organization of national production," while Maraviglia sought to "spiritualize the matter of society."[71] When D'Annunzio organized his syndicates in September, among his supporters (including de Ambris) were some of the leading nationalists: Corradini, Forges-Davanzati, Rocco, and Dino Grandi. Support was by no means unanimous, however—Francesco Coppola, editor of *Politica,* found any suggestion of syndicalism too "materialistic."[72]

As Mussolini's republicanism became more dubious, opportunities for closer collaboration between the Nationalist and Fascist parties arose.[73] They supported each other's candidates in the elections of 1921, but the alliance proved premature. At Udine on September 20, 1922, Mussolini definitely proclaimed himself a monarchist, announcing that the only trouble with the king was that he was not king enough. The alliance, accordingly, was re-established. The proclamation ordering the March on Rome was, in fact, nationalist in tone. It asserted that the Blackshirts were not marching against the army, the police, or the king, nor against the "productive bourgeoisie" or the "masses that work in fields and offices." They marched against "a political class of weaklings and defectives who for four years had been unable to give the nation a government." The Blueshirts protected the flanks of the Blackshirts on their "march." The following year the Fascist party absorbed the far smaller Nationalist party.

The nationalist press by no means overlooked the relation between nationalism and Sorelismo. The *Idea nazionale* had republished Sorel's "Giustizia all'Italia," which had appeared in Missiroli's *Resto del Carlino* in May 1919. Sorel was hailed as a friend of Italy. Patriotic societies had sent telegrams of thanks.[74] Articles in *Politica* dealt with the issue of Sorelismo directly.

Politica had been founded by Coppola and Rocco. Prominent among its contributors was Corradini, as well as the former syndicalists Federzoni, Maraviglia, and Forges-Davanzati. Notwithstanding their origins, they exhibited no serious interest in Sorel. Moreover, the journalist Filippo Carli declared Sorel's writing to be alien and inimical to the nationalist idea.[75] He defended syndicalism only in its corporate form, as contributing to the formation of an "equilibrium between capital and labor," to the elimination of crises in production, and to the development of a *"cultura professionale."* Oreste Ranelletti identified Sorel with "traditional syndicalism," which he pronounced "destructive."[76] He found objectionable the "proletarian" and "revolutionary" cast in which Sorel presented his ideas. No note was taken of Sorel's later development nor of the ways in which his ideas had been or could be useful to nationalism. Again, as in the prewar years, most nationalist writers would admit of no foreign influence; they insisted that their corporatism was uniquely Italian.

Corradini and Prezzolini, the prewar nationalists who had been closest to Sorelismo, had by now embarked on rather different courses. Something of their prewar Sorelian involvement, however, was still in evidence in their work, although without acknowledgment.

As director of the *Idea nazionale* and the leading figure in the Italian nationalist movement, Corradini's writing continued to demonstrate preoccupation with problems raised by Sorel. In a collection of addresses delivered in 1916 he spoke of "another Italian irredenta: that of production."[77] He extended the meaning of Sorel's phrase, the *valore morale* of production," beyond the social and economic to include "thought," "creations of the mind," and "culture." *La Marcia dei produttori,* published that same year, viewed the capitalist bourgeoisie, "inventive and productive," as the true aristocracy of modern times.[78] But, he asserted, no revolution today could be made without or against the proletariat. The working class (particularly in view of the war experience) was an overriding fact of modern existence. The socialist movement had attempted to distort the historic mission of the worker: it viewed the worker as "a man of class struggle," the soldier as "a man of national struggle" and the two as irreconcilable adversaries; but the war had established the essential identity of the worker and soldier. The socialist movement, Corradini argued, was largely the making of bourgeois intellectuals and had little to do with what workers either wanted or needed. Articles in the *Idea nazionale,* meanwhile, saw in the Bolshevik Revolution and in Wilsonian internationalism common roots—the triumph of the "materialistic," "rational-istic," and "antidivine."[79] By 1922, in *L'Unità e la potenza delle nazioni,* Corradini had gone far in his acceptance of fascism.[80] The decadence of the ruling democratic and socialist bourgeoisie, their neglect of nation and state, had determined the origins of fascism. "The state stands for the will of the united nation transcending the warring wills of its component parts."

In contrast, Prezzolini did not take the road to fascism. He had joined with Mussolini in founding the *Popolo d'Italia* late in 1914 and had relinquished the direction of the *Voce.* Though he hurled literary darts and invective at the lethargy of Italians in general and the shabbiness of politicians in particular, Sorel had largely been superseded by Croce in his philosophy.[81] Notwithstanding his displeasure at the failure of Italy to entrust the government to those capable of commanding, he was critical of the postwar fascist movement. Prezzolini had founded the Casa Editrice of the *Voce* after the war and soon devoted himself to the study of fascism. Once again he returned to the Vocist themes of the prewar years. In his first major work, published in 1923, he saw in the triumph of fascism evidence of a Sorelian *ricorso,* a *"grande forza"* in Italian life, but he nevertheless thought the movement a threat to Italian culture.[82] The intransigence of fascism, the facile manner in which it took on the most difficult problems, its habit of resolving by force what could not be resolved by thought, its disdain for public opinion—all these qualities would militate against cultural renewal. Prezzolini, often considered a precursor of fascism,[83] was reluctant to accept some of its hard consequences. After the March on Rome (and once again more clearly under the aegis of Sorelismo), he remained critical of the new regime, though by no means did he join the "opposition" to it.

Unlike Corradini or Prezzolini, Missiroli's development took still another turn; although Sorel's articles in the *Resto del Carlino* and the correspondence between them testify to their personal ties, their intellectual ties became rather blurred. From a prewar national syndicalism Missiroli had gravitated by 1914 to theocracy. In his *La Monarchia socialista* of 1914 and *Il Papa in guerra* of 1915 he urged Italy to abandon its quasi-atheistic liberalism and "return" to Catholicism for moral and political direction.[84] A restored "national spirit" was required for this transformation, to do battle with alien ideologies imported from abroad and propagated by Italian universities. Sorel figured only marginally in this design. By 1918, when Missiroli became director of the *Resto del Carlino,* he had turned "liberal."[85] In newspaper articles published between 1919 and 1921 and in a collection of "notes" on a variety of personalities and issues (in which he discussed Sorel's "purity of morals"), he expressed fears of Mussolini's autocratic proclivities. The *Resto del Carlino* under Missiroli's direction became, in fact, a highly regarded liberal daily that published Sorel's pro-bolshevik articles and was opposed to fascism. In 1921, for reasons of local Bolognese politics, the fascists became enraged at Missiroli.[86] The newspaper was forced to take a line more agreeable to fascism and Missiroli was obliged to leave. In May 1922 Missiroli and Mussolini fought a duel. But Missiroli was to change his political faith once again within a few years, becoming a vigorous champion of the fascist regime and asserting once again the Sorelian origins of his political and social thought.

As for the fascist movement itself, its origin is a problem in the merger of intellectual and political currents animated by a substantially similar spirit but separated by sentiments of class and the weight of tradition. The Fasci of 1915 and of 1919, both comprised of disparate elements, were successful efforts on a small scale to bridge the gap. Many of those who played leading roles in the merger had come from Sorelismo.

Prominent among the contributors to the *Popolo d'Italia* and in the Fasci d'Azione Rivoluzionaria of 1915 were Lanzillo, Panunzio, Longobardi, Olivetti, Orano, and Mantica, who all came from syndicalism, while Prezzolini and Papini came by way of nationalism.[87] Moreover, the syndicalist organizers Corridoni, de Ambris, Rossoni, and Bianchi broke with the USI to form an interventionist syndicalist group. All had, either directly or marginally, been involved in the Sorelian ferment. That Sorel was hardly mentioned in the early issues of the *Popolo d'Italia* should come as no surprise. It should be recalled that he had publicly declared his opposition to intervention in the *Avanti!* In the early issues of the *Popolo d'Italia* was a notion, however, that had already appeared among some Sorelians in the agitation preceding the Libyan war—the notion that war would complete the revolutionary preparation of the masses.

Sorelismo was somewhat less pronounced in the reactivated Fasci di Combattimento, which met in Milan in March 1919.[88] The group was comprised of survivors of the prewar Fasci, for the most part syndicalist, plus a generous sprinkling of republicans and futurists.[89] Among Mussolini's chief aides were again Lanzillo, Orano, and Bianchi. Though the Fasci of 1919 had marked accents of the extreme left, it was clear from its origins that there were no boundaries or limits to its future development—this time Mussolini kept his options open.

In the final years before the March on Rome the fascists displayed remarkable "flexibility"; much of the rhetoric and tactics of fascism were now in the hands of futurists—students and intellectuals who tended toward a cynical activism and opportunism.[90] The evolution of fascism from 1919 to 1922 is a story of the progressive sacrifice of syndicalism to the interests of nationalism, of the proletariat to the interests of the bourgeoisie. The transition appears to have been dictated by circumstances that limited Mussolini's opportunities (electoral and otherwise) on the left, even the interventionist left, while improving those on the right. After the factories occupied in September 1920 had been evacuated, Mussolini was convinced that the Socialist party had allowed to pass a revolutionary opportunity that would not return. He was also quick to note that Italian conservative organizations, both agricultural and industrial, had been sufficiently frightened by the episode to see in fascism the possible savior of Italy.

Fascist organs that demonstrated any considerable interest in Sorel before the March on Rome were slow in appearing. The *Popolo d'Italia,* the party newspaper, was primarily concerned with the day-to-day struggle and little given to matters of doctrine; on the occasion of Sorel's death the obituary (attributed to Mussolini), though suggesting that Sorel was somewhat out of date, nevertheless admitted that "some of the most cherished ideas of the Sorelian conception of life and history" were to be found in fascism.[91] In January 1922, however, Mussolini had founded (and initially edited) *Gerarchia,* a doctrinal review and supplement to the *Popolo d'Italia.*[92]

Gerarchia was broadly interested in philosophies of revolt, and though the review was by no means Sorelian, Sorel was in 1922 a very frequent subject of discussion. The principal contributors included Orano, Lanzillo, "Volt" (nom de plume of Count Vincenzo Fani), Soffici, and Massimo Rocca. "Volt" in an article on Pareto designated Sorel as the prime spiritual source of fascism and applauded him for having foreseen as early as 1912 the role that Mussolini would someday play in Italian history.[93] A more critical view of Sorel's work was taken by Rocca (who as a syndicalist had written under the pseudonym of "Libero Iancredi").[94] Sorel's contributions to fascism were readily enumerated: his "pessimistic voluntarism" comparable to the Mazzinian ethic of sacrifice, his Bergsonian preference for the *homo faber,* his notion of the "historical continuity of revolutions" fundamental for Renan and Pareto, his concept of the *"morale* of producers"—all this had passed into fascism. But whatever in Sorel was no longer relevant to the needs of fascism must be "buried." Rocca singled out Sorel's concept of "producer": a producer has nothing to do with class. It was Lanzillo who published Sorel's obituary in *Gerarchia*.[95] Though Sorel had been drawn to Lenin, Lanzillo asserted, the Bolshevik Revolution had soon crushed what Sorel had admired in it: "Perhaps fascism will have the good fortune to fulfill the mission which was the implicit aspiration of the entire work of the *Maestro* of syndicalism."[96]

Whether Sorel was any longer necessary either to Mussolini or to his following after 1919 was doubtful. What they had taken from Sorel himself or from Sorelismo was largely the product of the prewar years, now altered to meet the requirements of postwar conditions and opportunities.

During the years from 1919 to 1922 Mussolini frequently expressed his revolutionism in terms that smacked of Sorelismo,[97] but he had more recently been influenced by the rhetoric of futurism and had become far more "Machiavellian." He now endeavored to pose as an adroit political artist who had mastered the craft of manipulating the masses: only to him could the fate of Italy be entrusted. In the March 1919 issues of the *Popolo d'Italia* concerning the reactivation of the Fasci he declared that fascism had no formal principles. "We accept whatever means may become necessary, the legal and the so-called illegal."[98] On the role of myth, he asserted that fascism was neither republican nor monarchist, neither Catholic nor anti-Catholic, socialist nor antisocialist. Fascists were "problemists, realists, realizers." At Trieste in September 1920 he declared that the two "pillars" of fascism were the "flexibility" of its technique, that is, its aversion to absolutes, and the "revived consciousness of the ancient glories of Italy," that is, the Roman Empire, the Renaissance, the Risorgimento, and the continuation of this tradition by intervention in the World War, seizure of Fiume by d'Annunzio, and fascist efforts to create a new imperial Rome.[99] In March 1921 he asserted that fascism had a horror of everything that was "hypothetically arbitrary" regarding the future.[100] In August he wrote to Bianchi that fascism needed a doctrine but that it was not necessary to be committed to it for all eternity.[101] Tomorrow was mysterious and unforeseeable. Rules were necessary merely to orient political and individual action. Early in September 1922 Mussolini drew distinctions between syndicalism of the "red" and of the "tricolor" variety and described their implications for the *"morale* of producers."[102] The need to produce, demonstrated by the war, he considered overriding in modern society, but he saw no sign that capitalism was on the verge of collapse. He denied too that the proletariat was the embodiment of all that was progressive and virtuous. The demands of modern production, as the war had made clear, required close collaboration of all social and economic groups. Fascism, therefore, was unalterably opposed to the class struggle. It was determined to preserve all that was vital in the social order. It did not promise an indefinite increase in riches to any group. It required "sacrifices" and "heroism" from all. In his well-known "Discorso di Udine" on September 20 he announced his immediate goals: "We wish to govern Italy."[103] When violence resolved a "gangrenous situation," it was eminently moral, sacrosanct, and necessary. When old elites failed, they had to be replaced by new. On the eve of the March on Rome, he proclaimed:

We have created a Myth, a Myth that is a Faith, a passion. It does not need to be a reality, it is a stimulus and a hope, belief and courage. Our Myth is the Nation, the grandeur of the Nation, which we will make a concrete "reality."[104]

These assertions were made without specific reference to Sorel. After 1922 Mussolini was to be far more explicit concerning his debt to him.

With the incorporation of syndicalist and nationalist elements, a Sorelian current entered the fascist movement. Mussolini aside, the Sorelians who became fascists came almost exclusively from syndicalism. Among them were Lanzillo, Panunzio, Orano, and, within a few years, Olivetti. With them, though not as closely identified with Sorel, were the organizers Rossoni and Bianchi (de Ambris became an antifascist exile). All were to rise to high rank in the party or to receive positions of prominence in the new regime. Among nationalists, no prewar figures had maintained clear-cut ties with Sorelismo and no new figures had yet appeared. Corradini, however, had accepted fascism, while Prezzolini and Missiroli opposed it.

The fascism of 1922 was indebted to Sorelismo. Mussolini had been a participant in the Sorelian ferment before the war. It may be that he had little ideological baggage. It may also be that he was without scruples. Mussolini may or may not have needed Sorel, but fascism had needed Sorelismo, particularly in the prewar form, with its aim of national syndicalism and its cult of heroic violence. The chaos of the postwar years created multiple revolutionary opportunities, better for the right than the left. What fascism now devised were the appropriate slogans, organization, and modes of action—it was *squadrismo,* fascist violence, that forced the decisive nationalization or neutralization of what remained of proletarian revolutionism and of opposition to fascism generally. Seen in this light, Mussolini's fascism, come to power in 1922, may be regarded, to a considerable degree, as an organized and vulgarized transformation of the prewar Sorelian movement.[105] If Mussolini could boast that fascism had no ideology, it was because for him Sorel's myth could be a lie, the role of an elite could be assumed by a gang of toughs, and violence could degenerate into gangsterism.

The appearance of Sorelians unwilling to accept fascism, however, was to have rather curious consequences. The Sorelian syndicalists who had accepted fascism were to constitute something of a "school" within the regime. Those drawn to bolshevism, joined by those who opposed fascism for other reasons, were now to form the nucleus of a Sorelian opposition to fascism.

Sorelians
after
Sorel

Sorel had professed no interest in establishing a "school." He had wanted to be free of disciples. Even during his Action Française interlude he had demonstrated a remarkable independence of his admirers. Yet, it is indisputable that a Sorelian movement had in fact appeared in both France and Italy, however blurred in its changing character and dimensions. Sorel himself had by 1922 arrived at a view of communism, and possibly fascism, as *ricorsi,* and saw them, it is very likely, as revolutionary alternatives. His following had arrived at similar or related conclusions, also inclined, for the most part, toward the new communist or fascist regime. In any case, the outstanding feature of the movement thus far was a political indeterminacy limited to the extremes and marked by attempts to bridge the gap between them. Its adherents had demonstrated an extraordinary freedom of action, not only with respect to the master but with respect to each other. For most, no position was maintained for very long (though there were exceptions), and at no time was Sorel's following all to be found at any one place in the spectrum of extremism.

The Sorelian movement persisted, at times in even greater vigor, in the two decades after Sorel's death. What impelled it were events that gave continuing relevance to Sorel's thought. To be sure, France was spared some of the more onerous postwar difficulties, but a generalized mood of dissatisfaction continued in France, particularly in the mid-twenties, in which the new communist and fascist regimes abroad figured prominently in discussion and activity. Italy, moreover, now possessed a professedly revolutionary regime. Internal conflict concerning the orientation of that regime, as well as the growth of opposition to it, sustained interest in Sorel. By the early 1930s these developments had been fortified by the deepening world economic, political, and international crisis.

In these circumstances, not only did the Sorelian movement persist, it continued to proliferate. Mounting dissatisfaction with both communism and fascism was to lead some of Sorel's following—both old and new—to professions of faith in still other revolutionary possibilities—some old, some new.

Chapter
14
The 1920s

During the 1920s Sorelian activities in both France and Italy took unusual turns. In France Berth dominated Sorelian activities on the left. French communism at first provided ample opportunity for the activities of fellow-travelers, but the evolution of the party soon led to disillusionment for Berth and his associates. Meanwhile, Valois, as always on the margin of the Action Française and now much impressed by the success of Italian fascism, was to experiment with his own brand of "French fascism," and was to experience the same disenchantment. In both cases, disillusionment led to new departures. In France Sorelian activity was able to develop in virtually complete freedom, but in Italy this was soon no longer possible. Within a few years the new regime imposed obstacles on all sides. Until the mid-twenties, however, before a full-blown dictatorship was established, Sorelismo flourished in both fascist and antifascist camps.

I

In France whatever Sorelian tendencies may have been in evidence in the *Revue communiste* disappeared when Sorel's articles ceased to appear shortly before his death. Moreover, though Delesalle and Louzon continued on the staff of *Humanité* and *Vie ouvrière,* now organs of the Communist party and trade-union federation respectively, Sorelian notions were not for long destined to received currency in these quarters. Prewar syndicalists found it increasingly difficult to work with communists.

Clarté, however, did become Sorelian. It had been founded in 1919 by the antiwar novelist Barbusse, but for several years lacked firm doctrinal orientation.[1] Under Barbusse it had tried to be communist without being Marxist. It was not until Berth was appointed to the editorial board in 1922 that a Sorelian line was adopted (briefly, Berth assumed the pseudonym "Édouard Darville"). As Barbusse gradually withdrew from the publication, Berth was joined by Marcel Fourrier, Georges Michael, and Jean Bernier, all avowedly Sorelians; even Bloch of the prewar *Effort* contributed. Berth and his associates now undertook not only the elaboration of a proletarian moral system but also the delineation of the principles of a proletarian culture, both in accordance with Sorel's ideas.[2]

Articles in *Clarté* by Berth's associates rejected fascism's claims to Sorel and discussed the problem of rallying the communist proletariat in France to "a civilization rich in quiritarian values,"[3] presented an analysis of Sorel's efforts to restore to Marxism its "Hegelian sense of struggle" (though the bolshevik experience, it was acknowledged, had effectively destroyed Sorel's argument concerning the merits of abstention from political activity),[4] and considered the continuing relevance of Sorel's thought, particularly his idea of a "society of heroes" as manifested in the Soviet regime.[5] Berth's articles were of special interest.[6] He condemned Jouhaux and the CGT for their disavowal of the Soviet regime—Lenin struck Berth as a "Sorelian" and "Nietzschean" hero.[7] He urged a "Holy Alliance" of "proletarian nations" against the "Anglo-Saxon plutocracies"—the struggle in history had always been between "Rome and Carthage."[8] He remained convinced that France was "decadent,"[9] but he persisted in the hope that a *ricorso* would return her "to instinct, poetry, faith, force, and the sublime." The French worker in the socialist society of the future would be the successor, as Sorel had hoped, to the "saint and hero" of past ages. By October 1925, however, *Clarté* was breaking up.[10] Barbusse had departed the year before, complaining that it had become a "little communist review." When the editorial board decided to change the propaganda line to reach the "middle classes" (as distinct from the bourgeoisie), Berth too left; his ideological ties with the Soviet regime were also loosening.[11] The remaining staff had in the interim shifted its interests from ethics to art and from Sorel to surrealism. Surrealism was declared to be a passionate Freudian revolt against everything rational and bourgeois in both art and politics and not at all in conflict with the previous interests of the group. In the final issues of *Clarté* a new periodical was planned. It never appeared, however, and the group broke up.

The *Révolution prolétarienne* succeeded *Clarté* as a center of Sorelian activity, and again Berth played a central role. The periodical appeared in 1925 with a staff composed of prewar syndicalists who had first rallied to the Communist party and the CGTU and had then either left voluntarily or been excluded.[12] From the very beginning (in view of Lenin's death and the ensuing struggle between Stalin and Trotsky for the succession) the review demonstrated a marked Trotskyite flavor. Both the editor Monatte and one of his principal collaborators, Louzon, had served with Sorel on the prewar *Mouvement socialiste*.

Berth joined the *Révolution prolétarienne* in 1926, after he had left *Clarté* and after he too had broken with the communists. Berth was now convinced that the *ricorso* initiated by Lenin had been sabotaged by a Stalinist bureaucracy both in the Soviet Union and in the French Communist party.[13]

The *Révolution prolétarienne* now attempted a revival of "classical" prewar revolutionary syndicalism. Both Monatte and Louzon argued for a syndicalism that was rigidly proletarian. Though their interests were practical rather than theoretical, they were concerned with such themes as *"le facteur morale,"* a "society of heroes," and "revolution as a law of life."[14] A persistent concern in their writings was the danger to the worker of an all-powerful state, socialist, capitalist, communist, or fascist.[15] Berth's articles went much further and deeper in their defense of Sorel[16] and in their attack on the "vulgar Marxism" which had become the hallmark of Russian bolshevism, German social democracy, and French communism alike.[17] Under Stalin, bolshevism had become pure autocracy, a "Russian deviation" of Marxism. In its worship of the state it was no better than fascism. What Berth and his associates wanted was the autonomous development of the trade unions. "The hour has come for western socialism, that is, revolutionary syndicalism, to seize the torch of European revolution as it falls from the failing hands of communism."[18]

Above all, Berth defended Sorel, determined to win for him a secure place in the history of the proletarian cause. In 1931, the *Critique sociale,* a Trotzkyite review edited by Boris Souvarine, Berth's associate on *Clarté,* published a selection of Sorel's letters to Croce which had recently appeared in Croce's *Critica,*[19] and accused Sorel of not being a socialist, of not knowing Marxism, of being anti-Semitic, and of being sympathetic to nationalism and fascism. Berth denied all this, particularly the last charge.[20] Sorel, he said, had never attached himself to any group, but had always remained an observer, an outsider. His relationship with Valois and the Action Française was "cultural." As for fascism, Sorel never relented in his opposition to dictatorship, left or right.

In nationalist circles Sorelian activity in the early twenties was confined largely to the margins of the Action Française. Berth was the most active propagator of Sorel's ideas on the left; Valois played the same role on the right, and Valois was by no means alone. Among some men of letters, Sorel's influence was still very much in evidence. For all of them the traditional right as represented by the Action Française, now, as in the prewar years, left something to be desired. They were increasingly drawn to Mussolini and the fascist experiment as the only alternative to communism.

Bourget, a member of the Academie Française, was the best known of these men. It was Bourget who had brought Valois to Maurras's attention in 1907.[21] Three years later Bourget had established Sorel as a celebrity with the production of *La Barricade.* In an interview in 1926 Bourget asserted that the books he most often reread were Sorel's *Réflexions* and Pascal's *Mystère de Jesus.*[22] As for the *Réflexions,* Bourget claimed, "They explain the conception and the forms of present-day social conflict, the action as well as the reaction, Lenin as well as Mussolini."[23] Bourget's interview had followed the publication of his novel of 1926, *Nos actes nous suivent,* in which the protagonist preached "integral revolution"—he demanded "either Lenin or Mussolini." Like his creator, the protagonist really wanted Mussolini. Variot, Sorel's associate on the prewar *Indépendance,* also saw the significance of Sorel in the same light. Bolshevism and fascism had both derived from the *Réflexions.*[24] Variot now turned to an exaltation of French imperialism.[25] Drieu La Rochelle, however, in his search for the meaningful and heroic life had shifted to the surrealism of André Breton, which itself appeared oriented toward Moscow; the Action Française had become for Drieu an anachronism.[26] "By the time of Locarno" the choice for him lay between decadence and heroism, between "Geneva or Moscow."

When Johannet published his *Éloge* in 1924, he touched off a controversy, the *"querrel des bourgeois,"* especially with Valois. In this final version of his articles of 1920, Johannet wrote that nothing great had ever come from the masses.[27] The bourgeoisie were, in fact, a "natural elite" and their "greatest hero" had been Joan of Arc! The bourgeoisie had never known decadence for long. They had repeatedly renewed themselves. Sorel's *Réflexions* had not only revealed their "flabbiness," but also the cure.[28] It was Sorel also who had inspired the *Éloge.* Of Sorel's letters during the war Johannet wrote, "Even when you wrote to justify the bombardment of the cathedral of Reims, I adored getting them."[29] For France in the mid-twenties, Johannet urged bourgeois renewal, neither *"avidité plutocratique"* nor *"stupidité manuelle."* What was required was a "French Mussolini."

Valois's formidable organizational talents provided the focus of Sorelian activity in these political quarters; he aspired to be the "French Mussolini."[30] By 1922–1923, Valois, in addition to directing the monarchist publishing-house, wrote a daily column on social and economic affairs in the *Action française* and headed a variety of projects that aimed at the corporate organization of society and industry. Late in 1922 he undertook a campaign to convoke an "États-Généraux," an economic parliament, and soon another campaign to stabilize the franc.[31] By 1924 he was directing an entire section of the monarchist newspaper, the "Revue hebdomadaire de la production française" which, among other matters, carried items on the workings of fascism in Italy. Moreover, he had persuaded François Coty, the perfume magnate and director of the conservative newspapers *Figaro* and *Gaulois,* to support his activities.[32] Daudet pronounced Valois's work the most striking *"actualité."* Dimier noted that the *ligueurs* regarded him as "the equal of Maurras."

Valois had long been unhappy with the monarchists. In his published work, notably *La Révolution nationale* of 1924, he argued for a technocratic hierarchy, but he never strayed far from Maurrasian orthodoxy—the revolution, he wrote, required a monarch.[33] But he also wrote, "I owe to Sorel my definitive direction."[34] Nor could he conceal his enthusiasm for Italian fascism (earlier that year Valois and several of his friends had visited Italy and had met Mussolini and other officials). He saw Western civilization threatened by an "Asiatic bolshevism."[35] Submission or fascism were the alternatives. He published Pietro Gorgolini's study of fascism, the first work on the Italian movement to appear in France.[36] He commented frequently and favorably on Italian affairs in his articles. Moreover, he took exception to Johannet's arguments: "I have never loved the bourgeoisie."[37] No class, as such, could constitute an elite. Valois feared a bourgeoisie that would turn the state against the working class. He urged an intellectual and technocratic elite leading both worker and bourgois. Since the end of the war he had clamored for action, particularly in *La Révolution nationale*. After the defeat of the Action Française in the elections of 1924 and the victory of the Cartel des Gauches, Valois threatened to resign if there were further electoral involvements and if Maurras failed to "act."[38] A break with Pujo came that same year when Valois's plans for future monarchist activity were turned down. It is likely that Valois was tolerated because he brought "big money" (in 1924, Coty) into the Action Française.[39] But in October 1925 Valois announced his decision to leave the *Action française* and to join the *Nouveau siècle*, a weekly he had founded with Coty's support in February.[40] The evidence is conclusive that Valois's departure was prearranged.

The *Nouveau siècle* had appeared in February 1925 with a "Déclaration" that France had "saved civilization on the Marne."[41] The victory, however, had been lost by the Republic. The veterans had been forgotten. There remained the German menace as well as that of communism. This announcement demanded a regime headed by a "*Chef nationale.*" It was signed by Valois and a number of colleagues associated with his multifarious postwar projects, notably Arthuys, Philippe Barrès, and Serge André, as well as his prewar associates Benjamin, Marsan, and the Tharaud brothers. Coty provided the funds—according to some sources, 1.5 million francs.[42] At first Maurras had nothing but praise for Valois's enterprise.[43] Valois, it was explained, was attempting to work outside the Action Française while still in it. But there were soon signs of acrimony. The stage was set for the emergence of the Faisceau, the first serious attempt to establish a French fascist movement. Valois's final article in the monarchist newspaper appeared on October 11, 1925.

On Armistice Day, November 11, 1925, Valois announced in the *Nouveau siècle* the establishment of the Faisceau, replete with strong-arm veterans' units, the Blueshirts.[44] The declared goal of these units was "the conquest of the state." Prominent among them was the much-decorated Marcel Bucard (who was to lead the Francistes in the following decade). By the end of the year the organization was thriving. Coty was now by no means the sole backer of the Faisceau. There were others prominent in French industry. The newspaper had meanwhile become a daily; it proclaimed itself an organ of "veterans and producers."[45] Within two months of its formation the Faisceau possessed, according to Valois, 25,000 paid subscribers and 100,000 sympathizers.[46]

Almost simultaneously, the *Action française* launched a vigorous attack on Valois and all his works.[47] Maurras charged Valois with spreading lies in the Italian press, and the *camelots* broke up a meeting in Paris at which a "Faisceau *universitaire*" was being established—Valois had asserted at the meeting that for his purposes a republic was as good as a monarchy. Then came further charges and litigation as the Action Française opened its heavy artillery: Maurras, Daudet, and Pujo. Valois was charged with stealing membership lists, preparing comic-opera plots, being in the pay of Mussolini, conspiring with communists or the Sûrété Générale, as well as maintaining nefarious connections with the world of finance.[48] There were periodic clashes between *camelots* and Blueshirts, not only in Paris but in Strasbourg, Lyon, and elsewhere. On one occasion the Blueshirts wrecked the Paris offices of the Action Française on the Rue de Rome.[49]

The conflict turned doctrinal when Valois insisted that Sorel was the founder of both Italian and French fascism.[50] The controversy was promptly taken up by the *Action française*. Monarchist spokesmen roundly denounced Sorel: "And this is the *maître*, Hegelian, Philo-*Boche*, and *proboche*, that Gressent-Valois proposes to French veterans." Responding to the argument that Mussolini had been influenced by Sorel, the *Action française* asserted that even if Mussolini took his tactics from Sorel, it was not from Sorel that he derived his strategy. "And in fact, while Sorel ended up with Lenin, Mussolini ended up with the king."

In the meantime, Valois had transformed the Faisceau, more or less on the Italian model (though with emphasis on economic regionalism); resplendent in uniform and with appropriate gestures, he posed as the "French Mussolini."[51] The Faisceau groups were being organized throughout France as Valois undertook an intensive money-raising campaign and prepared for action. He planned a massive "National Assembly" at Reims on June 27, 1926, to be followed by a "March on Paris" by Blueshirts.[52] He appealed to the workers, in fact, to "all revolutionaries" against plutocracy for support.[53] He made much of several communists who had joined the Faisceau. The preparations were made in an atmosphere of national emergency created by the fall of the franc and the subsequent ministerial crisis.[54] Throughout Europe—in Portugal, Spain, and Greece, in the Pilsudski coup in Poland, even in the general strike in Britain— Valois saw fascism on the march. The time had come to seize power.

In the months preceding the assembly Valois continued to speculate on his own intellectual formation and the origins of the Faisceau. He announced that the "*querrel des bourgeois*" had ended. Johannet had appeared to be defending the bourgeoisie, while Valois was against them, but their differences, he concluded, were largely semantic.[55] Both he and Johannet opposed the current bourgeois parliamentary Republic, and that was what mattered. Johannet now joined the editorial staff of the *Nouveau siècle*. Valois wrote in February 1926 to Johannet:

> We have recalled, at the same time the conversations of our youth with our old *maître* and friend, Georges Sorel. Sorel believed that proletarian violence would oblige the bourgeoisie to climb up the hill democracy made it descend. . . . It is certainly the memory of our conversations with Sorel which led us to write, you your *Éloge du bourgeois* and I the *Révolution nationale*.[56]

In Sorel's *Réflexions,* Valois maintained, was the key to modern history—it was the statement concerning the relation between proletarian violence and bourgeois revival, the action and the reaction.[57] This was the idea that had produced in Russia the dictatorship of the proletariat and in Italy the fascist dictatorship. But the Russian regime had been destined to founder because it denied one of the great human impulses, the acquisition of property. He noted that the NEP had put Moscow on the "road to fascism," with the restoration of property and inheritance.[58]

Fascism required leadership from both the workers and the "captains of industry." It required an "elite open to all," "*un État syndicale et corporatif.*" It meant the salvation of European civilization. Fascism's originality lay in its combination of socialism and nationalism, according to Valois.[59] In a parliamentary regime these two most revolutionary and creative forces of the nineteenth century had fought each other; in fascism they worked together. "We are neither right nor left. These words have absolutely no meaning for us."

Although Valois dominated the *Nouveau siècle,* he was by no means the only one to express these views or to invoke the name of Sorel. Some of Valois's supporters had been prewar associates of Sorel on the *Revue critique* or the Cercle Proudhon (de Barral, Benjamin, Maire); others had been habituées of Péguy's shop (Johannet and the Tharaud brothers as well as the above); still others were recent associates in the Action Française (Arthuys, Barrès, and André Fourgeaud).[60]

After considerable fanfare the "National Assembly" at Reims, the "first organic assembly" outside the parliament, finally took place. Some 12,000 participated, representing, according to Valois (probably an exaggeration), 500,000 Faisceau.[61] Valois issued a call for a "republic of veterans and producers." When he began his "March on Paris" a number of serious street brawls erupted. Moreover, the road to Paris was blocked by Marcel Déat and some 3,000 socialists (*Humanité* claimed 10,000).[62] The "march" failed.

Valois soon planned another assembly "to commence the national revolution,"[63] but it was already too late. Poincaré had "saved" the franc, and the Faisceau quickly lost its appeal. In December 1926 the *Nouveau siècle* became a weekly again and Valois began a new campaign to raise money.[64] Coty had decided to withdraw his support; a split developed between a militarist, reactionary "right" around Arthuys and a syndicalist and revolutionary "left" around Valois; and a good part of the leadership, including Bucard, turned against Valois.[65] Valois maintained that he and Coty had never agreed on a working-class policy.[66] For more than a year, he complained, he had fought off attempts to transform the Blueshirts into an organization of anticommunists and strikebreakers. There was also disagreement on the international danger of communism, for Valois saw no immediate danger in Europe.

Valois tried to save himself. There were further frantic fund-raising campaigns and dramatic public ceremonies at Joan of Arc's birthplace at Domrémy and at Péguy's tomb, but Valois's following quickly dissolved. In December 1927 the *Nouveau siècle* declared itself for the "République syndicale."[67] His move to the "left," Valois asserted, was not "new." He had been moving to the left since he had founded the Cercle Proudhon in 1912. Valois now publicly regretted the use of the term "fascist" to designate his movement. "There is fascism and fascism," he maintained, "plutocratic" and "revolutionary."[68] Italian fascism he now denounced as "reactionary." On April 1, 1928, the *Nouveau siècle* ceased publication. Valois blamed Coty for his misfortunes. Coty, deciding to "fly with his own wings," had established the daily *Ami du peuple,* abandoning both Maurras and Valois.

By August 1928 Valois was back in business again, this time publishing the *Cahiers bleus,* at first a monthly and then a weekly review treating one or a very select number of political topics.[69] He now headed the "Parti Républicaine Syndicaliste," rather vaguely described as an organization that aimed to establish a "society of producers," opposed to all "parasitism," and based on "work and justice." It aimed at a "technical state," politically neutral. Valois published a list of over one hundred supporters of the new organization.[70] Many had not only backed the Faisceau, but also his postwar monarchist activities, and still others were associates from prewar days. The doctrinal position of the party was declared to be "Georges Sorel applied to present-day reality."[71]

Among those participating were Arthuys and Fourgeaud, plus a number of new figures: Bertrand de Jouvenal, Pierre Dominique, Gustave Rodriguez, and the young Serbian Sammy Béracha. Lagardelle of the prewar *Mouvement socialiste,* Berth more recently of the *Révolution prolétarienne,* and Labriola, now living in exile in Paris, also contributed (and even the young Pierre Mendès-France). All these figures demonstrated more than a casual interest in Sorel. If de Jouvenal called Sorel the "prophet" of the greatest economic transformation in human history, namely, the coming of the "controlled economy," Fourgeaud saw in Sorelian syndicalism the basis for an entirely new "juridical development of society."[72] If Dominique viewed Sorel as the *maître* of both Lenin and Mussolini and the key to "creative revolution" in the twentieth century, Béracha saw in him the idea of the "*morale* of producers" and the key to the social order of the future.[73] There was discussion of a "republic of producers," the First Five Year Plan, the electrification of Toulouse, and the dangers and opportunities occasioned by the beginning of the world economic depression. What Valois really attempted in the *Cahiers bleus,* according to Berth, was to rally "an intellectual company...around syndicalist conceptions [consisting of] the world of technicians and intellectuals who float between the poles of capital and labor."[74] Valois's new venture, this time as the apostle of a syndicalist and cooperative "revolution," was hardly a success. Politically, he was in a "no-man's-land." The *Cahiers bleus* ceased publication in 1932. It was to be followed by the equally ephemeral and "cultural" *Chantiers coopératifs,* which appeared from 1932 to 1934.[75]

II

Within Italian fascism after the March on Rome there was no clear "party line" regarding Sorel's contribution to the making of the fascist movement or what role his ideas might yet play in the future of the regime. The "line," if it did exist, was by no means hard enough to establish uniformity of opinion. The result was continuing controversy between Sorelian and anti-Sorelian currents within the movement. Differences on the subject of Sorel were, of course, symptomatic of deeper divisions, both long-standing and current.

Mussolini's own pronouncements on Sorel were clear enough. To be sure, *Gerarchia,* Mussolini's doctrinal review, no longer evinced any great interest in Sorel. After its foundation in January 1922 the review had attracted Orano and Lanzillo. Although Sorel was a frequent subject of discussion, the review was never Sorelian. When Margherita Sarfatti (at whose Milan salon Mussolini had been a frequent guest) succeeded him to the directorship shortly after the March on Rome, Sorel's name virtually disappeared from *Gerarchia*'s pages for the remainder of the decade. But Mussolini himself continued to speak of Sorel as his foremost mentor (others included Nietzsche, Pareto, and James). In an address in the Chamber of Deputies in November 1923 he asserted that Sorel had helped form his "*mentalità.*"[76] That same year the first of the "official" studies on the origins of fascism appeared. There was, the author Gorgolini insisted, "no substantial difference in ideas and programme between fascists and Sorelian socialists."[77] A French edition was published by the Nouvelle Librairie Nationale of the Action Française, then under Valois's direction. In a widely quoted interview that Mussolini gave in April 1926 to the *A.B.C.* of Madrid he asserted that neither Nietzsche nor James had been his principal mentor:

It is to Georges Sorel that I owe the most. It is to this master of syndicalism who, ... by his theories on the technique of revolution, contributed most to form the discipline, the energy and power of the fascist cohorts.[78]

An "official biography" by Sarfatti and the studies of Gentile, the "official philosopher" of fascism, also affirmed Sorel's influence on Mussolini's "first intellectual education": the former stressed Sorel's notion of the "utility" of myths; the latter emphasized Sorel's "Mazzinian conception of life."[79]

Apart from Mussolini's own pronouncements on Sorel, Sorelismo in the twenties showed both gains and losses. Croce, Pareto, and Michels no longer presented a "united front." Pareto, who had seen in fascism a "splendid confirmation" of Sorel's views, was appointed a senator by Mussolini in 1923 but died that same year.[80] Croce, after several years of defending fascism, eventually broke with it and later (in a sense) with Sorelismo. Michels never renounced either.

At the advent of fascism Croce at first accepted it as both inevitable and beneficial. In an article of October 1923, though he still called himself a "liberal," he favored Mussolini as a remedy for the "anarchy of 1922."[81] As a senator (he was so named in 1910), he supported the government even after the assassination of socialist-deputy Matteotti. Croce believed liberals ought now to recognize that they had failed to save Italy. He suggested that they could best serve her in the future by acting as a friendly and understanding elder generation. In an interview early in 1924 he refused to be alarmed by increasing fascist violence and censorship.[82] Even a month after the Matteotti murder, Croce still did not turn definitively against the regime—he was viewed as a precursor "in spite of himself" in *Gerarchia*.[83] He stated that he "had always maintained" that fascism was devoid of new institutions, but he paid tribute to its constructive contributions. The public was determined "not to return to all the weakness and all the inconclusiveness which had preceded it."

By 1925, however, Croce had found fascism "lawless and immoral."[84] Early that year Gentile, who had broken with Croce and other "liberals" in 1921–1922, issued a "fascist manifesto" signed by intellectuals who supported the regime. Croce, in turn, issued a "counter-manifesto" in which faith in "liberalism" was proclaimed by some forty men of culture. The break with fascism was now clear-cut. Even Sorelismo now came in for criticism: it had ended in a "cynical and reactionary nationalism." Croce never went into exile and was never persecuted, possibly because of his immense intellectual stature. His monthly *Critica* now became a vehicle of antifascism and remained so until the fall of the regime.

From January 1927 to May 1930 the *Critica* published Sorel's letters to Croce. In a comment introducing the series, Croce announced that he had reserved the right to omit passages, "especially ... those written during the last years."[85] Though there can be no certainty, it is likely that Croce chose to leave out comments favorable to the fascist movement and its leader, though several such statements nevertheless appeared. Some twenty years after the event, Croce responded to an inquiry regarding the excisions by replying:

They could not have contained any allusions against fascism, for in that case I would have been obliged to publish them.... Sorel, being the impressionable man he was, in principle was favorable to Mussolini. He hated the professional politicos, and saw mistakenly in Mussolini a spontaneous and beneficial force.[86]

By publishing Sorel's letters so soon after his own break with the regime Croce had evidently chosen to leave out comments by Sorel that might have suggested an even more enthusiastic support of nascent fascism.

Michels was honored by Mussolini personally in 1928 with an appointment to the University of Perugia.[87] The fascist movement provided him with raw material for his subsequent studies of charismatic leadership and the role of elites in mass movements.[88] Mussolini's role he viewed as a "living and active incarnation" of fascism; he was not only "the leader of a great party, he has become also the leader of a great state." Sorel received credit for having defined and elaborated the qualities of elites in general in his description of workers' syndicates. These Michels enumerated as the homogeneous unity of elements, "communalization of political ideals," premarital sexual purity and monogamic integrity of the family, and high productive capacities developed from work-discipline in factories and syndicates.[89] These qualities Michels saw operative in both communism and fascism.

Since the World War, two new parties inspired ... by the severe and diversified conceptions of the French syndicalist movement under the spiritual direction of Georges Sorel (Pareto's friend) have arisen. These parties have a new basis, that of the elite. Both consequently find themselves in deep-seated contrast with the current democratic and electionistic theories. In Russia, bolshevism ... has imposed ... the domination of a proletarian minority. In Italy, fascism, gifted with the same *élan vital*, snatched the power from weak hands and called to itself, in the name of the country, the minority of active and energetic men who are always to be found.[90]

High rank and honors were the rewards of the syndicalist professors who came to the support of fascism—some were even given membership in the Commission of Eighteen charged in 1925 with the organization of a corporate state. But their power and prestige carried a price tag: renunciation of previously held doctrinal positions and support of a regime over whose evolution they soon exercised little control. With the exception of Orano, long one of Mussolini's lieutenants, these exercises were performed more or less convincingly. Orano received in 1925 the directorship of the Rome edition of the *Popolo d'Italia,* the official mouthpiece of the regime, and he was subsequently appointed Rector of the University of Perugia.[91] His *Mussolini da vicino* of 1928, though arguing that Mussolini owed much to "classical revolutionary syndicalism" in the "solution" of the social problem, was little more than a piece of simplistic propaganda of the most unscholarly and uncritical variety.

Lanzillo had expected the class struggle to continue within the fascist regime.[92] Emerging from the conflict would be a new "juridical order," a uniquely fascist system. But evidence of a syndicalist militancy progressively disappeared from his writing as he rose to positions of prominence. As had Orano, he had been close to Mussolini, having served as correspondent of the *Popolo d'Italia* since its foundation. After 1922 he taught political economy at the University of Milan, served as deputy in the Chamber, was appointed to the Commission of Eighteen, and was finally appointed to the National Council of Corporations.[93] Though among the fascists who had admonished Mussolini during the Matteotti affair, his faith in the regime appeared unshaken. Not until the thirties did Lanzillo undertake a serious study of the relations, both past and future, between syndicalism and the corporatist regime.

Olivetti and Panunzio earnestly endeavored from the start to establish the Sorelian origins of fascism as well as the credibility of their own credentials as fascists. Since their careers had been devoted to the promotion of proletarian syndicalism, they were now obliged to make the appropriate sacrifices. What they now asserted, in substance, was that they and Sorelismo generally had "always" been fascist.

The former secretary of the UIL, Olivetti, remained militantly syndicalist. Syndicalism, he held in 1924 when he joined the Fascist party, was more "a state of mind" than a doctrine, "passionate, critical, constructive" and based on the Mazzinian notion of "association."[94] In this sense, even nationalism possessed syndicalist origins. The source of that *élan* required protection. Without "freedom of labor" there could be "neither political liberty, nor spiritual liberty, nor moral liberty." Olivetti too was appointed to the Commission of Eighteen, but by 1926 he was on the defensive against the assault of nationalists.[95] He insisted that Italian fascism could be traced to the "heroic syndicalism" that dated from his foundation of the *Pagine libere* in 1907. It was syndicalism that had launched the idea of the "organic state." The negation of ideology, the doctrine of elites, the role of direct action—all these had their origins in prewar syndicalism. In 1930 he defended Sorel against the charge of the *Critica fascista*, a leading doctrinal review of the regime, that Sorelismo had culminated in bolshevism.[96] Sorel's entire evolution, his involvement with both right and left, Olivetti declared, had to be taken into account. Moreover, he recalled that as early as 1912 the *Pagine libere* had been not only nationalist but imperialist. From the beginning, he asserted, Sorel had followed and supported the evolution that culminated with the UIL and, in his final letters and conversations, had applauded the "corporate state." There were no contradictions, as had been charged, in Sorel or in Sorelismo. The contradictions were to be found in those who accepted a fictitious and artificial opposition between the bourgeoisie and the proletariat, an opposition that was the product of rationalism and materialism. Sorel and his Italian disciples had worked for a "moral revolution" that was not necessarily related to class: "Contemporary Italian society is *il più bel frutto del pensiero soreliano,* without which there would have been in Italy neither the intervention, the war, nor . . . the fascist revolution."[97]

The same argument appeared in the work of Panunzio, professor of law at Rome, deputy, and member of the national party directorate, who also served as a member of the National Council of Corporations. In *Che cose' è il fascismo?* of 1924 he asserted that the root of the fascist regime was to be found in prewar national syndicalism, to which the war had given final shape.[98] Sorel, as its founder, had initiated a *"ricorso mediterraneo."* Probing more deeply into fascist origins in an article in the *Civiltà fascista,* he argued that its roots were to be found in the revision of Marx, first by Bernstein and then definitively by Sorel.[99] Revisionism began in Italy with the publication of Sorel's "L'Avenir," the "bible" of the New School, and its elaboration by Labriola in the *Avanguardia socialista* and by Leone in the *Divenire sociale.* The syndicalism of Sorel and the fascism of Mussolini were in opposition only if viewed logically, statically. Psychological and dynamic identities bound them together. Long before the triumph of fascism, syndicalism had already become nationalist. The "old" syndicalism had been economic; the "new" was political. And the new was superior because the state took precedence over society. The demonstration of this verity, according to Panunzio, was Mussolini's greatest achievement. In studies published in 1929 and 1930, Panunzio was more explicit.[100] Fascism had, quite properly, turned Sorel inside out. Instead of the syndicates absorbing the state, the state had absorbed the syndicates. Panunzio now rejected categorically the "sovereignty" of the syndicates.

In syndicalist circles in the 1920s something of a "legal opposition" to the policies of the regime appeared. Several periodicals, though professing loyalty to Mussolini, were in open disagreement with fascist labor policies. Among these was the *Stirpe.*

The *Stirpe* called itself a review of "fascist corporatism."[101] To dispel any doubts, it began publication in December 1923 with a letter from Il Duce to Rossoni, its director. What *Stirpe* preached was "integral syndicalism." It urged the regime to assume an orientation more favorable to the proletariat. Frequent contributors included Olivetti and Panunzio, who never failed to assert fascism's debt to Sorel.[102] "Integral syndicalism," beyond arguments asserting the autonomy of the syndicates, was never clearly defined, and the relations between the syndicates and the state remained obscure.[103] Articles asserted the primacy of the state and deplored the survivals of class war. The *Stirpe* never really clarified its purposes or challenged the regime.

A far more original enterprise was undertaken by Curzio Suckert (later "Malaparte").[104] Malaparte was a "fascist of the first hour" who had published *L'Europa vivente* in 1923 and in the following year established a weekly, the *Conquista dello stato*. At 16 he had been a republican and interventionist, an associate of Corridoni who joined the Garibaldi Brigade in France. By 1922 he was a secretary of a Florentine federation of fascist syndicates and a member of the local Vocist group.

L'Europa vivente viewed Italian fascism as the revival of a long-established Latin tradition that had been temporarily submerged by northern movements since the Reformation.[105] The decadence of Europe Malaparte attributed to liberalism, democracy, socialism, and "modernism," which, he argued, had all stemmed from the Reformation. The restoration of "Catholic virtues" (social and moral rather than "religious") was therefore vital. Malaparte's Maurrasian-like thesis was sustained by an argument with a Sorelian origin. Sorelian violence had initiated the "Counter-Reformation": the fanatics of violence had first thrown Italy into the war. The fascist revolution, too, was born of the Sorelian ethic. Sorel's celebrated statement in the *Réflexions* on bourgeois renewal was the *raison déterminante* of fascism: all might be saved if proletarian violence were to reinforce class divisions and restore in the bourgeoisie something of its former energy. In Italy Sorelismo had partly detached itself from its creator "by transforming the concept of social classes into that of national classes and economic presuppositions into historical ones." Malaparte saw in Sorel something of a prophet.[106] Who but Sorel could have compared Mussolini as early as 1912 with the *condottieri* of the fifteenth century? Who but Sorel could have recognized that what Italy really needed was a "hero-tyrant"? Fascism was the beginning of a new civilization:

We are sure that it will be neither bourgeois nor proletarian. We hate both equally.... We have seen how Italian syndicalism took the class myth of the general strike from Sorel and transformed it into that of a revolutionary war for Italian liberty, for us an historic concept; and today we see how fascism has made use of its own revolutionary spirit of syndicalist violence in order to complete that profound transformation of the modern social order...from which will rise a single powerfully organized national class. Fascism already represents this new class.[107]

Malaparte's *Italia barbara,* published in 1926, continued the attack on "modernism."[108] Italians were by their "nature" unfit to become modern. What had long been needed was a revolution that would return Italians to their natural and historic modes of civilization. Fascist violence, he noted, had spread from Italy's central provinces, the most characteristically Italian, and turned against the liberal, Bonapartist regime shot through with French and German culture: "the provinces . . . against the city of profiteers and shirkers." The *Conquista dello stato*, Malaparte's Roman weekly, appeared from 1924 until his arrest in 1928.[109] The revolutionary conquest, Malaparte announced, had been achieved. The problem now was the creation of a unitary government. Malaparte won to his cause a small group of *fascisti* including Soffici, who sought the fundamental principles of fascism in Catholicism, and "Volt," who had served on the *Gerarchia* and was associated with the Gentile school of idealism. By 1928 Missiroli and Olivetti had also become contributors. The *Conquista* engaged in heated arguments with the *Rivoluzione liberale* and the *Resto del Carlino*. Malaparte himself was obliged to fight several duels, notably one with Rossoni.

Conquista demonstrated a serious interest in Sorel, though it was by no means exclusively Sorelian. Sorel's work was viewed as forming a vital link in the inheritance of the new regime. From the pages of the weekly emerged the argument that Mazzini was the prophet of fascism, that Sorel's vision of the historic mission of the syndicalist movement was closer to the spirit of Mazzini and therefore more meaningful for Italy than Marx's, that Corridoni suffered martyrdom in the cause of national syndicalism, and that Mussolini's fascism was the fulfillment of Corridoni's dream.[110] Fascism was a *"nuova 'democrazia eroica.'"* Its failure would mean the triumph of communism—the *Conquista* demonstrated no apparent sympathy for this alternative. Interest in Sorel, however, was not limited to discourses on the origins or nature of fascism.[111] Pareto's obituary on Sorel in the *Ronda* was published, as was an unpublished letter by Sorel in 1921 (probably to Missiroli) declaring his interest in and sympathy for fascism as a movement "defending the national independence conquered by Garibaldi."

Malaparte's highly individualistic brand of fascism led eventually to friction with the regime.[112] As early as 1925 the very title of an article indicated growing dissatisfaction with Mussolini: "*Mussolini si proclama integralista: ma quando attueremo il Fascismo integrale?*"[113] Moreover, Malaparte tended to become increasingly critical of the squadrist, jingoist, and imperialist fascism represented by the *Impero* of Rome. Nor was he sufficiently cautious in his criticism of Roberto Farinacci, from 1925 to 1926 secretary of the Fascist party and leader of the *duri,* or toughs. The *Italia barbara* had been published in 1926 by Piero Gobetti, who was clearly identified with the opposition to the regime. Malaparte appeared to be moving in the same direction. He was arrested in June 1928, and the *Conquista* ended publication.[114] By 1929, however, he was editor of the *Stampa* of Turin, writing of the "revolutionary genius" of Lenin[115]—an exercise not necessarily in conflict with fascist censorship. It was evidence of his growing fascination with all political extremism.

During the twenties in the new Italian regime hostility to anything that smacked of proletarian revolutionism, hostility promoted by the general evolution of the regime, was on the increase. Though syndicalists within fascism led a campaign against traditional liberalism and dreamed of a radical transformation of the social and economic order, their cause was hopeless. Adherents of the former Nationalist party declared against all experimentation; behind them were the conservatives who wanted in fascism a movement of reaction. Attitudes toward Sorelismo, in these circumstances, were bound to be affected. Even before the March on Rome and, in fact, even before the war, suspicion of Sorelismo had been marked in nationalist quarters. As then, Sorelismo was now invariably associated with proletarian syndicalism and was only grudgingly admitted (if at all) to have had any influence on the coming of fascism or any relevance to its future course.

The policy of opportunism and concessions to industry came at the beginning of the fascist regime. It was launched with agreements reached at the Palazzo Chigi (1923) and Palazzo Vidoni (1925).[116] These established permanent liaison between the government and big industry. All strikes and lockouts, moreover, were prohibited by the law of 1926. During these years the battle was also fought within the fascist syndicates. The outcome of the contest between Rossoni and the Commission of Eighteen on a "mixed syndicalism" that provided for some measure of syndicalist autonomy was a foregone conclusion. Rossoni's position progressively deteriorated, representing the defeat of the "revolutionary" element in fascism stemming from syndicalism and left-wing interventionism.[117]

When the system of corporatism began to take shape in 1926, the assault on Sorelismo began in earnest, a fact that suggests that Sorel's influence was regarded as no small matter and was identified with proletarian syndicalism.[118] In a series of articles and reports from 1926 to 1928 (two climactic years of the corporate state) Giuseppe Bottai, minister of corporations and later minister of culture, expressed the utmost disdain for the syndicalism that still remained under Sorel's influence.[119] It was foolish, he argued, to look for the origins of fascism or fascist syndicalism in these circles. At the heart of the matter was the role of the state. Proletarian syndicalism had opposed the state; fascism demanded it. In an editorial in the influential and outspoken *Critica fascista* (founded in 1927 by Bottai) syndicalist organizers were excoriated for failing to see the difference between a corporatism that had fascist origins and a syndicalism whose origins were socialist.[120]

In 1928 the journalist Ugo d'Andrea, writing in the *Giornale d'Italia,* rejected the assertion that Italian nationalism had ever borne any relation to the syndicalism of Corridoni.[121] All they had in common was a contempt for the liberal democratic regime. Never had Corradini, Rocco, or Coppola the slightest sympathy for Sorel. Gramsci noted an even more marked hostility to

Sorel in the Italian press about 1929, after Croce in 1927 began the publication of Sorel's letters in the *Critica*.[122] There were particularly violent responses in letters to the *Critica* and in an article by Arturo Stranghellini, novelist and journalist, in the *Italia letteraria*. Lorenzo Giusso in the *Critica fascista* in 1929 could see in Sorel's work no more than the demolition of bourgeois ideologies and in Sorel "a dark and ominous horseman of the Apocalypse."[123] Others were even more explicit in their criticism. Arnaldo Fioretti in the *Lavoro fascista*, organ of the fascist labor movement, wrote in 1930, "We derive neither from Sorel nor Marx.... Syndicalism is and can be no more than an aspect of the general organization of fascism."[124] Somewhat more perceptively, Carlo Curcio in the *Resto del Carlino* in 1930 recognized that eight years earlier Sorel had been viewed as an apostle and liberator.[125] This was no longer the case. Sorel's criticism of democracy remained fundamental but his career had concluded with Lenin and the International. It was Mussolini who had worked the "miracle." He had brought syndicalism and the state together. "He went far beyond Sorel."

The "Rossoni affair" took place in the midst of the fray. The battle between Rossoni and Il Duce occurred in the winter of 1928–1929 over the leadership and direction of the fascist syndicates.[126] The break in the party over the issues was serious because it developed along class lines. By January 1929 Rossoni was beaten. He was deprived of the leadership of the syndicates and was "promoted" to membership in the Fascist Grand Council. The national organization of syndicates was dissolved and in its place appeared six organizations, each representing a branch of economic activity and tied closely to corresponding employers' organizations. With the resignation of Rossoni, every element of freedom that had remained in fascist syndicalism was broken.

Among groups opposed to the fascist regime there were also signs of Sorelismo, though by no means in all quarters of antifascism. Communism had been embattled against the established order even before 1922. With the arrival of fascism to power, elements in the entire spectrum from communism to liberalism were in opposition. Communism had been revolutionary since its origin. The same tendency now more or less appeared in a radical liberalism— not without the invocation of Sorel's name. Any sustained and systematic challenge to fascism within Italy (Sorelian or otherwise), however, was not destined to survive the censorship and repression that came after 1925.

After it was burned out by the fascists in 1922, the *Ordine nuovo* of Turin ceased publication for two years. Gramsci himself left Italy to work for the Communist International in Moscow and Vienna, returning in 1924.[127] He was joined by Amadeo Bordiga and Antonio Graziadei in re-establishing the *Ordine nuovo* as a bimonthly review. Berth promptly appeared as one of its contributors.[128] The review attempted to breathe new life into the communist movement but was so harassed that it appeared only intermittently before it ceased publication altogether in 1925. Arrested in 1926 after the passage of the Exceptional Laws, Gramsci was found guilty of treason in 1928 and sentenced to twenty years' imprisonment.[129] In 1927 he began to plan his celebrated *Quaderni del carcere.* There were studies applying Marxism to Italian history and culture. By the 1930s his "prison notebooks" were to reveal an even deeper interest in Sorel than in his younger years.

Another indication of the persistence of Sorelismo in Italian communist quarters was evidenced in the *Stato operaio* of Milan, which under the direction of Togliatti briefly attempted in 1923 to continue Gramsci's work.[130] Gramsci, in fact, occasionally published there. The 1924 issue announcing Lenin's death republished in full Sorel's "Pour Lénine."[131] Sorel's friendship for the Italian proletariat, it was asserted, was "beyond dispute." His prophecy, moreover, had come true: Russian bolshevism had overcome the assault of the "international capitalist brigands." In 1925 the *Stato operaio* and in 1926 the *Quarto stato,* also of Milan (which appeared only for several months), were forced to end publication. In 1927 the *Stato operaio* reappeared as a monthly published by Italian communists in exile in Paris, where Togliatti continued the struggle against fascism, though without demonstrating any interest in Sorel.

The *Rivoluzione liberale,* though not communist, was in some respects the true successor to the *Ordine nuovo;* moreover, its interest in Sorel was marked. It was established in February 1922 by the twenty-one-year-old Piero Gobetti, the drama critic of the burned-out *Ordine nuovo.* Gobetti proclaimed himself a "liberal."[132] But he had inherited, he wrote, the "Sorelian spirit," at least the "healthy part of it." He aimed to "radicalize" liberalism. Gobetti assembled an elite of antifascists of all persuasions that included Max Ascoli, Gaetano Salvemini, Guido de Ruggerio, Carlo Rosselli, and Luigi Salvatorelli. His contributors also included Berth, Labriola, Prezzolini, and Missiroli, all (at the moment) also hostile to fascism.

Gobetti took as the foundation of the *Rivoluzione* an integral and vigorous vision of the Risorgimento.[133] Liberalism must aim at the renewal of the Risorgimento by the active participation of the masses in the life of the state and nation. Italian liberalism thus far had failed not only to produce a ruling class, but to create a modern economy and to provide vehicles for a direct expression of liberty. Though no Marxist or socialist, Gobetti saw a "liberating" spirit at work in the Bolshevik Revolution. For these reasons, he admired Gramsci and other communists who in 1920 and 1921 had worked for freely elected workers' councils in the factories of Turin. Gobetti, moreover, hoped that the common threat from fascism would bring liberals and Marxists together.

On December 14, 1922, the *Rivoluzione* published a memorial issue devoted entirely to Sorel as a "liberator of the human spirit." The issue included the first comprehensive bibliography of Sorel's works ever published, listing some 114 items.[134] Notwithstanding the common admiration for Sorel, a wide diversity of opinion was expressed by the contributors. All recognized Italy's special debt to Sorel for having determined the character of current political and intellectual debate.[135] Berth, Cesare Spellanzon, and Natalino Sapegno each claimed Sorel for the proletariat, praised him for supporting the bolsheviks in their darkest hour, and berated both French and Italian socialism for having ignored him. Pareto and Lanzillo, who also contributed to the memorial issue, were little concerned with the proletariat. Both exhibited far greater interest in Sorel's "search for truth," his flexibility and "lack of program." Both studiously avoided any reference to fascism.

Gobetti's interest in Sorel did not extend beyond the general outlines of Sorel's thought. The most vital aspect of a movement, Gobetti agreed, was the creation of "myths of action" and the accompanying "tragic revolutionary faith."[136] As Sorel had labored to point out, the most energetic force in the modern world was the workers' movement, the sole force capable of the conquest of "a new civilization." How the working-class movement was to be won over to liberalism, even a radical liberalism, was never clear in Gobetti's writing. Sorel continued to be a frequent subject of discussion in the *Rivoluzione,* and a number of his articles were published posthumously.[137] The claims made on Sorel by fascists were denied, most vigorously by Salvatore Vitale in May 1924.[138] Fascist syndicalism was at the "opposite pole" of *"sindacalismo sorelliano."* Where in fascism was "the scission, the new spiritual values, and the *morale* of producers"?

The *Rivoluzione* progressively assumed a more hostile antifascist posture. It engaged in lively polemics not only with Malaparte's *Conquista* but also with leading fascist hierarchs.[139] Mussolini would not tolerate this for long, nor would he tolerate the formation of "Rivoluzione liberale" groups in Turin, Milan, Rome, and Naples. Gobetti was beaten several times by fascist police. On November 25, 1925, the *Rivoluzione liberale* was suppressed.[140] Gobetti fled to Paris into exile. He died within a few months (in February 1926) of influenza.

Beyond the activities of Gramsci and Gobetti there was little sign of a systematic or organized antifascist Sorelismo in the twenties. The prewar Sorelians who opposed fascism after the March on Rome were to turn in rather different directions. Each in his own way, however, remained faithful to Sorel.

Leone was an intransigent antifascist from the start, who had also turned against the new Russian regime. In *Il Neo-Marxismo: Sorel e Marx,* published in 1923, he once again held up Sorel as an object of veneration, as the man who had brought an "end to all schools," an end to all ideologies, and a transposition of Marx's doctrines from a "logico-economic basis" to the terrain of "practical psychology."[141] Leone now considered the Communist party as something inimical to the development of the "soviet" or "syndicalist" element in the Russian regime. He saw conflict ahead between the state, run by the party and dedicated to a program of "state capitalism," and the workers' soviets. Leone had never really abandoned his prewar syndicalism and remained as opposed as ever to statism, whether fascist or communist. He was to perish at the hands of the fascists.[142]

In contrast, Labriola took the road to exile, at least for the moment. He had for some years also asserted his opposition to the new Russian regime, while as parliamentary deputy (from 1924 to 1926) he also continued to be critical of the fascist dictatorship—he had now arrived at the acceptance of "democracy."[143] His *Studio su Marx con appendice di Giorgio Sorel* of 1926 revealed nostalgia for prewar syndicalism, and dwelt on the war and postwar events that had rendered it obsolete.[144] Labriola fled to Paris in 1927.[145] Mussolini had refused a passport and had also opposed his appointment to the University of Messina; Labriola was dismissed from all academic posts, and his home was wrecked. "Those who believe fascism is defending Europe against communism do not reflect that fascism in already communism," he reflected bitterly. Abroad, he quarreled incessantly with antifascists of all kinds. In 1928 Labriola joined Valois in Paris in the establishment of the neo-syndicalist *Cahiers bleus*.

Though Prezzolini, like Labriola, had collaborated with Gobetti's *Rivoluzione liberale,* he soon withdrew, reluctant to be identified with a full-blown antifascism. For several years he continued to direct the Voce publishing-house in Florence, emphasizing works on the origins of Mussolini's regime. His own study, published in 1925, viewed fascism as a postwar revolt of the middle class, characterized by nationalism and conversatism.[146] Fascism, he argued, was nevertheless led by those who had matured under the spell of prewar syndicalism and Sorelismo. Prezzolini had little more to say about Sorel, and although it was critical of fascism, the study was by no means an antifascist polemic. Prezzolini, nevertheless, left for Paris in 1925, remaining until 1929 and departing shortly thereafter for New York to head the Casa Italiana at Columbia University.[147]

Still another response to the coming of fascism was that of Missiroli. He had explicitly identified himself with Gobetti's "Manifesto" in 1922. "My support," he asserted, "is unconditional."[148] The problems that tortured Gobetti, he noted, were identical with those that had troubled him in *La Monarchia socialista* of 1914. A "modern state" can be created only in those nations that had surpassed the Catholic idea by way of the Reformation. Those states not the direct and genuine product of a spiritual revolution were obliged to oscillate between an abstract democracy that degenerated into demagogy and a class authoritarianism that negated the idea of liberty. Needless to say, Missiroli was engaged during the twenties in lively debate with Malaparte.[149] Like Malaparte, Missiroli proclaimed the need for renewal, and renewal could be only the work of Sorelian myths. Missiroli, nevertheless, was to experience a change of heart: from a liberal opponent of fascism he became a fellow-traveler and supporter of the regime.[150] What appeared to be crucial in this transformation (no mean feat, for Missiroli's opposition had been not only to fascism but to Mussolini personally) were the Lateran Treaties of 1929. *Date a Cesare* of that year, concerned with Mussolini's solution of the Roman problem, was followed by *Cosa deve l'Italia a Mussolini* the following year.[151] Mussolini had found a way out of the impasse. Missiroli now became an active propagandist of the fascist regime, soon to present a new view of the role Sorel had played in its formation.

Chapter

15

The 1930s

The principal factors operative in the development of Sorelian thought and activity in the 1930s are easily delineated: the introduction of Soviet planning, the world economic crisis, Hitler's arrival to power and the general spread of fascism, and the danger once again of war. All combined to provide renewed stimulus to the conviction of a *"crise totale de la civilisation."* Yet, it was during the course of the 1930s that the Sorelian movement began to exhibit serious weaknesses in France, while it all but disappeared by the end of the decade in Italy. In France it seems clear that, for Sorelians, communism had led to unacceptable statist distortions. While the same may be partially true of fascism in France, something of a Sorelian ferment did continue in this quarter. During the thirties fascist and pseudo-fascist movements proliferated. Valois's Faisceau had "peaked" too soon; the Sorelian ferment was now to be more dispersed. Sorelian activity now appeared also in the movements of neo-syndicalism and *"planisme."* Only here were new recruits to be found in any number. Here, moreover, interest in Sorel changed markedly in quality. In Italy, apart from official ritualistic references to Mussolini's origins, the repression of the regime effectively ruled out new departures in Sorelismo in either fascism or antifascism. Meanwhile, the ranks of Sorelismo in France and Italy had been reduced by disillusionment or death. With comparatively few new recruits, by the eve of the war it was clear that the Sorelian movement had failed to extend itself much beyond the generation that had known Sorel personally.

I

In revolutionary circles on the French left the *Révolution prolétarienne* continued substantially unchanged the editorial policy initiated in the twenties. Given the times, its rigidity was remarkable. New groups and reviews, of course, periodically appeared in the thirties to explore alternative modes of thought and action, but their doctrinal foundations were uncertain, a weakness of considerable consequence in an age of ideologies.

Monatte and Louzon, both prewar syndicalists, refused to alter the course of the *Révolution prolétarienne*. The title of an article by Monatte (whose work dominated the review), "Le Syndicalisme de 1906 ne peut pas mourir," published in 1937, was symptomatic of the policy and character of the review.[1] Throughout the thirties the review carried on its inside cover the proclamation: "Neither parliamentarism nor fascism. All power to the workers! All power to the syndicates! Down with national defense! Down with military alliances! Down with communist treason!"[2] The militants idealized the syndicalism of the first decade of the century, which Sorel had himself admired and which had inspired his *Réflexions*. The leading theme in the pages of the review, however, was Trotsky's case against Stalin. Again, it was Berth's numerous articles, published until 1937, that continued to give to the review a Sorelian aspect.

Berth seemed always to be defending his *maître* against attack from all sides, but his views are not without interest. With Hitler's arrival to power, he saw the coming of "a new Middle Ages" of which bolshevism, fascism, and the new Nazi regime were the foretaste.[3] Bolshevism he called the "twin brother" of fascism, and fascism was the exaltation of the state.[4] The choice for France after the riots of February 6, 1934, Berth thought was between "caesarism" and "anarchy," and by anarchy he meant the syndicalism of Pelloutier and Griffuelhes. Noting that Sorel had been charged with being sympathetic to fascism, Berth asserted that Sorel had regarded Russia, Italy, and Germany since the war as "proletarian countries." The proletariat had so asserted itself here that nationalism was obliged to be "socialist." Only in this sense, he averred, could Sorel be regarded as a champion of "fascism." As a tribute to his *maître* he published in 1935 a collection of Sorel's early essays, under the title *D'Aristote à Marx*.[5] Also in that year he denounced efforts to create a "popular front" of the left as "a new fraud"—a purely political unity could be no substitute for working-class unity.[6]

In 1935 the *Révolution prolétarienne* became deeply involved in an altercation with Valois.[7] Valois, who now considered himself a man of the left, was attempting to participate in a union of proletarian interest groups that were against war.[8] The *Révolution prolétarienne* objected to Valois because of his background. Berth, however, came to Valois's defense in Valois's own newspaper, the *Nouvel âge*. In the last years before the war there were indications that Berth was suffering from deep despair and isolation. His last article in the *Révolution prolétarienne*, signed May 1938, argued the existence of a competition between a "Paris-London Axis" and a "Rome-Berlin Axis" to save capitalism.[9] Under these circumstances, what hope was there for the proletarian revolution? During his years with Monatte's group he had written little in direct support of their policies. In any case, Berth's final studies before his death were to appear in Valois's *Nouvel âge*.

The *Nouvel âge* was another of Valois's enterprises, starting as a monthly in January 1931, a somewhat literary successor to the *Cahiers bleus*.[10] As contributors Valois had now acquired an assortment of international literary celebrities, among them Ilya Erenbourg, Knut Hamsun, Eugene O'Neill, John Dos Passos, Upton Sinclair, and André Malraux. Except for Valois and Berth, only a few contributors demonstrated any appreciable interest in Sorel.[11] At the outset Valois demanded a "society of producers" led by an elite of workers, technicians, and intellectuals opposed to both bolshevism and fascism as unacceptable statist solutions to problems of the modern world.[12] The February 1934 riots he denounced as a plutocratic and fascist plot, and he urged a temporary alliance with parliamentary democracy and socialism.[13] By 1936, however, the review addressed itself more directly to current affairs. It gave at least lukewarm support to the Popular Front; it was unqualified, however, in its demands for aid to Loyalist Spain. It also demanded "a social democracy of consumers by communes and federation of communes, then of peoples, then of humanity itself." It demanded a "constructive revolutionary socialism." The debt to Sorel was once again explicit: "The movement represented by the *Nouvel âge* owes most to Sorel."[14]

The monthly ceased publication in 1936, but since May 8, 1934, a weekly newspaper had been appearing under the same name and organized, as the monthly had been, as a cooperative. The principal contributors and mainstays of what Valois now called a "movement" were Berth, Béracha, and Rodriguez (who had all served on the *Cahiers bleus* and *Chantiers coopératifs*) and the newcomer Jacques Rennes. The demand was for the "République syndicale," the banner Valois had raised after the collapse of the Faisceau.[15] Valois was against capitalism and fascism. Once again he declared his movement "revolutionary" and engaged in organizational activities with groups established at Nantes, Nancy, and Reims, among others. The *Nouvel âge,* meanwhile, attacked the *grande presse,* banks, and trusts, holding them responsible for the February riots. Valois's support of the Popular Front continued, though grudgingly, as the elections of May 1936 approached. He demanded nationalization of credit and basic industries and promoted a planned and rational organization of the economy. Here, as elsewhere during the thirties, the *planisme* of Henri de Man aroused considerable interest.

The years 1935 and 1936 were years of controversy for the *Nouvel âge* over what came to be called the "*cas* Valois."[16] In May 1935 the *Révolution prolétarienne* attempted to organize a "union against war" among groups of the left.[17] Some twenty organizations responded by forming a committee, but at a "national conference" in August 1935 at St. Denis a near-riot took place when the *Révolution prolétarienne* refused to participate because Valois had been nominated for a committee position. Valois refused to withdraw, and was in fact elected.[18] Monatte and Chambelland, representatives of the syndicalist review, nevertheless succeeded in wrecking the organization by refusing to cooperate; they then resigned. Valois, meanwhile, had become once again the object of a vituperative campaign launched by the *Révolution prolétarienne.*

His prewar and postwar activities on behalf of the Action Française were reviewed, as was his Faisceau interlude. He was denounced as a cynical adventurer who could not be trusted, whose entire career had been devoted to the destruction of the workingmen's movement. Moreover, he was one of those responsible for the murder of Jaurès, he was Mussolini's disciple, and his Faisceau was the spiritual ancestor of the Croix de Feu.

Berth, whose relations with the *Révolution prolétarienne* were strained (it had refused to publish his "letter" on the "*cas* Valois"), came to Valois's defense in an open letter in the *Nouvel âge* on March 5, 1936.[19] Valois introduced him to his readers: Berth and he were "the two most fervent friends of the thought of Georges Sorel." The "*cas* Valois" had issued directly from the immense deception which followed the Dreyfus affair and the tendency for antidemocrats of all kinds inspired by Sorel to join forces. In his letter Berth asserted that he had known Valois for twenty-five years and had never doubted his soundness of character. They had founded the Cercle Proudhon together, which Berth now admitted was a mistake (it should be recalled that Berth had used the pseudonym "Jean Darville" during his monarchist period). Throughout his career Valois had pursued one goal, that of emancipation of the workers. Even within the Action Française, Valois had always fought for the working class. Valois's politics were a direct product of the Dreyfus era, as was Péguy's invective against Jaurès. Valois may have been naive, but he was not perfidious. The fact that he turned from right to left was proof enough. Passing from left to right was what was common, almost banal. Berth maintained that he had tried to convince Valois not to try to impose himself as a leader in the "union against war," but had failed. It was not easy, Berth concluded, for certain men to be happy with a secondary rank.

The interest demonstrated in Sorel by the "school" of the *Nouvel âge* was consistent and considerable. Valois himself continued to publish widely and asserted once again that, notwithstanding his political "transformations," he had always remained a "Sorelian syndicalist" and a friend of the worker.[20] A collection of open letters suggested that fascism was a "passing phenomenon," that the future would belong to some form of socialism. The open letter to Déat, the socialist turned Neo-Socialist and later fascist, claimed that Valois had dissolved the Faisceau because "revolution was impossible with the middle classes," a class whose politics could only be antiproletarian, one that had emasculated every movement of which it had been a part—Boulangism, Briandism, Millerandism, radicalism:[21]

Do you know, Déat, the number of men that I have led from the right to syndicalist, cooperative, or socialist positions where I now am? . . . I know exactly, a dozen at the most.[22]

Whoever relied on the "middle classes," he warned Déat, was inevitably at the mercy of secret subscribers.[23] The cashbox can be filled only by the plutocracy.

Then "the game is over." One ends like Mussolini or Hitler. A letter reminded Jouhaux, the CGT leader who had been among Valois's attackers, that Valois had been a comrade of Pelloutier and a disciple of Sorel.[24] He doubted, however, that Jouhaux had revolutionary intentions. Valois suggested, sarcastically, the multiplication of strikes and the training of shock troops. As for the abuse he had received at the hands of Monatte, Louzon, and other syndicalists, he wrote: "I am the more satisfied for having fought ... under capitalism under a variety of flags than having been its ally or servant under the flag of the Revolution."[25] An article on violence occasioned by Nazi violence maintained that Europeans in the past twenty years had grown accustomed to the "odor of massacre."[26] This "animal violence" was not what Sorel or he had been preaching. Violence must be directed at institutions, at the banks and trusts, which must be struck down mercilessly. As the international and domestic crisis worsened, Valois attacked the Blum government: Blum's non-interventionist policies had endangered the Spanish Loyalists, and he had "abolished" the right to strike.[27] His hopes for revolution waning while the danger of war increased, Valois demanded a "popular blockade" of the "racist bloc" and the eventual reorganization of Europe along federalist lines.[28]

Berth, too, in the *Nouvel âge,* in response to European events of the late thirties, seemed utterly despondent. He speculated that had Sorel known of more recent communist or fascist violence, he would not have approved of these regimes.[29] For Sorel, violence was intransigence, a way of separating two worlds, two orders. The vulgarities committed by Stalin and Hitler had nothing to do with Sorelian violence. When late in 1938 the *Révolution prolétarienne* had refused to publish his articles on the Munich Agreement, Berth published them instead in the *Nouvel âge.*[30] Working-class internationalism had been defeated. Not only had France, he cried, capitulated before Hitler but so too had the revolution itself. "Our pacifist syndicalists do not seem to understand." Berth's break with the *Révolution prolétarienne* seemed complete. On January 25, 1939, shortly after his return to Catholicism, Berth died. "I can say," wrote Valois, "that insofar as I am concerned, ... Berth has been the conscience of the *Nouvel âge.*"[31]

Younger members of the *Nouvel âge* group were far less preoccupied with defending Sorel than with searching for continuing relevance in his thought. Béracha, for example, who had been Valois's associate on the *Cahiers bleus,* considered himself a disciple of both Sorel and Valois. In a study of 1931 he saw in Valois's *"démocratie syndicale"* an advance over Sorelian syndicalism— Valois was far closer to present-day realities.[32] Another work by Béracha, the *Marxisme après Marx* of 1937, was based on notes prepared for a projected "École de Georges Sorel" in Toulouse.[33] In it he attempted to revise both Marx and Sorel.[34] The struggle between social systems, he asserted, placed "generations," not classes, in opposition. What was required was a "myth" capable of commanding conviction, a myth capable of implementing the solution to practical problems for no more than a quarter of a century, a generation. Rennes, on the other hand, in a dispute in 1934 with the *Homme réel,* a syndicalist review that had turned *"planiste,"* took issue with the argument that Sorel's myth of the general strike might be transformed into a "myth of the plan."[35] No myth constructed around a plan should mean the abandonment of the strike in the interests of the plan. What would happen to the proletariat if it were confronted by an adversary armed to the teeth? Rennes published a full-length study of Sorel in 1936.[36] In it he wrote only of Sorel as a syndicalist. Neither Lenin nor Mussolini could be regarded as his disciple, and under no circumstances could the bourgeoisie claim Sorel as one of their own. Studies Rennes published in 1938 and 1939 paralleled the evolution of the *Nouvel âge*: Sorel and Valois were the most authentic interpreters of Marx on the contemporary scene; their movement aimed at a federation of communes constituting a republic of consumers and producers; and the "heroism" which in the past was devoted to war must in the future be directed toward peaceful pursuits. This, he asserted, Sorel had "always wanted."[37]

In its final years of publication the *Nouvel âge* changed rapidly in quality and temper. Though it became a daily in 1938, it possessed only a modest circulation. It turned against the Popular Front government as a "prisoner" of capitalism.[38] It remained "revolutionary" or "Sorelian" only in the vaguest way: its principal concern was the double danger of fascism and war. Valois was *"anti-Munichois"*—he accused Daladier of trying to wreck the Franco-Soviet pact—and he still demanded a *"blocus économique"* as the only way to prevent the fascist powers from making war.[39] With the Nazi-Soviet pact, he demanded that the French Communist party be outlawed and bitterly turned on the Soviet Union.[40] In the months after the outbreak of war, reviewing the rapid spread of "totalitarianism" (both left and right) throughout Europe, he openly proclaimed his faith in "democracy": he hoped eventually for the federation of Europe and the establishment of regimes that would assure the "liberty" and the "dignity of the human person."[41] The *Nouvel âge* continued publication into 1940. Notwithstanding the heavy hand of the censor, it was clear that Valois had renounced most of his past. At the end, though with faint hope, he looked to a postwar world in which syndicalism would triumph.[42] The *Nouvel âge* ended publication in June 1940.

The *"planisme"* in vogue in the thirties also owed something to Sorel.[43] In reviews that sometimes lasted no more than a few years and never possessed more than a few thousand subscribers, both contributors and ideas circulated more or less freely. Here was a response to the economic and attendant intellectual crisis that focused not only on Soviet planning but on Italian, German, and even American efforts to deal with the ravages of the Great Depression. On the subject of planning it was de Man's writing that frequently served as the center of attention, but for the most part Proudhon and, especially, Sorel (although one encounters frequent references to Nietzsche) provided the intellectual tone of planist reviews. These reviews generally endeavored to be politically open-ended. Their aim was "*renouvellement*," to liberate nationalism from its "bourgeois" character and socialism from its "proletarian" cast. On close examination it is clear that planist reviews, especially after the February 1934 riots, were unable completely to sever ties with the traditional left or right. The reviews were all more or less "revolutionary." They demonstrated no liking for the methods of republican democracy and were unconvinced that planning could be undertaken in a capitalist regime, but they possessed no clear idea of how the revolution was to take place and no clear conception of what might serve as the vehicle of the revolution.

Plans, which appeared in January 1931, was the first of these reviews. It was edited by Philippe Lamour, a former member of the Faisceau, and Lagardelle was its chief financial support and leading contributor. Others included Le Corbusier and Walter Gropius, who published articles on modern architecture and city planning. The first issue, carrying quotations from Lenin and Mussolini, introduced the review as an effort to fuse various aspects of the Soviet system, Italian fascism, and lessons drawn from industrial America.[44] The focus was on planning, and technocratic overtones were prominent, but *Plans* also professed to be the heir of the prewar *Mouvement socialiste* of Lagardelle and Sorel.

Lagardelle's articles dominated *Plans.* By 1914 he had become a reformist socialist and since the war he had become interested in regionalism and syndicalism within the existing state. He had in 1929 published a work on southwest France, a study of how the Aquitaine region could be developed by means of electrification.[45] Something of his prewar solicitude for the proletariat remained, but little of his former preoccupation with revolution was now in evidence. He continued to demand the end of "abstract man" and to urge the founding of a new social order characterized by syndicalism and regionalism.[46] Moreover, his prewar syndicalist disdain of the state was also very much in evidence: syndicalism and regionalism would culminate in a "nonpolitical state" reduced in function to accountability, control, and administration. A Sorelian emphasis (without reference to Sorel) also persisted in his coupling of the need for a "general line" with the role of creative minorities and the importance of "action," and in his conception of work as a "creative act." Above all, it was in industry that Lagardelle saw the hope of the future: "Industrial civilization will save the world from material and moral exhaustion."

When Lagardelle was asked by the Daladier government in 1933 to join the French embassy in Rome in a non-official capacity, *Plans* terminated publication.[47] Mussolini, in a well-known article on fascism in the *Enciclopedia italiana,* had recently named Sorel, Péguy, and Lagardelle as having played the leading part in the prewar origins of the Italian regime.[48] Lagardelle during the next several years came to know Mussolini personally. He participated in the final discussions which led to the establishment of the corporatist regime in Italy, no longer seeing any conflict between syndicalism and corporatism. In 1935 Lagardelle's article on "fascism" in the *Encyclopédie française* argued that fascism was a new creation transcending both liberalism and socialism: from liberalism it took the virtue of initiative and private property and from socialism the requirements of a collective order.[49] Individual interests were in this way placed at the service of the collectivity and the "citizen" was replaced by the "real man." As for Sorel, Lagardelle wrote that only a "spiritual thread" united fascism and prewar syndicalism; the rest had been translated into modern terms. After the Ethiopian war, Lagardelle's position at the French embassy deteriorated and he returned to France in 1937.

The *Homme réel* appeared in 1934 as a review dedicated to a "constructive syndicalism"; after a few issues it turned planist.[50] Though it stressed ties with the *Révolution prolétarienne,* it claimed to be above Marxian sectarian controversy.[51] Its editor, Pierre Ganivet, and its leading contributors, René Belin, Robert Lacoste, and Jean Duret, were CGT officials. Several of Valois's supporters in the twenties, as well as Berth (listed as a "principal collaborator") and Lagardelle, also published here—Lagardelle, in fact, may have exercised "considerable influence" on the review during his service in Rome.[52]

A series of editorials asserted (as Lagardelle had in *Plans*) that the "abstract man" must give way to the "real man."[53] The abstract man was the "citizen," the creation of parliamentary liberalism, who was consulted and who governed in the name of philosophical principles. The real man was rooted in *"métier, commune, region."* A syndicalism which was antistatist, neither exclusive nor separatist, but aimed at a "new humanism" and "industrial democracy" was required.[54] When the review became planist, Le Corbusier also became a frequent contributor. Entire issues were devoted to planning in October 1934 and June 1935. By now both anticommunist and antifascist, the review was pro-Loyalist during the Spanish Civil War and against the Munich agreement in 1938.

The *Homme réel* demonstrated considerable interest in Sorel. Duret, especially, though he considered the myth of the general strike outmoded, nevertheless regarded Sorel's concept of myth of continuing relevance:

> To employ Sorelian terminology, the realization of the plan must become a "social myth," arousing the energy of the ... masses and permitting them to triumph over the formidable obstacles they will encounter.[55]

"The plan" might serve as a guide after power had been taken, but it was also an indispensable instrument in its conquest. Lagardelle also edited and published in the *Homme réel* the letters Sorel had written to him before their break (which had appeared the previous year in Italy in the *Educazione fascista*).[56] If Berth's articles repeated what he had written elsewhere,[57] those of Lacoste affirmed the review's relation to Sorel: its economic federalism resting on a syndicalist base had been Sorel's invention—"all power to the syndicates."[58] The *Homme réel's planisme,* and eventually its federalism, bore little relation to the *Révolution prolétarienne,* but its interest in Sorel persisted.[59] What was unusual, however, was that Sorel was acclaimed in a review that professed to be "humanistic" and "democratic." This was, indeed, novel, though not more so than Valois's *Nouvel âge* in its final years. As the war approached, issues of the periodical appeared less and less regularly; in 1939 publication ceased.

Somewhat less *planiste* in emphasis, though still preoccupied with a reordering of society, were two reviews, one initially federalist, the other corporatist. In both, characteristically, though there was little sympathy for liberal democracy or bourgeois capitalism, the politics at the start were open-ended, but the riots of February 1934 were decisive in producing a turn to the right.

The *Ordre nouveau* appeared in 1933 as the heir to *Plans,* directed by Arnaud Dandieu and Robert Aron, who were joined by Alexandre Marc, Pierre Dominique, and Denis de Rougement. Although Dandieu's death at 35 came soon after the review's inception, his efforts had led to its establishment and his work initially inspired it.[60]

The review avoided all statist temptations and maintained a strict independence of political parties.[61] The review called for the spontaneous creation of syndical and federal groupings and the division of the economy into private and planned sectors: "The *Ordre nouveau* places institutions at the service of personality, subordinates the state to man." As for Sorel, Dandieu wrote: "In the shadow of Jaurès, the . . . public . . . could not distinguish Sorel any better than Baudelaire could be distinguished in the shadow of Victor Hugo."[62] "Pessimism," Dandieu believed, was at the center of Sorel's thought.[63] Sorel had reintroduced the link between the principle of "violence" and that of the "sublime" in human action. He had simultaneously announced bolshevism and fascism. Dandieu was, nevertheless, repelled by the oppression and distortions produced by the state in these regimes. If the revolution were to aim at syndicalist and federalist goals, then the economic transformation underway would promote the process of human liberation.[64] The machine and the division of labor were, in fact, creating a new kind of worker. The more work became mechanical, the more man could develop his intelligence and personality. Dandieu's arguments opened the way to the "personalism" of Emmanuel Mounier. Indeed, some of his collaborators left after his death to join the *Esprit,* which had been established in 1932.[65]

No single source of inspiration was claimed by the *Ordre nouveau* after Dandieu's death. A "Bibliography of Revolution" listed as sources Robespierre, Nietzsche, Lenin, Proudhon, Marx, and the Fascist Labor Charter, as well as Sorel. Sorel, however, consistently received the most attention.[66] The passage in the *Réflexions* in which Sorel spoke of "unlearning" was cited as a necessary precondition to any great revolutionary effort: "One who does not at first learn how to unlearn cannot aid us in clearing the road to the new order."

After 1934 the review became more openly hostile to the Republic, and its syndicalism and federalism were transformed into full-blown corporatism.[67] The *Ordre nouveau* now not only preached the virtues of a managerial elite and became explicitly planist; it also extended its federalism from the national to the international arena. Though interest in Sorel persisted, it tended henceforth to be somewhat perfunctory. Sorel's view of the working class no longer applied, it was asserted, for class conflict had become depersonalized and had lost its heroic character.[68] On the other hand, the review stressed Sorel's admonition regarding the dangers to a revolutionary movement from participation in democratic institutions, even the vote—it urged its readers not to vote.[69] It reaffirmed Sorel's strictures concerning the dangers of decadence and urged the pursuit of the "heroic life." The review continued publication until 1938, remaining to the end opposed to communist and fascist statism.

In 1934 the *Homme nouveau* began publication. It was economically anticapitalist but politically open-ended. It was also planist and technocratic but its director, Georges Roditi, declared himself for the "national and social revolution," "the economic and social politics of the extreme left," and "the intellectual and moral universe of traditionalism."[70] Its contributors included Drieu La Rochelle, Andreu, and Déat. Articles here abounded on the Soviet and Italian fascist regimes, as well as on the American New Deal. In general, Sorel was viewed as a link between Proudhon and de Man.[71] Déat especially saw in "the plan" a new conception of action, neither reformist nor insurrectionary socialism, both of which were "old-fashioned." A survey initiated in the first issue of the review indicated something of its essential thrust: "Do you believe that a new social order can take as its task not only the work of economic liberation, but, even more, the creation of a superior type of humanity, of a new man?"[72]

It was the young Pierre Andreu whose studies contributed most to the Sorelian bent of the review. Andreu was then also a contributor to *Esprit* and *Combat,* deploring the failure of the Action Française to continue its prewar efforts to win working-class support.[73] In the *Homme nouveau* Andreu reviewed Sorel's long-forgotten study of 1889 on the trial of Socrates.[74] Socrates had appeared to Sorel, argued Andreu, as an "anti-Homer," the destroyer of heroic myths. Sorel, to be sure, was on the side of Socrates' accusers, but Sorel had also maintained, asserted Andreu, that conservatives had always erred in their insistence that "heroic generations" could be formed only by "traditional myths." Conservatives still failed to understand the way in which the hatred of the working class for their bourgeois employers could also serve the purposes of conservation. Andreu also noted that Sorel had disliked socialist intellectuals because they destroyed the purity of the working-class movement.[75] "He is against socialist intellectuals, he is not against bourgeois intellectuals, . . . Renan, . . . Bergson, . . . Maurras." The *Homme nouveau* appeared until 1938, when it was reconstituted under a new title and dropped all interest in Sorel.

What remained of Sorelian activity in France in the thirties was to be found largely among several prewar friends and associates whose politics had long been somewhat marginal to the monarchist movement. They had been drawn to Italian fascism in the twenties and, except for Valois, they had been interested in literary rather than organizational activities. Among them one may cite Bourget, who still sang the praises of Sorel and Mussolini (rather more so than Maurras) and who continued to deplore the "decadence" of the French bourgeoisie.[76] There was also Johannet, who looked to fascism of the Mussolini or Hitler variety to solve the working-class problem—it was the "politicized and socialized proletariat," not the "worker," who was to be suppressed.[77] Still another was the novelist and playwright Variot, who published the *Propos de Georges Sorel* in 1935; an interview showed him to be sympathetic though critical of the Action Française and rather partial to Italian fascism.[78] Perhaps only in the review *Combat* was there evidence of more recent figures who seemed drawn to Sorel along similar or related lines.

Combat was an intellectual review founded in 1936. Its directors, Jean de Fabrègues and Thierry Maulnier, had recently arrived from the *Réaction,* a monarchist and Catholic effort that had unsuccessfully attempted an "*ouverture à gauche.*" They were joined by Drieu La Rochelle, J.-P. Maxence, Robert Francis, and Andreu in a second effort, this time from a "nationalist" rather than a monarchist standpoint.[79] *Combat* recognized the "social question" and was accordingly "anticapitalist" and "antibourgeois," but it expressed little or no interest in planning.[80] "Nationalism," it asserted, "must resolve the problems from which socialism is born." Its nationalism, moreover, was revolutionary: "A revolutionary attitude in the most complete sense, the most demanding and the most brutal which the word can have, has become the only possible attitude for nationalism."[81] The review demonstrated more than a casual interest in Maurras, La Tour du Pin, Drumont, Proudhon, and, especially, Sorel. Needless to say, it was intensely hostile to the Franco-Soviet pact, the imposition of sanctions on Italy during the Ethiopian war, and the Popular Front government. There was talk in it also of a "solution" to the "Jewish question" that could only be achieved by the suppression of the "democratic and mercantile state."[82]

Here, again, Andreu was the most consistently interested in Sorel. In "Fascisme, 1913" he discussed the prewar Cercle Proudhon, observing that in August 1914 its members had contributed by their heroism to the "*triomphe insolent des démocraties*" and "the ruin of their own hopes."[83] Lagrange, one of the more colorful members of the Cercle whose rigor and violence "terrified" Maurras, was the subject of another article.[84] Andreu also published excerpts from Sorel's writings on "the incomparable treasures of classical culture and the Christian tradition."[85] Andreu's doctrinal position insisted that what was required was a corporatism organically related to the process of production—neither the anarchy of liberalism nor an autocratic state socialism.[86] In neither the CGT nor the CGTU (merged in October 1935) did he perceive any sign that the workers understood their true situation. Andreu expressed little hope that the efforts of *Combat* to reach the workers would succeed.

Drieu La Rochelle, both in *Combat* and elsewhere, continued to acknowledge the leading role that Sorel had played in his intellectual formation. His "lyrical and warlike pessimism" had started with Sorel and by the mid-thirties appeared to end with Mussolini and Hitler.[87] He called himself a "syndicalist" in the manner of Sorel. He admitted that Italian and German fascism had at the outset helped certain economic groups, but these regimes had initiated a process whereby capitalism would eventually be weakened and ultimately destroyed. Moreover, he claimed to see in the heart of the regimes of Mussolini and Hitler "new revolutionary waves" which would restore the syndicalist impulse. "I mean a revolutionary syndicalism of which Sorel and Proudhon are the initiators."[88] By 1937 Drieu had joined Jacques Doriot and the Parti Populaire Française.[89] But when Doriot turned "*Munichois,*" Drieu denounced the PPF in Doriot's newspaper as a "false fascism" subservient to the Nazi: France could not hold her own against Germany without herself becoming truly fascist. "Everything that is alive and acts in this world takes the form of fascism."[90]

The leading theorist of *Combat,* Maulnier, considered the work undertaken by the review as a continuation of the efforts of the Cercle Proudhon.[91] The goal remained unchanged: the formation of an elite to improve the condition of the oppressed, to restore order, and to undertake once again the pursuit of "national grandeur." There are "two violences," the violence of the oppressed and the violence of those who defend their just rights—"it is up to us to unite the two."

II

The 1930s were marked by a continuing decline in Sorelian activities in Italy. Whatever organized elements there may have been in either fascist or antifascist Sorelismo now rapidly dissolved. Sorel's name did not drop entirely out of sight, however; it continued to be invoked, and it remained a subject of controversy. Sorel was also becoming a subject of scholarly study in Italy, long before anything comparable appeared in France. Mussolini was still talking about Sorel. In his celebrated article on fascism under his signature in the *Enciclopedìa italiana* in 1932 Mussolini asserted:

In the great river of fascism are to be found the streams which had their source in Sorel, Péguy, . . . Lagardelle, . . . and groups of Italian syndicalists, in [the] *Pagine libere* of Olivetti, *La Lupa* of Orano and *Divenire sociale* of Enrico Leone.[92]

Though it has been asserted that Gentile may have authored the article (at least in part) one can assume that the argument was not in conflict with Il Duce's own view of fascist origins.[93] In widely publicized newspaper interviews that same year, Mussolini told Émile Schreiber that "Georges Sorel was my *maître*."[94] Aware of the opposition to Sorel within the ranks of the party, Mussolini asserted that he personally could never have demanded the "hemlock" of Sorel. To Émil Ludwig he said much the same.[95] These references to Sorel and others by Mussolini were never supported by an extended discussion of the nature of the indebtedness or that of the fascist movement generally. When they were accompanied by additional comments (on the role of myth or violence, for example), these were neither very deep nor very faithful to the master.[96] "Official biographies," nevertheless, rarely missed an opportunity to insist that Sorel was the "prophet" of fascism and Mussolini was his foremost "disciple."[97] Claims were sometimes made that were without apparent foundation: that the two corresponded, that they had numerous "conversations," that Sorel was one of Mussolini's favorite authors (which might have briefly been true in the first decade of the century). What purpose was to be served by these assertions, in view of the regime's general hostility to Sorel, remains unclear.

There was little, in any case, to support these efforts. Pareto had died in 1923 and Michels had turned to other studies before his death in 1936. Croce had joined the ranks of antifascism. Though he never turned on his former friend, Croce noted in lectures delivered in 1931 before the Academy of Moral and Political Sciences of Naples that irrationalism and activism had caused the disintegration and moral chaos of the twentieth century.[98] Of Sorel's work Croce wrote that it was "born of violence" in pursuit of the "sublime." It was

the construction of a poet thirsting for . . . austerity, . . . sincerity, . . . stubbornly trying to find a hidden fount from which the fresh pure stream would well forth; and tested by reality, his poetry vanished even in his own eyes.[99]

The books of Sorel, he was willing to admit in an interview, had in fact been the "breviary of fascism."[100] "It is there that Mussolini . . . studied the technique of the coup d'état, as M. Malaparte pointed out."

The ranks of the syndicalist professors were now depleted. Olivetti had died. Orano had been elevated to the Senate; he had become an admirer of the Nazis, supported the Italian regime's anti-Semitic campaign, and now rarely mentioned Sorel.[101] But Lanzillo, who held high rank in the Supreme Council on Education in the thirties, was still determined to salvage something of his prewar syndicalism.[102] Suspicious of the all-powerful state, he looked to the formation of "syndicalist consciousness" in the emerging corporate system. There were hints of disillusionment with fascism. In Panunzio's writings, too, in the *Popolo d'Italia,* in scholarly studies, and elsewhere, one finds echoes of the same disillusionment.[103] Though he served as councillor in the Chamber of Fasces and Corporations, Panunzio continued to look back with nostalgia on prewar syndicalism. In it he saw the roots of the fascist regime and, particularly, the source of its concern with moral renovation. Panunzio by 1939 had little to say of Sorel. He wrote only in praise of Mussolini, the "great builder" of fascist institutions.

At least one new source of interest in Sorel appeared within the regime. Lagardelle, it should be recalled, had been assigned to the French embassy in Rome at Mussolini's invitation, and had participated from 1933 to 1937 in discussions leading to the establishment of the corporatist regime.[104] Lagardelle was now identified with the movements of neo-syndicalism and planism.

The same tendencies were now also in evidence in the *Problemi del lavoro* of Milan. In 1927 Rinaldo Rigola, former head of the CGL, supported by a Milanese coterie of former CGL organizers who professed loyalty to Mussolini, attempted a revival of serious discussion of the role of the proletariat in the fascist regime.[105] By 1933 the *Problemi* had also turned its attention to neo-syndicalism and planism. The move was accompanied by considerable interest, evinced in Parisian periodicals of the same tendencies, attempting simultaneously a revival of Sorelian fundamentals.[106] These were the *Homme réel,* with which Lagardelle was associated, and the "national and social" *Homme nouveau.* By 1935 there were even exchange visits between the Italian and French groups.

Although he was by no means the only social theorist to receive attention, Sorel was discussed often and seriously in the *Problemi.*[107] He was regarded as the essential link between Marx and de Man. It was he who had broken with an exclusively proletarian syndicalism. It was his defense of Lenin and bolshevism that had led him, though reluctantly, to statism. His *"morale* of producers" opened the way to a thoroughly modern industrial order. All this made Sorel relevant today. What the *Problemi* rejected in Sorel was the exclusively proletarian syndicalism of the *Réflexions.* As for the fascist regime, the *Problemi* had no problems.[108] In his polemic with the Parisian reviews, Rigola defended class collaboration, the special role of the Fascist party, and the overriding interests of the state.

A few Sorelians rallied late to fascism or otherwise made their peace with the regime; of these, Missiroli alone continued without limit in his admiration for Sorel. The Lateran Treaties had finally brought Missiroli around to fascism.

"L'Ultimo Sorel," a lengthy article he published in 1931 in Coppola's *Politica,* served the following year as a preface to *L'Europa sotto la tormenta,* an anthology of Sorel's articles that had appeared in the Italian press mainly in the years immediately after the war.[109] Missiroli presented Sorel in his final years, notwithstanding his "exaltation of Lenin," as a defender of Italy's "most extreme" national aspirations.[110] To say that Sorel contradicted himself, Missiroli asserted, was no explanation of his doctrines. He belonged to all extremist groups. His "contradictions" were transcended by "a rigorous internal unity," the product of his personality. "By instinct, he was a Jansenist tormented by the problem of evil."[111] As for Sorel's attraction to fascism, Missiroli cited one of the articles in the collection (originally published in November 1919), as well as Sorel's correspondence in 1921, to establish Sorel's interest in and approval of the nascent fascist movement.[112] In his *Studi sul fascismo* of 1934 and in later works during the decade, Missiroli more than made his peace with the fascist regime, addressing himself largely to the "injustices" of 1919 and to the grandeur of Mussolini's foreign policy.[113]

Prezzolini remained in New York, while Labriola returned to Italy. Although their attitude toward fascism was now somewhat ambiguous, their Sorelismo had become a thing of the past. Prezzolini, as head of the Casa Italiana, was now engaged in literary and bibliographical studies.[114] He was, nevertheless, obliged to comment on personalities and events of his Vocist days as well as his current activities. There were claims by a colleague at Columbia that the *Voce* had prepared the way for the great Italian renewal that came with fascism.[115] From the *Nation* of New York and the antifascist *Giustizia e libertà* of Paris came charges that the Casa Italiana was a center of fascist propaganda subventioned by the Italian government and that antifascists were not invited to speak at the Casa.[116] What is alone certain is that Prezzolini was not publicly antifascist during these years.

Though Labriola continued to publish with the Librairie Valois in Paris, he criticized Sorel severely in his *Au delà du capitalisme et du socialisme* of 1932.[117] He now proposed a socialism limited to the enlargement of economic elites and the rational development of economic life, but he did retain his prewar syndicalist suspicion of the state and remained an active antifascist in exile. The Fascist party, he wrote the following year, ruled in Italy like an army of occupation.[118] Again, in a work of 1936 marked by Spenglerian overtones, he saw in Lenin, Stalin, Hitler, and Mussolini the "classic" manifestations of a "vast tragedy of human history."[119] Labriola nevertheless returned to Italy in December 1935, during the Italo-Ethiopian War.[120] In the Ethiopian war he saw something of the Libyan war. The hostility of the world to Italy's "glorious" endeavor required this act of "complete solidarity" with his native land, notwithstanding his "political preferences." Once returned, Labriola lived in virtual silence and isolation. His "support" had come too late.

Malaparte's attitude had also become ambiguous. He left the party in 1931 and migrated to France, where he published the celebrated *Technique du coup d'état* that year.[121] This was a study (in the style of Machiavelli) of methods of both the conquest and the defense of the state that had been employed from the Bolshevik coup to the nascent Nazi movement. Malaparte insisted that he had no preferences; he did not write of Sorel. His concern was solely with revolutionary tactics and countertactics. He nevertheless focused on a theme familiar to Sorelians: the assault against the liberal democratic state by the "*catilinaires* of right and left"—fascism and communism. Returning to Italy in 1933, he was arrested for antifascist activity abroad; he was not released until 1938.

The few traces of Sorelismo in evidence within the regime were more than matched by the persistence of opposition to it. At a 1931 congress of agricultural workers, Luigi Razza, president of the national confederation, announced the "funeral oration" of Sorelian syndicalism: "We Sorelians of yesterday proclaim that our syndicalism has nothing to do with Sorel and his theories."[122] To be sure, Sorelian syndicalism had served to instill in the proletariat contempt for parliamentary procedures, a taste for violence, and disdain for international socialism. But beyond this the Sorelians had accomplished nothing. The Commission of Eighteen, moreover, had declared any kind of freedom of class action incompatible with the dictatorship. Razza stood high in the fascist hierarchy as a member of the Fascist Grand Council, the National Council of Corporations, and co-director of the *Lavoro fascista,* which after 1936 became a daily and the official organ of fascist labor.

The *Lavoro fascista* itself never ceased to admonish those who demonstrated any sympathy for a syndicalism that was contrary to the interests of or set limits to the supremacy of the state.[123] Coppola, too, editor of the *Politica,* dissented in an editorial footnote from Missiroli's opinion of Sorel.[124] Coppola did not share his admiration for Sorel, nor did he believe him to be a "great thinker." An article in *Gerarchia* was more charitable. Bruno Biagi, also high in the corporatist hierarchy, argued that what fascist syndicalism owed to Sorelismo was neither doctrine nor method.[125] It was, rather, its ardent revolutionary and heroic spirit and its moral austerity. This was Sorel's great contribution. Moreover, the *Archivio di studi corporativi,* established in 1930 as the official organ devoted to the study of the legal and institutional aspects of corporatism and directed by Bottai, rarely mentioned Sorel.[126] Other sources made only oblique or passing references:[127] fascism was born in "idea and fact" with the establishment of the Fasci of 1919; it was the work of Italians; even the idea of myth had a Mazzinian origin; Sorel's contribution to fascism was the notion of scission; "Mussolini started where Sorel finished."

As for antifascism, little if anything now remained of a Sorelian opposition to fascism. Leone was dead. Gramsci's *Ordine nuovo* and Gobetti's *Rivolu-*

zione liberale had been suppressed. Gobetti, too, was dead. Labriola, Prezzolini, and Missiroli could no longer be identified (for one reason or another) with the opposition. Gramsci alone, in fragmentary writings (letters and notes on literary, historical, and philosophical studies during his nine years in prison), commented often and significantly on Sorel.

The volumes that comprise the *Quaderni del carcere* were written from 1929 to 1933.[128] In them Gramsci endeavored to translate the Mazzinian tradition into socialist terms. What had drawn him initially to Sorel was what the latter had written about workers' councils, but it was clear at the start (from their common admiration for Croce and Bergson, for example) that there were deeper bonds.[129] From a study of Croce, whom he considered the greatest living philosopher, Gramsci developed a voluntaristic and subjective approach to history and the repudiation of whatever smacked of historical determinism. A more intensive study of Sorel was, therefore, not without relevance and not without results. In his "notebooks" Gramsci speculated, for example, on communist slogans as "vital illusions" that were historically creative, on the nature and purposes of an avant-garde party elite, and on the role of violence in history.[130] In all these he recognized Sorel as the foremost theoretician.

Gramsci invariably commented on publications by or relating to Sorel, particularly Sorel's recently published correspondence with Croce, Michels, and Lagardelle, Sorel's articles in Missiroli's collection, and the study of Michael Freund, the German scholar who in a major work on Sorel had labelled him a "conservative revolutionary."[131] Gramsci noted that in his letters to Croce, Sorel had revealed a far greater "intellectual subordination" to the younger man than Gramsci had anticipated.[132] Though it may have been the other way around, Gramsci commented, "*Vivere senza religione*" was the essence of what Sorel drew from his reading of Croce.[133] Gramsci also noted the "coolness" of Sorel's relations with Michels and Lagardelle.[134] He denied Missiroli's argument that Sorel had figured in the genesis of the fascist movement, but he was willing to concede that there was considerable "irresponsibility" in Sorel's own political affiliations.[135] He denied, however, that there were more than a few points in Sorel's work that might have conservative implications—Sorel belonged to the proletariat, and his final testament was his defense of Lenin.[136]

Gramsci, as his earlier writings indicated, did not consider himself a disciple of Sorel, though he held him in the highest regard. Without a party elite (which as a defender of bolshevism Sorel had rejected) Sorelian syndicalism would prevent the transformation of the working class from the "economic-corporatist" stage to the establishment of an "ethical-political" state. If to anyone, Gramsci continued to look to Croce. He saw in Croce a way of transforming socialism into a movement that would fulfill the promise of the

Risorgimento. It is likely that Gramsci did not appreciate the extent to which Croce during his youth had himself fallen under the spell of Sorel.

Gramsci died of tuberculosis in a Roman clinic in 1937, a few days after the expiration of his reduced twenty-year sentence.[137] For reasons of propaganda Mussolini had let him die a free man. Gramsci's notebooks, transmitted by the party faithful in rather devious ways, were not published until 1948 to 1951.

With the deaths of Gramsci and Gobetti, the Sorelian current in Italian antifascism (what there was of it) had also died. Both had helped to prepare the ground for Carlo Rosselli's *Giustizia e libertà,* the Parisian newspaper of anti-fascist exiles that included Labriola, Malaparte, and Ascoli and began publication in 1934. Rosselli had himself contributed to the *Rivoluzione liberale.* The new review was supported by both socialist and liberal antifascists, but there was no sign in its pages of explicit interest in Sorel. Tasca's article of 1937, "Ritorno a Gramsci e a Gobetti," however, suggests something of the tenor of the review, as well as its tenuous relation to Sorelismo.[138]

By the thirties a new genre of literature on Sorel had begun to appear. Almost from the very start, Sorel had been the subject of scholarly study in Italy, but these prewar efforts had been primarily the work of disciples. Though distinctions are not always possible, a new kind of literature, the work primarily of academicians and essentially devoid of partisan feeling, had also appeared. Cesare Goretti's studies during the twenties had been concerned with the juridical implications of Sorel's work.[139] Two brief studies on the 1920s by Giuseppe La Ferla were followed by his *Ritratto di Georges Sorel* of 1933.[140] Sorel was presented as a severe and unrelenting moralist who detested the new plutocratic bourgeoisie that threatened to corrupt the traditional class structure. Giuseppe Santonastaso's studies begun in 1929 continued into the thirties.[141] Like La Ferla, Santonastaso saw *"antiborghesismo"* as the most powerful impulse behind Sorel's work. A somewhat different note was struck by Renzo Peccarini at the beginning of the war.[142] The theme of Sorel's work was, he asserted, the battle of *"serietà e austerità"* against demagoguery and oppression. None of these studies, one might point out, had as yet a French counterpart. None of them, moreover, addressed itself in any detail to the study of Sorel's following.

Chapter

16

The War Years and Conclusion

By the beginning of World War II little remained in either France or Italy of an organized or structured Sorelian movement; the war years constituted an apparent conclusion and epilogue to the work of Sorel and the Sorelians. Sorel's name was still invoked occasionally, but such invocations were increasingly rare. Massimo Rocca, the Italian politico and journalist, wrote of Sorel in 1943 in the Belgian collaborationist weekly, *Cassandre,* that the "entire atmosphere of Europe is impregnated with his ideas, . . . revolutionary as well as counterrevolutionary."[1] It is doubtful that they were Sorel's ideas; if they were, they had merged with others and had been vulgarized in a form that would hardly have been recognizable to Sorel. One could argue that for many of Sorel's followers, especially those who had been devoted to him since the pre-World War I years, the heroic values Sorel had espoused had by World War II either failed to materialize or turned destructive (there were, of course, a few exceptions).

For France the long-awaited Apocalypse came finally with the Fall of France. How did the most devoted of Sorel's following react? Berth had become a convert to Catholicism and died just before the war.[2] Valois joined the Resistance, was arrested first by the Vichy police, then by the Gestapo, and died in Bergen-Belsen.[3] On the other hand, Lagardelle, who participated in the formulation of the Vichy Charte de Travail, was appointed Minister of Labor in 1942. After the war he was sentenced to hard labor for life.[4] Drieu La Rochelle, an admirer of Hitlerian Germany, became the director of Gide's *Nouvelle revue française* in 1940, and committed suicide in 1945 after becoming convinced that Hitler was not the apostle of Europe.[5] Some served Vichy: Dominique, Variot,[6] and Johannet. Others joined the Resistance: Aron and Lacoste. The rest remained inconspicuous or silent: Monatte, Delesalle, Louzon, and Duret, among the syndicalists; Fourgeaud, Rennes, and Béracha, in Valois's group; and Andreu, of the nationalists.[7]

In Italy the Apocalypse, if it came at all, did so in 1922. By 1943, with the fall of fascism, virtually all of Sorel's following had become its victims. Mussolini's end in the Piazzale Loreto in Milan is well known. Lanzillo, Orano, Panunzio, and Labriola survived the war, but each in his own way had become a casualty.

254

All of them had compromised their integrity by settling for considerably less than they had for so long struggled. Others too survived, though in circumstances that suggest that they had not entirely abandoned Sorel. Malaparte developed a frank sympathy for the Soviet regime (with Sorelian overtones) when he served as war correspondent on the Russian front for the *Corriere della sera*.[8] Expelled in 1941 by the Gestapo, he survived the war as an officer in the Italian army of liberation, thereafter defending himself against charges of having been a fascist or a communist at one time or another. Missiroli's eulogies of Mussolini during the war were followed after the war by a second anthology of Sorel's post-World War I newspaper articles and a collection of his letters, this time endeavoring to show that Sorel's career had reached its apogee not with Mussolini but with Lenin.[9] Prezzolini's departure (in "disgrace") from the Casa Italiana came at the end of 1940. Though he spent the war and postwar years defending himself against the charge of fascism, he still identified himself after the war as a *"sorelista."*[10] Leone, Gobetti, and Gramsci had fallen victim to fascism before their own apocalyptic expectations could come to pass. Croce alone survived the war in Italy as an opponent of the regime, though his reputation as an antifascist was somewhat tarnished.

What followed the Second World War has been, for the most part, a steady though circumscribed fascination in France and Italy (and elsewhere), with Sorel's work. Reminiscences, anthologies, and works of scholarship have appeared almost without interruption.[11] What has sustained this interest? For some it is partly nostalgia, partly also the allure of a problem whose understanding may illuminate a severely troubled and not too distant era. Most recently, however, it may also be due to the conviction that something in the world against which Sorel and the Sorelians rebelled, as well as their response to that something, are still very much with us. The "conclusion" to this study may be more apparent than real.

》　》　》

A number of paradoxes stand at the beginning of Sorel's career. There were "mystical tendencies," we have been told, in his Catholic family environment (and his own long-standing record of defending the "miraculous" in Catholicism), yet he turned to a career as an engineer. His was an intensely bourgeois appearance and demeanor, yet he lived for over twenty-two years with an illiterate working-class woman whom he considered the inspiration of his work. His sympathies were royalist after the fall of the Second Empire, yet his reading and re-education in social thought drew him to the anarchist Proudhon.

It would be desirable to know more about his youth, but there is not enough data to undertake a psychological study in any depth. It is worth hazarding a guess, however, as to the possible resolution of these paradoxes.

Sorel's powerful moralizing predilections were rooted in the rigidly Catholic environment of his boyhood years. Moreover, his illicit relationship with Marie-Euphrasie may have been the source of guilt-feelings which reinforced an initially puritanical outlook. His concern with morality was to be powerfully conditioned, however, by unusual class ties. By family origin he was drawn to the middle class. Throughout his life he presented to those who knew him the aspect of one who in manner and appearance belonged to the petite bourgeoisie. Through Marie-Euphrasie, however, he was drawn to the proletariat. She did not in any sense "convert" him; rather, she made it possible for him to escape his class origins and thereby prepared the way for his curious class ambivalence. It may be significant that Proudhon, also a severe and uncompromising moralist, had a wife named Marie-Euphrasie who was also of working-class origin. Sorel's intellectual bent, however, was perhaps most decisively shaped by schooling in the engineering sciences. His training and career as an engineer convinced him that true knowledge was not abstract Cartesianism or its multifarious derivatives, but empirical conclusions drawn from experience. Throughout his work was to be found the imprint of a technical mind constantly on the search for hidden "supports" underlying ideological constructions, religious or secular. This predisposition undoubtedly explains not only his alienation from the Sorbonne but also his resentment against rationalistic intellectuals in the church. Beyond the engineering sciences his education was based on random omnivorous reading. To be sure, he possessed in time an immense general culture and encyclopedic erudition, but his preparations were haphazard, a factor which was to count for much in shaping his career. It is worth re-emphasizing, however, that in matters concerning his youth (as in other respects throughout his career) not everything about Sorel can be "explained."

What drew Sorel to Proudhon was rooted in Sorel's fear of decadence. In Proudhon he found a "*sens guerrier.*" The Greek city-state idealized by Proudhon as a community of warriors devoted to its patrimony became Sorel's model society. The warriors of antiquity were transformed into contemporary equivalents. The society envisaged by Sorel was from the start a "society of heroes" based on work. Before he had read Marx or Vico he had begun to look for a moral transformation, though he was by no means yet a revolutionary. Even before he knew of James, he was a pragmatist in attributing a functional value to tradition, and, by implication, regarded production as a moral equivalent of war. And before Bergson had appeared on the scene, Sorel was well on his way to becoming a Bergsonian in his disdain of rationalism and intellectualism.

The initial impact of Marxian socialism in 1893 on Sorel must have been powerful, but he did not for long accept orthodoxy. He soon found himself engaged in the Revisionist controversy. Almost simultaneously with his perception of the inadequacies of Marxism, his reading led him to Bergson and Vico. Out of an amalgam of Proudhon, Marx, Bergson, and Vico emerged the first indications of the Sorelian *ricorso*. Marx, he maintained, had to be translated into a modern language. The essence of Marxism lay in the concept of class consciousness, the view of society divided into two hostile camps. Marxism was not a science but "social poetry," a reflection of the state of mind of a militant proletariat. The most authentic manifestation of the proletarian movement was syndicalism: hence the significance of "L'Avenir," in which Sorel, with his eye on Pelloutier's movement, first elaborated the virtues of syndicalism as an isolated and homogeneous sect embarked on the creation of a "society of producers" by way of a peaceful *ricorso*.

The Dreyfus affair persuaded Sorel in 1898 to re-evaluate his position once again. It attracted his attention just as he had perceived a proletarian *ricorso* in the syndicalist movement. He viewed the affair as a great moral issue which the socialists, with the notable exception of Jaurès, had failed to discern. The workers were now urged to support the politicians and intellectuals who constituted the mainstay of the Dreyfusards. He attacked the church, the army, and the anti-Semites and for the first and only time defended the parliamentary Republic. But when the Dreyfusards triumphed, it was not long before Sorel once again had misgivings; the very thing that had drawn him to the Dreyfusards now repelled him. He was outraged by the vindictiveness of socialists and republicans determined to punish the church and the army. He hated the university socialists and others who supported Dreyfus for electoral reasons. He deplored the increased involvement of French socialism in the routine politics of the Third Republic. He denounced Jaurès, particularly, as the great demagogue who had stirred up the baser passions and who threatened to turn socialism into a sophistical degeneration of the ideology of 1789. In all this, his reversal was conclusive—he never went back.

By 1903 the caesarism of the Second Empire, the "opportunist" democracy of the Third Republic, and the radicalism of the Dreyfusards thoroughly convinced Sorel that the French bourgeoisie were decadent. The bourgeois order had to be destroyed by revolution, for a fundamental transformation could not be the work of piecemeal reforms. He now urged syndicalists to reject reformism and achieve their goals by the methods of direct action, by the general strike. Simultaneously (and characteristically), he cautioned Catholics to be wary of "modernism." Reformism and modernism were linked as debasers of their respective doctrines. The path which Sorel had taken was a most unusual one. He did not arrive at revolution by "Jacobin ways." He never had any real sympathy for the French Revolution nor was he much interested in 1830, 1848, or 1871. The critique of bourgeois society which he presented stemmed from an essentially conservative standpoint—he was, with Proudhon, a "man of Old France." He condemned bourgeois society for its morals, that is, its sexual license and disregard for the sacred institutions of the community. He condemned its political organization, which corrupted all parliamentarians and made the state the scene of irresponsible chatter by rationalistic intellectuals. He condemned its ultimate goals, that is, its individualism and materialism, uninspired by a collective ideal consonant with the needs of an industrial age. Sorel was looking for primordial forces to destroy the old order and to create a new.

» » »

The career of Sorel from 1903 to his death raises a number of biographical problems centering on his activities in behalf of the revolutionary movements which he supported. In these activities one may take the measure of the man and his work.

Sorel's personality and the character of his work were related. His was the life of an isolated and sorely troubled intellect attempting to assume the role of a man of letters—he had not at all the aspect of a revolutionary. In any event, he was not altogether successful. There was much that suggests that his work was that of a highly gifted and dedicated amateur.

The personality of Sorel was that of a secluded intellectual who had a horror of noise, public places, and politics. One is struck by his fierce independence. He was well aware of the unorthodox route by which he had become a man of letters and of the shortcomings of his work. Undoubtedly, he resented those who were more conventionally equipped for the task by learning and position. Yet, he did desire recognition. He was disheartened when his work failed to evoke a favorable reaction among those for whom he battled, and he was not so independent that he could resist for long the blandishments of an opposing political and intellectual camp. Most striking was his hypersensitive temperament, which kept him (as his letters reveal) in a perpetual state of inquietude, a condition aggravated by old age and frequent illness. Most of his studies were based on works the authors of which he wished to belittle, even though he borrowed from them. He was never happier than when he could show someone to be at fault. He quarreled with Antonio Labriola, with Lagardelle and the staff of the *Mouvement socialiste,* with his associates of the projected *Cité française,* and then with Benda, Péguy, Barrès, and the staff of the *Indépendance.* Always suspicious, he was chronically troubled by "intrigues" of politicians and "plots" to boycott his books, in his early as well as in his later years. There was also something of a vicious streak in his make-up. His reversal with regard to the innocence of Dreyfus was hardly typical even of "repentant Dreyfusards"—Péguy and Halévy never doubted Dreyfus's innocence. His attacks on Jaurès and even Péguy after their deaths are those of a man lacking in compassion. His violent language—hurled against politicians, intellectuals (especially Sorbonnards), Jews, the entire Western world—demonstrated a capacity for deep hatred.

The work of Sorel gave little evidence of systematic or thorough scholarship, or, for that matter, of consistent intellectual orientation and growth. The studies he published were little more than confused collections of annotations on a variety of matters, divided by no apparent system into paragraphs and chapters. The book review was generally the first form in which an argument was presented, followed by an article, and, if it proved to be worth elaborating, by a book. Moreover, he was invariably content to use second-hand sources. His work was frequently punctuated by citations from Renan and Ferrero on ancient history and Taine and de Tocqueville on modern. Cournot, Bergson, and James served him well in philosophy, as did Le Play, Le Bon, and Durkheim in sociology. Brunetière, de Rousier, Reinach, Croce, Pareto, Bernstein, Kautsky, and, of course, Marx and Proudhon were useful for any number of purposes. That these sources were frequently in conflict on vital matters disturbed him not at all. They were employed primarily to illustrate or to confirm his own conceptions. Moreover, the development of Sorel's ideas presented the appearance of an intellect not only self-taught but erratic. Assuming that the main outlines of his development can be defended, his work still leaves much to be desired. The case for proletarian movements was always developed, both from the standpoint of volume and passion, more thoroughly and convincingly, thereby creating the widespread impression that Sorel was always a man of the left. Yet, his ambivalence was constant. While supporting one movement he never completely gave up his hope for another. Also, no one movement was delineated quite like another, thereby leaving a multitude of questions unanswered at every stage of his career.

The method Sorel employed revealed an unusual approach to intellectual problems. He believed his method to be rigorously "scientific." Pareto, however, accurately observed that Sorel's approach to history was in essence "metaphysical." Though there was little that was fundamentally consistent, his method was grounded in a combination, not ordinarily found, of historical pessimism and historical materialism. Basically, he was not a Marxist. Indeed, there is some question if Sorel was ever a Marxist except for a brief period during his formative years. Quite apart from the overall development of his thought, which can hardly be called Marxist, was the centrality of his notion of myth. Sorel saw movements as impelled by a variety of myths throughout history. To be sure, in describing contemporary movements he used such terms as "proletarian" and "bourgeois" rather freely, but these were not so much class designations as states of mind. For Sorel what impelled the historical process was the struggle of a revolutionary sect animated by a value system containing expectations of apocalyptic success. Nothing demanded that the myth be based on class grievances or class grievances alone.

Sorel's historical pessimism was rooted in the belief that the historical process, if left to itself, results in decadence. He fervently believed that the idea of automatic progress was an illusion. One senses a profound sadness in him.

Sorel believed that each period of history produced a certain structure of institutions and values, but that these become prisons for the future. The germ of decadence is to be found in the tendency to stop—at certain times in history there was an enormous accumulation of dead things. Sorel did not resolve his pessimism by a sterile negation of life. Pessimism justified itself and was transformed into an enthusiasm for whatever possessed faith. There was, in fact, something biblical in his outlook, something in the tradition of Pascal. Though formed of different matter than former religionists and though he was closer to this world, the essence was identical. For Sorel the unique value of life resided in instances of fervor, of revolt, of faith. It was periodically necessary to renew this faith that had dried up in a decadent elite. He saw this effort assume the aspect of revolutionary action. The action of a genuine revolutionary was, therefore, at bottom conservative. Only by revolutionary action could the work of conservation be realized.

His historical materialism was rooted in the notion that every action must be explained by the material conditions in which men live. He believed every action to have an idea or ideology which justified or pretended to justify itself. These ideologies tended always to pass themselves off as eternal and universal, but these constructions were mere devices by which men persuaded themselves and others of the historical rightness of their cause. He did not, however, take historical materialism to be a determinism of any kind. A major role in history was attributed to the will, to the subconscious, to the mystical. Everything, moreover, was quite fluid. Science had no way of foreseeing. Only in retrospect was there logical truth in history. He saw material conditions as indispensable auxiliaries of the will. They established the limits within which wills may act effectively. The great popular movements of history were always polarized toward a faith which was at once false and sincere.

Sorel's quest was for something "strong"; that was the constant in the variety and confusion of his career. He was on the lookout for a revolutionary movement which presaged a politico-spiritual conquest, similar to those which he found at certain stages of history. His quest, however, must be viewed in a twofold light. He was simultaneously an observer and a participant.

Sorel was, in a sense, "outside" the movements he supported. A stranger to the world of labor as well as to the bourgeois society, he never inscribed himself as a member of the CGT, the Action Française, or the Communist party. These groups were studied "from a distance" by an intellectual who was more interested in the play of ideas than in practical politics. Sorel attempted to fathom the various movements with which he identified himself. These were already in existence; his theories came later. His purpose was to reveal to the militants their historic mission. There was no attempt to lead or to impose a theory on them. Sorel wanted to make his observations a reflection of the movements. He frequently expressed views hardly calculated to increase his popularity among the leaders or the following of these groups, but that was because his allegiance was not to a doctrine or to persons but to an heroic state of mind. It was not his job to believe or to disbelieve. It was for the actors in the drama itself to have faith in order to overcome all obstacles. His freedom of action permitted him to criticize without stint and to take his departure when he perceived that the revolutionary temperament of the movement had weakened.

He was at the same time a partisan. He was a moralist, and as such could be no passive recorder of the movements which he studied. There can be no doubt of his personal emotional involvement. He pretended to see things in the movements which frequently were not there. He was caught in the same dilemma as Marx. During each of his "periods" he became so completely taken up with a movement (though not always to the same degree) that he adopted not only many of its ideas but often its language as well. Sorel attempted to rationalize his behavior. The mission of the philosopher, he maintained, was to understand the movements which seemed important to him. To do this one had to immerse oneself in them—Renan had said that in order to understand Christianity one must have been a Christian. Without this involvement it would be impossible to get to the bottom of things. He was not in any sense, however, a propagandist. The role of the scholar, if he understood the movement, was not to write words in which he did not believe. His role was to understand and respect the fecundity of the movement, to encourage its adherents, who were unconsciously making historical advances. The function Sorel assumed was that of an evocator of energies.

The fact that Sorel gave his allegiance to a succession of revolutionary movements was not a mark of intellectual immaturity or instability. He was always opposed to the same thing, to the "decadent" bourgeoisie, and his "contradictions," that is, his periodic reversals after 1903, were not fundamental. His behavior was understandable in terms of his own preconceptions.

Sorel loved all passions; hence the comparative ease with which he moved from one revolutionary faith to another. New energies had to be discovered and released. These were to be found in *ricorsi,* revolutionary movements dedicated to the violent displacement of a society which had exhausted all spirituality and creativity. However they might vary, they all appeared to be devoted to the establishment of a "society of heroes." He found in the temper and goals of the "extreme left" and "extreme right," therefore, not only marked similarities but alternatives as well. It would appear that when he turned to the left he did so believing that he perceived a sign of a fresh historical creation. When he turned to the right he seemed to be convinced that he had discovered evidence of a reassertion of traditional values and institutions. What is generally called the "extreme left" and the "extreme right" were for him aspects of a single system of thought, a single mood of revolt. Sorel identified himself spontaneously with these movements during their "heroic" period. Before the war, in his tour first among the partisans of revolutionary syndicalism and of integral nationalism, he soon found them not far enough removed from the corruption of the real world to meet his very rigorous demands. When he perceived that the strength of these movements was illusory, he re-embarked on his search. In the postwar years, when bolshevism and fascism appeared on the scene, he also greeted them (certainly the former) with undisguised enthusiasm. It is conceivable that had Sorel lived longer, though he had started with the same hope, he might very well have ended with the same deception.

His changing attitude toward France also clarifies Sorel's "contradictions." Sorel assumed at the outset that France was decadent, but he did not consider her irretrievably lost. When he identified himself with revolutionary syndicalism and integral nationalism he was essentially thinking of a French *ricorso*. The CGT and the Action Française appeared to him to be the most promising movements of their kind. Either seemed capable of restoring France to her leading role in Western society. To be sure, even before the war he periodically had doubts, expressing the hope that Italian syndicalism or nationalism would succeed where their French counterparts had failed. He viewed France in a far different light, however, during the war and postwar years. His published work and especially his correspondence with Croce and Missiroli were now characterized by continual disparagement of France. To the failure of prewar French syndicalism and nationalism was added the role of France during the war and after. Nothing delighted him more than a barb hurled at his own country. The war had also changed his focus: not only France but the Western world in general was decadent. The *ricorsi* he now sought were immeasurably broadened. When he turned to bolshevism he was convinced that everything was "rotten" in Europe; almost concurrently with Spengler, he was convinced of the "decline of the West." Bolshevism was for him "Russian" rather than "European." To bolshevism was assigned the task of burying the corpse and starting all over again with a "new Middle Ages." When he appeared to turn to fascism he viewed the merger of the traditional and the revolutionary as a possible alternative. He seemed to say that the West might still save itself.

》　》　》

There were no schematically conceived notions in Sorel's formulation of *ricorsi*. As an anti-intellectual he abhorred abstractions. The fluidity of his thought gave him a certain freedom, but it was not anarchy. Without claiming to be a logician, Sorel commanded a logic as perfect and as rigorous as Proudhon's. For him logic was not the effect of some abstract schema, it was the product of the intimate continuity of life and thought. But Sorel is not readily understood if some structure is not imposed on him. The structure here employed has been devised primarily to provide boundaries. Within these he has been permitted to speak freely. From his formulations emerge the outlines of revolutionary sects embarked on a great historic conquest. Both the sect and the regime it creates are organized for conquest, for "violence." Nevertheless, Sorel's *ricorsi* changed in quality. The apocalyptic idea was always evident in his work, but it tended to deteriorate. Though never vulgarized, it lost much of its initial subtlety. The *ricorso* became less an essay in Christian pessimism and more a problem in social engineering.

Sorel wanted a violent displacement of democratic idols. Revolutionary movements were *ricorsi* which served as instruments of destruction and presented also a preview of the regimes they could be expected to establish. Two broad types of movement were delineated by him, a proletarian and a bourgeois. The proletarian movement was a reaction to bourgeois decadence. Whether the bourgeoisie were capable of an original revolutionary creation or whether they became revolutionary only as a defensive reaction to proletarian revolutionism was not always clear. These conceptions, in any case, were introduced in Sorel's prewar discussion of revolutionary syndicalism and integral nationalism. They were retained in substance for bolshevism and fascism, but were there treated with far greater realism.

The motivation of revolutionary movements was attributed to revolutionary myths. Sorel did not discover the concept of myth. There was much in French nineteenth-century history with its succession of revolutionary efforts which suggested it. In German Protestant exegesis of the nineteenth century (notably in the work of David Friedrich Strauss) the concept of myth held an important place, and it was subsequently introduced into Catholicism by the modernist Abbé Loisy. Hegel had maintained that nothing great in history had been accomplished without passion. In Carlyle's hero-worship and Gobineau's racism there was much that suggested the myth. Sorel, however, probably encountered myth in Renan's studies on the origins of Christianity. He was familiar with the concept when he published his first two books in 1889, but not until his consideration of Marxism as "social poetry" did he put it to effective use. The notion of myth permitted Sorel to respect the principles of a revolutionary movement at the same time that it gave him complete freedom of action.

The myth was the fulcrum of Sorel's political theory. Sorel viewed the revolutionary myth as a value system containing expectations of apocalyptic success. It was anonymous, a fact born of daily struggle. It was for its adherents an article of faith. The ideology of a movement possessed no objective validity. It was a mere translation of its myths into an abstract form. Ideology was, according to Sorel, something of a facade for class or national self-interest, an argument which has been supported by the distinction made by psychoanalysis between the "real" and the "social" self. Sorel saw in the myth simultaneously a cohesive element and a directive force: it convinced its adherents of the historical and moral rightness of their cause; it permitted the individual to escape the bondage of the immediate and lend his efforts to a work which was at once destructive and creative; and it made action possible while it delimited the field of action. The core of Sorel's argument was an important one, symptomatic of the new century and the debility of the liberal rationalist tradition: it was the assumption that men were moved not by their reason but by their passion.

The myth was a product peculiar to a revolutionary group, its quality differing from place to place, from era to era. Sorel at the outset saw in the social and national myths of his day something in the nature of "myth" and "counter-myth." In the first instance, conviction derived from the daily struggle of the workers against bourgeois society, while in the second they had their origin in an "instinct of preservation" among the bourgeoisie. The future society was envisaged as a totally new creation or as the traditional order restored in its purity and vigor. The first tended toward the destruction of the existing order, while the second made for the expulsion of alien and aberrant elements. The two appeared to be, for him, in almost total opposition in revolutionary syndicalism and integral nationalism; but Sorel ultimately discovered that they were not entirely irreconcilable. Syndicalist notions were introduced, though not very clearly, into his conception of integral nationalism. Both bolshevism and fascism, though viewed substantially as representing "revolution" and "counterrevolution," respectively, were thought to be impelled by myths compounded in varying degrees of both the social and the national. Sorel was ultimately obliged to recognize the extremely heterogeneous quality of the motivation of these movements, impelled simultaneously by the revolutionary and the traditional.

The organization of revolutionary movements was based on an elite. As in the case of myth, Sorel did not derive his conception of an elite from any single source. Though he learned much from the Marxian view of a proletarian elite, he did not hold that a revolutionary elite was automatically the consequence of the structure of society. There are indications that at times Sorel was thinking in terms of Nietzschean heroes, though he seldom referred to Nietzsche's work. With Pareto and Michels Sorel shared the notion of a voluntaristic elite, the result of a will-to-power, cultivating a sense of the sublime and the highest revolutionary virtues. Sorel drew largely upon the history of religion in elaborating his conception of a revolutionary elite. In religious sects and monastic orders he found model "fighting institutions," linking thereby modern revolutionary elites and specially dedicated religious groups.

Sorel's conception of a revolutionary elite took the form of a political sect. He feared large-scale organization, which he thought led to the formation of leaders interested in self-aggrandizement, and who fell prey to enervation and corruption. He denied the validity of any consensual ethic. Instead, he lauded the elite of a sect, living in the midst of crisis, which stressed purity and feared contamination from the decadent world without. He saw in such an elite the only instrument capable of fostering the ideals of the movement and making preparations for the future. The revolutionary sect expected an ever-deepening crisis which would be resolved ultimately by a transformation in which the old order would be destroyed. It had, therefore, to prepare for the new: hence his concern for the development of new mores, customs, rights, and duties.

His view of an elite was not consistently based on class. The syndicates were class organs but the *camelots* were less clearly so—they were more like a "national" elite. The soviets appeared to be class organs but included both peasants and workers as "producers." The Blackshirts, though hardly discussed at all, appeared to have no necessary class origin. Evidently, Sorel believed (especially after the war) that movements rooted in both the social and the national might be more broadly based. "Proletarian" and "bourgeois" became more obviously (as in fact they had always been) states of mind.

He also began to view the preparation of a revolutionary movement in more realistic terms after his experience with revolutionary syndicalism. The role of leadership first became apparent to him in the Action Française, and thereafter never failed to receive emphasis. Moreover, the importance of the *camelots* and similar paramilitary or military organizations such as the Red Army and the Blackshirts was now also stressed. It is evident that he was now much more concerned with the practical problems revolutionaries were likely to encounter.

The technique of revolutionary movements was that of violence. Sorel derived his conception of violence essentially from his reading of Proudhon and Marx. Proudhon had suggested that historical movements occurred by the play of antagonisms, the shock of absolutes, the opposition of powers. This conflict resulted in a kind of residue which became an acquisition of civilization. There was danger, therefore, in the absence of conflict. Marx had also impressed Sorel with the notion that force was the "midwife" of progress. For Sorel this was the real Marx, the Marx of the *Manifesto,* the Marx of 1848. However, Sorel felt obliged to detach the Marxian idea of class struggle from its economic base. Sorel grounded his conception of violence on what was an essentially evolutionary notion transported to the social question, though he did not expressly say so. That society which ceased to struggle, he seemed to say, ceased to grow. Even more, it began to decay, for its weaknesses had not been weeded out. Violence and war were positive symptoms in the healthy struggle for survival. The gravest fault of democracy was that it permitted one to sink into an easy philanthropy, a lazy altruism, and social peace. No modern writer of stature has gone further in attributing a moral and historical value to violence.

The violence Sorel advocated was a normal expression of social war. For him, it was a primordial manifestation, objectionable only when not clearly an "act of war." He did not want violence for its own sake. The emphasis was placed on the symbolic and psychological aspects of violence. So broadly was it conceived that Christian non-violent resistance was held to be compatible with it. For Sorel violence was an instrument of social scission. Struggle was the only means of communication possible between hostile groups. The "word" was corrupt and engendered corruption. He saw movements triumph by means of unforeseen paths. Preconceived plans were, therefore, of little value. The "movement" was everything and it was violence that sustained the movement.

The role Sorel assigned to violence also underwent important changes. Sorel regarded violence in a new light after his association with revolutionary syndicalism. Syndicalist violence largely took the form of strikes, a mode of action functionally related to syndicalist organization. A new note was sounded when violence became the function of groups expressly organized and prepared for physical combat, such as the *camelots,* the Red Army, and the Blackshirts. He came to hope for the appearance of a "Cromwellian army" of dedicated revolutionaries. Sorel also eventually viewed the ultimate purpose of violence in a more practical light. The coming of the syndicalist general strike had been only vaguely delineated; he did not speculate as to how or when it would come about, and implied that these factors mattered little. The violence of succeeding movements was conceived in terms more concretely goal-oriented. There was no talk of a revolution in the remote future. For the *camelots* and the Blackshirts he was thinking in terms of a more or less calculated seizure of power by means of an armed coup.

Sorel sought the establishment of a revolutionary society. He carried over the concepts of myth, elite, and violence from the revolutionary movement to the postrevolutionary order. The regime established by the movement, therefore, would be no fortuitous development. It would be a pragmatic elaboration of the revolutionary movement. He apparently had also the notion of "permanent revolution" in mind. The revolution had for its purpose the creation of new values and institutions. Since these derived from heroic action, the revolutionary regime would have to be impelled by a continuing heroic state of mind. He viewed the revolutionary society as, essentially, "integral" or "totalitarian." Each regime might possess its own moral system, its own mode of organization, and a technique peculiar to its needs, but all of them would be permeated by an essential principle, and all of them would be, in their own way, societies of heroes. He vastly expanded his conceptions after the war, well beyond the rather simplistic structures of a syndicalist order. There was, he ultimately believed, no necessary conflict between the social and the national. The nationalization of socialism and the socialization of nationalism were, indeed, important developments of the new century with which Sorel was directly associated.

The motivation of the revolutionary order was attributed by Sorel to new moral values. He drew his moralism primarily from the works of Proudhon, Renan, and Le Play. Although these commentators differed in detail, Sorel seized upon their common point of departure. They were equally disturbed by the moral future of humanity. They saw religion lose ground daily as a moral force and worried lest there be nothing to replace it. The *morale* of democracy was no morality at all. An organic society was being destroyed by the preachers of "emancipation." Among bourgeois and proletarian alike a spirit of sacrifice had almost disappeared. Sorel was, moreover, a moral "conservative." It was by this bent that most of his sympathies were to be explained. If he venerated Proudhon, if he loved Pelloutier or Lucien Jean, or spoke with respect of Bureau or de Rousiers, it was because of their preoccupation with *morale*. If he was a revolutionary it was because he saw in a revolutionary *ricorso* the only possibility of moral renewal.

The moral catastrophe produced by the revolution, he thought, would be greater than the material one. Sorel held that the moral values of the future would derive from and reflect the revolutionary myth. After the revolution the new values would pervade all the institutions of society. Espousal of a *morale* based on enthusiasm and instinct rather than on rationalism was, of course, thoroughly Bergsonian. Sorel gave to the new revolutionary *morale* the task of curbing the passions and overcoming the tendency toward individualism, for human nature, when left to itself, tended toward evil. A new *morale* would discipline the instincts and direct them along socially constructive lines. A social order maintained its vigor only by maintaining its virtue. There was no "progress" in moral principles—a libertarian moral system repelled him.

The various moral systems Sorel was prepared to accept may have been substantially of the same kind, but the details varied with the nature of the regime. For Sorel revolutionary syndicalism would be a "*morale* of producers." Integral nationalism would derive its morality from traditional sources. Bolshevik and fascist values would be fashioned of various elements, both social and national. For Sorel morality would have to meet varying needs. A syndicalist society required values which inspired the perfection of machinery and increased the productivity of labor. A nationalist society required those which inspired a spirit of sacrifice on behalf of the fatherland. Again, bolshevism and fascism would be inspired by values which were both social and national. Morality, therefore, would play a role unique in each regime. In any case, for Sorel the morality of the individual was his abnegation in favor of the group, while the *morale* of the group was the morality of success.

The organization of the revolutionary order would be based on the new elites elevated by the revolution. His conception of social organization had multiple roots. The theories of the elitists Pareto and Michels, as well as those of

Le Play on "social authorities," found their way into his work. Moreover, Proudhon's federalism had undoubtedly had an influence from the beginning of his career. The purely functional role which he attributed to government derived implicitly from the utopian socialists whom he, for the most part, contemptuously berated.

The revolutionary society was variously conceived, but certain principles tended to persist. He stressed the role of a ruling minority in a collectivist society organized in accordance with overriding goals. The concept of such a society managed by an elite was for him a constant. Only a disciplined elite absolutely devoted to its mission could govern in the interests of the masses. An elite, therefore, was not a luxury but a primordial necessity. He also stressed the authoritarian character of government and the merits of varying degrees of local autonomy. Authoritarianism entailed the political "neutralization" of the community. This would mean the end of the party system and the apparatus of parliamentary government. Instead, government would be reduced to its essential role and placed in the hands of responsible functionaries. Federalism or regionalism seemed to him necessary in order to avert the dangers of excessive centralization and the stifling of local initiative and differences. But the prospects for decentralization, he seemed to think, were none too good.

The structure of the revolutionary order underwent important changes in Sorel's thinking. He did not give emphasis to leadership or admit the value of the state until after his experience with revolutionary syndicalism. Revolutionary syndicalism was conceived as a society based on voluntary contractual agreements between federated labor organizations. Only when Sorel turned to integral nationalism did he perceive the value of a leader; Lenin and Mussolini ultimately revealed to him the potential of charismatic leadership. As for his initial antistatism, Sorel was not so much opposed to the state per se as to the traditional "bourgeois" or "political" state. Revolutionary syndicalism was viewed in virtually anarchistic terms, for the state and the struggle for its control, he held, inspired needless controversy and conspiracy. In integral nationalism he envisaged a regime without parties which effectively depoliticized the state. In the bolshevik regime and in the fascist movement, moreover, he saw the emergence of orders in which the apparatus of the bourgeois parliamentary state had been or would be destroyed. Sorel did not long view the revolutionary society in the exclusively proletarian and economic terms of revolutionary syndicalism. Syndicalist society had been conceived as a "society of producers," and producers were only those who participated directly in the processes of production. Nationalist society, however, was more broadly conceived. It was dedicated primarily to political advancement, but it was organized, presumably, along corporate lines and was devoted to matters of production as well. Bolshevik society was visualized in essentially syndicalist terms as a "society of producers," but bolshevism was thought to be inspired by political as well as economic goals. Fascism was based on the idea of a corporate society with both a political and an economic mission. In brief, Sorel was obliged to modify his conceptions considerably. The nationalist society had to find an honorable place for the workers in some kind of corporate structure and could not ignore production in an industrial age. And the proletarian society could not be conceived without the apparatus of the state (as long as it was not the "bourgeois" state) in an international community of states.

The technique of the revolutionary order prescribed by Sorel derived from a variety of sources. The Bergsonian admonition that reality was fluid and that those who wished to act effectively must be free from prejudice and prepared to cope with unforeseen problems was basic to his outlook. The "Romanism" in Sorel, that is, his concern with "juridical sentiments" and his glorification of war, derived essentially from Proudhon. The idea of a cult of production as a "moral substitute" for war stemmed from James, while the notion of art as the highest form of work derived largely from his reading of the utopian socialists.

Sorel's ultimate goal was the creation of a "society of heroes." He repeatedly emphasized the need to awaken "juridical sentiments" proper to each society. Each society operated in accordance with its own imperatives, the primacy of which had to be universally admitted. These imperatives constituted the "force" which gave direction and purpose to justice, and justice entailed a continuing search for and elaboration of the forms and norms required by each society. He looked, essentially, to the establishment of a permanently heroic state of mind. What he envisaged for the twentieth century was a society after the Roman prototype. It would be a society in which the "striving for perfection" characterized its producers, its artists, its warriors. Such a society allowed natural genius to play the leading role. A society thus devoted to "violence," to the "sublime," in short, a "society of heroes," would assure the continued progress of humanity.

Sorel's conception of the character of a "society of heroes," however, tended to vary. His emphasis in revolutionary syndicalism was on the primacy of production. In integral nationalism it was on the primacy of the national interest. Both bolshevism and fascism were conceived as rooted in one fashion or another in the two imperatives, with bolshevism grounded mainly on the syndicalist prototype and fascism, presumably, on the nationalist. His ultimate goal, in each case, was the creation of a cult of work or a cult of the nation or some combination of the two. "Violence" or "conquest" was, in any case, the essential, whatever the combination. The "worker-inventor," virtually equated with the "artist," was the hero of syndicalism. The heroes of nationalism would be "warriors" and "artists." To bolshevism, however, was ascribed the heroism of both "producers" and "soldiers of socialism." As for fascism, though much remains unclear, one suspects that it too was called to "grandeur," both domestic and international.

» » »

The problem of Sorel's impact is partly one of distinguishing an influence that can be attributed to him, as against from the influence of a number of other sources. From about the 1890s the new science and scholarship fostered rebellion not only in political thought and movements but in philosophy, literature, and art. The new view of the physical universe that emerged from Einsteinian relativity, of nature that derived from Darwinian evolutionism, or of man himself implied in the work of Pavlov and Freud drained much of the meaning of the accepted absolutes. In political thought and movements alone, developments were striking. Perhaps of major importance was the "discovery" of mass politics and the role of the irrational in moving the masses. New currents were in evidence throughout Europe, to some extent even in conventional politics, but primarily in a variety of revolutionary movements—anarchist, syndicalist, socialist, racist, nationalist, and imperialist. A new value was placed on voluntarism, activism, and the will-to-power. Until 1914 these views, though widely circulated, did not extend much beyond minority groups, and Sorel's work was clearly only part of this rebellion. What the war did, however, was to remove many of the restraints of civilized life, and by doing so, seemed to confirm the prewar intellectual and political currents of irrationalism. These, moreover, were now provided with a mass basis. The passions aroused by the war revealed the extraordinary energies in the masses available for collective purposes. In the social engineering employed during the war to sustain morale was to be found the first modern effort at systematic, nationwide manipulation of collective passions. Even the regimes that "won the war" experienced no full "recovery" from the intellectual and emotional orgy that had accompanied it. But again, what Sorel wrote during the immediate postwar years constituted no more than a small component of the postwar mood of rebellion.

There is also the problem of determining Sorel's influence at various levels of organizational activity. Sorel appears to have reached a large reading public in France between 1908 and 1910 and an even larger one in Italy throughout the prewar and postwar period, but there can be no certainty of the size of this public or the extent of his influence. One might argue that his ideas were incapable of appealing to the great masses in revolutionary movements. If accepted by rank-and-file revolutionaries, his ideas could not have inspired them to action. The worm of reflection must not touch them. Should they come to realize the mythical character of their constructions they might abandon them. One must not rule out the possibility, however, that his ideas may have at times reached the rank-and-file in a vulgarized form. Sorel did win notice among diverse smaller groups on the periphery of revolutionary movements. These were mainly comprised of intellectuals or those with intellectual pretensions who propagated their views through the media of more or less Sorelian publications. Though at this level his influence is more readily established, problems nevertheless remain. At no time were these periodicals to be found in any one place on the political spectrum. Moreover, these organs often identified themselves with rival political camps and admitted to other influences. Basically, however, it was their common indebtedness to Sorel that made it possible for their participants to join together at times to form new and unusual combinations of both persons and ideas. Sorel wielded his greatest influence on a limited number of individuals. At this level his influence is somewhat more easily established. Extremists and dissidents of all sorts could readily find something congenial in him. They were, for the most part, marginal to the main revolutionary currents, "outsiders among outsiders." While some were proletarian in orientation, others were nationalist, and still others moved freely among the extremes or attempted an accommodation between them. Having taken the essentials from Sorel, they went their separate ways, sometimes anticipating or even influencing their *maître*'s next move. They combined periodically to form groups and to publish reviews, frequently picking up several newcomers, only to break up within a few years. All expressly considered Sorel to have been more or less the major (or a major) intellectual force in their lives, though for some this might be true for no more than a few years. All had essentially similar apocalyptic political conceptions. All tended to view revolutionary movements as impelled by "myths," though they were more aware than Sorel of the possibilities of manipulation of these myths. All saw in extremes the only alternatives, and all wanted a "society of heroes." These were the Sorelians.

In France one is struck by Sorel's failure to evoke any marked reaction to his work during his lifetime, though there were exceptions of importance. Perhaps the prime factor here was the absence of a powerful and sustained revolutionary ferment. With the liquidation of the Dreyfus affair the Republic was saved from those who had most threatened it since its foundation. The successful prosecution of the war of 1914–1918, moreover, served further to confirm the legitimacy of the Republic. A generalized atmosphere of revolt (such as in Italy), which might have given greater relevance to Sorel's work, did not exist in France. Moreover, Sorel's ideas did not fit into the traditional political categories so sharply divided in France. Except for marginal persons and activities, Sorel became largely suspect to both the revolutionary left and right. Yet, the marginality of these efforts was significant. Their novelty lay precisely in their marginality. These activities point to at least one Sorelian current during the prewar years, modest to be sure but more or less uninterrupted and "prefascist," leading to the formation of a French postwar fascism.

One looks in vain for evidence of any appreciable influence in France on the major organizations to which Sorel was drawn. In virtually all cases— the CGT and the Action Française before the war and the Communist party and the Action Française after the war—Sorel seems hardly to have made a significant impression. These were movements that possessed more or less strong direction and well-defined orientation: the CGT (notwithstanding its rhetoric) was reformist even during its "heroic" period; Maurras dominated the monarchists (if not most of the French right) both before and after the war; and the Communist party had Moscow behind it.

All of the Sorelian enterprises, such as Lagardelle's *Mouvement socialiste*, Bloch's *Effort*, Sorel's own *Indépendance*, Berth and Valois's *Cahiers du Cercle Proudhon*, all before the war, and Valois's organizational activities on behalf of the Action Française after the war were marginal to larger organizations. The activities of these reviews—with the exception of the *Mouvement socialiste*, which in its day was a very substantial enterprise—though transient were nevertheless important. With the exception, again, of the *Mouvement socialiste*, which asserted a militantly proletarian syndicalism, the reviews were attempts to transcend the traditional categories of left and right. Bloch's *Effort* and *Effort libre*, briefly and not very successfully, undertook the enterprise from the left. In most of this activity, it was Valois's initiative from the right that was most striking in the effort to bridge the gap between antidemocrats. Beginning with the publication of *L'Homme qui vient* in 1906, and continuing through the activities of the *Revue critique* in 1908, the ill-fated *Cité française* in 1910, and the Cercle Proudhon in 1911, Valois's activities were virtually unbroken (except for the war years), continuing up to the *Nouveau siècle* and the Faisceau twenty years later.

Sorel succeeded in influencing individuals in France rather than movements, and the number he persuaded to follow his lead was not impressive. Perhaps the most powerful factor operating against him was his flagrant violation of French intellectual tradition. Whether educated at the *université* or by the Bons Pères, French intellectuals were more or less under the discipline of Descartes. For centuries tradition had favored the abstract, the general, and the formal. Clarity of exposition came to be equated with truth. Because he flouted this tradition, Sorel could not for long hope to receive a sizable audience of readers in France. The two disciples Sorel found in the *Mouvement socialiste*, Lagardelle and Berth, by no means marked the limits of his influence, however. At least partially under his spell were Péguy and Halévy, as well as lesser figures such as Delesalle and Louzon. There were perhaps others, but it is indeed remarkable that only two who came from the left completely identified themselves with his conceptions and with one (Lagardelle) Sorel in 1908 parted company. Berth alone followed his master in his "contradictions." The monarchists, however, were more responsive. Valois (who had had a brief encounter with anarchism and syndicalism before he joined the Action Française) led the way. By 1910, joined by Berth and Variot, Valois had brought not only Bourget but twenty to thirty young monarchists active on the *Revue critique* and in the Cercle Proudhon under Sorel's tutelage, and engaged in what can only be described as proto-fascist activities. Bourget was perhaps the most distinguished member of the group; he was the only one among the original founders of the Action Française to fall under Sorel's sway. Though many of the prewar Sorelians in the monarchist movement did not survive the war, some of the names reappear as participants in Valois's postwar activities. Berth alone followed his *maître* into the communist camp, joined by Delesalle and Louzon, who had never left the fold of proletarian revolutionism.

In Italy Sorel's ideas took a stronger hold. The most significant factor here may have been the existence of a generalized mood of rebellion on all levels of Italian life. His revolt against materialistic and mechanistic thought drew him into a current of irrationalism and activism already present. His preoccupation with decadence and heroism found receptive ground in the widespread conviction that the Risorgimento had satisfied neither the spiritual nor the material aspirations of numerous elements. His idea of periodic rejuvenations was a familiar one, for in Italian thought the Renaissance and Risorgimento were so regarded, and even before the war there was the feeling that Italy was getting stale and needed a new start. What was of special interest in Italy was that the antagonism between left and right was not as acute as in France. The most recent historical experience for Italians had been the Risorgimento, and it had been impelled by a social as well as a national impulse. Something of that tradition was retained by the revolutionary movements which appeared at the beginning of the twentieth century. There was undoubtedly a sustained and significant Sorelian movement in Italy from about 1903 to 1922 and even beyond.

On the level of mass organization, the conditions necessary for some kind of influence clearly existed in Italy, if not in France. The Italian syndicalist movement as a whole was directly under the influence of Sorelismo. In the activities of Labriola and others in the Segretariato Nazionale up to 1906, in Corridoni's Comitato Nazionale della Resistenza to 1910, in Corridoni's USI after the Libyan war, and in Rossoni's UIL after the World War Sorelians endeavored to implant the Sorelian idea among the workers. How they attempted to do so is clear enough: as propagandists, agitators, organizers, and participants at syndicalist meetings and congresses. It is equally clear (especially in their articles in provincial newspapers) that they were able to urge workers to give to their activities an "heroic" aspect only at the loss of some subtlety in Sorel's notions of myth, elite, and violence. Though the impact of Sorelian activity on rank-and-file syndicalists cannot readily be measured, one can nevertheless assume that it was not without effect. Moreover, the activities of Corradini and Prezzolini until 1910 in the nationalist movement, Gramsci in the Communist party, and especially Mussolini and the syndicalist professors and organizers in the Fascist party suggest the possibility of a more or less comparable impact on other organizations.

Sorelian publications possessed a range that was seemingly unlimited, from Croce's *Critica* to obscure workers' weeklies in the provinces. At the center were major Sorelian syndicalist enterprises such as Labriola's *Avanguardia socialista,* Leone's *Divenire sociale,* and Olivetti's *Pagine libere,* and at least fifteen others, mostly provincial publications. Among the most important publications were those experimenting with a proletarian nationalism, first the *Pagine libere* and later Orano's *Lupa.* Somewhat less successful were the nationalist organs—Corradini's *Regno* and Prezzolini's *Voce* (though from 1908 to 1910 of major importance), and Viana's *Tricolore,* which attempted from the right what *Lupa* undertook from the left. It was the diversity of these periodicals that undoubtedly made possible the dissemination of Sorel's ideas on virtually all intellectual levels and in virtually every political quarter. Sorelian tendencies were to be found not only in various forms of proletarian revolutionism but also (though weaker) in revolutionary nationalism, as well as in attempts to combine the two. Sorelismo could be for war in Libya or against it, for intervention or against it, and in communism and in fascism, as Gramsci's *Ordine nuovo* and (to a degree) Mussolini's early *Gerarchia* testify.

Sorel succeeded in reaching a far greater number of individuals in Italy than in France. These "carriers" fell into several categories: intellectuals of first rank who did not expressly identify themselves with revolutionary movements but who were nevertheless sympathetic toward them, theoreticians both syndicalist and nationalist who served these movements, and syndicalist agitators and organizers devoted to practical revolutionary work. They were all well placed—from scholarship to agitation. It was among them (particularly in the writing and activities of Labriola, Olivetti, Orano, Panunzio, Lanzillo, and Corridoni on the one hand, and Corradini and Prezzolini on the other) that Sorelismo became a symptom and, unwittingly, an effective agent in the prewar preparation of fascism: by its vogue of "creative violence," in its proletarian revolutionism inclined toward nationalism, in its nationalist revolutionism inclined toward a "solution" of the social problem, and in its precedent for a coup set by the Fasci of 1915. The extent to which Italian fascism was in its origins a Franco-Italian enterprise is striking. Moreover, it may be true that some individuals arrived at fascism by other routes, and it may also be true that not all Sorelians ended in fascism, but for those partisans of Sorel, both named and nameless, who joined Mussolini in these fateful years immediately after the war, Sorelismo was the "root" of their fascism.

» » »

After 1922, one might argue, France rather than Italy became the center of Sorelismo. Within a few years the fascist dictatorship had effectively smothered any free-wheeling political debate, while France began to experience in the mid-twenties and certainly by the thirties something of the disorders that had beset postwar Italy. Sorelian activities during the interwar years, nevertheless, have something of the character of epilogue. It is not so much that the *maître* was no longer available for direction—in point of fact, he had no longer been much needed by war's end, if not before. Moreover, it would be useless to speculate about Sorel's reaction to the interwar years. Events continued to give relevance to the Sorelian movement but at the same time prepared the way for its demise.

Most striking in France in the twenties was Berth's disillusionment with communism and Valois's with fascism—not that the Faisceau is of only incidental importance. As a movement of half a million members in 1926 (Valois's figure) and origins that could be traced to the prewar Cercle Proudhon and beyond, it can hardly be dismissed. Its growth, interestingly, had paralleled that of the Italian fascist movement; in both the Sorelian component had been crucial. But the abandonment of communism by Berth and fascism by Valois was ironic, for Sorel's own development had culminated, it should be recalled, in the communist-fascist alternative. Bourget, Variot, and Johannet, although inclined toward fascism, also saw the choice as similarly limited, though they remained monarchists; but for Berth and Valois new departures were in order. Henceforth communism and fascism were bereft of French Sorelian activity (with the exception of Drieu La Rochelle and a few others). Both Berth and Valois eventually turned to neo-syndicalism, somewhat humanized and democratized in Valois's *Nouvel âge*. What remained of Sorelian activity by the late thirties was confined to small groups of avant-garde planist and technocratic reviews, more or less humanitarian, more or less authoritarian (anticipating a post-World War II development), for the most part as critical as the *Nouvel âge* of communist, fascist, or Nazi totalitarianism, though still vaguely interested in a "society of heroes." It is likely that the full realization of the nature of totalitarianism (especially in its Stalinist and Hitlerian form) and the impact of the war were decisive in the demise of Sorelian activity in France.

In Italy, whether Sorelismo was fascist (Malaparte's *Conquista*) or antifascist (Gobetti's *Rivoluzione liberale*), it was effectively terminated by the mid-twenties. The syndicalist professors of the prewar years had been tamed by high rank. They turned, accordingly, to scholarship, a good part of which was devoted to asserting the syndicalist origins of fascism. In any event, they had been effectively neutralized. Sorelismo was now virtually exhausted. Nevertheless, something of Sorel had entered the fascist regime, and it remained there. The doctrinal quality of Sorelismo, especially in the form that aimed to transcend the conventional categories of left and right, rendered Sorelismo's transformation into a non-ideology or even an anti-ideology no great intellectual feat. In this form Sorelismo may very well have survived to the end as the one continuous "ideological" thread in fascism.

The cult of violence, the quest of Sorel and the Sorelians for the Apocalypse, comes close to revealing the character of the crisis among intellectuals in the twentieth century, the fear of "decadence." Sorel's importance in this regard, however, was not primarily as a "mover." There are not many innovative giants in history—Sorel himself recognized that many of his ideas were "in the air." To be sure, the movement he inspired was novel in its vision of what was required to break with the decadence of its time, especially its recognition of alternative paths to a "society of heroes" and the possibility of bridging the gaps among a variety of movements that seemed to be engaged in the same pursuit. One cannot search for meaning in the twentieth century without crossing his path. The real importance of Sorel and the Sorelians, however, was of another order. Their work was symptomatic of a profound intellectual and moral disturbance—the desertion by intellectuals (and those with intellectual pretensions) of the democratic idea. And their story was something of a tragedy. They had sought to evoke the "sublime." But their efforts, purposefully or not, had worked from 1914 to Auschwitz (along with others) to unleash the "beast."

What role they may have played since World War II is difficult to assay. Though little or no sign of a cult of violence (Sorelian or otherwise) survived the war in Europe (there were hints in the work of Jean-Paul Sartre and Albert Camus that Sorel's ideas were by no means dead), within a few years it had clearly reappeared in the Third World. With the writings on violence of Frantz Fanon (a West Indian educated in French schools who worked for Algerian independence) the possibility of a link with Sorel became increasingly a subject for scholarly debate.[12] Moreover, beginning with the demonstrations against the Vietnam war, links have been perceived between the violence of the protest movements of the sixties and after on the American-European scene and the continued struggles of the Third World for "liberation" in which the ideas of Herbert Marcuse and Régis Debray have figured prominently. It is likely that much in the world against which Sorel and the Sorelians rebelled has persisted into our own time. Moreover, it is likely that something of the Sorelian vision of the role of violence in history has also persisted. It may be that "Sorel's ghost" has not been entirely laid to rest. In the post-World War II "Time of Troubles," arising in places and contexts that would have been recognizable to Sorel, a cult of violence has reappeared, traces of which may be attributable to Sorel and the Sorelians. One may legitimately speculate whether apocalyptic politics—the pursuit of the "sublime"—may yet, if it has not already done so, lead to unleashing the "beast" anew.

Notes

Preface

1. Raoul Narsy, "Georges Sorel," *Journal des débats,* September 1, 1922.
2. Georges Guy-Grand, "Georges Sorel," *Action,* September 7, 1922.
3. Paul Souday, "Les Livres: Georges Sorel," *Temps,* September 7, 1922.
4. Émile Buré, "Péguy et Sorel," *Éclair,* September 7, 1922.
5. Robert Louzon, "Georges Sorel," *Vie ouvrière,* September 8, 1922.
6. Paul Delesalle, "Georges Sorel," *Humanité,* September 1, 1922.
7. Georges Valois, "Georges Sorel," *Action française,* September 4, 1922.
8. "Commento alla corrispondenza da Parigi: la morte di Giorgio Sorel," *Popolo d'Italia,* August 31, 1922. The article, though unsigned, is attributed to Mussolini. See Benito Mussolini, "Dalla conferenza di Cannes alla Marcia su Roma, 14 gennaio 1922–30 ottobre 1922," *Opera omnia di Benito Mussolini,* ed. Edoardo Susmel and Dulio Susmel (33 vols., Florence: La Fenice, 1951), 18, p. 494.
9. A more spectacular introduction to a study of Sorel and the Sorelians might have begun with the story (too good to be true) that in the early 1930s the ambassadors of the Soviet Union and fascist Italy in Paris, having heard that Sorel's grave was in disrepair, independently and almost simultaneously informed the director of the Bibliothèque Nationale in Paris of the desire of their respective governments to erect a monument to Sorel. Rolland Marcel, the director of the library, who had himself known Sorel, asked Daniel Halévy, the well-known littérateur, for guidance in this delicate matter. Halévy, who had known Sorel since the turn of the century, was also perplexed, but after inquiries to Sorel's friends and relatives Halévy returned with the response that Sorel's tomb was a family matter which concerned no one else. He speculated, "*Sorel l'aurait ainsi donné.*" The incident is reported by Daniel Halévy, "Préface" to Pierre Andreu, *Notre maître: M. Sorel* (Paris: Grasset, 1953), pp. 19–20. Cf. Neil McInnes, "The Revolutionary Conservative," *Times Literary Supplement,* October 1, 1976, p. 1226.
10. The inclusion of Italy is important in dealing with the argument that fascism was a "French invention": see Zeev Sternhell, *La Droite révolutionnaire, 1885–1914: les origines françaises du fascisme* (Paris: Seuil, 1978). Perhaps the only attempt to explore Sorel's impact outside of France and Italy (in Spain, Latin America, Britain, the United States, Russia, Germany, Austria, and Hungary) is in Michel Charzat, *Georges Sorel et la révolution au XXᵉ siècle* (Paris: Hachette, 1977), pp. 217–26. The result, some nine pages of virtually undocumented text, is skimpy at best (especially in its comments on the "Frankfort School") and only reinforces

the conviction that nothing very solid is to be found in these quarters. A better case is presented (though without extended reference to Sorel) in Jens Petersen, "Il Fascismo italiano visto dalla Repubblica di Weimar," *Storia contemporanea,* 9 (June 1978):497–529.

11. Cf. a recent essay in which the same question is raised: Richard Vernon, *Commitment and Change: Georges Sorel and the Idea of Revolution* (Toronto: University of Toronto Press, 1978), pp. 61–74. It is unfortunate that Vernon has chosen to translate only five excerpts of Sorel's work dating from 1894 to 1909. Sorel can be properly understood only against the entire sweep of his career (which extends to within two months of the March on Rome in 1922) as well as the work of his followers (from about 1903 to the Second World War). Vernon's arguments (pp. 61–74) on the possible persistence of Sorelian ideas on the subject of violence since the Second World War are suggestive.

Chapter 1. Introduction

1. See Andreu, *Notre maître,* pp. 23–44. Much of the material on the family and youth of Sorel has its source in T. Quoniam, "Notre compatriote: Georges Sorel" (Unpublished address to the Société Nationale Académique de Cherbourg, November 6, 1946), which is also cited by Andreu. Quoniam was a long-time friend of Charles Péguy.

2. Andreu, *Notre maître,* pp. 23–24, 26.

3. Ibid., p. 27; see also Albert-Émile Sorel, "Souvenirs de Georges Sorel," *Echo de Paris,* September 8, 1922. On details of interest concerning Sorel's youth and career as an engineer see Andreu, *Notre maître,* annexes I–III, pp. 315–19.

4. Andreu, *Notre maître,* p. 32. See also Édouard Berth, *Du "Capital" aux "Réflexions sur la violence"* (Paris: Rivière, 1932), pp. 172–73n, and Jean Variot, ed., *Propos de Georges Sorel* (Paris: Gallimard, 1935), p. 189.

5. "Mes raisons du syndicalisme" (1910), *Matériaux d'une théorie du prolétariat* (3rd ed., Paris: Rivière, 1929), p. 249.

6. The following is based largely on Andreu, "Du nouveau sur Georges Sorel," *Figaro littéraire,* July 1948; see the more recent Félicien Gallet, "À la recherche de Georges Sorel et de Marie David: le double miracle d'un amour," *Visage de l'Ain,* 18 (January/February 1965):38–43.

7. The present writer has seen the death certificates of both Marie-Euphrasie David and Georges Sorel, in which their marital status was denoted *"célébataire."* Édouard Berth, Sorel's closest friend in later years, does not appear to have commented on Sorel's relationship with Marie-Euphrasie at all. Jean Variot has written that Sorel ran off with the wife of one of his superiors and that her husband would not grant her a divorce: see "Georges Sorel et la révolution nationale," *Revue universelle,* N.S. 16 (August 25, 1941):226. Édouard Dolléans and Quoniam also long held Variot's views: see Dolléans, *Proudhon* (3rd ed., Paris: Rivière, 1948), p. 496; and Quoniam, "Notre compatriote," p. 5. See also Andreu, *Notre maître,* annex V, p. 324.

8. "Lettre à Daniel Halévy," July 15, 1907, in *Réflexions sur la violence* (10th ed., Paris: Rivière, 1946), pp. 7–8.

9. See Andreu, *Notre maître*, annex IV, pp. 320–23.
10. "Sur les applications de la psycho-physique," *Revue philosophique*, 22 (October 1886):374, 375; "Le Calcul des probabilités et l'expérience," ibid., 23 (January 1887):66; "Correspondance," ibid., 25 (April 1888):462; "De la cause en physique," ibid., 26 (November 1888):479. Sorel also published in the *Bulletin de la Société agricole, scientifique et littéraire des Pyrénées-Orientales;* also see his *Les Girondins du Rousillon* (Perpignan: Charles Latrobe, 1889). For a recent study of these works see Erica Boffi, "Dalla polemica antipositivistica al socialismo," *Georges Sorel: studi e ricerche* (Florence: Olschki, 1974), p. 14.
11. See Halévy, "Préface" to Andreu, *Notre maître*, p. 15; Jules Monnerot, "Georges Sorel ou l'introduction aux mythes modernes," *Science et conscience de la société: mélange en l'honneur de Raymond Aron* (Paris: Calmann-Lévy, 1971), p. 380; Mario Missiroli, "Prefazione," *Lettere a un amico d'Italia* (hereafter cited as Sorel to Missiroli) (San Casciano: F. Cappelli, 1963), pp. 14–17. On controversies concerning the origin of the two books of 1889 see Boffi, "Dalla polemica antipositivistica al socialismo," p. 19, and Georges Goriely, *Le Pluralisme dramatique de Georges Sorel* (Paris: Rivière, 1962), p. 30.
12. *Contribution à l'étude profane de la Bible* (Paris: A. Ghio, 1889), pp. vii, viii, 2.
13. *Le Procès de Socrate* (Paris: F. Alcan, 1889), pp. 85, 121–22, 172, 238; for the argument that "social rationalism" today threatens only those institutions unable to bear open confrontation, see Neil McInnes, "Georges Sorel on the Trial of Socrates," *Politics*, 10 (1975):37–44.
14. *Le Procès*, pp. 11, 13, 21, 72n, 150–61, 183, 186, 210–11.
15. Ibid., p. 31.
16. See especially articles by Sorel in *Revue philosophique* (1890), *Revue Scientifique* (1891), and the *Annales de philosophie chrétienne* (1892).
17. See "Lettera auto-biografica," February 20, 1910, in Agostino Lanzillo, *Giorgio Sorel* (Rome: Libreria Editrice Romana, 1910), pp. 5–6. It was probably Marie-Euphrasie (Sorel certainly thought so) who made it possible for him to transcend his own class outlook and who inspired him to dedicate the remaining years of his life to the study of society. In the "lettera auto-biografica" he wrote: "Our intellectual life depends in large part on a chance meeting."
18. "Essai sur la philosophie de Proudhon," *Revue philosophique*, 34 (July 1892): 44–46, 67–68; Andreu, *Notre maître*, p. 48.
19. "Lettera auto-biografica," pp. 5–8; Andreu, *Notre maître*, pp. 35–36; Variot, *Propos*, p. 251n.
20. Andreu, *Notre maître*, p. 36.
21. See Sorel's articles in *Revue scientifique* (1892 and 1893) and *Annales de philosophie chrétienne* (1892).
22. "Lettre à Daniel Halévy," p. 8.
23. Berth, *Du "Capital" aux "Réflexions sur la violence*," pp. 170–71; Henri Clouard, "Des souvenirs sur Georges Sorel," *Progrès civique*, 4 (September 16, 1922):24.
24. "Mes raisons du syndicalisme," p. 249.
25. "Science et socialisme," *Revue philosophique*, 35 (1893):509–11.
26. "La Crime politique, d'après M. Lombroso," *Revue scientifique*, 51 (May 6, 1893):561, 563, 564–65 [also published as "Une Faute du crime politique," *Archivio*

di psichiatria, scienze penali ed antropologia criminale, 14 (1893):450–55]. For a bibliography of Sorel's publications in Italy, see Gian Biago Furiozzi, "Sorel e l'Italia: bibliografia ragionata," *Annali della facoltà di scienze politiche* (Perugia: 1968–1970).

27. "Mes raisons du syndicalisme," p. 252; "Introduzione," May 1, 1901, to *Saggi di critica del Marxismo* (Milan: R. Sandron, 1903), pp. 5–6.

28. *D'Aristote à Marx* (Paris: Rivière, 1935), pp. 95–96, 149–51, 167, 217, 226–27 [first published as: "L'Ancienne et la nouvelle métaphysique," *Ère nouvelle*, 2 (March-June 1894):392–51, 461–82, 51–87 and 180–205]. Sorel was to take up the theory of knowledge a second time only at the end of his career in *De l'utilité du pragmatisme* (Paris: Rivière, 1921). See Paolo Pastori, "Scienza e metafisica in Sorel," *Storia e politica*, 8 (October/December 1969):602–616, and "Socialità e conoscenza in Sorel," *Rivista internazionale di filosofia del diritto*, 47 (1970): 409–410.

29. *D'Aristote à Marx*, pp. 161*n*, 177, 226, 263.

30. Ibid., p. 134.

31. *La Ruine du monde antique* (3rd ed., Paris: Rivière, 1933), pp. 41, 132–35, 142–43, 179; first published as "La Fin du paganisme," *Ère nouvelle*, 2 (August-October 1894):338–64; 33–72, and 170–99.

32. *La Ruine*, pp. 44, 88–89, 137, 140, 176–77, 186–87.

33. "Mes raisons du syndicalisme," pp. 249–51; "Introduzione" to *Saggi*, p. 6.

34. "Mes raisons du syndicalisme," pp. 249–51.

35. René Johannet, *Itinéraires d'intellectuels* (Paris: Nouvelle Librairie Nationale, 1921), p. 188*n*; Gian Biagio Furiozzi, *Sorel e l'Italia* (Florence: D'Anna, 1975), pp. 20–53.

36. "Mes raisons du syndicalisme," pp. 249–51; "Introduzione" to *Saggi*, pp. 6–7; *Introduction à l'économie moderne* (2nd ed., Paris: Rivière, 1922), p. 59. On Sorel and Durkheim, see Michele Maggi, *La Formazione dell'egemonia in Francia: l'ideologia sociale nella Terza Repubblica tra Sorel e Durkheim* (Bari: De Donato, 1977).

37. "Lettere di Georges Sorel a Benedetto Croce" (herafter cited as Sorel to Croce), December 20, 1895, in *Critica*, 25 (1927):45. A far less intensive correspondence was begun with Guglielmo Ferrero concerning the *Divenir social*: see "Georges Sorel e Guglielmo Ferrero fra 'cesarismo' borghese e socialismo (con 27 lettere inedite di Sorel a Ferrero 1896–1921)" (hereafter cited as Sorel to Ferrero), July 21, 1896, in *Pensiero politico*, 5 (1972):132.

38. Croce, "Antonio Labriola," *Marzocco*, February 14, 1904; Croce, *Storia dell'Italia da 1871 al 1915* (Bari: Laterza, 1928), p. 161; Croce, *Contribution à ma propre critique*, trans. J. Chaix-Ruy (Paris: Nagel, 1949), p. 48. Croce has also given an extended account of these activities in an essay, "Come nacque e come morì il marxismo in Italia: 1895–1900," published originally in the *Critica* and later as an appendix both to his own *Materialismo storico ed economia marxistica* (Bari: Laterza, 1946), and to his edition of Antonio Labriola, *La Concezione materialistica della storia* (Bari: Laterza, 1938). On the relations between Sorel and Labriola see Franco Bozzi, "Il Mancato incontro tra Sorel e Antonio Labriola," *Georges Sorel: studi e ricerche*, pp. 113–39.

39. The publication of Sorel's 343 letters to Croce was the first of such collections to appear. Boris Souvarine, in introducing selections from the correspondence, notes that Sorel did not want his letters to be published after his death. Sorel carefully destroyed copies of his own letters as well as the originals of his correspondents'. Souvarine wonders if Sorel forgot to express this wish to Croce, and also raises the question of whether Croce could have published the entire correspondence under the fascist regime in Italy [see "Lettres de Georges Sorel à Benedetto Croce," *Critique sociale*, 1 (March 1939):9]. On Sorel's relations with Croce see Salvatore Onufrio, "Considerazioni su Croce e Sorel," *Georges Sorel: studi e ricerche*, pp. 141–53. The appearance of this collection was followed by the publication of Sorel's correspondence (in whole or part) with Roberto Michels (1927), Hubert Lagardelle (1933), Paul Delesalle (1947), Vilfredo Pareto (1962), Mario Missiroli (1963), Guglielmo Ferrero (1972), and Napoleone Colajanni (1976). Sorel's correspondence with Édouard Berth has yet to be published in full. The entire correspondence (in the possession of Pierre Andreu) was accessible to Jules Levey for his Ph.D. thesis, published in 1967; for bibliographical details see below. Extracts of this correspondence with particular reference to Charles Péguy appeared in 1960; see "Lettres: Georges Sorel à Édouard Berth, extraits," ed. A. Martin, in *Amitié Charles Péguy*, no. 77 (May 1960):23–33.
40. "Superstition socialiste?" *Devenir social*, 1 (November 1895):739, 743, 748, 750.
41. "La Science dans l'éducation," *Devenir social*, 2 (February–May 1896):129, 219–20, 365, 460.
42. Signed "B," "Progrès et développement," *Devenir social*, 2 (March 1896):193–94, 200–201, 206–207.
43. "Étude sur Vico," *Devenir Social*, 2 (October–December 1896):796–809, 876, 934–35, and 1046. See Monnerot, "Georges Sorel ou l'introduction aux mythes modernes," p. 382, a comparison of Durkheim and Lévy-Bruhl; Hans Barth, *Masse und Mythos: die ideologische Krise an der Wende zum 20. Jahrhundert und die Theorie der Gewalt: Georges Sorel* (Hamburg: Rowohlt, 1959), on Sorel's relation to Proudhon, Renan, and Vico; and Giovanna Cavalleri, "Le Idee giuridiche e la trasformazione della società democratico-borghese," *Georges Sorel: studi e ricerche*, pp. 60–64, on the crucial role of Vico in Sorel's thought. On the application of Vico in France from Michelet to Sorel and beyond, see Patrick H. Hutton, "Vico's Theory of History and the French Revolutionary Tradition," *Journal of the History of Ideas*, 37 (1976):241–56; on Vico and modern theories of revolution, see Isaiah Berlin, "Corsi e ricorsi," *Journal of Modern History*, 50 (1978):480–89.
44. Antonio Labriola, *Essai sur la conception matérialiste de l'histoire*, with "Préface" by G. Sorel (hereafter cited as "Préface" to Labriola) (Paris: V. Giard and E. Brière, 1897), pp. 1, 5n, 5–7, 9, 12–15.
45. Studies in the *Devenir social* from May 1895 to December 1896 prepared the way for his drastic critique of Marxism.
46. Sorel to Croce, June 2, 1897, 25, p. 45.
47. Signed "H," "Contre une critique anarchiste," *Devenir social*, 3 (May 1897):453.
48. Review of Vilfredo Pareto's *Cours d'économie politique* in *Devenir social*, 3 (May 1897):473. See Gabriele de Rosa, ed., *Carteggi Paretiani, 1892–1923* (Rome: Banca Nazionale del Lavoro, 1962), p. 196; the correspondence was almost com-

pletely lost, leaving only the seventeen letters from Sorel to Pareto included in this collection. See also Giuseppe La Ferla, "Giorgio Sorel e Vilfredo Pareto: due spiriti inattuale," *Nuova antologia*, 488 (1963):303–312, for a general discussion of their relations.

49. "Sur la théorie marxiste de la valeur," *Journal des économistes*, 29 (May 1897): 224, 228–29, 231; also published as "Ueber die Marx'sche Werttheorie," *Sozialistische Monatshefte*, 1 (June 1897):345–53.

50. Signed "X," "Sociologie de la suggestion," *Devenir social*, 3 (August/September 1897):688.

51. "Die Entwickelung des Kapitalismus," *Sozialistische Monatshefte*, 1 (October 1897):544, 547.

52. "Der Ursprung des Staatssozialismus in Deutschland," *Sozialistische Monatshefte*, 1 (November 1897):610.

53. "Pro e contro il socialismo," *Devenir social*, 3 (October 1897):855, 864, 869, 879, 884; see "Mes Raisons du syndicalisme," pp. 252–53. Sorel and Merlino engaged in an intensive correspondence which has been entirely lost: see Furiozzi, *Sorel e l'Italia*, p. 65n. For Croce's differences with Labriola, see Gian Luca Casanuovi, "Materialismo e storiografia in Croce neglianni 1896–97," *Archivio storico italiano*, 135 (1977):3–100.

54. "Correspondance," *Devenir social*, 3 (December 1897):952.

55. Sorel to Croce, November 30 and December 27, 1897, 25, pp. 48, 51–52; see also "Introduzione" to *Saggi*, p. 1.

56. Sorel to Croce June 2, 1897, 25, p. 44; "Lettera auto-biografica," pp. 5–6; and Andreu, *Notre maître*, pp. 38–39, 56, and annex V, p. 324.

57. "Mes raisons du syndicalisme," p. 253.

58. Georges Valois, *D'un siècle à l'autre* (Paris: Nouvelle Librairie Nationale, 1921), pp. 131–33. "Georges Valois" was the pen name of Alfred Georges Gressent; others in the group included Lucien Jean, Gabriel de la Salle, Jean Grave, and Charles Albert. See also Robert Louzon, "Introduction" to Georges Sorel, *Lettres à Paul Delesalle* (hereafter cited as Sorel to Delesalle) (Paris: Grasset, 1947), p. 53; Dora Marucco, *Arturo Labriola e il sindacalismo revoluzionario in Italia* (Turin: Einaudi, 1970), p. 98.

59. Valois, *D'un siècle a l'autre*, p. 133.

60. "L'Avenir socialiste des syndicats," *Matériaux*, pp. 79–80, 87 [first published in *Humanité nouvelle*, 2 (March-May 1898):294–307 and 432–45].

61. Ibid., pp. 87–88, 98.

62. Ibid., pp. 80–82, 101, 114, 133.

63. Ibid., p. 112.

64. Ibid., pp. 121–23, 132.

65. Ibid., p. 127. See Goriely, *Le Pluralisme*, p. 11, on "Sorel as a Jansenist."

66. Ibid., pp. 85, 87, 92–96, 114–16, 121–22, 129–30.

67. Valois, *D'un siècle à l'autre*, pp. 131–32.

68. See Marucco, *Arturo Labriola*, p. 10.

69. Bernstein to Sorel, June 14, 1890, quoted in Uberto Lagardelle, ed., "Lettere de Giorgio Sorel a Uberto Lagardelle" (hereafter cited as Sorel to Lagardelle), *Educazione fascista*, 11 (March 1933):236.

70. Sorel to Croce, January 20, April 1, and April 23, 1898, 25, pp. 103, 106–107, 169–70.

71. See especially "Ein sozialistischen Staat?" *Sozialistische Monatshefte*, 2 (Febru-

ary 1898):60; "Was man von Vico lernt," 2 (June 1898):270–71; "Nuovi contribuiti alla teoria marxistica de valore," *Giornale degli economisti,* 2 (July 1898):17, 30.
72. Johannet, *Itinéraires d'intellectuels,* p. 191; Berth, *Du "Capital" aux "Réflexions sur la violence",* p. 174.
73. "Mes raisons du syndicalisme," pp. 254–56.
74. Saverio Merlino, *Formes et essences du socialisme,* with "Préface" by G. Sorel (hereafter cited as "Preface" to Merlino) (Paris: V. Giard and E. Brière, 1898), pp. xix–xv.
75. Ibid., p. xlii. The reference to Nietzsche is interesting. Although Sorel read Nietzsche, he never discussed him at length; for him Proudhon sufficed.
76. Ibid., pp. xvi–xvii.
77. Sorel to Lagardelle, August 10 and 15, 1898, pp. 239–43.
78. See also "La Necessità e il fatalismo nel marxismo," *Riforma sociale,* 8 (August 15, 1898):708–709.
79. In September 1898 Sorel suggested a program for the *Mouvement socialiste:* it was to be reformist and Dreyfusard (Sorel to Lagardelle, September 20, 1898, p. 323).
80. La Crise du socialisme," *Revue politique et parlementaire,* 18 (December 1898): 597, 600, 607, 612.
81. "Der amerikanische Kapitalismus," *Sozialistische Monatshefte,* 2 (December 1898):543.
82. Sorel to Croce, December 27, 1898, and February 23 and June 16, 1899, 25, pp. 175, 301, 307. The *Discorrendo* was translated as *Socialisme et philosophie: lettres à G. Sorel* (Paris: V. Giard and E. Brière, 1899); see pp. iv–v, 207–224. On Sorel's controversy with Antonio Labriola see Furiozzi, "La Fortuna italiana di Sorel," *Georges Sorel: studi e ricerche,* pp. 96–97; Bozzi, "Il Mancato incontro tra Sorel e Antonio Labriola," pp. 113–39; and Furiozzi, *Sorel e l'Italia,* pp. 121–31.
83. Sorel to Lagardelle, January 8, 1906, p. 769; "Lettera auto-biografica," p. 7. See also Johannet, *Itinéraires d'intellectuels,* p. 191, and Berth, *Du "Capital" aux "Réflexions sur la violence",* p. 174.
84. "L'éthique du socialisme," *Morale sociale* (Paris: F. Alcan, 1899), pp. 136–39 [also published in *Revue de métaphysique et de morale,* 8 (May 1899):280–301].
85. "Morale et socialisme," *Mouvement socialiste,* 1 (March 1, 1899):207, 209.
86. "Y a-t-il de l'utopie dans le marxisme?" *Revue de métaphysique et de morale,* 7 (March 1899):158–59, 167, 171–74.
87. "Église, évangile et socialisme," *La Ruine,* p. 311 [first published as: "Chiesa, van-gelo e socialismo," *Rivista critica del socialismo,* 1 (April-May 1899):295–304, 385–94].
88. Sorel to Croce, June 7, 1899, 25, p. 306. On Sorel's activities on Italian reviews to 1903 see Furiozzi, *Sorel e l'Italia,* pp. 65–141.
89. "L'Evoluzione del socialismo in Francia," *Riforma sociale,* 9 (June 15, 1899):524.
90. "Quelques objections au matérialisme économique," *Humanité nouvelle,* 3 (June-July 1899):659 and 42.
91. Sorel to Lagardelle, July 15 and 19, 1899, pp. 326–27, 347; Sorel to Croce, August 4, 1899, 25, p. 310.
92. "La Scissione socialista in Francia in rapporto con la teoria socialista," *Rivista critica del socialismo,* 1 (October 1899):869.
93. "Socialismo e democrazia: conclusione sulla faccenda Dreyfus," *Rivista critica del socialismo,* 1 (November-December 1899):874, 965–69, and 980.
94. "Préface pour Colajanni," *Matériaux,* pp. 175–200 [first published in Napoleone

Colajanni, *Le Socialisme* (Paris: V. Giard and E. Brière, 1900), pp. i–xxl]; "La Science et la morale," *Questions de morale* (Paris: F. Alcan, 1900), pp. 1–25. The transformation in Sorel's thinking is detailed in some seventeen recently published letters by Sorel to Colajanni, who was also editor of the *Rivista popolare*, to which Sorel contributed: see S. Massimo Ganci, ed., "I Rapporti Sorel-Colajanni nella 'crisi del marxismo' (1896–1905)," *Annuali dell'Istituto Giangiacomo Feltrinelli*, 17 (1976):191–217.

95. "Préface pour Colajanni," pp. 177, 179; "Les Facteurs moraux de l'évolution," *Questions de morale*, pp. 93–100.

96. "Préface pour Colajanni," pp. 184–85, 188–89; "La Science et la morale," pp. 15, 22–25.

97. "Préface pour Colajanni," p. 199; "Les Facteurs moraux de l'évolution," pp. 93, 100.

98. "Préface pour Colajanni," p. 199.

99. Valois, *D'un siècle à l'autre*, pp. 135–36.

100. Daniel Halévy, *Péguy and Les Cahiers de la Quinzaine* (New York: Longmans, Green, 1947), p. 47; Romain Rolland, *Péguy* (2 vols., Buenos Aires: Viau-Feugere, 1946), 1, p. 42.

101. Halévy, *Péguy and Les Cahiers de la Quinzaine*, pp. 54–56, 59, 67, 71, 75.

102. Ibid., p. 67.

103. "Les Polémiques pour l'interprétation du marxisme: Bernstein et Kautsky," *Revue internationale de sociologie*, 7 (April-May 1900):264, 275, 284, and 369n.

104. "Les Dissensions de la social démocratie en Allemagne: à propos des écrits de M. Bernstein," *Revue politique et parlementaire*, 25 (July 1900):38–42, 44, 49–51, 55, 63, 66.

105. A number of articles published by Sorel in 1900–1901 are of less interest; see *Riforma sociale* (1900), *Mouvement socialiste* (1900 and 1901), and *Pages libres* (1901).

106. *La Valeur sociale de l'art* (Paris: Jacques, 1901), pp. 11, 27, 29; "Économie et agriculture," *Revue socialiste*, 33 (April 1901):427, 440–41; "Proudhon," *Pages libres*, 1 (May 4, 1901):399, 402; "Quelques mots sur Proudhon," *Cahiers de la quinzaine*, 2, no. 13 (1901):25.

107. "Introduzione" to *Saggi*, pp. 8–9, 13, 15.

108. Ibid., p. 15.

109. "Pour Proudhon," *Pages libres*, 1 (June 8, 1901):504.

110. *La Ruine*, pp. 319–20. This study was essentially a re-edition of "La Fin du paganisme" of 1894 with a new "Avertissement," additional notes, and a conclusion.

111. Sorel to Lagardelle, August 21 and September 14, 1901, 328–30.

112. "De l'église et de l'état," *Cahiers de la quinzaine*, 3, no. 3 (1901):4, 29, 55 [also published in *Revue socialiste*, 34 (August-October, 1901):129–54, 325–42, and 402–420].

113. Ibid., pp. 58, 61–64.

114. Halévy, *Péguy and Les Cahiers de la Quinzaine*, pp. 71–74; Jérôme and Jean Tharaud, *Notre cher Péguy* (2 vols., Paris: Plon, 1926), 1, p. 261; and René Salomé, "Le Lyrisme de M. Sorel," *Revue des jeunes*, 13 (January 25, 1923):151.

115. Tharaud, *Notre cher Péguy*, 1, p. 255.

116. Halévy, *Péguy, and Les Cahiers de la Quinzaine*, p. 76. Tharaud, *Notre cher Péguy*, 2, p. 138.

117. Halévy, *Péguy and Les Cahiers de la Quinzaine*, pp. 77–78. See Johannet, *Itinéraires d'intellectuels*, p. 202; Raïsa Maritain, *We Have Been Friends Together*, trans. J. Kernan (New York: Longmans, Green, 1947), p. 83.
118. Sorel to Croce, October 11, 1901, 25, p. 365; Sorel to Lagardelle, October 18 and November 2, 1901, pp. 330–31.
119. *L'Avenir socialiste des syndicats* (2nd ed., Paris: G. Jacques, 1901), pp. vii-viii, xv, xvl, xvii-xix.
120. "Préface pour Gatti," *Matériaux*, pp. 201–237 [first published in G. Gatti, *Le Socialisme et l'agriculture* (Paris: V. Giard and E. Brière, 1902), pp. 7–38, and simultaneously printed as "Socialismes nationaux," *Cahiers de la quinzaine*, 3, no. 14 (1902)].
121. Ibid., p. 202.
122. "Préface" to Fernand Pelloutier, *Histoire des bourses du travail* (Paris: Schleicher Frères, 1902), pp. 1–5, 26, 32.
123. "Idées socialistes et faits économiques au XIXᵉ siècle," *Revue socialiste*, 35 (March-May 1902):297, 303, 306, 317, 402–403, and 540.
124. "Storia e scienze sociale," *Rivista italiana de sociologia*, 6 (March/June 1902): 224–25.
125. "Le Matérialisme historique," *Bulletin de la Société française de philosophie*, 2 (May 1902):105; "Les Syndicats industriels et leur signification," *Revue socialiste*, 36 (July/August 1902):179.
126. "Le Matérialisme historique," p. 110.
127. "La Crise de la pensée catholique," *Revue de métaphysique et de morale*, 10 (September 1902):531–32, 550.
128. See especially "Observations sur le régime des chemins de fer," 1 (January/February 1903):3–5; "Le Compagnonnage," 1 (March/April 1903):88; "Nouveaux réquisitoires de M. Brunetière," 1 (May/June 1903):150; "À propos d'anticlericalisme," 1 (July/August 1903):248; and "Leon XIII," 1 (November/December 1903): 377–78.
129. Sorel to Croce, May 9, 1903, 36, p. 31; Sorel to Lagardelle, August 10 and 23, 1903, pp. 507, 508–509.
130. Sorel to Croce, April 28, 1903, 25, p. 372.
131. Cf. Boffi, "Della polemica antipositivistica al socialismo," p. 35, and Andreu, *Notre maître*, pp. 139–40. See also Goriely, *Le Pluralisme*, p. 104; L. P. Rouanet, "Irrationalism and Myth in Georges Sorel," *Review of Politics*, 26 (1964):45–69; and, especially, Andreu, "Bergson et Sorel," *Études bergsoniennes*, 3 (Paris: Michel, 1952), p. 68.

Revolutionary Syndicalism

Chapter 2. The Man

1. Between 1899 and 1901 Sorel contributed several articles to the *Mouvement Socialiste*.
2. *Introduction*, p. 12.

3. Ibid., pp. 3–4, 232, 251, 390–97. On controversies concerning this work see Cavallari, "Le Idee giuridiche e la trasformazione della società democratico-borghese," pp. 80–84, and Monnerot, "Georges Sorel ou l'introduction aux mythes modernes," pp. 380, 385, 403, 411.

4. *Introduction*, pp. 390–97. See Sorel to Croce, November 27, 1903, and December 27, 1905, 26, pp. 34, 93.

5. Sorel to Croce, November 27, 1903, 26, p. 34.

6. Sorel developed at length a theory of mechanics from Bergsonian metaphysics: see "Sur les divers aspects de la mécanique," *Revue de métaphysique et de morale*, 11 (November 1903):734; see also the very abstruse "Les Préoccupations métaphysiques de physiciens modernes," ibid., 13 (November 1905):859–89, which was also published in the *Cahiers de la quinzaine*, 8, no. 16 (1907).

7. Sorel also attended the lectures of the physician Georges Castex at the Collège de France. See Georges Castex, *La Douleur physique*, with preface by G. Sorel (Paris: Jacques, 1905); in 1919 the preface was revised and appended to the second edition of the *Introduction* as "L'Humanité contre la douleur," pp. 399–421.

8. "Le Développement des états mystiques chez sainte Thérèse," *Bulletin de la Société française de philosophie*, 6 (January 1906): esp. p. 26. Jacques Maritain probably overheard Sorel's remarks after this meeting when Maritain stopped in at Péguy's and heard Sorel say: "Those people do not know the real sources. There are two books which must be read on the subject: *Le catéchisme spirituel* by Father Surin, a seventeenth-century Jesuit and. . . ." Raïsa Maritain has written that Jacques seized only upon the first title, "and thus we came to know this masterpiece of spirituality. The reading of this book at once had a decisive effect on us. . . ." See Maritain, *We Have Been Friends Together*, p. 153.

9. The name of the institution had been changed in 1901.

10. Sorel's reviews appeared in the *Revue générale de bibiographie française*, 2–3 (1904–1905), and continued to appear when the periodical was renamed *Revue générale de critique et de bibliographie*, 4–5 (1906–1907).

11. Sorel to Croce, January 23, 1904, 26, p. 35.

12. "Due anni de anticlericalismo in Francia," *Rivista popolare di politica, lettere e scienze social*, 10 (May 31, 1904):259–63; and "La Restaurazione giacobina in Francia," ibid., 11 (February 15, 1905):74–76.

13. Sorel to Lagardelle, November 1, 1904, p. 514; see also Furiozzi, *Sorel e l'Italia*, pp. 184–85.

14. Sorel to Croce, January 10, 1905, 26, p. 39, and Sorel to Lagardelle, June 10, 1905, p. 764.

15. *Insegnamenti sociali della economia contemporanea* (Milan: R. Sandron, 1907), pp. 4–6, 388.

16. Ibid., pp. 53–55, 278n, 389–98.

17. *Le Système historique de Renan* (Paris: Jacques, 1905–1906), pp. 2, 198–208; see also Sorel to Croce, November 20, 1912, 26, p. 439.

18. *Système*, pp. 207–208.

19. Ibid., p. 2.

20. Sorel to Michels, November 13, 1905, in Roberto Michels, ed., "Lettere de Georges Sorel a Roberto Michels," *Nuovi studi di diritto, economia e politica*, 2 (September/October 1929):289.

21. "Préface de 1905," *Matériaux*, p. 58. This edition was never published, for he had also in 1905 begun to think of a series of articles on violence which would have appeared incongruous beside a study written in 1898. The "Préface de 1905" is of interest because of his opposition to sabotage as well as to collaboration between mutualities and cooperatives and the syndicates (see pp. 59, 63–64n, 66–67, 75, 145–51, and 153–60).

22. Berth, *Du "Capital" aux "Réflexions sur la violence"*, p. 175.

23. Sorel's first articles published in Lagardelle's review were the "Conclusioni" of the *Insegnamenti*["Conclusions aux *Enseignements sociaux de l'économie moderne*," *Mouvement socialiste*, 7 (July 1, 1905):289–99], and the "Préface de 1905" ["Le Syndicalisme révolutionnaire," *Mouvement socialiste*, 7 (November 1 and 15, 1905):265–80].

24. Sorel's first article published in Leone's review was the "Conclusioni" of the *Insegnamenti* ["Insegnamenti sociali dell'economia moderna," *Divenire sociale*, 1 (August 1, 1905):232–35].

25. See below, Chapter 4.

26. *Divenire sociale*, 1–2 (October 1, 1905–April 1, 1906), and *Mouvement socialiste*, 7 (January 15–June 15, 1906).

27. See below.

28. Rolland, *Péguy*, 1, p. 321.

29. Sorel to Lagardelle, January 8, 1906, pp. 769–70.

30. Michels, ed., "Lettere," pp. 288n–289n.

31. For good general treatments of revolutionary syndicalism during these years see Peter Stearns, *Revolutionary Syndicalism and French Labor* (New Brunswick: Rutgers University Press, 1971), and Daniel L. Horowitz, *The Italian Labor Movement* (Cambridge: Harvard University Press, 1963).

32. *Insegnamenti*, p. 278n.

33. Sorel to Lagardelle, May 3, 1906, p. 771.

34. Ibid., May 26, 1906, pp. 772–73.

35. Ibid., June 11 and August 6, 1906, pp. 773–76; Sorel to Croce, October 12, 1906, 26, p. 96.

36. "La Démocratie," *Bulletin de la Société française de philosophie*, 7 (March 1907): 105.

37. See below, Chapter 4.

38. "A Proposito del Congresso di Roma," *Divenire sociale*, 2 (October 15, 1906): 308–310.

39. "Le Déclin du parti socialiste international," *Mouvement socialiste*, 8 (February 15, 1906):194–202 [also *Divenire sociale*, 2 (January 1, 1906):3–6].

40. "Les *Droits acquis* de Lassalle," *Mouvement socialiste*, 8 (April 15, 1906):476–85 [also *Divenire sociale*, 2 (April 16, 1906):115–18].

41. *Mouvement socialiste*, 8 (August-December 1906):289–328, 65–129, 219–49, and 314–46.

42. "La Storia ebraica ed il materialismo storico," *Divenire sociale*, 2 (May 1, 1906): 131–33; "Robert Owen," ibid., 2 (June 1, 1906):164–67; "Le Elezioni generali in Francia," ibid., 2 (June 16, 1906):177; "C'è qualche cosa di religiosa nel socialismo?" ibid., 2 (November 1, 1906):325–28; "I cattolici contro la chiesa," ibid., 2 (December 16, 1906):369–72.

43. Sorel to Croce, January 10, March 16, June 10, September 10, and October 23, 1907, and May 15 and 27, 1908, 26, pp. 98-106.
44. "Le Prétendu 'socialisme juridique,'" *Mouvement socialiste*, 9 (April 1907): 321-47.
45. "La Crise morale et religieuse," *Mouvement socialiste*, 9 (July 15, 1907):13-32.
46. "Lettre à Daniel Halévy," *Mouvement socialiste*, 9 (August 15/September 15, 1907):137-65.
47. Review of C. Maurras's *Le Dilemme de Marc Sangnier* in *Mouvement socialiste*, 9 (August 15/September 15, 1907):251.
48. "L'*Évolution créatrice*," *Mouvement socialiste*, 9-10 (October 15, 1907-April 15, 1908):257-82, 478-94, 34-52, 184-94, and 276-94.
49. "Le Idee di libertà," *Divenire sociale*, 3 (January 1, 1907):2-5; "Le Idee di uguaglianza," ibid., 3 (March 16, 1907):81-84; "La Rivoluzione dreyfusarda," ibid., 3 (March 5, 1907):65-68; "Modernismo nella religione e nel socialismo," ibid., 3 (November 16, 1907):339-45; "Morale e socialismo," ibid., 4 (May 1, 1908):152-54; "La Decadenza parlementare," ibid., 4 (May 16, 1908):169-71. Many of the articles published in the *Divenire sociale* did not appear in the *Mouvement socialiste*.
50. *La Décomposition du Marxisme* (Paris: Rivière, 1908), p. 60. The study is presented in English translation in Irving L. Horowitz, *Radicalism and the Revolt against Reason* (New York: Humanities Press, 1961), pp. 207-254.
51. *Décomposition*, pp. 22, 58-59, 60.
52. *Réflexions*, p. iii.
53. *Lo Sciopero generale e la violenza*, trans. S. Piroddi (Rome: Tipografia Industria e Lavoro, 1906).
54. Johannet, "Un Précurseur de la Révolution nationale: Georges Sorel," *Candide*, 17 (July 16, 1941):5; Variot, "Georges Sorel," *Nouvelles littéraires*, 10 (October 3, 1931):1; see also J. H. Meisel, *The Genesis of Georges Sorel* (Ann Arbor: George Wahr, 1951), p. 18.
55. *Réflexions*, p. 6.
56. See *Matériaux*, p. 189n. On Sorel and Le Bon see Horowitz, *Radicalism and the Revolt against Reason*, pp. 36-39 (Sorel had reviewed Le Bon's *Psychologie des foules* in 1895 in the *Devenir social*); see also Robert A. Nye, "Two Paths to a Psychology of Social Action: Gustave Le Bon and Georges Sorel," *Journal of Modern History*, 45 (September 1973):411-38.
57. *Réflexions*, pp. 61, 130.
58. Ibid., p. 51.
59. *Considerazioni sulla violenza*, trans. A. Sarno, with preface by B. Croce (Bari: Laterza, 1907); Sorel to Croce, May 6, 1907, 26, p. 100; also Sorel to Halévy, July 7, 1907, in Halévy, "Georges Sorel: introduction à deux lettres inédites," *Fédération*, no. 34 (November 1947):3-4.
60. *Réflexions*, pp. 107, 110, 332.
61. *Les Illusions du progrès* (4th ed., Paris: Rivière, 1927), pp. 7-8. An Italian edition was published several years later: *Le Illusioni del progresso* (Milan: R. Sandron, 1910). A recent English translation has also appeared, trans. J. and C. Stanley (Berkeley: University of California Press, 1969).
62. *Illusions*, pp. 3-6, 49, 137.

63. Tharaud, *Notre cher Péguy*, 1, pp. 258-59.
64. "Apologie pour la violence," *Matin*, May 18, 1908; the article was included in the appendix to later editions of the *Réflexions*, beginning with the second edition of 1910.
65. "Les Illusions du progrès," *Petite République*, June 12, 1908.
66. See below, Chapter 4.
67. "Modernisme dans la religion et dans le socialisme," *Revue critique des idées et des livres*, 2 (August 10, 1908):177-204.
68. Sorel to Croce, September 18, 1908, 26, p. 108.
69. Louzon, "Introduction" to Sorel to Delesalle, p. 108n.
70. Sorel to Lagardelle, March 2, 1908, p. 970.
71. Sorel to Croce, June 24, 1908, 26, p. 108.
72. Pierre Angel, *Essais sur G. Sorel* (2 vols., Paris: Rivière, 1936), 1, p. 271.
73. Louzon, "Introduction" to Sorel to Delesalle, pp. 107-108n.
74. Sorel to Lagardelle, September 27, 1908, pp. 966-67; Louzon, "Introduction" to Sorel to Delesalle, p. 109n.
75. "Lettera auto-biografica," p. 8.
76. Sorel to Lagardelle, October 31, 1908, p. 968.
77. Sorel to Delesalle, November 2, 1908, p. 108.
78. Sorel to Lagardelle, p. 328.
79. "La Politique américaine," *Mouvement socialiste*, 10 (June 15, 1908):449-56; "Grandeur et décadence de Rome: la république d'Auguste," ibid., 10 (July 15, 1908):36-51; and "Les intellectuels à Athènes," ibid., 10 (September 15, 1908): 214-35.
80. *La Révolution dreyfusienne* (2nd ed., Paris: Rivière, 1910), pp. 14-16, 31, 51, 54, 64, 72.
81. Sorel to Croce, June 27, 1909, 26, p. 195.
82. See, for example, Sorel's enthusiastic letter on the Parma strike of 1908, "which applied his doctrine" published in the Bolognese *Internazionale*, July 21, 1908.
83. Arturo Labriola, *Karl Marx*, with preface by G. Sorel (hereafter cited as "Préface" to Labriola) (Paris: Rivière, 1910), pp. i, xxxiii.
84. See some seven articles in the *Divenire sociale* from July 16 to December 31, 1909, including: "La Disfatta dei 'mufles,'" 5 (July 16, 1909):177-81; "La letteratura sindacalista," 5 (September 1, 1909):219-20; "I dolori dell'ora presente," 5 (September 16/October 1, 1909):236-40; "La Maturità del movimento sindicale," 5 (December 16, 1909):257-61; and "Gl'intellettuali control gli operai," 5 (December 31, 1909):295-97. See also Furiozzi, "Quattro lettere inedite di Sorel a Pouget e Dolléans," *Pensiero politico*, 10 (1977):423-24.
85. "Socialistes antiparlementaires," *Action française*, August 22, 1909 [this is the same as "La Disfatta dei 'mufles,'" *Divenire sociale*, 5 (July 16, 1909):177-81].
86. Lanzillo, *Giorgio Sorel*, pp. 68-70.
87. Pierre Gilbert, "Une Conversation avec M. Georges Sorel: Ferrer et Briand," *Action française*, September 29, 1909.
88. Lanzillo, *Giorgio Sorel*, pp. 68-69; Furiozzi, *Sorel e l'Italia*, pp. 242-43.
89. Lanzillo, *Giorgio Sorel*, p. 70.
90. "Préface" to Victor Griffuelhes and Louis Niel, *Les Objectifs de nos luttes de classes* (Paris: La Publication Sociale, 1910), p. 5.

91. "Unité et multiplicité," *Réflexions*, pp. 407, 415–416.
92. See below; see also discussion in H. Stuart Hughes, *Consciousness and Society* (New York: Vintage Books, 1961), pp. 92–93, 173–76.
93. "Le Confessioni," *Divenire sociale*, 6 (March 1–May 16, 1910):45–47, 66–68, 84–86, 113–114, 131–133; also published as a brochure, *Le Confessioni: come divenni sindacalista* (Rome: Libreria Editrice del Divenire sociale, 1910); see also "Mes raisons du syndicalisme," pp. 239–86. The version in *Matériaux* does not include the introduction to the original, due to Sorel's renewed allegiance to a proletarian movement when it was published in 1918 (*Matériaux*, pp. 239–40n). See also Vito Mercadante, *Le Ferrovie ai ferrovieri: con prefazione di Vilfredo Pareto e lettera di Giorgio Sorel* (Milan: Tipografia Koschitz, 1911), pp. 6–8 (for which Sorel refused to write a preface).
94. *Le Confessioni*, p. 3.
95. "Giorgio Sorel e i monarchici francese," *Giornale d'Italia*, November 20, 1910.
96. A. Pezzotti, "Une Parti syndicaliste in Italie," *Mouvement socialiste*, 13 (March 1911):184.
97. Ibid., p. 185.

Chapter 3. The Idea

1. On Sorel as systematizer see Édouard Dolléans, "Le Visage de Georges Sorel," *Revue d'histoire économique et sociale*, 26 (1947):49.
2. In the *Réflexions* Sorel speaks of the society of the future as "syndicalism," while in the *Illusions* and generally elsewhere he calls it "socialism."
3. "Préface de 1905," p. 66.
4. *Réflexions*, pp. 35–36, 44, 177–178, 179; see also Monnerot, "Georges Sorel ou l'introduction aux mythes modernes," p. 393.
5. *Réflexions*, pp. 50, 182. For a recent study see Rouanet, "Irrationalism and Myth in Georges Sorel," pp. 45–69.
6. *Réflexions*, pp. 32, 50, 177–78, 180, 182; *Système*, pp. 305–312; *Décomposition*, p. 50; *Insegnamenti*, p. 95. In "Le Prétendu 'socialisme juridique,'" p. 331, Sorel wrote that the feeling for revenge for the Commune was stronger than that for the defeat of 1870.
7. *Réflexions*, p. 182.
8. *Décomposition*, pp. 5–8, 64; *Réflexions*, p. 196; *Introduction*, pp. 394–95; and "Préface" to Labriola, pp. xxxvii–xxxviii.
9. *Introduction*, p. 396; *Réflexions*, pp. 32–33, 46, 181; and "L'*Évolution créatrice*," 10, p. 288.
10. Review of E. Dolleans' *Le Caractère religieux de socialisme*, in *Mouvement socialiste*, 8 (November 1906):285–86.
11. *Réflexions*, p. 49.
12. *Système*, pp. 305–312; *Réflexions*, pp. 46–47; "Préface" to Labriola, p. vi; and "Préface de 1905," p. 67. See also Paolo Pastori, "Il Mito sociale in Sorel," *Storia e politica*, 7 (October/December 1968):662–68.
13. *Réflexions*, p. 181.
14. Ibid., pp. 45n, 46–47, 218, 316–17.
15. Ibid., p. 12.

16. Ibid., pp. 149, 173, 230; "Mes raisons du syndicalisme," pp. 249–50.
17. Ibid., p. 184.
18. "L'*Évolution créatrice*," 10, p. 294; *Décomposition*, p. 59; *Réflexions*, pp. 16–18, 316–17; *Introduction*, p. 6; *Illusions*, pp. 5–6, 276; *Insegnamenti*, p. 9.
19. *Réflexions*, p. 21.
20. Ibid., pp. 46, 176, 199, 201; "Apologie de la violence," pp. 433–36.
21. "Unité et multiplicité," p. 432.
22. *Réflexions*, pp. 35–36, 44, 358–60; "La Crise morale et religieuse," p. 13.
23. *Décomposition*, p. 64.
24. "Unité et multiplicité," pp. 429–32; *Réflexions*, pp. 72, 75, 106–108, 200, 324–25; "Conclusions aux *Enseignements sociaux de l'économie moderne*," p. 298; *Décomposition*, p. 68; *Insegnamenti*, pp. 5–47; "Préface" to Griffuelhes and Niel, p. 6; *La Révolution dreyfusienne*, p. 28; and "Gl'intellettuali contro gli operai," pp. 296–97.
25. *Réflexions*, p. 240n; the emphasis is Sorel's.
26. "Unité et multiplicité," p. 429.
27. "Conclusions aux *Enseignements sociaux de l'économie moderne*," p. 299; *Réflexions*, p. 350.
28. "Unité et multiplicité," pp. 429–32; *Décomposition*, pp. 51–52; "Robert Owen," p. 66; "I Dolori dell'ora presente," p. 240; *Insegnamenti*, p. 38; *La Révolution dreyfusienne*, pp. 20–21; *Introduction*, p. 73; *Réflexions*, p. 173; "Le Prétendu 'socialisme juridique,'" p. 342; "Conclusions aux *Enseignements sociaux de l'économie moderne*," pp. 292–93.
29. "Unité et multiplicité," pp. 430–31; "Préface de 1905," pp. 73–74.
30. "Préface de 1905," p. 431.
31. Ibid., pp. 429–32; *Réflexions*, pp. 202, 278; *Système*, pp. 165, 377; Review of E. Boutroux's *Science et religion dans la philosophie contemporaine* in *Mouvement socialiste*, 10 (May 15, 1908):389; "Préface de 1905," p. 146; *Décomposition*, p. 64.
32. *Réflexions*, pp. 113–14, 192; "Conclusions aux *Enseignements sociaux de l'économie moderne*," pp. 292–93; "Préface de 1905," pp. 155, 158; *Introduction*, p. 172.
33. Ibid., p. 268.
34. "Apologie de la violence," pp. 433–36; *Réflexions*, pp. 22–24, 35–36, 136, 247, 434. For a recent interpretation of Sorel's conception of violence see Claude Polin, "La Violence de Sisyphe ou Georges Sorel et sa logique," *Réflexions* (Paris: Rivière, 1972), vii–xliv; see also Albert Garreau, "Georges Sorel et la bourgeoisie," *Ordre français*, 145 (November 1971):48. For a theological and historical assessment of Sorel's theory of violence (from ancient Christian heresies to modern "liberation" movements, see George W. Huntston, "Four Modalities of Violence, with Special Reference to the Writings of Georges Sorel," *Journal of Church and State*, 16 (Winter–Spring 1974):237–45 and 248–61.
35. *Décomposition*, p. 66; "Le Déclin du parti socialiste international," p. 198; *Réflexions*, p. 434.
36. *Réflexions*, pp. 166, 257, 263.
37. "Apologie de la violence," p. 435.
38. "Préface de 1905," p. 70; *Réflexions*, pp. 62, 118, 278; "Unité et multiplicité," pp. 418–23; *Système*, pp. 198–208.
39. "Préface de 1905," p. 67; "A Proposito de Congresso di Roma," p. 310; "Les *Droits*

acquis de Lassalle," p. 485; *Décomposition*, p. 66; "L'*Évolution créatrice*," p. 279; "La Letteratura sindacalista," p. 219; "Préface" to Griffuelhes and Niel, pp. 7–8; *Réflexions*, pp. 381, 389.

40. *Système*, pp. 198–208, 316; *Réflexions*, pp. 97–98, 190; *Décomposition*, p. 12; "La Maturità del movimento sindacale," p. 257; "Unité et multiplicité," p. 424; "La Storia ebraica ed il materialismo storico," p. 133; "Les *Droits acquis* de Lassalle," p. 484; "Conclusions aux *Enseignements sociaux de l'économie moderne*," pp. 297–98; and "Le Prétendu 'socialisme juridique,'" p. 332.

41. *Réflexions*, p. 120.

42. Ibid., pp. 71, 96–98, 115–16; *Illusions*, p. 134.

43. *Réflexions*, p. 94.

44. Ibid., pp. 115–16, 118–19, 130, 191. In the *Illusions*, pp. 210–11, 212n, and 213–14, as well as in the "Préface de 1905," p. 74, Sorel wrote that bourgeois cowardice served only to increase the revolutionary ardor of the proletariat and intensify the class struggle.

45. *Réflexions*, p. 168.

46. "Conclusions aux *Enseignements sociaux de l'économie moderne*," p. 299.

47. *Réflexions*, pp. 21, 96, 100, 130, 168, 193, 202, 204, 226, 230, 233, 236–37; *Système*, pp. 335–36; *Décomposition*, pp. 24, 48, 56n, 58, 66–68; "Préface de 1905," p. 61; "Conclusions aux *Enseignements sociaux de l'économie moderne*," p. 298.

48. See above, Chapter 3, note 2.

49. "Préface de 1905," p. 74.

50. *Réflexions*, pp. 346, 351–54.

51. Ibid., pp. 39, 319, 346, 387.

52. Ibid., p. 354; "La Crise morale et religieuse," pp. 27–35.

53. *Réflexions*, pp. 318–19; "La Crise morale et religieuse," pp. 23–24, 30, 35; "Préface de 1905," p. 147.

54. *Réflexions*, pp. 343, 371; "La Démocratie," p. 103.

55. "Morale e socialismo," p. 152; "La Crise morale et religieuse," p. 36.

56. *Réflexions*, p. 365; *Insegnamenti*, p. 29; Review of L. Garriguet's *Régime de la propriété* in *Mouvement socialiste*, 10 (January 15, 1908):151; and "La Crise morale et religieuse," p. 23.

57. *Réflexions*, pp. 313n, 386; "Morale e socialismo," pp. 152–54.

58. *Réflexions*, pp. 17, 313, 315, 262–63, 384–85; *Illusions*, p. 274; and "La Crise morale et religieuse," p. 13.

59. *Insegnamenti*, pp. 172–73.

60. "La Crise morale et religieuse," p. 13; Review of J. Lemaître's *Jean-Jacques Rousseau* in *Mouvement socialiste*, 9 (June 1907):507; *Réflexions*, pp. 212–13.

61. *Réflexions*, p. 364.

62. Ibid., pp. 316–17, 322, 345, 365, 386; "La Crise morale et religieuse," p. 35; "Le Prétendu 'socialisme juridique,'" p. 328; "Unité et multiplicité," p. 405; and "Morale e socialismo," pp. 152–54.

63. *Illusions*, p. 136; "Le Idee di uguaglianza," pp. 83–84; "La Rivoluzione dreyfusarda," pp. 67–68; *Décomposition*, pp. 44, 49.

64. "Préface de 1905," p. 70; "La Rivoluzione dreyfusarda," pp. 67–68; *Décomposition*, pp. 53–54, 68; *Illusions*, p. 10; *Réflexions*, pp. 91, 154.

65. *Réflexions*, pp. 324–25.

66. *Illusions*, p. 123; "Préface de 1905," p. 70.

67. *Réflexions,* pp. 113, 163, 299; "La Restaurazione giacobina in Francia," pp. 74–75; "La Démocratie," pp. 104–105; *Insegnamenti,* p. 31; Review of G. Ferrero's *Grandeur et décadence de Rome* in *Mouvement socialiste,* 8 (July 1906):266–67; *Décomposition,* pp. 27–28. See also Preston King, *Fear of Power: An Analysis of Anti-Statism in Three French Writers* (London: Frank Cass, 1967), p. 91.

68. *Introduction,* pp. 160–61; "Préface de 1905," p. 70.

69. *Introduction,* p. 161.

70. *Réflexions,* p. 240; "Préface de 1905," pp. 70–71; *Illusions,* pp. 276–77; *Insegnamenti,* pp. 18–20. The views presented in the *Insegnamenti* on the future of property, nowhere considered in any detail, are the most elaborate treatment of the problem to be found in Sorel's works. In the *Introduction,* p. 11, he considers the continued existence of private property as beyond discussion. In the *Réflexions,* p. 48, he states that socialism will mean the suppression of private property.

71. *Introduction,* p. 349.

72. *Introduction,* p. 251; "Préface de 1905," p. 60; "Le Déclin du parti socialiste international," p. 200; *Réflexions,* p. 215.

73. "Préface de 1905," pp. 59–60.

74. *Introduction,* pp. 250–51.

75. "Le Idee de libertà," p. 5.

76. *Introduction,* pp. 131, 137.

77. *Illusions,* pp. 171, 284; *Décomposition,* p. 42.

78. "Les Préoccupations métaphysiques des physiciens modernes" in *Cahiers de la quinzaine,* p. 57; *Illusions,* pp. 280–84.

79. *Illusions,* p. 285; *Introduction,* pp. 72–73; *Réflexions,* p. 377.

80. *Réflexions,* pp. 377–78.

81. Ibid.

82. Ibid., pp. 24–28, 378; *Insegnamenti,* p. 71; "Préface de 1905," p. 70; "Le Prétendu 'socialisme juridique,'" pp. 335–41; "Sur les divers aspects de la mécanique," p. 716; *Introduction,* pp. 15–16.

83. *Réflexions,* pp. 26–27.

84. Ibid., p. 27; "La Démocratie," p. 102; *Insegnamenti,* p. 32.

85. *Réflexions,* pp. 214, 217; *Insegnamenti,* pp. 251–52, 278n.

86. *Illusions,* pp. 276–77.

87. *Réflexions,* pp. 125–26.

88. Ibid., p. 126.

89. Ibid., p. 129.

90. Ibid., pp. 129, 385–87; *Illusions,* pp. 276–77, 283.

91. Ibid., pp. 382, 384–85.

92. Ibid., p. 382.

93. Ibid., pp. 382, 386; "L'*Évolution créatrice,*" p. 52.

94. Review of G. Alfassa's *La Crise de l'apprentissage* in *Mouvement socialiste,* 10 (April 15, 1908):299; *Réflexions,* pp. 378, 381–84, 388; and "Le Idee di libertà," p. 5.

95. *Réflexions,* pp. 384–85.

Chapter 4. The Impact

1. "Courte déclaration," *Pages libres* 1 (January 5, 1901):1–2. The *Pages libres* published excerpts from all of Sorel's works from *La Ruine* (1901) to *Réflexions*

(1908); the first French edition of the *Réflexions* was published there. Only one post-1901 article was published, "Le Modernisme et le nouveau Syllabus," *Pages libres,* 7 (September 7, 1907):246–49. On the syndicalist press and reviews in general see Félicien Challaye, "Journaux et revues syndicalistes," *Pages libres,* 8 (March 7, 1908):249–67.

2. Lagardelle, "Avant-propos à la table des matières de la première serie," *Mouvement socialiste,* 6 (January 1, 1904):2–8; Berth, *Du "Capital" aux "Réflexions sur la violence,"* p. 175.

3. See above, Chapter 2.

4. See below.

5. See below for activities of Italian syndicalists.

6. Lagardelle, "Enquête sur l'idée de patrie et la classe ouvrière," *Mouvement socialiste,* 7 (August 1/25, 1905):430–70, and (September 1/15, 1905):36–71.

7. Lagardelle, "Chronique politique et sociale," *Mouvement socialiste,* 7 (January 15, 1906):121.

8. For descriptions of some of these ephemeral publications see the Appendix to Félicien Challaye, *Syndicalisme révolutionnaire et syndicalisme réformiste* (Paris: F. Alcan, 1909); Jean Claude Peyrounet, "Un Exemple de journal militant: *La Guerre sociale* de Gustave Hervé, 1906–1914," (*Doctorat,* Faculté des Lettres et Sciences Humaines de l'Université de Paris, 1964), pp. 118, 122.

9. See especially Lagardelle, "La Grève générale," 1 (February 4, 1908):1–2; and Editorial, "A nos lectures," 1 (February 4, 1908):1; also Amédée Dunois, "Les Livres: *Réflexions sur la violence,*" 1 (August 12, 1908):3.

10. Delesalle, *Les Deux méthods du syndicalisme* (Paris: Société Ouvrière d'Imprimerie, 1903); *La Confédération générale du travail* (Paris: La Publication Sociale, 1907); and *Les Bourses du travail et la C.G.T.* (Paris: Rivière, 1910).

11. See Louzon, "La Faillite du dreyfusisme ou le triomphe du parti juif," *Mouvement socialiste,* 8 (July 1906):180–204.

12. See Halévy, *Péguy and Les Cahiers de la Quinzaine,* p. 76; Péguy, *Situations* (Paris: Gallimard, 1940), p. 118; and Péguy, "Notre jeunesse," *Cahiers de la quinzaine,* 11, no. 12 (1910).

13. Halévy, "Apologie pour notre passé," *Luttes et problèmes* (Paris: Rivière, 1911), p. 97.

14. See above, Chapter 1.

15. Lagardelle, ed., *La Grève générale et le socialisme: enquête internationale* (Paris: E. Cornély, 1905), pp. 45, 419, 420, and *Syndicalisme et socialisme* (Paris: Rivière, 1908), p. 5.

16. Lagardelle, "Mannheim, Rome, Amiens," *Mouvement socialiste,* 8 (October/November 1906):256; see also Lagardelle's *Le Socialisme ouvrier* (Paris: V. Giard and E. Brière, 1911), p. 57.

17. Lagardelle, "Les Intellectuels et le socialisme ouvrier," *Mouvement socialiste,* 9 (February 1907):105, 118.

18. Lagardelle, *Le Parti socialiste et la C.G.T.* (Paris: Rivière, 1908), p. 24; "À propos de Marx," *Mouvement socialiste,* 10 (March 15, 1908):201.

19. Sorel to Lagardelle, p. 232.

20. Lagardelle, "Le Mouvement politique et social: monarchistes et syndicalistes," *Mouvement socialiste*, 13 (January 1911):54; *Le Socialisme ouvrier*, pp. 203–204, 223–224.

21. See Jules Levey, "The Sorelian Syndicalists: Édouard Berth, Georges Valois, and Hubert Lagardelle" (Ph.D. dissertation, Faculty of Political Science, Columbia University, 1967), p. 34.

22. Berth, "Les Revues socialistes allemandes," *Mouvement socialiste*, 7 (November 1/15, 1905):377.

23. Berth, *Les Méfaits des intellectuels*, with "Préface" by G. Sorel (Paris: Rivière, 1914), pp. 148, 167–168, 211, 226.

24. Berth, *Les Nouveaux aspects du socialisme* (Paris: Rivière, 1908), pp. 18, 28, 35–49, 51.

25. Berth, "Le Centenaire de Proudhon, 1809–1909," *Mouvement socialiste*, 11 (January 15, 1909):53.

26. Berth, "Avant-propos" (March 1913), *Les Méfaits des intellectuels*, p. 13.

27. This widely held view has been maintained not only by contemporaries closely associated with the syndicalist movement but by more recent writers as well: Challaye, *Syndicalisme révolutionnaire et syndicalisme réformiste*, p. 79; Maxim Leroy, *La Coutume ouvrière* (2 vols., Paris: Rivière, 1913), 1, pp. 522, 539; Gaëtan Pirou, "A propos du syndicalisme révolutionnaire: théoriciens et militants," *Revue politique et parlementaire*, 70 (October 10, 1911):134; Philippe Serre, *Les Atteintes à la notion moderne de l'état en France au début du XXᵉ siècle* (Paris: Presses Universitaires de France, 1925), pp. 2–3; Dolléans, *Histoire du mouvement ouvrier* (2 vols., 5th ed., Paris: A. Colin, 1957), 2, p. 135; Robert Goetz-Girey, *La Pensée syndicale française: militants et théoriciens* (Paris: A. Colin, 1948), pp. 38, 43–44; J.-J. Chevallier, "Le Dernier mot de Georges Sorel," *Politique*, 5 (September/October, 1948):716. Many others might be mentioned, the most recent being Stearns, *Revolutionary Syndicalism and French Labor*, p. 6.

28. The name Sorel, apparently, was hardly mentioned in any of the issues examined from 1903 to 1908; see Émile Pouget, "Sur la sellette," *Voix du peuple*, 7 (May 19/26, 1907):1 (where Pouget expresses his disdain for a syndicalism tied to politics or intellectualism).

29. See below, Chapter 5.

30. Dolléans, *Histoire du mouvement ouvrier*, 2, pp. 126–27.

31. See Stearns, *Revolutionary Syndicalism and French Labor*, a most useful survey of syndicalist activities, especially pp. 35–72 on the "moderation" of the French movement before the war; also valuable is Goetz-Girey, *La Pensée syndicale française*, pp. 38 and 43–44, and Guy Thorel, *Chronologie du mouvement syndical ouvrier en France* (Paris: Temps Present, 1947), pp. 61–67 and Appendix.

32. Stearns, *Revolutionary Syndicalism and French Labor*, pp. 21–33.

33. See ibid., pp. 73–102, on the "failure" of syndicalism.

34. See these studies of leading syndicalist militants and leaders of the CGT: Pouget, *La C.G.T.* (Paris: Rivière, 1908), p. 38; Griffuelhes, *L'Action syndicaliste* (Paris: Rivière, 1908), p. 32; Griffuelhes, "La Confédération générale du travail," *La Grève générale et le socialisme*, ed. H. Lagardelle (Paris: Rivière, 1905), pp. 26,

61; Pouget, *Les Bases du syndicalisme* (Paris: Rivière, 1906), pp. 10, 17; Pouget, *Le Sabotage* (Paris: Rivière, 1910), pp. 7-8. The issues of the *Voix du peuple* from 1903 to 1908 reveal little or no interest in Sorel.

35. Émile Pataud and Émile Pouget, *Comment nous ferons la révolution* (Paris: Rivière, 1909), pp. 141-42; Pouget, *Le Syndicat* (Paris: Rivière, 1907), p. 18; Griffuelhes, "La Confédération générale du travail," pp. 34, 51; Pirou, *Proudhonisme et syndicalisme révolutionnaire* (Paris: Librairie Nouvelle de Droit et de Jurisprudence, 1910), pp. 225, 230-33.

36. Louis Niel, "Vers le centre," *Humanité,* August 20, 1908; see also Stearns, *Revolutionary Syndicalism and French Labor,* Appendix B, pp. 121-35.

37. For an early attempt to establish the character of "Sorelismo" see Bruno Facinelli, *Sindacalismo Soreliano* (Florence: Vallecchi, 1938); for a brief contemporary view see Giuseppe A. Borgese, *La Vita e il libro* (3 vols., Turin: Fratelli Bocca, 1910-1913), 1, pp. 335, 338-39. For the general discontent with "Giolittismo" see A. William Salomone, *Italian Democracy in the Making* (Philadelphia: University of Pennsylvania Press, 1945).

38. See above, Chapter 1; see also Onufrio, "Considerazione su Croce e Sorel," p. 149, and Croce, *Critica,* 25 (1927):368. Croce invited Sorel in 1903 to contribute to his newly established *Critica.* Sorel submitted only three reviews: see Furiozzi, *Sorel e l'Italia,* p. 154.

39. Croce, "Il Pensiero di Giorgio Sorel" in G. Sorel, *Considerazioni sulla violenza,* trans. A. Sarno (Bari: Laterza, 1909), p. v; this introduction first appeared as "Cristianesimo, socialismo e metodo storico," *Critica,* 5 (July 20, 1907):317-30. On Croce and the *Réflexions* see Furiozzi, "La Fortuna italiana di Sorel," p. 103.

40. Croce, "Il Pensiero di Giorgio Sorel," pp. xxvi-xxvii.

41. Ibid., pp. vi, xxi.

42. Croce, "Le Droit comme économie pure," *Mouvement socialiste,* 11 (May 1909): 349.

43. Croce, "Hegel e Marx," *Cultura,* 29 (January 1, 1910):7, 10; also "Hegel et Marx," *Mouvement socialiste,* 12 (March 1910):181-89.

44. Croce, "Socialismo e massoneria," *Giornale d'Italia,* October 6, 1910.

45. See Furiozzi, *Sorel e l'Italia,* p. 135n; Pareto, *Les Systèmes socialistes* (2 vols., 2nd ed., Paris: Giard, 1926), 2, pp. 398-99n, 408, 413. On Sorel and Pareto see D.C. Band, "The Question of Sorel," *Journal of European Studies,* 7 (1977):207.

46. Pareto, *Manuel d'économie politique,* trans. A. Bonnet (Paris: V. Giard and E. Brière, 1909), pp. 115, 134, 360n, 480n, 495, 499.

47. "*Les Antagonismes économiques* de M. Effertz," *Mouvement socialiste,* 9 (August 15/September 15, 1907):170-78.

48. Guido Sensini, ed., *Corrispondenza di Vilfredo Pareto* (hereafter cited as Pareto to Sensini) (Padua: C.E.D.A.M., 1948), p. 38; the letter is dated November 14, 1907.

49. Pareto to Sorel, November 11, 1909, in *Carteggi Paretiani, 1892-1923,* p. 48; this is the only letter from Pareto to Sorel in the collection. See also Andreu, "Une lettre inédite de Pareto à Georges Sorel," *Nation française,* no. 121 (January 29, 1958):11.

50. See above, Chapter 2.

51. Michels, *L'Allemagne, le socialisme et les syndicats* (Paris: V. Giard and E. Brière, 1906), pp. 1–5.
52. Michels, *Le Prolétariat et la bourgeoisie dans le mouvement socialiste italien,* trans. G. Bourgin (Paris: M. Giard, 1921), p. 318.
53. Michels, "Le Syndicalisme et le socialisme en Allemagne" in *Syndicalisme et socialisme,* p. 28.
54. See *Ente per la storia del socialismo e del movimento operaio italiano: bibliografia del socialismo del movimento operaio italiano,* ed. G. E. Modigliani, vol. I (Turin: Edizioni E.S.M.O.I., 1956), for excellent brief sketches of many of these periodicals. One of the earliest centers of discussion of Sorel's ideas during the revisionist controversy was Merlino's *Rivista critica del socialismo;* see Marucco, *Arturo Labriola,* pp. 113–14. Marucco, however, argues for the Neapolitan origins of Italian syndicalism and sees its beginnings in the *Propaganda* of Naples in 1898, as did Antonio Gramsci. On the same subject see Furiozzi, *Sorel e l'Italia,* pp. 143–44.
55. For the general line of the newspaper see Arturo Labriola, "Perché siamo repubblicani," *Avanguardia socialista,* August 23, 1903, and "Siamo noi anarchici?" ibid., April 7–8, 1904; Sergio Panunzio, "Socialisti ed anarchici," ibid., July 30, 1904; and "Psicologia dello sciopero," ibid., January 14, 1905. In 1905 Labriola hailed the appearance of the *Avant-garde* in Paris: see "Un'Altra 'Avanguardia' in Francia con lo stesso programma dell' 'Avanguardia' italiana," ibid., April 22, 1905. For a general discussion of the *Avanguardia socialista* see Furiozzi, *Sorel e l'Italia,* pp. 143–86.
56. See issues of 1905. For comparisons between the general strike of 1904 and the Russian Revolution of 1905 see Labriola, "La Rivoluzione russa e il grandiosa manifestazione di Milano," *Avanguardia socialista,* January 28, 1905.
57. Published in brief installments from no. 27, June 28, 1903, to no. 48, November 22, 1903. On January 4, 1903, the *Avanguardia socialista* published a list of eighteen Italian socialist periodicals "that follow our direction"; see Furiozzi, *Sorel e l'Italia,* p. 149n.
58. See Editorial, "Siamo noi anarchici?" *Avanguardia socialista,* April 7/8, 1904; G. Allevi, "Il Sindacalismo è la pratica del marxismo," ibid., November 4, 1905; see also Marucco, *Arturo Labriola,* pp. 153–54.
59. For Mussolini's articles discussing Sorel see "Atei!" *Avanguardia socialista,* March 13, 1904, and "La Teppa," ibid., December 10, 1904. Mussolini also published during this period in the *Lima,* the *Popolo,* and the *Lotta di classe* (Forlì): see below.
60. Mussolini in *Avanguardia socialista,* March 13 and December 10, 1904.
61. For Leone's views on Sorel see his "Prefazione" to Georges Sorel, *Lo Sciopero generale e la violenza* (Rome: Tipografia Industria e Lavoro, 1906), pp. iii–iv. Sorel's disciples who published in this review were Lagardelle, Berth, and Delesalle. On Leone and the *Divenire sociale* see Furiozzi, *Sorel e l'Italia,* pp. 187–220.
62. A frequent contributor signed his articles "Soreliano." For views of Sorel see Panunzio, "Alcuni pregiudizi socialisti," *Divenire sociale,* 2 (January 1, 1906): 12–15. For defense of Sorel's opposition to a general strike in the Ferrer affair see "Asterische polemici," *Divenire sociale,* 5 (December 16, 1909):275–76. Some syndicalists, especially those with anarchist tendencies, were disturbed by Sorel's

opposition to a general strike in protest against the execution of the Barcelona anarchist.

63. See above, Chapter 2.

64. It declared itself "against every endeavor of social pacifism"; see La Redazione, "Programma," *Lotta proletaria,* July 1, 1905. Lagardelle published there frequently.

65. Editorial, "Il Sindacato," *Sindacato operaio,* July 30, 1905; both Sorel and Lagardelle published there. See "La Solidarità di Giorgio Sorel," ibid., September 30, 1906.

66. *Propaganda* invoked the names of both Sorel and Labriola (as Sorel's leading Italian exponent); see F. B., "Il Sindacalismo," *Propaganda,* June 9/10, 1906.

67. See Sorel, "Apologia della violenza," *Guerra sociale,* May 30, 1908.

68. For a discussion of the reaction to Sorel's position on the Ferrer affair, see "Everyone," "Asterische polemici," *Divenire sociale,* 5 (December 16, 1909):275-76.

69. A. O. Olivetti, "L'Anti-Marxismo di Giorgio Sorel," *Stirpe,* 8 (January 1930):8.

70. Olivetti, "Presentazione," *Pagine libere,* 1 (December 1906):1-3; see Olivetti's collection of articles from 1906 to 1911 in *Cinque anni di sindacalismo e di lotta proletaria in Italia* (Naples: Società Editrice Partenopea, 1914), pp. 39-45, 47-49, 123-27, 149-67, 253-58. For Olivetti's views of the history of the periodical see his "Quindici anni di vita di una rivista independente," *Pagine libere,* 8 (August/ September, 1921):247-80.

71. Horowitz, *The Italian Labor Movement,* pp. 53-54, 79; Robert Paris, *Histoire du fascisme en Italie* (Paris: Maspero, 1962), p. 44; see Marucco, *Arturo Labriola,* pp. 121 and 130-42, on Labriola and Leone on the "question *meridionale.*"

72. On the classification of Italian syndicalists on the basis of their attitude toward the "use" of the Socialist party see Armando Borghi, *Mezzo secolo di anarchia (1898-1945)* (Naples: ESI, 1954), p. 87.

73. Panunzio, "Il Sindacalismo," *La Civiltà fascista,* ed. G. Luigi (Turin: Unione Tipografico Editrice, 1928), p. 355; Facinelli, *Sindacalismo Soreliano,* p. 141; Borgese, *La Vita e il libro,* 1, pp. 338-39; and Marucco, *Arturo Labriola,* pp. 81-103.

74. Labriola, "La Fonction des idéologues," *Études socialistes,* 1 (January/ February 1903):54, 56-58.

75. Labriola, *Riforme e rivoluzione sociale* (Milan: R. Sandron, 1904), p. 154; see also Furiozzi, *Sorel e l'Italia,* pp. 165-70.

76. Labriola, *L'État et la crise* (Paris: Rivière, 1933), p. 279. See Labriola's articles in the *Pagine libere* after 1907, when he became co-director; also Marucco, *Arturo Labriola,* pp. 188-89.

77. Labriola, *Karl Marx* (Paris: Rivière, 1910), p. 211; *Storia di dieci anni, 1899-1909* (Milan: Il Viandate, 1910), p. 174.

78. Leone, *L'Économia sociale in rapporto al socialismo* (Genoa: Libreria Moderna, 1904), pp. 21-29.

79. Leone, "Prefazione" to Sorel, pp. iii-vi, viii; cf. Furiozzi, *Sorel e l'Italia,* pp. 201-204.

80. Leone, *Il Sindacalismo* (Milan: R. Sandron, 1907), p. 192. See also "L'Azione elettorale e il sindacalismo," *Sindacata operaio,* January 28, 1907, and "Le Matérialisme économique dans l'histoire," *Mouvement socialiste,* 13 (July 1910):16. Cf. Marucco, *Arturo Labriola,* pp. 180, 200.

81. Olivetti, "Presentazione," December 1, 1906, in *Cinque anni di sindacalismo e di lotta proletaria in Italia*, p. 7; *Problemi del socialismo contemporaneo* (Lugano: Società Editrice "Avanguardia," 1906), pp. 208, 212, 296.

82. Olivetti, "Il Misticismo e noi," January 1, 1907, in *Cinque anni*, p. 45.

83. Olivetti, "Tutti contro tutti!" January 15, 1907, in *Cinque anni*, p. 49.

84. Olivetti, "Il Congresso della dedizione," June 1, 1909, in *Cinque anni*, pp. 262-63.

85. Olivetti, "I Sindacalisti e la élite," July 1, 1909, in *Cinque anni*, p. 268.

86. Olivetti, "Cinquantenario," May 1, 1911, in *Cinque anni*, pp. 354-55.

87. On Orano in general see Michels, *Le Prolétariat et la bourgeoisie dans le mouvement socialiste italien*, p. 318; on Orano's special role in the origins of revolutionary syndicalism in Italy see L. Rosenstock-Franck, *L'Économie corporative fasciste en doctrine et en fait* (Paris: Librarie Universitaire J. Gamber, 1934), p. 14; on Sorel's rather critical view of Orano see Furiozzi, *Sorel e l'Italia*, p. 229.

88. Orano, "Giorgio Sorel e i suoi studi sul Cristianesimo," May 1907, in *Cristo e quirino* (Florence: A. Quattrini, 1911), pp. 287-306; "Le Syndicat et le Parti socialiste en Italie," *Mouvement socialiste*, 9 (December 15, 1907):448, 462.

89. See below, Chapter 7.

90. Panunzio, "Socialisti ed anarchici," *Avanguardia socialista*, July 30, 1904; "Le Socialisme syndicaliste," *Mouvement socialiste*, 8 (January 15, 1906):57. See also Michels, *Le Prolétariat et la bourgeoisie dans le mouvement socialiste italien*, pp. 336-37n. On Panunzio's general ideas on violence see Furiozzi, *Sorel e l'Italia*, pp. 180-86.

91. Panunzio, "Le Socialisme italien après le congrès de Rome," *Mouvement socialiste*, 9 (February 1907):147.

92. Panunzio, *La Persistenza del diritto* (Pescara: Casa Editrice Abruzzese, 1910), pp. 12, 41, 261. See also Panunzio, "Syndicalisme et représentation ouvrière," *Mouvement socialiste*, 12 (May/June 1910):322.

93. Michels, *Le Prolétariat et la bourgeoisie dans le mouvement socialiste italien*, pp. 336-37n; Pietro P. Trampeo, "Una Pagine inedita di G. Sorel," *Cultura*, 2 (February 15, 1923):190.

94. Lanzillo, "Le Congrès de Florence et le socialisme italien," *Mouvement socialiste*, 10 (November 15, 1908):378.

95. Lanzillo, "Sorel e la democrazia," preface to G. Sorel's *Le Illusioni del progresso*, (Milan: R. Sandron, 1910), pp. 9, 15.

96. Lanzillo, *Le Mouvement ouvrier en Italie* (Paris: Rivière, 1910), p. 59.

97. Lanzillo, *Giorgio Sorel*, pp. 43, 84-85, 87, 90-98.

98. For articles by Arcà and Longobardi see *Divenire sociale*, *Pagine libere*, *Azione sindacalista*, and *Propaganda*; for articles by de Pietri-Tonelli see *Avanguardia socialista*, *Pagine libere*, *Lotta proletaria*, and *Bandiera del popolo*. For a general discussion of Longobardi see Furiozzi, *Sorel e l'Italia*, pp. 173-74.

99. For articles by de Ambris, Bianchi, and Rossoni see *Avanguardia socialista*, *Divenire sociale*, *Pagine libere*, *Gioventù*, *Gioventù socialista*, *Sindacato operaio*, *Guerra sociale*, and *Bandiera del popolo*.

100. Ivon de Begnac, *L'Arcangelo sindacalista: Filippo Corridoni* (Verona: Casa Editrice Mondadori, 1943), pp. 115-212.

101. Ibid., pp. 101, 108, 110; see also Sorel to Corridoni, April 19, 1907, in ibid., p. 883.

102. See Corridoni's articles in *Bandiera proletaria*: "Gli insegnamenti di una rivoluzione," August 7, 1909; "La Tecnica rivoluzionaria," September 4, 1909; "Il Sin-

dacalismo," September 23, 1909; and "Sciopero generale," October 23, 1909; see also de Begnac, *L'Arcangelo sindacalista*, p. 103.

103. Corridoni, "Maggio di raccoglimento," *Gioventù socialista*, n.d., 1910 (photographed in part in de Begnac, *L'Arcangelo sindacalista*, p. x.).

104. Mussolini to Adrian Wyss (a socialist deputy of the Grand Council of Geneva), May 5, 1904, quoted in Gaudens Megaro, *Mussolini in the Making* (London: Unwin Brothers, 1938), p. 67. See Renzo de Felice, *Mussolini il rivoluzionario* (Turin: Einaudi, 1965), pp. 40–41; and Furiozzi, *Sorel e l'Italia*, pp. 177–80. De Felice cites two occasions when Mussolini in fact declared himself a "revolutionary syndicalist": see *Mussolini il rivoluzionario*, p. 45. For Sorel's influence on the "young Mussolini" see Band, "The Questions of Sorel," p. 210.

105. Mussolini, "Dagli inizi all'ultima sosta in Romagna" in vol. 1 of *Opera omnia di Benito Mussolini*, pp. 46–97.

106. ["Vero Eretico"], "L'Attuale momento politico (considerazione inattuali)," *Lima*, 16 (April 18, 1908), "Dagli inizi all'ultima sosta in Romagna," pp. 119–22 in vol. 1 of *Opera omnia*.

107. Mussolini, "Per finire," *Lima*, 16 (June 6, 1908):1, 147–49 in vol. 1 of *Opera omnia*; also de Felice, *Mussolini il rivoluzionario*, p. 52n.

108. Mussolini, "La Teoria sindacalista," *Popolo*, May 27, 1909, "Il Periodo Trentino verso la fondazione de *La Lotta di classe*," pp. 123–28 in vol. 2 of *Opera omnia*. On Mussolini and Prezzolini see de Felice, *Mussolini il rivoluzionario*, pp. 66–67.

109. Mussolini, "Lo Sciopero generale e la violenza," *Popolo*, June 25, 1909, pp. 163–68. Mussolini apparently read the *Réflexions* for the first time while in Lausanne: see F. Hayward, "Lorsque Mussolini avait vingt-ans . . . ," *Petit Parisien*, August 20, 1926.

110. Mussolini, "Ai compagni!" *Popolo*, October 1, 1909, p. 255.

111. Atti della Direzione del Partito Socialista Italiano, *Resconto stenografico del IX Congresso nazionale: Roma: 7–8–9–10 ottobre 1906* (Rome 1907), p. 207; Rinaldo Rigola, *L'Évoluzione della Confederazione generale del lavoro* (Florence: Edizione della Critica Sociale, 1921), pp. 5–20; Salomone, *Italian Democracy in the Making*, pp. 102–114; Michels, *Le Prolétariat et la bourgeoisie dans le mouvement socialiste italien*, pp. 319–20, 336; and Horowitz, *The Italian Labor Movement*, p. 75.

112. See Horowitz, *The Italian Labor Movement*, pp. 66–67, 75–80; see also Lanzillo, *Le Mouvement ouvrier en Italie*, p. 27; Michels, *Le Prolétariat et la bourgeoisie dans le mouvement socialiste italien*, p. 336; Francesco Ferrari, *Le Régime fasciste italien* (Paris: Éditions Spes, 1928), p. 235; and Facinelli, *Sindacalismo Soreliano*, p. 142. See especially Alfredo Gradilone, *Storia del sindacalismo: Italia* (2 vols., Milan: A. Giuffrè, 1959), 1, pp. 1–2, 4n; and Marucco, *Arturo Labriola*, p. 174.

113. Horowitz, *The Italian Labor Movement*, pp. 66–67, 75–80; Rigola, *Manualetto di tecnica sindacale* (Florence: Edizioni U-Biblioteca di Critica Sociale, 1947), p. 26.

114. Panunzio, "Il Sindacalismo," p. 355; Horowitz, *The Italian Labor Movement*, p. 75; and Gradilone, *Storia del sindacalismo*, pp. 438–48. Cf. Marucco, *Arturo Labriola*, p. 171n.

115. Croce, "Cristianesimo, socialismo e metodo storico," p. 317; Atti della Direzione del Partito Socialista Italiano, *Resconto stenografico, 1906*, p. 206; Rigola,

Manualatto di tecnica sindacale, pp. 5–23; and Panunzio, "Il Sindacalismo," p. 355.

116. Panunzio, "Il Sindacalismo," p. 355; Michels, *Le Prolétariat et la bourgeoisie dans le mouvement socialiste italien*, pp. 335–37.

117. See below, Chapter 5.

118. Panunzio, "Il Sindacalismo," p. 355; Facinelli, *Sindacalismo Soreliano*, p. 142; Ferrari, *Le Régime fasciste italien*, p. 235; Rosenstock-Franck, *L'Économie corporative fasciste*, p. 14; and Paolo Basevi, "Lo Sciopero agrario a Parma nel 1908," *Emilia*, 3 (1951):145–47.

119. Horowitz, *The Italian Labor Movement*, p. 79; Marucco, *Arturo Labriola*, p. 183; and Biagio Riguzzi, *Sindacalismo e riformismo nel Parmese* (Bari: Laterza, 1931), p. 119. For an excellent treatment of origins, see Thomas R. Sykes, "Revolutionary Syndicalism in the Italian Labor Movement: The Agrarian Strikes of 1907–08 in the Province of Parma," *International Review of Social History*, 22 (1976): 186–211.

120. Quoted in Horowitz, *The Italian Labor Movement*, p. 79.

121. Atti della Direzione del Partito Socialista Italiano, *Resconto stenografico del X Congresso nazionale: Firenze, 19-20-21-22 settembre 1908* (Rome, 1908), pp. 334–36; Michels, *Storia critica del movimento socialista italiano dagli inizi fin al 1911* (Florence: La Voce, 1926), p. 344; Marucco, *Arturo Labriola*, p. 185; Riguzzi, *Sindacalismo e riformismo nel Parmese*, pp. 133–35; Basevi, "Lo Sciopero agrario a Parma nel 1908," p. 147; and Furiozzi, *Sorel e l'Italia*, p. 234.

122. Rosenstock-Franck, *L'Économie corporative fasciste*, pp. 9–10; and Lanzillo, *Le Mouvement ouvrier en Italie*, pp. 47, 49.

123. Pezzotti, "Une Parti syndicaliste en Italie," p. 184.

124. *Le Confessioni*, p. 3, and "Giorgio Sorel e i monarchici francesi," *Giornale d'Italia*, November 20, 1910.

Integral Nationalism

Chapter 5. The Man

1. See above, Chapter 1.

2. *Réflexions*, p. 110.

3. Valois, *D'un siècle à l'autre*, p. 108; Fréderic Lefèvre, "Une Heure avec M. Georges Valois," *Nouvelles littéraires*, 3 (February 16, 1924):1; for details see Yves Guchet, *Georges Valois* (Paris: Éditions Albatros, 1975), pp. 20–25. For recent studies that concern in part Sorel's relations with the Action Française see: Paul Mazgaj, "The Social Revolution or the King: The Initiatives of the Action Française toward the Revolutionary Left, 1906–1914" (Ph.D. dissertation, University of Iowa, 1976); and Paul Sérant, *Les Dissidents de l'Action Française* (Paris: Copernic, 1978), pp. 13–36.

4. Valois, *D'un siècle à l'autre*, pp. 208, 134–35.

5. Valois, *L'Homme qui vient: philosophie de l'autorité* (2nd ed., Paris: 1909), pp. xx, xxiv, xxvii, xxxix–xlii.

6. Valois, *D'un siècle à l'autre*, pp. 247–48.

7. Valois, *Basile, ou la politique de la calomnie* (Paris: Librairie Valois, 1927), p. x.

8. Valois, *D'un siècle à l'autre,* pp. 247–48.
9. Guchet, *Georges Valois,* pp. 75–77; Eugen Weber, *Action Française: Royalism and Reaction in Twentieth-Century France* (Stanford: Stanford University Press, 1962), p. 76; and Edward Tannenbaum, *The Action Française: Die-Hard Reactionaries in Twentieth-Century France* (New York: John Wiley, 1962), pp. 182–86.
10. Valois, *D'un siècle à l'autre,* p. 249; Guchet, *Georges Valois,* p. 61.
11. See *Action française,* September 15, October 15, November 15, and December 15, 1907.
12. "A nos lecteurs," *Revue critique des idées et des livres,* 1 (April 25, 1908):5–6.
13. Valois, "Enquête sur la monarchie et la classe ouvrière: quelques réflexions de M. Georges Sorel," *Revue critique des idées et des livres,* 1 (May 10, 1908):145 [the inquiry was published separately as *La Monarchie et la classe ouvrière* (Paris: Nouvelle Librairie Nationale, 1909)].
14. Ibid., pp. 145–46, 155.
15. Ibid., p. 149.
16. For the complete series see Valois, *La Monarchie et la classe ouvrière,* pp. 59–364.
17. "Modernisme dans la religion et dans le socialisme," *Revue critique des idées et des livres,* 2 (August 10, 1908):177–204; see Chapter 2, fn. 49, for the Italian source.
18. Ibid., pp. 184, 189.
19. Ibid., pp. 191, 198.
20. Valois, *D'un siècle à l'autre,* p. 253.
21. See Valois, *Basile,* p. xi.
22. Valois, *D'un siècle à l'autre,* p. 257.
23. Variot, *Propos,* p. 24. The question of the authenticity of the *Propos* is raised by Variot himself (p. 8). He states that he took notes while Sorel spoke. After organizing them he showed them to Sorel, who made additions and corrections. He followed this procedure throughout except for Sorel's comments on Lenin in 1922 (pp. 66–86), which were made the last time he saw Sorel. Sorel demanded only that Variot promise not to publish the collection until ten years following his death. (On two occasions in the *Propos,* Variot was in error by giving the date of Sorel's death as 1924—pp. 8 and 14—whereas Sorel died in 1922. For someone who knew Sorel well, the error is surprising.) In any case, Variot kept his commitment to Sorel. Portions of what in 1935 was published as the *Propos* first appeared in 1932 as "Entretiens avec Georges Sorel: sur l'Europe d'avant 1914," *Nouvelles littéraires,* February 27, March 5, March 12, March 19, and March 26, 1932. The question of the credibility of the *Propos* is also something of a problem. Variot became a monarchist shortly after meeting Sorel. He was still one in 1935 when the *Propos* was published and is therefore hardly a disinterested editor. The views expressed by Sorel in the *Propos* are, however, substantially corroborated by other sources.
24. Variot, *Propos,* pp. 24–27.
25. Sorel to Croce, June 27, 1909, 26, p. 196. On nationalism in Sorel's letters to Croce see Annamaria Andreasi, "Il Nazionalismo nelle lettere di Sorel a Benedetto Croce," *Georges Sorel: studi e ricerche,* pp. 155–58.
26. Sorel to Croce, August 22, 1909, 26, pp. 334–35.
27. Sorel to Maurras, July 6, 1909, in Andreu, *Notre maître,* annex VI, p. 326.

28. The article was "La Disfatta dei 'mufles,'" pp. 177-81; the whole appeared under the title "Socialistes antiparlementaires," *Action française,* August 22, 1909.
29. Pierre Gilbert, "Une Conversation avec M. Georges Sorel: Ferrer et Briand," *Action française,* September 29, 1909.
30. Paul Bourget, *La Barricade* (Paris: Librairie Plon, 1910), p. 1-li.
31. Ibid., p. 1.
32. Ibid., p. 234.
33. Anon., "La Barricade," *Gaulois,* January 8, 1910.
34. G. de Maizière, "Aux armes, les bourgeois!" *Gaulois,* January 11, 1910.
35. Anon. "L'Apôtre de la violence," *Temps,* January 13, 1910; Jacques Morland, "Les Idées de M. Georges Sorel," *Opinion,* 3 (January 15, 1910):75-77; Henri Massis, "Les Idées sociales de M. Georges Sorel," *Mercure de France,* 83 (February 16, 1910):610-21; G. Sorbets, "La Barricade," *Illustration théâtrale,* March 5, 1910.
36. Enrico Corradini, "Per Coloro che risorgono," *Regno,* November 29, 1903; Giuseppe Prezzolini, "Marx era collettivista?" *Regno,* May 24, 1904. See Papini and Prezzolini, *Vecchio e nuovo nazionalismo* (Milan: Studio Editoriale Lombardo, 1914), for a collection of articles written by the two for the *Regno*; see also Maffio Maffii, "Corradini e il Regno," *Politica,* 41 (August 1937):81. For a good general study of Italian nationalism see John A. Thayer, *Italy and the Great War* (Madison: University of Wisconsin Press, 1964), pp. 192-232; also Delia Frigessi, "Introduzione" to *"Leonardo," "Hermes," "Il Regno"* ["La Cultura italiana del 1900 attraverso le riviste" (Turin: Einaudi, 1960), pp. 11-85]. For article by Giovanni Papini critical of Sorel see "Il Sindacalismo è pericoloso," *Regno,* June 25, 1905. On Italian nationalism see Alexander J. De Grand, *The Italian Nationalist Association and the Rise of Fascism in Italy* (Lincoln: University of Nebraska Press, 1978).
37. Prezzolini, *Cos' è il modernismo* (Milan: Fratelli Treves, 1908), pp. 16-17, 19; Sorel to Croce, May 15, 1908, 26, p. 106.
38. Panunzio, "Il Sindacalismo," p. 355; Rosenstock-Franck, *L'Économie corporative fasciste,* p. 14.
39. For additional articles see *Avanguardia socialista, Lotta proletaria,* and *Propaganda*; for discussion see Thayer, *Italy and the Great War,* pp. 198, 206, 216-18, as well as Panunzio, "Il Sindacalismo," p. 355.
40. For general discussion see Maurice Vaussard, *De Pétrarque à Mussolini* (Paris: A. Colin, 1961), p. 165; see especially Corradini, "Sindacalismo, nazionalismo, imperialismo" (December 1909), *Discorsi politici, 1902-1924* (Florence: Vallecchi, 1925), pp. 51-71, and *Il Volere d'Italia* (Naples: Perrella, 1911).
41. Sorel to Croce, May 4, 1909, 26, p. 195; see also Sorel to Delesalle, May 19, 1918, p. 145.
42. "Presentazione," *Tricolore,* April 3, 1909; "Il Primo nazionalista d'Italia," ibid., p. 4. See also Gradilone, *Storia del sindacalismo,* 2, p. 114; Vaussard, *De Pétrarque à Mussolini,* pp. 178-80; and Gioacchino Volpe, "Genesi del fascismo," in *Il Fascismo,* ed. C. Casucci (Bologna: Il Mulino, 1961), p. 71. Furiozzi, *Sorel e l'Italia,* pp. 246-47, quotes brief letters from Sorel and Corradini to Viana.

43. For a good general study see Angelo Romanò, "Introduzione" to *La Voce (1908–1914)*["La Cultura italiana del 1900 attraverso le riviste" (Turin: Einaudi, 1960), pp. 11–79]; see Papini and Prezzolini, *Vecchio e nuovo nazionalismo,* pp. vi–x; also Peter M. Riccio, *On the Threshold of Fascism* (New York: Columbia University Press, 1929), pp. 69–70.

44. See Sorel to Croce, December 9, 1908, and February 3, 1909, 26, pp. 192–93.

45. Prezzolini, "Giorgio Sorel," *Voce,* December 20, 1908; Paolo Mazzoldi, "Il Valore morale del sindacalismo," ibid., January 3, 1909; Alfredo Gargiulo, "Giorgio Sorel," ibid., June 10, 1909; and Agostino Lanzillo, "Colloquio con Giorgio Sorel," ibid., December 9, 1909.

46. Prezzolini, *La Teoria sindacalista* (Naples: Perrella, 1909), pp. 217–64, 335.

47. Ibid., pp. 231, 334–35.

48. Sorel to Croce, April 5, 1909, 26, pp. 194–95.

49. See Salomone, *Italian Democracy in the Making,* pp. 92–94.

50. Atti del Congresso di Firenze, *Il Nazionalismo italiano* (Florence, 1911), pp. 3–9.

51. Corradini, *Il Nazionalismo italiano* (Milan: Fratelli Treves, 1914), pp. 67–69. This address is dated December 3, 1910, and was presented at the Congress of Florence. It should be recalled that the syndicalist Labriola had also in 1910 begun to write of an "imperialism of the poor." See Furiozzi, *Sorel e l'Italia,* pp. 245–50; and M. Isnenghi, *Il Mito della grande guerra de Marinetti a Malaparte* (Bari: Laterza, 1970), p. 11.

52. Sorel to Croce, June 9 and December 9, 1908, 26, pp. 107, 192.

53. Sorel to Croce, May 4, 1909, 26, p. 195.

54. "La Religion d'aujourd'hui," *Revue de métaphysique et de morale,* 17 (March and May 1909), 240–73 and 413–47; also *La Religione d'oggi,* trans. A. Lanzillo (Lanciano: Carabba, 1911). Borgese argues in *La Vita e il libro,* 1, p. 14, that instead of the distinction between good and evil, Sorel presented here a distinction between *"l'attività e l'inerzia."*

55. Some of these articles published early in 1910 were later modified and expanded for the *Indépendance.*

56. Marguerite Sarfatti, "Georges Sorel," *Figaro littéraire,* January 21, 1939.

57. Borgese, *La Vita e il libro,* 1, p. 335. Santarelli argues that Sorel as a "precursor of fascism" was later to be dated as of about 1910: see his "Sorel e il Sorelismo in Italia," *Rivista storica del socialismo,* 10 (May/August 1960):301.

58. See Halévy, *Péguy and Les Cahiers de la Quinzaine,* chapt. 8, on the origins of the work.

59. Sorel to Croce, February 11 and 28, 1910, 26, pp. 337–38.

60. "Le Réveil de l'âme française," *Action française,* April 14, 1910; "Il Risveglio dell'anima francese," *Voce,* 2 (April 14, 1910):303.

61. Sorel to Croce, April 22, 1910, 26, p. 339.

62. Sorel to Berth, March 27, April 1, April 24, and May 6, 1910, cited in Levey, "The Sorelian Syndicalists," p. 132.

63. Variot, *Propos,* June 17, 1910, pp. 121–22, and 125–27.

64. "Grandeur et décadence," *Illusions,* pp. 287–336. The first version of this article was "Evoluzione e decadenza," *Divenire sociale,* 6 (January 1–March 1, 1910): 4–7, 24, 27, 55–56. See Sorel to Croce, January 25, 1911, 26, pp. 343–45.

65. Sorel to Missiroli, May 6, 1910, p. 69, and Sorel to Croce, June 28, 1910, 26, p. 342. The correspondence between Sorel and Missiroli began on May 6, 1910. It should

be recalled that Missiroli had been a contributor to the short-lived nationalist-socialist *Tricolore*. Missiroli eventually published two collections of Sorel's newspaper articles (for the most part originally in the *Resto del Carlino*): *L'Europa sotto la tormenta* (Milan: Corbaccio, 1932), and *Da Proudhon a Lenin* (Florence: L'Arco, 1949). It is very likely that Missiroli and Sorel met; see Sorel to Missiroli, May 6, 1910, p. 71.

66. "La Politica degli immortali," *Resto del Carlino,* June 6, 1910.
67. "Il Nazionalismo francese," *Resto del Carlino,* August 7, 1910.
68. "La Rivincita del patriotismo," *Resto del Carlino,* September 28, 1910.
69. "Barbarie o civiltà?" *Resto del Carlino,* December 27, 1910.
70. "Vues sur les problèmes de la philosophie," *Revue de métaphysique et de morale,* 18 (September 1910):581–613, and 19 (January 1911):64–99; see also Sorel to Croce, June 28, 1910, 26, p. 341.
71. "Vues sur les problèmes de la philosophie," p. 613.
72. Valois, *D'un siècle à l'autre,* p. 256. The *Terre libre* was published intermittently as a bi-monthly from November 1909, to March 1912, and from December 1913, to May 1914, by Émile Janvion; see Sternhell, *La Droite révolutionnaire, 1885–1914,* pp. 385–90.
73. Variot, *Propos,* pp. 260–61.
74. Ibid.; Johannet, *Itinéraires d'intellectuels,* p. 205; Valois, *D'un siècle à l'autre,* p. 256.
75. Valois to Berth, June 3, 1910, quoted in Levey, "The Sorelian Syndicalists," p. 113; Sorel to Missiroli, November 1, 1910, p. 85.
76. Variot, *Propos,* p. 261; Sorel to Croce, June 28 and September 5, 1910, 26, pp. 340–41, 342.
77. "Déclaration," *Cité française* (Paris: Rivière, 1910), p. 4; for full text see Andreu, *Notre maître,* annex VII, pp. 327–28.
78. "L'Indépendance française," *Cité française,* pp. 1, 3–4; for full text see Andreu, *Notre maître,* annex VIII, pp. 329–31.
79. Berth, "Vers un ordre social antidémocratique," *Cité française,* pp. 4–7.
80. Gilbert and Valois, "L'Union contre la démocratie," *Cité française,* p. 8.
81. Variot, *Propos,* p. 262; Maurice Reclus, "Au tour d'une 'conversion': le cas de Charles Péguy," *Gil Blas,* May 23, 1910.
82. Variot, *Propos,* p. 262; Marcel Péguy, *La Rupture de Charles Péguy et de Georges Sorel d'après des documents inédits* (Paris: Cahiers de la Quinzaine, 1930), pp. 17–18.
83. Lagardelle, "Le Mouvement politique et social: monarchistes et syndicalistes," *Mouvement socialiste,* 13 (January 1911):52–55; see also his "Quelques précisions," *Le Socialisme ouvrier* (Paris: Rivière, 1911), pp. 264–66.
84. Anon., "Giorgio Sorel e i monarchici francesi," *Giornale d'Italia,* November 20, 1910.
85. Ibid.
86. Sorel to Croce, January 25, February 15, and February 19, 1911, 26, pp. 345, 347.
87. E. R. A. Seligman, *L'Interprétation économique de l'histoire,* trans. H. E. Barrault (Paris: Rivière, 1911), pp. ii, xviii–xxix.
88. Sorel to Berth, July 9, 1910, cited in Levey, "The Sorelian Syndicalists," p. 134; see also Sorel's "Minute: conditions de ma collaboration à *La Cité française*," November 15, 1910, cited in Levey, "The Sorelian Syndicalists," pp. 134–35. Sorel

did begin the preparation of a study of religion intended for the *Cité française*: see Sorel, "L'Expérience religieuse: préface pour une oeuvre nouvelle," *Liberté de l'esprit*, no. 28 (February 1952):33–35, and Andreu, "Un Inédit de Georges Sorel," ibid., p. 36. Cf. Andreu, "Un Inédit de Georges Sorel," *Table ronde*, no. 12 (December 1948):2128–36.

89. Sorel to Berth, November 17 and 27, 1910, cited in Levey, "The Sorelian Syndicalists," pp. 135–36; Sorel to Croce, January 25, 1911, 26, p. 344; Variot, *Propos*, p. 262; and Valois, *D'un siècle à l'autre*, p. 256.

90. Sorel to Maurras, December 19, 1910, cited in Levey, "The Sorelian Syndicalists," p. 136.

91. Valois, "Syndicalisme et démocratie: une note de M. Hubert Lagardelle," *Revue critique des idées et des livres*, 12 (January 10, 1911):89; Lagardelle, "Monarchistes et syndicalistes," *Mouvement socialiste*, 13 (January 1911):52–54; see Levey, "The Sorelian Syndicalists," pp. 134–39.

92. See above.

93. See Halévy, *Péguy and Les Cahiers de la Quinzaine*, p. 221n; Péguy, *Situations*, pp. 118, 154.

94. Variot, *Propos*, pp. 253, 260; cf. Ardengo Soffici, "Schizzo di Péguy e Sorel," *Riccordi di vita artistica e letteraria* (Florence: Vallecchi, 1942), pp. 325–29.

95. See Sorel to Croce, October 24, 1908, November 27, 1909, and September 21 and November 24, 1912, 26, pp. 190, 336–438, and 439–40; Variot, *Propos*, p. 256; Sorel to Missiroli, March 12, 1911, p. 87.

96. Variot, *Propos*, p. 256.

97. Ibid., p. 258.

98. Péguy, "Notre jeunesse"; see Halévy's reaction in *Péguy and Les Cahiers de la Quinzaine*, pp. 138–51.

99. Variot, *Propos*, p. 264; Halévy, *Péguy and Les Cahiers de la Quinzaine*, p. 138.

100. "Préface pour la deuxième édition," *La Révolution dreyfusienne*, pp. 3–7. See also Variot, *Propos*, p. 263.

101. Variot, *Propos*, p. 262.

102. "Avertissement," *Indépendance*, 1 (March 1, 1911):1. See also Andreu, *Notre maître*, annex IX, p. 332.

103. "Avertissement," p. 1.

104. Albert-Émile Sorel, "Souvenirs de Georges Sorel," *Echo de Paris*, September 8, 1922.

105. Variot, *Propos*, pp. 153–54.

106. Ibid., pp. 242–43.

107. Ibid., p. 176.

108. See below, Chapter 7.

109. Dolléans, "Le Visage de Georges Sorel," *Revue d'histoire économique et sociale*, 26 (1947):106.

110. "L'Oeuvre de défense française," *Indépendance*, 1 (May 1, 1911):194.

111. "Les Cours du Général Bonnal à l'Institut d'Action Française," *Indépendance*, 1 (May 15, 1911):233.

112. See *Indépendance*, 2 (December 15, 1911):299–300, and ibid. (January 1, 1912): 334–36; see also Variot, "Deux mots au *Bulletin de la semaine*," *Indépendance*, 4

(January 15, 1913):322, and "*Le Bulletin de la semaine*," ibid., 5 (April/May, 1913): 146.

113. "Le Monument de Jules Ferry," *Indépendance*, 1 (March 1, 1911):1–16.
114. "L'Abandon de la revanche," *Indépendance*, 1 (April 1, 1911):71–92.
115. "Lyripipii sorbonici moralisationes," *Indépendance*, 1 (April 15, 1911):111–25.
116. "Responsabilités de 1870," *Indépendance*, 1 (May 1, 1911):167–87.
117. "Sur la magie moderne," *Indépendance*, 2 (September 1, 1911):1–11.
118. "Si les dogmes évoluent," *Indépendance*, 2 (September 15, 1911):33–44.
119. "Un Critique des sociologues," *Indépendance*, 2 (October 1, 1911):73–84.
120. "À la mémoire de Cournot," *Indépendance*, 2 (October 15, 1911):97–114.
121. "Trois problèmes," *Indépendance*, 2 (December 1 and 15, 1911):221–40 and 261–79.
122. "Urbain Gohier," *Indépendance*, 2 (January 1, 1912):305–320.
123. "Aux ordres d'Arthur Meyer," *Indépendance*, 2 (February 1, 1912):414–16.
124. "D'un écrivain prolétaire," *Indépendance*, 3 (March 1, 1912:19–36. The first version appeared as "Uno Scrittore proletario: l'opera de Luciano Jean," *Divenire sociale*, 6 (June 1, 1910):146–149.
125. "La *Rivolta ideale*," *Indépendance*, 3 (April 15, 1912):161–77.
126. "Quelque prétentions juives," *Indépendance*, 3 (May 1–June 1, 1912):217–36, 277–95, and 317–36; a preliminary version appeared as "Gli Ebrei," *Divenire sociale*, 6 (July 16, 1910):196–98.
127. "Aux temps dreyfusiens," *Indépendance*, 4 (October 10, 1912):29–56.
128. Sorel to Croce, September 23 and October 14, 1911, 26, esp. p. 43; Sorel to Missiroli, September 23 and November 6, 1911, and September 20, 1912, pp. 97, 107.
129. Sorel to Croce, July 8 and August 18, 1911, and August 11, 1912, 26, pp. 432, 433, 437.
130. "Le Democrazia antiche," *Rassegna contemporanea*, 4 (November 1911): 210–11.
131. See below, Chapter 7; see also Andreu, *Notre maître*, p. 85.
132. Variot, *Propos*, p. 153.
133. Variot, "Quelques souvenirs: le père Sorel," *Éclair*, September 11, 1922.
134. "Avertissement pour la troisième édition," *Réflexions* (3rd ed., Paris: Rivière, 1912), p. 1.
135. Sorel to Dolléans, October 13, 1912, quoted in Dolléans, "Le Visage de Georges Sorel," p. 107.
136. Bergson to Gilbert Maire, ca. 1912, quoted in "Correspondance," *Indépendance*, 4 (November 15, 1912):167.
137. Tharaud, *Notre cher Péguy*, 2, p. 139. Berth confirms that Sorel did not believe in Péguy's conversion: see Berth, "Notre cher Péguy," *Révolution prolétarienne*, 2 (June 1926):14.
138. Sorel to Joseph Lotte, January 8, 1913, quoted in Marcel Péguy, *La Rupture*, p. 58; Sorel to Lotte, ca. 1912, quoted in Tharaud, *Notre cher Péguy*, 2, p. 140.
139. Sorel to Lotte, January 14, 1913, quoted in Marcel Péguy, *La Rupture*, p. 38; Dolléans, "Le Visage de Georges Sorel," p. 109.
140. Tharaud, *Notre cher Péguy*, 2, p. 140; Variot, *Propos*, p. 260.
141. Variot, *Propos*, pp. 265–68. For a recent interpretation of the break, see Jean

Onimus, "Péguy et Sorel," *Amitiés Charles Péguy*, no. 77 (May 1960):9, 13, 15, 21-22.

142. Originally published in the *Ère nouvelle* (1894) and republished by Péguy's *Cahiers* in 1907.

143. Sorel to Croce, September 3, 1912, 26, p. 437.

144. Sorel to Croce, November 24, 1912, 26, p. 439.

145. Tharaud, *Notre cher Péguy*, 2, p. 414; Variot, *Propos*, pp. 265-68.

146. Variot, *Propos*, pp. 265-68 (Variot must be considered a witness favorable to Sorel, but he is the sole source for the conversation); cf. Marcel Péguy, *La Rupture*, p. 19.

147. Rolland, *Péguy*, 2, p. 284.

148. Péguy to Sorel, ca. December 1912, quoted in Marcel Péguy, *La Rupture*, p. 14; Variot, *Propos*, p. 250. It is not possible to date exactly the *petit bleu*; it was in all probability sent several days before December 12, 1912 (see Halévy, *Péguy and Les Cahiers de la Quinzaine*, p. 222).

149. Rolland, *Péguy*, 2, p. 53.

150. Quoted in Halévy, *Péguy and Les Cahiers de la Quinzaine*, p. 223.

151. Rolland, *Péguy*, 2, p. 53.

152. Roger Secrétain, *Péguy, soldat de la liberté* (New York: Brentano, 1941), p. 145.

153. Quoted in Halévy, *Péguy and Les Cahiers de la Quinzaine*, p. 222; the entry was dated December 12, 1912.

154. Marcel Péguy, *La Rupture*, p. 19.

155. Variot, *Propos*, p. 251.

156. Halévy, *Péguy and Les Cahiers de la Quinzaine*, p. 223.

157. Marcel Péguy, *La Rupture*, pp. 14-15; Émile Buré, "Péguy et Sorel," *Éclair*, September 7, 1922.

158. Variot, *Propos*, p. 267.

159. Halévy, *Péguy and Les Cahiers de la Quinzaine*, pp. 222-23.

160. Marcel Péguy, *La Rupture*, p. 17; Dolléans, "Le Visage de Georges Sorel," p. 106; Variot, "Georges Sorel et la révolution nationale," p. 229.

161. Sorel to Lotte, December 21, 1912, quoted in Marcel Péguy, *La Rupture*, pp. 49, 56-57.

162. Sorel to Lotte, January 8, 10, and 20, 1913, quoted in ibid., p. 47.

163. Sorel to Croce, January 12, 1913, 26, p. 440; Sorel to Lotte, April 30, 1913, quoted in Marcel Péguy, *La Rupture*, p. 42.

164. Sorel to Croce, June 22, 1913, 26, p. 442. See also Andreu, "Bergson et Pascal: lettre inédite de Georges Sorel," *Nef* (July 1947):59-60; the view concerning miracles was expressed in a letter dated April 8, 1913, to an unknown addressee.

165. Lefèvre, "Une Heure avec Jean Variot," *Nouvelles littéraires*, 12 (February 4, 1933):2.

166. Sorel to Croce, November 20, 1912, 26, pp. 438-39; Variot, *Propos*, p. 41.

167. Variot, *Propos*, "Easter 1913," pp. 41, 43-44.

168. Ibid., pp. 43-44.

169. Ibid., pp. 45-46.

170. Tharaud, *Notre cher Péguy*, 2, p. 142.

171. Sorel to Lotte, February 25, 1914, quoted in Marcel Péguy, *La Rupture*, p. 49; see also Sorel to Pareto, May 27, 1914, in *Carteggi Paretiani, 1892-1923*, pp. 3-4,

concerning his comments on Michels and Missiroli. Sorel added, "I ask myself if Italy possesses a national idea."

172. Sorel to Croce, March 20, 1914, 27 (1929):48.
173. "Préface" to Berth, *Les Méfaits des intellectuels,* pp. i–xxxvii.
174. Ibid., p. xxix.
175. Ibid., pp. viii–ix, xxxiii.

Chapter 6. The Idea

1. Variot, *Propos,* p. 28.
2. See especially Richard Vernon, "Rationalism and Commitment in Sorel," *Journal of the History of Ideas,* 34 (July/September 1973):419.
3. "Aux temps dreyfusiens," p. 55.
4. Variot, *Propos,* November 12, 1908, p. 25; review of A. Chevrillon's *Nouvelles études anglaises,* in *Indépendance,* 1 (June 15, 1911):338; review of H. Van Laak's *Harnack et le miracle* in ibid., 1 (April 1, 1911):108; review of P. Lasserre's *La Philosophie de M. Bergson* in ibid., 1 (May 1, 1911):191; and review of P. A. Gardeil's *La Crédibilité et l'apologétique* in ibid., 4 (November 15, 1912):157.
5. Variot, *Propos;* review of *La Philosophie de M. Bergson,* p. 191; review of *La Crédibilité et l'apologétique,* p. 157.
6. Variot, *Propos,* November 12, 1908, and December 11, 1912, pp. 25, 28; "L'Abandon de la revanche," p. 91.
7. "La Réveil de l'âme française"; "Sur la magie moderne," pp. 5–6; review of P. A. de Poulpiquet's *L'Objet intégral de l'apologétique* in *Indépendance,* 3 (August 1/ 15, 1912):565; "Vues sur les problèmes de la philosophie," p. 583; "Si les dogmes évoluent," pp. 41–42; "La Religion d'aujourd'hui," pp. 245 and 421; and review of A. Houtin's *Un Prêtre marié: Charles Perraud* in *Indépendance,* 2 (August 15, 1911):481.
8. "Si les dogmes évoluent," p. 38; Variot, *Propos,* January 13, 1910, p. 113; review of A. Leclère's *Pragmatisme, modernisme, protestantisme* in *Indépendance,* 1 (April 1, 1911):108–109; "Un Critique des sociologues" in ibid., 2 (October 1, 1911):80; review of A. Schinz's *Antipragmatisme* in ibid., 1 (March 1, 1911):30.
9. "Si les dogmes évoluent," p. 38.
10. "Aux ordres d'Arthur Meyer," p. 414; "À la mémoire de Cournot," p. 113.
11. "L'Indépendance française," p. 2; "Avertissement," *Indépendance,* p. 1.
12. "Si les dogmes évoluent," pp. 41–42; "La Politica degli immortali."
13. "La Religion d'aujourd'hui," pp. 423–25; "Grandeur et décadence," p. 325; review of R. Eucken's *Les Grands courants de la pensée contemporaine* in *Indépendance,* 1 (May 15, 1911):230–32.
14. "Sur la magie moderne," pp. 5–6; "Quelques prétentions juives," p. 336; "La Politica degli immortali."
15. Variot, *Propos,* January 13, 1910, p. 113.
16. "Avertissement," *Indépendance,* p. 1; "L'Indépendance française," p. 1.
17. "Quelques prétentions juives," p. 320; "D'un écrivain prolétaire," p. 32; "Urbain Gohier," pp. 318–20; "Aux temps dreyfusiens," p. 56.
18. Variot, *Propos,* March 27, 1910, pp. 147, 150; "Quelques prétentions juives," pp. 334–35.

19. "Urbain Gohier," p. 320.
20. Variot, *Propos,* November 14, 1908, and February n.d., 1909, pp. 91, 139; "Il Nazionalismo francese."
21. "Il Nazionalismo francese"; Variot, *Propos,* February n.d., 1909, p. 139.
22. "La Politica degli immortali"; "La Rivincita del patriotismo"; Variot, *Propos,* June 17, 1910, p. 123.
23. Variot, *Propos,* June 13, 1910, pp. 114–15; "Socialistes antiparlementaires"; "La Politica degli immortali"; "La Rivincita del patriotismo."
24. Variot, *Propos,* June 17, 1910, p. 124.
25. Ibid., June 13, 17, and 18, 1912, pp. 116, 125–26, 170.
26. Ibid., "Easter 1913," p. 43.
27. "Aux armes, les bourgeois!" Variot, *Propos,* June 17, 1910, p. 122.
28. Ibid.
29. Variot, *Propos,* June 17, 1910, p. 124.
30. Ibid., and February n.d., 1909, p. 139.
31. Ibid., June 13, 1910, p. 116; "Grandeur et décadence," p. 317.
32. Variot, *Propos,* p. 116.
33. Ibid., pp. 122–23.
34. Ibid., p. 124.
35. Ibid., and June 1, 1909, pp. 87 and 125.
36. Ibid., January 13, 1910 and June 5, 1909, pp. 114 and 94; "Aux temps dreyfusiens," pp. 29–32.
37. "Grandeur et décadence," pp. 335–36; "Si les dogmes évoluent," pp. 34–39; "Aux temps dreyfusiens," pp. 29–32, 55; "Quelques prétentions juives," p. 284; "Urbain Gohier," p. 317.
38. "Si les dogmes évoluent," pp. 34, 38; "Un Critique des sociologues," pp. 75–76; "Aux temps dreyfusiens," p. 55; "La *Rivolta ideale,*" p. 172.
39. Variot, *Propos,* March 27, 1910, p. 151.
40. "Aux temps dreyfusiens," p. 56.
41. "Quelques prétentions juives," pp. 285, 333.
42. "Trois problèmes," pp. 238, 238n.
43. "La Religion d'aujourd'hui," pp. 261–64; "Trois problèmes," p. 279; review of P. Gaultier's *La Pensée contemporaine* in *Indépendance,* 1, (July 1, 1911):373.
44. "D'un écrivain prolétaire," pp. 21–24, 25, 26; "La *Rivolta ideale,*" p. 165.
45. "Grandeur et décadence," pp. 318, 329, 332.
46. "Trois problèmes," p. 221.
47. "Aux temps dreyfusiens," pp. 29, 32, 39; "Grandeur et décadence," pp. 302, 307; "Préface pour la deuxième édition," *Révolution dreyfusienne,* p. 4; "D'un écrivain prolétaire," pp. 25–26.
48. "D'un écrivain prolétaire," pp. 24–25; "Sur la magie moderne," pp. 2–5.
49. "D'un écrivain prolétaire," pp. 24–25; review of A. Vincent's *Les Instituteurs de la démocratie* in *Indépendance,* 5 (March 15, 1913):37–39.
50. Variot, *Propos,* October n.d., 1908, and December 18, 1912, pp. 16, 19, 29.
51. Ibid., June 16, 1909, January 12 and June 13, 1910, pp. 99, 109, 119.
52. Review of *Les Instituteurs de la démocratie,* p. 37.
53. Variot, *Propos,* June 1, 1909, p. 88.

54. Ibid., June 1, 1909, p. 90.
55. "*Pages Choisies* de Jules Lemaître," *Indépendance,* 3 (March 1, 1912):42; Variot, *Propos,* June 1, 13, and 16, 1910, pp. 92, 98–99, 106n, 117–20; "Trois problèmes," p. 227; review of D. Marcault's *L'Art de tromper, d'intimider et de corrompre l'électeur* in *Indépendance,* 4 (January 15, 1913):305; "L'Abandon de la revanche," p. 90.
56. Variot, *Propos,* June 13, 1910, p. 117.
57. Review of J. Charles-Brun's *Le Régionalisme* in *Indépendance,* 2 (November 1, 1911):165; "Le Monument de Jules Ferry," p. 5.
58. "Grandeur et décadence," p. 297; "Lyripipii sorbonici moralisationes," p. 116; "Trois problèmes," p. 225n.
59. "Le Monument de Jules Ferry," pp. 3–5.
60. Ibid.; "Lyripipii sorbonici moralisationes," p. 125.
61. Variot, *Propos,* June 16, 1909, pp. 104, 106–107.
62. Ibid., February 26 and June 16, 1909, pp. 106–108, 135.
63. Ibid., June 5 and 16, 1909, pp. 95, 104, 106–107.
64. Review of P. Harmignie's *L'État et ses agents: étude sur le syndicalisme administratif* in *Indépendance,* 3 (September 1, 1911):30–31.
65. Variot, *Propos,* June 16, 1909, p. 106.
66. Ibid., February n.d., 1909, and June 17, 1910, pp. 123, 140; see also Sorel's remarks to Variot on corporatism and professionalism in April and July 1911 (Variot, "Quelques souvenirs: le père Sorel," *Éclair,* September 11, 1922).
67. "Déclaration," *Cité française,* p. i.
68. Variot, *Propos,* January 4, 1911, p. 178.
69. Ibid., December 14, 1912, pp. 30–31.
70. Variot, "Quelques souvenirs: le père Sorel"; Variot, *Propos,* June 17, 1910, and January 4, 1911, pp. 123, 178.
71. "Avertissement," *Indépendance,* p. 1; review of *Annales de l'Institut supérieur de philosophie de Louvain* in ibid., 4 (November 15, 1912):164.
72. "Grandeur et décadence," pp. 335–36; "Si les dogmes évoluent," p. 33; "Quelques prétentions juives," p. 336; "Urbain Gohier," p. 320; Variot, *Propos,* April 15, 1911, p. 232. See especially Sorel to Lotte, April 30, 1913, and February 25, 1914, in Marcel Péguy, *La Rupture,* pp. 43, 46.
73. "Lyripipii sorbonici moralisationes," pp. 111, 113, 122–23, 125; "Le Monument de Jules Ferry," p. 14; "Quelques prétentions juives," pp. 290–92, 336; review of A. Loisy's *À propos d'histoire des religions* in *Indépendance,* 2 (December 1, 1911): 260.
74. Review of G. Maze-Sencier's *L'Erreur primaire* in *Indépendance,* 1 (June 1, 1911): 286; "Lyripipii sorbonici moralisationes," p. 125; Variot, *Propos,* October 11, 1912, p. 236.
75. Review of J. Ruskin's *Praeterita, souvenirs de jeunesse* in *Indépendance,* 1 (May 15, 1911):229; review of L. Cazamian's *L'Angleterre moderne: son évolution* in ibid., 1 (May 1, 1911):193–94. See also Lanzillo, "Idee letterarie di Giorgio Sorel (con pagine inedite)," *Opere e i giorni,* 2 (February 1923):53.
76. Variot, *Propos,* January 12, 1910, pp. 109–113; "Urbain Gohier," p. 320.
77. Variot, *Propos,* March 27, 1910, p. 152.

78. Ibid., November 8 and December 11, 1912, pp. 22–23, 28.
79. Ibid., December 11, 1912, p. 28; see also ibid., June 16, 1909, pp. 97–98; and "Socialistes antiparlementaires."
80. Variot, *Propos,* January 4 and April 15, 1911, and November 18, 1912, pp. 179, 232, 248.
81. Ibid., November 18, 1912, p. 248.
82. Ibid., January 5, 1911, and October 11, 1912, pp. 183, 237.
83. "L'Indépendance française," *Cité française,* p. 2. See also Sorel to Lotte, April 30, 1913, in Marcel Péguy, *La Rupture,* p. 43; Variot, *Propos,* April 15, 1911, p. 232.
84. Variot, *Propos,* January 4, 1911, p. 178.
85. Review of *Annales de l'Institut supérieur de philosophie de Louvain,* p. 164.
86. Variot, *Propos,* June 16, 1909, pp. 101–104.
87. Ibid., June 5 and 16, 1909, pp. 96, 100.
88. Ibid., June 5, 1909, p. 96.
89. "Grandeur et décadence," pp. 315–17; Variot, *Propos,* June 16, 1909, p. 108.
90. Variot, *Propos,* December 14, 1912, p. 37; review of E. Ollivier's *L'Empire libérale: étions nous prêts?* in *Indépendance,* 2 (September 15, 1911):71; "Responsabilités de 1870," pp. 186–87.
91. "L'Abandon de la revanche," pp. 72, 82–84, 88, 90–91; Variot, *Propos,* June 1, 1909, p. 91.
92. "Préface pour la deuxième édition," *Révolution dreyfusienne,* pp. 5–7; "Trois problèmes," p. 227; "Urbain Gohier," p. 314; "La Rivincita del patriotismo."
93. "L'Abandon de la revanche," pp. 86n, 91.
94. Variot, *Propos,* December 14, 1912, pp. 34, 35, 37.
95. "Le Monument de Jules Ferry," pp. 10–11; review of O. Maynier's *L'Afrique noire* in *Indépendance,* 2 (October 1, 1911):95; "Barbarie o civiltà?"
96. "Trois problèmes," p. 277.

Chapter 7. The Impact

1. See above, Chapter 5, and below, this chapter and Chapters 11, 13, 14, 15, 16. The argument that fascism is a prewar French "invention" of a "revolutionary right," though not new and not without merit, is overstated in Sternhell, *La Droite révolutionnaire, 1885–1914,* pp. 364–72, 385–90.
2. Valois, *D'un siècle à l'autre,* p. 256; Berth, *Guerre des états ou guerre des classes,* p. 19. On the argument that Maurras's "conception of monarchy" may have been and could be viewed as comparable to Sorel's "myth of the General Strike," see Stephen Wilson, "The Action Française in French Intellectual Life" in John C. Cairns, ed., *Contemporary France: Illusions, Conflict, and Regeneration* (New York: New Viewpoints, 1978), pp. 141, 144.
3. Valois, "Pourquoi nous rattachons nos travaux à l'esprit proudhonnien," *Cahiers du Cercle Proudhon,* 1 (January/February 1912):34–38; Sorel to Berth in Levey, "The Sorelian Syndicalists," p. 142.
4. Valois, *D'un siècle à l'autre,* p. 256; Berth, *Guerre des états ou guerre des classes,* p. 19.
5. See "Déclaration," *Cahiers du Cercle Proudhon,* 1 (January/February 1912):2.

6. Ibid., p. 1.
7. "Hommage à Georges Sorel," *Cahiers du Cercle Proudhon*, 1 (May/August 1912):109–110.
8. Henri Lagrange, "L'Oeuvre de Sorel et le Cercle Proudhon," *Cahiers du Cercle Proudhon*, 1 (May/August 1912):129.
9. Sorel to Berth, ca. end of 1911, quoted in Andreu, *Notre maître*, p. 85.
10. Charles Maurras, "À Besançon," *Cahiers du Cercle Proudhon*, 1 (January/February 1912):4–8.
11. Valois, *Basile*, pp. xi, xiii.
12. Gilbert Maire, "La Philosophie de Georges Sorel," *Cahiers du Cercle Proudhon*, 1 (March/April 1912):65.
13. Ibid., pp. 65, 69–80. Maire cites an undated letter he received from Bergson on Sorel: "He is not a disciple. But he accepts some of my views and when he cites me, he does so as a man who has read me attentively and who has perfectly understood me" (p. 65).
14. Weber, *The Action française*, p. 76n.
15. Henri Lagrange, "L'Oeuvre de Sorel et le cercle Proudhon, précisions et prévisions," *Cahiers du Cercle Proudhon*, 1 (May/August 1912):129, 132.
16. René de Marans, "Grandes rectifications soréliennes," *Cahiers du Cercle Proudhon*, 1 (May/August 1912):118–122.
17. Valois, *La Révolution nationale* (2nd ed., Paris: Nouvelle Librairie Nationale, 1926), p. 9.
18. Pierre Drieu La Rochelle, "Modes intellectuels," *Nouvelles littéraires*, January 6, 1934, pp. 1–2.
19. Valois, *L'Homme contre l'argent* (Paris: Librairie Valois, 1928), pp. 21, 62.
20. Variot, "Sur Minerva," *Indépendance*, 2 (February 15, 1912):441.
21. Robert Havard de la Montagne, "Revue de la presse," *Action française*, September 8, 1922.
22. Berth ["Jean Darville"], "Proudhon," *Cahiers du Cercle Proudhon*, 1 (January/February 1912):27–28.
23. Berth, "Proudhon en Sorbonne," *Indépendance*, 2 (April 1, 1912):129–30, 140.
24. Berth ["Jean Darville"], "Satellites de la ploutocratie," *Cahiers du Cercle Proudhon*, 1 (1913):179.
25. Ibid., p. 209.
26. Berth, *Les Méfaits des intellectuels*, p. 11; see also "La Monarchie de la classe ouvrière," *Cahiers du Cercle Proudhon*, 2 (January/February 1914):15, 19, and 29.
27. Berth, *Les Méfaits des intellectuels*, p. 80.
28. Ibid., pp. 15, 54, 65, 75.
29. Valois, "Pourquoi nous rattachons nos travaux à l'esprit proudhonien," pp. 37–39, 41.
30. Valois, "Sorel et l'architecture sociale," *Cahiers du Cercle Proudhon*, 1 (May/August 1912):111–12.
31. Valois, "La Bourgeoisie capitaliste," *Cahiers du Cercle Proudhon*, 1 (1913):215.
32. Ibid., p. 245.
33. Valois, *Le Père* (Paris: Nouvelle Librairie Nationale, 1913).
34. See above, Chapter 5.

35. Valois, *Basile*, p. xi. Valois is hardly a disinterested observer, having parted company with the Action Française after most bitter recriminations; see below, Chapter 14.

36. Ibid., p. ix; Archives nationales, *Action française*, March 25, 1912, cited by Tannenbaum, *The Action Française*, p. 278.

37. Valois, *Basile*, p. 62; de la Montagne, "Revue de la presse," *Action française*, September 8, 1922.

38. Sorelian activities seemed limited to Parisian students on the right: see above, Chapter 5.

39. Tannenbaum, *The Action française*, pp. 86, 126, 232, 278; Weber, *The Action française*, pp. 43, 73–76; and Mazgaj, "The Social Revolution or the King," pp. 302–356.

40. J.-R. Bloch, "La Théâtre du peuple," *Effort*, 1 (June 1910):3–4. For studies of Bloch and his circle see Avriel Goldberger, *Visions of a New Hero: The Heroic Life according to André Malraux and Earlier Advocates of Human Grandeur* (Paris: Lettres Modernes, 1965).

41. "La 'Second manière' de M. Georges Sorel," *Effort*, 1 (August 15, 1910):4.

42. Bloch, "L'Irrédentisme française," *Effort*, 1 (Christmas 1910):1–2.

43. Bloch, "Renaissance classique ou renaissance révolutionnaire?" *Effort*, 2 (March 11, 1911):67.

44. Bloch, "Examen de conscience," *Effort*, 3 (January 1913):94.

45. Bloch, *Carnival est mort* (3rd ed., Paris: Éditions de la Nouvelle Revue Française, 1920), p. 263.

46. Henri Franck, "Réflexions sur la Sorbonne," *Effort libre*, 4 (March 1914):329–42.

47. Charles Albert, "Chroniques: la vie politique et sociales," *Effort libre*, 4 (June 1914):438.

48. Croce, "La Morte del socialismo," *Voce*, 3 (February 9, 1911):196; see also his *Cultura e vita morale: intermezzi polemici* (Bari: Laterza, 1914), pp. 176, 178.

49. Croce, *La Philosophie de Jean-Baptiste Vico*, trans. H. Buriot-Darsiles and G. Bourgin (Paris: V. Giard and E. Brière, 1913), p. 312.

50. Ibid., pp. 263–64, 266.

51. Pareto to Sensini, January 16, 1910, p. 47; on the parallel development of Sorel and Pareto see Gabriele de Rosa, "Prefazione," *Carteggi Paretiani, 1892–1923*, pp. xxvi, xxviii–xix.

52. Pareto, "Rentiers et spéculateurs," *Indépendance*, 1 (May 1, 1911):166.

53. Pareto, *Il Mito virtuista e la letteratura immorale* (Rome: Bernado Lux, 1914), pp. 220–21; see Sorel to Missiroli, October 22, 1910, p. 84.

54. Pareto, *Il Mito virtuista e la letteratura immorale*, p. 244.

55. Michels, *Les Parties politiques*, trans. S. Jankelevitch (Paris: E. Flammarion, 1914), pp. 48, 256.

56. Ibid., pp. 170, 308.

57. Michels, *L'Imperialismo italiano* (Milan: Società Editrice Libreria, 1914), pp. 92, 180.

58. See Anon., "Il Problema morale dell'Italia e il nazionalismo," *Idea nazionale*, August 31, 1911, for a favorable review of Missiroli in "*la bella rivista di Giorgio Sorel.*"

59. Labriola, "L'Europa contro l'Italia," *Idea nazionale*, October 12, 1911; see also Sorel to Missiroli, November 19, 1912, p. 107.

60. Gradilone, *Storia del sindacalismo,* 2, p. 114; see also Viana, *Sindacalismo* (Bari: Laterza, 1923).
61. Prezzolini, "Bottettino bibliografico: lavori su e di Giorgio Sorel," *Voce,* November 10, 1910; see also articles published in 1911.
62. See general index of the *Voce,* in Romanò, "'La Voce' (1908–1914)," 721–84; Thayer, *Italy and the Great War,* p. 257.
63. Enrico Paresce, *Giorgio Sorel ed altri saggi* (Palermo: Gustavo Travi, 1934), p. 12.
64. Corradini, *Il Volere d'Italia* (Naples: Perrella, 1911), passim.
65. Ibid., p. 206.
66. See Corradini, *La Patria lontana* (Milan: Fratelli Treves, 1911), p. 244; *Il Nazionalismo italiano* (Milan: Fratelli Treves, 1914), pp. 5, 35.
67. Prezzolini, "La Fine del nazionalismo," *Voce,* 4 (May 23, 1912):87.
68. Prezzolini, "Prefazione," *Vecchio e nuovo nazionalismo,* p. x.
69. Prezzolini, "Collaborazione al mondo," *Voce,* 7 (April 28, 1914):2.
70. Sorel to Missiroli, May 6, 1910, pp. 69–71.
71. Missiroli, "Le Nationalisme italien," *Indépendance,* 1 (August 1, 1911):426–27, 433–35.
72. Missiroli, "Giorgio Sorel per Alfredo Oriani," *Resto del Carlino,* May 4, 1912.
73. Atti del Congresso di Firenze, pp. 129–36; see also Salomone, *Italian Democracy in the Making,* pp. 129–36; Thayer, *Italy and the Great War,* pp. 207–209; P. L. Occhini, *Enrico Corradini e la nuova coscienza nazionale* (Florence: Vallecchi, 1924), p. 121; and Corradini, *Il Nazionalismo italiano,* pp. 67–69. For brief sketches of the syndicalists who joined the nationalist movement in 1906 and who thereafter identified themselves completely with nationalism (Forges-Davanzati, Maraviglia, Federzoni, and Monicelli) see Prezzolini, *Fascism,* trans. K. Macmillan (New York: Dutton, 1926). See also Sorel to Missiroli, May 3, 1911, p. 88.
74. For a general treatment see Salomone, *Italian Democracy in the Making,* p. 94.
75. Gioacchino Volpe, *L'Italia in cammino* (Milan: Fratelli Treves, 1931), pp. 134–35.
76. Rosenstock-Franck, *L'Économie corporative fasciste,* pp. 16–17. Sorel was much impressed by the possibility that conservative Catholics might rally to the cause of nationalism: see Sorel to Pareto, May 27, 1914, *Carteggi Paretiani, 1892–1925,* p. 4, and Sorel to Missiroli, June 16, 1914, p. 116.
77. Alfredo Rocco, *Idea nazionale,* May 23, 1914, quoted in Herbert W. Schneider, *Making the Fascist State* (New York: Oxford, 1928), p. 150. In Rocco's articles and speeches dating from 1913 there is not a single reference to Sorel: see *Scritti e discorsi politici* (3 vols., Milan: A. Giuffrè, 1938).
78. Guido Pedroli, *Il Socialismo nella Svizzera italiana, 1880–1912* (Milan: Feltrinelli, 1963), p. 101. Gradilone, *Storia del sindacalismo,* 2, p. 98.
79. See Giulio Barni, "Tripoli e il sindacalismo," *Pagine libere,* 5 (December 1/15, 1911):481–96.
80. Giulio Colamarino, "Angustie sindacalista," *Pagine libere,* 5 (December 1/15, 1911):568.
81. Orano, "La Lupa," *Lupa,* October 16, 1910, p. 1. See Sorel to Missiroli, September 23 and October 16, 1910, pp. 81, 82.
82. B. Fabre, "Monarchici e sindacalisti contro la Repubblica," *Lupa,* October 16, 1910, p. 3; Giovanni Diotallevi and Raffaello Giolli, "Il Dibatto sul sindacalismo e il nazionalismo," *Lupa,* October 30, 1910, p. 3; cf. Corradini, "Nazionalismo e sindacalismo," *Lupa,* October 16, 1910, p. 1.

83. See Orano, "Verso Tripoli," *Lupa,* September 10, 1911, and "Dobbiamo avere Tripoli," *Lupa,* September 24, 1911.

84. These are the most prominent of such reviews.

85. On Mussolini's position concerning Sorel and the monarchists see below.

86. See, for example: Lanzillo, "Il Crepuscolo di un idea," *Avanti!* February 28, 1913, and "Nuove tendenze di vita in Francia: l'Action Française," *Avanti!* March 11, 1913; Labriola, "Le Parti socialiste italien et le syndicalisme," pp. 72–78; Colamarino, "Angustie sindacaliste," pp. 563–71; de Pietri-Tonelli, "I Capricci della lotta politica," *Bandiera del popolo,* February 25, 1911; Aflredo Poggi, "Soddisfatti?" *Lupa,* July 2, 1911; and Lanzillo, *Giorgio Sorel,* p. 80.

87. Lanzillo, "Nazionalismo italico," *Conquista,* November 22, 1910; Labriola, "L'Europa contro l'Italia," *Idea nazionale,* October 12, 1911; Orano, "Dobbiamo avere Tripoli"; Olivetti, *Pro e contro Tripoli,* pp. 11, 14, 22, 57, 91. See also Marucco, *Arturo Labriola,* pp. 203–207, on Labriola's position on the Libyan war; Labriola, *La Guerra di Tripoli e l'opinione socialista* (Naples: Morano, 1912), pp. 20, 104.

88. Labriola, "Le Parti socialiste italien et le syndicalisme," pp. 72–78.

89. De Pietri-Tonelli, "I Capricci della lotta politica."

90. Lanzillo, "Il Crepuscole di un idea"; Panunzio, *Il Socialismo giuridico* (Genoa: Libreria Moderna, 1910), pp. 8–15; Olivetti, "Dobbiamo avere Tripoli"; and Panunzio, *La Persistenza del diritto* (Pescara: Casa Editrice Abruzzese, 1910), p. 12.

91. Olivetti, *Cinque anni,* p. 2.

92. Lanzillo, *Giorgio Sorel,* p. 36n; see also Marucco, *Arturo Labriola,* p. 203. See Leone, *Espansionismo e colonie* (Rome: Tipografia Editrice Nazionale, 1911), and "Irredentismo borghese ed antipatriottismo operaio," *Gioventù,* September 7, 1913.

93. Corridoni ["Leo Celvisio"], "Cortigiani," *Conquista,* February 15, 1911. For further informaton on Corridoni as a hero and martyr see Ivon de Begnac, *L'Arcangelo sindacalista,* especially the appendix.

94. Corridoni, "Cortigiani."

95. De Begnac, *L'Arcangelo sindacalista,* p. 307.

96. Ibid., appendix, nos. 21–35.

97. Attracted to the *Voce,* Mussolini wrote on irredentism in the Trentino; here, perhaps, are to be found the earliest traces of a "proletarian nationalism" in his work. See Mussolini, "Il Trentino," *Voce,* 2 (December 15, 1910):461.

98. Mussolini, "L'Ultima capriola," *Lotta di classe,* 1 (November 26, 1910):263–64; see also *Dalla fondazione de "La Lotta di classe" al primo comploto contro Mussolini,* 3, pp. 271–72.

99. Mussolini, "Fine stagione," *Lotta di classe,* 1 (December 17, 1910); *Dalla fondazione,* p. 289.

100. Mussolini, "Note e letture," *Lotta di classe,* 2 (July 8, 1911):264; see also *Dal primo complotto contro Mussolini alla sua nomina a direttore dell'Avanti!* 4, pp. 45–46.

101. Mussolini's address at the congress was published as "Sull'azione de gruppo parlementare," *Lotta di classe,* 2 (July 8, 1912); see *Dal primo complotto,* p. 166. Cf. Croce, *Storia d'Italia dal 1871 al 1915* (Bari: Laterza, 1942), pp. 279ff., on Mussolini and the Congress of Reggio Emilia.

102. Mussolini, "Da Guicciardini a ... Sorel," *Avanti!* July 18, 1912; see de Felice, *Mussolini il rivoluzionario*, p. 141, on the participation of *syndacalisti* and *meridionalisti* on the *Avanti!*

103. Mussolini, "Lo Sviluppo del partito," *Avanti!* March 9, 1913.

104. Piétro Nenni, "La Faillite du syndicalisme fasciste," *Cahier bleus*, no. 25 (July 27, 1929):7; see also de Felice, *Mussolini il rivoluzionario*, p. 120.

105. Mussolini, *La Mia vita* (Rome: Faro, 1947), pp. 191–92 (from an address at the Teatro Comunale of Cesena, May 3, 1914). See also Domenico Settembrini, "Mussolini and the Legacy of Revolutionary Socialism," *Journal of Contemporary History*, 11 (1976):239–68, comparing "Mussolinianism" and "Leninism," especially between 1912 and 1917.

106. Gradilone, *Storia del sindacalismo*, 2, pp. 96–97; Ferrari, *La Régime fasciste italien*, p. 235; de Begnac, *L'Arcangelo sindacalista*, pp. 281–307.

107. W. Hilton-Young, *The Italian Left* (London: Longmans, Green, 1949), pp. 67–69; Horowitz, *The Italian Labor Movement*, pp. 56–57.

108. See Horowitz, *The Italian Labor Movement*, pp. 86–94, for a discussion of the relations between syndicalism and the Socialist party from Reggio Emilia to "Red Week."

109. Ibid., p. 86; Gradilone, *Storia del sindacalismo*, 2, p. 100; de Begnac, *L'Arcangelo sindacalista*, p. 324; and Bruno Buozzi and Vincenzo Nitti, *Fascisme et syndicalisme*, trans. S. Priacel (Paris: Librairie Valois, 1930), p. 16.

110. Leonardo Paloscia, *La Concezione sindacalista di Sergio Panunzio* (Rome: Casa Editrice Gismondi, 1949), p. 26; Horowitz, *The Italian Labor Movement*, p. 88; Armando Borghi, *Mezzo secolo di anarchia, 1898-1945*, p. 92; and Tullio Masotti, *Corridoni* (Milan: Fratelli Treves, 1932), pp. 57–60.

111. Paloscia, *La Concezione sindacalista;* Adolfo Pepe, *Storia della CGdL dalla guerra di Libia all'intervento, 1911-1915* (Bari: Laterza, 1971), p. 189.

112. On the subject of Red Week see Horowitz, *The Italian Labor Movement*, p. 92; Gradilone, *Storia del sindacalismo*, 2, pp. 31–34; and Orietta Lupo, "I Sindacalisti rivoluzionari nel 1914," *Rivista storica del socialismo*, 10(1967):73–79. For Sorel's comments on Red Week see Sorel to Missiroli, June 16, 1914, pp. 115–16. Settembrini argues that in the years just before World War I, "Voluntarism, idealism, anarchism—something of all of these [was] to be found in the ... 'new' extreme Left which was developing around the young Mussolini, and from which were to come the leading groups of both fascism and communism.... Gramsci ... once described him as 'our leader.'" (Settembrini, "Mussolini and the Legacy of Revolutionary Socialism," p. 251.)

Bolshevism

Chapter 8. The Man

1. "Avant-propos," *Matériaux*, pp. 1–52; see Monnerot, "Georges Sorel ou l'introduction aux mythes modernes," p. 411; Richard Vernon, "Rationalism and Commitment in Sorel," p. 419.

2. "Avant-propos," *Matériaux*, pp. 2, 4.

3. Ibid., p. 3.
4. See Berth, *Du "Capital" aux "Réflexions sur la violence,"* p. 177; Johannet, *Itinéraires d'intellectuels,* p. 230; de Rosa, "Prefazione," *Carteggi Paretiani, 1892–1923,* pp. xix–xx; and Sorel to Missiroli, August 10, 1914, p. 117.
5. Sorel to Croce, September 22, 1914, 27, p. 51. See Sorel to Berth, September 11, 1914, in Andreu, *Notre maître,* annex X, pp. 333–35, where Sorel argues that Prussian "discipline" is upholding the "principles" of "Rome"; also Sorel to Missiroli, October 24 and November 10, 1914, pp. 130, 136.
6. Sorel to Croce, September 22, 1914, 27, p. 51.
7. Sorel to Delesalle, November 22, 1915, pp. 111–12.
8. Sorel to Croce, October 26 and November 14, 1914, and April 8, 1915, 27, pp. 52, 114, 120; Sorel to Missiroli, August 10, 1914, pp. 117–18.
9. Sorel to Croce, April 25, 1915, 27, p. 120.
10. Sorel to Croce, May 5, 1915, 27, p. 121. Johannet was to write during the Vichy period that Sorel wanted a German victory in 1914 ("Un Précurseur de la Révolution nationale: Georges Sorel," p. 5); see Salvo Mastellone, "Sorel e la Guerra Mondiale," *Georges Sorel: studi e ricerche,* p. 173.
11. Sorel to Croce, January 28, 1915, and May 30, 1916, 27, pp. 117, 358.
12. Sorel to Croce, January 30, 1915, 27, p. 117.
13. Sorel to Missiroli, August 10 and 24 and November 10, 1914, pp. 117, 119, 136; Sorel to Croce, November 2, 1914, 27, p. 52; see also Sorel to Pareto, November 24 and December 3, 1914, *Carteggi Paretiani, 1892–1923,* pp. 5–6. See Mastellone, "Sorel e la Guerra Mondiale," pp. 170, 172–73.
14. Sorel to Croce, November 28, 1914, 27, p. 115; Sorel to Missiroli, December 9, 1914, pp. 141–42.
15. Sorel to Croce, December 3, 1914, and January 19, 1915, 27, pp. 115, 117; Sorel to Missiroli, December 23, 1914, p. 143. See Furiozzi, *Sorel e l'Italia,* pp. 281–85.
16. "Un Giudizio de Giorgio Sorel su l'intervento dell'Italia," *Avanti!* May 15, 1915, and "Il Destino dell'Austria," *Avanti!* May 16, 1915. Sorel had already published three articles in Italy in late 1914 and early 1915 on the likely consequences the war would have on the Vatican, on Slavic expansion, and on the future of Europe: see "Francia, Vaticano e Italia durante e dopo la guerra," *Giornale d'Italia,* December 6, 1914; "L'Avvenire degli slavi," ibid., January 24, 1915; and "Quarantottate," ibid., February 5, 1915.
17. Sorel to Croce, May 26, 1915, 27, p. 121. See also Sorel to Pareto, May 30, 1915, *Carteggi Paretiani, 1892–1923,* pp. 6–7. For further discussion of Sorel's reaction to Italian intervention and the origins of fascism see below, Chapter 11.
18. Sorel to Pareto, November 15, 1915, *Carteggi Paretiani, 1892–1923,* p. 39; see also Sorel to Croce, December 5, 1915, 27, p. 295.
19. Sorel to Croce, December 5, 1915, 27, pp. 295–96.
20. Sorel to Croce, January 9, 1916, 27, p. 354.
21. Sorel to Croce, December 27, 1916, 27, p. 441.
22. "Prefazione: crisi cattolica" to Missiroli, *Il Papa in guerra* (Bologna: Zanichelli, 1915), p. 21.
23. "Germanismo e storicismo di Ernesto Renan: saggi inedito di Giorgio Sorel," *Critica,* 29 (May 20, 1931):199–207; see Sorel to Missiroli, December 27, 1914, and February 26 and April 30, 1915, pp. 144, 155–56, 164.

24. Jean Labadie, ed., *L'Allemagne a-t-elle le secret de l'organisation?* (Paris: Bibliothèque de l'Opinion, 1916), pp. 11–19.

25. Ibid., p. 19.

26. Sorel to Missiroli, September 8, 1916, p. 208. According to Johannet, however, Sorel had expressed the belief in 1916 that the tsar would end on the scaffold (*Itinéraires d'intellectuels,* p. 230). See also Sorel to Missiroli, January 5, 1916, and March 5 and May 15 and 28, 1917, pp. 198, 214, 220, 221.

27. "Avant-propos," *De l'utilité du pragmatisme* (hereafter cited as *Pragmatisme*) (Paris: Rivière, 1922), pp. 1–2, 8, 20*n*, 21.

28. Sorel to Michels, April 9, 1917, p. 291; Sorel to Delesalle, August 6, 1917, p. 115. See A. Paris, "Note critique: Georges Sorel en Italia," *Mouvement social,* 50 (January/March 1965):134.

29. Sorel to Croce, October 25 and December 8, 1917, 28, p. 43. In a letter to Halévy dated October 16, 1917, he also speculated that the "*tyrannie de l'or*" could be held in check only by a strict military tradition; the German socialism fashioned by the experience of the war might someday become a more formidable power than Prussian militarism. See Halévy, "Georges Sorel: introduction à deux lettres inédites," p. 4.

30. Sorel to Delesalle, August 17 and December 22, 1917, and January 27 and February 6, 1918, pp. 117, 120–21, 125–26; see also Johannet to Pareto, March 21, 1918, *Carteggi Paretiani, 1892–1923,* p. 72.

31. Sorel to Croce, February 5, 1918, 28, pp. 44–45.

32. Sorel to Delesalle, February 6, 1918, pp. 127–28.

33. Sorel to Delesalle, March 14, 1918, p. 151; Sorel to Croce, March 15, 1918, 28, p. 45.

34. Late in April 1918, on the insistence of his "niece," who feared the bombardment, Sorel fled Boulogne again for Malix, the area from which Marie-Euphrasie had come; there he remained until late in September (see Sorel to Delesalle, April 23 and September 22, 1918, pp. 134, 170).

35. Sorel to Delesalle, June 23, 1918, pp. 153–55.

36. Ibid., August 1, 1918, p. 162.

37. Ibid., August 18, 1918, p. 164.

38. Ibid., p. 165.

39. Ibid., August 26, 1918, p. 168.

40. Ibid, pp. 167, 169–70.

41. Ibid., p. 170.

42. Ibid., pp. 168–69.

43. See "Avant-propos" and "Post-Scriptum," *Matériaux,* pp. 52–53; Sorel to Delesalle, December 2, 1918, p. 174.

44. Sorel to Delesalle, December 2, 1918, p. 175.

45. "Post-Scriptum," *Matériaux,* p. 53. Sorel's attitude toward the new Russian regime was paralleled by the fear of the imminent "Americanization" of Western Europe: see Sorel to Croce, December 16, 1918, 28, p. 48.

46. Sorel to Croce, February 1, 1919, 28, p. 50; Sorel to Delesalle, February 20, 1919, p. 177.

47. Variot, *Propos,* June 28, 1919, p. 46.

48. Andreu, *Notre maître,* p. 110. See also Sorel to Delesalle, February 20, 1919,

p. 178; de Rosa, "Prefazione," *Carteggi Paretiani, 1892–1923,* p. xvi; and Sorel to Missiroli, March 15, 1919, p. 231.

49. "Dubbi sull'avvenire intelletuale," *Tempo,* January 24, 1919.
50. "Le Neutralità belga," *Tempo,* March 2, 1919.
51. "Charles Péguy," *Ronda,* 1 (April 1919):58–63; see especially "editorial note" of Auguste Martin in Sorel, "Charles Péguy," *Amitié Charles Péguy,* no. 77 (May 1960):34–37. It was Johannet who wrote to Sorel of Péguy's death early in the war. When Johannet met Sorel in the beginning of 1915, Sorel said, "*C'est un suicide.*" Johannet remarked that Sorel was not the only one who thought so. See Johannet, *Vie et mort de Péguy* (Paris: Flammarion, 1950), p. 444; see also Sorel to Missiroli, January 30, 1921, p. 303.
52. "Guerra e borghesia," *Resto del Carlino,* April 30, 1919; "Zarismo e bolscevismo," ibid., May 9, 1919; "Futuri oppressori," ibid., May 21, 1919; "Luce ed ombre bolsceviche," *Tempo,* May 11, 1919. Cf. Sorel to Croce, February 1, 1919, 28, p. 50.
53. "Clemenceau," *Resto del Carlino,* June 1, 1919.
54. "Le Guerra di brigantaggio," *Resto del Carlino,* June 7, 1919.
55. "L'Avvenire dell'Italia," *Resto del Carlino,* June 11, 1919.
56. "I Guai della democrazia," *Resto del Carlino,* June 25, 1919.
57. "Chiarimenti su Lenin," *Resto del Carlino,* July 23, 1919.
58. "Gli arditi della borghesia," *Resto del Carlino,* August 15, 1919.
59. "Perché si processa il kaiser," *Resto del Carlino,* August 29, 1919.
60. "La Morte di Jaurès," *Resto del Carlino,* September 2, 1919.
61. "Le Idee di libertà," *Resto del Carlino,* September 10, 1919.
62. "Paralleli," *Resto del Carlino,* September 15, 1919.
63. "Proudhon," *Ronda,* 1 (September 1919):5–17.
64. "Socialisti e conservatori," *Resto del Carlino,* October 5, 1919; "Foche presidente?" ibid., November 2, 1919; and "Bisanzio," ibid., November 6, 1919.
65. "Una Formula equivoca," *Resto del Carlino,* November 18, 1919; "Ricordi e confronti," ibid., December 23, 1919.
66. "Pour Lénine," *Réflexions,* pp. 437–54.
67. Paul Seippel, "L'Autre danger," *Journal de Genève,* February 4, 1918.
68. "Pour Lénine," p. 442.
69. Ibid., p. 452.
70. Ibid., p. 449.
71. Ibid., p. 451.
72. Ibid., p. 453.
73. Ibid., pp. 453–54. In a footnote he paid his final tribute to Marie-Euphrasie, to whose memory the first edition of the *Réflexions* had been dedicated (p. 454*n*).
74. "Avertissement pour la troisième édition," *Introduction,* pp. i, ix. See Paris, "Note critique: Georges Sorel en Italie," p. 38, arguing that though Sorel was poorly informed on Russia, the comparison between the soviets and "worker's councils," "factory councils," and "syndicates" was "common" during the period.
75. "L'Humanité contre la douleur," *Introduction,* pp. 400, 410; see also "Préface" to Castex.
76. Sorel to Delesalle, May 19, 1920, pp. 190–91.
77. Ibid., August 12, 1920, p. 193.
78. Sorel to Croce, August 13, 1920, 28, p. 193.

79. Sorel to Delesalle, August 15, 1920, p. 195.
80. Ibid., April 28, 1920, p. 189.
81. Charles Rappoport, "Pourquoi et comment nous sommes communistes," *Revue communiste*, 1 (March 1920):4.
82. "La Chine," *Revue communiste*, 1 (July 1920):429–34.
83. "Le Bolchevisme en Egypte," *Revue communiste*, 2 (September 1920):27–32.
84. "Le Travail dans la Grèce ancienne," *Revue communiste*, 2 (November 1920): 215–22.
85. "I Popolari," *Resto del Carlino*, January 6, 1920; "Proudhon disfattista," ibid., January 17, 1920; "Contro la servitù," ibid., January 29, 1920; "I Presidenti," ibid., February 21, 1920; and "Nitti e la Russia," ibid., March 14, 1920.
86. "I Monarchici in Francia," *Resto del Carlino*, March 16, 1920; "Crisi socialista in Francia," ibid., March 25, 1920.
87. "La Borghesia in Francia," *Resto del Carlino*, July 16, 1920.
88. "La Diplomazia e la Russia," *Resto del Carlino*, July 24, 1920.
89. "Il Presidente Millerand," *Resto del Carlino*, August 30, 1920.
90. "La 'Barbarie' Moscovita," *Resto del Carlino*, October 8, 1920.
91. "Dio ritorno," *Resto del Carlino*, October 13, 1920.
92. "Antimarxismo francese," *Resto del Carlino*, November 14, 1920.
93. "Crepe nel socialismo francese," *Resto del Carlino*, December 30, 1920.
94. Sorel to Delesalle, August 21, 1920, p. 199.
95. "Exégèses proudhoniennes," *Matériaux*, pp. 443–44.
96. Ibid., pp. 422, 423n.
97. "La Marche au socialisme," *Illusions*, pp. 350, 373, 381–84.
98. "Ultime meditazioni: scritto postumo inedito," *Nuova antologia*, 63 (December 1, 1928):292–93.
99. Bourget, *Quelques témoignages: hommes et idées* (Paris: Plon, 1933), p. 9; Anon., "Georges Sorel," *Revue universelle*, 10 (September 15, 1922):769.
100. Variot, *Propos*, January n.d., 1921, p. 49.
101. Ibid., p. 48.
102. Ibid., p. 49.
103. Ibid., March n.d., 1921, pp. 53–55.
104. Sorel to Delesalle, February 2 and July 7, 1921, pp. 203, 233–34.
105. Sorel to Croce, July 8, 1921, 28, pp. 194–95.
106. "Lénine d'après Gorki," *Revue communiste*, 2 (January 1921):401–413; also "Lenin secondo Gorki," *Ordine nuovo*, February 27, 1921. Sorel was not at first very enthusiastic about the *Ordine nuovo;* see Sorel to Missiroli, November 4, 1919, p. 262.
107. Quoted in Dolléans, *Proudhon*, p. 507.
108. "Le Génie du Rhin," *Revue communiste*, 3 (April 1921):96–110.
109. "I Cattolici contro Bergson," *Resto del Carlino*, January 23, 1921.
110. "Le Istituzioni musulmane," *Resto del Carlino*, May 1, 1921; "Napoleone e i socialisti," *Tempo*, May 21, 1921.
111. "Calvinismo politico," *Resto del Carlino*, June 12, 1921.
112. "Testimonianza competenti," *Tempo*, June 19, 1921; "La Neutralità del Belgio in teoria e nella realità," *Ronda*, 3 (June 1921):357–72; "Bertrand Russell in Russia," *Resto del Carlino*, July 8, 1921.

113. "Sull'orlo dell'abisso," *Tempo,* August 13, 1921; "Il Tramonto dell'autorità," *Resto del Carlino,* August 26, 1921. See Sorel to Ferrero, February 24, 1921, pp. 147–48.

114. "Burocrazia e autonomia locali," *Tempo,* September 13, 1921; "Industrializ-zazione della guerra," *Resto del Carlino,* September 15, 1921; "Il Mito della Comune," ibid., October 14, 1921; "Guerra e rinascenza religiosa," ibid., November 15, 1921; "La Decadenza degli Absburgo," ibid., November 24, 1921.

115. "La Produzione moderna," *Resto del Carlino,* December 10, 1921; "Proudhon e la rinascita del socialismo," *Ronda,* 3 (November/December 1921):727–45.

116. On Sorel's quarrel with Ferrero see Sorel to Ferrero, March 5, March 13, and June 26, 1921, pp. 148–51; see "Avertissement, deuxième édition," *La Ruine,* pp. xxiii–xxv.

117. Bernard Lecache, "Chez Georges Sorel, apôtre du syndicalisme révolutionnaire, ami de la Russie des Soviets," *Humanité,* March 9, 1922.

118. Michels, "Lettere di Georges Sorel a Roberto Michels," p. 293n (from a note in Michels's diary dated March 22, 1922).

119. Ibid.

120. L. Auriant, *Fragments ... mélanges et souvenirs* (Brussels: Nouvelle Revue Belgique, 1943), pp. 9–16.

121. "Jeremy Bentham et l'indépendance de l'Égypte," *Mercure de France,* 145 (April 15, 1922):397, 405–407, 410 ("L. Auriant" appears as co-author of the article). See Auriant, *Fragments ... mélanges et souvenirs,* pp. 15–16.

122. Balandes to Valois, June 11, 1922, cited in Valois, *Basile,* p. 684 (Sorel inquired after the Action Française on this occasion).

123. Johannet, "Un Précurseur de la Révolution nationale: Georges Sorel," p. 5. This curious admission was made in an article designed to establish Sorel as a "precursor" of the Vichy regime.

Chapter 9.   The Idea

1. "Lénine d'après Gorki," pp. 401, 404–405, 407; "Le Caractère religieux du social-isme," *Matériaux,* p. 337.

2. "Lénine d'après Gorki," pp. 402–405.

3. "Chiarimenti su Lenin"; "Lénine d'après Gorki," p. 405; "Pour Lénine," p. 443; "Post-Scriptum," *Matériaux,* p. 53; "Clemenceau"; review of V. Serge's *Les Anarchistes et l'expérience de la révolution russe* in *Revue communiste,* 3 (August/September 1921):390; "La Marche au socialisme," pp. 381–84; and "Il Mito della Commune."

4. Variot, *Propos,* n.d., 1922, p. 67; "Pour Lénine," p. 448; "Lénine d'après Gorki," p. 406.

5. "Socialisti e conservatori"; "Zarismo e bolscevismo"; "Pour Lénine," p. 448; "Futuri oppressori."

6. "Lénine d'après Gorki," pp. 403–404, 407–409.

7. Ibid., p. 408.

8. Ibid.

9. Variot, *Propos,* n.d., 1922, p. 82; "Lénine d'après Gorki," p. 413.

10. "Lénine d'après Gorki," p. 413.
11. "Le Caractère religieux du socialisme," pp. 355–56; "Lénine d'après Gorki," p. 409.
12. "Lénine d'après Gorki," p. 408; Variot, *Propos,* March n.d., 1921, p. 65.
13. "Lénine d'après Gorki," p. 408; "Exégèses proudhoniennes," p. 432n.
14. "Lénine d'après Gorki," p. 408.
15. "Bertrand Russell in Russia"; "Lénine d'après Gorki," pp. 408–409.
16. "Lénine d'après Gorki," p. 408.
17. Ibid., pp. 409–413.
18. Ibid., pp. 412–13.
19. "Exégèses proudhoniennes," pp. 423, 428; review of *Les Anarchistes,* pp. 390, 393.
20. "Socialisti e conservatori"; "La Diplomazia e la Russia"; "Il Mito della Comune."
21. Review of *Les Anarchistes,* pp. 390–92.
22. Ibid., p. 392.
23. "Bertrand Russell in Russia"; "Socialisti e conservatori"; "Contro la servitù"; Variot, *Propos,* March n.d., 1921, p. 55; "Pour Lénine," p. 451n.
24. Review of *Les Anarchistes,* p. 393; Variot, *Propos,* March n.d., 1921, p. 55; "Pour Lénine," pp. 450–52; review of P. Pascal's *En Russie rouge* in *Revue communiste,* 3 (August/September 1921):393; Variot, *Propos,* n.d., 1922, p. 81.
25. "Lénine d'après Gorki," p. 408.
26. Review of *Les Anarchistes,* p. 393.
27. Variot, *Propos,* March n.d., 1921, p. 55; "Zarismo e bolscevismo"; "Pour Lénine," pp. 450–51.
28. "Socialisti e conservatori"; "La Marche au socialisme," pp. 385–86.
29. "La Marche au socialisme," pp. 385–86.
30. Variot, *Propos,* March n.d., 1921, pp. 55, 82.
31. Ibid., p. 61; "Le Travail dans la Grèce ancienne," p. 217; "Le Guerra di brigantaggio"; "Pour Lénine," p. 451.
32. "Le Bolschevisme en Égypte," p. 32; "Avertissement," *Introduction,* p. ii.
33. Variot, *Propos,* n.d., 1922, pp. 67–68; "La 'Barbarie' Moscovita"; review of R. Labry's *L'Industrie russe et la révolution* in *Revue communiste,* 3 (April–June 1921):137 and 270.
34. Review of *Les Anarchistes,* p. 392.
35. Variot, *Propos,* n.d., 1922, p. 83.
36. Ibid.; review of *Les Anarchistes,* p. 392; "Pour Lénine," pp. 445–47; "Socialisti e conservatori."
37. "Chiarimenti su Lenin"; "Lénine d'après Gorki," p. 410; "L'Organisation de la démocratie," *Matériaux,* p. 386.
38. Ibid.
39. "L'Organisation de la démocratie," p. 386.
40. Variot, *Propos,* n.d., 1922, p. 84; "Pour Lénine," pp. 452–53.
41. "Pour Lénine," p. 444n.
42. Ibid., pp. 434–44; "Proudhon e la rinascita del socialismo," p. 744; and "Le Istituzioni musulmane."
43. "Una Formula equivoca."
44. Variot, *Propos,* n.d., 1922, p. 69; "Crisi socialista in Francia"; "Contro la servitù."

45. Variot, *Propos,* n.d., 1922, pp. 82, 85; "Pour Lénine," p. 442; "Chiarimenti su Lenin"; "Lénine d'après Gorki," p. 401.
46. "Zarismo e bolscevismo."
47. "Bertrand Russell in Russia"; "Chiarimenti su Lenin"; "Pour Lénine," p. 444*n*; "La Marche au socialisme," pp. 344–45, 348, 355, 357*n*; "Socialisti e conservatori."
48. "Chiarimenti su Lenin."
49. "La Marche au socialisme," pp. 355, 357*n*; "Bertrand Russell in Russia."
50. "Chiarimenti su Lenin."
51. Ibid.; "Lénine d'après Gorki," p. 401; "Pour Lénine," p. 422; Variot, *Propos,* n.d., 1922, pp. 82, 85.
52. "Socialisti e conservatori."
53. "Pour Lénine," p. 444*n*; "Una Formula equivoca."
54. "Una Formula equivoca"; "Socialisti e conservatori"; "La Marche au socialisme," p. 359; "Crepe nel socialismo francese."
55. "Avant-propos, Post-Scriptum," p. 53.
56. "La March au socialisme," pp. 344–45, 348.
57. "Avertissement," *Introduction,* p. ii; "Socialisti e conservatori"; "La Marche au socialisme," p. 359.
58. "Le Travail dans la Grèce ancienne," pp. 221–22.
59. Variot, *Propos,* n.d., 1922, pp. 69–70; "Socialisti e conservatori"; "Chiarimenti su Lenin."
60. "Chiarimenti su Lenin"; Variot, *Propos,* n.d., 1922, pp. 82–83; "Lénine d'après Gorki," p. 410.
61. "La Marche au socialisme," p. 382; Variot, *Propos,* n.d., 1922, p. 70.
62. "Lénine d'après Gorki," p. 410; "Socialisti e conservatori."
63. "Le Travail dans la Grèce ancienne," p. 220; "Chiarimenti su Lenin," and cf. "Grèves et droit au travail," *Matériaux,* p. 404*n*, where Sorel takes an unfavorable view of the Taylor System; "Una Formula equivoca"; review of S. Zagorsky's *La République des Soviets* in *Revue communiste,* 3 (April 1921):135.
64. Variot, *Propos,* n.d., 1922, p. 84; "Chiarimenti su Lenin"; review of *La République des Soviets,* p. 135; "La Produzione moderna"; "La Marche au socialisme," p. 359; "Le Travail dans la Grèce ancienne," pp. 221–22.
65. "Il Tramonto dell'autorità"; "Una Formula equivoca"; "Le Travail dans la Grèce ancienne," pp. 216, 221–22; "Avertissement," *Introduction,* pp. xiii, xix.
66. "La Marche au socialisme," pp. 383–84; "La Diplomazia e la Russia"; "Il Mito della Commune"; "Il Crepuscolo dell'Internazionale"; "Industrializzazione della guerra"; "Crisi socialista in Francia"; Variot, *Propos,* n.d., 1922, p. 72.
67. "Lénine d'après Gorki," pp. 409–411; "Le Bolchevisme en Égypte," pp. 29, 31–32; "La Chine," pp. 432–33; "Le Istituzioni musulmane."
68. *Pragmatisme,* p. 384; "Le Idee di libertà"; "L'Humanité contre la douleur," p. 420; "Pour Lénine," pp. 443–44; "Chiarimenti su Lenin"; "Le Travail dans la Grèce ancienne," p. 222.
69. "Chiarimenti su Lenin"; "Avertissement," *Introduction,* p. ix; "Exégèses proudhoniennes," pp. 427–34.
70. "Dubbi sull'avvenire intellectuale"; "Lénine d'après Gorki," p. 409; "Ricordi e confronti."

71. "La Produzione moderna"; "Avertissement," *La Ruine,* p. xxv; "Lénine d'après Gorki," p. 409; "Nitti e la Russia"; "Avertissement," *Introduction,* pp. iv–v; "Bisanzio"; Variot, *Propos,* n.d., 1922, p. 82.

72. "Futuri oppressori"; "Zarismo e bolscevismo"; "La Chine," p. 143; "La Marche au socialisme," p. 377; "Lénine d'après Gorki," p. 409; "La 'Barbarie' Moscovita."

73. "La Chine," p. 433; "Futuri oppressori"; "Le Bolchevisme en Égypte," p. 31.

74. "Pour Lénine," p. 453. The quotation here cited is viewed as summarizing Sorel's correspondence with Missiroli on the Bolshevik Revolution: see Giuseppe La Ferla, "Georges Sorel e gli amici Italian," *Nuova antologia,* 94 (January 1964):85.

Chapter 10. The Impact

1. Delesalle, "Bibliographie sorélienne," *International Review for Social History,* 4 (1939):463–87.

2. V. I. Lenin, *Materialism and Empirio-Criticism,* trans. David Kvitka (New York: International Publishers, 1930), p. 58.

3. Ibid., 13, p. 249. Cf. Carlo Carini, "Lenin e la rivoluzione russa negli scritti italiani di Sorel," *Georges Sorel: studi e ricerche,* pp. 210–13, on the changing character of Lenin's views on the utility of spontaneous strikes.

4. Anon., "Georges Sorel," *Revue universelle,* 10 (September 15, 1922):770; Variot, "Georges Sorel," *Nouvelles littéraires,* 10 (October 3, 1931):1, 4; Johannet, *Itinéraires d'intellectuels,* p. 222n; Variot, *Propos,* p. 174.

5. A. Maletsky, "Georges Sorel," *Internationale communiste,* 4 (March 1923):112.

6. Ibid., p. 113.

7. For a general treatment see R. Tiersky, *French Communism, 1920–70* (New York: Columbia University Press, 1974).

8. Sorel to Delesalle, April 28, 1920, p. 189; Lecache interview in *Humanité,* March 9, 1922.

9. Anon., "Georges Sorel," *Humanité,* August 31, 1922.

10. Delesalle, "Georges Sorel," *Humanité,* September 1, 1922.

11. Anon., "Réflexions sur la pessimisme," *Humanité,* September 3, 1922.

12. Louzon, "Héroisme prolétarien et lâcheté fasciste," *Humanité,* June 14, 1923.

13. Louzon, "Georges Sorel," *Vie ouvrière,* September 8, 1922.

14. Anon., "Une Autre page de Sorel," *Vie ouvrière,* September 1 and 8, 1922.

15. Charles Rappoport, "Pourquoi et comment nous sommes communistes," *Revue communiste,* 1 (March 1920):4.

16. Marcel Fourrier, "Éditorial: de *Clarté* à *La Guerre civile,*" *Clarté,* 5 (December 1925):1, 8.

17. Berth, "Georges Sorel," *Clarté,* 2 (September 15, 1922):495–96.

18. See below, Chapter 14.

19. See Berth's contributions to *Charles Maurras: poèmes, portraits, jugements* (Paris: Nouvelle Librairie Nationale, 1919).

20. Sorel to Berth, March 19, 1919, cited in Levey, "The Sorelian Syndicalists," p. 163.

21. Berth, "Avant-propos" to Max Ascoli, *Georges Sorel* (Paris: Librairie Delesalle, 1921), pp. 3–5; Berth, *Guerre des états ou guerre des classes,* pp. 55–56, 66, 197–99.

22. Berth, "Georges Sorel," pp. 495–96.

23. Berth, "Le Tertullien du socialisme," *Rivoluzione liberale,* 1 (December 14, 1922): 139–40.

24. See below, Chapter 13.

25. For a general treatment see John M. Cammett, *Antonio Gramsci and the Origins of Italian Communism* (Stanford: Stanford University Press, 1967).

26. See Gradilone, *Storia del sindacalismo,* 2, pp. 102–103; Borghi, *Mezzo secolo di anarchia, 1898–1945,* p. 164. See also Borghi, *La Rivoluzione mancata* (Milan: Edizioni Azione Comune, 1964), on the role of the USI in the factory occupations of September 1920. Eventually, the USI announced that it could not accept political domination by any party or any state.

27. See Antonio Gramsci, *Scritti giovanili, 1914–1918* (Turin: Einaudi, 1958), pp. 74–75, 86; *Passato e presente* (3rd ed., Turin: Einaudi, 1953), pp. 55–59. See also *Elementi di politica,* ed. Mario Spinella (Rome: Riuniti, 1964), pp. 94–95n. Sorel did not think the first issues of the *Ordine nuovo* "very original": see Sorel to Missiroli, November 4, 1919, p. 262. On the Turinese group see G. Bergami, "Sorel e i giovani rivoluzionari di Torino," *Ponte* (1970):1062–64.

28. Palmiro Togliatti, "La Battaglia delle idee," *Ordine nuovo,* July 12, 1919; Angelo Tasca, "Perché siamo comunisti?" *Ordine nuovo,* September 6, 1919. For complete bibliography and selected items see *L'Ordine nuovo (1919–1920),* ed. Paolo Spriano ["La Cultura italiana del '900 attraverso le riviste" (Turin: Einaudi, 1963)].

29. On the young Gramsci see Fabrizio F. Bracco, "Il Giovane Gramsci e Sorel," *Georges Sorel: studi e ricerche,* pp. 177–95; F. S. Romano, *Antonio Gramsci* (Turin: Einaudi, 1965); G. Nardone, *Il Pensiero di Gramsci* (Bari: Laterza, 1971); and Settembrini, "Mussolini and the Legacy of Revolutionary Socialism," p. 257, who argues that Gramsci came from the "Mussolinianism" of the immediate prewar years.

30. Gramsci, "Cronache dell'*Ordine nuovo*," *Ordine nuovo,* October 11, 1919. Sorel's article, "Socialisti e conservatori," had appeared on October 5. See also Gramsci, "Il Partito comunista," *Ordine nuovo,* September 4 and October 9, 1920; "Il Programma dell'*Ordine nuovo,*" ibid., August 28, 1920; "Bergsoniano!" ibid., January 2, 1921. See also Maggi, *La Formazione dell'egemonia in Francia,* pp. 262–69, on Sorel and Gramsci.

31. See especially Sorel, "Sindacati e soviet," *Ordine nuovo,* November 15, 1919.

32. Gramsci, "Il Partito comunista," September 4, 1920.

33. See especially Charles Rappoport, "Giorgio Sorel," *Ordine nuovo,* February 26, 1921, which preceded the publication of Sorel's "Lenin secondo Gorki" on February 27, 1921.

34. "m.s.," "La Morte di Giorgio Sorel," *Ordine nuovo,* September 1, 1922 ("m.s." was possibly Mario Stragiotti).

35. Sorel, "Una Pagina di Sorel: pessimismo e rivoluzione," *Ordine nuovo,* September 18, 1922.

36. Cited in Sorel to Delesalle, March 23, 1919, p. 180. Leone alone, according to Sorel, remained faithful to the "syndicalist idea": see Sorel to Missiroli, November 4, 1919, p. 292.

37. Leone to Delesalle, March 6, 1921, quoted in *Lettres à Paul Delesalle,* p. 222.

Within two years Leone's break with communism was to be complete. During these years Leone was under attack from communist quarters: see Amadeo Bordiga, "Sindacalismo e stato," *Comunista,* October 29, 1921.

38. Labriola, *Spiegazioni a me stesso: note personali e colturale* (Naples: Edizioni Centro Studi Sociali, 1945), p. 163; also Marucco, *Arturo Labriola,* pp. 209–220, for Labriola's career as a deputy. See Sorel to Missiroli, June 18, 1920, pp. 287–88, for Sorel's reaction to Labriola as a minister; also Marucco, *Arturo Labriola,* pp. 267–77.

39. Labriola, *Il Socialismo contemporaneo* (Naples: Morano, 1922), pp. 344, 381.

40. Ibid., p. 361. See Marucco, pp. 231–48, on Labriola's participation in a mission to Russia in 1917.

41. Labriola, *Le Due politiche: fascismo e riformismo* (Naples: Morano, 1923), p. 195.

42. Ibid.

43. Ibid., pp. 176, 196; see Marucco, *Arturo Labriola,* pp. 280–81.

Fascism
Chapter 11. The Man

1. Variot, "Quelques souvenirs: le père Sorel." The quotation does not appear in any of the conversations recorded in the *Propos* for 1912, but it is corroborated by other sources. See Furiozzi, "La Fortuna italiana di Sorel," p. 108; Onufrio, "Considerazioni su Croce e Sorel," p. 149; Furiozzi, *Sorel e l'Italia,* p. 352; and Pierre Angel, *Essais sur G. Sorel* (Paris: Rivière, 1936), pp. 310–11.

2. An exception must be made with respect to his irredentism: see Mussolini, "Il Trentino," *Voce,* 2 (December 15, 1910):461.

3. Variot, *Propos,* December 14, 1912, p. 32.

4. Lanzillo, "Idee letterarie di Giorgio Sorel (con pagine inedite), pp. 49–50.

5. Sorel to Barrès, n.d. (before the outbreak of war in 1914), quoted in Giorgio Pini, *The Official Life of Benito Mussolini,* trans. L. Villari (London: Unwin Brothers, 1939), p. 245.

6. Sorel to Croce, November 28, 1914, 27, p. 115; Sorel to Missiroli, December 27, 1914, and June 14 and 16, 1915, pp. 115, 145–46, 173; Sorel to Pareto, June 19, 1915, *Carteggi Paretiani, 1892–1923,* p. 13. See also Ugo Piscopo, "I Futuristi e Sorel," *Georges Sorel: studi e ricerche,* pp. 159–67, on the views of D'Annunzio, Vocists, and futurists on intervention.

7. See above, Chapter 8.

8. Sorel to Croce, May 26, 1915, 27, p. 354. See also Sorel to Pareto, August 9, 1915, *Carteggi Paretiani, 1892–1923,* p. 29.

9. Sorel to Michels, August 28, 1917, p. 292; Sorel to Pareto, October 15, 1915, *Carteggi Paretiani, 1892–1923,* p. 37; and Sorel to Missiroli, April 16, 1921, p. 306.

10. Sorel to Delesalle, May 19, 1918, p. 145.

11. "Grèves et droit au travail," pp. 395n, 412, 412n.

12. Sorel to Croce, December 6, 1918, 28, p. 47.

13. Ibid., December 28, 1918, and January 6, 1919, 28, p. 49.

14. Ibid., February 1, 1919, 28, p. 50.

15. Ibid., April 4, 1919, 28, p. 51.
16. Sorel to Delesalle, September 6, 1917, and April 28, 1920, pp. 186, 188; Sorel to Missiroli, October 16 and 30, 1920, pp. 294, 296.
17. Sorel to Croce, July 30, 1920, 28, p. 192.
18. "La Dalmazia," *Tempo,* February 14, 1919; "Giustizia all'Italia!" *Resto del Carlino,* May 12, 1919; "L'Avvenire dell'Italia," ibid., June 11, 1919; "La Rocca della reazione," ibid., August 4, 1919; "I Malentesi tra Italia e Francia," ibid., August 9, 1919; unpublished article, September 1919, quoted in Missiroli, "Prefazione," *L'Europa sotto la tormenta,* pp. xxxiii–xxxv; "Sonnino," *Resto del Carlino,* September 28, 1919. See also the brochure Sorel published jointly with Leone: *La Dalmazia è terra d'Italia: socialisti francesi e italiani per l'italianità della Dalmazia* (Rome: Evarsto Armoni, 1919).
19. "Guerra e borghesia," *Resto del Carlino,* April 30, 1919; "Socialisti e conservatori," ibid., October 5, 1919; "Nuovo temporalismo," ibid., October 17, 1919; "Giolitti," ibid., November 12, 1919; "Una Formula equivoca," ibid., November 18, 1919; "Ricordi e confronti," ibid., December 23, 1919.
20. "Stato e proprietà rurale," *Resto del Carlino,* November 10, 1919.
21. "I Popolari," *Resto del Carlino,* January 6, 1920; "I Presidenti," ibid., February 21, 1920; "Nitti e la Russia," ibid., March 14, 1920; "La Plutocrazia contro l'Italia," ibid., April 4, 1920; "La Diplomazia e la Russia," ibid., July 24, 1920. See also "Cristianesimo greco e Europa moderna," *Ronda,* 2 (August/September 1920): 549; "Ultime meditazioni: scritto postumo inedito," *Nuova antologia,* 63 (December 1, 1928):289–307.
22. Sorel to Delesalle, February 26, 1921, p. 210; cf. Sorel to Croce, March 25, 1921, 28, p. 195, and Sorel to Missiroli, March 11, 1921, p. 304.
23. Sorel to Delesalle, March 19, 1921, p. 215.
24. Sorel to Missiroli, January 30, 1921, p. 303; Sorel to Delesalle, March 24, 1921, p. 217.
25. Variot, *Propos,* March n.d., 1921, pp. 53–54; on this question see Band, "The Question of Sorel," p. 211.
26. Ibid., p. 55.
27. Ibid., p. 56.
28. Ibid.
29. Ibid., p. 57.
30. Sorel to Delesalle, April 9 and 18 and July 13, 1921, pp. 218–19, 223, 236. See also Sorel to Missiroli, March 11, 1921, p. 304; Sorel to Ferrero, March 13, 1921, p. 149.
31. Sorel to Delesalle, April 18, 1921, p. 223.
32. Sorel to Delesalle, July 13, 1921, p. 236.
33. Sorel to Croce, August 26, 1921, 28, p. 195. This was the last letter Croce received from Sorel. Croce continued to write but Sorel's health, according to Croce, did not permit him to reply. When Croce announced publication of the letters, he reserved the right to omit passages from them, "especially those written during the last years" ["Lettere di Giorgio Sorel," 25 (January 20, 1927):38]. In a letter to James H. Meisel dated May 14, 1950, Croce explained that he did not recall what passages he had omitted some twenty years earlier, but he felt certain that the passages in question "could not have contained any allusions against Fascism, for in that case I would have been obliged to publish them.... Sorel, being the impres-

sionable man he was, in principle was favorable to Mussolini. He hated the professional politicos, and saw mistakenly in Mussolini a spontaneous and beneficial force" (quoted in Meisel, *Genesis of Georges Sorel,* p. 225). The evidence appears to indicate that if the complete collection of letters were available, a stronger case could be made in support of the view that Sorel was in these years strongly attracted to Italian fascism.

34. Sorel to Missiroli, April 16, 1921, pp. 306–307. Cf. Furiozzi, *Sorel e l'Italia,* pp. 353–69; but see also Roberto Vivarelli, ed., "Introduzione" to *Georges Sorel: Scritti politici* (Turin: Unione Tipografico Editrice, 1963), p. 48, on Sorel's attraction to Mussolini and the fascist movement.

35. Sorel to Missiroli, September n.d., 1921, in Missiroli, "Prefazione" to *L'Europa sotto la tormenta,* pp. xxxii–xxxiii. This letter, for reasons unexplained, is not included in Missiroli's *Lettere a un amico d'Italia*; cf. Sorel to Missiroli, June 21, 1921, p. 308. The letter was first published in Curzio Malaparte's review, dated September 30, 1921, and signed "Spectator": "Mussolini e il fascismo nel '21: una lettera inedita di Giorgio Sorel," *Conquista dello stato,* December 15, 1928, p. 1.

36. Sorel to Missiroli, September n.d., 1921, in Missiroli, "Prefazione" to *L'Europa sotto la tormenta,* p. xxxiii.

37. "Il Crepuscolo dell'Internazionale," *Tempo,* March 22, 1921.

38. "I Consigli operai," *Resto del Carlino,* March 22, 1921.

39. "Burocrazia e autonomie locali," *Tempo,* September 13, 1921.

40. Michels, "Lettere di Georges Sorel a Roberto Michels," p. 293*n.*

41. Variot, *Propos,* n.d., 1922, p. 66. On Sorel's "simultaneous enthusiasm" for Lenin and Mussolini see Vivarelli, "Introduzione," p. 48.

Chapter 12. The Idea

1. "Ultime meditazioni: scritto postumo inedito," p. 307.

2. See Sorel to Delesalle, April 9 and 18 and July 13, 1921, pp. 218–19, 223, 236. For a recent study of the relation of Sorel's myth to fascism see Helmut Berding, *Rationalismus und Mythos: geschichts Auffassung und politische Theorie bei Georges Sorel* (Munich: R. Oldenbourg, 1969), p. 147.

3. Variot, *Propos,* March n.d., 1921, p. 56.

4. Sorel to Missiroli, September n.d., 1921, in Missiroli, "Prefazione" to *L'Europa sotto la tormenta,* pp. xxxii–xxxiii.

5. "La Plutocrazia contro l'Italia"; "La Rocca della reazione"; "L'Avvenire dell'Italia"; "Sonnino"; "I Malintesi tra Italia e Francia."

6. Sorel to Missiroli, September n.d., 1921, in Missiroli, "Prefazione" to *L'Europa sotto la tormenta,* pp. xxxii–xxxiii.

7. Sorel to Delesalle, April 9, 1921, p. 220.

8. "Stato e proprietà rurale"; "Ultime meditazioni: scritto postumo inedito," p. 306.

9. "La Rocca della reazione"; Sorel to Delesalle, March 19 and 24 and April 9, 1921, pp. 215, 217, 219.

10. Variot, *Propos,* March n.d., 1921, p. 55.

11. Sorel to Croce, August 26, 1921, 28, p. 195; "Stato e proprietà rurale"; Sorel to Delesalle, April 9, 1921, p. 219.

12. Variot, *Propos,* March n.d., 1921, p. 55.
13. Ibid., p. 56.
14. Sorel to Missiroli, September n.d., 1921, in Missiroli, "Prefazione" to *L'Europa sotto la tormenta,* pp. xxxii–xxxiii; Sorel to Delesalle, March 19 and April 9, 1921, pp. 215, 218–19.
15. Variot, *Propos,* March n.d., 1921, p. 55.
16. "Stato e proprietà rurale."
17. Variot, *Propos,* n.d., 1922, p. 66.
18. "Guerra e borghesia."
19. Sorel to Missiroli, September n.d., 1921, in Missiroli, "Prefazione" to *"L'Europa sotto la tormenta,"* pp. xxxii–xxxiii.
20. "Ultime meditazioni: scritto postumo inedito," p. 307.
21. "Stato e proprietà rurale."
22. "Il Presidenti."
23. Variot, *Propos,* n.d., 1922, p. 86.
24. Ibid., p. 86.
25. "Stato e proprietà rurale."
26. "Giolitti."
27. Sorel to Missiroli, September n.d., 1921, in Missiroli, "Prefazione" to *L'Europa sotto la tormenta,* pp. xxxii–xxxiii.
28. "Giolitti"; "I Consigli operai"; "Socialisti e conservatori."
29. "Grèves et droit au travail," pp. 410–11; see also "I Consigli operai."
30. "Stato e proprietà rurale."
31. Sorel to Missiroli, September n.d., 1921, in Missiroli, "Prefazione" to *L'Europa sotto la tormenta,* p. xxxiii.
32. "Nuovo temporalismo"; Variot, *Propos,* n.d., 1922, pp. 73–74; "Giustizia all'Italia!"; "Nitti e la Russia"; "Sonnino"; "La Diplomazia e la Russia."
33. "L'Avvenire dell'Italia."
34. "La Diplomazia e la Russia."
35. "Sonnino"; "I Malintesi tra Italia e Francia."
36. "Cristianesimo greco e Europa moderna," p. 549.

Chapter 13. The Impact

1. For Valois's activities during the war years see Valois, *Basile,* p. xvi; for his attitude toward the Action Française at war's end see his *L'Homme contre l'argent* (Paris: Librairie Valois, 1928), pp. 20–22, 26–30, 63.
2. Valois, *L'Économie nouvelle* (Paris: Nouvelle Librairie Nationale, 1919), p. 95.
3. Ibid., p. 283.
4. Ibid., p. 136.
5. Ibid., "Les Semaines économiques, préface des états," *Cahiers des états généraux,* 1 (September 15, 1923):306. The movement was launched with the publication of the *Production française* in April 1920 (it became a weekly in April 1922).
6. See the curious obituary on Sorel by Jacques Tible, "Georges Sorel est mort," *Production française,* September 2, 1922.

7. See Louis Dimier, *Vingt ans d'Action française* (Paris: Nouvelle Librairie Nationale, 1926), p. 224.

8. Valois, *Basile,* pp. xviii–xx.

9. Valois, "Lettre à Marcel Déat," August 18/September 27, 1933, quoted in Valois, *Technique de la révolution syndicale* (Paris: Librairie Valois, 1935), p. 23.

10. Valois, "Georges Sorel," *Action française,* September 4, 1922.

11. Quoted by Jean Bourdeau in "Les Idées de Georges Sorel," *Journal des debats,* September 15, 1922.

12. Variot, "Quelques souvenirs: le père Sorel."

13. Johannet, *Itinéraires d'intellectuals,* pp. 193, 215.

14. Johannet, *Éloge du bourgeois française* (Paris: Grasset, 1924), pp. 201, 221, 298, 333.

15. Drieu La Rochelle, "Modes intellectuelles."

16. Quoted in Pierre-Henri Simon, *Procès du héros: Montherlant, Drieu La Rochelle, Jean Prévost* (Paris: Seuil, 1950), p. 116.

17. Drieu La Rochelle, *État-civil* (Paris: Nouvelle Revue Française, 1921).

18. Drieu La Rochelle, *Mesure de la France* (Paris: Grasset, 1922), pp. 109–115, 119.

19. See above, Chapter 11; see also Pietro P. Trompeo, "George Sorel," *Cultura,* 2 (December 15, 1922):94–95. The argument that Sorel was to Italy during the years from 1905 to 1915 what Herbert Marcuse was to American students in the 1960s is presented by Giuseppe Goisis in "Sorel e i Soreliani italiani," *Mulino,* 22 (July/August 1973):615; see also Daniel Guerin, *Sur le fascisme* (Paris: Maspero, 1969), chapt. 7.

20. Croce, "Cultura tedesca e politica italiana," *Italia nostra,* December 27, 1914.

21. Quoted in Croce, *Contribution à ma propre critique,* p. 51.

22. Croce, "La Guerra italiana," *Giornale d'Italia,* September 24, 1917.

23. Croce, *Pagine sparse: pagine sulla guerra* (Naples: Laterza, 1919), p. 311.

24. Ibid., pp. 86–87, 89–91, 102, 106–107, 114, 124–25, 127, 237–43, 296–300.

25. Croce, "'Tener fede al liberalismo e aiutare cordialmente il fascismo' dice Benedetto Croce in una nostra intervista," *Giornale d'Italia,* October 27, 1923.

26. Pareto, *The Mind and Society,* trans. A. Bongiorno and A. L. Livingston (4 vols., New York: Harcourt, Brace, and Co., 1935), 3, esp. pp. 885–989.

27. Ibid., 4, p. 1527.

28. Ibid., 4, p. 1530.

29. Ibid., 4, pp. 1530–36.

30. See Pareto, *Trasformazione della democrazia* (Milan: Corbaccio, 1921), pp. 11–12.

31. Pareto, "Georges Sorel," *Ronda,* 4 (September/October 1922):541–48. See also Pareto to Vittore Pansini, July 31, 1919, *Carteggi Paretiani, 1892–1923,* p. 164; also cited in Carlo Mongardini, "Considerazioni sull'interesse sociologico dell'opera di Sorel," *Cultura e scuola,* no. 10 (April/June 1964):189. Pareto noted that during his career Sorel had appeared to "oscillate like a pendulum."

32. Pareto, "Georges Sorel," pp. 541–42, 546.

33. Ibid., p. 542.

34. Ibid., p. 546.

35. Ibid., pp. 544–45.
36. Michels, *Le Prolétariat et la bourgeoisie dans le mouvement socialiste italien*, pp. 344–45.
37. Michels, "Lettere di Georges Sorel a Roberto Michels," p. 293n.
38. See below; see especially Michels' articles in the 1920s and 1930s on fascism in *First Lectures in Political Sociology*, trans. A. de Grazia (Minneapolis: University of Minnesota Press, 1949).
39. Gradilone, *Storia del sindacalismo*, 2, pp. 100, 103–104; Brunello Vigezzi, *L'Italia di fronte alla prima guerra mondiale: L'Italia neutrale*, (2 vols., Milan: Longanesi, 1966), 1, p. 390; Borghi, *Mezzo secolo di anarchia, 1898-1945*, pp. 158–59, and *L'Italia tra due Crispi* (Paris: Liberia Internazionale, 1924), p. 78. For the general development of fascism from intervention to the March on Rome see de Felice, *Mussolini il rivoluzionario*, chapts. 10–14, and *Mussolini il fascista* (2 vols., Turin: Einaudi, 1966 and 1968, 1, chapts. 1–4. Cf Charles L. Bertrand, "Italian Revolutionary Syndicalism and the Crisis of Intervention: August-December, 1914," *Canadian Journal of History*, 10 (1975):349–68.
40. Panunzio, "Il Sindacalismo," p. 358; Rosenstock-Franck, "L'Économie corporative fasciste," pp. 14–15.
41. Rossoni, *Le Idee della ricostruzione* (Florence: R. Bemporad, 1923), p. 59.
42. Gradilone, *Storia del sindacalismo*, 2, p. 104; Horowitz, *The Italian Labor Movement*, pp. 177–78. See de Felice, *Mussolini il rivoluzionario*, p. 385, dating the UIL from the USI break on intervention in 1914–1915.
43. Italo M. Sacco, *Storia del sindacalismo* (2nd ed., Turin: Societá Editrice Internazionale, 1947), pp. 231–32.
44. Gradilone, *Storia del sindacalismo*, 2, p. 105. The *Italia nostra* had been founded by the Unione Sindacale Milanese and the Comitato Sindacale Italiana in April 1918 and became an organ of the UIL; see issues of June 1918. See below for the *Pagine libere*.
45. Horowitz, *The Italian Labor Movement*, p. 178; Rosenstock-Franck, *L'Économie corporative fasciste*, pp. 26–30. See especially Fernando Cordova, "Le Origini dei sindacati fascisti," *Storia contemporanea*, 1 (December 1970):957–58.
46. Gradilone, *Storia del sindacalismo*, 2, pp. 105, 108–111; Cordova, "Le Origini dei sindacati fascisti," p. 969.
47. Gradilone, *Storia del sindacalismo*, 2, p. 191; Cordova, "Le Origini dei sindacati fascisti," p. 988; see also Schneider, *Making the Fascist State*, p. 146.
48. Gradilone, *Storia del sindacalismo*, 2, pp. 191–92; Schneider, *Making the Fascist State*, p. 146; and de Felice, *Mussolini il fascista*, 1, pp. 191–92.
49. Quoted in Schneider, *Making the Fascist State*, p. 146.
50. Cordova, "Le Origini dei sindacati fascisti," pp. 992, 1007; Gradilone, *Storia del sindacalismo*, 2, pp. 105, 108–111; and Rosenstock-Franck, *L'Économie corporative fasciste*, p. 29.
51. Editorial, "Quindici anni di vita di una rivista indipendente," *Pagine libere*, 8 (August/September 1921):284; see also de Felice, *Mussolini il rivoluzionario*, p. 234n.
52. Olivetti, "Ripresa," *Pagine libere*, 6 (February 15, 1920):1–3; Panunzio, "Socialismo in ritardo," ibid., 8 (August/September 1921):289–96; Anon., "Il Mito

comunista—la realtà sindacale," ibid., 7 (March 15, 1920):51–55; Olivetti, "La Questione della proprietà," ibid., 7 (March 15, 1920):41–42; Olivetti, "Sindacalismo e mazzianismo," ibid., 9 (April 1922):121–29.

53. Ascoli, "Giorgio Sorel," *Pagine libere*, 7 (July 31, 1920):295–312; Editorial, "Quindici anni di vita di una rivista indipendente," ibid., 8 (August/September 1921): 279; Panunzio, "Socialismo in ritardo," ibid., p. 289; "Swift," "Letteratura sindacalista," ibid., 9 (April 1922):134–39; and Olivetti, "Un Nome–una bandiera," ibid., 9 (October 1922):321–26.
54. Ascoli, "Giorgio Sorel," p. 312.
55. Labriola, "Giorgio Sorel," *Pagine libere*, 9 (September 1922):281–85.
56. Olivetti, "Nel labirinto," *Pagine libere*, 9 (May/June 1922):164. See de Felice, *Mussolini il rivoluzionario*, p. 660.
57. Lanzillo, *La Disfatta del socialismo* (Florence: Libreria della Voce, 1918), pp. 14, 226, 281.
58. Lanzillo, *Le Rivoluzioni del dopoguerra* (Città di Castello: Il Solco, 1922), pp. 102–104, 219–20, 223.
59. Lanzillo, "Giorgio Sorel," *Gerarchia*, 1 (September 25, 1922):529.
60. Panunzio, "Socialismo in ritardo," 289–90.
61. Panunzio, *Diritto, forza e violenza* (Bologna: Licino Cappelli, 1921), p. 17.
62. Ibid., *Che cos'è il fascismo* (Milan: Editrice Alpes, 1924), p. 79.
63. See Orano's articles on the war years, *La Spada sulla bilancia* (Milan: Fratelli Treves, 1917); see Schneider, *Making the Fascist State*, pp. 145–46.
64. See Orano, *Crisi* (Cagliari: Casa Editrice, 1922).
65. Olivetti, "Il Manifesto dei sindacalisti," *Pagine libere*, 8 (April/May 1921):143, 156–58; de Felice, *Mussolini il fascista*, 1, p. 604.
66. Olivetti, "Internazionalismo psichico," *Pagine libere*, 8 (October 1921):350.
67. On nationalism and intervention see Thayer, *Italy and the Great War*, especially the final chapter.
68. "Manifesto," *Politica*, 1 (December 1918):1–17.
69. Ibid., p. 17.
70. Associazione Nazionalista Italiana, *Il Nazionalista Italiano e i problemi del lavoro e della scuola* (Rome: Società Editrice "L'Italiana," 1919), p. 34.
71. Ibid., pp. 37–42, 73.
72. Rosenstock-Franck, *L'Économie corporative fasciste*, pp. 30–32.
73. See de Felice, *Mussolini il fascista*, 1, pp. 312–13; cf. Schneider, *Making the Fascist State*, p. 80.
74. Anon., "Consensi all'articolo di Sorel," *Resto del Carlino*, May 14, 1919.
75. Filippo Carli, "Sindacati e ricostruzione," *Politica*, 2 (April 24, 1919):8.
76. Oreste Ranelletti, "I Sindacati e lo stato," *Politica*, 2 (July 31, 1920):262–63.
77. Corradini, *Discorsi nazionali* (Rome: "L'Italiana," 1917), pp. 17–18.
78. Corradini, *La Marcia dei produttori* (Rome: "L'Italiana," 1916), pp. 53, 164, 169.
79. Corradini, "Nazionalismo e internazionalismo," *Idea nazionale*, March 23, 1919.
80. Corradini, *L'Unità e la potenza delle nazioni* (Florence: Vallecchi, 1922), p. 93.
81. See Prezzolini, *Amici* (Florence: Libreria della Voce, 1922), chapt. 1.
82. Prezzolini, *La Cultura italiana* (Florence: Libreria della Voce, 1923), p. 360.
83. On Prezzolini as a precursor of fascism see Peter M. Riccio, *On the Threshold of Fascism*.

84. Sorel to Missiroli, May 27, 1914, facing p. 45. See also Missiroli, *La Monarchia socialista* (Bari: Laterza, 1914), and *Il Papa in guerra* (Bologna: Zanichelli, 1917), which was dedicated to Sorel.

85. Missiroli, *La Repubblica degli accattoni* (Bologna: Zanichelli, 1920), and *Opinioni* (Florence: La Voce, 1921), pp. 81–83.

86. Sorel to Missiroli, April 7 and 16, 1921, pp. 305–308; Sorel to Delesalle, November 8, 1921, p. 237. See also Missiroli, *Il Fascismo e la crisi italiani* (Bologna: Cappelli, 1923), and Mussolini, "Il Fascismo e Mario Missiroli," *Popolo d'Italia,* September 18, 1921.

87. On the origin of the *Popolo d'Italia* and the Fasci of 1915 see de Felice, *Mussolini il rivoluzionario,* pp. 40, 249–87, and especially chapt. 10, entitled "Il Mito della guerra rivoluzionaria." Mussolini had recently quoted Sorel on the relationship between war and socialism in *Lavoro,* December 30, 1914; see Furiozzi, *Sorel e l'Italia,* pp. 272n, 273–74.

88. On the Fasci of 1919 see de Felice, *Mussolini il rivoluzionario,* p. 460. For Mussolini's own views on the subject (and on Sorel) in 1939 see de Begnac, *Palazzo Venezia: storia di un regime* (Rome: Editrice la Rocca, 1950), pp. 159–60.

89. F. T. Marinetti, *Futurismo e fascismo* (Foligno: E. Campitelli, 1924), pp. 24–27. This collection of articles dates from 1909. Marinetti was an important figure in the Milan *fascio* when it was founded in 1919. When Mussolini a year later turned "monarchist" and "Catholic," Marinetti temporarily withdrew his support from fascism.

90. See de Felice, *Mussolini il rivoluzionario,* pp. 590–91; for details see de Felice, *Mussolini il fascista,* 1, pp. 3–387 where the period 1919 to 1922 is considered.

91. "La Morte di Giorgio Sorel," *Popolo d'Italia,* August 31, 1922 (according to the editors of the *Opera omnia di Benito Mussolini,* the obituary is "attributed" to Mussolini).

92. "Breve preludio," *Gerarchia,* 1 (January 25, 1922):2.

93. "Volt," "Vilfredo Pareto e il fascismo," *Gerarchia,* 1 (October 25, 1922):598.

94. Massimo Rocca, "L'Errore di Sorel," *Gerarchia,* 1 (July 25, 1922):370–75.

95. Lanzillo, "Giorgio Sorel," *Gerarchia,* 1 (September 25, 1922):529.

96. Ibid.

97. The best sources for Mussolini's general development during this period are de Felice's *Mussolini il rivoluzionario,* chapts. 12–14, and *Mussolini il fascista,* 1, chapts. 1–3.

98. Mussolini, "23 marzo," *Popolo d'Italia,* March 18, 1919. This article and others in February and March concerning the reactivation of the Fasci on March 23, 1919, are discussed in de Felice, *Mussolini il rivoluzionario,* pp. 501–504; see also Mussolini's article in the *Popolo d'Italia* on the following day, March 19, 1919.

99. Mussolini, "Discorso di Trieste," September 20, 1920, in *Scritti e discorsi di Benito Mussolini* (8 vols., Milan: Hoepli, 1934), 2, p. 107.

100. Mussolini, "Dopo due anni," *Popolo d'Italia,* March 23, 1921.

101. Mussolini to Bianchi, August 27, 1921, in Mussolini, *Messaggi e proclami* (Milan: Imperia, 1929), p. 29.

102. Mussolini, "Sindacalismo," *Popolo d'Italia,* September 2, 1922. See de Felice, *Mussolini il rivoluzionario,* p. 412.

103. Mussolini, "Discorso di Udine," September 20, 1922, in *Scritti e discorsi di Benito Mussolini*, 2, p. 315.

104. Mussolini, "Discorso di Napoli," October 24, 1922, in *Scritti e discorsi di Benito Mussolini*, 2, p. 345; de Felice, *Mussolini il fascista*, 1, p. 346. See also de Felice, *Mussolini il fascista*, 2, pp. 365–67, and George W. Mosse, "The Genesis of Fascism," *Journal of Contemporary History*, 1 (1966):15–16, where emphasis is placed on both Sorel and Le Bon and the role of myth in moving the masses; see also Nye, "Two Paths to a Psychology of Social Action," pp. 411–38.

105. See, for example, de Felice, *Mussolini il fascista*, 1, p. 165; on the "varieties" of fascism in 1922 see ibid., 1, pp. 12–13. Cf. Furiozzi, "La Fortuna italiana di Sorel," pp. 110–112.

Sorelians after Sorel

Chapter 14. The 1920s

1. For the general development of *Clarté* see Marcel Fourrier, "Éditorial: de *Clarté* à *La Guerre civile*," pp. 1–10. See also Jean Bernier, "Rectifications," *Clarté*, 4 (October 15, 1925):30. It should be recalled that Berth used the pseudonym "Jean Darville" during his monarchist days.

2. Fourrier, "Editorial: de *Clarté* à *La Guerre civile*," pp. 8–9.

3. Editorial, "Une Apologie de M. Jourdain," *Clarté*, 3 (June 1, 1924):247–48.

4. Michael, "Révolutionaires français," *Clarté*, 3 (November 1, 1924):450–54; also Michael, "Qu'est-ce que fut le Sorelisme?" *Clarté*, 4 (January 1, 1925):16n, 18, 18n.

5. Michael, "Sorelisme au Léninisme," *Clarté*, 4 (March 1, 1925):9, 11–13, 22.

6. Most of Berth's articles published from 1923 to 1925 in *Clarté* were republished in new editions of former studies or in collections; for greater detail see Levey, "The Sorelian Syndicalists," chapt. 6.

7. Berth, "Bolshevisme et syndicalisme," *Les Derniers aspects du socialisme* (Paris: Rivière, 1923), pp. 4, 16, 29.

8. Berth, *La France au milieu du monde* (Turin: Piero Gobetti, 1924), pp. 31–32, 36; also *Guerre des états ou guerre des classes* (Paris: Rivière, 1924), pp. 71–72, 79–80, 84.

9. Berth, *La Fin d'une culture* (Paris: Rivière, 1927), pp. 28, 216.

10. Fourrier, "Éditorial: de *Clarté* à *La Guerre civile*," pp. 9–10.

11. Berth, "Le Passage du Rubicon ou le retour de l'enfant prodigue," *Clarté*, 5 (May 1925):195; Berth here uses the term "*classes moyennes.*"

12. V. Delagarde, P. Monatte, and A. Rosmer, *Lettres aux membres du Parti communiste* (Paris: La Cootypographie, 1924), pp. 5–11.

13. Berth, "Avant-propos," *La Fin d'une culture*, p. 12.

14. Louzon, "Les Conditions matérielles de la révolution," *Révolution prolétarienne*, 3 (March 1927):3; also "La Révolution: loi de la vie," ibid., 7 (April 5, 1931):9–10; Editorial, "La Ligne syndicaliste," ibid., 6 (January 1, 1930): inside cover.

15. See especially Monatte, "Le Syndicalisme de 1906 ne peut pas mourir," *Révolution prolétarienne*, 13 (March 10, 1937):9–10.

16. Berth, "Notre cher Péguy," *Révolution prolétarienne*, 2 (June 1926):12–14.

17. Berth, "Proudhon et Marx," *Révolution prolétarienne*, 2 (September-November 1926):14–21, 13–19, and 16–20; also "Du 'Capital' aux 'Réflexions sur la violence,'" *Révolution prolétarienne*, 5 (March 15 and April 1, 1929):3–7 and 3–6. These and other essays appeared in Berth's collection, *Du "Capital" aux "Réflexions sur la violence."*

18. Berth, "Le Syndicalisme révolutionnaire est-il encore possible?" *Révolution prolétarienne*, 6 (June 15, 1930):5.

19. "Lettres de Georges Sorel à Benedetto Croce," *Critique sociale*, 1 (March-July 1931):9–15 and 56–65; also P. K. and L. L. [Pierre Kaan and Lucien Lurat], "À propos des lettres de Sorel," *Critique sociale*, 1 (October 1931):107.

20. Berth, "Sorel ... pas socialiste!" *Révolution prolétarienne*, 8 (February 1932): 25–28.

21. See above, Chapter 5.

22. Alberic Cahuet, "Notre nouveau roman," *Illustration*, 84 (December 18, 1926): 685–86; see also Bourget, "L'Éducation par la résistance," *Figaro*, March 25, 1929.

23. Cahuet, "Notre nouveau roman," p. 685.

24. See above, Chapters 5 and 7.

25. Variot, "Apologie pour l'impérialisme," *Lettre à l'anglais* (Paris: Stock, 1923), pp. 75–138. Variot, who was a novelist and playwright, devoted himself particularly to the collection of Alsatian legends: see *Legendes et traditions orales d'Alsace* (2 vols., Paris: Georges Crès), and *L'Alsace éternelle: récits légendaires de l'Alsace* (Paris: Les Oeuvres Représentatives, 1929).

26. See Drieu La Rochelle, "Modes intellectuelles," *Nouvelles littéraires*, January 6, 1934, on his position in the 1920s; for Drieu's journalism and fiction during the 1920s and 1930s see Robert Soucy, "Romanticism and Realism in the Fascism of Drieu La Rochelle," *Journal of the History of Ideas*, 31 (January/ March 1970): 78–79. For Drieu's writing during the period see *Écrits de jeunesse, 1917–27* (Paris: Gallimard, 1941).

27. Johannet, *Éloge du bourgeois français*, pp. 8–9, 60, 259.

28. Ibid., pp. 270, 283, 303.

29. Ibid., pp. 201, 221, 298, 303.

30. For a general treatment of Valois's break with the Action Française and the formation of the Faisceau see Guchet, *Georges Valois*, pp. 145–201; Weber, *The Action Française*, pp. 208–211; and Jules Levey, "Georges Valois and the Faisceau: The Making and Breaking of a Fascist," *French Historical Studies*, 7 (Fall 1973): 279–304.

31. On Valois and his campaign for the États-Généraux see Guchet, *Georges Valois*, pp. 125–36.

32. Valois, "La Bataille des journaux," *Nouveau siècle*, April 1, 1928; Daudet, "Le Mystère de la rue de Rivoli," *Action française*, February 19, 1924; and Dimier, *Vingt ans de L'Action française*, p. 224.

33. Valois, *La Révolution nationale* (2nd ed., Paris: Nouvelle Librairie Nationale, 1924), pp. 50–51.

34. Valois, *D'un siècle à l'autre*, p. 134.

35. Valois, *La Révolution nationale*, pp. 34–35.

36. Pietro Gorgolini, *La Révolution fasciste*, trans. E. Marsan with "Préface" by G. Valois (Paris: Nouvelle Librairie Nationale, 1924).
37. Fréderic Lefèvre, "Une Heure avec M. Georges Valois," *Nouvelles litteraires*, February 16, 1924; Valois, *La Révolution nationale*, pp. 52, 55–56.
38. Valois, *Basile*, pp. xvi–xviii, xx, xxiii.
39. See Anon., "La Conférence de St. Denis," *Révolution prolétarienne*, 11 (August 25, 1935):3–13. Valois's ties with Coty were to be brought up in the mid-thirties during the "*cas* Valois": see Guchet, *Georges Valois*, p. 153n.
40. Valois, "L'Action Française économique et sociale: nouvelle étape," *Action française*, October 11, 1925; see also "La Bataille des journaux," *Nouveau siècle*, April 1, 1928.
41. "Déclaration," *Nouveau siècle*, February 26, 1925.
42. On Coty's financial aid, see Guchet, *Georges Valois*, p. 195.
43. Maurras, "La Politique: Georges Valois," *Action française*, October 12, 1925.
44. "Discours prononcé le 11 Novembre à la réunion donné a la Salle Wagram pour la création du 'Faisceau des Combattants et des Producteurs,'" *Nouveau siècle*, November 12, 1925; for Valois's address see "La politique de la victoire" in the same issue. On the Faisceau and battle with the Action Française see Serant, *Les Dissidents de l'Action Française*, pp. 28–32.
45. The *Nouveau siècle* became a daily on December 7, 1925.
46. Valois, "Lettre à Déat," August 18/September 27, 1933, quoted in *Technique de la révolution syndicale* (Paris: Édition Liberté, 1935), p. 25.
47. The attack on Valois began in Maurras's column of December 15, 1925; see "La Politique: une éxecution," *Action française*, December 15, 1925; see also Anon., "Georges Valois chassé par les étudiants" in the same issue. Valois's interviews had appeared in the *Momento* (Turin), November 7, 1925, and the *Tribuna* (Rome), December 8, 1925. Valois had argued there that the Action française was not interested in "action"; he had wanted to launch the movement in a clearly revolutionary direction.
48. See Maurras's daily column, "La Politique," throughout January 1926; Daudet, "Le Cas de Georges Valois," *Action française*, January 8, 1926; Pujo, "Revue de la presse," *Action française*, April 28, 1926.
49. Valois, "Sur l'aggression de l'Action française," *Nouveau siècle*, December 15, 1925; "Une Infamie," ibid., January 14, 1926; "À Strasbourg, gros succès du Faisceau," ibid., April 17, 1926. See also "Gressent-Valois envoie ses amis à l'assaut de l'Action française et les fait massacrer," *Action française*, November 16, 1926.
50. Valois, "Origines françaises du fascisme," *Nouveau siècle*, April 27, 1926; also "Caractère universel du fascisme," ibid., April 28, 1926. See also Pujo, "Revue de la presse: pour 'Valois,'" *Action française*, April 28, 1926; and G. Larpent, "Revue de la presse: Mussolini et Georges Sorel," ibid., April 26, 1926.
51. On similarities with Italian fascism see Guchet, *Georges Valois*, pp. 154–56.
52. Valois, "Sur la route de Reims," *Nouveau siècle*, March 14, 1926; see also Valois, "L'Assemblée de Reims," ibid., April 10, 1926; and Valois, "À Reims! À Reims!" ibid., June 26, 1926.
53. "Appel aux travailleurs français," *Nouveau siècle*, May 12, 1926.
54. On Valois and the crisis of the franc see Guchet, *Georges Valois*, pp. 106–124.

55. Valois, "Fin de 'la querelle du bourgeois,'" *Nouveau siècle*, February 4, 1926.
56. Valois, "Lettre de Georges Valois à René Johannet," *Nouveau siècle*, February 5, 1926; see also *La Révolution nationale*, p. 193.
57. Valois, *Le Fascisme* (Paris: Librairie Valois, 1927), pp. 7–8, 24, 68; this work is a revision of *Il Fascismo francese* (Rome: Marino, 1926).
58. Valois, "Erreurs et verités sur le fascisme," *Nouveau siècle*, April 24, 1926.
59. Valois, *Le Fascisme*, p. 68.
60. See their articles in *Nouveau siècle*.
61. "L'Assemblée nationale de Reims," *Nouveau siècle*, June 28, 1926. For Guchet's estimates concerning the circulation of the daily and membership, see *Georges Valois*, pp. 166–67.
62. "10,000 travailleurs manifeste contre le fascisme," *Humanité*, June 28, 1926; see also "Au sujet des bagarres de dimanche," *Nouveau siècle*, June 29, 1926.
63. Valois, "À tous les membres du Faisceau," *Nouveau siècle*, July 4, 1926.
64. "Pour le nouveau quotidien et pour le mouvement," *Nouveau siècle*, December 5, 1926.
65. See Guchet, *Georges Valois*, pp. 185–90; Levey, "Georges Valois and the Faisceau," p. 296.
66. Valois, "La Bataille des journaux," *Nouveau siècle*, April 1, 1928.
67. Valois, "Vers l'état syndical et le fédéralisme économique," *Nouveau siècle*, January 1, 1928; see also "Premier manifeste pour la République syndicale," ibid., March 18, 1928.
68. Valois, "Il y a fascisme et fascisme," *Nouveau siècle*, February 25, 1928.
69. Valois, "Pour la République syndicale," *Cahiers bleus*, no. 1 (August 15, 1928): 1; see Sérant, *Les Dissidents de l'Action Française*, p. 33.
70. Valois, *L'Homme contre l'argent* (Paris: Librairie Valois, 1928), p. iii.
71. Sammy Béracha, "La Rationalisation intégrale," *Cahiers bleus*, no. 15 (May 18, 1929):19.
72. Both also published with the Librairie Valois during this period: see de Jouvenal, *L'Économie dirigée* (Paris: Librairie Valois, 1928), pp. 18 and 194, and Fourgeaud, *Du code individualiste au droit syndical* (Paris: Librairie Valois, 1929), p. 174. Both de Jouvenal and Fourgeaud considered themselves at this time disciples of Valois.
73. Dominique and Béracha also published with the Librairie Valois and considered themselves disciples of Valois, though they were drawn to certain of Sorel's ideas. See Dominique, *La Révolution créatrice* (Paris: Librairie Valois, 1928) pp. 77–78, 127, 194–95, 208; and Béracha, *Rationalisation et révolution* (Paris: Librairie Valois), pp. 181 and chapt. 7. On Sorel's influence on Béracha see his "Introduction au marxisme réaliste," *Cahiers bleus*, no. 48 (February 8, 1930):7–15.
74. Berth, *Du "Capital" aux "Réflexions sur la violence,"* p. 83n.
75. For details see Guchet, *Georges Valois*, pp. 212–13.
76. Mussolini, "Dal viaggo negli Abruzzi al delitto Matteotti, 23 agosto 1923–13 giugno 1924," *Opera omnia*, 20, p. 123.
77. See English edition of Pietro Gorgolini, *The Fascist Movement in Italian Life*, trans. M. D. Petre (London: F. Fischer, 1923), p. 52; and the French edition, *Le Fascisme*, trans. Eugene Marsan (Paris: Nouvelle Librairie Nationale, 1923).

78. The quotation was cited soon afterward in the French press; see particularly Jean Bertholin, "Le Fascisme est de formation française: Mussolini et Georges Sorel," *Gaulois du dimanche,* April 24, 1926.

79. Marguerite Sarfatti, *Mussolini: l'homme et le chef,* trans. M. Croci and E. Marsan (Paris: Albin Michel, 1927), p. 117; Giovanni Gentile, *Origini e dottrina del fascismo* (Rome: Libreria del Littorio, 1929), pp. 20–21.

80. Pareto, "Georges Sorel," pp. 544–45.

81. Croce, " 'Tener fede al liberalismo e aiutare cordialmente il fascismo' dice Benedetto Croce in una nostra intervista," *Giornale d'Italia,* October 27, 1923.

82. Croce, "Le Elezioni e il ritorna alla vita politica normale," *Corriere Italiano,* February 1, 1924, in *Pagine sparse* (2 vols., Naples: Riccardo Ricciardi Editore, 1943), 2, pp. 374–76.

83. Croce, "La Situazione politica," *Giornale d'Italia,* July 10, 1924, in *Pagine sparse,* 2, pp. 376–79; Lorenzo Giusso, "Il Fascismo e Benedetto Croce," *Gerarchia,* 3 (October 1924):529.

84. Cecil Sprigge, Benedetto Croce: Man and Thinker (Cambridge: Bowes and Bowes, 1952), pp. 17–19. See also Onufrio, "Considerazioni su Croce e Sorel," p. 152n; and de Felice, *Mussolini il fascista,* 2, p. 118n.

85. In Sorel to Croce (January 20, 1927), 25, p. 38.

86. Croce to Meisel, May 14, 1950, quoted in Meisel, *Genesis of Georges Sorel,* p. 225.

87. Michels had been barred for many years from academic appointment in Germany because of his attraction to socialism: see Seymour Lipset's "Introduction" to Michels, *Political Parties,* trans. Eden and Cedar Paul (New York: Collier Books, 1962), p. 33.

88. Michels, *First Lectures in Political Sociology,* trans. Alfred de Grazia (Minneapolis: University of Minnesota Press, 1949), pp. 126, 137, 166; this study is composed of a number of Michels' articles published in the 1920s and 1930s.

89. Michels, *Corso di sociologia politica* (Milan: Vallardi, 1927), p. 93.

90. Michels, "The Sociological Character of Political Parties," *American Political Science Review,* 21 (November 1927), quoted in *First Lectures in Political Sociology,* pp. 151–52.

91. See Federico Perini, *Paolo Orano: saggio bibliografico* (Tolmezzo: Stabilimento Grafico "Carnia," 1937), p. 5; see also his *Crisi* of 1922.

92. Lanzillo, *Le Rivoluzione del dopoguerra* (Città di Castello: Il Solco, 1922), pp. 225–26, 231.

93. Alfonso de Pietri-Tonelli, *Agostino Lanzillo, 31 ottobre 1886–3 marzo 1952,* Estratto dalla *Rivista di politica economica* (Rome: Tip. delle Terme, 1952), p. 7.

94. Olivetti, *Il Sindacalismo come filosofia e come politica* (Milan: Alpes, 1924), pp. 10, 480.

95. Olivetti, "Sindacalismo eroica: ricordando Filippo Corridoni," *Augustea,* 2 (December 15, 1926):5–6.

96. Olivetti, "L'Antimarxismo di Giorgio Sorel," *Stirpe,* 8 (January 1930):7–11.

97. Ibid., p. 11.

98. Panunzio, *Che cose' è il fascismo?* (Milan: Alpes, 1924), pp. 19, 35–41, 79.

99. Panunzio, "Il Sindacalismo," pp. 352–54, 356–57, 364.

100. Panunzio, *Il Sentimento dello stato* (Rome: Littorio, 1929), p. 98; *Il Diritto sindacale e corporativo* (Perugia: "La Nuova Italia," 1930), pp. 24-25.

101. Rossoni, "La Corporazione fascista," *Stirpe,* 1 (December 1923):9-11.

102. See Panunzio, "Iposesi ed eventi," *Stirpe,* 1 (December 1923), 19-20; Olivetti, "Sindacalismo integrale," ibid., 2 (April 1924): 277-79.

103. Rossoni, "Sviluppi giuridici della rivoluzione nel campo sociale," *Stirpe,* 6 (January 1928):1-2.

104. See De Grand, "Curzio Malaparte: The Illusion of the Fascist Revolution," *Journal of Contemporary History,* 7 (1972):73-89; Benjamin Crémieux, "Préface" to Curzio Malaparte, *L'Italie contre l'Europe,* trans. M. Y. Lenoir (Paris: Alcan, 1927), pp. i-xiv.

105. Suckert [Malaparte], *L'Europa vivente: teoria storica del sindacalismo nazionale* (Florence: Libreria della Voce, 1923), pp. 48, 70.

106. Ibid., p. xlvii.

107. Ibid., pp. 115-16.

108. Malaparte, *Italia barbara* (Turin: Gobetti, 1926), pp. 20-23, 32, 38-40; see also Ludovico Incisa, "La Rivolta dell'ordine" (1954) in *Il Fascismo,* ed. C. Casucci (Bologna: Il Mulino, 1961), p. 415.

109. Suckert [Malaparte], "I Problema fondamentale," *Conquista dello stato,* July 10, 1924; see also De Grand, "Curzio Malaparte," pp. 82-84.

110. Silvio Galli, "Sorel e Marx," *Conquista dello stato,* August 30, 1924; Suckert [Malaparte], "Filippo Corridoni, martire operaio," ibid., October 1, 1924; and Suckert [Malaparte] "Che cosa intendiamo per rivoluzione fascista," ibid., January 25, 1925.

111. Pareto, "Giorgio Sorel," *Conquista dello stato,* May 24, 1925; "Spectator," "Mussolini e il fascismo nel '21: una lettera inedita di Giorgio Sorel," ibid., December 15, 1928. The letter is quoted at length in Missiroli's preface to *L'Europa sotto la tormenta* (1932), pp. vii-lxiv.

112. Cf. De Grand, "Curzio Malaparte," p. 84.

113. See the *Conquista dello stato,* March 22, 1925, and issues of 1926 to 1928.

114. Anon., "L'Arresto di Malaparte," *Conquista dello stato,* June 1, 1928.

115. A collection of these articles was published as *Intelligenza di Lenin* (Milan: Treves, 1930).

116. See de Felice, *Mussolini il fascista,* 1, pp. 403-404, and 2, pp. 98-101.

117. See ibid., 2, pp. 48-101, for a general treatment of this subject. On the controversy concerning de Felice's distinction between "fascism-movement" and "fascism-regime" see Michael A. Ledeen, "Renzo De Felice and the Controversy over Italian Fascism," *Journal of Contemporary History,* 11 (1976):269-82, esp. p. 277. See also Giuseppina and Ughetta Cavallucci and Oscar Bandini, "Torquato Nanni: un socialista nella crisi del primo dopoguerra," *Storia contemporanea,* 9 (April 1978):265.

118. De Felice, *Mussolini il fascista,* 2, p. 48.

119. Bottai, *L'Expérience corporative* [Paris: Nouvelles Éditions Latines, n.d. (ca. 1929-1930)], pp. 9, 32; see De Grand, "Giuseppe Bottai e il fallimento del fascismo revisionista," *Storia contemporanea,* 6 (December 1975):697-731, and *Giuseppe Bottai e la cultura fascista* (Bari: Laterza, 1978).

120. Bottai, "In fondo alla rivoluzione," *Critica fascista,* July 15, 1927.

121. Ugo d'Andrea, "Nazionalismo e sindacalismo nel nuovo secolo," *Giornale d'Italia,* April 10, 1928.

122. Gramsci, *Il Materialismo storico e la filosofia di Benedette Croce* (2nd ed., Turin: Einaudi, 1949), Note 3, pp. 110–111.

123. Lorenzo Giusso, "Giorgio Sorel e il terzo stato francese," *Critica fascista,* 7 (August 1929):292–94.

124. Arnaldo Fioretti, "Il Compito degli organizzatori," *Lavoro fascista,* April 24, 1930.

125. Carlo Curcio, "Oltre Sorel," *Resto del Carlino,* February 26, 1930.

126. See de Felice, *Mussolini il fascista,* 2, pp. 329–36.

127. Cammett, *Antonio Gramsci,* pp. 163ff.

128. See, e.g., Berth, "Anatole France," *Ordine nuovo,* March 1, 1925.

129. Cammett, *Antonio Gramsci,* pp. 181–82; Bracco, "Il Giovane Gramsci e Sorel," pp. 177, 182–83.

130. See Gramsci, "Il Nostro indirizzo sindacale," *Stato operaio,* October 18, 1923; see also Furiozzi, *Sorel e l'Italia,* p. 368.

131. Sorel, "Apologia di Lenin," *Stato operaio,* January 29, 1924.

132. See articles by Gobetti in the *Rivoluzione liberale:* "Manifesto," February 12, 1922; "Storia dei comunisti torinesi scritta da un liberale," April 2, 1922; and "Postilla," April 29, 1924.

133. See Gobetti's articles cited above, no. 132. On Sorel's influence on Gobetti see G. Arfè, "La Rivoluzione liberale di Piero Gobetti," *Rivista storica italiana,* 74 (1962):320.

134. S. Caramella and N. Sapegno, "Bibliografia delle opere di Sorel," *Rivoluzione liberale,* December 14, 1922.

135. See December 14, 1922, issue of *Rivoluzione liberale,* especially: Cesare Spellanzon, "Giorgio Sorel in Italia"; Pareto, "Sorel"; and Berth, "Le Tertullien du socialisme."

136. Gobetti, "Per una Società degli Apoti," *Rivoluzione liberale,* September 28, 1922.

137. Sorel, "Quand Israel est roi: articolo inedito," *Rivoluzione liberale,* March 8, 1923. The article is dated October 22, 1922; it discusses the prevalence of Jews in postwar revolutionary movements.

138. Vitale, "Sorel ed il fascismo," *Rivoluzione liberale,* May 20, 1924.

139. See Suckert [Malaparte], "Il Dramma della modernità," *Rivoluzione liberale,* June 4, 1944; Carlo A. Di Gualtieri, "Controriforma," *Rivoluzione liberale,* April 19, 1925. See also de Felice, *Mussolini il fascista,* 1, p. 674n.

140. Gobetti, *La Rivoluzione liberale: saggio sulla lotta politica in Italia,* ed. G. de Caro (Turin: Einaudi, 1964), pp. xxxvi–xxxvii.

141. Leone, *Il Neo-Marxismo: Sorel e Marx* (Bologna: Sindacato Ferrovieri, 1923), pp. 10, 70, 113n, 134n.

142. Louzon, "Introduction" to Sorel, *Lettres à Paul Delesalle, 1914–1921,* p. 55.

143. Marucco, *Arturo Labriola,* pp. 289–98.

144. Labriola, *Studio su Marx con appendice di Giorgio Sorel* (2nd ed., Naples: Morano, 1926).

145. Marucco, *Arturo Labriola,* pp. 304–309; also Labriola, "Why I Fled from Italy," *Review of Reviews,* 75 (September 15/October 15, 1927): 221–27. He also engaged in antifascist activities in Belgium, the United States, and Argentina until the mid-thirties.
146. Prezzolini, *Le Fascisme,* trans. G. Bourgin (Paris: Bossard, 1925), pp. 70, 93–94, 182.
147. Prezzolini, *L'Italiano inutile* (Milan: Longanesi, 1953), pp. 235–50.
148. Missiroli, "La Rivoluzione liberale," *Rivoluzione liberale,* February 12, 1922; "La Monarchia socialista," ibid., May 14, 1922.
149. By 1928 Missiroli had become a regular contributor to the *Conquista dello stato.* See also his *Il colpo di stato* (Turin: Gobetti, 1924).
150. Massimo Rocca, *Le Fascisme et l'antifascisme en Italie* (Paris: Alcan, 1930), p. 192; de Felice, *Mussolini il fascista,* 2, p. 116n.
151. Missiroli, *Date a Cesare: la politica religiosa di Mussolini* (Rome: Littorio, 1929), and *Cosa deve l'Italia a Mussolini* (Rome: Novissima, 1930). See also de Felice, *Mussolini il fascista,* 2, p. 417n.

Chapter 15. The 1930s

1. See *Révolution prolétarienne,* 13 (March 10, 1937):9–11. The year 1906 was that of the Charte d'Amiens and the general strike for the eight-hour workday; Monatte argues that the syndicalism of 1906 would not have joined a "popular front."
2. *Révolution prolétarienne,* inside covers, esp. 11 (January 10, 1935).
3. Berth, "En fin, nous avons Hitler! ou la fin de l'Europe libérale," *Révolution prolétarienne,* 9 (October 10, 1933):3–4.
4. Ibid. (October 25, 1933):3.
5. Sorel, *D'Aristote à Marx.*
6. Berth, "Vers une nouvelle mystification," *Révolution prolétarienne,* 11 (November 10 and 25, 1935):1–4 and 1–4.
7. For the beginning of the *"cas* Valois" see Louzon, "La Conférence nationale de Saint-Denis," *Révolution prolétarienne,* 11 (August 10, 1935):1–2.
8. See above, Chapter 14.
9. Berth, "Clan des ya? Clan des da?" *Révolution prolétarienne,* 14 (August 25, 1938): 2–3.
10. The *Chantiers coopératifs* was published almost concurrently from 1932 to 1934; it often directed itself explicitly to political problems.
11. See Victor Crastre, "Les Livres: *Guerre ou révolution* par Georges Valois," *Nouvel âge,* no. 8 (August 1931):755–76.
12. See *Nouvel âge* during the period 1931–1934.
13. Valois, "Vers la constituante syndicale," *Chantiers coopératifs,* April 18, 1934; *Technique de la révolution syndicale* (Paris: Éditions Liberté, 1935), pp. 36–39. See also Guchet, *Georges Valois,* pp. 217–19.
14. "Le Mouvement de Nouvel âge est de ceux qui doivent le plus à Sorel," *Nouvel âge,* no. 69 (April 16, 1936):27.

15. "Nouvel âge," *Nouvel âge*, Numéro spécial, autumn 1934; see also issue of March 5, 1936.

16. A special issue of the original *Nouvel âge* presented Valois's side of the "*cas* Valois"; see Valois, "'Le Cas Valois' exposé par Georges Valois," *Nouvel âge*, nos. 101–104 (September 20–27, 1936):1–31.

17. See issue of *Révolution prolétarienne* of June 10, 1935.

18. "La Conférence nationale de Saint-Denis," *Révolution prolétarienne*, 11 (August 25, 1935):3–13; see countercharges in Anon., "Le Cas de la 'Révolution prolétarienne,'" *Nouvel âge*, no. 51 (October 10, 1935):4.

19. Berth, "Lettre ouverte aux camarades de la R. P. à propos du 'cas Valois,'" *Nouvel âge*, no. 65 (March 5, 1936):3–4.

20. Valois, *Technique de la révolution syndicale* (Paris: Éditions Liberté, 1935), pp. 8–12, 22.

21. Valois, "Lettre à Marcel Déat," pp. 18–21: Valois speaks here of the "*classes moyennes.*"

22. Ibid., p. 25.

23. Ibid., pp. 29–30.

24. Valois, "Lettre à Léon Jouhaux," pp. 110, 136–37.

25. Valois, "'Le Cas Valois' exposé par Georges Valois," p. 29.

26. Valois, "Quelques refléxions sur la violence," *Nouvel âge*, May 22, 1937.

27. See Valois's articles in the *Nouvel âge*, August 2 and 16 and December 3 and 4, 1936.

28. See Valois's articles in the *Nouvel âge* (now a daily) on January 28, March 15 and 23, and September 27, 1938; these arguments were published in his *Guerre ou blocus économique* (Paris: Valois, 1938).

29. Berth, "Réflexions à propos des 'Réflexions sur la violence,'" *Nouvel âge*, May 6 and 10, 1938.

30. Ibid., "L'Accord de Munich," *Nouvel âge*, December 22, 23, 24–30, 1938.

31. Valois, "Mort d'Édouard Berth," *Nouvel âge*, January 29–30, 1939. Valois incorrectly lists Mussolini as a contributor to the prewar *Mouvement socialiste*.

32. Béracha, *À la recherche d'une patrie* (Paris: Librairie Valois, 1931), p. 296.

33. Béracha, *Le Marxisme après Marx* (Paris: Rivière, 1937), p. 24.

34. Ibid., pp. 19–20, 22, 204–206, 219.

35. Rennes, "Du mythe de la grève générale à la mystique du plan," *Nouvel âge*, no. 18 (November 15, 1934):2.

36. Rennes, *Georges Sorel et le syndicalisme révolutionnaire* (Paris: Éditions Liberté, 1936), pp. 12–14, 183–84.

37. Rennes, *Exposé du marxisme* (Paris: Éditions Liberté, 1938), pp. 203–204, and *Thèses sociales du Nouvel âge* (Paris: Éditions Liberté, 1939), pp. 202, 204–205, 212–13.

38. See issues of *Nouvel âge* of October and November 1936.

39. Valois, "Ni guerre, ni la capitulation," *Nouvel âge*, September 26, 1938; "Le Blocus, le blocus, le BLOCUS," ibid., September 27, 1938, and "Les État-Unis d'Europe," ibid., October 1, 1938; see also Guchet, *Georges Valois*, pp. 234–35.

40. See *Nouvel âge*, August 27 and 28 and September 3, 1939.

41. *Nouvel âge,* September 4 to 11, 1939.

42. Valois, *Prométhée vainqueur, ou explication de la guerre* (Paris: Éditions Liberté, 1940), pp. 125–28.

43. For excellent studies of *planiste* and neo-syndicalist reviews of the thirties see the following: Jean Touchard, "L'Esprit des années 1930: une tentative de renouvellement de la pensée politique française," in *Tendances politiques dans la vie française depuis 1789,* ed. G. Michaud (Paris: Hachette, 1960); and Jean-Louis Loubet del Bayle, *Les Non-conformistes des années 30: une tentative de renouvellement de la pensée politique française* (Paris: Éditions du Seuil, 1969). Also of interest are Robert Soucy, "French Fascist Intellectuals in the 1930's: An Old New Left?" *French Historical Studies,* 8 (Spring 1974):445–58, and the more recent study by Andreu, *Le Rouge et le blanc: 1928–1944* (Paris: La Table Ronde, 1977), esp. pp. 45, 66.

44. Editorial, "La Ligne générale," *Plans,* 1 (January 1931):7–9; see also Loubet del Bayle, *Les Non-conformistes,* p. 100.

45. Lagardelle, *Sud-Ouest: une région française* (Paris: Librairie Valois, 1929), pp. 90, 164, 166–67.

46. Lagardelle in *Plans:* "De l'homme abstrait à l'homme réel," 1 (January 1931):25, 32; "L'homme réel et le syndicalisme," 1 (March 1931):11–12, 16; "La Fin d'une culture," 1 (May 1931):16; "Supercapitalisme," 1 (December 1931):12; "Ententes internationales de producteurs," 2 (January 1932):122; and "Sources du syndicalisme," 2 (February 1932):18, 21.

47. Andreu, "L'Itinéraire spirituel d'Hubert Lagardelle," *Nation française,* October 1, 1958; see also Lagardelle, *Mission à Rome: Mussolini* (Paris: Plon, 1955), pp. 260–62.

48. See below.

49. Lagardelle, "Le Fascisme: doctrines, institutions," *Encyclopédie française,* 10 (June 1935): chapt. 3, pt. 2, pp. 5–15.

50. The review initially carried the subtitle *Revue du syndicalisme et de l'humanisme.*

51. E. E., "Revues syndicalistes," *Homme réel,* 1 (May 1934):110.

52. Andreu, "L'Itinéraire spirituel d'Hubert Lagardelle."

53. Editorial, "Lignes de force," *Homme réel,* 1 (January 1934):1–2.

54. Ibid., 2 (March/April 1935):5.

55. Duret, "Le Syndicalisme et la notion de plan," *Homme réel,* 1 (May 1934):69; see also Georges Lefranc, "Le Plan d'action d'Henri de Man," ibid., 1 (January 1934): 20–23.

56. Lagardelle, ed., "Lettres de Georges Sorel à Hubert Lagardelle," *Homme réel,* 1 (February-September 1934):117–22, 188–91, and 41–44. A letter from Bernstein to Sorel dated June 14, 1898, was also published: "Lettre d'Édouard Bernstein à Sorel," *Homme réel,* 4 (May 1937):92–95.

57. Berth, "Variations sur quatre themes proudhoniens," *Homme réel,* 1 (September 1934):8–21, and "La Propriété, selon Proudhon," ibid., 4 (January 1937):9–31.

58. Lacoste, "Le Syndicalisme et la réforme de l'état," *Homme réel,* 1 (October 1934):46–47, 50; see also Lacoste, "Syndicalisme et économie," *Visage du syndicalisme* (Paris: Librairie Syndicale, 1937), p. 46.

59. See Édouard Dolléans, "Les temps héroiques du syndicalisme, 1892–1909," *Homme réel*, 4 (May 1937):7–23.

60. The principal works expressing the ideas of the *Ordre nouveau* began to appear around 1931: Robert Aron and Arnaud Dandieu, *Décadence de la nation française* (Paris: Rieder, 1931); Aron and Dandieu, *Le Cancer américain* (Paris: Rieder, 1931); and Aron and Dandieu, *La Révolution nécessaire* (Paris: Grasset, 1933).

61. Editorial, "Premiers principes," *Ordre nouveau*, 1 (May 1933):i.

62. Dandieu, *Anthologie des philosophes français contemporains* (3rd ed., Paris: Éditions du Sagittaire, 1931), p. 32.

63. Ibid.

64. Aron and Dandieu, *La Révolution nécessaire*, pp. 294–97.

65. By the beginning of 1936 the break between *Esprit* and the *Ordre nouveau* was complete. The *Ordre nouveau* "is clearly oriented toward an antiworking-class fascism and a petit-bourgeois technocracy we cannot support," wrote Mounier; cited in Touchard, "L'Esprit des années 1930," p. 109.

66. Anon., "Essai de bibliographie révolutionnaire," *Ordre nouveau*, 1 (July 1933): 2–6, 7–12.

67. Touchard, "L'Esprit des années 1930," pp. 106–107.

68. Albert Ollivier, "Violence collective," *Ordre nouveau*, 4 (June 15, 1936):14; see also Loubet del Bayle, *Les Non-conformistes*, pp. 84–85.

69. Alexandre Marc, "Georges Sorel et le syndicalisme," *Ordre nouveau*, 5 (March 1, 1937):59–60.

70. Georges Roditi, "L'Homme nouveau," *Homme nouveau*, 2 (June 1935): n.p.

71. Déat, "Le 'Planisme' et la tradition française," *Homme nouveau*, 2 (January 1, 1935):1–2.

72. "Enquête," *Homme nouveau*, 1 (January 1939): n.p.

73. See above, Chapters 5 and 7; see also Andreu, *Le Rouge et le blanc: 1928–1944*, esp. pp. 100–104.

74. Andreu, "Sorel et le procès de Socrate," *Homme nouveau*, 2 (May 1, 1935): n.p.

75. Andreu, "Le Socialisme de Sorel," *Homme nouveau*, 2 (June 1935): n.p.

76. Bourget, *Au service de l'ordre* (2 vols., Paris, 1929–1933), 2, pp. 175–76.

77. Johannet, *Voyage à travers le capitalisme* (Paris: Éditions Spes, 1934), p. 224.

78. Frédéric Lefèvre, "Une Heure avec Jean Variot," *Nouvelles littéraires*, February 4, 1933. It is entirely possible that Variot's bias was reflected in his editing of the *Propos*: see the first published version of part of the *Propos* in Variot, "Entretiens avec Georges Sorel: sur l'Europe d'avant 1914," *Nouvelles littéraires*, February 27, March 5, March 12, March 19, and March 26, 1932.

79. Touchard, "L'Esprit des années 1930," p. 91.

80. Fabrèguez, "Liberer le prolétariat," *Combat*, 3 (May 1938):3.

81. Maulnier, "Il faut refaire un nationalisme en dépit de la nation," *Combat*, 2 (April 1937):2.

82. Fabrèguez, "Liberer le prolétariat."

83. Andreu, "Fascisme, 1913," *Combat*, 1 (February 1936):5–6. Andreu's first writings had appeared in *Esprit*, where he demonstrated great affection for the prewar Action Française when, for example, Maurras had taken the side of the workers

against the Clemenceau government; see Andreu, "Chronique sociale," *Esprit*, 2 (May 1934), 284-93.

84. Andreu, "Demain sur notre tombeaux," *Combat*, 1 (April 1936):5.

85. Andreu, "Textes à relire: Georges Sorel," *Combat*, 1 (July 1936):6-7.

86. Andreu, "Capitalisme et corporatisme," *Combat*, 1 (Summer 1936):6-7, and "État du syndicalisme français," *Combat*, 1 (December 1936):5.

87. Drieu La Rochelle, "Modes intellectuelles," *Nouvelles littéraires*, January 6, 1934; Gilbert Comte, "Enquête sur le rajeunissement de la France," *Grand review*, 38 (March 1934):14-17. See also Pierre-Henri Simon, *Procès du héros*, pp. 115-16; Drieu La Rochelle, *Socialisme fasciste* (Paris: Gallimard, 1934), pp. 66-67, 112.

88. Comte, "Enquête sur la rajeunissement de la France," p. 15.

89. Drieu La Rochelle, *Avec Doriot* (Paris: Gallimard, 1937).

90. Drieu La Rochelle, "Mourir en démocrates ou survivre en fascistes," October 28, 1938, in *Chronique politique, 1934-1942* (Paris: Gallimard, 1943), p. 192.

91. Maulnier, "Les Deux violences," *Combat*, 1 (February 1936):4; *Mythes socialistes* (Paris: Gallimard, 1936), p. 23; and *Au delà du nationalisme* (Paris: Gallimard, 1938), p. 232.

92. Mussolini, "La Dottrina del fascismo," *Scritti e discorsi* (12 vols., Milan: Hoepli, 1934), 8, pp. 67-69. See de Felice, *Mussolini il rivoluzionario*, p. 41.

93. See Marcel Prélot, *L'Empire fasciste* (Paris: Librairie du Recueil Sirey, 1936), p. 76.

94. Schreiber, *Rome d'après Moscou* (Paris: Plon, 1931), p. 114. Schreiber reports incorrectly that Sorel and Mussolini had "numerous conversations" (p. 92).

95. Émile Ludwig, *Entretiens avec Mussolini*, trans. R. Henry (Paris: Albin Michel, 1932), p. 169; a difference of opinion between Sorel and Mussolini on the subject of moral progress is cited (p. 140).

96. See, for example, de Begnac, *Palazzo Venezia: storia di un regime*, pp. 129, 130, 184, 396, 552.

97. Giorgio Pini, *The Official Life of Benito Mussolini*, trans. L. Villari (London: Unwin Brothers, 1939), pp. 58, 241; see also Schreiber, *Rome d'après Moscou*, p. 92.

98. Croce, *History of Europe in the Nineteenth Century*, trans. H. Furst (New York: Harcourt, Brace and World, 1933), pp. 341-50.

99. Ibid., p. 306.

100. Louis Gillet, "Naples nouvelle," *Revue des mondes*, 103 (February 15, 1933):786.

101. Orano, *Gli Ebrei in Italia* (Rome: Pinciana, 1937); see Perini, *Paolo Orano: saggio bibliografico*, p. 6.

102. Lanzillo, *Studi di economia applicata* (Padua: La Garangola, 1933), p. xiii; de Pietri-Tonelli, *Agostino Lanzillo, 31 ottobre 1886-3 marzo 1952*, p. 7.

103. Panunzio, *L'Economia mista: dal sindacalismo giuridico al sindacalismo economico* (Milan: Hoepli, 1936), pp. 10, 208; "Teoria e storia del sindacato," *Estratto dalla Rivista del lavoro* (Rome: Rocca S. Casciano, 1938), p. 6; *Le Camere dei fasci e delle corporazioni* (Rome: Collana di Studi della Confederazione Fascista dei Commercianti, 1939).

104. See above.
105. Rigola, "Punti fermi," *Problemi del lavoro,* 1 (March 25, 1927):1–2, and "La Vitalità del capitalismo," *Problemi del lavoro,* 1 (August 1, 1927):1–2.
106. See especially Rigola, "Giovani revisionisti francesi," *Problemi del lavoro,* 9 (August 1, 1935):1–3; see also Andreu, "L'Itinéraire spirituel d'Hubert Lagardelle," *Nation française,* October 1, 1958.
107. Anon., "Critica e superamento del materialismo storico," *Problemi del lavoro,* 7 (June 1, 1933):9–13; Rigola, "Constatazioni," ibid., 8 (January 1, 1934):1–4; A. de C., "Libri nuovi: Sorel e Proudhon," ibid., 9 (February 1, 1935):11–12; Anon., "Vecchi e nuovi problemi socialisti," ibid., 9 (March 1, 1935):6–9; Anon., "Politica ed economia," ibid., 10 (June 1 and August 1, 1936):8–10 and 6–8.
108. Rigola, "Giovani revisionisti francesi," pp. 1–3; Anon., "La Dottrina dei neosindacalisti francesi," *Problemi del lavoro,* 11 (December 1, 1937):9–10.
109. Missiroli, "Prefazione" to *L'Europa sotto la tormenta,* pp. vii–lxiv; also "L'Ultimo Sorel," *Politica,* 13 (February/April 1931):272–303.
110. Missiroli, "Prefazione" to *L'Europa sotto la tormenta,* pp. ix, x, xlvi–xlviii.
111. Ibid., p. xlix.
112. Sorel, "Stato e proprietà rurale," *L'Europa sotto la tormenta,* pp. 87–92 (originally published in the *Resto del Carlino,* November 10, 1919); see also Missiroli's "Prefazione" to the collection, in which he quotes from a letter by Sorel dated September 1921, pp. xxxii–xxxiii.
113. Missiroli, *Studi sul fascismo* (Bologna: Nicola Zanichelli Editore, 1934), and *Da Tunisi a Versailles* (Rome: Società Editrice di "Novissima," 1939).
114. Carlo Martini, *"La Voce": storia e bibliografia* (Pisa: Nistri-Lischi, 1956), p. 235.
115. Riccio, *On the Threshold of Fascism;* see Prezzolini's review, "La Voce," *Stampa,* January 3, 1930.
116. Anon., "Will Dr. Butler Act?" *Nation,* 139 (November 7, 1934):523–24; Anon., "Prezzolini, Butler e la Casa degli italiani," *Giustizia e libertà,* January 4, 1935.
117. Labriola, *Au delà du capitalisme et du socialisme,* trans. S. Priacel (Paris: Librairie Valois, 1932), pp. 75*n*, 105, 132–133*n*, 148, 284. See also Marucco, *Arturo Labriola,* p. 306.
118. Labriola, *L'État, la crise* (Paris: Rivière, 1933), p. 276.
119. Labriola, *Le Crépuscule de la civilisation* (Paris: G. Mignolet et Storz, 1936), p. 334.
120. Marucco, *Arturo Labriola,* pp. 316–18.
121. Malaparte, *Technique du coup d'état,* trans. J. Bertrand (Paris: Bernard Grasset, 1931), p. 708; see De Grand, "Curzio Malaparte," pp. 86–87.
122. See Ministero delle Corporazioni, *Informazioni corporative,* 4 (July/December 1931):509, for address of Luigi Razza on September 27, 1931.
123. See Riccardo del Guidice, "La Fine del sindacato," *Lavoro fascista,* January 10, 1936; Rafaelle Mastrostefano, "Sindacalismo fascista," ibid., February 29, 1936.
124. See Missiroli, "L'Ultimo Sorel," p. 303*n*.

125. Bruno Biagi, "La Corporazione," *Gerarchia,* 13 (May 1933):357.
126. Only one article on Sorel appeared in the ten volumes published from 1930 to 1931, and that one was critical: see Andrea Billi, "G. Sorel e la critica," *Archivio di studi corporativi,* 4 (1933):143–58.
127. Edoardo Malsuardi, *Elementi di storia del sindacalismo fascista* (Lanciano: R. Carabba, 1938), pp. 2, 5; Simone Malvagna, "Il Pensiero politico di Sorel e il fascismo," *Rivista internazionale di filosofia del diritto,* 19 (January/April 1939): 69, 81, 90, 93.
128. Gramsci, *Quaderni del carcere* (6 vols., Turin: Einaudi, 1964). See Cammett, *Antonio Gramsci,* pp. 187–212, on the origins and general nature of the *Quaderni.*
129. See Bracco, "Il Giovane Gramsci e Sorel," p. 182, on Togliatti's article of 1963 that argued that Gramsci and Sorel had only the idea of the workers' or factory councils (*"consigli di fabbrica"*) in common.
130. Gramsci, *Passato e presente* (3rd ed., Turin: Einaudi, 1953), pp. 156–57, and *Note sul Machiavelli, sulla politica e sullo stato moderno* (3rd ed., Turin: Einaudi, 1953), pp. 4–5. See Edmondo Cione, *Benedetto Croce* (2nd ed., Milan: Longanesi, 1953), p. 446; E. J. Hobsbawm, "The Great Gramsci," *New York Review of Books,* 21 (April 4, 1974): 42; Bracco, "Il Giovane Gramsci e Sorel," esp. pp. 178–83.
131. Gramsci, *Il Materialismo storico e la filosofia de Benedetto Croce* (2nd ed., Turin: Einaudi Editore, 1949), pp. 106, 176; *Lettere del carcere* (7th ed., Turin: Einaudi, 1950), pp. 180–82; *Gli Intellecttuali e l'organizzazione della cultura* (5th ed., Turin: Einaudi, 1953), pp. 44, 197; *Note sul Machiavelli, sulla politica e sullo stato moderno,* pp. 99–100; *Passato e presente,* pp. 54, 111–12.
132. Gramsci, *Il Materialismo storico e la filosofia de Benedetto Croce,* p. 176.
133. Ibid., p. 225.
134. Gramsci, *Note sul Machiavelli, sulla politica e sulla stato moderno,* pp. 99–100; *Passato e presente,* p. 54.
135. Gramsci, *Il Materialismo storico e la filosofia de Benedetto Croce,* pp. 109–110.
136. Gramsci, *Passato e presente,* pp. 186–87; *Note sul Machiavelli, sulla politica e sullo stato moderno,* pp. 4–5, 53.
137. Cammett, *Antonio Gramsci,* p. 136; Frank Rosengarten, *The Italian Anti-Fascist Press (1919–1945)* (Cleveland: Case Western Reserve Press, 1968), pp. 47–48.
138. Angelo Tasca, "Ritorno a Gramsci e a Gobetti," *Giustizia e libertà,* May 7, 1937.
139. Cesare Goretti, *Il Sentimento giuridico nell'opera di Giorgio Sorel* (Città di Castello: Il Solco, 1922), and *Sorel* (Milan: Edizioni Athena, 1928).
140. La Ferla, "L'Antintellettualismo di Georges Sorel," *Annuario del R. Istituto Magistrale 'R. Bonghi' (1925–26),* 4 (1927):53–69; "Introduzione allo studio delle opera di Georges Sorel," *Estratto dall'Annuario del R. Istituto Magistrale di Assisi, 1926–27* (Assisi: Tipografia Metastasio, 1929):45; and *Ritratto di Georges Sorel* (Milan: Società Editrice "La Cultura," 1933).
141. Santonastaso, *Giorgio Sorel* (Palermo: Edizioni del Ciclope, 1929); "Pensieri postumi di Sorel," *Nova Italia,* 2 (January 20, 1931):15–20; "Da Marx a Sorel," ibid., 2 (April 20, 1931):142–45; *Georges Sorel* (Bari: Laterza, 1932); *Studi di pensiero politico* (Udine: Istituto delle Edizioni Accademiche, 1939).

142. Peccerini, "L'Opera di G. Sorel," *Nuova rivista storica,* 24–25 (January 1940–
January 1941):25–45, 200–215, 352–77, 473–94, and 50–73.

Chapter 16. The War Years and Conclusion

1. Massimo Rocca, "Georges Sorel et le syndicalisme," *Cassandre,* 10 (September
5, 1943):5.
2. See above, Chapter 15.
3. For Valois's activities during the war years see G. L. Fréjafon, *Bergen-Belsen: les
derniers jours de Georges Valois* (Paris: Librairie Valois, 1947); see also Valois,
L'Homme devant l'éternal (Paris: Librairie Valois, 1947), for essays written from
1941 to 1943. For several years after the war (1945–1948) Valois's following revived the prewar *Nouvel âge.*
4. J. M. Aimot, "Hommage à Hubert Lagardelle," *Révolution nationale,* May 3,
1942; Lagardelle, *La Charte du travail et son application* (Paris: Office des Comités
Sociaux, 1943); and Andreu, "L'Itinéraire spirituel d'Hubert Lagardelle," *Nation
française,* October 1, 1958.
5. Commenting on the Fall of France, Drieu wrote in 1940: "The France that had
read Sorel, Barrès, Maurras, Péguy, Bernanos, Céline, Giono, Malraux, Petitjean
was not strong enough to impose itself on the France that had read A. France,
Duhamel, Giraudoux, Mauriac, Maurois"; see *Notes pour comprendre le siècle*
(Paris: Gallimard, 1941), p. 173. See also Pierre-Henri Simon, *Procès du héros,* p.
175, and Pol Vandromme, *Drieu La Rochelle* (Paris: Éditions Universitaires,
1958), p. 107.
6. But Variot denied that Sorel was in any way one of the founders of the National
Revolution; see Variot, "Georges Sorel et la révolution nationale," *Revue universelle,* no. 16 (August 25, 1941):321.
7. Andreu continued to be interested in and to publish on Sorel well after the war; see,
for example: "Notes et documents: Bergson et Sorel," *Études bergsoniennes,* 2
(Paris: Albin Michel, 1949); "Bergson et Sorel," ibid., 3 (Paris: Albin Michel,
1952); *Notre maître, M. Sorel* (Paris: Bernard Grasset, 1953); "Une Lettre inédite
de Pareto à Sorel," *Nation française,* January 29, 1959; "Une Lettre inédite de
Georges Sorel à Pierre Lassere," ibid., April 2, 1958; and *Le Rouge et le blanc:
1928–1944* (1977).
8. Collected, translated, and published in French after the war; see Malaparte, *La
Volga naît en Europe,* trans. J. Bertrand (Paris: Éditions Denoël, 1948), pp. 7, 21;
see also Malaparte's *Kaputt,* trans. J. Bertrand (Paris: Éditions Denoël, 1946),
"Note bibliographique," pp. 5–7.
9. Missiroli, *L'Italia d'oggi* (2nd ed., Bologna: Zanichelli Editore, 1942); Sorel, *Da
Proudhon a Lenin,* ed. M. Missiroli (Florence: L'Arco, 1949), p. 7; Sorel, *Lettere
a un amico d'Italia* (San Casciano: Cappelli Editore, 1963). In Missiroli's collection of letters from Sorel he failed to include a letter dated September 1921 that
was highly favorable to the fascist movement; he had quoted it at length in the
"Prefazione" to his collection of Sorel's articles published in 1932. See Sorel,
L'Europa sotto la tormenta, pp. xxxii–xxxiii; the final letter included in the *Lettere*

a un amico d'Italia is dated June 21, 1921. For a critique of Missiroli's *Lettere* see Alexandre Croix, "Georges Sorel et l'Italia," *Révolution prolétarienne*, no. 591 (March 1973):55–58, and no. 592 (April 1973):91–95.

10. See Prezzolini, *L'Italiano inutile*, pp. 130–33 and appendix, pp. 363–88.

11. Much of this postwar literature has been employed in this study and is cited in the documentation. See Neil McInnes, "The Revolutionary Conservative," p. 1226. This is a review of two recent collections of excerpts from Sorel's work, one sponsored by the Italian Communist party and the other by an American academician of "conservative patronage": Annamaria Andreasi, ed., *Sorel: democrazia e rivoluzione* (Rome: Reuniti, 1976), and John L. Stanley, ed., *Essays in Socialism and Philosophy* (Oxford: Oxford University Press, 1976).

12. On possible links between Sorel and post-World War II violence, especially in the sixties, see, for example: Isaiah Berlin, "Georges Sorel," *Times Literary Supplement*, December 31, 1971, pp. 1617–22; McInnes, "The Revolutionary Conservative," p. 1226; Jean-Paul Sartre, "Preface" to Frantz Fanon, *The Wretched of the Earth*, trans. C. Farrington (New York: Grove Press, 1966), pp. 12–13; Hannah Arendt, *On Violence* (New York: Harcourt, Brace, and World, 1970), pp. 12, 20, 65, 69–72, 89–90, on Sorel, Sartre, and Fanon on violence. Cf. Irene L. Gendzier, *Frantz Fanon: A Critical Study* (New York: Vintage Books, 1974), p. 203. On Sorel's conception of violence and modern "liberation" movements, see Williams, "Four Modalities of Violence, with Special Reference to the Writings of Georges Sorel," pp. 248–61. For other recent attempts to establish links with Third World movements, liberation movements, or the violence of the sixties, see also: Hutton, "Vico's Theory of History," on Daniel Cohn-Bendit; Charzat, *Georges Sorel*, pp. 251–82, on Sorel and the politics of "*autogestion*"; and Vernon, *Commitment and Change*, pp. 61–71.

Index

Designer:	Phoenix Publishing Services, Inc.
Compositor:	Phoenix Publishing Services, Inc.
Printer:	Thomson-Shore, Inc.
Binder:	Thomson-Shore, Inc.
Text:	Comp/Edit Times Roman
Display:	Photo Typositor Trump Medieval Bold
Cloth:	Kivar 9 Butternut Corinth Bright
Paper:	50 lb P&S offset